DogFriendly.com's

California and Nevada Dog Travel Guide

3rd Edition

by
Tara Kain

DogFriendly.com's California and Nevada Dog Travel Guide, 3rd Edition
by Tara Kain, President of DogFriendly.com, Inc.

DogFriendly.com, Inc.
4570 Pleasant Valley Road #J55
Placerville, California 95667 USA
1-877-475-2275
email: email@dogfriendly.com
http://www.dogfriendly.com

PLEASE NOTE
Although the author and publisher have tried to make the information as accurate as possible, they do not assume, and hereby disclaim, any liability for any loss or damage caused by errors, omissions, misleading information or potential travel problems caused by this book, even if such errors or omissions result from negligence, accident or any other cause.

CHECK AHEAD
We remind you, as always, to call ahead and confirm that the applicable establishment is still "dog-friendly" and that it will accommodate your pet.

DOGS OF ALL SIZES
If your dog is over 75-80 pounds, then please call the individual establishment to make sure they allow your dog.

OTHER PARTIES DESCRIPTIONS
Some of the descriptions have been sent to us by our web site advertisers or other parties.

ISBN 0-9718742-4-7

Printed in the United States of America

Cover Photographs (clockwise, from top left):
Marriott San Diego Marina, San Diego, CA
Top Hand Ranch Carriage Rides, Sacramento, CA
Carmel City Beach, Carmel, CA
The Park Bench Cafe, Huntington Beach, CA

California Regions

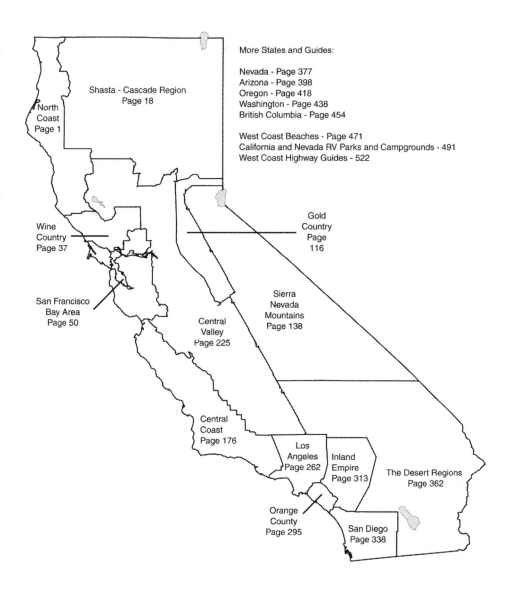

Shasta - Cascade Region
Page 18

North
Coast
Page 1

More States and Guides:

Nevada - Page 377
Arizona - Page 398
Oregon - Page 418
Washington - Page 438
British Columbia - Page 454

West Coast Beaches - Page 471
California and Nevada RV Parks and Campgrounds - 491
West Coast Highway Guides - 522

Wine
Country
Page 37

Gold
Country
Page
116

San Francisco
Bay Area
Page 50

Central
Valley
Page 225

Sierra
Nevada
Mountains
Page 138

Central
Coast
Page 176

Los
Angeles
Page 262

Inland
Empire
Page 313

The Desert Regions
Page 362

Orange
County
Page 295

San Diego
Page 338

Table of Contents

California and Nevada Dog Travel Guides

Additional Guides

Introduction by the Author and President of DogFriendly.com, Inc.

I grew up with dogs and have always loved dogs. When I moved away from home, I discovered a whole new world through traveling. But whenever I traveled, the last thing I wanted to do was leave my best friend behind. I practically spent the whole time worrying about my beloved pooch. So I began taking my dog with me. It was much tougher than I originally thought. I would often spend several days researching and planning where my dog and I would be accepted and what else I could do with my dog, aside from just staying in a hotel room. Unfortunately, many places did not allow dogs, especially a large dog like my standard poodle. Many times when I found a supposedly "dog-friendly" hotel or motel, they would allow pets only in smoking rooms. In my opinion, just because I have a dog should not limit me to a smoking room. So in June of 1998, I began to compile my list of dog-friendly places, notes and photos and began to post them on a web site called DogFriendly.com. This allowed me to easily keep track of my research and also help other dog lovers know about these dog-friendly places. I was devoted to finding the best pet-friendly places and then letting the rest of the world know about them.

In search of the best places, I have traveled over 100,000 miles across the United States and Canada with my dog. Today I continue to travel with my best friend. Together we scout out not just lodging but also great places to dine, sightsee, walk and shop. I believe it's important to make a complete travel guide which does not just list places to stay, but also fun and exciting places like dog-friendly attractions, parks, hikes, beaches, outdoor restaurants and retail stores. I still continue the tradition of focusing on establishments that allow all well-behaved dogs, regardless of size or breed as well as only listing places that allow dogs in your choice of smoking or non-smoking rooms. By using this guide, I hope you will spend less time researching and more time actually going places with your dog. We at DogFriendly.com believe that well-behaved dogs are an integral and wonderful part of people's lives and they should be as welcome as anyone, anywhere. And last, but not least, thank you! We know you have a choice when looking for dog-friendly resources. We want to thank you for choosing DogFriendly.com as your source for finding great dog-friendly vacation getaways.

Tara Kain, Author and President of DogFriendly.com, Inc.

Your Comments and Feedback

We value and appreciate your feedback and comments. If you want to recommend a dog-friendly place or establishment, let us know. If you find a place that is no longer dog-friendly, allows small dogs only or allows dogs in smoking rooms only, please let us know. You can contact us using the following information.

Mailing Address and Contact Information:
DogFriendly.com, Inc.
4570 Pleasant Valley Road #J55
Placerville, California 95667 USA
toll free phone: 1-877-475-2275
email: email@dogfriendly.com
website: http://www.dogfriendly.com

How To Use This Guide

General Guidelines

1. Please only travel with a well-behaved dog that is comfortable around other people and especially children. Dogs should also be potty trained and not bark excessively.

2. Always keep your dog leashed unless management specifically tells you otherwise.

3. Establishments listed in this book should allow well-behaved dogs of ALL sizes (at least up to 75 pounds) and in non-smoking rooms. If your dog is over 75-80 pounds, then please call the individual establishment to make sure they will allow your dog. We have listed some establishments which only allow dogs up to 50 pounds, but we try our best to make a note in the comments about the restrictions. All restaurants and attractions we list should allow dogs of all sizes.

4. Accommodations listed do not allow dogs to be left alone in the room unless specified by hotel management. If the establishment does not allow pets to be left alone, try hiring a local pet sitter to watch your dog in the room.

5. All restaurants listed as dog-friendly refer to outdoor seating only. While dogs are not permitted to sit in a chair at a restaurant's outdoor dining table, they should be allowed to sit or lay next to your table. We do not list outdoor restaurants that require your dog to be tied outside of a fenced area (with you at the dining table on one side and your dog on the other side of the fence). In our opinion, those are not truly dog-friendly restaurants. Restaurants listed may have seasonal outdoor seating.

6. Pet policies and management changes often, especially within the lodging and restaurant industries. Please always call ahead to make sure an establishment still exists and is still dog-friendly.

7. After purchasing your book, please visit http://www.dogfriendly.com/updates for FREE book updates. We will do our best to let you know which places may no longer be dog-friendly.

Preparation for a Road Trip

A Month Before

If you don't already have one, get a pet identification tag for your dog. It should have your dog's name, your name and phone number. Consider using a cell phone number, a home number and, if possible, the number of where you will be staying.

Get a first aid kit for your dog. It comes in very handy if you need to remove any ticks. The kits are usually available at a pet store, a veterinary office or on the Internet.

If you do not already have a dog harness for riding the car, consider purchasing one for your dog's and your own safety. A loose dog in the car can fly into the windshield, out of the car, or into you and injure you or cause you to lose control of the car. Dog harnesses are usually sold at pet stores or on the Internet.

Make a trip to the vet if necessary for the following:

- A current rabies tag for your dog's collar. Also get paperwork with proof of the rabies vaccine.
- Dogs can possibly get heartworm from mosquitoes in the mountains, rural areas or on hikes. Research or talk to your vet and ask him or her if the area you are traveling to has a high risk of heartworm disease. The vet may suggest placing your dog on a monthly heartworm preventative medicine.
- Consider using some type of flea preventative for your dog, preferably a natural remedy. This is out of courtesy for the dog-friendly hotels plus for the comfort of your pooch.

- Make sure your dog is in good health. See your vet if necessary.

Several Days Before

Make sure you have enough dog food for the duration of the trip.

If your dog is on any medication, remember to bring it along.

Some dog owners will also purchase bottled water for the trip, because some dogs can get sick from drinking water they are not used to. Talk to your vet for more information.

The Day Before

Do not forget to review DogFriendly.com's Etiquette for the Traveling Dog!

Road Trip Day

Remember to pack all of your dog's necessities: food, water, dog dishes, leash, snacks and goodies, several favorite toys, brush, towels for dirty paws, plastic bags for cleaning up after your dog, doggie first aid kit, possibly dog booties if you are venturing to an especially cold or hot region, and bring any medicine your dog might be taking.

Before you head out, put on that doggie seat belt harness.

On The Road

Keep it cool and well ventilated in the car for your dog.

Stop at least every 2-3 hours so your dog can relieve him or herself. Also offer him or her water during the stops.

Never leave your pet alone in a parked car - even in the shade with the window cracked open. According to the Los Angeles SPCA, on a hot day, a car can heat up to 160 degrees in minutes, potentially causing your pet (or child) heat stroke, brain damage, and even death.

If your dog needs medical attention during your trip, check the yellow pages phone book in the area and look under Veterinarians. If you do not see an emergency vet listed, call any local vet even during the evening hours and they or their answering machine can usually inform you of the closest emergency vet.

Etiquette for the Traveling Dog

So you have found the perfect getaway spot that allows dogs, but maybe you have never traveled with your dog. Or maybe you are a seasoned dog traveler. But do you know all of your doggie etiquette? Basic courtesy rules, like your dog should be leashed unless a place specifically allows your dog to be leash-free. And do you ask for a paper bowl or cup for your thirsty pooch at an outdoor restaurant instead of letting him or her drink from your water glass?

There are many do's and don'ts when traveling with your best friend. We encourage all dog owners to follow a basic code of doggie etiquette, so places will continue to allow and welcome our best friends. Unfortunately all it takes is one bad experience for an establishment to stop allowing dogs. Let's all try to be on our best behavior to keep and, heck, even encourage new places to allow our pooches.

Everywhere...

- Well-Behaved Dogs. Only travel or go around town with a well-behaved dog that is friendly to people and especially children. If your dog is not comfortable around other people, you might consider taking your dog to obedience classes or hiring a professional trainer. Your well-behaved dog should also be potty trained and not bark excessively in a hotel or other lodging room. We believe that dogs should be kept on leash. If a dog is on leash, he or she is easier to bring under control. Also, many establishments require that dogs be on leash and many people around you will feel more comfortable as well. And last, please never leave your dog alone in a hotel or other lodging room unless you have the approval from the establishment's management.

- Leashed Dogs. Please always keep your dog leashed, unless management specifically states otherwise. Most establishments (including lodging, outdoor restaurants, attractions, parks, beaches, stores and festivals) require that your dog be on leash. Plus most cities and counties have an official leash law that requires pets to be leashed at all times when not on your property. Keeping your dog on leash will also prevent any unwanted contact with other people who are afraid of dogs, people who do not appreciate strange dogs coming up to them, and even other dog owners who have a leashed dog. Even when on leash, do not let your pooch visit with other people or dogs unless welcomed. Keeping dogs on leash will also protect them from running into traffic, running away, or getting injured by wildlife or other dogs. Even the most well-behaved and trained dogs can be startled by something, especially in a new environment.

- Be Considerate. Always clean up after your dog. Pet stores sell pooper scooper bags. You can also buy sandwich bags from your local grocery store. They work quite well and are cheap!

At Hotels or Other Types of Lodging...

- Unless it is obvious, ask the hotel clerk if dogs are allowed in the hotel lobby. Also, because of health codes, dogs are usually not allowed into a lobby area while it is being used for serving food like continental breakfast. Dogs may be allowed into the area once there is no food being served, but check with management first.

- Never leave your dog alone in the hotel room. The number one reason hotel management does not allow dogs is because some people leave them in the room alone. Some dogs, no matter how well-trained, can cause damage, bark continuously or scare the housekeepers. Unless the hotel management allows it, please make sure your dog is never left alone in the room. If you need to leave your dog in the room, consider hiring a local pet sitter.

- While you are in the room with your dog, place the Do Not Disturb sign on the door or keep the deadbolt locked. Many housekeepers have been surprised or scared by dogs when entering a room.

- In general, do not let your pet on the bed or chairs, especially if your dog sheds easily and might leave pet hair on the furniture. Some very pet-friendly accommodations will actually give you a sheet to lay over the bed so your pet can join you. If your pet cannot resist coming hopping onto the furniture with you, bring your own sheet.

- When your dog needs to go to the bathroom, take him or her away from the hotel rooms and the bushes located right next to the rooms. Try to find some dirt or bushes near the parking lot. Some hotels have a designated pet walk area.

At Outdoor Restaurants...

- Tie your dog to your chair, not the table (unless the table is secured to the ground). If your dog decides to get up and move away from the table, he or she will not take the entire table.

- If you want to give your dog some water, please ask the waiter/waitress to bring a paper cup or bowl of water for your dog. Do not use your own water glass. Many restaurants and even other guests frown upon this.

- Your pooch should lay or sit next to your table. At restaurants, dogs are not allowed to sit on the chairs or tables, or eat off the tables. This type of activity could make a restaurant owner or manager ban dogs. And do not let your pooch beg from other customers. Unfortunately, not everyone loves dogs!

At Retail Stores...

- Keep a close eye on your dog and make sure he or she does not go to the bathroom in the store. Store owners who allow dogs inside assume that responsible dog owners will be entering their store. Before entering a dog-friendly store, visit your local pet store first. They are by far the most forgiving. If your dog does not go to the bathroom there, then you are off to a great start! If your dog does make a mistake in any store, clean it up. Ask the store clerk for paper towels or something similar so you can clean up any mess.

At Festivals and Outdoor Events...

Make sure your dog has relieved himself or herself before entering a festival or event area. The number one reason that most festival coordinators do not allow dogs is because some dogs go to the bathroom on a vendor's booth or in areas where people might sit.

Customs Information for Traveling Between the United States and Canada

If you will be traveling between the United States and Canada, identification for Customs and Immigration is required. U.S. and Canadian citizens traveling across the border need the following:

People

- Proof of citizenship such as your passport or a certified copy of your birth certificate issued by the city, county or state/province where you were born.

- Photo identification such as a current valid driver's license.

- People with children need to bring their child's birth certificate. Single parents, grandparents or guardians traveling with children often need proof or notarized letters from the other parent authorizing travel.

Dogs

- Dogs must be free of evidence of diseases communicable to humans when possibly examined at the port of entry.

- Valid rabies vaccination certificate (including an expiration date usually up to 3 years from the actual vaccine date and a veterinarian's signature). If no expiration date is specified on the certificate, then the certificate is acceptable if the date of the vaccination is not more than 12 months before the date of arrival. The certificate must show that the dog had the rabies vaccine at least 30 days prior to entry.

- Young puppies must be confined at a place of the owner's choosing until they are three months old, then they must be vaccinated. They must remain in confinement for 30 days after the vaccination.

Chapter 1

California Dog-Friendly Travel Guide North Coast

Albion Dog Travel Guide
Accommodations - Vacation Home Rentals

Albion

The Doors
North Hwy 1
Albion, CA 95410
707-937-9200
This vacation home rental is dog-friendly. There are no additional pet fees. Please call to make reservations.

Arcata Dog Travel Guide
Accommodations

Arcata

Best Western Arcata Inn
4827 Valley West Boulevard
Arcata, CA 95521
707-826-0313
There is a $10 per dog per day pet charge. Amenities include free continental breakfast, an indoor/outdoor pool and spa, large deluxe rooms including Jacuzzi® rooms and complimentary cable television with HBO.

Hotel Arcata
708 Ninth Street
Arcata, CA 95521
707-826-0217
This hotel comes highly recommended from one of our readers who says "In Arcata, just north of Eureka, we stayed in an old refurbished hotel, the Hotel Arcata. It's in the center of town, right on the town square. Ask for a room that doesn't face the square, as it can get noisy at night. Bringing a dog into the elevator is fun." There is a $5 per day additional pet fee.

Quality Inn
3535 Janes Rd
Arcata, CA 95521
707-822-0409
There is a $10 per day pet fee.

Super 8
4887 Valley W. Blvd
Arcata, CA 95521
707-822-8888
There are no additional pet fees.

Beaches

Arcata

Mad River Beach County Park
Mad River Road
Arcata, CA
707-445-7651
Enjoy walking or jogging for several miles on this beach. Dogs on leash are allowed. The park is located about 4-5 miles north of Arcata. To get there, take Highway 101 and exit Giuntoli Lane. Then go north onto Heindon Rd. Turn left onto Miller Rd. Turn right on Mad River Road and follow it to the park.

Parks

Arcata

Arcata Community Forest
11th and 14th Streets
Arcata, CA
707-822-3619
Leashed dogs are allowed on this 600+ acre park which offers 18 trails. The trails range from 1/10 of a mile to almost 2 miles long. The park is located on the east side of the City of Arcata, accessible from Redwood Park located at the east ends of 11th and 14th Streets; on the southern side from Fickle Hill Road, which begins at the east end of 11th and 7th Streets at Bayside Road; and from the east end of California Street which connects with L.K. Wood Blvd. north of Humboldt State University.

Boonville Dog Travel Guide
Accommodations

Boonville

Boonville Hotel
Highway 128
Boonville, CA 95415
707-895-2210
This historic hotel was built in 1862. Dogs and children are allowed in the Bungalow and the Studio rooms which are separate from the main building. Both of these rooms are in the Creekside building with private entrances and yards. Room rates start at $225 per night and there is a $15 per day pet charge. Please note that their restaurant is closed on Tuesdays and Wednesdays. This hotel is in Anderson Valley, which is located 2 1/2 hours north of San Francisco.

Crescent City Dog Travel Guide

Accommodations

Crescent City

Gardenia Motel
119 L Street
Crescent City, CA
707-464-2181
There is a $5 per day additional pet fee.

Super 8
685 Hwy 101 S.
Crescent City, CA 95531
707-464-4111
There is a $10 per day pet fee.

Town House Motel
444 US Highway 101 South
Crescent City, CA 95531
707-464-4176
They offer one non-smoking pet room for well-behaved dogs. There is no pet charge.

Accommodations - RV Parks and Campgrounds

Crescent City

Jedediah Smith Campground
Highway 199
Crescent City, CA
707-464-6101
This campground is located in the Jedediah Smith Redwoods State Park and offers 106 RV or tent sites in an old growth redwood forest. RVs must be 36 feet or less. Camp amenities include restrooms, showers, fire pits, dump station and bear-proof lockers. While dogs are not allowed on any park trails, they are allowed in the campground. They are also allowed to walk on or along Walker Road which is just west of the campground. Pets must be leashed and attended at all times. Please clean up after your pets.

Beaches

Crescent City

Beachfront Park
Front Street
Crescent City, CA
707-464-9507
Dogs are allowed at park and the beach, but must be leashed. Please clean up after your pets. To get there, take Highway 101 to Front Street. Follow Front Street to the park.

Crescent Beach
Enderts Beach Road
Crescent City, CA
707-464-6101
While dogs are not allowed on any trails in Redwood National Park, they are allowed on a couple of beaches, including Crescent Beach. Enjoy beachcombing or bird watching at this beach. Pets are also allowed at road accessible picnic areas and campgrounds. Dogs must be on a 6 foot or less leash and people need to pick up after their pets. The beach is located off Highway 101, about 3 to 4 miles south of Crescent City. Exit Enderts Beach Road and head south.

Parks

Crescent City

Redwood National and State Parks
1111 Second Street
Crescent City, CA 95531
707-464-6101
This park does not allow dogs on any trails but some of the beaches and campgrounds welcome dogs. Pets are allowed on Crescent Beach, Gold Bluffs Beach and the Freshwater Spit Lagoon. The campgrounds that allow pets include Jedediah Smith Redwoods State Park campground, Prairie Creek Redwoods State Park campground and Gold Bluffs Beach campground. Dogs are also allowed along some gravel roads including Cal Barrel Road which usually does not have many cars on it. Pets must be leashed and attended at all times and please clean up after them.

Restaurants

Crescent City

Beacon Burger
160 Anchor Way
Crescent City, CA
707-464-6565
Well-behaved leashed dogs are allowed at the outdoor seating area.

Betterbean Espresso
315 M Street
Crescent City, CA
707-465-1248
Well-behaved leashed dogs are allowed at the outdoor seating area.

Big Louie's Pizza
389 M Street
Crescent City, CA
707-464-8573
Let them know that you want to sit outside and they will bring out a table. Well-behaved leashed dogs are welcome at the outdoor seating area.

Bistro Gardens
938 K Street
Crescent City, CA
707-464-5627
Let them know that you want to sit outside and they will bring out a table. Well-behaved leashed dogs are welcome at the outdoor seating area.

Glen's Bakery and Restaurant
722 3rd Street
Crescent City, CA
707-464-2914
This restaurant has one outdoor table and well-behaved leashed dogs are allowed.

Good Harvest Cafe
700 Northcrest Drive
Crescent City, CA
707-465-6028
Well-behaved leashed dogs are allowed at the outdoor seating area.

Los Compadres Mexican Food
457 Highway 101
Crescent City, CA
707-464-7871
Well-behaved leashed dogs are allowed at the outdoor seating area.

Surfside Grill & Brewery
400 Front Street
Crescent City, CA
707-464-7962
Well-behaved leashed dogs are allowed at the outdoor seating area.

Eureka Dog Travel Guide
Accommodations

Eureka

Best Western Bayshore Inn
3500 Broadway
Eureka, CA 95503
707-268-8005
There are no pet fees if paying by credit card. If you pay with cash, a $100 refundable deposit is required.

Discovery Inn
2832 Broadway
Eureka, CA
707-441-8442
There is a $7 per day additional pet fee.

Motel 6
1934 Broadway
Eureka, CA 95501
707-445-9631
One large dog is allowed per room.

Quality Inn
1209 Fourth Street
Eureka, CA 95501
707-443-1601
You must pay for the room with a major credit card when traveling with a pet.

Ramada Inn
270 5th Street
Eureka, CA 95501
707-443-2206
There is an $8 per day pet fee. Dogs up to 50 pounds are allowed.

Red Lion Hotel
1929 Fourth Street
Eureka, CA 95501
707-445-0844
This hotel offers spacious guest rooms, with amenities like data ports, room service, hairdryers, fitness center and outdoor pool. There is a $30 one time fee for dogs.

The Eureka Inn
518 Seventh Street
Eureka, CA 95501
707-442-6441
This inn has been named a National Historical Place, and is a member of Historic Hotels of America. Dogs are allowed on the first floor and there is no pet fee. They have allowed well-behaved St. Bernards here before.

Accommodations - RV Parks and Campgrounds

Eureka

Eureka KOA
4050 North Highway 101
Eureka, CA 95503
707-822-4243
Pets are allowed in the campgrounds and RV spaces, but not in the cabins. Well-behaved leashed dogs of all sizes are allowed. People

need to clean up after their pets. There is no pet fee. Site amenities include 50 amp service available and cable TV and telephone service for an extra fee. Other amenities include a swimming pool open during the summer, hot tub/sauna, LP gas, snack bar and free modem dataport. They are open all year.

Beaches

Samoa

Samoa Dunes Recreation Area
New Navy Base Road
Samoa, CA
707-825-2300
The Bureau of Land Management oversees this 300 acre sand dune park. It is a popular spot for off-highway vehicles which can use about 140 of the park's acres. Dogs are allowed on leash or off-leash but under voice control. Even if your dog runs off-leash, the park service requests that you still bring a leash just in case. To get there, take Highway 255 and turn south on New Navy Base Road. Go about four miles to the parking area.

Parks

Eureka

Fort Humboldt State Historic Park
3431 Fort Avenue
Eureka, CA 95503
707-445-6567
This old military post was established in 1853 to assist in resolving conflicts between Native Americans and settlers who were searching for gold. Dogs are not allowed inside any buildings but they can walk through the outdoor exhibits and view historic logging equipment. There is also a grassy bluff area where you can walk your dog. Pets must be on leash and please clean up after them. The park is located south of Eureka off Highway 101. Go east on Highland Avenue for one block.

Six Rivers National Forest
1330 Bayshore Way
Eureka, CA
707-442-1721
This national forest covers almost 1 million acres of land which ranges in elevation from sea level to almost 7,000 feet. Please see our listings in this region for dog-friendly hikes and/or campgrounds.

Restaurants

Eureka

Los Bagels
403 Second Street
Eureka, CA 95501
707-442-8525
This bakery offers a variety of breads, bagels and pastries. It is located in Eureka's historic Old Town. Well-behaved, leashed dogs are allowed at the outside tables.

Ramone's Drive-Thru Bakery & Cafe
430 N Street
Eureka, CA 95501
707-442-3307
At this drive-thru bakery, you can get coffee and baked goodies on the go.

Spoons Deli
1036th 5th Street
Eureka, CA 95501
707-443-2968
Located inside the North Coast Co-Op natural foods store, this deli serves a variety of foods including vegan, vegetarian and meats. They usually have a few small outdoor tables. Well-behaved, leashed dogs are allowed at the outside tables.

Starbucks Coffee
1117 Myrtle Avenue
Eureka, CA 95501
707-445-2672
Fuel up with some coffee and pastries at Starbucks. Well-behaved, leashed dogs are allowed at the outside tables.

Tomo Deli
2120 4th Street
Eureka, CA 95501
707-444-3318
Well-behaved dogs are welcome this Japanese restaurant's outdoor seating area. Dogs need to be leashed.

Fort Bragg Dog Travel Guide
Accommodations

Fort Bragg

Beachcomber Motel
1111 N. Main Street
Fort Bragg, CA 95437
707-964-2402
This ocean front motel is next to a walking,

jogging, and cycling trail that stretches for miles along the coast. Many rooms have ocean views. They allow well-behaved dogs up to about 75-80 pounds. There is an additional $10 per day pet charge.

Cleone Gardens Inn
24600 N. Hwy 1
Fort Bragg, CA 95437
707-964-2788
This park-like inn is on 5 acres. There are three pet rooms and an additional pet charge of $6 per day.

Delamere Cottages
16821 Ocean Drive
Fort Bragg, CA 95437
707-964-9188
This establishment comes highly recommended from one of our readers who says: "They are located in Fort Bragg just minutes away from Mendocino. Last weekend my boyfriend and I stayed there with our two dogs. The stay was wonderful. The hostess was nice and the overall feeling was downright friendly and warm. The cottage we stayed in had dog treats for the dogs and a gazebo out the back for a peaceful breakfast. You had your own private walk down to a secluded beach. Your dog could romp freely at the beach. Mendocino is just a short drive away." There are no additional pet fees.

Accommodations - Vacation Home Rentals

Fort Bragg

Harbor View Seasonal Rental
Call to arrange.
Fort Bragg, CA
760-438-2563
Watch the boats go in and out of the harbor and listen to the sea lions and fog horns from this dog-friendly vacation rental. This 3,000 square foot house is entirely furnished. The main floor has a living room, dining room, kitchen, 2 bedrooms, 1 bathroom and a deck with a view of the harbor. The upstairs has a large master suite with a deck and a view of the bridge and ocean. The downstairs level has an apartment with a sofa bed and full bathroom. The yard has redwood trees and even deer wandering through. This area is popular for year-round fishing. The rental is available throughout the year. Please call to inquire about rates and available dates at 760-438-2563 or 760-809-8889 (cell phone).

Attractions

Fort Bragg

Mendocino Coast Botanical Gardens
18220 N. Highway 1
Fort Bragg, CA 95437
707-964-4352
This botanical garden is the only public garden in the continental United States fronting directly on the ocean. Well-behaved, leashed dogs are welcome. The gardens offer everything from colorful displays to thunderous waves. The mild maritime climate makes it a garden for all seasons, attracting gardeners and nature lovers alike. You are welcome to bring a picnic lunch to enjoy on the grounds.

Beaches

Fort Bragg

MacKerricher State Park
Highway 1
Fort Bragg, CA
707-964-9112
Dogs are allowed on the beach, but not on any park trails. Pets must be leashed and people need to clean up after their pets. Picnic areas, restrooms and campsites (including an ADA restroom and campsites), are available at this park. The park is located three miles north of Fort Bragg on Highway 1, near the town of Cleone.

Restaurants

Fort Bragg

Cafe One
753 N Main Street
Fort Bragg, CA
707-964-3309
This cafe has a few outdoor tables and well-behaved leashed dogs are allowed.

Home Style Cafe
790 S. Main Street
Fort Bragg, CA
707-964-6106
This cafe has two outdoor picnic tables and well-behaved leashed dogs are allowed.

Laurel Deli
401 N Main Street
Fort Bragg, CA
707-964-7812

Well-behaved leashed dogs are allowed at the outdoor seating area.

Piaci Pub and Pizzeria
120 W. Redwood Avenue
Fort Bragg, CA
707-961-1133
Alcohol drinks are not allowed outside but you are welcome to dine at the outdoor tables with your well-behaved leashed dog.

Fortuna Dog Travel Guide
Accommodations

Fortuna

Best Western Country Inn
2025 Riverwalk Drive
Fortuna, CA 95540
707-725-6822
There are no extra pet fees. Dogs are allowed in certain pet rooms. Large dogs are okay if they do not bark.

Super 8
1805 Alamar Way
Fortuna, CA 95540
707-725-2888
There is a $10 per day pet fee.

Attractions

Fortuna

Fortuna Depot Museum
3 Park St
Fortuna, CA 95540
707-725-7645
The museum contains the history of the Eel River Valley. Museum collections include memorabilia from railroad, farm and war eras. There is also a doll collection. Well-behaved, leashed dogs are allowed, just keep them right next to you.

Garberville Dog Travel Guide
Accommodations - RV Parks and
Campgrounds

Redway

Dean Creek Resort
4112 Redwood Drive
Redway, CA 95560
707-923-2555
Located on the Eel River, this campground is located just 3 miles from the Avenue of the Giants attraction. Riverfront sites are available for both RVs and tent camping. Many of the RV sites have full hookups with 50 amp service available. All sites have picnic tables and barbecue grills. Other amenities include a pool, spa, sauna, coin laundry, mini-mart, meeting room, game room, playground and restrooms. Pets are allowed but must be leashed at all times. The camp is open year round.

Parks

Garberville

Benbow Lake State Recreation Area
1600 Highway 101
Garberville, CA 95542
707-923-3238
Leashed dogs are allowed. The park consists of about 1,200 acres with campsites and a large day-use picnic area. Hiking, picnicking and camping are popular summer time activities, while salmon and steelhead fishing are popular in the winter.

Gasquet Dog Travel Guide
Accommodations - RV Parks and
Campgrounds

Gasquet

Panther Flat Campground
Highway 199
Gasquet, CA
707-442-1721
This campground is located in the Smith River National Recreation Area and is part of the Six Rivers National Forest. The campground offers 39 tent and RV sites. RVs up to 40 feet are allowed and there are no hookups. Amenities include flush restrooms, pay shower, potable water, picnic tables, grills, fishing and sites with river and scenic views. There is a $15 per night fee. Pets on leash are allowed and please clean up after them. The campsite is located 2.5 miles east of Gasquet on Highway 199.

Parks

Gasquet

Myrtle Creek Trail
Highway 199
Gasquet, CA
707-442-1721

This trail is located in the Smith River National Recreation Area and is part of the Six Rivers National Forest. The trail is an easy 1 mile interpretive hiking path. The elevations range from 250 to 500 feet. From this trail you can also access the Smith River. Pets on leash are allowed and please clean up after them. The trail is located 8 miles west of Gasquet at Milepost 7.0. Park on the south (river) side of the highway. Use caution when crossing Highway 199 to reach the trailhead.

Gualala Dog Travel Guide
Accommodations

Gualala

Mar Vista Cottages
35101 South Highway One
Gualala, CA 95445
just north of Anchor Bay
707-884-3522
They are very pet-friendly. Well-behaved pets are welcome and there are lots of paths (and a beach) where you can walk with them. The owners have remodeled their twelve cottages specifically with pets in mind, creating a pet and child friendly environment. They have hardwood floors, country furniture, slipcovers, and things that dogs need as well as humans, like beds, or a dog sheet if they sleep with you, a dog bath and towels. There is no additional pet charge and they have no designated smoking or non-smoking cottages, but they discourage guests from smoking inside the cottages.

Surf Motel
39170 S. Highway 1
Gualala, CA 95445
707-884-3571
There is a $10 per day pet charge.

Accommodations - RV Parks and Campgrounds

Gualala

Gualala Point Regional Park Campgrounds
42401 Coast Highway 1
Gualala, CA
707-785-2377
This dog-friendly park offers sandy beaches, hiking trails and 20 campsites. RVs are permitted and there is a dump station, but no hookups. Dogs are allowed but must be on a 6 foot or less leash and proof of a rabies vaccination is

required.

Accommodations - Vacation Home Rentals

Gualala

Ocean View Properties
P.O. Box 1285
Gualala, CA 95445
707-884-3538
Ocean View Properties offers vacation home rentals on The Sea Ranch and Mendocino Coast. Some of their vacation homes are pet-friendly. They offer a wide variety of special vacation home rentals, located on the oceanfront, oceanside and hillside at The Sea Ranch. Each of the rental homes has a fully equipped kitchen, a fireplace or wood stove, blankets, pillows, and telephones. Most have hot tubs, televisions, VCR's, radios, CD/cassette players, and washer/dryers. Guests provide kindling, bed linens, and towels. With advance notice, linens can be rented and maid service can be hired. Please call and ask them which rentals are dog-friendly.

Sea Ranch Vacation Homes
P.O. Box 246
Gualala, CA 95445
707-884-4235
Rent a vacation home for the weekend, week or longer along the coast or on a forested hillside. Some of their 50 homes allow well-behaved dogs.

Serenisea Vacation Homes
36100 Highway 1 S.
Gualala, CA 95445
707-884-3836
Serenisea maintains and manages a number of vacation homes and cottages in this community on the Mendocino coast. Some of them allow dogs of all sizes.

Beaches

Gualala

Gualala Point Regional Park Beach
42401 Coast Highway 1
Gualala, CA
707-565-2041
This county park offers sandy beaches, hiking trails, campsites, picnic tables and restrooms. Dogs are allowed on the beach, on the trails, and in the campground, but they must be on a 6 foot or less leash. People also need to clean up after

their pets. There is a $3 day use fee.

Parks

Gualala

Gualala Point Regional Park
42401 Coast Highway 1
Gualala, CA
707-785-2377
The 195 acre park has open meadows mixed with coastal forest. The park contains a campground, trail system, Visitors Center, coastal vistas, and sandy beaches. The park is located adjacent to the Gualala River, which offers limited seasonal fishing. Dogs are allowed but they must be on a leash no longer than 6 feet and have a rabies tag or proof of rabies vaccination. There is a $1 per day pet charge.

Hyampom Dog Travel Guide
Accommodations

Hyampom

Ziegler's Trails End
1 Main St, P.O. Box 150
Hyampom, CA 96046
530-628-4929
These cabins are on the South Fork of the Trinity River. This is in the middle of the dog-friendly Six Rivers National Forest.

Jenner Dog Travel Guide
Accommodations - RV Parks and Campgrounds

Jenner

Stillwater Cove Regional Park Campgrounds
22455 Highway 1
Jenner, CA
707-565-2041
This 210 acre park offers 17 campsites. RVs are permitted and there is a dump station, but no hookups. The park also features a small beach, great views of the Pacific Ocean, picnic tables and restrooms. Dogs are allowed but must be on a 6 foot or less leash and proof of a rabies vaccination is required. The park is located off Highway 1, about 16 miles north of Jenner.

Beaches

Jenner

Stillwater Cove Regional Park
22455 Highway 1
Jenner, CA
707-565-2041
This 210 acre park includes a small beach, campground, picnic tables, and restrooms. The park offers a great view of the Pacific Ocean from Stillwater Cove. Dogs are allowed on the beach, and in the campground, but they must be on a 6 foot or less leash. People also need to clean up after their pets. There is a $3 day use fee. The park is located off Highway 1, about 16 miles north of Jenner.

Klamath Dog Travel Guide
Attractions

Klamath

Trees of Mystery
15500 Highway 101 N.
Klamath, CA 95548
800-638-3389
Located in the center of the Redwood National and State Parks, this attraction allows leashed dogs everywhere people are welcome. They have an 8/10ths of a mile groomed interpretive trail through the awe-inspiring Redwoods of California. Also located here is a world-class Native American Museum and a gondola which takes you and your pooch on an aerial ride through the redwood forest canopy. They are located along Highway 101 in Klamath. Klamath is 36 miles south of the Oregon border and 260 miles north of Santa Rosa.

Leggett Dog Travel Guide
Accommodations - RV Parks and Campgrounds

Leggett

Standish-Hickey State Recreation Area Campground
69350 Highway 101
Leggett, CA 95455
707-925-6482
This campground offers tent sites. Dogs are not allowed on the park trails, but they are allowed on a few fire roads. The fire roads are not passable during the winter because of the river, but are fine during the summer months. The fire roads are located near the campground and near the main swimming hole. Dogs are also allowed in the water. Pets must be on leash and please clean up

after them. The park is located 1.5 miles north of Leggett on Highway 101.

Parks

Leggett

Standish-Hickey State Recreation Area
69350 Highway 101
Leggett, CA 95455
707-925-6482
While dogs are not allowed on the trails, they are allowed on a few fire roads. The fire roads are not passable during the winter because of the river, but are fine during the summer months. The fire roads are located near the campground and near the main swimming hole. Dogs are also allowed in the water. Pets must be on leash and please clean up after them. The park is located 1.5 miles north of Leggett on Highway 101.

Lindsay Dog Travel Guide
Accommodations

Lindsay

Super 8
390 Hwy 65
Lindsay, CA 93247
559-562-5188
There is a $10 per visit one time pet charge.

McKinleyville Dog Travel Guide
Beaches

McKinleyville

Clam Beach County Park
Highway 101
McKinleyville, CA
707-445-7651
This beach is popular for fishing, swimming, picnicking and beachcombing. Of course, there are also plenty of clams. Dogs on leash are allowed on the beach and at the campgrounds. There are no day use fees. The park is located off Highway 101, about eight miles north of Arcata.

Mendocino Dog Travel Guide
Accommodations

Mendocino

Inn at Schoolhouse Creek
7051 N. Highway 1

Mendocino, CA 95456
707-937-5525
With 8+ acres of ocean view gardens, meadows, forest, hiking trails and a secluded beach cove you and your pets will truly feel like you've gotten away from it all. To help your pets get in the vacation mood they will be welcomed with their own pet basket that includes a bed, towel, blanket and a treat. At the end of your day, relax in the ocean view hot tub.

MacCallum House
45020 Albion Street
Mendocino, CA 95460
707-937-0289
Pets of all varieties are welcomed at the MacCallum House Inn and Restaurant, located in the heart of the Mendocino Village. Pets are allowed in the cottages and Barn and are provided with blankets and sheets. The original Victorian mansion, built in 1882 by William H. Kelley, was a wedding gift to his daughter, Daisy MacCallum, and is a historic landmark. Rooms include a full breakfast and a complimentary wine hour is served in the Grey Whale Bar featuring wines from throughout the California wine country. Children are also welcomed.

McElroys Cottage Inn
Main and Evergreen Streets
Mendocino, CA
707-937-1734
All of the four rooms at this bed and breakfast inn have private baths and all rooms are non-smoking. There is a $15 per day pet charge. Dogs must be on leash and never left unattended in the room. Dogs are not allowed on the furniture or beds, so you might want to bring your own pet bedding.

Mendocino Seaside Cottages
10940 Lansing St
Mendocino, CA
707-485-0239
Accommodations have jacuzzi spas, wet bars,& fireplaces. It is located within easy walking distance of Mendocino.

Stanford Inn by the Sea
44850 Comptche-Ukiah Rd
Mendocino, CA 95460
707-937-5615
This is a very dog friendly inn. It is known both as the Stanford Inn by the Sea and Big River Lodge. In the room there are doggie dishes, pet sheets and upon arrival, a ribbon wrapped biscuit. For the humans, all rooms are non-smoking, have fireplaces, VCRs, refrigerators and CD

players/stereos. The only places dogs aren't allowed on this 10 acres are the lobby (they have resident cats), the restaurant and the pool area. Other than that, you and your pooch are more than welcome to stroll the 10 acre grounds which have several gardens as well as several llamas. Room rates are $245 and up. There is a $25 charge per stay, for the first pet. Additional pets are $12.50. If you are into adventure, walk over to the canoe rentals, take one of the canoes and spend an hour or all day going up the river with your pup (see Attractions).

Accommodations - Vacation Home Rentals

Mendocino

Coastal Getaways
10501 Ford Street POB1355
Mendocino, CA 95460
707-937-9200
Coastal Getaways has over 5 vacation homes that allow dogs. Most of the homes have ocean front views and one is located in the quaint village of Mendocino. The rates range from $140 to $250 and up per night. They also have weekly rates. For more information, please call 800-525-0049.

Sweetwater Spa & Inn
44840 Main Street
Mendocino, CA 95460
707-937-4076
Sweetwater Spa & Inn offers a unique variety of accommodations, including cabin and vacation home rentals. They give dog treats at check-in as well as sheets for the guests to cover furniture and towels for wet paws in the rainy season. Some of the rentals are located in the village of Mendocino. The other rentals are located around the Mendocino area. There is a two night minimum on weekends and three night minimum on most holidays. All units are non-smoking. Your well-behaved dog is welcome. Room rates start at

the low $100s and up. There is a $15 per day additional pet fee.

Whitegate Inn Village Retreat
P.O. Box 150, 499 Howard St.
Mendocino, CA 95460
707-937-4892
Pets are welcome in this Victorian house in the heart of Mendocino on the rugged Pacific coast. The Whitegate Inn Village Retreat includes the main house and cottage with 4 bedrooms and 3 baths. The house has ocean views, TV, VCR, fine linens, deck, BBQ, gas fireplace, hot tub, sauna, phone, washer and dryer. Stroll with your dog in beautiful Mendocino and nearby state parks.

Yorkville

Sheep Dung Estates
P.O. Box 49
Yorkville, CA 95494
off Highway 128
707-894-5322
This unique country hideaway has five private cottages on 320 acres in beautiful Anderson Valley. It is located about 1 1/2 hours from Mendocino and 2 hours north of San Francisco. The property has hiking trails and a swimming pond. The cottages are solar powered and eco-friendly. Each cottage is at the end of its own private driveway on l0 to 40 acres. This is such a popular spot for dogs and dog owners that the cottages usually book out well in advance. Dogs and children are welcome. There are no size restrictions for dogs, and the only requirement is that you place a sheet to cover the down comforter if your canine gets on the bed. Dogs are welcome off leash as long as they are under voice control.

Attractions

Mendocino

Catch a Canoe Rentals
44850 Comptche-Ukiah Rd
Mendocino, CA 95460
Highway 1
707-937-5615
This canoe rental shop is located on the grounds of the dog-friendly Stanford Inn by the Sea. Feel free to walk into the shop with your pooch. If you are staying at the inn, it's a five minute walk to the shop. If you are staying at another hotel, there is ample parking. If your pup is over 50 pounds., he or she is more than welcome, but the folks at the

shop will warn you that if your dog is a land-lover or decides to make a quick turn in the canoe, the whole party may become very wet. However, this dog-friendly rental shop has even modified a Mad River Winooski to create an incredibly stable canoe especially designed for dogs. Interior carpet, water bowl and a dog biscuit is included. The river you will be canoeing on is close to the ocean and it does contain a lot of salt water, so make sure you bring separate water for you and your dog. Check with the shop for water conditions, but in general this is a calm river - no white water rafting here.

Beaches

Mendocino

Big River Beach
N. Big River Road
Mendocino, CA 95460
Highway 1
707-937-5804
This small beach is located just south of downtown Mendocino. There are two ways to get there. One way is to head south of town on Hwy 1 and turn left on N. Big River Rd. The beach will be on the right. The second way is to take Hwy 1 and exit Main Street/Jackson heading towards the coastline. In about 1/4-1/2 mile there will be a Chevron Gas Station and a historic church on the left. Park and then walk behind the church to the trailhead. Follow the trail, bearing left when appropriate, and there will be a wooden staircase that goes down to Big River Beach. Dogs must be on leash.

Van Damme State Beach
Highway 1
Mendocino, CA 95460
Little River (city)

This small beach is located in the town of Little River which is approximately 2 miles south of Mendocino. It is part of Van Damme State Park which is located across Highway 1. Most California State Parks, including this one, do not allow dogs on the hiking trails. Fortunately this one allows dogs on the beach. There is no parking fee at the beach and dogs must be on leash.

Parks

Mendocino

Mendocino Headlands State Park
off Hesser Drive
Mendocino, CA 95460
Mendocino Peninsula

This trail (1-2 miles each way) is located next to the village of Mendocino and it follows the Mendocino peninsula and coastline on bluffs above the beach. The trail is part of the Mendocino Headlands State Park. To get there, take Hwy 1, exit Main Street/Jackson toward the coastline. When Main Street ends, turn right onto Hesser Drive. Go 4 blocks and turn left to continue on Hesser Drive. There are many trailheads or starting points along Hesser Drive, but in the summer, watch out for foxtails.

10483 Lansing Street
Mendocino, CA 95460
Albion Street
707-937-0836
This is a nice spot for breakfast if you want fresh pastries or bagels. They are also open for lunch. The bakery is located in the small village of Mendocino.

Restaurants

Mendocino

Lu's Kitchen
45013 Ukiah Street
Mendocino, CA
707-937-4939
Dogs are allowed at the outdoor tables.

Mendo Burgers
10483 Lansing Street
Mendocino, CA 95460
Albion Street
707-937-1111
Look carefully or you might miss it. This place is located behind the Mendocino Bakery and Cafe. This very dog-friendly place usually has a water bucket for dogs next to the front door. If they don't, ask them and they'll be happy to get your pooch some water.

Mendocino Bakery & Cafe

Mendocino Cafe
10451 Lansing Street
Mendocino, CA 95460
Albion Street
707-937-6141
Lunch and dinner are served at this cafe. The food is great, but if you go for dinner, come early as they may not serve outside when it gets dark and chilly. They do have food to go if you arrive too late.

Mendocino Cookie Co.
10450 Lansing Street
Mendocino, CA 95460
Albion Street
707-937-4843
This place has no outdoor seats, but it's worth noting because you can order cookies or coffee from the outside window. Not to mention the delicious cookies.

Tote Fete
10450 Lansing
Mendocino, CA
707-937-3383
Dogs are allowed at the outdoor tables.

Miranda Dog Travel Guide
Accommodations

Miranda

Miranda Gardens Resort
6766 Avenue of the Giants
Miranda, CA 95553
707-943-3011
The cottages are surrounded by flowering gardens and surrounded by ancient redwoods. From this resort, you can take day trips to the Avenue of the Giants or the Lost Coast. All cottages are non-smoking. Children are welcome and the resort has a children's play area. Pets are allowed in certain cabins and there is a $50 one time pet charge.

Orick Dog Travel Guide
Accommodations - RV Parks and Campgrounds

Orick

Elk Praire Campground
Newton B. Drury Scenic Parkway
Orick, CA
707-464-6101
This campground is located in Prairie Creek Redwoods State Park. While dogs are not allowed on any park trails, they are allowed at this campground. There are 75 RV or tent sites which are next to a prairie and old growth redwood forest. RVs must be less than 27 feet. There are no RV hookups. Camp amenities include restrooms, showers, fire pits, dump station and

bear-proof lockers. Located just north of the campground is Cal Barrel Road. Dogs can walk on or along this 3 mile gravel road. There are not too many cars that travel along this road. Pets must be leashed and attended at all times. Please clean up after your pet. The campsite is located on Newton B. Drury Scenic Parkway off Highway 101.

Freshwater Lagoon Spit Overnight Use Area
Highway 101
Orick, CA
707-464-6101
Dogs are allowed at this overnight use area and in the water. The overnight tent use is located south of the southern most vehicle access point. Amenities include picnic areas with grills, chemical toilets and fire pits. Vehicles are $10 per night and people are $3 per night. Fees are payable at the self-registration kiosks. Overnight stays are limited to 15 consecutive days. Pets must be leashed and attended at all times. Please clean up after your pet. This tent area is located 1 mile south of Orick on Highway 101.

Gold Bluffs Beach Campground
Davison Road
Orick, CA
707-464-6101
This campground is located in Prairie Creek Redwoods State Park. While dogs are not allowed on any park trails, they are allowed at this campground and the adjoining beach. There are 29 tent sites and 25 RV sites at the beach. RVs must be less than 24 feet long and 8 feet wide. There are no RV hookups. All sites are on a first-come, first-served basis. Camp amenities include restrooms, solar showers and fire pits. Pets must be leashed and attended at all times. Please clean up after your pets. The campground is located on Davison Road, off Highway 101.

Beaches

Orick

Gold Bluffs Beach
Davison Road
Orick, CA
707-464-6101
Dogs are allowed on this beach, but not on any trails within this park. Picnic tables and campgrounds are available at the beach. Pets are also allowed at road accessible picnic areas and campgrounds. Dogs must be on a 6 foot or less leash and people need to pick up after their pets. The beach is located off Highway 101. Take

Highway 101 heading north. Pass Orick and drive about 3-4 miles, then exit Davison Rd. Head towards the coast on an unpaved road (trailers are not allowed on the unpaved road).

Phillipsville Dog Travel Guide
Attractions

Phillipsville

Avenue of the Giants
Highway 101
Phillipsville, CA
707-722-4291
This 33 mile drive offers spectacular views of redwoods and some very unique redwood trees, including some of the biggest trees in the world. You and your pooch might be able to drive your car through a redwood tree or two (depending on the size of your car). There is a fee to drive through some of the trees. The auto tour can be taken from the northbound or southbound direction. Allow about 1-2 hours, depending on stops and any traffic. From the north start at the Pepperwood/Jordan Creek exit off Highway 101 and from the south, start at the Phillipsville exit off Highway 101. The auto tour map can be picked up at either entrance. Dogs are not allowed on the trails in the state park, but they are allowed on fire roads and access roads in the Humboldt Redwoods State Park. One of the access points to the fire roads is at Albee Creek Campground.

Salmon Creek Dog Travel Guide
Beaches

Salmon Creek

Sonoma Coast State Beach
Highway 1
Salmon Creek, CA
707-875-3483
Dogs on leash are allowed at some of the beaches in this state park. Dogs are allowed at Shell Beach, Portuguese Beach and Schoolhouse Beach. They are not allowed at Goat Rock or Salmon Creek Beach due to the protected seals and snowy plovers. Please clean up after your pets. While dogs are allowed on some of the beaches and campgrounds, they are not allowed on any hiking trails at this park.

Trinidad Dog Travel Guide
Beaches

Trinidad

Trinidad State Beach
Highway 101
Trinidad, CA
707-677-3570
Dogs are unofficially allowed at College Cove beach, as long as they are leashed and under control. The residents in this area are trying keep this beach dog-friendly, but the rules can change at any time. Please call ahead to verify.

Ukiah Dog Travel Guide
Accommodations

Ukiah

Days Inn
950 North State St
Ukiah, CA 95482
707-462-7584
There is a $5 per day pet fee.

Motel 6
1208 S State Street
Ukiah, CA 95482
707-468-5404
There are no additional pet fees.

Parks

Ukiah

Lake Mendocino Recreation Area

Ukiah, CA
707-462-7581
Dogs on leash are allowed on many of the trails and in the lake.

Weott Dog Travel Guide
Accommodations - RV Parks and Campgrounds

Weott

Humboldt Redwoods State Park Campgrounds
Avenue of the Giants
Weott, CA
707-946-2409
There are several campgrounds located in this park including Albee Creek, Burlington and Hidden Springs Campgrounds. Tent and RV sites are available. There are no hookups. Camp amenities include picnic tables, fire rings,

showers and flush toilets. While dogs are not allowed on the trails, they are allowed in the campgrounds and on miles of fire roads and access roads. These paths are used mainly for mountain biking, but dogs are allowed too. There are both steep and gently sloping fire roads. Some of the fire roads are located next to the Albee Creek Campground. Pets on leash are allowed and please clean up after them. The park is located along the Avenue of the Giants, about 45 miles south of Eureka and 20 miles north of Garberville.

Parks

Weott

Humboldt Redwoods State Park
Avenue of the Giants
Weott, CA
707-946-2409
This park is located along the scenic Avenue of the Giants. While dogs are not allowed on the trails, they are allowed in the campgrounds and on miles of fire roads and access roads. These paths are used mainly for mountain biking, but dogs are allowed too. There are both steep and gently sloping fire roads. Some of the fire roads are located next to the Albee Creek Campground. Pets on leash are allowed and please clean up after them. The park is located along the Avenue of the Giants, about 45 miles south of Eureka and 20 miles north of Garberville.

Westport Dog Travel Guide
Accommodations

Westport

Howard Creek Ranch Inn B&B
40501 N. Highway 1
Westport, CA 95488
(north of Mendocino)
707-964-6725
Howard Creek Ranch is a historic, 40 acre ocean front farm located about 5-6 hours north of San Francisco. Accommodations include cabins, suites and rooms. It is bordered by miles of beach and mountains. They offer award winning gardens, fireplaces or wood stoves, farm animals, a hot tub, and a sauna. Dog-friendly beaches nearby include Westport Union Landing State Beach in Westport, MacKerricher State Park 3-4 miles north of Fort Bragg and the 60 mile Sinkyone Wilderness Area (Lost Coast). Outdoor restaurants nearby are Jenny's Giant Burgers and

Sea Pal (in Fort Bragg). Room rates are $80 and up (includes a full hearty ranch breakfast). There is a $10 plus tax per day pet charge. Certain dog rules apply: don't leave your dog alone in the room, dogs must be supervised and attended at all times, bring towels to clean up your pooch if he/she gets dirty from outside, clean up after your dog, and if your dog will be on the bed, please use a sheet to cover the quilt (sheets can be provided). The inn is located 3 miles north of Westport.

Picture is Courtesy of Howard Creek Ranch

Beaches

Westport

Westport-Union Landing State Beach
Highway 1
Westport, CA
707-937-5804
This park offers about 2 miles of sandy beach. Dogs must be on a 6 foot or less leash at all times and people need to clean up after their pets. Picnic tables, restrooms (including an ADA restroom) and campsites are available at this park. Dogs are also allowed at the campsites, but not on any park trails. The park is located off Highway 1, about 2 miles north of Westport or 19 miles north of Fort Bragg.

Whitethorn Dog Travel Guide
Accommodations - RV Parks and Campgrounds

Whitethorn

Nadelos Campground
Chemise Mountain Road
Whitethorn, CA
707-825-2300
This campground offers 8 walk-in tent sites ranging from 50 to 300 feet from the parking lot. The sites are shaded by Douglas fir trees and are

set along a small mountain stream. Campground amenities include picnic tables, vault toilets, drinking water and fire rings. Day use parking for the dog-friendly Chemise Mountain Trail is located at this campground. Sites are $8 per day with a maximum of 14 days per stay. Pets are allowed but must be leashed in the campground. To get there, take Highway 101 to Redway. Go west on Briceland/Shelter Cove Road for 22 miles and then head south on Chemise Mountain Road for 1.6 miles. Travel time from Highway 101 is about 55 minutes.

Wailaki Campground
Chemise Mountain Road
Whitethorn, CA
707-825-2300
This campground offers 13 tent and trailer sites along a small mountain stream amidst large Douglas fir frees. Day use parking for the dog-friendly Chemise Mountain Trail is located at this campground. Camp amenities include picnic tables, grills, water and restrooms. There are no RV hookups. Sites are $8 per day with a maximum of 14 days per stay. Pets are allowed but must be leashed in the campground. To get there, take Highway 101 to Redway. Go west on Briceland/Shelter Cove Road for 22 miles and then head south on Chemise Mountain Road for 1.7 miles. Travel time from Highway 101 is about 55 minutes.

Parks

Whitethorn

Chemise Mountain Trail
Chemise Mountain Road
Whitethorn, CA
707-825-2300
This trail is about 1.5 miles long and involves an 800 foot climb. At the top of the trail you will see vistas of the coastline and inland mountain ranges. This trail is popular with hikers and mountain bikers. Pets are required to be leashed in the campgrounds. On the trails there is no leash requirement but your dog needs to be under direct voice control. There is a $1 day use fee. To get there, take Highway 101 to Redway. Go west on Briceland/Shelter Cove Road for 22 miles and then head south on Chemise Mountain Road for just over 1.5 miles. Trailhead parking is available at the Wailaki or Nadelos Campgrounds. Travel time from Highway 101 is about 55 minutes.

Chapter 2

California Dog-Friendly Travel Guide
Shasta – Cascade Region

Alturas Dog Travel Guide
Accommodations

Alturas

Best Western Trailside Inn
343 North Main Street
Alturas, CA 96101
530-233-4111
There is a $5 per day pet charge.

Hacienda Motel
201 E 12th St
Alturas, CA
530-233-3459
There are no additional pet fees.

Parks

Alturas

Modoc National Forest

Alturas, CA
530-233-5811
Dogs are allowed on leash. This forest offers lake basins, mountains and a high plateau. Within this forest, you can find Fort Bidwell in Surprise Valley which was the site of a cavalry unit established in the1860's to protect settlers against Indian attack. In the valley are abandoned homesteads, stone circles, rock piles, and petroglyphs (rock art). Also be sure to try one of the hiking trails, like the Blue Lake Trail. This trail is 1.5 miles long. It begins at the Blue Lake Campground and continues around the west side of the lake to the boat ramp. At least 90 percent of the trail is shaded by white fir and ponderosa pine trees. Squirrels, ducks, geese, loons and hawks are frequently seen by hikers while walking on the trail. Blue Lake, at an elevation of about 6,000 feet, is a beautiful deep-blue 160 acre lake and is located approximately 15 miles east of Likely and 35 miles south of Alturas in the South Warner Mountains. Information about more trails in this forest can be found at the Ranger's Office located at 800 West 12th Street in Alturas (Monday through Friday).

Anderson Dog Travel Guide
Accommodations

Anderson

AmeriHost Inn
2040 Factory Outlets Dr
Anderson, CA 96007
530-365-6100
There are no additional pet fees.

Best Western Knight's Inn
2688 Gateway Drive
Anderson, CA 96007
530-365-2753
Well-trained, leashed dogs are allowed. There is no extra pet charge.

Belden Dog Travel Guide
Parks

Belden

Yellow Creek Trail
Highway 70
Belden, CA
530-283-0555
This trail is located in the Plumas National Forest and is an easy one way 1.4 mile trail. This day hike ends in a box canyon. Dogs on leash or off-leash but under direct voice control are allowed. Please clean up after your pets. The trailhead is location about 25 miles west of Quincy on Highway 70. It is to the right of the Ely Stamp Mill rest area, across from Belden.

Blairsden Dog Travel Guide
Parks

Blairsden

Plumas-Eureka State Park
Johnsonville Road
Blairsden, CA
530-836-2380
Dogs are allowed on one trail which is called the Grass Lake Trail. This 3.8 mile trail climbs steadily to the Pacific Crest Trail passing several lakes. Pets must be on leash and please clean up after them. The trailhead is at the Jamison Mine. To get there take Johnsonville Road (County Road A14) off Highway 89 in Graeagle. Go about 4.5 miles to the unimproved Jamison Mine Road. There should be a sign on the left for the Jamison Mine/Grass Lake Trail. Continue another 1.5 miles to the parking area.

Bucks Lake Dog Travel Guide
Accommodations - RV Parks and Campgrounds

Bucks Lake

Silver Lake Campground
Forest Road 24N29X
Bucks Lake, CA
530-283-0555
This campground is located in the Plumas National Forest and offers 8 campsites. They are on a first-come, first-served basis. The trailhead for the Gold Lake Trail is located at this campground. In the campground dogs must be on leash. On the trails, dogs on leash or off-leash but under direct voice control are allowed. To get there from Quincy, go west 9.2 miles on Bucks Lake Road. Turn right on a gravel road, 24N29X (Silver Lake sign). Go 6.4 miles to the campground.

Parks

Bucks Lake

Gold Lake Trail
Forest Road 24N29X
Bucks Lake, CA
530-283-0555
This trail is located in the Plumas National Forest and is an easy one way 1.5 mile trail. This trail provides access to the Bucks Lake Wilderness and the Pacific Crest Trail. At Bucks Lake swimming and fishing are popular activities. Dogs on leash or off-leash but under direct voice control are allowed. Dogs are allowed on the trails and in the water. Please clean up after your pets. To get there from Quincy, go west 9.2 miles on Bucks Lake Road. Turn right on a gravel road, 24N29X (Silver Lake sign). Go 6.4 miles to the lake and the Silver Lake Campground. The trail begins at the campground.

Burney Dog Travel Guide
Accommodations

Burney

Shasta Pines Motel
37386 Main Street
Burney, CA
530-335-2201
Dogs of all sizes are allowed. There are no additional pet fees.

Cedarville Dog Travel Guide
Accommodations

Cedarville

Sunrise Motel & RV Park
54889 Highway 200 West
Cedarville, CA 96104
530-279-2161
Located at the base of the dog-friendly Modoc National Forest, this motel offers all non-smoking rooms. There are no pet fees. If you are out during the day and cannot bring your pooch with you, they do have an outdoor kennel available for an extra $5.

Attractions

Cedarville

Surprise Valley Back Country Byway
Highway 299
Cedarville, CA
530-279-6101
If you are up for some adventure, try this 93 mile driving tour which traverses by many points of interest in the Great Basin Desert. The loop begins and ends in Cedarville and takes a minimum of three hours and longer if you make any stops. The Bureau of Land Management offers a 32 page self-guided Byway Tour Guide which tells about the historic and prehistoric stories of Surprise Valley. It includes details about fossils and wildlife. The byway is paved in California and is a gravel road in Nevada which can be passable by all vehicles when the road is dry. Dogs on leash are allowed. Please clean up after your dog. Contact the following BLM office for a map and more details: BLM, Surprise Field Office, 602 Cressler Street, Cedarville, CA 96104, 530-279-6101. The office is open Monday through Friday.

Chico Dog Travel Guide
Accommodations

Chico

Esplanade Bed & Breakfast
620 The Esplanade
Chico, CA 95926
530-345-8084
Built in 1915, this Craftsman Bungalow has been completely restored. This B&B is located just steps from downtown Chico and Chico State University. Each room has a private bathroom and cable television. Enjoy their hearty breakfast served in the dining room or on the patio. Well-

behaved dogs are allowed with a $20 refundable deposit. Children are also allowed.

Holiday Inn
685 Manzanita Ct
Chico, CA 95926
530-345-2491
There is a $25 one time pet fee per visit.

Motel 6
665 Manzanita Ct
Chico, CA 95926
530-345-5500
One pet per room is permitted.

Music Express Inn Bed and Breakfast
1091 El Monte Avenue
Chico, CA 95928
530-891-9833
This B&B is located near the dog-friendly Bidwell Park, the third largest municipal park in the United States. The B&B offers nine rooms all with private baths, refrigerators and microwaves. All rooms are non-smoking. A well-behaved dog is allowed, but must be leashed when outside your room. Pets must be attended at all times. There are no pet fees. Children are also allowed.

Super 8
655 Manzanita Ct
Chico, CA 95926
530-345-2533
There is a $4 per day additional pet fee.

Parks

Chico

Bidwell Park
Highway 99
Chico, CA
530-895-4972
This park exceeds 3,600 acres, making it the third largest municipal park in the United States. The park is comprised of three major sections: Lower Park, Middle Park and Upper Park. Lower Park has children's playgrounds, natural swimming areas, and vehicle-free roads for runners, cyclists, rollerbladers and walkers. Middle Park features ball-playing fields, picnic areas, the "World of Trees" walk, which is accessible to the physically challenged, and the park's environmental and informational headquarters. Upper Park remains relatively untouched with majestic canyons overlooking Big Chico Creek, which contains some of the most spectacular swimming areas in Northern California. Dogs on leash are allowed.

Please clean up after them.

Restaurants

Chico

Baja Fresh Mexican Grill
2072 E. 20th St.
Chico, CA
530-896-1077
This Mexican restaurant is open for lunch and dinner. They use fresh ingredients and making their salsa and beans daily. Some of the items on their menu include Enchiladas, Burritos, Tacos Salads, Quesadillas, Nachos, Chicken, Steak and more. Well-behaved leashed dogs are allowed at the outdoor tables.

Beachfront Deli
160 Convair Avenue
Chico, CA
530-898-1020
This deli welcomes leashed dogs to their outdoor tables and they even have doggie treats.

Bean Scene Coffee House
1387 E 8th Street
Chico, CA
530-898-9474
Well-behaved leashed dogs are allowed at the outdoor seating area.

Bellachinos
800 Bruce Road
Chico, CA
530-892-2244
This restaurant welcomes dogs on their outdoor patio which has music and a fountain. Dogs should be leashed.

Bombers Baja Grill
973 East Avenue
Chico, CA
530-343-2247
Well-behaved leashed dogs are allowed at the outdoor seating area.

Cafe Flo
365 E 6th Street
Chico, CA
530-892-0356
Well-behaved leashed dogs are allowed at the outdoor seating area.

Cafe Max
101 Salem Street
Chico, CA

530-345-6655
Leashed dogs are allowed at the outdoor seating in the front but not in the back.

Cal Java
2485 Notre Dame Blvd.
Chico, CA
530-893-2662
Leashed dogs are welcome at their outdoor tables.

California Pasta Production
118 W East Ave
Chico, CA
530-343-6999
Well-behaved leashed dogs are allowed at their perimeter tables.

Casa Bonita
305 Nord Avenue
Chico, CA
530-891-6097
Well-behaved leashed dogs are allowed at the outdoor seating area.

Celestino's Pasta and Pizza
1354 East Ave
Chico, CA
530-345-7700
Well-behaved leashed dogs are allowed at the outdoor seating area.

Dog House
1008 W Sacramento Avenue
Chico, CA
530-894-3641
Well-behaved leashed dogs are allowed at the outdoor seating area.

El Cantarito
244 Walnut Street
Chico, CA
530-891-3591
Well-behaved leashed dogs are allowed at the outdoor seating area.

First Street Deli
215 W First Street
Chico, CA
530-895-8462
Well-behaved leashed dogs are allowed at the outdoor seating area.

French Gourmet Bakery & Deli
1910 Esplanade
Chico, CA
530-345-2257
Well-behaved leashed dogs are allowed at the

outdoor seating area.

La Cantera
3524 State Highway 32
Chico, CA
530-345-1048
Well-behaved leashed dogs are allowed at the outdoor seating area.

Leftcoast Pizza Co
800 Bruce Road
Chico, CA
530-892-9000
Well-behaved leashed dogs are allowed at the outdoor seating area.

Moxie's Cafe & Gallery
128 Broadway Street
Chico, CA
530-345-0601
Well-behaved leashed dogs are allowed at the outdoor seating area.

Nagels Bagels
1722 Mangrove Avenue
Chico, CA
530-345-3900
Well-behaved leashed dogs are allowed at the outdoor seating area.

S & S Organic Produce and Natural Foods
1924 Mangrove Avenue
Chico, CA
530-343-4930
This natural food store has an onsite deli. Well-behaved leashed dog are allowed at the outdoor tables.

Spiteri's Delicatessen
971 East Avenue
Chico, CA
530-891-4797
Well-behaved leashed dogs are allowed at the outdoor seating area.

Yummy's Homemade Ice Cream
2500 Floral Avenue
Chico, CA
530-893-2663
Well-behaved leashed dogs are allowed at the outdoor seating area.

Corning Dog Travel Guide
Accommodations

Corning

Best Western Inn-Corning
2165 Solano Street
Corning, CA 96021
530-824-2468
Amenities include a free continental breakfast and an outdoor swimming pool. There is a $5 per day pet charge.

Shilo Inn Suites
3350 Sunrise Way
Corning, CA 96021
530-824-2940
Your pet is welcome. The hotel has complimentary continental breakfast, Mini-suites with microwave, refrigerator & wet bar, in-room iron, ironing board, coffee maker & hair dryer, guest laundromat, seasonal outdoor pool & spa, sauna, steam room and a fitness center. Conveniently located off I-5 and Highway 99 at the South Avenue Exit, 18 miles from Red Bluff, 47 miles from Redding, and 30 miles from Chico.

Happy Camp Dog Travel Guide
Accommodations - RV Parks and Campgrounds

Happy Camp

Norcross Campground
Elk Creek Road
Happy Camp, CA
530-493-1777
This 6 site campground is located in the Klamath National Forest at an elevation of 2,400 feet. Amenities include vault toilets. The campground is open from May to October. This campground serves as a staging area for various trails that provide access into the Marble Mountain Wilderness. The trails are used by hikers and horseback riders. Dogs must be leashed in the campground. On trails, pets must be either leashed or off-leash but under direct voice control. Please clean up after your pets. The campsite is located 16 miles south of Happy Camp on Elk Creek Road.

La Porte Dog Travel Guide
Accommodations - RV Parks and Campgrounds

La Porte

Little Beaver Campground
off La Porte Road
La Porte, CA
530-534-6500

This campground is located at the Little Grass Valley Reservoir Recreation Area in the Plumas National Forest. There are 120 campsites, some of which offer prime lakeside sites. Amenities include water, flush toilets, trailer space and an RV dump station. Dogs are allowed in the campgrounds, on trails and in the water. In the campground dogs must be on leash. On the trails, dogs on leash or off-leash but under direct voice control are allowed. Reservations for the campsites can be made by calling 1-877-444-6777. The campground is located 3 miles north of La Porte off La Porte Road.

Lake Shasta Dog Travel Guide
Accommodations - RV Parks and Campgrounds

Shasta Lake

Hirz Bay Campground
Gilman Road
Shasta Lake, CA
530-275-1587
This campground is located in the Shasta-Trinity National Forest at an elevation of 1,100 feet. The campground offers 37 tent and RV campsites. RVs up to 30 feet are allowed and there are no hookups. Amenities include drinking water, accessible restrooms, flush toilets and boat ramp. Fishing, swimming and boating are popular activities at the campground. The camp is open year round. To make a reservations, call 1-877-444-6777. Dogs are allowed in the lake, but not at the designated swimming beaches. Pets must be leashed and please clean up after them. The campground is located 10 miles from Interstate 5 on Gilman Road.

Parks

Shasta Lake

Hirz Bay Trail
Gilman Road
Shasta Lake, CA
530-275-1587
This 1.6 mile easy rated trail is located in the Shasta-Trinity National Forest. The trail follows the shoreline and crosses several cool, shady creeks. It also provides scenic vistas of the lake. The trailhead is located at Hirz Bay Campground which is 10 miles from Interstate 5 on Gilman Road. Dogs are allowed in the lake, but not at the designated swimming beaches. Pets must be leashed and please clean up after them.

Lakehead Dog Travel Guide
Accommodations

Lakehead

Sugarloaf Cottages Resort
19667 Lakeshore Drive
Lakehead, CA 96051
800-953-4432
These cottages are located near the shore of
Lake Shasta and have air conditioning, heating,
bathrooms, linens and complete kitchens, but no
phones, televisions or maid service. They charge
a $5 per night pet fee and allow only one pet per
unit.

Tsasdi Resort Cabins
19990 Lakeshore Dr.
Lakehead, CA 96051
530-238-2575
All cabins have private baths, linens, cable TV, air
conditioning, heating, outdoor barbecue and
private decks, most of which overlook Shasta
Lake. There is a $10 per day pet fee. In order for
them to continuing being pet-friendly, they ask
that all pets be kept on a leash and not be left
unattended in the cabins or on the decks. Please
clean up after your pets.

Accommodations - RV Parks and Campgrounds

Lakehead

Lakeshore Inn & RV
20483 Lakeshore Drive
Lakehead, CA 96051
530-238-2003
This campground has tall pine and oak trees, and
overlooks Shasta Lake. All of the RV and tent
sites have electricity and water. Septic and cable
TV are available at some of the sites. Amenities
include a large swimming pool, mini store, gift
shop, playground, picnic area, video game room,
showers, laundromat, dump station and handicap
bathrooms. Well-behaved dogs are welcome.
Pets should be quiet and please clean up after
them. There is a $1 per day pet fee.

Shasta Lake RV Resort and Campground
20433 Lakeshore Drive
Lakehead, CA 96051
530-238-2370
This RV resort and campground is located on
Lake Shasta. The campground is on Shasta-
Trinity National Forest land. RV and tent sites are
available. RVs up to 60 feet are allowed.

Amenities include hot showers, swimming pool,
private boat dock, playground and more. Well-
behaved leashed dogs are allowed. Please clean
up after your pets.

Lassen National Park Dog Travel Guide
Accommodations

Fall River Mills

Lava Creek Lodge
1 Island Rd
Fall River Mills, CA
530-336-6288
The lodge is located on 60 wooded acres
interspersed with recent lava flows along the
banks of Eastman Lake (Little Tule River). They
offer eight rooms attached to the main lodge and
seven cabins, all with private, full bathrooms. This
lodge offers a full service restaurant including the
option of ordering a box lunch to enjoy on a trail
or riverside. There is a $10 per day pet charge
and dogs must be leashed.

Mill Creek

Child's Meadow Resort
41500 Highway 36E
Mill Creek, CA 96061
530-595-3383
Dogs are allowed in this all season resort.
Located between the towns of Susanville and
Red Bluff, this quiet resort is on 18 acres of
picturesque meadows and streams at the end of
the Shasta/Cascade Mountain Range. The resort
is just 9 miles from the southwest entrance to
Lassen Volcanic National Park. RV hookups are
available at the resort. There is no pet charge.

Susanville

Budget Host Frontier Inn
2685 Main St
Susanville, CA
530-257-4141
There are no additional pet fees.

River Inn
1710 Main St
Susanville, CA
530-257-6051
There is an $11 per day additional pet fee. One
large dog per room is allowed.

Accommodations - RV Parks and Campgrounds

Hat Creek

Hat Creek Campground
Highway 89
Hat Creek, CA
530-336-5521
This campground is located in the Lassen National Forest at an elevation of 4,300 feet. The camp offers 75 campsites. Camp amenities include water, fire rings, picnic tables and restrooms. Most sites are available on a first-come, first-served basis. Some sites can be reserved. Call 1-877-444-6777 to make a reservation. The camp is open from late April to October. Dogs on leash are allowed at the campground and on trails. Please clean up after your dog. The camp is located in Hat Creek on Highway 89.

Mineral

Lassen Volcanic National Park Campgrounds
PO Box 100
Mineral, CA 96063
530-595-4444
This park offers many campgrounds, with the largest campground having 179 sites. Tent and RV sites are available and trailers up to 35 feet are permitted. There are no hookups. All sites are on a first-come, first-served basis. Pets must be leashed and attended at all times. Please clean up after your pet. Dogs are not allowed on any trails or hikes in this park, but see our Lassen National Forest listing in Susanville for nearby dog-friendly hiking, sightseeing and additional camping.

Old Station

Cave Campground
Highway 89
Old Station, CA
530-336-5521
This campground is located in the Lassen National Forest near the Subway Cave where you and your pooch can explore an underground lava tube. The camp is at an elevation of 4,300 feet and offers 46 campsites. Camp amenities include water, fire rings, picnic tables and restrooms. Most sites are available on a first-served basis. Some sites can be reserved. Call 1-877-444-6777 to make a reservation. The camp is open from April to October. Dogs on leash are allowed at the campground and on trails. Please

clean up after your dog. The camp is located near the intersection of Highways 44 and 89.

Shingletown

Mt. Lassen/Shingletown
7749 KOA Road
Shingletown, CA 96088
530-474-3133
Located at an elevation of 3,900 feet, this twelve acre campground offers both tent and RV sites in the pines. Maximum length for pull through sites is 60 feet. Sites have 30 amp service available. Other amenities include LP gas, free modem dataport, snack bar, swimming pool during the summer and a deli. Well-behaved leashed dogs of all sizes are allowed. People need to clean up after their pets. The campgrounds are open from seasonally from March 1 through November 30.

Parks

Mineral

Lassen Volcanic National Park
PO Box 100
Mineral, CA 96063
530-595-4444
This national park does not really have much to see or do if you bring your pooch, except for staying overnight at the campgrounds. However, the dog-friendly Lassen National Forest surrounds the national park. At the national forest you will be able to find dog-friendly hiking, sightseeing and camping. See our Lassen National Forest listing in Susanville for more details. Pets must be leashed and attended at all times. Please clean up after your pet.

Susanville

Bizz Johnson Trail
Richmond Road
Susanville, CA
530-257-0456
This 25 mile trail follows the old Fernley and Lassen Branch Line of the Southern Pacific Railroad. It begins in Susanville at 4,200 feet and climbs 1,300 feet to a high point of 5,500 feet. Following the Susan River, the trail crosses over the river many times and passes through a former railroad tunnel. During the winter the trail's upper segment, located west of Highway 36, is used for cross-country skiing. Dogs on leash are allowed. Please clean up after your dog. To check on current trail conditions, call the Eagle Lake BLM

Field Office at 530-257-0456. To get there from Alturas, take Highway 36 to Susanville. Follow Main Street to the stop light at the bottom of the hill by historic Uptown Susanville. Turn left on Weatherlow Street which becomes Richmond Road. Follow Richmond Road .5 miles across Susan River to Susanville Railroad Depot Trailhead and Visitor Center.

Lassen National Forest
Highways 44 and 89
Susanville, CA
530-257-4188
Within this forest you can explore a lava tube, watch prong-horn antelope, drive four-wheel trails into high granite country or discover spring wildflowers on foot. Dogs are allowed on leash. If you want to check out a lava tube take a self-guided tour of the Subway Cave. Be sure to bring a flashlight, as there are no other sources of light underground. Subway Cave is located near the town of Old Station, 1/4 mile north of the junction of Highway 44 & 89 across from Cave Campground. The temperature inside the cave remains a cool 46 degrees F. year around. The cave is open late May through October and closed during the winter months. Or try a hike instead. Try the Spattercone Trail which explores the volcanic landscape and how life adapts to it. Three of the four kinds of volcanoes in the world can be seen along the Spattercone Trail. The trailhead and parking area are located at the Sanitary Dump Station across the highway form Hat Creek Campground on Highway 89 in Old Station. The trail has a round-trip distance of 1.5 miles. This trail is not shaded, so during the summer, try an early morning or late afternoon walk. For information about other miles of trails throughout this beautiful forest, stop by any National Forest Offices in Susanville including the Eagle Lake Ranger District Office located at 477-050 Eagle Lake Road in Susanville.

Lewiston Dog Travel Guide
Accommodations

Lewiston

Lewiston Valley RV Park
4789 Trinity Dam Blvd.
Lewiston, CA
530-778-3942
This RV park is on 8 acres and offers 7 pull through sites and 2 back-in sites. The sites have 50 amp service. Amenities include a seasonal heated pool. Within walking distance is a family style restaurant, gas station and mini-mart. Well-

behaved leashed dogs are allowed. There is no pet fee.

Accommodations - RV Parks and Campgrounds

Lewiston

Lakeview Terrace Resort
Lewiston, CA
530-778-3803
This resort overlooks Lewiston Lake and features an RV park and cabin rentals. RV spaces feature pull through sites, tables and barbecues. Most of the pull through sites offer a lake view. Other amenities include a laundry facility, restrooms and showers. Well-behaved quiet leashed dogs are welcome, up to two pets per cabin or RV. Pets are not allowed in the swimming pool area and cannot not be left alone at any time, either in your RV or at the cabins. Please clean up after your pet. There is no pet fee if you stay in an RV space, but there is a $10 per day fee for pets in the cabins.

Attractions

Lewiston

Trinity Alps Marina
Fairview Marina Rd.
Lewiston, CA 96052-0670
530-286-2282
Rent a houseboat on Lake Trinity with your well-behaved dog. There is a $75 one time pet fee.

Likely Dog Travel Guide
Accommodations - RV Parks and Campgrounds

Likely

Blue Lake Campground
Forest Service Road 64
Likely, CA
530-233-5811
This campground is located along Blue Lake at 6,000 foot elevation in the Modoc National Forest. There are 48 RV and tent sites, several of which are located directly on the lake. RVs up to 32 feet are allowed and there are no hookups. Amenities include picnic tables, fire pits, vault toilets and piped water. A boat ramp is located near the campground. Rowboats, canoes and low powered boats are allowed on the lake. The 1.5 mile Blue

Lake National Recreation Trail begins at this campsite. Dogs on leash are allowed at the campgrounds, on trails and in the water. Please clean up after your pets. The campground is usually open from June to October, weather permitting. There is a $7 per vehicle fee. The campground is located is 16 miles from the small town of Likely. From Highway 395 go east on Forest Service Road 64. At about 10 miles you will come to a road junction. Stay on Forest Service Road 64 for the remaining 6 miles.

Mill Creek Falls Campground
Mill Creek Rd.
Likely, CA
530-233-5811
This campground is located in the Modoc National Forest at an elevation of 5,700 feet. There are 19 RV and tent sites. There are no hookups. Amenities include picnic tables, fire pits, vault toilets and drinking water. The Clear Lake Trail begins here and provides access into the South Warner Wilderness. Dogs on leash are allowed at the campgrounds, on trails and in the water. Please clean up after your pets. The campground is usually open from June to October, weather permitting. There is a $6 per night fee. To get there from the town of Likely, go 9 miles east on Co. Rd. #64. Then go northeast on West Warner Road for 2.5 miles. Go east on Mill Creek access road for 2 more miles.

Parks

Likely

Blue Lake National Recreation Trail
Forest Service Road 64
Likely, CA
530-233-5811
This 1.5 mile one way trail is located at Blue Lake, in the Modoc National Forest, at an elevation of 6,000 feet. At least 90 percent of the trail is shaded by white fir and massive ponderosa pine trees. The trailhead begins at the Blue Lake Campground and ends at the boat ramp. Dogs on leash are allowed at the campgrounds, on the trail and in the water. Please clean up after your pets. The trail is located is 16 miles from the small town of Likely. From Highway 395 go east on Forest Service Road 64. At about 10 miles you will come to a road junction. Stay on Forest Service Road 64 for the remaining 6 miles.

Clear Lake Trail
Mill Creek Rd.
Likely, CA

530-233-5811
This trail is located in the Modoc National Forest at an elevation of 5,700 feet. At .5 miles into the trail, you will reach Mills Creek Falls. Beyond that the trail serves as a major entry way to the trails of the South Warner Wilderness. Dogs on leash are allowed on the trail and in the water. Please clean up after your pets. To get there from the town of Likely, go 9 miles east on Co. Rd. #64. Then go northeast on West Warner Road for 2.5 miles. Go east on Mill Creek access road for 2 more miles. The trailhead is located in the Mill Creek Falls Campground.

Mad River Dog Travel Guide
Parks

Mad River

Ruth Lake Recreation Area
Lower Mad River Rd, south of Hwy 36
Mad River, CA
800-500-0285
Dogs on leash are allowed on the trails and in the lake. RV and camp sites are available with reservations.

Modoc Dog Travel Guide
Parks

Modoc

Modoc National Forest
800 West 12th Street
Modoc, CA 96101
530-233-5811
This national forest covers over 1.9 million acres of land which ranges in elevation from 4,300 to 9,934 feet. Please see our listings in this region for dog-friendly hikes and/or campgrounds.

Mount Shasta Dog Travel Guide
Accommodations

Dunsmuir

Oak Tree Inn
6604 Dunsmuir Avenue
Dunsmuir, CA 96025
530-235-2884
There is a $6 per day pet charge.

Railroad Park Resort
100 Railroad Park Road
Dunsmuir, CA 96025

530-235-4440
Spend a night or more inside a restored antique railroad car at this unique resort. Dogs are allowed for an additional $10 per day. This resort also offers RV hookup spaces.

Travelodge
5400 Dunsmuir Ave
Dunsmuir, CA 96025
530-235-4395
There are no additional pet fees.

McCloud

Stony Brook Inn
309 Colombero
McCloud, CA
800-369-6118
There is a $15 per day pet fee. There are only 2 pet rooms so you need to call ahead.

Mount Shasta

Best Western Tree House Motor Inn
111 Morgan Way
Mount Shasta, CA 96067
530-926-3101
Hotel amenities include a complimentary full breakfast, heated indoor pool, room refrigerators, hair dryers, iron/ironing boards and more. There is an additional $10 per day pet charge.

Dream Inn Bed and Breakfast
326 Chestnut Street
Mount Shasta, CA 96067
530-926-1536
Dogs (and children) are welcome at this bed and breakfast inn. The Victorian home, built in 1904 and completely restored, is located at 3,500 ft. in downtown Mount Shasta. Lying at the base of 14,162 ft. Mount Shasta, they are surrounded by National Forest. The inn offers 4 bedrooms with shared bathrooms. The owners also have a dog on the premises. There are no pet fees.

Econo Lodge
908 S. Mt. Shasta Blvd.
Mount Shasta, CA 96067
530-926-3145
There is an additional $5 per day pet charge. There is a limit of one dog per room.

Mount Shasta Ranch Bed and Breakfast
1008 W. A. Barr Rd.
Mount Shasta, CA 96067
530-926-3870
Dogs are allowed at this ranch style house bed

and breakfast built in 1923. This B&B offers 12 bedrooms including a cottage. Five of the rooms have private bathrooms. There is a $10 one time per stay, per pet fee. Children are also welcome.

Mountain Air Lodge
1121 S Mount Shasta Blvd
Mount Shasta, CA 96067
530-926-3411
There is an additional $7 per day pet charge.

Swiss Holiday Lodge
2400 S. Mt. Shasta Blvd.
Mount Shasta, CA 96067
530-926-3446
There is an additional $5 per day pet charge.

Weed

Holiday Inn Express
1830 Black Butte Drive
Weed, CA 96094
530-938-1308
There is a $10 one time pet fee. A well-behaved large dog is okay.

Lake Shastina Golf Resort
5925 Country Club Drive
Weed, CA 96094
530-938-3201
Dogs are allowed in some of the condos at this 18 hole golf course resort. There is a $25 one time pet charge.

Attractions

Mount Shasta

Self Guided Audio Cassette Tour
204 West Alma St
Mount Shasta, CA
530-926-4511
This free audio cassette tour is available when you travel the Upper Sacramento River Canyon on Interstate 5, between Mt. Shasta and Anderson in scenic Northern California. The tape and its original sound track are keyed to I-5 exit signs traveling at 65 mph. The tapes tell a colorful story filled with details of more than a century of traveling and recreating in the canyon. Pick up and drop off the free "Then and Now" canyon history audio cassette tape. If you are traveling south on I-5, you can pick up a tape at the Mt. Shasta Ranger Station located at 204 West Alma St. in Mt. Shasta or the Upper Sacramento River Exchange located at 5819 Sacramento Ave. in

Dunsmuir. You can drop off your southbound tape at either the Shasta Lake Ranger Station on the east side of I-5 at the Mountain Gate exit or the California Welcome Center located at the Factory Outlet Stores in Anderson, adjacent to I-5. Going north, you can pick up a tape at the California Welcome Center in Anderson and drop it off at the Mt. Shasta Ranger Station. There is even an after hours drop box in Mt. Shasta.

Restaurants

Dunsmuir

Cafe Maddalena
5801 Sacramento Avenue
Dunsmuir, CA
530-235-2725
Well-behaved leashed dogs are allowed at the outdoor seating area.

Cornerstone Bakery & Cafe
5759 Dunsmuir Avenue
Dunsmuir, CA
530-235-4677
Well-behaved leashed dogs are allowed at the outdoor seating area.

Mount Shasta

Tolo Grill
107 Chestnut Street
Mount Shasta, CA
530-918-9091
Well-behaved leashed dogs are allowed at the outdoor seating area.

Pulga Dog Travel Guide
Parks

Pulga

Chambers Creek Trail
Highway 70
Pulga, CA
530-283-0555
This trail is located in the Plumas National Forest and is a moderate one way 4.2 mile trail. There are some great waterfalls at the bridge. It takes about 2 to 3 hours to reach the bridge and a total of 6 hours to the top of the trail. Dogs on leash or off-leash but under direct voice control are allowed. Please clean up after your pets. The trailhead is location about 40 miles west of Quincy on Highway 70, or about 40 miles from Oroville.

Quincy Dog Travel Guide
Accommodations

Quincy

Bucks Lake Lodge
23685 Bucks Lake
Quincy, CA
530-283-2262
There is a $10 per day additional pet fee. Dogs are allowed in the cabins, but not the motel section. The cabins are not designated as smoking or non-smoking. Thanks to one of our readers for this recommendation.

Accommodations - RV Parks and Campgrounds

Quincy

Pioneer RV Park
1326 Pioneer Rd.
Quincy, CA
530-283-0769
This pet-friendly RV park is located in the Sierra Nevada Mountains between Lassen National Park and Lake Tahoe. They have over 60 sites on 6.5 acres. RV sites have long wide pull through sites, picnic tables, 30 or 50 amp service and full hookups with satellite TV. Tent campers are also welcome. Other amenities include a laundry room, LP gas, rec room with modem hookup, big screen TV, books exchange and ping pong table. They are located about 1.5 miles from downtown Quincy and right next to a county park which has an Olympic size swimming pool and a playground. Well-behaved leashed dogs of all sizes are allowed. People need to clean up after their pets. There is no pet fee. The RV park is open all year.

Parks

Quincy

Plumas National Forest
159 Lawrence Street
Quincy, CA 95971
530-283-2050
This national forest covers over 1.1 million acres of land which ranges in elevation from around 2,000 to over 7,000 feet. Please see our listings in this region for dog-friendly hikes and/or campgrounds.

Red Bluff Dog Travel Guide

Accommodations

Red Bluff

Motel 6
20 Williams Ave
Red Bluff, CA 96080
530-527-9200
There are no additional pet fees.

Super 8
203 Antelope Blvd
Red Bluff, CA 96080
530-527-8882
A $100 refundable pet deposit is required only if paying with cash.

Travelodge
38 Antelope Blvd
Red Bluff, CA 96080
530-527-6020
There is a $6 per day pet fee.

Redding Dog Travel Guide
Accommodations

Redding

Best Western Ponderosa Inn
2220 Pine Street
Redding, CA 96001
530-241-6300
There is a $100 refundable pet deposit.

Comfort Inn
2059 Hilltop Drive
Redding, CA 96002
530-221-6530
There is a $15 one time pet fee.

Fawndale Lodge and RV Resort
15215 Fawndale Road
Redding, CA 96003
800-338-0941
Nestled in the pines, this lodge offers acres of lawn, a pool and easy access to many recreational activities. All rooms are non-smoking. There is a $50 refundable pet deposit and a $6 per day pet charge.

Holiday Inn Express
1080 Twin View Blvd
Redding, CA 96003
530-241-5500
There is a $30 one time pet fee or a $20 pet fee if you are an AAA or AARP member.

La Quinta Inn Redding
2180 Hilltop Drive
Redding, CA
530-221-8200
Dogs of all sizes are allowed at the hotel.

Motel 6
1640 Hilltop Dr
Redding, CA 96002
530-221-1800
There are no additional pet fees.

Motel 6 - North
1250 Twin View Blvd
Redding, CA 96003
530-246-4470
A well-behaved large dog is okay.

Motel 6 - South
2385 Bechelli Ln
Redding, CA 96002
530-221-0562
One pet is allowed per room.

Ramada Limited
1286 Twin View Blvd
Redding, CA 96003
530-246-2222
There is a $15 one time pet fee.

Red Lion Hotel
1830 Hilltop Drive
Redding, CA 96002
530-221-8700
Dogs up to 50 pounds are allowed. This full service hotel features room service, several pools and an exercise room.

River Inn
1835 Park Marina Drive
Redding, CA 96001
530-241-9500
This inn is adjacent to the Sacramento River and has a private grass area next to their lake. There is a $6 per day pet charge. Thanks to one of our readers for recommending this inn.

Shasta Lodge
1245 Pine Street
Redding, CA 96001
530-243-6133
There is a $20 refundable pet deposit. There is also a $5 per day pet fee.

Accommodations - RV Parks and Campgrounds

Redding

Mountain Gate RV Park
14161 Holiday Road
Redding, CA 96003
530-275-4600
This RV park's amenities include full RV hookups, lighted grounds, large pull through sites, convenience store, video rentals, cable TV, pool, rec room with pool table, email station, laundry, showers, restrooms, dump station, easy I-5 access and pet areas. Well-behaved leashed dogs are allowed. Please clean up after your pets. The park is located 7 miles north of Redding. From the south, take Interstate 5 and exit at Wonderland Blvd. Turn right and then make the first right (Holiday Road) and go .5 miles south. From the north, take Interstate 5 to the second Wonderland Blvd (Mountain Gate) Exit and turn left. Cross over I-5 and make the first right (Holiday Road). Then go .5 miles south.

Parks

Redding

Sacramento River Trail
North Market Street
Redding, CA
530-224-6100
This trail attracts people of all ages, from the walkers and joggers to bicyclists and fisherman looking for an ideal angling spot. The complete trail, round-trip, is approximately 6 miles and can easily be walked in a couple of hours. It is located along the Sacramento River from the North Market Street bridge to Keswick Dam. There are also several access points to the paved trail in Caldwell Park.

Shasta Lake

Redding, CA
530-365-7500
Dogs on leash are allowed on the trails and in the lake. There are miles of trails near this beautiful lake. The easiest trail to reach from Interstate 5 is the Bailey Cove Trail. For a map of all trails, stop at the Visitors Center and Ranger's Station located just south of the lake on Interstate 5 at the Wonderland Blvd exit in Mountain Gate. The Visitor's Center is about 8 miles north of Redding.

Shasta-Trinity National Forest
3644 Avtech Pkwy
Redding, CA 96002
530-226-2500
This national forest covers over 2 million acres of land which ranges in elevation from 1,000 to 14,162 feet. Please see our listings in this region for dog-friendly hikes and/or campgrounds.

Restaurants

Redding

Burrito Bandito
8938 Airport Road
Redding, CA
530-222-6640
Well-behaved leashed dogs are allowed at the outdoor seating area.

Chevys Fresh Mex
1691 Hilltop Drive
Redding, CA
530-223-5797
Well-behaved leashed dogs are allowed at the outdoor bar patio tables.

Chico's Tecate Grill
913 Dana Drive
Redding, CA
530-223-3299
Dogs are welcome at the outdoor tables and they give dogs a bowl of water. Pets should be on leash.

Coffee Creek Juice and Java
2380 Athens Avenue
Redding, CA
530-229-7500
Well-behaved leashed dogs are allowed at the outdoor seating area.

Corina's Ristorante Italiano
1630 Hilltop Drive
Redding, CA
530-221-6433
Well-behaved leashed dogs are allowed at the outdoor seating area.

Espresso Joe's
2143 Hilltop Drive
Redding, CA
530-223-1198
Well-behaved leashed dogs are allowed at the outdoor seating area.

La Gondola
632 N Market Street
Redding, CA
530-244-6321
Well-behaved leashed dogs are allowed at the

outdoor seating area.

La Palomar Mexican Dining
2586 Churn Creek Road
Redding, CA
530-222-1208
Well-behaved leashed dogs are allowed at the outdoor seating area.

Manhattan Bagel
913 Dana Drive
Redding, CA
530-222-2221
Well-behaved leashed dogs are allowed at the outdoor seating area.

Market St Pizza and Deli
871 N Market Street
Redding, CA
530-242-0675
Well-behaved leashed dogs are allowed at the outdoor seating area.

Nick's Bella Vista Grill
21442 Highway 299
Redding, CA
530-549-3042
Well-behaved leashed dogs are allowed at the outdoor seating area.

Sandwichery
1341 Tehama Street
Redding, CA
530-246-2020
Well-behaved leashed dogs are allowed at the outdoor seating area.

Sunset Cafe & Yogurt
3639 Eureka Way
Redding, CA
530-246-7954
Well-behaved leashed dogs are allowed at the outdoor seating area.

Wall Street Pizza
1165 Hartnell Avenue
Redding, CA
530-221-7100
Well-behaved leashed dogs are allowed at the outdoor seating area.

Tionesta Dog Travel Guide
Accommodations - RV Parks and Campgrounds

Tionesta

Eagle's Nest RV Park
off Highway 139
Tionesta, CA
530-644-2081
This RV park is located 24 miles south of the town of Tulelake and 2 miles off Highway 139. Amenities include 20 full hookup pull through sites, showers, restrooms, laundromat, clubhouse with pool table, satellite TV and a book exchange. Grassy tent sites are also available. Well-behaved leashed dogs are welcome. Please clean up after your pets.

Trinity Center Dog Travel Guide
Accommodations - RV Parks and Campgrounds

Trinity Center

Clark Springs Campground
Highway 3
Trinity Center, CA
530-623-2121
This campground is located in the Shasta-Trinity National Forest at an elevation of 2,400 fee. The campground offers 21 tent and RV campsites. RVs up to 25 feet are allowed and there are no hookups. Amenities include a swimming beach, boat ramp, drinking water, picnic sites, wheelchair access and flush toilets. Fishing, swimming, boating and hiking are popular activities at the campground. The Trinity Lakeshore trailhead is located here. The camp is open from the beginning of April to mid-September. To make a reservations, call 1-877-444-6777. The campground is located 18 miles north of Weaverville off Highway 3. Dogs are allowed on the trails and in the lake water but only on non-designated swimming areas. Pets must be leashed and please clean up after them.

Hayward Flat Campground
off Highway 3
Trinity Center, CA
530-623-2121
This campground is located on the west side of the East Fork arm of Trinity Lake in the Shasta-Trinity National Forest. The campground is at an elevation of 2,400 feet and offers 94 tent and RV campsites. RVs up to 40 feet are allowed and there are no hookups. Amenities include drinking water and flush toilets. Fishing, swimming and boating are popular activities at the campground. The camp is open from mid-May to mid-September. To make a reservations, call 1-877-444-6777. The campground is located 20 miles north of Weaverville and 2.5 miles off

Highway 3. Pets must be leashed and please clean up after them.

Wyntoon Resort
Highway 3
Trinity Center, CA 96091

This 90 acre wooded resort is located at the north end of Lake Trinity and offers both RV and tent sites. The RV sites are tree shaded, have full hookups with 30 or 50 amp service and RVs up to 60 feet. Tent sites are located under pine and cedar trees and have picnic tables and barbecues. Other camp amenities include a swimming pool, clubhouse, snack bar, ping pong, showers and laundry facilities. Well-behaved leashed pets are always welcome. Please clean up after your pet. There is a $1 per day pet fee.

Attractions

Trinity Center

Estrellita Marina
49160 State Highway 3
Trinity Center, CA 96091
530-286-2215
Rent a patio/pontoon boat with your pooch on Lake Trinity. There is a 4 hour minimum for boat rentals and pricing starts at about $75 for 4 hours. This full service marina includes a country store, launch ramp and gas. Well-behaved dogs are allowed on the boats. The marina also rent houseboats and well-behaved dogs are welcome on those too.

Parks

Trinity Center

Trinity Lakeshore Trail
Highway 3
Trinity Center, CA
530-623-2121
This easy to moderate hike follows the western shore of Trinity Lake. The four mile trail runs from Clark Springs Campground to a private resort. There are a few short, steep stretches along the route. The trail offers shade and goes through an old-growth forest. Please stay on the trail when walking through private facilities. The majority of this trail is in the Shasta-Trinity National Forest. The trailhead at the Clark Springs Campground which is located 18 miles north of Weaverville off Highway 3. Pets should be leashed and please clean up after them.

Trinity County Dog Travel Guide
Accommodations

Coffee Creek

Becker's Bounty Lodge and Cottage
HCR #2 Box 4659
Coffee Creek, CA 96091
530-266-3277
The lodge is a secluded mountain hideaway at the edge of the one-half million acre Trinity Alps Wilderness. Dogs are not allowed on the furniture. There is a $50 one time pet charge.

Accommodations - Vacation Home Rentals

Coffee Creek

Blackberry Creek Garden Cottage
On SR-3
Coffee Creek, CA 96091
530-266-3502
There is a $15 per day additional pet fee. According to a reader "We just spent a week at this wonderful cottage, and it is a little piece of heaven for you and your dog. Nestled under the pines, cedars and redwoods the cottage has everything you need for the perfect vacation in the woods. Down the road is the greatest swimming hole in the Trinity River, and great hikes await you in every direction. Our dogs did not want to leave and neither did we. "

Hayfork

Trinity County Vacation Rental
Call to Arrange.
Hayfork, CA
415-252-9590
Get away from it all at this lovely 800 square foot cabin on a year round creek. Enjoy seven acres of privacy with your best friend. There is a fenced yard around the house. The home has a fully equipped kitchen, washer dryer, garbage disposal and satellite television with VCR. Located in Trinity County about 5 hours from the Bay Area and 4 hours from Sacramento. The cabin is available for weekly rentals year round.

Tulelake Dog Travel Guide
Accommodations - RV Parks and Campgrounds

Tulelake

Indian Well Campground

1 Indian Well
Tulelake, CA 96134
530-667-2282
This campground, located in the Lava Beds National Monument, offers 40 campsites for tents and small to medium sized RVs. Amenities include water and flush toilets. Campsites are available on a first-come, first-served basis. Pets must be leashed and attended at all times. Please clean up after your pet. Dogs are not allowed on any trails or hikes in this park, but see our Modoc National Forest listings in this region for nearby dog-friendly hiking, sightseeing and additional camping.

Medicine Lake Campground

Forest Service Road 44N38
Tulelake, CA
530-233-5811
This campground is located on the shores of Medicine Lake at 6,700 foot elevation in the Modoc National Forest. There are 22 RV and tent sites. RVs up to 22 feet are allowed and there are no hookups. Amenities include picnic tables, fire pits, vault toilets and potable water. Dogs on leash are allowed at the campgrounds and in the water. Please clean up after your pets. The campground is usually open from July to October, weather permitting. There is a $7 per vehicle fee. To get there from the junction of Highway 139 and Co. Rd. 97, go about 18.5 miles west on Co. Rd. 97. Turn right on Forest Service Road 44N75. Go 1 mile to Forest Service Road 44N38. Go another .5 miles and then turn right and follow the signs to the Medicine Lake Campground.

Attractions

Tulelake

Medicine Lake Highlands

Forest Road 49
Tulelake, CA
530-233-5811
Medicine Lake is an area of moderately sloping to steep mountains. It was formed by a volcano and is one of North America's most unique geological areas. One feature is that it has no known outlets but yet its water remains clean and clear. It lies within the volcanic caldera of the largest shield volcano in North America. Obsidian and pumice are common in the highlands. For thousands of years Native Americans have used these substances to make tools and other objects. More recently astronauts prepared in the pumice fields for their first landing on the moon. To get there

from the town of Tulelake, take Highway 139 south and follow the signs to the Tulelake National Wildlife Refuge. Then go south through the Lava Beds National Monument. Follow the signs along Forest Road 49 to Medicine Lake. This route is part of the Modoc Volcanic Scenic Byway.

Volcanic Historic Loop

State Route 139
Tulelake, CA
530-233-5811
This self-guided auto tour takes you through an area of "rocks that float and mountains of glass" and into one of the most unique geological regions in North America. The tour begins in the town of Tulelake and heads south on State Route 139. At CR97 head west and go into the town of Tionesta. Head another 12 miles west and you will come to Glass Mountain. The glass flow is from glassy dacite and rhyolitic obsidian that flowed from the same vent simultaneously without mixing. At nearby Medicine Lake you can camp, sightsee, swim, fish or take photos. Medicine Lake was once the center of a volcano. Native Americans believed that the lake had special healing powers. About 4.5 miles southeast of the lake is the Burnt Lava Flow. It is estimated to be about 200 years old which makes it the youngest lava flow in the area. The tour continues, but goes into the Lava Beds National Monument which only allows dogs in parking lots and along roads. In the national forest, which is the majority of this tour, dogs on leash are allowed on trails and in lake waters. Please clean up after your pets. For more information including maps, contact the Modoc National Forest office at 800 West 12th Street, Alturas, CA 96101, 530-233-5811.

Parks

Tulelake

Lava Beds National Monument

1 Indian Well
Tulelake, CA 96134
530-667-2282
This national park does not really have much to see or do if you bring your pooch, except for staying overnight at the Indian Well Campground. However, the dog-friendly Modoc National Forest surrounds the national park. At the national forest you will be able to find dog-friendly hiking, sightseeing and camping. See our Modoc National Forest listing in this region for more details. Pets must be leashed and attended at all times. Please clean up after your pet.

Upper Lake Dog Travel Guide

Accommodations - RV Parks and Campgrounds

Upper Lake

Sunset Campground
County Road 301/Forest Road M1
Upper Lake, CA
916-386-5164
This campground is located in the Mendocino National Forest and is managed by Pacific Gas and Electric. Camp amenities include 54 tables, 54 stoves, 12 toilets, water, trailer space and 27 grills. The Sunset Nature Trail Loop begins at this campground. The campground is open from about May to September. There is a $12 fee per campsite and an extra $1 per night per pet fee. Dogs on leash are allowed and please clean up after them. To get there from Upper Lake, take County Road 301 north for 31 miles.

Parks

Upper Lake

Sunset Nature Trail Loop
County Road 301/Forest Road M1
Upper Lake, CA
530-934-3316
This self-guided interpretive trail is an easy .5 mile one way hike. Elevation begins at 1,800 feet and has a 100 foot climb. The trail is located in the Mendocino National Forest, adjacent to a campground. Pets on leash are allowed. Please clean up after your pets. To get there from Upper Lake, take County Road 301 north for 31 miles. The trail begins at the Sunset Campground.

Weaverville Dog Travel Guide

Accommodations

Weaverville

Best Western Weaverville Victorian Inn
1709 Main Street
Weaverville, CA 96096
530-623-4432
Amenities at this inn include a free continental breakfast and swimming pool. There is one non-smoking pet room and there is no pet fee.

Whiskeytown Dog Travel Guide

Accommodations - RV Parks and Campgrounds

Whiskeytown

Brandy Creek RV Campground
P.O. Box 188
Whiskeytown, CA 96095
530-246-1225
This campground is part of the Whiskeytown National Recreation Area which allows dogs on trails, in the lake and on non-swimming beaches only. The camp offers paved parking spots for RVs along an access road. There are no hookups and generators are allowed but not during the quiet time which is usually from 10pm to 6am. All sites are on a first-come, first-served basis. Dogs must be leashed and attended at all times. Please clean up after your pet. The campground is open all year.

Oak Bottom Campground
P.O. Box 188
Whiskeytown, CA 96095
530-359-2269
This campground offers tent sites next to Whiskeytown Lake. The campground is part of the Whiskeytown National Recreation Area which allows dogs on trails, in the lake and on non-swimming beaches only. The camp also offers RV sites but there are no hookups. Generators are allowed but not during the quiet time which is usually from 10pm to 6am. During the summer reservations are required and during the winter sites are on a first-come, first-served basis. Dogs must be leashed and attended at all times. Please clean up after your pet. The campground is open all year.

Parks

Whiskeytown

Whiskeytown National Recreation Area
P.O. Box 188
Whiskeytown, CA 96095
530-246-1225
The main highlight of this park is Whiskeytown Lake. Popular activities include swimming, sailing, water-skiing, scuba diving and fishing. The land surrounding the lake offers ample opportunities for hiking, mountain biking and horseback riding. Dogs are allowed on the trails, in the campgrounds and in the water at non-swim beaches which are beaches without sand. Pets are not allowed on the sandy swimming beaches or inside any buildings. Dogs must be leashed and attended at all times. Please clean up after your pet. This recreation area is located on

Highway 299 near Highway 5.

Yreka Dog Travel Guide
Accommodations

Yreka

Ben-Ber Motel
1210 S Main St
Yreka, CA 96097
530-842-2791
There is a $6 per day pet charge.

Best Western Miner's Inn
122 East Miner Street
Yreka, CA 95991
530-842-4355
There is a $10 one time pet charge. There is a self-guided walking tour of historic Yreka about one block from this motel. Ask the motel for more information.

Days Inn
1804 B Fort Jones Rd
Yreka, CA 96097
530-842-1612
There is a $20 refundable pet deposit.

Motel 6
1785 S Main Street
Yreka, CA 96097
530-842-4111
There are no additional pet fees.

Attractions

Yreka

Blue Goose Steam Excursion Train
300 East Miner Street
Yreka, CA 96097
530-842-4146
The Blue Goose excursion train rides on railroad tracks that were built in1888. The train travels over Butcher Hill in Yreka and then down through the scenic Shasta Valley with Mt. Shasta in the view. The train then crosses over the Shasta River and continues on to the old cattle town of Montague. The distance is about 7.5 miles one way and takes approximately 1 hour to arrive. Upon arrival in Montague, passengers disembark the train and will have about 1.5 hours for lunch and to explore the historic town of Montague. During lunchtime, the train is pushed back in preparation for the return trip to Yreka. The train returns to pick up passengers about 15 minutes

before departure. The total round trip time for this ride is about 3.5 hours. Trains run from Memorial Day Weekend to the end of October on a limited schedule. Well-behaved leashed dogs that are friendly towards people and children are welcome. They ask that you please keep your pooch out of the aisles once on the train.

Parks

Yreka

Klamath National Forest
1312 Fairlane Road
Yreka, CA 96097
530-842-6131
This forest has over 1,700,000 acres of land throughout Siskiyou County in California and Jackson County in Oregon. Dogs should be on leash. Hiking from East Fork Campground provides access to the lakes in the Caribou Basin, Rush Creek, and Little South Fork drainages. The campground is located 27 miles southwest of Callahan next to the East and the South Forks of the Salmon River, at a 2,600 foot elevation. From the Bridge Flat Campground, the historic Kelsey Trail offers excellent opportunities for scenic day hikes or longer trips into the Marble Mountain Wilderness. The campground is located on the Scott River approximately 17 miles from Fort Jones, at a 2,000 foot elevation. For more details, call or visit the Salmon River Ranger District, 11263 N. Highway 3,Fort Jones, (530) 468-5351. The Klamath National Forest offers miles of other hiking trails. For maps and more information on trails throughout this forest, please contact the forest office in Yreka.

Chapter 3

California Dog-Friendly Travel Guide
Wine Country

Napa Valley Dog Travel Guide

Accommodations

Calistoga

Hillcrest Bed and Breakfast
3225 Lake County Hwy.
Calistoga, CA 94515
707-942-6334
This inn is located near the base of Mt. St. Helena and within a five minute drive to downtown Calistoga. This bed and breakfast also offers swimming, hiking and fishing on 40 acres. Dogs are welcome. The owner also has two dogs. There is a $10 per day pet charge.

Pink Mansion Bed and Breakfast
1415 Foothill Blvd.
Calistoga, CA 94515
707-942-0558
This restored 1875 home offers modern amenities for wine country travelers. The Pink Mansion has been featured in The Wine Spectator, Best Places To Kiss and the New York Post. Dogs are allowed in one of their six rooms. Each room has a private bathroom. There is a $30 per day pet charge.

Napa

The Chablis Inn
3360 Solono Ave
Napa, CA 94558
707-257-1944
There is a 150 pound limit for dogs. There is a $10 per day additional pet fee. All rooms are non-smoking.

The Napa Inn Bed and Breakfast
1137 Warren Street
Napa, CA 94559
707-257-1444
Located on a quiet street in historic, downtown Napa, this inn is within an easy walking distance of shops and restaurants. Dogs are allowed in one room, the garden cottage. This private cottage is decorated in French Provincial prints. It has a queen size bed, sofa, fireplace, French doors overlooking a private flower garden, skylight, wet bar with refrigerator and microwave, and an outdoor spa. It sleeps up to four people. There is a $20 per day pet charge.

St Helena

El Bonita Motel
195 Main Street
St Helena, CA 94574
707-963-3216
Amenities at this motel include a continental breakfast, pool, whirlpool, sauna, and over two acres of peaceful gardens. Room amenities include microwaves, refrigerators, and more. Room rates start at about $130 per night and up. There is a $5 per day pet charge.

Harvest Inn
One Main Street
St Helena, CA 94574
707-963-9463
This inn is nestled among 8-acres of award winning landscape. Most guest rooms feature wet bars, unique brick fireplaces and private terraces. Amenities include two outdoor heated pools and whirlpool spas and jogging and bike trails bordering the grounds. Dogs are allowed in the standard rooms. There is a $75 one time pet charge.

Yountville

Vintage Inn
6541 Washington St.
Yountville, CA 94599
707-944-1112
This inn is located in the small town of Yountville and is located within walking distance of several dog-friendly restaurants. Amenities at this pet-friendly inn include a continental champagne breakfast, afternoon tea, coffee & cookies, a heated pool, two tennis courts, and award winning gardens. Room amenities include a wood burning fireplace in every room, refrigerator with a chilled welcome bottle of wine, terry robes, nightly turn down service, hair dryer, in room iron & ironing board and more. If you need to leave your room, but can't take your pooch with you, the concierge can arrange for a dog sitter. They also have a list of nearby dog-friendly outdoor restaurants. Room rates start at about $200 per night and up. There is a $30 one time pet charge.

Accommodations - RV Parks and Campgrounds

Calistoga

Napa County Fairgrounds Campground
1435 Oak Street
Calistoga, CA 94515
707-942-5111
Located at the fairgrounds, this campground offers 46 RV/tent sites. RV sites are parallel in the parking lot and tent sites are located on an adjacent lawn. RV sites have full hookups (some have sewer). Other amenities include restrooms, showers, potable water and disabled accessible. Dogs are allowed but must be on a 10 foot or less leash. Please clean up after your pet. The campground is open all year.

Attractions

Calistoga

Cuvaison Winery
4550 Silverado Trail
Calistoga, CA
707-942-6266
Well-behaved leashed dogs are allowed in the tasting room and at the outdoor picnic areas.

Dutch Henry Winery
4310 Silverado Trail
Calistoga, CA 94515
707-942-5771
This winery is very dog-friendly. They invite well mannered owners and well mannered pets to visit. Dutch Henry is a small, family-owned winery and they produce hand crafted wines including Cabernet Sauvignon, Merlot, Chardonnay, and Zinfandel. Their two dogs, Dutch and Buggsy serve as the official greeters of the winery and are more than happy to chase tennis balls or give your own well-behaved canine the "doggie tour".

Old Faithful Geyser
1299 Tubbs Lane
Calistoga, CA 94515
707-942-6463
Your well-behaved dog is welcome to accompany you to this natural phenomena. Just keep him or her away from the hot water. This geyser is one of only three Old Faithful geysers in the world, erupting about every 40 minutes on a yearly average. The water is 350 degrees hot and shoots about 60 feet into the air for about three to four minutes, then recedes. To see the geyser, you and your pup will need to walk through the main entrance and gift shop. Purchase the tickets at the gift shop and then walk to the geyser area to watch Old Faithful erupt. There is also a snack bar and picnic areas onsite. The admission price is $6 per adult, $5 per senior, $2 per children 6-12 and FREE for dogs. Prices are subject to change.

Petrified Forest
4100 Petrified Forest Rd.
Calistoga, CA 94515
707-942-6667
Geologists call this petrified forest, "one of the finest examples of a pliocene fossil forest in the world." The petrified forest was created from a long ago volcanic eruption, followed by torrential rains which brought giant mud flows of volcanic ash from the eruption site to entomb the felled giants/trees. The 1/2 mile round trip meadow tour shows some of the petrified trees. Your leashed dog is welcome. Admission prices are $5 for adults, less for seniors and children, and FREE for dogs. Prices are subject to change.

Rutherford

Sullivan Vineyards
1090 Galleron Rd
Rutherford, CA
707-963-9646
Well-behaved leashed dogs are allowed in the tasting room and at the picnic table. They have three dogs on the premises.

St Helena

Casa Nuestra Winery
3451 Silverado Trail North
St Helena, CA
866-844-WINE
Dogs are welcome in the picnic area. The winery has five dogs that "work" here as greeters, but they all work different days.

Rustridge
2910 Lower Chiles Valley Rd
St Helena, CA
707-965-2871
Well-behaved leashed dogs are allowed in the tasting room and in the picnic area. The owner also has four dogs on the premises.

V. Sattui Winery
1111 White Lane
St Helena, CA
Hwy 29
707-963-7774
Dogs are welcome in the picnic area. This winery also has an onsite deli. This winery has lawn picnic benches and a shaded area.

Parks

Napa

Canine Commons Dog Park
Alston Park - Dry Creek Road
Napa, CA
(near Redwood Rd)
707-257-9529
This fenced 3 acre dog park has water, benches, and pooper scoopers. The dog park is located in Alston Park which has about 100 acres of dog-friendly on-leash trails. Thanks to one of our readers for recommending this park. To get there from Napa, take Hwy 29 North and exit Redwood Rd. Turn left on Redwood Rd and then right on Dry Creek Rd. The park will be on the left.

Restaurants

Calistoga

Home Plate Cafe
Hwy 128 & Petrified Forest Rd.
Calistoga, CA 94515
707-942-5646
You and your pup can enjoy hamburgers or chicken sandwiches at this cafe. The restaurant is

located near the Old Faithful Geyser.

Rutherford

Rutherford Grill
1180 Rutherford Road
Rutherford, CA 94573
On Hwy 29/128
707-963-1792
This is definitely a dog-friendly restaurant. They usually bring out treats for your dog while you dine at the lovely outdoor patio. The food is great. Rutherford is north of Napa, just beyond Oakville and just south of St. Helena. Thanks to one of our readers for recommending this restaurant.

Yountville

29 Joes Coffee House
677 St. Helena Hwy S.
Yountville, CA 94574
707-967-0820
This coffee house serves a variety of coffee and some pastries. Your dog is welcome at the outdoor tables. You can order inside or through the drive-thru window.

Bistro Jeanty
6510 Washington St.
Yountville, CA 94599
707-944-0103
This restaurant can get pretty crowded during lunch and dinner, so come early to ensure an outdoor table.

Compadres Mexican Grill
6539 Washington St.
Yountville, CA 94599
707-944-2406
This restaurant has an enjoyable outdoor patio with heaters and shade umbrellas.

Napa Valley Grille

6795 Washington St.
Yountville, CA 94599
707-944-8686
Your pup is welcome to join you at the outdoor tables. There are outside heaters and shade umbrellas to keep you comfortable. This restaurant was selected as one of the "Hot Concepts" for 1998 by Nation's Restaurant News.

Stores

St Helena

Fideaux
1312 Main Street
St Helena, CA 94574
707-967-9935
Well-behaved leashed dogs are welcome to accompany you into Fideaux. The store boasts dog specialty items and gifts. It is located in the center of St. Helena.

Yountville

Best Friends of the Napa Valley
6525 Washington St
Yountville, CA 94599
707-945-0125
Dogs are welcome in this specialty gift store for

pets.

Sonoma Dog Travel Guide
Accommodations

Guerneville

Creekside Inn & Resort
16180 Neeley Rd
Guerneville, CA 95446
707-869-3623
Dogs are allowed in one of their cottages. During the summer it books up fast, so please make an early reservation. The inn will be able to help you find some pet-friendly hiking trails and beaches nearby.

River Village Resort and Spa
14880 River Road
Guerneville, CA 95446
800-529-3376
This inn is located just minutes from the Russian River. At this inn, dogs are allowed in certain cottages and there is a $10 per day pet fee. Please do not walk pets on the lawn. Children are also welcome.

Healdsburg

Best Western Dry Creek Inn
198 Dry Creek Road
Healdsburg, CA 95448
707-433-0300
Amenities include a Complimentary Continental Breakfast and a Gift bottle of Sonoma County Wine. There is a $20 one time pet charge.

Duchamp Hotel
421 Foss Street
Healdsburg, CA 95448
707-431-1300
This hotel, located in Healdsburg, allows dogs in two of their cottages. Every cottage features a king bed, oversized spa shower, private terrace, fireplace, mini bar, and more. Children over 16 years old are allowed. The entire premises is non-smoking. Dogs are not allowed in the pool area and they request that you take your dog away from the cottages and hotel when they go to the bathroom.

Monte Rio

Grandma's House Bed and Breakfast
20280 River Blvd
Monte Rio, CA 95462

707-865-1865

This dog-friendly bed and breakfast inn is located on the Russian River. The inn offers three rooms, all with private bathrooms. Each room also includes a private phone line, TV and VCR, refrigerator, microwave, and more. One of the rooms is handicapped accessible. Clean, well-behaved dogs may accompany their owners, with advance notice, for $10 per dog per day. There is a $75 damage and cleaning deposit, refundable (if not needed) at departure. Owners are expected to clean up behind their dog on the grounds. Pooper-scooper bags are available for this purpose. Dogs must not be left unattended in the room for long periods. Owners are responsible for not letting their dog disturb other guests and making sure their dog is not destructive to the property.

Rohnert Park

Motel 6
6145 Commerce Blvd
Rohnert Park, CA 94928
707-585-8888
A large well-behaved dog is okay. Dogs must be leashed when outside and never left alone in the room.

Santa Rosa

Comfort Inn
2632 Cleveland Ave
Santa Rosa, CA 95403
707-542-5544
There is a $10 per day pet fee.

Days Inn
3345 Santa Rosa Ave
Santa Rosa, CA
707-568-1011
There is a $10 per day additional pet fee.

Hilton Sonoma County
3555 Round Barn Blvd
Santa Rosa, CA 95403
707-523-7555
Located in the heart of Sonoma's wine country, this hotel is nestled on a hillside with 13 acres of landscaped grounds. There is a $15 per day pet charge.

Los Robles Lodge
1985 Cleveland Ave
Santa Rosa, CA 95401
707-545-6330
Dogs are allowed, but not in the poolside rooms

or executive suites. There is a $10 per day pet charge.

Motel 6 - North
3145 Cleveland Ave
Santa Rosa, CA 95403
707-525-9010
A large well maintained and well-behaved dog is okay.

Motel 6 - South
2760 Cleveland Ave
Santa Rosa, CA 95403
707-546-1500
One pet per room is permitted.

Santa Rosa Motor Inn
1800 Santa Rosa Ave
Santa Rosa, CA
707-523-3480
There is a $10 per day pet fee and a refundable pet deposit.

Sonoma

Best Western Sonoma Valley
550 Second St. West
Sonoma, CA 95476
707-938-9200
This motel is within walking distance of the small downtown shopping area in Sonoma. Amenities include a gift bottle of wine, complimentary continental breakfast delivered to your room, heated pool and more. Room amenities include refrigerators and a fireplace or jacuzzi. Room rates start at $130 per night and up. There is a $20 per day pet charge. The entire hotel is non-smoking.

Accommodations - RV Parks and Campgrounds

Guerneville

Fifes Guest Ranch
16467 Highway 116
Guerneville, CA 95446
707-869-0656
Located on 15 acres and among redwood trees, this guest ranch offers individual cabins, cottages and tent camping. Amenities include a pool, volleyball court, gym and onsite massages. Well-behaved dogs of all sizes are allowed in the campsites, cabins and cottages for an additional fee.

Santa Rosa

Spring Lake Regional Park Campgrounds
5585 Newanga Avenue
Santa Rosa, CA
707-785-2377
This 320 acre regional park with a 72 acre lake offers 27 campsites and miles of easy walking trails. RVs are permitted and there is a dump station, but no hookups. Dogs are allowed but must be on a 6 foot or less leash and proof of a rabies vaccination is required.

Accommodations - Vacation Home Rentals

Guerneville

Russian River Getaways
14075 Mill Street, P.O. Box 1673
Guerneville, CA 95446
707-869-4560
This company offers about 40 dog-friendly vacation homes in Russian River wine country with leash free beaches nearby. There are no pet fees and no size limits for dogs. There is a $75 refundable pet deposit.

Windsor

Villa Terra Bella
Call to Arrange
Windsor, CA 95492
707-838-3048
Enjoy a private cottage located on a 7 acre European-style estate in the heart of Sonoma County. The new 800 sq. ft. cottage at Villa Terra Bella has 2 bedrooms, private bath, full kitchen and patio for outdoor grilling. Enjoy the relaxing stone pool and spa or stroll along the grounds where one acre of zinfandel vines, palm trees and local vegetation abound. A children's playground and putting green provide additional relaxation. Villa Terra Bella is located in Windsor, the

Gateway to the Wine Country, just minutes from Healdsburg and Santa Rosa. There is a $50.00 pet fee per visit and pets must remain on leash or within the room at all times.

Attractions

Forestville

Topolos Vineyards
5700 Gravenstein Hwy N.
Forestville, CA 95436
707-887-1575
Dogs are allowed in the tasting room. The tasting room is open 11 am to 5:30 pm daily.

Guerneville

F. Korbel and Brothers Champagne Cellars
13250 River Road
Guerneville, CA 95446
707-824-7000
Well-behaved leashed dogs are allowed at the outdoor picnic area.

Healdsburg

Foppiano Vineyards
12707 Old Redwood Highway
Healdsburg, CA 95448
707-433-7272
Dogs are allowed at the picnic area and on the self-guided vineyard tour.

Lambert Bridge Winery
4085 W. Dry Creek Rd
Healdsburg, CA 95448
800-975-0555
Dogs are allowed in the wine tasting room and the large picnic grounds. The winery is open daily from 10:30 am to 4:30 pm.

Russian River Adventures
20 Healdsburg Avenue
Healdsburg, CA 95448
707-433-5599
Take a self-guided eco-adventure with your pooch. Rent an inflatable canoe and adventure along the Russian River. The SOAR 16 is the largest model and is great for taking children and dogs. There are many refreshing swimming holes along the way. Dogs and families of all ages are welcome. Be sure to call ahead as reservations are required.

Santa Rosa

Deloach Vineyards
1791 Olivet Road
Santa Rosa, CA 95401
707-526-9111
Dogs are allowed at the picnic area.

Hanna Winery
5353 Occidental Road
Santa Rosa, CA
707-575-3371
Well-behaved, leashed dogs are allowed in the tasting room and in the picnic area.

Martini and Prati Wines
2191 Laguna Road
Santa Rosa, CA 95401
707-823-2404
Well-behaved, leashed dogs area allowed at the picnic area.

Pacific Coast Air Museum
2330 Airport Blvd
Santa Rosa, CA 95403
707-575-7900
Well-behaved, leashed dogs are allowed in the museum. The museum offers both indoor and outdoor exhibits.

Sebastapol

Taft Street Winery
2030 Barlow Lane
Sebastapol, CA
707-823-2404
Dogs are allowed on the picnic deck.

Windsor

Martinell Vineyards
3360 River Road
Windsor, CA
707-525-0570
Dogs are allowed at the picnic area.

Beaches

Cloverdale

Cloverdale River Park
31820 McCray Road
Cloverdale, CA
707-565-2041
This park is located along the Russian River and offers seasonal fishing and river access for kayaks and canoes. There are no lifeguards at the beach area. Dogs are allowed, but must be on a 6 foot or less leash. They can wade into the water, but cannot really swim because pets must remain on leash. There is a $3 per car parking fee.

Healdsburg

Healdsburg Memorial Beach
13839 Old Redwood Highway
Healdsburg, CA
707-565-2041
This man-made swimming beach is located on the Russian River. Dogs are allowed at this park, but must be on a 6 foot or less leash. They can wade into the water, but cannot really swim because pets must remain on leash. People are urged to swim only when lifeguards are present, which is usually between Memorial Day and Labor Day. The beach area also offers picnic tables and a restroom. There is a $3 to $4 parking fee per day, depending on the season.

Sea Ranch

Sea Ranch Coastal Access Trails
Highway 1
Sea Ranch, CA
707-785-2377
Walk along coastal headlands or the beach in Sea Ranch. There are six trailhead parking areas which are located along Highway 1, south of the Sonoma Mendocino County Line. Access points include Black Point, Bluff Top Trail, Pebble Beach, Stengal Beach, Shell Beach and Walk on Beach. Dogs must be on a 6 foot or less leash. There is a $3 per car parking fee. RVs and vehicles with trailers are not allowed to use the parking areas.

Parks

Glen Ellen

Elizabeth Anne Perrone Dog Park
13630 Sonoma Highway
Glen Ellen, CA
707-565-2041
This one acre fenced dog run is located in the dog-friendly Sonoma Valley Regional Park. The dog park has a doggie drinking fountain, and a gazebo which provides shade for both people and dogs.

Jack London State Historic Park

2400 London Ranch Road
Glen Ellen, CA
707-938-5216
This park is a memorial to the famous writer and adventurer Jack London. He lived here from 1905 until his death in 1916. Dogs on leash are allowed around the ranch and historic buildings, but not inside. Pets are also allowed on the Wolf House Trail which is a 1.2 mile round trip trail. Please clean up after your pet. The park is located about 20 minutes north of Sonoma.

Sonoma Valley Regional Park
13630 Sonoma Highway
Glen Ellen, CA
707-565-2041
This 162 acre park offers both paved and dirt trails which are used for hiking, bicycling and horseback riding. Dogs are allowed but must be on a 6 foot or less leash. The Elizabeth Anne Perrone Dog Park is also located within this park and allows dogs to run leash-free within the one acre. There is a $3 parking fee.

Rohnert Park

Crane Creek Regional Park
5000 Pressley Road
Rohnert Park, CA
707-565-2041
Located just east of Sonoma State University, this 128 acre foothills park offers hiking and bicycling trails. There are picnic tables and restrooms at the trailhead. Dogs must be kept on a 6 foot or less leash. There is a $3 per car parking fee.

Santa Rosa

Hood Mountain Regional Park
3000 Los Alamos Road
Santa Rosa, CA
707-565-2041
This 1,450 acre wilderness park offers bicycling, equestrian and rugged hiking trails for experienced hikers in good physical condition. Dogs are allowed at this park, but must be on a 6 foot or less leash. Access to the park is on Los Alamos Road which is a very narrow and winding road. There is a $3 per car parking fee.

Northwest Community Dog Park
2620 W. Steele Lane
Santa Rosa, CA 95403
707-543-3292
Thanks to one of our readers who writes "Wonderful dog park. 2 separately fenced areas (one for little dogs too... It's all grassy and some

trees and right near the creek. Also a brand new childrens play area (one for big kids and one fenced for toddlers). This dog park is sponsored by the Peanut's comics creator Charles M. Schultz's estate."

Spring Lake Regional Park
391 Violetti Drive
Santa Rosa, CA
707-785-2377
This 320 acre park with a 72 acre lake offers miles of easy walking trails and a campground. Dogs are allowed but must be on a 6 foot or less leash and proof of a rabies vaccination is required.

Sebastopol

Joe Rodota Trail
Petaluma Avenue
Sebastopol, CA
707-565-2041
This is a 2.8 mile paved trail that runs parallel to an abandoned railway line. There are agricultural ranches and farms along the trail. Dogs are allowed, but must be on a 6 foot or less leash. Parking is available in the town of Sebastopol, at the trailhead located off of Petaluma Avenue.

Ragle Ranch Regional Park
500 Ragle Road
Sebastopol, CA
707-565-2041
This 157 acre park offers walking trails, sports courts, picnic areas and a children's playground. Dogs are allowed, but must be on a 6 foot or less leash. There is a $3 per car parking fee.

Sonoma

Maxwell Farms Regional Park
100 Verano Avenue
Sonoma, CA
707-565-2041
This 85 acre park offers meadow nature trails on 40 acres, multi-use fields for soccer and softball, a children's playground and picnic areas. Dogs are allowed but must be on a 6 foot or less leash. There is a $3 parking fee.

Windsor

Foothill Regional Park
1351 Arata Lane
Windsor, CA
707-565-2041

Hiking, bicycling, horseback riding and fishing are popular activities at this 211 acre park. Dogs must be kept on a 6 foot or less leash. No swimming, wading or boating is allowed on the lakes. There is a $3 per car parking fee.

Restaurants

Glen Ellen

Garden Court Cafe & Bakery
13875 Sonoma Highway 12
Glen Ellen, CA 95442
707-935-1565
Well-behaved dogs may accompany owners on the enclosed patio. They have a special dog menu as well. The restaurant is open 7 days a week for breakfast and lunch. Its hours are 7:30 am to 2 pm.

Guerneville

Andorno's Pizza
16205 First Street
Guerneville, CA
707-869-0651
Well-behaved leashed dogs are allowed at the outdoor seating area.

Korbel Deli & Market
13250 River Road
Guerneville, CA
707-824-7313
Well-behaved leashed dogs are allowed at the outdoor seating area.

Main Street Station
16280 Main Street
Guerneville, CA
707-869-0501
Alcohol drinks are not allowed outside but you are welcome to dine at the outdoor tables with your well-behaved leashed dog.

Mi Casita
16380 Mill Street
Guerneville, CA
707-869-9626
Well-behaved leashed dogs are allowed at the outdoor seating area.

Pasta Boys Cafe and Deli
16337 Main Street
Guerneville, CA
707-869-1665
Well-behaved leashed dogs are allowed at the outdoor seating area.

Healdsburg

Dry Creek General Store
3495 Dry Creek Rd
Healdsburg, CA 95448
707-433-4171
Dogs are allowed at the outdoor tables.

Giorgio's Pizzeria
25 Grant Avenue
Healdsburg, CA 95448
Healdsburg Avenue
707-433-1106
Dogs are allowed at the outdoor tables. The outdoor tables are on a covered deck.

Rohnert Park

Baja Fresh Mexican Grill
451 Rohnert Pk. Expressway West
Rohnert Park, CA
707-585-2252
This Mexican restaurant is open for lunch and dinner. They use fresh ingredients and making their salsa and beans daily. Some of the items on their menu include Enchiladas, Burritos, Tacos Salads, Quesadillas, Nachos, Chicken, Steak and more. Well-behaved leashed dogs are allowed at the outdoor tables.

Cafe Des Croissants
101 Golf Course Drive
Rohnert Park, CA 94928
707-585-6185
Dogs are allowed at the outdoor tables.

Santa Rosa

Chevy's Fresh Mex
24 4th Street
Santa Rosa, CA 95401
Railroad Square
707-571-1082
Dogs are allowed at the outdoor seats. The restaurant is in Railroad Square, next to the train station.

Flying Goat Coffee
10 4th Street
Santa Rosa, CA 95401
707-575-1202
Dogs are allowed at the outdoor seats. The coffee shop is in Railroad Square in Santa Rosa, next to the train station.

Sonoma Valley Bagel
2194 Santa Rosa Ave
Santa Rosa, CA 95407
707-579-5484
Dogs are allowed at the outdoor tables, which are covered.

Whole Foods Market
1181 Yulupa Ave.
Santa Rosa, CA 95405
707-575-7915
This natural food supermarket offers natural and organic foods. Order some food from their deli and bring it to an outdoor table where your well-behaved leashed dog is welcome.

Sebastopol

Whole Foods Market
6910 McKinley St.
Sebastopol, CA 95472
707-829-9801
This natural food supermarket offers natural and organic foods. Order some food from their deli and bring it to an outdoor table where your well-behaved leashed dog is welcome. They have a couple of small tables outside.

Stores

Santa Rosa

REI
2715 Santa Rosa Ave
Santa Rosa, CA
707-540-9025
This clothing and outdoor adventure store allows well-behaved, leashed dogs to accompany shoppers.

Chapter 4

California Dog-Friendly Travel Guide
San Francisco Bay Area

Marin - North Bay Dog Travel Guide
Accommodations

Novato

Inn Marin
250 Entrada Drive
Novato, CA 94949
415-883-5952
Inn Marin invites both business and leisure travelers. Nestled in a beautiful resort setting and richly restored, this inn welcomes your best friend. Amenities include a large outdoor heated pool and spa, garden patio area with barbecue, exercise facility, guest laundry facility and a continental breakfast. Rooms include data ports, voice mail and two line speaker phone, iron and ironing board, and handicapped rooms/facilities are available. They are located just off Highway 101, perfect for the business or tourist traveler. There is a $20 one time pet fee. You are required to bring a crate if you plan to leave your dog alone in the room.

Occidental

Occidental Hotel
3610 Bohemian Hwy
Occidental, CA 95465
707-874-3623
There is an $8.70 per day pet fee for each pet. Dogs must be on leash and may not be left alone in the rooms.

Travelodge
7600 Redwood Blvd
Novato, CA 94945
415-892-7500
There is a $10 per day pet fee. Dogs are allowed on the first floor only.

Olema

Ridgetop Inn and Cottage
9876 Sir Francis Drake Blvd.
Olema, CA 94950
415-663-1500
Dogs are allowed in the cottage. It is a non-smoking, one bedroom cottage with a private bathroom and a full kitchen. They stock the kitchen with breakfast items so you can serve yourself breakfast in the morning. The cottage is located above the Village of Olema, less than a mile from the Point Reyes National Seashore headquarters. There is a $25 one time pet fee. Children are also welcome.

Petaluma

Sheraton Sonoma County - Petaluma
745 Baywood Drive
Petaluma, CA 94954
707-283-2888
Dogs up to 80 pounds are allowed. There are no additional pet fees. The entire hotel is non-smoking.

Point Reyes Station

Point Reyes Station Inn Bed and Breakfast
11591 Highway One, Box 824
Point Reyes Station, CA 94956
415-663-9372
They offer private, romantic rooms with thirteen foot vaulted ceilings, whirlpool baths, fireplaces and views of rolling hills. This inn is located at the gateway of the Point Reyes National Seashore. Well-behaved dogs are welcome and there is no extra pet charge. Children are also welcome.

Tree House Bed and Breakfast Inn
73 Drake Summit, P.O. Box 1075
Point Reyes Station, CA 94956
415-663-8720
This inn offers a secluded and peaceful getaway in West Marin. It is located on the tip of Inverness Ridge with a view of Point Reyes Station. The Point Reyes National Seashore is nearby. All three rooms have a private bathroom. Pets and children are always welcome. Smoking is allowed outdoors. There are no pet fees.

Accommodations - RV Parks and Campgrounds

Bodega Bay

Doran Regional Park Campgrounds
201 Doran Beach Road
Bodega Bay, CA
707-875-3540
Walk to the beach from your campsite! There are over 100 campsites in this park which features 2 miles of sandy beach. RVs are permitted and there is a dump station, but no hookups. Dogs are allowed but must be on a 6 foot or less leash and proof of a rabies vaccination is required.

Westside Regional Park Campgrounds
2400 Westshore Road
Bodega Bay, CA
707-875-3540
This park offers 38 campsites. RVs are permitted but there are no hookups. Fishing is the popular activity at this park. Dogs are allowed but must be on a 6 foot or less leash and proof of a rabies vaccination is required. To get there from Highway 1, take Eastshore Road.

San Rafael

Samuel P. Taylor State Park Campgrounds
Sir Francis Drake Blvd.
San Rafael, CA
415-488-9897
This park offers campsites for tents and RVs up to 27 feet. There are no hookups. Amenities include water, tables, grills, flush toilets and showers. While dogs are not allowed on the hiking trails, they are allowed on the bike trail that runs about six miles through the park. The path is nearly level and follows the Northwest Pacific Railroad right-of-way. The trail is both paved and dirt and it starts near the park entrance. Dogs are also allowed in the developed areas like the campgrounds. Pets must be leashed and please clean up after your pet. The park is located north of San Francisco, 15 miles west of San Rafael on Sir Francis Drake Blvd.

Accommodations - Vacation Home Rentals

Inverness

Rosemary Cottage
75 Balboa Ave
Inverness, CA 94937
415-663-9338
Dogs are welcome at the Rosemary Cottage and The Ark Cottage. Families are also welcome. The Rosemary Cottage is a two room cottage with a deck and garden. It is adjacent to the Point Reyes National Seashore. The Ark Cottage is a two room cottage tucked in the forest a mile up the ridge from the village of Inverness. There is a $25 one time pet charge for one dog or a $35 one time pet charge for two dogs.

Stinson Beach

Beach Front Retreat
90 Calle Del Ribera
Stinson Beach, CA 94970
415-383-7870
This vacation home rental offers 3 bedrooms, 2 baths, a fireplace and a beach deck with BBQ. You can view the ocean from the balcony located next to the master bedroom. There is an additional $50 one time per stay pet charge

Attractions

Petaluma

Petaluma Adobe State Historic Park
3325 Adobe Road
Petaluma, CA
at Casa Grande
707-762-4871
This old adobe ranch building, the largest private hacienda in California between 1834 and 1846, was the center of activity on one of the most prosperous private estates established during the Mexican period. The park offers shaded picnic areas with views of farmland and oak-studded hills. Leashed dogs are allowed at the park, but not inside the buildings. Once a year, usually in May, is Living History Day at this park. Volunteers dress up in authentic clothing. You will find Mexican vaqueros, musicians, blacksmiths, carpenters and more. Try brick-making, basketry, corn-grinding, candlemaking and more. The park is located a twenty minute drive from Sonoma. It is at the east edge of Petaluma, off Highway 116 and Adobe Road.

Petaluma Self-Guided Film Walking Tour
Keller St. and Western Ave.
Petaluma, CA
707-769-0429
Commercial and feature film producers love to step back in time to Petaluma's town charm. Petaluma's iron front buildings are frequently the backdrop for film sets. The Film Tour will lead you through the streets to locations of films like American Grafitti, Peggy Sue Got Married, Heroes,Howard the Duck,Shadow of A Doubt, and Basic Instinct. To begin the tour, park in the city garage at the corner of Keller Street and Western Avenue. The Riverfront at the foot of Western Avenue was where the police car was hurled into the water in Howard the Duck. This was also a film site for Explorers. Nearby, 120 Petaluma Blvd. North (Bluestone Main Building) was the site of Bodell's Appliances in Peggy Sue Got Married where Charlie worked for his father. The Mystic Theater, 23 Petaluma Blvd. North near B St. starred as the State Movie Theater in American Graffiti. Walk down Petaluma Blvd. South to H Street. The end of H Street at the Petaluma River was Lovers Lane for Peggy Sue and her boyfriend. Head back to D Street, turning Left on D and head west to 920 D Street. The upstairs bedroom was used in Explorers, and a 20 foot tree was imported from Los Angeles for the boyfriend to climb to the girl's bedroom. Commercials for General Electric, Levi's, and catalog stills for the local Biobottoms company were shot here. At Brown Court off D Street, is an area that has a look that is a favorite with commercial producers, including Orville Redenbacher Popcorn. At 1006 D Street was Charlie's house in Peggy Sue Got Married. Backtrack down D Street to Sixth Street and go north towards town. St. Vincent's Church and neighborhood at Howard/Sixth and Liberty Streets were used for scenes in the TV remake of Shadow of a Doubt with Mark Harmon and Basic Instinct with Michael Douglas and Sharon Stone.

The big white house at 226 Liberty Street, on the east side of Liberty near Washington Street was Peggy Sue's house in Peggy Sue Got Married. For more information, please visit the Petaluma Visitor Center at 800 Baywood Drive, Suite #1 in Petaluma or call 707-769-0429. The Visitor Center is located a the northwest corner of Highway 116 (Lakeville Hwy.) and Baywood Drive next to the Petaluma Marina. Take the Lakeville Hwy 116 exit off Hwy 101.

Petaluma Village Factory Outlet
2200 Petaluma Blvd N.
Petaluma, CA 94952
707-778-9300
Dogs are allowed on leash in the shopping center. Whether they are allowed in the stores or not is up to the individual stores. Dogs may sit with you at the outdoor tables while you eat at some of the food places.

River Walk
Near D St. bridge and Washington St.
Petaluma, CA
707-769-0429
You and your pooch can take an almost 2.5 mile stroll on the River Walk. This walk will take you around the riverfront which was once a bustling river port, and is now a favorite weekend yachting destination. There are numerous species of birds that inhabit this area. For more details of the walk, pick up a brochure at the Petaluma Visitor Center at 800 Baywood Drive, Suite #1 in Petaluma or call 707-769-0429. The Visitor Center is located a the northwest corner of Highway 116 (Lakeville Hwy) and Baywood Drive next to the Petaluma Marina. Take the Lakeville Hwy 116 exit off Hwy 101.

Beaches

Bodega Bay

Doran Regional Park
201 Doran Beach Road
Bodega Bay, CA
707-875-3540
This park offers 2 miles of sandy beach. It is a popular place to picnic, walk, surf, fish and fly kites. Dogs are allowed but must be on a 6 foot or less leash and proof of a rabies vaccination is required. There is a minimal parking fee. The park is located south of Bodega Bay.

Bolinas

Agate Beach
Elm Road
Bolinas, CA
415-499-6387
During low tide, this 6 acre park provides access to almost 2 miles of shoreline. Leashed dogs are allowed.

Muir Beach

Muir Beach
Hwy 1
Muir Beach, CA

Dogs on leash are allowed on Muir Beach with you. Please clean up after your dog on the beach. To get to Muir Beach from Hwy 101 take Hwy 1 North from the north side of the Golden Gate Bridge.

Olema

Point Reyes National Seashore

Olema, CA
415-464-5100
Leashed dogs (on a 6 foot or less leash) are allowed on four beaches. The dog-friendly beaches are the Limantour Beach, Kehoe Beach,

North Beach and South Beach. Dogs are not allowed on the hiking trails. However, they are allowed on some hiking trails that are adjacent to Point Reyes. For a map of dog-friendly hiking trails, please stop by the Visitor Center. Point Reyes is located about an hour north of San Francisco. From Highway 101, exit at Sir Francis Drake Highway, and continue west on Sir Francis Drake to Olema. To find the Visitor Center, turn right in Olema onto Route 1 and then make a left onto Bear Valley Road. The Visitor Center will be on the left.

Stinson Beach

Upton Beach
Highway 1
Stinson Beach, CA
415-499-6387
Dogs not allowed on the National Park section of Stinson Beach but are allowed at Upton Beach which is under Marin County's jurisdiction. This beach is located north of the National Park. Dogs are permitted without leash but under direct and immediate control.

Parks

Bodega Bay

Westside Regional Park
2400 Westshore Road
Bodega Bay, CA
707-565-2041
Located on Bodega Bay, this park is a popular spot for fishing. Dogs are allowed but must be on a 6 foot or less leash and proof of a rabies vaccination is required. To get there from Highway 1, take Eastshore Road.

Fairfax

Deer Park
Porteous Avenue
Fairfax, CA
415-499-6387
Leashed dogs are allowed at this park including the nature trails. The 54 acre park is located in a wooded setting.

Mill Valley

Mill Valley-Sausalito Path
Almonte Blvd.
Mill Valley, CA

This multi-purpose path is used by walkers, runners, bicyclists and equestrians. Dogs on leash are allowed. The path is located in the Bothin Marsh Open Space Preserve.

Mount Tamalpais State Park
801 Panoramic Highway
Mill Valley, CA 94941
415-388-2070
While dogs are not allowed on most of the trails, they are allowed on the Old Stage Road. This path is about .5 to .75 miles and leads to the Marin Municipal Water District Land which allows dogs on their trails. Dogs must be leashed on both the state park and the water district lands. Please clean up after your pets. To get there, take Highway 101 north of San Francisco's Golden Gate Bridge. Then take Highway 1 to the Stinson Beach exit and follow the signs up the mountain.

Olema

Bolinas Ridge Trail
Drake Blvd
Olema, CA

Dogs on leash may accompany you on the Bolinas Ridge Trail. The trailhead is about 1 mile from the Pt Reyes National Seashore Visitor Center in Olema. Dogs are not allowed on trails in Pt Reyes (see Point Reyes National Seashore) so this is the closest trail available. The trailhead is one mile up Drake Blvd from Olema on the right. Parking is at the side of the road.

Petaluma

Rocky Memorial Dog Park
W. Casa Grande Road
Petaluma, CA
707-778-4380
Your dog can run leash-free in this 9 acre fenced dog park. To get there, take Lakeville Hwy. (Hwy 116) east, and turn west on Casa Grande Rd.

San Rafael

Civic Center Lagoon Park
Civic Center Drive
San Rafael, CA
415-499-6387
This 20 acre park has an 11 acre lagoon which is used for fishing and non-motorized boating. The park also has picnic areas and a children's playground. Leashed dogs are allowed.

John F. McInnis Park
Smith Ranch Road
San Rafael, CA
415-499-6387
This 440 acre parks offers nature trails, sports fields, and a golf course. Dogs are allowed not allowed on the golf course. Pets are allowed off

leash but must be under immediate verbal control at all times. Owners must also carry a leash and pick up after their pets.

Samuel P. Taylor State Park
Sir Francis Drake Blvd.
San Rafael, CA 415-488-9897

While dogs are not allowed on the hiking trails, they are allowed on the bike trail that runs about six miles through the park. The path is nearly level and follows the Northwest Pacific Railroad right-of-way. The trail is both paved and dirt and it starts near the park entrance. Dogs are also allowed in the developed areas like the campgrounds. Pets must be leashed and please clean up after your pet. The park is located north of San Francisco, 15 miles west of San Rafael on Sir Francis Drake Blvd.

Sausalito

Sausalito Dog Park
Bridgeway and Ebbtide Avenues
Sausalito, CA

This fenced dog park is 1.3 acres complete with lighting, picnic tables, benches, a dog drinking water area, and a scooper cleaning station. On some days, this very popular park has over 300 dogs per day.

Restaurants

Bolinas

Coast Cafe
46 Wharf Rd
Bolinas, CA 94924
415-868-2224
Dogs are allowed at the outside tables. Bolinas usually has a large number of dogs walking around with their owners. It is a bit off the beaten

path, about 10 minutes from Highway 1.

Corte Madera

A.G. Ferrari Foods
107 Corte Madera Town Ctr
Corte Madera, CA 94925
415-927-4347
Dogs are allowed at the outdoor tables. The restaurant is at the Corte Madera Town Center Shopping Center.

Baja Fresh Mexican Grill
100 Corte Madera Town Center
Corte Madera, CA
415-924-8522
This Mexican restaurant is open for lunch and dinner. They use fresh ingredients and making their salsa and beans daily. Some of the items on their menu include Enchiladas, Burritos, Tacos Salads, Quesadillas, Nachos, Chicken, Steak and more. Well-behaved leashed dogs are allowed at the outdoor tables.

Book Passage Bookstore and Cafe
51 Tamal Vista
Corte Madera, CA
415-927-1503
Dogs are allowed at the outdoor tables.

David's Wild Side
205 Corte Madera Town Center
Corte Madera, CA 94925
415-927-5849
Dogs are allowed at the outdoor tables. The restaurant is in the Corte Madera Town Center shopping center.

World Wrapps
208 Corte Madera Town Center
Corte Madera, CA
415-927-3663
Dogs are allowed at the outdoor tables. This is a quick service restaurant providing healthy and flavorful alternatives to traditional fast food. They offer gourmet low fat wrapped meals with multi-cultural ingredients. They also serve smoothies.

Inverness

Gray Whale Restaurant
12781 Sir Francis Drake Blvd.
Inverness, CA 94937
415-669-1244
Located in downtown Inverness, this restaurant serves pizza, pasta, sandwiches, salads, desserts and more. The outdoor seating offers a bay view. Dogs are allowed at the outdoor tables.

Vladimir's Czechoslovakian Restaurant
12785 Sir Francis Drake Blvd.
Inverness, CA 94937
415-669-1021
This restaurant is located in downtown Inverness and dogs are allowed at the outdoor tables. The restaurant has a well covered patio with heaters.

their salsa and beans daily. Some of the items on their menu include Enchiladas, Burritos, Tacos Salads, Quesadillas, Nachos, Chicken, Steak and more. Well-behaved leashed dogs are allowed at the outdoor tables.

Maya Palenque Restaurant
349 Enfrente Rd
Novato, CA 94949
near Ignacio Blvd
415-883-6292
Dogs are allowed at the outdoor tables, which are covered.

Ristorante Orsi
340 Ignacio Blvd
Novato, CA 94949
West of 101
415-883-0960
Dogs are allowed at the outside tables.

Novato

Baja Fresh Mexican Grill
924 Diablo Ave.
Novato, CA
415-897-4122
This Mexican restaurant is open for lunch and dinner. They use fresh ingredients and making

Petaluma

Apple Box
224 B Street
Petaluma, CA 94952
707-762-5222
Dogs are allowed at the outdoor seats on the patio. It overlooks the Petaluma River near the Riverwalk.

Arnaud's Deli
139 Petaluma Blvd N.
Petaluma, CA 94952
Downtown
707-763-6959
Dogs are allowed at the outdoor tables.

Whole Foods Market
340 Third Street
San Rafael, CA 94901
415-451-6333
This natural food supermarket offers natural and organic foods. Order some food from their deli and bring it to an outdoor table where your well-behaved leashed dog is welcome.

Sausalito

Scoma's
588 Bridgeway
Sausalito, CA
415-332-9551
Dogs are allowed at the outdoor tables. This restaurant is located on the waterfront and offers a great view of the San Francisco Bay. Seafood is their specialty.

San Rafael

Ristorante La Toscana
3751 Redwood Hwy.
San Rafael, CA 94903
415-492-9100
Dogs are allowed at the outdoor tables. This Italian restaurant features pasta, veal, seafood, rabbit and a full bar.

Sebastopol

Pasta Bella
796 Gravenstein Highway
Sebastopol, CA
707-824-8191
This Italian restaurant is open daily for lunch and dinner, and serves brunch on Sundays. Well-behaved leashed dogs are allowed at the outdoor tables. Thanks to one of our readers for recommending this dog-friendly restaurant!

Tiburon

Boudin's Bakery and Cafe
1 Main Street
Tiburon, CA 94920
Downtown Tiburon
415-435-0777
Dogs are allowed at the outdoor tables. They

request that you do not tie your dog to the table. Either hold the leash or tie them to your chair.

Shark's Deli
1600 Tiburon Blvd
Tiburon, CA 94920
415-435-9130
Dogs are allowed at the outdoor tables.

Tiburon Deli
110 Main Street
Tiburon, CA 94920
415-435-4888
Dogs are allowed at the outdoor tables.

Tomales

Emily B's Deli
27000 Highway 1
Tomales, CA 94971
707-878-2732
Dogs are allowed at the outdoor tables.

Tomales Bakery
27000 Highway One
Tomales, CA 94971
707-878-2429
This bakery offers a variety of breads and pastries plus calzones and more. They have a few outdoor tables and dogs are allowed at the outdoor tables.

Valley Ford

Route 1 Diner
14450 Highway 1
Valley Ford, CA 94972
707-876-9600
Dogs are allowed at the outdoor seats.

Stores

Corte Madera

REI

213 Corte Madera Town Center
Corte Madera, CA
415-927-1938
This clothing and outdoor adventure store allows well-behaved, leashed dogs to accompany shoppers.

Vets and Kennels

San Rafael

Pet Emergency & Specialty
901 Francisco Blvd E
San Rafael, CA 94901
415-456-7372
Monday - Friday 5:30 pm to 8 am, 24 hours on weekends.

Oakland - East Bay Dog Travel Guide
Accommodations

Benicia

Best Western Heritage Inn
1955 East Second Street
Benicia, CA 94510
707-746-0401
There is a $25 one time pet fee.

Berkeley

Beau Sky Hotel
2520 Durant Ave
Berkeley, CA 94704
510-540-7688
This small hotel offers personalized service. Some rooms have balconies. If your room doesn't, you can sit at the chairs and tables in the patio at the front of the hotel. Your small, medium or large dog will feel welcome here because they don't discriminate against dog size. It is located close to the UC Berkeley campus and less than a block from the popular Telegraph Ave (see Attractions). There aren't too many hotels in Berkeley, especially around the campus. So if you are going, be sure to book a room in advance. To get there from Hwy 880 heading north, take the Hwy 980 exit towards Hwy 24/Walnut Creek. Then take the Hwy 24 exit on the left towards Berkeley/Walnut Creek. Exit at Claremont Ave and turn left onto Claremont Ave. Make a slight left onto College Ave. Turn left onto Haste St. Turn right onto Telegraph Ave and then right onto Durant. The hotel will be on the right. There are no additional pet fees. All rooms are non-smoking.

Golden Bear Motel
1620 San Pablo Ave
Berkeley, CA 94702
510-525-6770
This motel has over 40 rooms. Eight of the rooms have two-bedroom units and there are four two-bedroom cottages with kitchens. Parking is free. To get there from Hwy 80 heading north, exit University Ave. Turn right onto University Ave, and then left on San Pablo Ave. The motel is on the left. There is a $10 per day additional pet fee.

Concord

Holiday Inn
1050 Burnett Ave
Concord, CA 94520
925-687-5500
There is a $100 refundable pet deposit and a $5 per day pet fee.

Emeryville

Woodfin Suite Hotel
5800 Shellmound
Emeryville, CA 94608
510-601-5880
All rooms are suites and all are non-smoking.

Hotel amenities include a pool, exercise facility, complimentary video movies or books and a complimentary breakfast buffet. There is a $5 per day pet fee and a $150 refundable pet deposit. All well-behaved dogs are welcome.

Fairfield

Motel 6
1473 Holiday Ln
Fairfield, CA 94533
707-425-4565
There are no additional pet fees.

Fremont

La Quinta Inn & Suites Fremont
46200 Landing Parkway
Fremont, CA
510-445-0808
Dogs of all sizes are allowed at the hotel.

Motel 6
46101 Research Ave
Fremont, CA 94539
510-490-4528
You may not leave your dog unattended in the room.

Residence Inn by Marriott
5400 Farwell Place
Fremont, CA 94536
510-794-5900
There is a $75 one time pet fee and an additional $10 per day pet fee. All rooms have full kitchens, irons/ironing boards, hairdryers, and data ports on phones. The inn has self-service laundry facilities, and dinner delivery service from local restaurants. To get there from Hwy 880 heading north, exit Mowry Ave towards central Fremont. Turn right onto Mowry Ave. Turn left on Farwell Drive, then left onto Farwell Place. There is a $75 one time pet fee and a $10 per day additional pet fee.

Hayward

Comfort Inn
24997 Mission Boulevard
Hayward, CA 94544
510-538-4466
Newly renovated guestrooms. Every room has a microwave & refrigerator, hairdryer, iron & ironing board, two 2-line phones with voice mail, coffeemaker, and 27" TV's with expanded cable & HBO.

Super 8 Motel - Hayward I-880
2460 Whipple Road
Hayward, CA 94544
510-489-3888
Motel amenities include a free 8 minute long distance call each night, a free continental breakfast and an on-site guest laundry. A Coffee maker, night light, clock/radio and safe is located in each room. Kids 12 and under stay free. There is a $10 pet fee per stay for up to 3 dogs in one room. From I-880, Exit Whipple Road East.

Vagabond Inn
20455 Hesperian Blvd.
Hayward, CA 94541
510-785-5480
This two story motel offers a heated pool and spa. To get there from Hwy 880 heading north, exit A Street/San Lorenzo. Turn left onto A Street. Then turn right onto Hesperian Blvd. There is a $10 per day additional pet fee per pet.

Livermore

Motel 6
4673 Lassen Rd
Livermore, CA 94550
925-443-5300
One large dog is permitted per room.

Residence Inn by Marriott

1000 Airway Blvd.
Livermore, CA 94550
925-373-1800
There is a $75 one time pet fee and an additional fee of $6 per day. Each room at this motel is a suite with a kitchen. Some of the rooms have loft bedrooms or two bedroom suites. To get there from Hwy 580 heading east, take the Airway/Collier Canyon Rd exit. Turn left onto Airway. There is a $75 one time pet fee and a $10 per day additional pet fee per pet.

Newark

Motel 6
5600 Cedar Ct
Newark, CA 94560
510-791-5900
A well-behaved large dog is okay. No dog barking allowed.

W Silicon Valley - Newark
8200 Gateway Boulevard
Newark, CA 94560
510-494-8800
Dogs of all sizes are allowed. There is a $50 one time additional pet fee.

Woodfin Suite Hotel
39150 Cedar Blvd.
Newark, CA 94560
510-795-1200
All well-behaved dogs are welcome. Every room is a suite with a full kitchen. Hotel amenities include free video movies and a complimentary hot breakfast buffet. There is a $50 one time per stay pet fee.

Oakland

Motel 6
1801 Embarcadero
Oakland, CA 94606

510-436-0103
Dogs may never be left alone in the rooms.

Pleasant Hill

Residence Inn
700 Ellinwood Way
Pleasant Hill, CA 94523
925-689-1010
There is a $75 one time pet fee and a $6 per day additional pet fee.

Pleasanton

Candlewood Suites
5535 Johnson Ct
Pleasanton, CA 94588
925-463-1212
There is a $75 one time pet fee. This suite motel has a kitchen in every room. To get there from Hwy 580 heading east, take the Hopyard Rd Exit. Turn right on Hopyard and then right on Owens Drive. Then turn right onto Johnson Ct. There is a $75 one time pet fee.

Motel 6
5102 Hopyard Rd
Pleasanton, CA 94588
925-463-2626
A well-behaved large dog is allowed.

Ramada Inn
5375 Owens Court
Pleasanton, CA 94588
925-463-1300
There is a $50 refundable pet deposit.

Residence Inn - Pleasanton
11920 Dublin Canyon Rd
Pleasanton, CA 94588
925-227-0500
There is a $100 one time pet fee and a $10 per day additional pet fee.

San Ramon

Residence Inn - San Ramon
1071 Market Place
San Ramon, CA 94583
925-277-9292
There is a $75 one time pet fee and a $5 per day additional pet fee.

San Ramon Marriott
2600 Bishop Drive
San Ramon, CA 94583
925-867-9200
This Marriott allows dogs of all sizes. They have had Great Danes stay here before. Amenities include room service, self service laundry facilities, gift shop, an outdoor pool, fitness room and more. Room amenities include hairdryers and iron/ironing boards. Thanks to one of our readers for recommending this dog-friendly hotel. There is a $75 one time pet fee for dogs.

Walnut Creek

Holiday Inn
2730 N Main Street
Walnut Creek, CA 94596
925-932-3332
There is a $25 one time pet fee.

Motel 6
2389 N Main Street
Walnut Creek, CA 94596
925-935-4010
A well-behaved large dog is okay. Dogs may not be left alone in the room.

Attractions

Alameda

Rosenblum Cellars
2900 Main Street
Alameda, CA 94501
510-865-7007
Well-behaved dogs are allowed at the outdoor tables. The tasting room hours are 12pm-5pm daily.

Berkeley

Telegraph Ave
Telegraph Ave
Berkeley, CA
Bancroft & Dwight Ways

Telegraph Avenue in Berkeley is a colorful multi-cultural center. There are numerous boutiques, street vendors, artists and street performers set up along the sidewalks of Telegraph Avenue between Bancroft Way and Dwight Way. It can be quite busy here, so make sure your pup is okay in crowds. Thanks to one of our readers for the following information: "There is an ordinance prohibiting more than two 'stationary' dogs within ten feet of each other on a certain part of Telegraph Avenue. This ordinance is aimed at the homeless, and I've never personally seen it enforced in the two or so years of existence... The most likely consequence of violating the ordinance is being asked to move your dog. A more serious concern to me would be bringing a not-yet-fully immunized young puppy to the area, where it might me more likely to get parvo, etc/ from a dog that has not received much if any veterinary care." To get there from Hwy 880 heading north, take the Hwy 980 exit towards Hwy 24/Walnut Creek. Then take the Hwy 24 exit on the left towards Berkeley/Walnut Creek. Exit at Claremont Ave and turn left onto Claremont Ave. Make a slight left onto College Ave. Turn left onto Dwight Way. Then turn right onto Telegraph Ave. Parking can be very difficult except maybe during the summer and University holidays.

Livermore

Marina Boat Rentals
Del Valle Road
Livermore, CA
In Del Valle Reg. Park
925-373-0332
Rent a patio boat with your dog and explore Lake Del Valle. Each patio boat holds up to 6 people. There is a 10 mph speed limit on the lake. It costs about $70 for 2 hours or less. All day rentals are available for $100. They do require a $100 refundable deposit (credit card okay). Prices are subject to change. The rentals are available from 6am-5pm, seven days a week, weather

permitting. This lake is about 5 miles long and is located in Del Valle Regional Park, about 10 miles south of Livermore. To get there from Hwy 580 heading east, exit S. Vasco Road. Turn right onto Vasco and head south. When Vasco ends, turn right onto Tesla Rd. Then turn left onto Mines Rd. Turn right onto Del Valle Road. Follow Del Valle Rd to the park entrance.

Oakland

Jack London Square
Broadway & Embarcadero
Oakland, CA 94607
510-814-6000
Historic Jack London Square was named after the famous author, who spent his early years in Oakland. In the 1800's, this waterfront was one of Oakland's main shipping ports. Today it is a shopping village with shops, restaurants, entertainment and more. While at the village, you and your dog can take a self-guided history walk by following the distinctive bronze wolf tracks in the walkway. The walk begins at Heinold's First and Last Chance Saloon. At the village you will also find musical entertainment Sunday afternoons in the courtyard. Be aware that on Sundays, from 10am-2pm, there is a Farmer's Market in the main walkway (center and north end of the village). Dogs are not allowed in the market and the security attendants will remind you. The market pretty much fills up the main walkway, so it is tough to walk around it. There are many dog-friendly outdoor restaurants located at the village (see Restaurants). To get there from Hwy 880 heading north, exit Broadway. Turn left onto Broadway. Follow Broadway into Jack London Square.

Western Aerospace Museum
8260 Boeing St., Building 621 Oakland Airport
Oakland, CA 94614
510-638-7100
The museum is located at historic Oakland Airport, North Field, in a 1940 wooden and corrugated metal military-type hanger. This site was the take-off point for many famous flights, including the first several flights across the Pacific. The museum has indoor and outdoor exhibit areas. Well-behaved, leashed dogs are welcome. Please make sure your pooch relieves himself before going into the museum, including the outdoor museum. The museum is open Wednesday through Sunday and on most holidays except for Christmas and New Year's Day). Hours are 10am to 4pm. There is a minimal admission fee.

Parks

Benicia

Benicia State Recreation Area
Interstate 780
Benicia, CA
707-648-1911
This park covers 720 acres of marsh, grassy hillsides and rocky beaches along the narrowest portion of the Carquinez Strait. Dogs on leash are allowed. Cyclists, runners, walkers and roller skaters enjoy the park's 2 miles of road and bike paths. Picnicking, bird watching and fishing are also attractions. The recreation area is 1.5 miles west of the outskirts of Benicia on I-780. Cars can enter the park through a toll gate.

Berkeley

Ohlone Dog Park
Hearst Avenue
Berkeley, CA

Martin Luther King Jr. Wy

This is a relatively small dog park. At certain times, there can be lots of dogs here. The hours are 6am-10pm on weekdays and 9am-10pm on weekends. The park is located at Hearst Ave, just west of Martin Luther King Jr. Way. There is limited street parking.

Tilden Regional Park
Grizzly Peak Blvd.
Berkeley, CA
510-562-PARK
This regional park has over 2,000 acres including Lake Anza. Dogs must be on leash in the parking areas, picnic areas, lawns and developed areas. Your dog can run off-leash in other areas and trails, just make sure they are under voice control and you must carry a leash. Your dog should be under voice control around bicyclists and equestrians - this has been the biggest area of conflict for unleashed dogs. At Lake Anza, dogs are not allowed at swimming pools or swim beaches. But you should be able to find a non-swim beach where your dog can play and swim in the water. The park can be reached via Canon Drive, Shasta Road, or South Park Drive, all off Grizzly Peak Boulevard in Berkeley.

Fremont

Central Park Dog Park
Stevenson Blvd
Fremont, CA
510-494-4800
Thanks to one of our readers who writes: "Fenced, fresh water on demand, plenty of free parking, easy to find, all grass." The park. located on one acre, is adjacent to the Central Park Softball Complex with access off of Stevenson Blvd.

Coyote Hills Regional Park
Patterson Ranch Rd.
Fremont, CA
near Paseo Padre Pkwy
510-562-PARK
This regional park has Ohlone Indian shellmound sites with fascinating archaeological resources. This Indian site can be viewed from the Chochenyo Trail. For a longer hike, try the 3.5 mile long BayView bike trail. There are many other numerous trails that wind through the park which offer scenic vistas of the San Francisco Bay. Dogs must be on leash. They are not allowed in the seasonal wetlands, marshes, or the Visitor Center lawn area. But there are plenty of dog-friendly trails around to satisfy you and your pup. Coyote Hills is at the west end of Patterson Ranch Road/ Commerce Drive in Fremont. From I-880, take Highway 84 west, exit at Paseo Padre Parkway and drive north. Turn left on Patterson Ranch Road (parking fee).

Sunol Regional Wilderness
Geary Rd.
Fremont, CA
Calaveras Rd.
510-562-PARK
This park is home to the Ohlone Wilderness Trail and Little Yosemite. The Wilderness Trail is at least 7 miles long in each direction. It spans the length of the park and connects up to the Mission Peak Regional Preserve. Hikers who cross into

the San Francisco Water Department lands that connect Mission Peak Regional Preserve, Sunol, Ohlone Regional Wilderness and Del Valle Regional Park must carry an Ohlone Wilderness Trail map/permit. Little Yosemite is a scenic gorge on the Alameda Creek. It is open to the public through a lease agreement with the San Francisco Water Department, who owns the property. The Canyon View Trail is about 1.5 miles each way and leads into Little Yosemite. There are approximately 6-7 other popular trails ranging from 1.2 miles to over 7 miles. Dogs must be on leash in the parking areas, picnic areas, lawns and developed areas. Your dog can run off-leash on most of the trails, just make sure they are under voice control and you must carry a leash. Check with the ranger as to which trails require your dog to be leashed. To get there from the Fremont area, drive north on I-680 and exit at Calaveras Road. Turn right on Calaveras and proceed to Geary Road, which leads directly into the park.

Hayward

Garin and Dry Creek Regional Parks
Garin Ave
Hayward, CA
Mission Blvd.

There are over 3,000 acres of land between these two parks. Combined, these parks have over 20 miles of unpaved trails. You'll also find several creeks that run through the parks. To get there from Mission Blvd, take Garin Rd to the park entrance. There is a minimal fee for parking.

Livermore

Bethany Reservoir State Recreation Area
off Grant Line Road
Livermore, CA
209-874-2056

This park offers activities like fishing and windsurfing. There is also a bike trail that follows the California Aqueduct. Leashed dogs are allowed on the trails. The person we spoke at the park office believes that dogs are also allowed in the lake. Please clean up after your pets. The recreation area is northeast of Livermore, 7 miles off Interstate 580 at the Grant Line Road exit.

Del Valle Dog Run
Del Valle Road
Livermore, CA
In Del Valle Regional Park
510-562-PARK

This dog run is located in Del Valle Regional Park. Here your dog can walk leash free along the trail with you. Del Valle Regional Park is over 3,997 acres of land and it includes a five mile long lake. To get there from Hwy 580 heading east, exit S. Vasco Road. Turn right onto Vasco and head south. When Vasco ends, turn right onto Tesla Rd. Then turn left onto Mines Rd. Turn right onto Del Valle Road. Follow Del Valle Rd to the park entrance. The dog run is to the right of the marina.

Del Valle Regional Park
Del Valle Road
Livermore, CA
510-562-PARK

This park is over 3,997 acres of land and it includes a five mile long lake. The park is in a valley surrounded by oak-covered hills. Miles of trails surround the lake. If you would rather view the scenery from the water, you and your dog can rent a patio boat at the Marina Boat Rentals (see Attractions). Dogs must be on leash in the parking areas, picnic areas, lawns and developed areas. Your dog can run off-leash in other areas and on trails, just make sure they are under voice control and you must carry a leash. Your dog should be under voice control around bicyclists and equestrians - this has been the biggest area of conflict for unleashed dogs. Dogs are not allowed at swimming pools or swim beaches. But with a 5 mile long lake, you should be able to find a non-swim beach where your dog can play in the water. To get there from Hwy 580 heading east, exit S. Vasco Road. Turn right onto Vasco and head south. When Vasco ends, turn right onto Tesla Rd. Then turn left onto Mines Rd. Turn right onto Del Valle Road. Follow Del Valle Rd to the park entrance.

Livermore Canine Park
Murdell Lane
Livermore, CA
In Max Baer Park

This dog park is located in Max Baer Park. It has several trees and a lawn. To get there from downtown Livermore, head west on Stanely Blvd. Turn left on Isabel Ave. Then turn left onto Concannon Blvd (if you reach Alden Ln, you've passed Concannon). Turn left on Murdell Lane and the park will be on the right.

Ohlone Regional Wilderness
Del Valle Rd
Livermore, CA
OR Geary Rd.
510-562-PARK
This park's centerpiece is the 3,817-foot Rose Peak, just 32 feet lower than Mount Diablo.

Surrounding Rose Peak are 9,156 acres of grassy ridges, flowered in season. Wildlife found at this park includes golden eagles, mountain lions, and tule elk. The wilderness trail through this park is 28 miles of mountain and canyon terrain in southern Alameda County. Your dog is allowed to run off-leash, as long as he or she is under voice control. There are several entrances to this park and the trail, including the Del Valle Regional Park (off Del Valle Rd) and the Sunol Regional Wilderness (off Geary Rd).

Sycamore Grove Park
Wetmore Road
Livermore, CA
Holmes Ave
510-373-5700
This park has over 360 acres and provides walking paths, jogging paths and picnic areas. There are many kinds of wildlife here such as deer, fox, bobcat, hawks and more. Dogs must be on leash. To get there from Hwy 580 heading east, take the First Street exit. Turn right and follow First Street until it turns into Holmes Ave. Then turn left onto Wetmore Road. The park entrance is on the right. There is a minimal fee for parking.

Martinez

John Muir National Historic Site
4202 Alhambra Avenue
Martinez, CA 94553
925-228-8860
While dogs are not allowed in any buildings or on the nature trails, they are allowed on the adjacent Mt. Wanda fire road trail. Hike up to the top and back with your pooch. Pets must be leashed and rangers actively patrol the area and will issue citations to anyone who has their dog off leash. To get to the trail, park at the historic site or at the Park and Ride lot on Franklin Canyon and Alhambra. Please clean up after your pet.

Oakland

Lake Merritt
Lakeside Drive
Oakland, CA

This park and lake is in the center of Oakland. Dogs are not allowed inside the park or lake. However, if you keep your dog leashed, you can walk the perimeter (furthest outside) sidewalk. You'll want to remember this rule, since a $270 ticket could be imposed if you venture into the park. It has a nice approximately 3 mile perimeter path that winds around the lake. It is a popular walking, jogging and biking path. To get there from Hwy 880 heading north, take the Oak Street exit towards Lakeside Drive. Turn right onto Oak Street. Oak Street becomes Lakeside Drive. There is ample parking.

Pleasanton

Shadow Cliffs
Stanley Blvd.
Pleasanton, CA
1 mi. fr downtown Pleasanton
510-562-PARK
Special thanks to one of our readers for the info on this great dog-friendly park. This 296-acre park includes an 80-acre lake. Dogs must be on leash in the parking areas, picnic areas, lawns and developed areas. Your dog can run off-leash in other areas and trails, just make sure they are under voice control and you must carry a leash. Your dog should be under voice control around bicyclists and equestrians - this has been the biggest area of conflict for unleashed dogs. Dogs are not allowed at swimming pools or swim beaches. But you should be able to find a non-swim beach where your dog can play and swim in the water. To get there, from I-580 take the Santa Rita Road south, turn left onto Valley Ave, then left onto Stanley Blvd. Turn right off Stanley into the park. There is a minimal entrance fee.

Richmond

Point Isabel Regional Shoreline
Isabel Street
Richmond, CA
510-562-PARK
The park has rules which state "dogs, except pit bulls, may be taken off leash." This 20 plus acre park is a dog park that is not completely fenced, but has paved paths, grass and beach access to the bay. If your pooch likes chasing birds, beware... dogs sometimes run over to the bird sanctuary which is close to the freeway. Nearby is a dog bathing place called Mudpuppy's which also has dog toys and treats. Other activities at this park include bay fishing, jogging and running trails, birdwatching, kite flying and picnicking. Thanks to one of our readers for providing us with this great information. From I-80 (the Eastshore Freeway) in Richmond, take Central Avenue west to Point Isabel, adjacent to the U.S. Postal Service Bulk Mail Center.

Restaurants

Albany

Cugini Restaurant

1556 Solano Ave
Albany, CA
Peralta Ave
510-558-9000
Your dog is welcome to join you for dinner at this restaurant. They serve a variety of wood-fired pizzas. It is located on Solano Ave, which is a shopping area.

Berkeley

Bel Forno
1400 Shattuck Ave
Berkeley, CA
Rose Street
510-644-1601
Open for breakfast and lunch, this cafe serves omelettes, pastries, salads, soups, sandwiches and more. They have 5-6 outdoor tables. It is located northwest of the UC Berkeley campus.

French Hotel Cafe
1538 Shattuck Ave
Berkeley, CA 94709
north of Cedar Street
510-548-9930
You and your dog are welcome at the outdoor tables. The cafe is located northwest of the UC Berkeley campus.

Whole Foods Market
3000 Telegraph Ave.
Berkeley, CA 94705
510-649-1333
This natural food supermarket offers natural and organic foods. Order some food from their deli and bring it to an outdoor table where your well-behaved leashed dog is welcome.

Dublin

Baja Fresh Mexican Grill
4550 Tassajara Rd.
Dublin, CA
925-556-9199
This Mexican restaurant is open for lunch and dinner. They use fresh ingredients and making their salsa and beans daily. Some of the items on their menu include Enchiladas, Burritos, Tacos Salads, Quesadillas, Nachos, Chicken, Steak and more. Well-behaved leashed dogs are allowed at the outdoor tables.

Fairfield

Baja Fresh Mexican Grill
1450 Travis Blvd
Fairfield, CA
707-432-0460
This Mexican restaurant is open for lunch and dinner. They use fresh ingredients and making their salsa and beans daily. Some of the items on their menu include Enchiladas, Burritos, Tacos Salads, Quesadillas, Nachos, Chicken, Steak and more. Well-behaved leashed dogs are allowed at the outdoor tables.

Lafayette

Baja Fresh Mexican Grill
3596 Mt. Diablo Blvd.

Lafayette, CA
925-283-8740
This Mexican restaurant is open for lunch and dinner. They use fresh ingredients and making their salsa and beans daily. Some of the items on their menu include Enchiladas, Burritos, Tacos Salads, Quesadillas, Nachos, Chicken, Steak and more. Well-behaved leashed dogs are allowed at the outdoor tables.

Livermore

Baja Fresh Mexican Grill
2298 Las Positas
Livermore, CA
925-245-9888
This Mexican restaurant is open for lunch and dinner. They use fresh ingredients and making their salsa and beans daily. Some of the items on their menu include Enchiladas, Burritos, Tacos Salads, Quesadillas, Nachos, Chicken, Steak and more. Well-behaved leashed dogs are allowed at the outdoor tables.

Bruno's Italian Cuisine
2133 First Street
Livermore, CA
925-371-3999
Well-behaved leashed dogs are allowed at the outdoor seating area.

Cafe Paradiso
53 Wright Brothers Avenue
Livermore, CA
925-371-2233
Well-behaved leashed dogs are allowed at the outdoor seating area.

Chevys Fresh Mex
4685 First Street
Livermore, CA
925-960-0071
Well-behaved leashed dogs are allowed at the outdoor seating area.

Me-N-Eds Pizza
4436 Las Positas Road
Livermore, CA
925-294-9333
Well-behaved leashed dogs are allowed at the outdoor seating area.

New York Pizza
853 E Stanley Blvd
Livermore, CA
925-447-4992
Well-behaved leashed dogs are allowed at the

outdoor seating area.

Noodle Express
4363 First Street
Livermore, CA
925-371-9038
Well-behaved leashed dogs are allowed at the outdoor seating area.

Panama Bay Coffee Co.
2115 First Street
Livermore, CA
925-245-1700
Well-behaved leashed dogs are allowed at the outdoor seating area.

Scardina' Deli
4084 East Avenue
Livermore, CA
925-443-0494
Well-behaved leashed dogs are allowed at the outdoor seating area.

Towns End Deli
7633 Southfront Road
Livermore, CA
925-960-0636
Well-behaved leashed dogs are allowed at the outdoor seating area.

Una Mas Taqueria
1476 First Street
Livermore, CA
925-606-5120
Well-behaved leashed dogs are allowed at the outdoor seating area.

Oakland

Heinolds First & Last Chance
56 Jack London Sq
Oakland, CA 94607
In Jack London Square
510-839-6761
Dogs are welcome at the outdoor tables of this bar. The saloon serves beer, wine and cocktails. Heinold's First and Last Chance Saloon is where the famous author, Jack London, borrowed his entrance fee for college from the proprietor. This bar is the starting point for the self-guided history walk of Jack London Square (see Attractions).

Italian Colors Ristorante
2220 Mountain Boulevard
Oakland, CA
510-482-8094
Dogs are allowed at the outdoor tables.

Le Boulanger Bakery
4039 Piedmont Ave
Oakland, CA 94611
between 40th & 41st St
510-597-1123
They are open for breakfast and lunch, serving baked goodies, bagels, sandwiches and a variety of coffee. There is street parking in front and a parking lot behind the restaurant. It is located on Piedmont Ave, east of the Hwy 580 and Hwy 980/24 intersections.

Tony Roma's
55 Washington St
Oakland, CA 94607
In Jack London Square
510-271-1818
This restaurant is famous for its BBQ ribs. They also serve chicken, steak, seafood and delicious desserts. It is located in the dog-friendly Jack London Square (see Attractions).

Zazoo's Restaurant
30 Jack London Sq
Oakland, CA 94607
In Jack London Square
510-986-5454
Located on the waterfront, this restaurant serves seafood, pasta, burgers, kabobs, omelettes, salads and more. Try the tasty kabobs. It is located in the dog-friendly Jack London Square (see Attractions).

Pleasanton

360 (Degrees) Gourmet Burritos
4220 Rosewood Drive
Pleasanton, CA
925-225-9306
Well-behaved leashed dogs are allowed at the outdoor seating area.

Baci Restaurant
500 Main Street
Pleasanton, CA
925-600-0600
Well-behaved leashed dogs are allowed at the outdoor seating area.

Baja Fresh Mexican Grill
2457 Stoneridge Mall Ste.

Pleasanton, CA
925-251-1500
This Mexican restaurant is open for lunch and dinner. They use fresh ingredients and making their salsa and beans daily. Some of the items on their menu include Enchiladas, Burritos, Tacos Salads, Quesadillas, Nachos, Chicken, Steak and more. Well-behaved leashed dogs are allowed at the outdoor tables.

Erik's Deli
4247 Rosewood Drive
Pleasanton, CA
925-847-9755
Well-behaved leashed dogs are allowed at the outdoor seating area.

High Tech Burrito
349 Main Street
Pleasanton, CA
925-462-2323
Well-behaved leashed dogs are allowed at the outdoor seating area.

New York Pizza
690 Main Street
Pleasanton, CA
925-484-4757
Well-behaved leashed dogs are allowed at the outdoor seating area.

New York Pizza and Deli
5321 Hopyard Road
Pleasanton, CA
925-847-1700
Well-behaved leashed dogs are allowed at the outdoor seating area.

Rising Loafer Cafe & Bakery
428 Main Street
Pleasanton, CA
925-426-0822
Well-behaved leashed dogs are allowed at the outdoor seating area.

TGI Fridays
3999 Santa Rita Road
Pleasanton, CA
925-225-1995
Well-behaved leashed dogs are allowed at the outdoor seating area.

Tomo Sushi Bar & Grill
734 Main Street
Pleasanton, CA
925-600-9136
Well-behaved leashed dogs are allowed at the seats on the front patio, but not on the back patio.

Twisted Pizza
6654 Koll Center Pkwy
Pleasanton, CA
925-249-6707
Well-behaved leashed dogs are allowed at the outdoor seating area.

San Ramon

Baja Fresh Mexican Grill
132 Sunset Drive
San Ramon, CA
925-866-6667
Your dog is welcome here! This Mexican restaurant is open for lunch and dinner. They use fresh ingredients and making their salsa and beans daily. Some of the items on their menu include Enchiladas, Burritos, Tacos Salads, Quesadillas, Nachos, Chicken, Steak and more. Well-behaved leashed dogs are allowed at the outdoor tables.

Whole Foods Market
100 Sunset Drive
San Ramon, CA 94583
925-355-9000
This natural food supermarket offers natural and organic foods. Order some food from their deli and bring it to an outdoor table where your well-behaved leashed dog is welcome.

Walnut Creek

Baja Fresh Mexican Grill
1271-1273 S. California Blvd.
Walnut Creek, CA
925-947-0588
This Mexican restaurant is open for lunch and dinner. They use fresh ingredients and making their salsa and beans daily. Some of the items on their menu include Enchiladas, Burritos, Tacos Salads, Quesadillas, Nachos, Chicken, Steak and more. Well-behaved leashed dogs are allowed at the outdoor tables.

Whole Foods Market
1333 E. Newell
Walnut Creek, CA 94596
925-274-9700
This natural food supermarket offers natural and organic foods. Order some food from their deli and bring it to an outdoor table where your well-behaved leashed dog is welcome.

Stores

Berkeley

Avenue Books
2904 College Avenue
Berkeley, CA
510-549-3532
Thanks to one of our readers who writes "So dog-friendly, they offer doggie biscuits!" They are located in the Elmwood district and are open 7 days a week.

Restoration Hardware
1733 Fourth Street
Berkeley, CA
510-526-6424

Concord

REI
1975 Diamond Blvd
Concord, CA
Willows Shopping Center
925-825-9400
This clothing and outdoor adventure store allows well-behaved, leashed dogs to accompany shoppers.

Fremont

REI
43962 Fremont Blvd
Fremont, CA
510-651-0305
This clothing and outdoor adventure store allows well-behaved, leashed dogs to accompany shoppers.

Livermore

Book Oasis
2369 First Street
Livermore, CA 94550
925-606-7876
Dogs are welcome at this book store. They usually have dog cookies at the front desk. The store is located in the historic Livermore Firehouse in an 1800 square foot space. The offer more than eighty different sections and subsections of books. Store hours are 10am to 7pm Monday through Saturday.

Walnut Creek

Restoration Hardware
1460 Mt Diablo Blvd
Walnut Creek, CA
925-906-9230
Your well-behaved leashed dog is allowed inside this store. They love having dogs in the store!

Vets and Kennels

Berkeley

Pet Emergency Treatment Service
1048 University Ave
Berkeley, CA 94710
San Pablo Ave
510-548-6684
Monday - Friday 6pm to 8am, Noon Saturday to 8 am Monday.

Concord

Veterinary Emergency Clinic
1410 Monument Blvd
Concord, CA 94520
925-798-2900
Monday - Friday 6pm to 8am, 24 hours weekends and holidays.

Fremont

Ohlone Veterinary Emergency
1618 Washington Blvd
Fremont, CA 94539
510-657-6620
Monday - Friday 6pm to 8am, 24 hours weekends and holidays.

San Leandro

Alameda County Emergency Pet Hospital
14790 Washington Ave
San Leandro, CA 94578
Hwy 880
510-352-6080
Monday - Friday 6pm to 8am, 24 hours weekends and holidays.

Palo Alto - Peninsula Dog Travel Guide
Accommodations

Belmont

Motel 6
1101 Shoreway Rd.

Belmont, CA 94002
650-591-1471
There is no extra pet charge in the regular rooms. There is a $25 one time pet charge in the studio rooms.

Burlingame

Embassy Suites
150 Anza Blvd.
Burlingame, CA 94010
650-342-4600
This majestic hotel which overlooks the San Francisco Bay has no size restrictions for your well-behaved dog. Inside, you will find a nine-story atrium filled with lush tropical palms, flowers and waterfalls. Amenities include a heated indoor pool and more. The hotel is located about two miles south of the San Francisco Airport and 16 miles from downtown San Francisco. There is a $50 one time pet fee.

Vagabond Inn
1640 Bayshore Highway
Burlingame, CA 94010
650-692-4040
This motel overlooks the San Francisco Bay. It is located just south of the airport and about 16 miles from downtown San Francisco. All rooms include coffee makers, cable television and air

conditioning. Pets are an additional $10 per day.

Half Moon Bay

Holiday Inn Express
230 S Cabrillo Hwy
Half Moon Bay, CA 94019
650-726-3400
Amenities at this motel include a deluxe complimentary continental breakfast. There is an additional $10 per day pet charge.

Ramada Limited
3020 N Cabrillo Hwy
Half Moon Bay, CA 94019
650-726-9700
There is a $15 per day pet fee.

Millbrae

Clarion Hotel
250 El Camino Real
Millbrae, CA 94030
650-692-6363
There is a $30 per day additional pet fee.

Mountain View

Residence Inn by Marriott

1854 W El Camino Real
Mountain View, CA 94040
650-940-1300
This is an apartment style inn that has suite style rooms. There is a $50 non-refundable room cleaning fee for pets and a $10 per day additional pet fee per pet.

Tropicana Lodge
1720 El Camino Real
Mountain View, CA 94040
650-961-0220
Pets may not be left alone in the rooms.

Palo Alto

Motel 6
4301 El Camino Real
Palo Alto, CA 94306
650-949-0833
There are no additional pet fees.

Sheraton Palo Alto Hotel
625 El Camino Real
Palo Alto, CA 94301
650-328-2800
Dogs up to 80 pounds are allowed. There are no additional pet fees.

Redwood City

Hotel Sofitel
223 Twin Dolphin Dr
Redwood City, CA 94065
650-598-9000
This nice 8 story dog-friendly hotel is located off Hwy 101 and Marine World Parkway. There is a $25 one time pet fee.

San Carlos

Inns of America
555 Skyway Road
San Carlos, CA 94070
650-631-0777
Amenities include a free continental breakfast, swimming pool, coin-op laundry, exercise room and more. They are located off Hwy 101 at the Holly Street Exit. Dogs are not allowed in the lobby except during check-in or check-out.

San Mateo

Residence Inn by Marriott
2000 Winward Way
San Mateo, CA 94404
650-574-4700
This is an apartment style inn that has suite style rooms. There is a $75 non-refundable room cleaning fee for pets and a $6 per day additional pet fee.

South San Francisco

Howard Johnson Express Inn
222 South Airport Blvd.
South San Francisco, CA 94080
650-589-9055
Dogs of all sizes are welcome. There is a $10 per day pet fee.

La Quinta Inn South San Francisco
20 Airport Blvd
South San Francisco, CA
650-583-2223
Dogs up to 75 pounds are allowed at the hotel.

Motel 6
111 Mitchell Ave.
South San Francisco, CA 94080
650-871-0770
Pets are allowed, but they are not to be left in the room alone. There is no extra pet charge.

Vagabond Inn
222 S. Airport Blvd
South San Francisco, CA 94080
650-589-9055
Amenities include microwaves and refrigerators in some rooms. There is a $10 per day pet charge. This inn was formerly a Howard Johnson Inn.

Accommodations - RV Parks and Campgrounds

Pescadero

Butano State Park Campground
Highway 1
Pescadero, CA
650-879-2040
The campground in this park offers both tent and RV sites. RVs up to 27 feet are allowed an there are no hookups. Camp amenities include picnic tables, water and vault toilets. While dogs are not allowed on the park trails, they are allowed in the campground and on miles of fire roads. Mountain biking is also allowed on the fire roads. Pets must be on a 6 foot or less leash. Please clean up after them. The park is located on the San Mateo Coast off Highway 1. To get there go 4.5 miles southeast of Pescadero via Pescadero and Cloverdale Roads.

Accommodations - Vacation Home Rentals

Pescadero

Estancia del Mar Cottages
San Mateo County Coastside
Pescadero, CA
650-879-1500
Enjoy a romantic getaway or a family vacation at one of the six cottages that overlook the ocean. Dogs are allowed as well as children. Estancia del Mar is also a working horse ranch where the owners breed, raise and train purebred Peruvian Paso horses.

Attractions

Half Moon Bay

Santa's Tree Farm
78 Pilarcitos Creek Road
Half Moon Bay, CA
650-726-2246
Well-behaved leashed dogs are allowed at this farm, but please note that the owners and/or employees reserve the right to request that your dog wait in the car if your pup misbehaves. Be watchful of others, especially children who may be frightened of dogs. They are open year-round. Santa's Tree Farm offers complimentary candy canes, hot apple cider, and of course, a great selection of Christmas trees. To get there from Hwy 280, take Hwy 92 West towards Half Moon Bay. Hwy 92 becomes Half Moon Bay Road. Go approximately 4 miles and then make a right turn onto Pilarcitos Creek Road.

Palo Alto

Downtown Palo Alto
University Ave
Palo Alto, CA
near El Camino Real

Downtown Palo Alto is a nice area to walk with your leashed dog. There are many shops and outdoor restaurants that line University Ave. Some of the stores allow dogs inside, like Restoration Hardware. However, please ask the store clerk before bringing your dog inside each store just in case their policies have changed. Enjoy lunch or dinner at one of the many nearby outdoor cafes (see Restaurants).

Hewlett-Packard Garage
367 Addison Ave
Palo Alto, CA

The HP Garage is known as the birthplace of Silicon Valley. You and your pup can see where William Hewlett and David Packard started HP. Please note that the house is now a private residence, so you'll need to view it from the

sidewalk only.

Stanford Shopping Center
680 Stanford Shopping Center
Palo Alto, CA 94304
near El Camino Real
650-617-8585
Stanford Shopping Center is the Bay Area's premier open-air shopping center. This dog-friendly mall has a beautiful outdoor garden environment. Thirty-five varieties of trees are represented by 1,300 specimens throughout the mall. There are hundreds of hanging baskets and flower-filled planters located in four microclimates. We have found that many of the stores do allow well-behaved dogs inside. For a list of dog-friendly stores, please look at our stores category. However, please ask the store clerk before bringing your dog inside each store just in case their policies have changed. Depending on the season, there will be many outdoor tables adjacent to the food stands and cafes. Here you can order the food inside and then enjoy it with your pup at one of the outside tables.

Beaches

Half Moon Bay

Blufftop Coastal Park
Poplar Street
Half Moon Bay, CA
650-726-8297
Leashed dogs are allowed at this beach. The beach is located on the west end of Poplar Street, off Highway 1.

Montara State Beach
Highway 1
Half Moon Bay, CA
650-726-8819
Dogs on leash are allowed at this beach. Please clean up after your pets. The beach is located 8

miles north of Half Moon Bay on Highway 1. There are two beach access points. The first access point is across from Second Street, immediately south of the Outrigger Restaurant. The second access point is about a 1/2 mile north on the ocean side of Highway 1. Both access points have steep paths down to the beach.

Surfer's Beach
Highway 1
Half Moon Bay, CA
650-726-8297
Dogs on leash are allowed on the beach. It is located at Highway 1 and Coronado Street.

Pacifica

Esplanade Beach
Esplanade
Pacifica, CA
650-738-7381
This beach offers an off-leash area for dogs. To get to the beach, take the stairs at the end of Esplanade. Esplanade is just north of Manor Drive, off Highway 1.

Pescadero

Bean Hollow State Beach
Highway 1
Pescadero, CA
650-879-2170
This is a very rocky beach with not much sand. Dogs are allowed but must be on a 6 foot or less leash. Please clean up after your pets. The beach is located 3 miles south of Pescadero on Highway 1.

Parks

Belmont

City of Belmont Dog Park
2525 Buena Vista Avenue
Belmont, CA
650-365-3524
This dog park is located at the Cipriani Elementary School.

Burlingame

Bayside Park Dog Park
1125 South Airport Blvd
Burlingame, CA
South of Broadway exit of 101

650-558-7300
This dog park is over 570 feet long. It is in the back of the parking area and then you have to walk about 1/8 mile down a path to the off-leash dog park.

Foster City

Foster City Dog Run
Foster City Blvd at Bounty
Foster City, CA
Bounty

There is a separate dog area for small dogs and large dogs at this off leash dog park.

Mountain View

Mountain View Dog Park
Shoreline Blvd at North Rd
Mountain View, CA
at Shoreline Park entrance

This fenced, off leash dog park is located across from Shoreline Ampitheatre at the entrance to Shoreline Park. Dogs are not allowed in Shoreline Park itself.

Pacifica

Pacifica State Beach
Highway 1
Pacifica, CA
650-738-7381
This wide crescent shaped beach is located off Highway 1 in downtown Pacifica. Dogs on leash are allowed and please clean up after them.

Palo Alto

Greer Dog Park
1098 Amarillo Avenue
Palo Alto, CA
West Bayshore
650-329-2261
This is a fenced off leash dog exercise park. Dogs on leash are allowed in the rest of the park.

Hoover Park
2901 Cowper St
Palo Alto, CA
near Colorado
650-329-2261
This is a small off leash dog exercise area. Dogs on leash are allowed in the rest of the park.

Mitchell Park/Dog Run
3800 Middlefield Rd
Palo Alto, CA
650-329-2261
Located in Mitchell Park at 3800 Middlefield Rd (between E. Charleston and E. Meadow) Note: It can be tough to find at first. The dog run is closer to E. Charleston by the baseball fields and over a small hill.

Palo Alto Baylands Preserve
San Antonio Road
Palo Alto, CA
Hwy 101
650-329-2506
The Palo Alto Baylands Preserve is a flat mostly unpaved 5 mile loop trail. Leashed dogs are allowed, unless posted in special bird nesting areas. There are several entrance points. One of the main starting points is from Hwy 101 heading north, exit San Antonio Road and turn right. San Antonio Road will bring you directly into the start of the Preserve. Please note that there is an adjacent park on the right which is a City of Mountain View park that does not allow dogs. However, no need to worry, the dog-friendly Palo Alto side has plenty of trails for you and your pooch to walk or run.

Stanford University
Palm Drive
Palo Alto, CA
El Camino Real
408-225-0225
Stanford University has miles of tree covered sidewalks and paths that wind through the campus. There is also a park at the end of Palm Drive which is a small but popular hang out for locals and their leashed dogs on warm days . To get there from downtown Palo Alto, take University Ave west toward the hills. University Ave turns into Palm Drive. There are tree lined walking paths along this street. The park is at the end of Palm. Ample parking is available.

Pescadero

Butano State Park
Highway 1
Pescadero, CA
650-879-2040
This 2,200 acre park is located in a secluded redwood-filled canyon. While dogs are not allowed on the trails, they are allowed in the campground and on miles of fire roads. Mountain biking is also allowed on the fire roads. Pets must be on a 6 foot or less leash. Please clean up after them. The park is located on the San Mateo

Coast off Highway 1. To get there go 4.5 miles southeast of Pescadero via Pescadero and Cloverdale Roads.

Portola Valley

Windy Hill Preserve
Hwys 84 and 35
Portola Valley, CA
650-691-1200
At this park there are views of the Santa Clara Valley, San Francisco and the ocean. This preserve features grassy meadows and redwood, fir, and oak trees. Leashed dogs are allowed on designated trails. Directions: From Hwy 280, take Hwy 84 west (La Honda Rd). Go about 2.3 miles to Hwy 35 (Skyline Blvd). The main parking is at the intersection of Hwys 84 and 35. Another starting option is to park at the Portola Valley Town Hall and begin there.

Redwood City

Pulgas Ridge Open Space Preserve
Edmonds Road
Redwood City, CA
Crestview Drive
650-691-1200
This park has about 293 acres and some great trails. There are are about 3 miles of trails that will provide moderate to strenuous exercise. Leashed dogs are allowed on the trails. The park offers some nice shade on warm days. To get there from Interstate 280, take the Edgewood Road exit. Travel 0.75 miles northeast on Edgewood Road toward San Carlos and Redwood City. Turn left (north) on Crestview Drive, and then immediately turn left on Edmonds Road. Limited roadside parking is available along Crestview Drive and Edmonds Road.

Shores Dog Park
Radio Road

Redwood City, CA
Redwood Shore Parkway

This dog park (opened Nov/Dec 98) was funded by Redwood City residents. To get there from Hwy 101, take Holly/Redwood Shores Parkway Exit. Go east (Redwood Shore Parkway). Turn right on Radio Road (this is almost at the end of the street). The park will be on the right. Thanks to one of our readers for this information.

Restaurants

Burlingame

Copenhagen Bakery and Cafe
1216 Burlingame Ave
Burlingame, CA 94010
650-342-1357
Dogs are allowed at the outdoor tables.

La Salsa Mexican Grill
1125 Burlingame Ave
Burlingame, CA 94010
650-579-3684
Dogs are allowed at the outdoor tables.

La Scala
1219 Burlingame Ave
Burlingame, CA 94010
650-347-3035
Dogs are allowed at the outdoor tables.

Left At Albuquerque
1100 Burlingame Ave
Burlingame, CA 94010
650-401-5700
Dogs are allowed at the outdoor tables.

Noah's Bagels
1152 Burlingame Ave
Burlingame, CA 94010
650-342-8423

Dogs are allowed at the outdoor tables.

Foster City

Baja Fresh Mexican Grill
1031 East Hillsdale Blvd.
Foster City, CA
650-358-8632
This Mexican restaurant is open for lunch and dinner. They use fresh ingredients and making their salsa and beans daily. Some of the items on their menu include Enchiladas, Burritos, Tacos Salads, Quesadillas, Nachos, Chicken, Steak and more. Well-behaved leashed dogs are allowed at the outdoor tables.

Half Moon Bay

Casey's Cafe
328 Main Street
Half Moon Bay, CA 94019
650-560-4880
Dogs are allowed at the outdoor tables.

Half Moon Bay Coffee Company
20 Stone Pine Rd #A
Half Moon Bay, CA 94019
650-726-3664
Dogs are allowed at the outdoor tables.

It's Italia Pizzeria
40 Stone Pine Rd
Half Moon Bay, CA 94019
650-726-4444
Dogs are allowed at the outdoor tables.

The 30 Cafe
46 Cabrillo Hwy N
Half Moon Bay, CA 94019
Half Moon Bay Airport
650-573-3701
This cafe is located in the airport terminal building adjacent to the parking lot. This dog-friendly place is popular with the locals. You can watch the small aircraft taking off from the outdoor seats. Thanks to one of our readers who recommended this cafe. The cafe is open for breakfast and lunch everyday except Mondays. The hours are 6:30 am to 2:00 pm, weekends to 4:00 pm.

Menlo Park

Cafe Borrone
1010 El Camino Real
Menlo Park, CA 94025
650-327-0830

There is a large outdoor seating area where dogs are welcome. There are umbrellas for shade. The coffee house is open for breakfast lunch and dinner except on Sunday when it is open until 5 pm.

Mountain View

Amici's East Coast Pizza
790 Castro Street
Mountain View, CA 94041
650-961-6666
Dogs are allowed at the outdoor tables.

Clarkes Charcoal Broiler
615 W El Camino Real
Mountain View, CA
650-967-0851
Enjoy their hamburgers, steak or chicken sandwiches.

La Salsa Restaurant
660 San Antonio Rd
Mountain View, CA
650-917-8290
This restaurant has several kinds of tacos and burritos to choose from.

Le Boulanger
650 Castro St #160

Mountain View, CA 94041
650-961-1787
Dogs are allowed at the outdoor tables.

Posh Bagel
444 Castro Street #120
Mountain View, CA 94041
650-968-5308
Dogs are allowed at the outdoor tables.

Palo Alto

Baja Fresh Mexican Grill
3990 El Camino Real
Palo Alto, CA
650-424-8599
This Mexican restaurant is open for lunch and dinner. They use fresh ingredients and making their salsa and beans daily. Some of the items on their menu include Enchiladas, Burritos, Tacos Salads, Quesadillas, Nachos, Chicken, Steak and more. Well-behaved leashed dogs are allowed at the outdoor tables.

Golden Wok
451 S California Ave
Palo Alto, CA
between El Camino & Mimosa
650-327-2222
Choose from a variety of Chinese appetizers and dishes like pot stickers, egg rolls, meat and vegetarians dishes, noodles and more. Then are open for lunch and dinner, but come early since they only have a few outdoor tables.

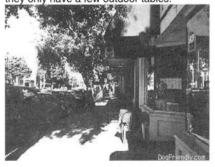

Izzy's Brooklyn Bagels
477 S California Ave
Palo Alto, CA
between El Camino & Mimosa
650-329-0700
This bagel shop has a wide variety of bagels and pastries.

Joanie's Cafe
447 S California Ave
Palo Alto, CA
between El Camino & Mimosa
650-326-6505
If you come here for breakfast, you can order a variety of dishes like belgium waffles, pancakes and more. They also serve sandwiches for lunch.

Kirk's
361 S. California Ave
Palo Alto, CA 94306
650-326-6159
Dogs are allowed at the outdoor tables.

Spalti Ristorante
417 S California Ave
Palo Alto, CA
between El Camino & Birch
650-327-9390
This nice Italian restaurant has outdoor heaters to keep you and your pup warm. Sidewalk and patio seating are available. They are open for lunch and dinner.

St. Michael's Alley
806 Emerson St.
Palo Alto, CA 94301
650-326-2530
This restaurant has dog-friendly outdoor seating and they love dogs. The owners also have two dogs. They serve brunch, lunch and dinner. For brunch they offer omelettes, French toast, pancakes and more. The lunch menu has a wide variety of appetizers, entrees, sandwiches and pizza. The dinner menu includes entrees like NY Steak, chicken, pasta and much more.

Taxi's Hamburgers
403 University Ave
Palo Alto, CA
650-322-8294
If you like burgers, then you'll definitely need to have lunch or dinner here. They serve big juicy hamburgers, great fries, and shakes (lowfat and nonfat shakes too.)

Whole Foods Market
774 Emerson Street
Palo Alto, CA 94301
650-326-8676
This natural food supermarket offers natural and organic foods. Order some food from their deli and bring it to the outdoor table where your well-

behaved leashed dog is welcome. They have one square picnic table located under an awning.

World Wrapps
201 University Ave.
Palo Alto, CA
650-327-9777
This restaurant has a variety of wrapps with veggies or meat and a selection of fruit smoothies.

San Carlos

Ciao Amore
788 Laurel Street
San Carlos, CA 94070
650-802-8808
This restaurant is dog-friendly and serves some delicious Italian food. They recently added more outdoor seats and the seating area is covered. After lunch or dinner, you can walk over to the pet store which is about 1/2 block away.

Princeton

Half Moon Bay Brewing Company
390 Capistrano Rd
Princeton, CA
650-728-BREW
Thanks to one of our readers who writes: "A great setting south of San Francisco to spend the day walking your dog on the beautiful San Mateo Coastal Beaches. You can enjoy an open air meal with your furry friend sitting beside you in a fun and relaxed patio with music and friendly service."

Redwood City

City Pub
2620 Broadway
Redwood City, CA 94063
650-363-2620
Dogs are allowed at the outside tables. They will bring your dog a bowl of water as well. They serve burgers, other food and many beers.

Diving Pelican Cafe
650 Bair Island Rd #102
Redwood City, CA 94063
415-368-3668
According to a reader "Great outdoor deck-like seating. Awesome place for brunch." Dogs need to be leashed at the outdoor deck.

Ristorante Piacere
727 Laurel Street
San Carlos, CA 94070
650-592-3536
This fine Italian restaurant serves you outside either at the tables next to the sidewalk or if you prefer, up on the patio. The seating area is covered and has outdoor heaters. If you are looking for an elegant place to take your pooch, this is it. Afterwards, you can stroll down to the pet store that is about 1/2 block away.

San Mateo

Whole Foods Market
1010 Park Place
San Mateo, CA 94403
650-358-6900

This natural food supermarket offers natural and organic foods. Order some food from their deli and bring it to an outdoor table where your well-behaved leashed dog is welcome.

Stores

Palo Alto

Bang & Olufsen
Stanford Shopping Center
Palo Alto, CA 94304
650-322-2264
Your well-behaved leashed dog is allowed inside this store.

Bloomingdale's
Stanford Shopping Center
Palo Alto, CA 94304
650-463-2000
Your well-behaved leashed dog is allowed inside this store.

Books Inc.
Stanford Shopping Center
Palo Alto, CA 94304
650-321-0600
Your well-behaved leashed dog is allowed inside this store.

Giants Dugout
Stanford Shopping Center
Palo Alto, CA 94304
650-323-9790
Your well-behaved leashed dog is allowed inside this store.

Going in Style Travel Accessories
Stanford Shopping Center
Palo Alto, CA 94304
650-326-2066
Your well-behaved leashed dog is allowed inside this store.

Hear Music
Stanford Shopping Center
Palo Alto, CA 94304
650-473-9142
Your well-behaved leashed dog is allowed inside this store.

Kenneth Cole Mens & Womens Shoes & More
Stanford Shopping Center
Palo Alto, CA 94304
650-853-8365
Your well-behaved leashed dog is allowed inside this store.

Lady Foot Locker
Stanford Shopping Center
Palo Alto, CA 94304
650-325-2301
Your well-behaved leashed dog is allowed inside this store.

Macy's and Macy's Mens Store
Stanford Shopping Center
Palo Alto, CA 94304
650-326-3333
Your well-behaved leashed dog is allowed inside this store.

Neiman Marcus
400 Stanford Shopping Center
Palo Alto, CA 94304
Stanford Shopping Center
650-329-3300
This famous department store, which sells everything from clothing to home furnishings, allows your well-behaved leashed dog to shop with you. It is located in Stanford Shopping Center, which is very dog-friendly.

Nordstrom
Stanford Shopping Center
Palo Alto, CA 94304
650-323-5111
Your well-behaved leashed dog is allowed inside this store.

Postal Annex
Stanford Shopping Center
Palo Alto, CA 94304
650-324-8082
Your well-behaved leashed dog is allowed inside this store.

Pottery Barn
Stanford Shopping Center
Palo Alto, CA 94304
650-473-0449
Your well-behaved leashed dog is allowed inside this store.

Restoration Hardware
281 University Avenue
Palo Alto, CA
650-328-4004
They love having dogs in the store!

The Discovery Channel Store
Stanford Shopping Center
Palo Alto, CA 94304
650-321-9833
Your well-behaved leashed dog is allowed inside

this store.

The Sharper Image
Stanford Shopping Center
Palo Alto, CA 94304
650-322-5488
Your well-behaved leashed dog is allowed inside this store.

San Carlos

REI
1119 Industrial Rd, Suite 1-B
San Carlos, CA
650-508-2330
This clothing and outdoor adventure store allows well-behaved, leashed dogs to accompany shoppers.

Vets and Kennels

Palo Alto

Emergency Veterinary Clinic
3045 Middlefield Rd
Palo Alto, CA 94306
650-494-1461
Monday - Thursday 6 pm to 8 am, Friday 6 pm - Monday 8 am.

San Francisco Dog Travel Guide
Accommodations

San Francisco

Best Western Tuscan Inn
425 Northpoint Street
San Francisco, CA
415-561-1100
Well-behaved dogs of all sizes are allowed on the first floor only, which consists of half smoking and half non-smoking rooms. There is a $50 one time per stay pet fee.

Campton Place Hotel
340 Stockton Street
San Francisco, CA 94108
415-781-5555
This dog-friendly hotel holds many awards including "Top 100 Hotels in the World" by Conde Nast Traveler. Room rates are approximately $230 to $345 a night. There is a $35 per day additional pet fee.

Days Inn - Lombard St
2358 Lombard Street
San Francisco, CA 94123
415-922-2010
There is a $10 per day pet fee. A well-behaved large dog is okay. Dogs may not be left alone in the rooms and you are responsible for any damage to the room by your pet.

Harbor Court Hotel
165 Steuart Street
San Francisco, CA 94105
415-882-1300
Well-behaved dogs of all sizes are welcome at this pet-friendly hotel. Amenities include a complimentary evening wine reception, and an adjacent fitness room. There are no pet fees, just sign a pet liability form.

Hotel Cosmo
761 Post Street
San Francisco, CA 94109
415-673-6040
Well-behaved dogs of all sizes are welcome at this pet-friendly hotel. The boutique hotel offers both rooms and suites. Hotel amenities include a complimentary evening wine service. There are no pet fees, just sign a pet liability form.

Hotel Juliana
590 Bush Street
San Francisco, CA 94108
415-392-2540
Well-behaved dogs of all sizes are welcome at this pet-friendly hotel. The luxury boutique hotel offers both rooms and suites. Hotel amenities include a complimentary evening wine reception, and a 24 hour on-site fitness room. There are no pet fees, just sign a pet liability form.

Hotel Palomar
12 Fourth Street
San Francisco, CA 94103

415-348-1111
Well-behaved dogs of all sizes are welcome at this pet-friendly hotel. The boutique hotel offers both rooms and suites. Hotel amenities include room service, an on-site 24 hour fitness room and complimentary high speed Internet access. There are no pet fees, just sign a pet liability form. Pets cannot be left alone in the room.

Hotel Triton
342 Grant Avenue
San Francisco, CA 94108
415-394-0500
Well-behaved dogs of all sizes are welcome at this pet-friendly hotel. The boutique hotel offers both rooms and suites. Hotel amenities include a complimentary evening wine reception, room service, and a 24 hour on-site fitness room. There are no pet fees, just sign a pet liability form.

Marina Motel - on Lombard Street
2576 Lombard St.
San Francisco, CA 94123
415-921-9406
All friendly dogs welcome regardless of size. Walk to the Golden Gate Bridge along Crissy Field beach five blocks away. Miles of pastoral hiking trails in the historical Presidio Park two blocks away. Numerous outdoor dog-friendly cafes around the corner. All rooms have refrigerators, coffee makers, irons and hair dryers. There is no pet fee for stays of one week or longer otherwise there is a $10/night pet fee. Dogs may not be left unattended in the room at any time. There is free garage parking.

Monticello Inn
127 Ellis Street
San Francisco, CA 94102
415-392-8800
Well-behaved dogs of all sizes are welcome at this pet-friendly hotel. The boutique hotel offers both rooms and suites. Hotel amenities include complimentary evening wine service, evening room service, hotel library with magazines, newspapers and books, and a Borders Books and Music room service. There are no pet fees, just sign a pet liability form.

Palace Hotel
2 New Montgomery Street
San Francisco, CA 94105
415-512-1111
There is a $75 one time pet fee. This is a Sheraton Hotel.

Prescott Hotel
545 Post Street

San Francisco, CA 94102
415-563-0303
Well-behaved dogs of all sizes are allowed at this pet-friendly hotel. The luxury boutique hotel is located in Union Square and offers both rooms and suites. Hotel amenities include room service and an on-site 24 hour fitness room. There are no pet fees, just sign a pet liability form.

Residence Inn
Oyster Point Blvd & 101
San Francisco, CA 94080
650-837-9000
There is a $75 one time pet fee and a $10 per day additional pet fee.

Serrano Hotel
405 Taylor Street
San Francisco, CA 94102
415-885-2500
Well-behaved dogs of all sizes are welcome at this pet-friendly hotel. The luxury boutique hotel offers both rooms and suites. Hotel amenities include an evening hospitality hour, and a 24 hour on-site fitness room. There are no pet fees, just sign a pet liability form.

The Laurel Inn
444 Presidio Ave.
San Francisco, CA 94115
415-567-8467
This pet-friendly hotel is a boutique hotel in San Francisco's atmospheric Pacific Heights neighborhood. This newly renovated hotel includes a classic 1960's modern architectural design. Amenities include a complimentary continental breakfast served daily in the lobby, free indoor parking, laundry and valet service, room service from Dine-One-One and more.

W San Francisco
181 Third Street
San Francisco, CA 94103
415-777-5300

Dogs up to 80 pounds are allowed. There is a $25 per day additional pet fee.

Attractions

San Francisco

Barbary Coast Trail

San Francisco, CA
415-775-1111
The Barbary Coast Trail is a 3.8-mile walk through historic San Francisco. Bronze medallions and arrows in the sidewalk mark the trail and guide you to 20 of the City's most important historic sites. It was created by the San Francisco Historical Society. Begin the self-guided walking tour at the Old U.S. Mint building on the corner of Mission and 5th Street. Along the trail you will find historic Union Square, the oldest Chinatown in North America, Plymouth Square, the Pony Express site and more.

Fisherman's Wharf Shopping
Jefferson Street
San Francisco, CA

Fisherman's Wharf is a classic tourist attraction. The walkways follow the bayshore and are complete with all types of street vendors and performers. It's a great dog-friendly place to walk your dog as long as your pup doesn't mind crowds. You can start at Ghirardelli Square and walk along the bayshore to Jefferson Street. Some of the piers don't allow dogs, but there are plenty of things to see and do on Jefferson Street.

Ghirardelli Square Shopping Center
900 North Point Street
San Francisco, CA 94109
(between Polk and Larkin)
415-775-5500
Back in 1893, the famous Ghirardelli chocolate factory occupied these buildings. Today, it is a popular shopping center with numerous shops including the dog-friendly Beastro By the Bay (your dog is welcome inside this unique animal motif gift store). At Ghirardelli Square, you and your pup can take the self-guided outside walking tour and learn about the area's history. Just pick up a free map at the information booth at the west end of Fountain Plaza.

Golden Gate Bridge Walk
Hwy 1/Hwy 101
San Francisco, CA

You and your dog can walk across this famous California and San Francisco landmark. The Golden Gate Bridge has been heralded as one of the top ten construction achievements of the 20th Century. The bridge was constructed in 1937 and is 1.7 miles long. Make sure your dog (and kids) stay away from the small gaps between the walking path and the road which go the water below. And don't forget to take a jacket, because it can get windy. There is a parking lot off Marine Street by Fort Point which is at the south end of the bridge (San Francisco side). You'll walk along a dirt and/or paved bike path to get to the Bridge Walk.

Pac Bell Park

24 Willie Mays Plaza
San Francisco, CA 94107
415-972-2000
There is a viewing deck along the water where you can view a few minutes of the game from way out in right field without entering the ballpark. You may take a leashed and well-behaved dog here. Also, one game a year the bleachers are open to you and your well-behaved pup. It is usually in August and is known as Dog Days of Summer. Get tickets early.

Red and White Fleet
Pier 43 1/2 at Fisherman's Wharf
San Francisco, CA 94133
415-673-2900
Take a one hour narrated Bay Cruise on the San Francisco Bay with your pooch. You will sail under the Golden Gate Bridge, around Alcatraz Island and past the city skyline. A snack bar is available on the boat. Cruise narration is available in English, Japanese, German, Mandarin, French and Spanish.

Waterfront Carriage Rides
Jefferson Street
San Francisco, CA
Pier 41
415-771-8687
Want to tour San Francisco in style? Take an

elegant horse and carriage ride with your well-behaved dog. They'll take you and your pup on a tour of Fisherman's Wharf. The carriages are located by Pier 41.

Beaches

San Francisco

Baker Beach
Golden Gate Natl Rec Area
San Francisco, CA
Lincoln Blvd/Bowley St

This dog-friendly beach in the Golden Gate National Recreation Area has a great view of the Golden Gate Bridge. The beach is located approx. 1.5 to 2 miles south of the Golden Gate Bridge. From Lincoln Avenue, turn onto Bowley Street and head towards the ocean. There is a parking lot next to the beach.

Fort Funston/Burton Beach
Skyline Blvd./Hwy 35
San Francisco, CA
John Muir Drive

This is a very popular dog-friendly park and beach. In the past, dogs have been allowed off-leash. However, currently all dogs must be on leash. Fort Funston is part of the Golden Gate National Recreation Area. There are trails that run through the dunes & ice plant from the parking lot above with good access to the beach below. It overlooks the southern end of Ocean Beach, with a large parking area accessible from Skyline Boulevard. There is also a water faucet and trough at the parking lot for thirsty pups. It's located off Skyline Blvd. (also known Hwy 35) by John Muir Drive. It is south of Ocean Beach. Thanks to one of our readers for this info. Expect to see lots and lots of dogs having a great time. But not to worry, there is plenty of room for everyone.

Ocean Beach
Great Hwy
San Francisco, CA
Sloat Blvd.
415-556-8642
You'll get a chance to stretch your legs at this beach which has about 4 miles of sand. The beach runs parallel to the Great Highway (north of Fort Funston). There are several access points including Sloat Blvd., Fulton Street or Lincoln Way. This beach has a mix of off-leash and leash required areas. Thanks to the San Francisco Dog Owners Group (SFDOG) for providing the following information: Dogs must be on leash on Ocean Beach between Sloat Blvd and Stairwell #21 (roughly at Fulton). North of Fulton to the Cliff House and South of Sloat for several miles are still okay for off-leash dogs, however parts of these areas may be impassible at high tide. The Golden Gate National Rec Area (GGNRA) strictly enforces the on-leash area between Sloat and Fulton. They usually give no warning tickets ($50 fine). As with all other leash required areas, we encourage dog owners to comply with the rules.

Parks

San Francisco

Alta Plaza Park
Clay Street
San Francisco, CA

This park is bordered by Jackson, Clay, Steiner and Scott streets. It is across from the tennis courts. The first Sunday of every month is Pug Day at this dog park. It's a casual meeting of pug owners which takes place at the north end of park, usually between 3:30 - 5:00, weather permitting. At the gathering, there can be 20-50 pugs.

Candlestick Point State Recreation Area
next to 3Com Park
San Francisco, CA
415-671-0145
This park offers views of the San Francisco Bay. Amenities include hiking trails, picnic areas and fishing. Dogs are allowed at the park and on the trails. Pets must be on a 6 foot or less leash, with the exception of the leash free areas. The off-leash areas are the big dirt lots near 3Com Park where sports fans park on game days. The off-leash areas are not available on game days. Please clean up after your pet. The park is located next to 3Com Park. Take the 3Com Park exit from Highway 101.

Crissy Field
Mason Street
San Francisco, CA
415-561-4700
This 100 acre shoreline park is part of the Golden Gate National Recreation Area. Enjoy views of the Golden Gate Bridge while you walk or jog along the paved paths. Dogs on leash are allowed at the park and along the water. The park

is located north of Mason Street and southeast of the Golden Gate Bridge.

Golden Gate National Recreation Area

San Francisco, CA
415-556-0560
This dog-friendly Recreation Area spans 76,500 acres of land and water. It starts at the coastline south of San Francisco, goes into San Francisco and then north of the Golden Gate Bridge. Many of the San Francisco beaches and parks are part of this Rec Area including Baker Beach, Fort Funston and Ocean Beach. One of the trails is located south of Baker Beach. From Lincoln Avenue, turn onto Bowley Street and head towards the ocean. There is a parking lot next to the beach.

Golden Gate Park Dog Run

Fulton Street
San Francisco, CA
38th Avenue

This dog run is completely fenced in with water bowls. Located at 38th Ave & Fulton Street.

Lafayette Park

Sacramento St
San Francisco, CA
Gough St/Laguna St
415-831-2700
Lafayette Park allows leashed dogs. It's located on Sacramento Street and about two blocks west of Van Ness Ave.

Presidio of San Francisco

Hwy 1/Park Presidio Blvd.
San Francisco, CA
Lake Street
415-561-4323
This land was an Army base and is now a dog-friendly national park (borders up to the Golden Gate Recreation Area.) The park has over 500 historic buildings and miles of nice hiking trails. Leashes are required. It's located south of the Golden Gate Bridge. From the Bridge and Hwy101, take Hwy 1 south. It will turn into Park Presidio Blvd. You can also enter the park from Arguello Blvd.

Restaurants

San Francisco

24th Street Cafe and Grill

3853 24th Street
San Francisco, CA 94114
415-282-1213
Dogs are allowed at the outdoor tables.

B44 Bistro

44 Belden Place
San Francisco, CA 94104
415-986-6287

This restaurant specializes in Spanish dishes and serves seafood, chicken and steak entrees as well as a vegetarian sandwich. They are open for lunch Monday through Friday from 11:30am until 2 :30pm. They serve dinner Monday through Saturday from 5:30pm until midnight. Well-behaved leashed dogs are allowed at the outdoor tables. The restaurant is located near Union Square on Belden Place which is a pedestrian only alley (no cars allowed).

Baja Fresh Mexican Grill
30 Fremont St
San Francisco, CA
415-369-9760
This Mexican restaurant is open for lunch and dinner. They use fresh ingredients and making their salsa and beans daily. Some of the items on their menu include Enchiladas, Burritos, Tacos Salads, Quesadillas, Nachos, Chicken, Steak and more. Well-behaved leashed dogs are allowed at the outdoor tables.

Bechelli's
2346 Chestnut St
San Francisco, CA 94123
415-346-1801
Dogs are allowed at the outdoor tables.

Blue Danube Coffee House
306 Clement St
San Francisco, CA 94118
Richmond District
415-221-9041
There is an outside counter where you can sit with your dog.

Cafe Bastille
22 Belden Place
San Francisco, CA 94104
415-986-5673
This French cafe and bistro serves crepes, quiche, mussels and more. They are open for lunch and dinner Monday through Saturday from 11:30am to 10pm. Well-behaved leashed dogs are allowed at the outdoor tables. The restaurant is located near Union Square on Belden Place which is a pedestrian only alley (no cars allowed).

Cafe De La Presse
352 Grant Ave
San Francisco, CA 94108
Bush St(by Chinatown)
415-398-2680
It is located next to the Hotel Triton and Chinatown. This cafe also serves beer. Dogs are allowed at the outdoor tables.

Cafe Niebaum-Coppola
916 Kearny Street
San Francisco, CA 94133
415-291-1700
Dogs are allowed at the outdoor tables.

Cafe Triste
1465 25th Street
San Francisco, CA 94107
415-550-1107
Dogs are allowed at the outdoor tables.

Calzone's
430 Columbus Ave
San Francisco, CA 94133
North Beach
415-397-3600
Located in North Beach, this Euro bistro features pasta, pizza and much more. Well-behaved, leashed dogs are allowed at the outdoor tables. The restaurant is open everyday from 9am-1am.

Cioppino's
400 Jefferson Street
San Francisco, CA
(Fisherman's Wharf)
415-775-9311
Cioppino's offers soups, salads, pastas, pizzas, entrees with fish, meat and chicken, and of course Cioppino. Well-behaved leashed dogs are

allowed at the outdoor tables. The restaurant is located in the Fisherman's Wharf area, on the corner of Jefferson and Leavenworth Streets across from the historic Cannery Building. They serve food 365 days of the year, from 11am to 10pm.

Coffee Bean and Tea Leaf
2201 Fillmore St
San Francisco, CA 94115
Fillmore District
415-447-9733
This coffee shop is very popular with the dogs. Dogs are allowed at the outdoor tables.

Coffee Roastery
2191 Union Street
San Francisco, CA 94123
415-922-9559
Dogs are allowed at the outdoor tables.

Crepes a Go Go
2165 Union St
San Francisco, CA 94123
415-928-1919
Dogs are allowed at the outdoor tables.

Dolores Park Cafe
18th and Dolores
San Francisco, CA

at Dolores Park
415-621-2936
Dogs are allowed at the outdoor tables.

Expo Family Restaurant
160 Jefferson St
San Francisco, CA 94133
(Fisherman's Wharf)
415-673-9400
Expo is located in the Fisherman's Wharf area on Jefferson by Taylor Street. Dogs are allowed at the outdoor tables.

Flippers
482 Hayes Street
San Francisco, CA 94102
415-552-8880
Dogs are allowed at the outdoor tables.

Ghirardelli Ice Cream Fountain
Ghirardelli Square
San Francisco, CA
Beach Street
415-771-4903
Come here to taste some of the best ice cream around. It's in Ghirardelli Square by the Clock Tower on the first floor (by Larkin Street). This place is almost always crowded, but there are several outdoor tables. You'll need to order inside and then grab one of the outdoor tables.

I Love Chocolate
397 Arguello Blvd
San Francisco, CA 94118
415-750-9460
Dogs are allowed at the outdoor tables.

Judy's Cafe
2269 Chestnut St #248
San Francisco, CA 94123
415-922-4588
Dogs are allowed at the outdoor tables.

Lou's Pier 47 Restaurant
300 Jefferson St
San Francisco, CA 94133
(Fisherman's Wharf)
415-771-5687
This Cajun seafood restaurant opens daily at 11am. Lou's is located in the Fisherman's Wharf area on Jefferson by Jones Street. They have live bands seven days a week and you might be able to hear the music from outside. Well-behaved leashed dogs are allowed at the outdoor tables.

Martha & Brothers Coffee Company
1551 Church Street
San Francisco, CA 94131
415-648-1166
Dogs are allowed at the outdoor tables.

Meze's
2373 Chestnut Street
San Francisco, CA 94123
415-409-7111
Dogs are allowed at the outdoor tables.

Mona Lisa
353 Columbus Ave
San Francisco, CA 94133
415-989-4917
Dogs are allowed at the outdoor tables.

Noe's Bar

1199 Church Street
San Francisco, CA 94114
415-282-4007
Dogs are allowed at the outside tables and may be allowed inside as well.

Park Chow
9th and Irving
San Francisco, CA
Sunset District
415-665-9912
Dogs are allowed at the outdoor tables.

Peet's Coffee
2156 Chestnut St
San Francisco, CA 94123
415-931-8302
Dogs are allowed at the outdoor tables.

Peet's Coffee and Tea
2197 Fillmore St
San Francisco, CA 94115
Fillmore District
415-563-9930
This coffee shop is very popular with pups and their people.

Plouf
40 Belden Place
San Francisco, CA 94104

415-986-6491
This French seafood bistro specializes in mussels, unique appetizers, salads, seafood entrees and grilled meats. They are open Monday through Wednesday for lunch from 11:30am to 3pm and for dinner from 5:30pm to 10pm. On Thursday through Saturday, they are open for lunch from 11am to 3pm and for dinner from 3pm to midnight. Well-behaved leashed dogs are allowed at the outdoor tables. The restaurant is located near Union Square on Belden Place which is a pedestrian only alley (no cars allowed).

Pluto's Fresh Food
3258 Scott St
San Francisco, CA 94123
Chestnut
415-775-8867
Dogs are allowed at the outdoor tables.

Pompei's Grotto
340 Jefferson St
San Francisco, CA
(Fisherman's Wharf)
415-776-9265
This restaurant specializes in seafood but also serves meat and chicken entrees. Pompei's Grotto is located in the Fisherman's Wharf area on Jefferson Street by Jones Street. Well-behaved leashed dogs are allowed at the outdoor tables.

Royal Ground Coffee
2060 Fillmore St
San Francisco, CA 94115
Fillmore District
415-567-8822
Dogs are allowed at the outdoor tables.

Ti Couz
3108 16th St
San Francisco, CA
Mission/Castro
415-252-7373

Dogs are allowed at the outdoor tables.

Stores

San Francisco

Le Video
1231 and 1239 9th Avenue
San Francisco, CA 94122
415-566-3606
Your well-behaved leashed dog is allowed inside this store.

Macy's
170 O'Farrell Street
San Francisco, CA 94102
415-397-3333
This Macy's store offers clothing, housewares, electronics and much more. Well-behaved leashed dogs are allowed in the store. It is located on O'Farrell between Powell and Stockton Streets at Union Square.

Neiman Marcus
150 Stockton Street
San Francisco, CA 94108
877-634-6264
This famous department store, which sells everything from clothing to home furnishings, allows your well-behaved leashed dog to shop with you.

Saks Fifth Avenue
384 Post Street
San Francisco, CA 94108
415-986-4300
This upscale department store at Union Square allows well-behaved dogs, but they need to be kept on a short leash.

Williams-Sonoma
340 Post Street
San Francisco, CA 94108
415-362-9450
Located at Union Square, this store offers cookware, cutlery, electronics, food and more. Well-behaved leashed dogs are allowed in the store.

Transportation Systems

San Francisco

Blue & Gold Fleet Ferry
San Francisco and Marin County
San Francisco, CA

415-773-1188
Both small and medium to large dogs are allowed on the ferry. Pets must be leashed and require a muzzle if they are not in a carrier. Dogs are not allowed on the boats to Alcatraz.

SF Municipal Railway (MUNI)
Throughout City
San Francisco, CA
415-673-6864
Both small and large dogs are allowed on cable cars, historic streetcars and trolley buses. People must pay the same fare for their dog that they do for themselves. Dogs are allowed to ride on Muni vehicles from 9 a.m. to 3 p.m. and from 7 p.m. to 5 a.m. on weekdays, and all day on Saturdays, Sundays, and holidays. Only one of dog may ride per vehicle. Dogs must be muzzled and on a short leash or in a small closed container.

Vets and Kennels

San Francisco

All Animals Emergency Hospital
1333 9th Ave
San Francisco, CA 94122
415-566-0531
Monday - Friday 6 pm to 8 am, Saturday noon - Monday 8 am.

San Jose Dog Travel Guide
Accommodations

Campbell

Residence Inn by Marriott
2761 S Bascom Ave
Campbell, CA 95008
408-559-1551
Every one of their 80 suites offers separate living and sleeping areas, complete with a full kitchen. There is a $75 one time pet charge and a $10 per day additional pet fee per pet.

Cupertino

Cypress Hotel
10050 S. DeAnza Blvd.
Cupertino, CA 95014
408-253-8900
Well-behaved dogs of all sizes are welcome at this pet-friendly hotel. The boutique hotel offers both rooms and suites. Hotel amenities include complimentary evening wine service, an a 24 hour on-site fitness room. There are no pet fees, just sign a pet liability form.

Milpitas

Best Western Brookside Inn
400 Valley Way
Milpitas, CA 95035
408-263-5566
This motel has over 70 renovated rooms. Some rooms have a private balcony, refrigerator and microwave. The motel also offers a heated pool. There is a $15 per day pet charge. To get there from Hwy 880 heading north, exit Hwy 237/Calaveras Blvd towards Milpitas-Alviso Rd. Merge onto Calaveras Blvd and then turn left at the first street which is Abbott Ave. Then turn left onto Valley Way.

Residence Inn by Marriott
1501 California Circle
Milpitas, CA 95035
408-941-9222
There is a one time pet fee of $75 and an additional daily pet charge of $10. All rooms have full kitchens, irons/ironing boards, hairdryers, and data ports on phones. They have self-service laundry facilities, and dinner delivery service from local restaurants. To get there from Hwy 880 heading north, exit Dixon Landing Rd. Turn right onto California Circle and the motel will be on the

right. There is a $75 one time pet fee and a $10 per day additional pet fee.

San Jose

Doubletree Hotel
2050 Gateway Pl
San Jose, CA
408-453-4000
Dogs are allowed on the first floor only.

Hilton San Jose
300 Almaden Blvd
San Jose, CA
408-287-2100
Dogs up to 50 pounds are ok. There is a $100 refundable pet deposit required.

Homewood Suites
10 W Trimble Rd
San Jose, CA 95131
408-428-9900
This inn is located in north San Jose, near Milpitas. The inn offers kitchens in each room. There are about half a dozen restaurants next door in a strip mall, many of which have outdoor seating. They require a $275 deposit, and $200 is refundable. The $75 fee is a one time pet charge.

Motel 6

2081 N 1st Street
San Jose, CA 95131
408-436-8180
There are no additional pet fees.

Motel 6 - South
2560 Fontaine Rd
San Jose, CA 95121
408-270-3131
There are no additional pet fees.

Residence Inn - South
6111 San Ignacio Ave
San Jose, CA 95008
408-559-1551
There is a $75 one time pet fee and a $10 per day additional pet fee.

Santa Clara

Guesthouse Inn & Suites
2930 El Camino Real
Santa Clara, CA 95051
408-241-3010
All rooms have microwaves and refrigerators. There is a $10 per day additional pet fee.

Marriott Hotel
2700 Mission College Blvd
Santa Clara, CA
408-988-1500
Dogs are allowed on the first floor only. There is a $100 refundable pet deposit.

Motel 6 - Santa Clara
3208 El Camino Real
Santa Clara, CA 95051
408-241-0200
One large dog is permitted per room.

Sunnyvale

Maple Tree Inn

711 E. El Camino Real
Sunnyvale, CA 94087
408-720-9700
Dogs of all sizes are allowed. There are no additional pet fees.

Residence Inn - SV I
750 Lakeway
Sunnyvale, CA 94086
408-720-1000
There is a $75 one time pet fee and a $10 per day additional pet fee. This hotel is called Residence Inn, Sunnyvale - Silicon Valley I.

Residence Inn - SV II
1080 Stewart Dr
Sunnyvale, CA 94086
408-720-8893
There is a $75 one time pet fee and a $10 per day additional pet fee. This hotel is called Residence Inn - Sunnyvale, Silicon Valley II.

Summerfield Suites
900 Hamlin Court
Sunnyvale, CA
408-745-1515
There is a $150 one time pet fee. 1 and 2 bedroom suites are available.

Woodfin Suite Hotel
635 E. El Camino Real
Sunnyvale, CA 94087
408-738-1700
All well-behaved dogs are welcome. All rooms are suites with full kitchens. Hotel amenities include a heated pool. There is a $5 per day pet fee.

Attractions

San Jose

Ron's Tours / Pedicab Service
Call to Arrange.
San Jose, CA
408-859-8961
Providing pedicab taxi and tour services for the downtown area of San Jose. The pedicab can also be hired for weddings and other special events. Dogs ride free.

Parks

Campbell

Los Gatos Creek Park
Dell Avenue

Campbell, CA
Hacienda Avenue
408-356-2729
This 80 acre park has a small lake, a couple of ponds, picnic benches, barbecues and restroom facilities. The Campbell-Los Gatos Creek Trail runs through the park which goes to the Los Gatos Vasona Park and downtown Los Gatos. Leashed dogs are welcome at this park and on the Creek Trail.

Los Gatos Creek Trail
various-see comments
Campbell, CA
408-356-2729
The Los Gatos Creek Trail is about 7 miles long each way. Most of it is paved until you enter the path at downtown Los Gatos heading towards the Lexington Reservoir County Park. You can gain access to the trail at numerous points. Some of the popular starting sites are at the Campbell Park in Campbell (Campbell Ave & Gilman Ave), Los Gatos Park in Campbell (Dell Ave & Hacienda Ave), Vasona Lake Park in Los Gatos (Blossom Hill Rd between Highway 17 & University Ave), and downtown Los Gatos (Main Street & Maple Ln-near Hwy 17).

Cupertino

Fremont Older Preserve
Prospect Road
Cupertino, CA
1.5 miles from Stelling Rd
650-691-1200
This preserve offers excellent views of the Santa Clara Valley. There are about 9 miles of trails. Dogs must be leashed. One of the popular hikes starts at Prospect Road, goes to Hunter's Point and then continues to Seven Springs Loop. On a hot day, you may want to bring some water with you. Here are directions to the park: From Hwy 280, take DeAnza Blvd south towards Saratoga. After crossing Hwy 85, you will soon come to Prospect Road. Turn right onto Prospect. Go about 1.5 miles on Prospect. Before Prospect Road ends, turn left onto a one lane road (should be signs to Fremont Older). There is parking for approximately 15 cars.

Los Gatos

Los Gatos Creek Trail
University Avenue
Los Gatos, CA
Hwy 17 (no Hwy exit here)
408-356-2729
This is a popular hike with about 5-7 miles of trails. There is a nice combination of fire roads and single track trails with streams. A loop trail begins at University Ave (by Hwy 17). The fire road trail parallels Hwy 17 for a while until you reach the Lexington Reservoir. Across the street from the parking lot (the one w/the portable restrooms) by the Reservoir, the trail continues. You'll hike uphill to the top and then back towards the bottom where you started. There are several forks in the trail. Always stay to the left and you'll be back where you started.

Vasona Lake Park
Blossom Hill Rd
Los Gatos, CA
408-356-2729

Your dog is welcome at this 151 acre park. This is a very popular park during the summer because of the nice lake, green landscape, walking trails and picnic tables. There are six miles of paved trails that wind through the park. The paved trails join the Los Gatos Creek Park to the south and the Los Gatos Creek Trail to the north. In the summer, there is usually a hot dog stand by the childen's playground. Your pup can also get his or her paws wet in the lake. The easiest spot is near the playground. The park is located on Blossom Hill Road between University Ave and Hwy 17 (no Hwy exit here). From southbound Hwy 17, take the Saratoga-Los Gatos (Hwy 9) exit and head east/right. At University Avenue, turn right. Turn right again at Blossom Hill and the park will be on the left. There is a fee for parking.

Milpitas

Dixon Landing Park
Milmont Drive
Milpitas, CA
Jurgens Dr

Dixon Landing Park is a relatively small park, but has much to offer. There are numerous picnic tables, a children's playground, tennis courts and a basketball court. You can grab food to go at one of the restaurants near Dixon Landing Rd and Milmont Drive, then bring it back to enjoy at the picnic tables. This park is a few blocks away (heading west) from the Levee Path. To get there from Hwy 880 heading north, exit Dixon Landing Rd. At the light, turn left then make a right onto Dixon Landing Rd. Turn right onto Milmont Dr/California Circle. The park will be on the right.

Morgan Hill

Anderson Lake/Park
Cochrane Rd.
Morgan Hill, CA
408-779-3634
The 2,365 acre Anderson Lake/Park also features the Coyote Creek Parkway's multiple use trails. Dogs on a 6 foot leash are allowed. Anderson Lake and the picnic areas along the Coyote Creek are located off of Cochrane Road in Morgan Hill, east of Highway 101.

San Jose

Almaden Quicksilver
McAbee Ave.
San Jose, CA
408-268-8220
This park encompasses over 3900 acres. Dogs are allowed on a 6 foot leash. During early spring the park offers a wildflower display. Remnants of the mining era also offer a look at the mining operations of the 1800's. The park may be accessed from three areas. The McAbee entrance at the north end of the park can be accessed off McAbee Road. This entrance is accessible to pedestrians and equestrians only. Turn south off Camden Avenue and follow McAbee Road until it ends (.6 miles). Only street parking is available. The Mockingbird Hill entrance is accessed off Mockingbird Hill Lane. This entrance is accessible to pedestrians and equestrians only. From Highway 85, take the Almaden Expressway exit south 4.5 miles to Almaden Road. Proceed .5 miles on Almaden Road to Mockingbird Hill Lane, turn right and continue .4 miles to the parking entrance is accessible to all users, including bicyclists. From Almaden Expressway, proceed 3 miles along Almaden Road through the town of New Almaden to the unpaved staging area on the right.

Coyote Creek Parkway
various-see comments
San Jose, CA
408-225-0225
The Coyote Creek Trail is approximately 13 miles each way. The north end is paved and popular with bicyclists, rollerbladers and hikers. The sound end (south of Metcalf Rd) has an equestrian dirt trail that parallels the paved trail. Leashed dogs are allowed on both the paved and dirt trails. You can gain access to the trail at numerous points. The south trail access has parking off Burnett Ave. From Hwy 101 South, exit Cochrane Rd. Turn right on Cochrane. Then turn right on Monterey Hwy (Hwy 82). Right on Burnett Ave and the parking will be at the end of Burnett. The north trail access has parking at Hellyer Park. From Hwy 101, exit Hellyer Ave and head west. Continue straight, pay at the booth and then park. There is also parking at Silver Creek Valley Blvd for north trail access. Take Hwy 101 and exit Silver Creek Valley Blvd. Head east (toward the hills). Parking will be on the right.

Hellyer Park/Dog Run
Hellyer Ave
San Jose, CA
408-225-0225
This two acre dog park has a nice lawn and is completely fenced. It is closed Wednesdays for maintenance. The dog park is located at the northeast end of Hellyer Park, near the Shadowbluff group area. There is a minimal fee for parking. To get there, take Hwy 101 to Hellyer Ave. Exit and head west on Hellyer. Continue straight, pay at the booth and drive to the parking lot where the dog park is located.

Miyuki Dog Park
Santa Teresa Boulevard
San Jose, CA
east of Cottle Road
408-277-4573
This dog park is almost one half acre. There is a rack where dog owners can leave spare toys for other pups to use. All dogs that use this off-leash park must wear a current dog license and proof of the rabies vaccine. The park is open from sunrise to one hour after sunset.

Santa Teresa County Park
San Vicente Avenue
San Jose, CA
408-268-3883
Dogs are allowed on a 6 foot leash. This diverse 1,688 acre park, located ten miles south of downtown San Jose, is rich in history and offers spectacular views from its trails located above the Almaden and Santa Clara Valleys. The secluded upland valleys of the park provide a quiet place for exploring the natural environment minutes away from the surrounding developed areas. From San Jose, follow Almaden Expressway until it ends. Turn right onto Harry Road, then turn left onto McKean Road. Travel approximately 1.3 miles to Fortini Road. Turn left onto Fortini Road toward the Santa Teresa Hills. At the end of Fortini Road, turn left onto San Vicente Avenue. A ten car parking area is located on the right about 500 feet from Fortini Road.

Watson Dog Park
East Jackson and 22nd St.
San Jose, CA
408-277-4661
This dog park opened in August of 2003 and offers a nice grassy area complete with benches. It even has a special puppy and older dog area. Thanks to one of our readers for recommending this park.

Santa Clara

Santa Clara Dog Park
3450 Brookdale Drive
Santa Clara, CA
close to Homestead Rd.
408-615-2260
The Santa Clara Dog Park was originally located on Lochnivar Ave. but has moved to a new location at 3450 Brookdale Drive. This park is completely fenced. Weekday hours are from 7am to a 1/2 hour after sunset and weekend hours are from 9am to a 1/2 hour after sunset.

Sunnyvale

Las Palmas Park/Dog Park
850 Russett Drive
Sunnyvale, CA
408-730-7506
After your pup finishes playing with other dogs at this dog park, you can both relax by the pond at one of the many picnic tables. It's located at 850 Russett Drive (by Remington Avenue and Saratoga-Sunnyvale Rd).

Restaurants

Campbell

Baja Fresh Mexican Grill
1976 S. Bascom Ave
Campbell, CA
408-377-2600
This Mexican restaurant is open for lunch and dinner. They use fresh ingredients and making their salsa and beans daily. Some of the items on their menu include Enchiladas, Burritos, Tacos Salads, Quesadillas, Nachos, Chicken, Steak and more. Well-behaved leashed dogs are allowed at the outdoor tables.

Le Boulanger Bakery
1875 S Bascom Ave
Campbell, CA 95008
Campbell Ave
408-369-1820
This bakery is located in the Pruneyard Shopping Center. The Campbell-Los Gatos path is within walking distance.

Noah's Bagels
715 E. Hamilton
Campbell, CA 95008
Bascom Ave
408-371-8321
The Campbell-Los Gatos path is within walking distance (off Hamilton Ave).

Pollo Rey
1875 S Bascom Ave
Campbell, CA 95008
Campbell Ave
408-377-3100
You can get burritos or roasted chicken at this Mexican Rotisserie. It's located in the Pruneyard Shopping Center. The Campbell-Los Gatos path within walking distance.

Rock Bottom Restaurant & Brewery
1875 S Bascom Ave
Campbell, CA 95008
Campbell Ave
408-377-0707
This restaurant is located in the Pruneyard Shopping Center. The Campbell-Los Gatos path is within walking distance.

The Kings Head Pub & Restaurant
201 Orchard City Drive
Campbell, CA 95008
408-871-2499
Thanks to one of our readers for recommending this dog-friendly restaurant, "They have lots of outdoor seating, including a big, shady deck with shade trees and umbrella seating. They'll cheerfully bring your doggie a bowl of water. There is also a resident dog there who hangs out on the deck, and who is very sweet and kind to

other doggies."

Whole Foods Market
1690 S. Bascom Avenue
Campbell, CA 95008
408-371-5000
This natural food supermarket offers natural and organic foods. Order some food from their deli and bring it to an outdoor table where your well-behaved leashed dog is welcome.

Yiassoo
2180 S Bascom Ave
Campbell, CA 95008
Shady Dale Ln (s. of Pruneyard Center)
408-559-0312
Delicious Greek food.

Cupertino

Baja Fresh Mexican Grill
20735 Stevens Creek Blvd
Cupertino, CA
408-257-6141
This Mexican restaurant is open for lunch and dinner. They use fresh ingredients and making their salsa and beans daily. Some of the items on their menu include Enchiladas, Burritos, Tacos Salads, Quesadillas, Nachos, Chicken, Steak and more. Well-behaved leashed dogs are allowed at the outdoor tables.

Whole Foods Market
20830 Stevens Creek Blvd.
Cupertino, CA 95014
408-257-7000
This natural food supermarket offers natural and organic foods. Order some food from their deli and bring it to an outdoor table where your well-behaved leashed dog is welcome.

Los Gatos

Whole Foods Market
15980 Los Gatos Blvd.
Los Gatos, CA 95032
408-358-4434
This natural food supermarket offers natural and organic foods. Order some food from their deli and bring it to an outdoor table where your well-behaved leashed dog is welcome.

Willow Street Pizza
20 S. Santa Cruz Ave
Los Gatos, CA
408-354-5566
There is a large outdoor seating area with heat lamps. The hours are 11:30 am to 10 pm, 11 pm on Friday and Saturday.

Milpitas

Bento Xpress
23 N. Milpitas Blvd
Milpitas, CA
408-262-7544
This restaurant offers quick Japanese cuisine. Dogs are allowed at the outdoor tables.

Erik's Deli Cafe
595 E. Calaveras Blvd.
Milpitas, CA
408-262-7878
This cafe offers sandwiches, soup, stew, chili and more. Dogs are allowed at the outdoor tables.

San Jose

Baja Fresh Mexican Grill
1708 Oakland Road
San Jose, CA
408-436-5000
This Mexican restaurant is open for lunch and dinner. They use fresh ingredients and making their salsa and beans daily. Some of the items on their menu include Enchiladas, Burritos, Tacos Salads, Quesadillas, Nachos, Chicken, Steak and more. Well-behaved leashed dogs are allowed at the outdoor tables.

Bill's Cafe
1115 Willow Street
San Jose, CA
at Lincoln Ave.
408-294-1125
Bill's cafe has outdoor seating for you and your dog. Dogs sometimes get biscuits and water.

Sonoma Chicken Coop
31 North Market Street

San Jose, CA
408-287-4098
Located in San Pedro Square, this restaurant allows dogs at their outdoor tables. Thanks to one of our readers for recommending this restaurant.

Santa Clara

Baja Fresh Mexican Grill
3950 Rivermark Plaza
Santa Clara, CA
408-588-4060
This Mexican restaurant is open for lunch and dinner. They use fresh ingredients and making their salsa and beans daily. Some of the items on their menu include Enchiladas, Burritos, Tacos Salads, Quesadillas, Nachos, Chicken, Steak and more. Well-behaved leashed dogs are allowed at the outdoor tables.

Pizz'a Chicago
1576 Halford Ave
Santa Clara, CA 95051
El Camino/Lawrence Expwy
408-244-2246
They have delicious deep dish style pizza. They only have 3 outdoor tables, so try to arrive before the lunch or dinner rush. Once there, you and your pup can enjoy being served pizza at the covered tables. This is a good place to go even if it's raining, because the tables are well covered.

Tony & Alba's Pizza & Pasta
3137 Stevens Creek Blvd
Santa Clara, CA 95050
Winchester Avenue
408-246-4605
Great food and nice outdoor seating. They have warm outdoor heat lamps. If for some reason they don't have them turned on, just ask one of the folks working there and they'll be happy to turn them on.

Sunnyvale

Fibbar Magees Irish Pub
1565 Murphy Avenue
Sunnyvale, CA 94086
W. Evelyn Ave
408-749-8373
You and your dog are welcome at the outdoor tables at this Irish Pub. It is located in the Murphy's Station area, across from the Sunnyvale Town Center Mall.

Scruffy Murphys Irish Pub
187 S Murphy Ave
Sunnyvale, CA 94086
W. Evelyn Ave
408-735-7394
Enjoy the great Irish food at this pub. They have just one outdoor table, so arrive early to ensure a seat with your pup. This restaurant is located in the Murphy's Station area, across from the Sunnyvale Town Center Mall. You can eat at the outdoor table, but the pub cannot server drinks outside.

Stores

San Jose

Hahn's Lighting Store
260 E Virginia St
San Jose, CA 95112
408-295-1755
Your well-behaved leashed dog is allowed inside this store.

Wilson Motor Sports
1980 Kingman Avenue
San Jose, CA 95128
408-371-9199
Your well-behaved leashed dog is allowed inside this store. We are a dog-friendly environment and welcome all animal owners.

Vets and Kennels

Campbell

United Emergency Animal Clinic
1657 S Bascom Ave
Campbell, CA 95008
Hamilton Ave
408-371-6252
Monday - Friday 6 pm to 8 am, 24 hours on weekends.

San Jose

Emergency Animal Clinic
5440 Thornwood Dr.
San Jose, CA 95123
Santa Teresa Blvd and Blossom Hill Rd
408-578-5622
Monday - Friday 6 pm to 8 am, 24 hours on weekends.

Guardian Petsitting Service
Please Call or Email at robinrmh@aol.com .
San Jose, CA 95123
408-394-3320
Visits start at $20. Dog walking available. Mid-day dog walking and overnight petsitting available upon special request. Member Better Business Bureau, Licensed, Bonded, and Insured.

Santa Cruz Dog Travel Guide
Accommodations

Aptos

Apple Lane Inn B&B
6265 Soquel Drive
Aptos, CA 95003
831-475-6868
You and your well-behaved dog are allowed at this Victorian farmhouse built in the 1870s. It is situated on over 2 acres with fields, gardens, and apple orchards. There are also many farm animals such as horses, chickens, goats, ducks and geese. They have three double rooms and two suites with antique furniture. Each of the five rooms have private baths. Room stay includes a full breakfast, and afternoon and evening refreshments. Rates are $120 per night and up. There is a $25 charge for a dog, extra person or crib. No smoking is allowed indoors. This bed and breakfast is located on Soquel Drive, near Cabrillo Jr. College. From Hwy 17 south, exit Hwy 1 south towards Watsonville. Take the Park Avenue/New Brighton Beach exit. Turn left onto Park Ave. Turn right onto Soquel. It will be near Atherton Drive and before Cabrillo College.

Bonny Doon

Redwood Croft B&B
275 Northwest Drive
Bonny Doon, CA 95060
831-458-1939
This bed and breakfast, located in the Santa Cruz Mountains, is set on a sunny hill amidst the redwood forest. It is the perfect country getaway, especially since they allow dogs. They are very dog-friendly. This B&B has two rooms each with a private bath and full amenities. The Garden Room has its own entrance, private deck with a secluded 7 foot Jacuzzi spa, full-size bed, woodburning stone fireplace and a skylit loft with a queen futon. The West Room is sunny and spacious, has a California king bed and large bathroom with a double shower and roman tub. Room stay includes a lavish country breakfast.

Room rates are $145 per night. The dog-friendly Davenport Beach (see Parks) is only about 10-15 minutes away. Call the inn for directions or for a brochure.

Capitola

Best Western Capitola By-the-Sea
1435 41st Ave
Capitola, CA 95010
831-477-0607
There is a $10 per day pet fee.

Capitola Inn
822 Bay Ave
Capitola, CA 95010
831-462-3004
This inn is located a few blocks from Capitola Village. They offer 56 rooms with either a private patio or balcony. There is a $20 per day pet charge.

Santa Cruz

Edgewater Beach Motel
525 Second Street
Santa Cruz, CA 95060
831-423-0440
This motel has ocean views, beach views, and 17 uniquely designed suites (for one to eight people). Some of the rooms have ocean views, microwaves, refrigerators. A couple of the rooms have fireplaces, private lawns and full kitchens. Non-smoking rooms are available. While dogs are not allowed on the Boardwalk or on the nearby beach, they are allowed on the West Cliff Drive Walkway. Walk to the waterfront, then go north (away from the Boardwalk) along the sidewalk on the street closest to the ocean. It will become a walkway that is used by walkers, joggers and bicyclists. If you walk about 1 1/2 - 2 miles, you'll reach several dog beaches (see Parks). To get to the motel, take Hwy 17 south. Take the Hwy 1

North exit. Then take the Ocean St exit on the left towards the beaches. Head towards the beach on Ocean St and then turn right on San Lorenzo Blvd. Turn left on Riverside Ave and then right on 2nd St. The motel will be on the left. Ample parking is available in their parking lot. There is a $20 one time additional pet fee.

Guesthouse International
330 Ocean Street
Santa Cruz, CA 95060
831-425-3722
There is a $10 per day pet fee.

Scotts Valley

Hilton Scotts Valley
6001 La Madrona Dr
Scotts Valley, CA 95066
831-440-1000
There is a $25 per day pet fee.

Soquel

Blue Spruce Inn Bed and Breakfast
2815 Main Street
Soquel, CA 95073
831-464-1137
A well-behaved dog is allowed in the Secret

Garden Room. This room offers a private enclosed garden that includes an outdoor hot tub for two, a small sitting area with gas fireplace and comfortable reading chairs, private bathroom and more. There is a $25 one time pet charge. Please abide by the following pet rules. If your dog will be allowed on the furniture, please cover it first with a sheet. If you take your pooch to the dog beach, please rinse him or her off in the outside hot and cold shower before entering the room. This bed and breakfast does offer a VIP (Very Important Pets) program for your pooch. This includes a dog bone, water bowl and poop bags upon arrival.

Accommodations - Vacation Home Rentals

Santa Cruz

1600 West Cliff
1600 West Cliff Drive
Santa Cruz, CA 95060
Swift Street
408-266-4453
Want to stay across the street from the ocean in beautiful Santa Cruz? 1600 West Cliff is a private 3 bedroom, 2 bath vacation rental home with lodging for 1 to 8 people. Relax on the enclosed back patio, or grab a chair and sit on the front yard patio and enjoy the beautiful ocean view. The living room faces the ocean and the kitchen is fully stocked. The West Cliff Drive Walkway is located directly across the street on the ocean side. This is a nice 2 mile walking and running path. West Lighthouse Beach, a leash free dog beach, is also located nearby. The owners of this vacation home are true dog lovers and believe the family dog should be welcome. Rates start at $350 per night and up. There is a 2 day minimum. A $500 security deposit is required, but can be charged on a credit card. To get there, head south on Hwy 17. Take the Hwy 1 North exit, heading towards Half Moon Bay and Hwy 9. Merge onto Mission Street (Hwy 1). Turn left onto Swift Street, and then turn right on West Cliff Drive.

Redtail Ranch by the Sea
Call to Arrange.
Santa Cruz, CA 95060
831-429-1322
This 3 bedroom, 1 1/2 bath ranch house is located on a 72 acre horse ranch, the Redtail Ranch. The house features a 180 degree ocean view of the Monterey Bay and views of the coastal hills. The house sleeps 1 to 8 people and comes with a complete full kitchen. The home is

located about a 5 minute drive to local beaches, a 1 hour drive to Monterey, Carmel and Big Sur, and a 1 1/2 hour scenic coastal drive to San Francisco. The rental is available year-round for nightly, weekly, and extended vacation rentals.

Sunset Beach

Seashell Cottage
84 Sunset Drive
Sunset Beach, CA 95076
831-722-0202
This cottage is perched 100 feet above the sand with a view of the Monterey Bay Marine Sanctuary. Pets not only allowed but welcomed. The cottage is next to a dog-friendly private beach. Walk miles of beaches and paths in the area. There are no additional pet fees.

Attractions

Bonny Doon

Bonny Doon Vineyard Tasting Room
10 Pine Flat Road
Bonny Doon, CA
831-425-4518
Dogs are allowed in this wine tasting room. There is no wine tasting fee. The wine tasting room is open daily from 11 am to 5 pm except on most holidays.

Felton

Roaring Camp & Big Trees RR
P.O.Box G-1
Felton, CA 95018
near Mount Hermon Rd
831-335-4484
Please note: As of the summer of 1999, dogs are required to wear muzzles on this train ride. A conductor was bitten and now all dogs need to wear muzzles on the train only, but not on the grounds. They have free muzzles you can borrow. At Roaring Camp you will find daily musical entertainment (Old Western style) and a couple of outdoor cafes that serve burgers, chicken sandwiches and more. They also hold many seasonal events here like a Harvest Fair and Steam Festival. The train ride takes you into the beautiful Santa Cruz Mountains. This is America's last steam-powered passenger railroad with year-round passenger service. They operate daily from 11am to 5pm. To get there, take Hwy 17 to the Scotts Valley Mount Hermon Road exit. Stay on Mount Hermon Road until it ends. Turn left onto

Graham Hill Road. Roaring Camp is 1/4 mile ahead on the right.

Santa Cruz

De Laveaga Park Disc Golf
Branciforte
Santa Cruz, CA
by De Laveaga Golf Course

Santa Cruz is quickly gaining recognition for being home to one of disc golf's premier courses. Disc golf is similar to golf with clubs and balls, but the main difference is the equipment. Discs are shot into elevated baskets/holes. Your leashed dog is allowed to go with you on this course (pick up after your pooch). Rangers patrol the park frequently and will fine any dog owner that doesn't have their dog on a leash or doesn't clean up after their pup. This course has 27 baskets and is part of an over 1200 acre park which allows dogs. If you do not have any discs, you can purchase them at various locations in the Santa Cruz area. You can purchase discs at Play it Again Sports in Soquel, on Soquel Ave right past Capitola Ave. Another place that sells discs is Johnny's Sports in downtown Santa Cruz. New discs cost about $8.00 to $12.00 depending on the make and model. To get to the park, take Hwy 17 south to Santa Cruz and exit Hwy 1 south (towards Watsonville). Take the first exit, Morrissey Blvd (the exit has a sharp 90 degree turn). Turn right at the stop sign, and then go to the end of the street where it dead ends at Branciforte. Turn right. Go over Hwy 1, stop at the stop sign, and continue straight up the hill. Follow the signs to the De Laveaga Golf Course. Go approx. 1/4 mile past the club house and the disc golf parking will be on the right. The first hole is across the road in the Oak Grove. Maps should be available.

Harbor Water Taxis
Lake Avenue
Santa Cruz, CA 95062
Santa Cruz Harbor
831-475-6161
The water taxis run inside the Santa Cruz Harbor only. The taxis are small barges (flat-bottomed boats). They have several very short hops across and around the harbor. It's something fun to do while walking around the harbor. If you are on the east side of the harbor by Lake Ave., you and your dog can take the taxi across the harbor to dine at Aldo's Restaurant (see Restaurants). There is more parking by Lake Ave than by Aldos. The taxi's are seasonal, usually running from May through October. There are several spots around the harbor where you can catch the water taxis and there is a minimal fee for the taxi. To get there from Hwy 17 heading south, take the Ocean Street exit on the left towards the beaches. Turn left onto East Cliff Drive. Go straight to go onto Murray Street. Turn right on Lake Avenue (East Santa Cruz Harbor). Take Lake Ave until it ends near Shamrock Charters. There is a minimal fee for parking.

Lighthouse Point Surfer's Museum
W. Cliff Dr
Santa Cruz, CA

831-420-6289
This lighthouse is home to California's first surfing museum. Well-behaved, leashed dogs are allowed inside. It is open from noon to 6pm daily, except it is closed on Tuesdays. The museum is located on West Cliff Drive, about a 5-10 minute drive north of the Santa Cruz Boardwalk.

Santa Cruz Harley Davidson Motorcyles
1148 Soquel Ave
Santa Cruz, CA 95062
831-421-9600
Well-behaved, leashed dogs are allowed in the store and the museum. They have dogs come into the store all the time. The museum, located inside the store, features vintage motorcycles, memorabilia, photos and more. Located at the corner of Soquel and Seabright.

Beaches

Aptos

Rio Del Mar Beach
Rio Del Mar
Aptos, CA
831-685-6500
Dogs on leash are allowed at this beach which offers a wide strip of sand. From Highway 1, take the Rio Del Mar exit.

Davenport

Davenport Beach
Hwy 1
Davenport, CA
831-462-8333
This beautiful beach is surrounded by high bluffs and cliff trails. Leashes are required. To get to the beach from Santa Cruz, head north on Hwy 1 for about 10 miles.

Manresa

Manresa State Beach
San Andreas Road
Manresa, CA
831-761-1795
Surfing and surf fishing are both popular activities at this beach. Dogs are allowed on the beach, but must be leashed. To get there from Aptos, head south on Highway 1. Take San Andreas Road southwest for several miles until you reach Manresa. Upon reaching the coast, you will find the first beach access point.

Santa Cruz

East Cliff Coast Access Points
East Cliff Drive
Santa Cruz, CA
12th to 41st Avenues
831-454-7900
There are many small dog-friendly beaches and coastal access points that stretch along East Cliff Drive between 12th Avenue to 41st Avenue. This is not one long beach because the water comes up to cliffs in certain areas and breaks it up into many smaller beaches. Dogs are allowed on leash. Parking is on city streets along East Cliff or the numbered avenues. To get there from Hwy 17 south, take the Hwy 1 exit south towards Watsonville. Take the exit towards Soquel Drive. Turn left onto Soquel Avenue. Turn right onto 17th Avenue. Continue straight until you reach East Cliff Drive. From here, you can head north or south on East Cliff Drive and park anywhere between 12th and 41st street to access the beaches.

Its Beach
West Cliff Drive
Santa Cruz, CA
near Columbia St
831-429-3777

Your dog can go leash free from sunrise to 10am and 4pm until sunset. It is not a large beach, but enough for your water loving dog to take a dip in the water and get lots of sand between his or her paws. According to the sign, dogs are not allowed between 10am and 4pm. It is located on West Cliff Drive, just north of the Lighthouse, and south of Columbia Street. It is also across from the Lighthouse Field off-leash area. To get there, head south on Hwy 17. Take the Hwy 1 North exit, heading towards Half Moon Bay and Hwy 9. Merge onto Mission Street (Hwy 1). Turn left onto Swift Street. Then turn left on West Cliff Drive. The beach and limited parking will be on the right.

Seabright Beach
Seabright Ave
Santa Cruz, CA
East Cliff Drive
831-429-2850
This beach is located south of the Santa Cruz Beach Boardwalk and north of the Santa Cruz Harbor. Dogs are allowed on leash. Fire rings are available for beach bonfires. It is open from sunrise to sunset. To get there from Hwy 17 south, exit Ocean Street on the left towards the beaches. Merge onto Ocean Street. Turn left onto East Cliff Drive and stay straight to go onto Murray Street. Then turn right onto Seabright Ave. Seabright Ave will take you to the beach (near the corner of East Cliff Drive and Seabright).

Twin Lakes State Beach
East Cliff Drive
Santa Cruz, CA
7th Avenue
831-429-2850
This beach is one of the area's warmest beaches, due to its location at the entrance of Schwann Lagoon. Dogs are allowed on leash. The beach is located just south of the Santa Cruz Harbor where Aldo's Restaurant is located. Fire rings for beach bonfires, outdoor showers and restrooms are available. It is open from sunrise to sunset. To get there from Hwy 17 south, exit Ocean Street on the left towards the beaches. Merge onto Ocean Street. Turn left onto East Cliff Drive and stay straight to go onto Murray Street. Murray Street becomes Eaton Street. Turn right onto 7th Avenue.

Parks

Aptos

Forest of Nisene Marks
Aptos Creek Road
Aptos, CA
Soquel Drive
831-763-7062
Dogs on leash are allowed in part of this park. They are allowed on a beautiful wooded trail that parallels the gravel Aptos Creek Road (on the left or west side of the road only). A good starting point is at the park entrance booth. Park after paying the minimal day use fee and then join the trail next to the parking lot. On this trail, head into the park (north). Dogs are allowed on the dirt trail up to the Steel Bridge (about 1 mile each way). You can continue on Aptos Creek Rd to the Porter Family Picnic Area, but dogs need to stay on the road (cars also allowed). The dirt trail up to the bridge is usually the best hiking trail that

allows dogs and it includes several trails that divert towards the creek. Here your pup can enjoy playing in the water. To get there from Hwy 17, exit Hwy 1 south towards Watsonville. Drive through Santa Cruz and Capitola on Hwy 1 and then exit at the Seacliff Beach/Aptos exit. Turn left onto State Park Drive. Then turn right on Soquel Avenue. After going under the train bridge, you'll soon turn left onto Aptos Creek Rd. It's a small street, so be careful not to miss it. Drive up this road until you reach the park entrance booth.

Felton

Henry Cowell State Park
Highway 9
Felton, CA
831-335-4598
Dogs are allowed in the picnic area, the campground, and on Pipeline Road, Graham Hill Trail, and Meadow Trail. They are not allowed on any other trails or interior roads. Dogs must be leashed. The park is near Felton on Highway 9 in the Santa Cruz Mountains. Traveling from San Jose to the main entrance: Take Highway 17 towards Santa Cruz. After you go over the mountains, turn right on Mt. Hermon Road. Follow Mt. Hermon road until it ends at Graham Hill Road. Turn right, and go to the next stop light (Highway 9). Turn left on Highway 9 and go through downtown Felton. The park entrance will be a half mile down on your left. You can park outside and walk a half mile into the park, or you can drive in and pay a fee.

Santa Cruz

Lighthouse Field
West Cliff Drive
Santa Cruz, CA
near Columbia St
831-429-3777
Your dog can go leashless from sunrise to 10am

and 4pm until sunset. Leashes are required between 10am and 4pm. This open field is across from the West Lighthouse Beach where dogs can run leashless during certain hours. This field is not fenced and there are several busy streets nearby, so if your dog runs off-leash, make sure he or she is very well trained. It is located on West Cliff Drive, just north of the Lighthouse, and south of Columbia Street. It is also across from the West Lighthouse Beach. To get there, head south on Hwy 17. Take the Hwy 1 North exit, heading towards Half Moon Bay and Hwy 9. Merge onto Mission Street (Hwy 1). Turn left onto Swift Street. Then turn left on West Cliff Drive. Limited parking will be on the right or on other sides of the field.

West Cliff Drive Walkway
West Cliff Drive
Santa Cruz, CA
north of Boardwalk
831-429-3777
This is a popular paved walking path that follows the beautiful Santa Cruz coastline. It is about 2 miles long each way and is frequented by walkers, runners, bicyclists and of course, dogs. It is located on West Cliff Drive, north of the Santa Cruz Beach Boardwalk and south of Natural Bridges State Beach. While dogs are not allowed on either the Boardwalk or the State Beach, there is a dog beach along this path called West Lighthouse Beach. There are several areas where you can park near the path. The easiest is by the north end of the path: Heading south on Hwy 17, take the Hwy 1 North exit towards Half Moon Bay and Hwy 9. Merge onto Mission Street (Hwy 1). Turn left onto Swift Street. Then turn right on West Cliff Drive. Turn right onto Swanton Blvd. Parking is available on Swanton Blvd. If you prefer to park closer to the Boardwalk, follow these directions: From Hwy 17 heading south, take the Hwy 1 North exit towards Half Moon Bay and Hwy 9. Merge onto Chestnut Street. Turn left onto Laurel Street, then right onto Center Street.

Make a slight left onto Washington Street and Washington will become Pacific Avenue. Then turn right onto Beach Street. There is limited metered parked available near the Municipal Wharf.

Restaurants

Aptos

Britannia Arms Restaurant
8017 Soquel Drive
Aptos, CA 95060
near State Park Drive
831-688-1233
Britannia Arms Restaurant and Pub serves some great British food and beer. They have one table in front, but the majority of tables are in the back. The seats on the back patio have shade umbrellas. This restaurant is located close to the Forest of Nisene Marks State Park (see Parks). To get there from Hwy 17, exit Hwy 1 south towards Watsonville. Drive through Santa Cruz and Capitola on Hwy 1 and then exit at the Seacliff Beach/Aptos exit. Turn left onto State Park Drive. Then turn right on Soquel Avenue. The restaurant will be on the left.

Capitola

Caffe Lido
110 Monterey Avenue
Capitola, CA 95060
near Capitola State Beach
831-475-6544
Caffe Lido is near the Capitola State Beach. While dogs are not allowed on this beach, you and your pup can walk around the nearby downtown shopping village. They have a few tables which are close together. Limited metered parking is available. To get there from Hwy 17 south, exit Hwy 1 south towards Watsonville. Exit on Bay Avenue towards Porter Street. Turn right onto Bay Avenue. Turn slight right onto Capitola Ave. Turn right onto Stockton Ave, and then left onto Esplanade. Esplanade becomes Monterey Ave. During the summer and weekends, parking can be very limited.

Davenport

La Cabana Taqueria
Hwy 1
Davenport, CA 95060
corner of Ocean Street
831-425-7742
This taqueria is located in the small town of Davenport which is about 10-15 minutes north of Santa Cruz. The Davenport Beach (see Parks) is across the highway from the restaurant. To get there from Hwy 17 south, exit Hwy 1 north. Drive about 10-15 minutes until you reach the town of Davenport. The restaurant will be on the right at the corner of Hwy 1 and Ocean Street.

Whale City Bakery
490 Hwy 1
Davenport, CA 95060
near Ocean Street
831-423-9803
This bakery, bar and grill is located in the small town of Davenport which is about 10-15 minutes north of Santa Cruz. They are open early for breakfast. The Davenport Beach (see Parks) is across the highway from the restaurant. To get there from Hwy 17 south, exit Hwy 1 north. Drive about 10-15 minutes until you reach the town of Davenport. The restaurant will be on the right near Ocean Street.

Santa Cruz

Aldo's Harbor Restaurant
616 Atlantic Avenue
Santa Cruz, CA 95060
by the Santa Cruz Harbor
831-426-3736
Aldo's outdoor dining area overlooks the Santa Cruz Harbor. They are open for breakfast and lunch. After dining here, you can go for a walk around the harbor. To get there from Hwy 17 south, exit Ocean Street on the left towards the beaches. Merge onto Ocean Street. Turn left onto East Cliff Drive and stay straight to go onto

Murray Street. Then turn right onto Seabright Ave. Turn left on Atlantic Ave. The road ends by the restaurant. Limited street parking or harbor parking lots are available.

Cheese Factory
21620 East Cliff Drive
Santa Cruz, CA 95060
17th Avenue
831-476-6111
This cafe and deli serves breakfast and lunch. They have seating at the picnic tables or on the patio. It is located near the East Cliff Coastal Access Points/Beaches (see Parks). To get there from Hwy 17 south, exit Hwy 1 south towards Watsonville. Take the Soquel Drive exit. Turn left onto Soquel Ave and then right onto 17th Ave. Turn right on East Cliff Drive and left on Johans Beach Drive.

Michael's Pizza
1700 Portola Drive
Santa Cruz, CA 95060
17th Avenue
831-477-0456
Michael's Pizza is located near the East Cliff Coastal Access Points/Beaches. To get there from Hwy 17 south, exit Hwy 1 south towards Watsonville. Take the Soquel Drive exit. Turn left onto Soquel Ave and then right onto 17th Ave.

Turn right left onto Portola Ave.

Pleasure Pizza
4000 Portola Drive
Santa Cruz, CA 95060
41st Avenue
831-475-4999
This pizza place serves slices and whole pizzas.
It is located near the East Cliff Coastal Access
Points/Beaches (see Parks). To get there from
Hwy 17 south, exit Hwy 1 south towards
Watsonville. Take the 41st Avenue exit. Turn right
onto 41st Avenue and the restaurant will be at
Portola Drive.

Vets and Kennels

Santa Cruz

Santa Cruz Veterinary
2585 Soquel Dr
Santa Cruz, CA 95065
Stanley
831-475-5400
24 hours for emergencies. 8 - 5 pm for routine
visits.

Vallejo Dog Travel Guide
Accommodations

Vallejo

Holiday Inn
1000 Fairgrounds Dr
Vallejo, CA 94589
707-644-1200
There is a $25 one time pet fee. Dogs are allowed
only on the first floor.

Chapter 5

California Dog-Friendly Travel Guide
Gold Country

Altaville Dog Travel Guide
Restaurants

Altaville

Mrs B's Frosty
22 N. Main Street
Altaville, CA 95221
209-736-4312
Dogs are allowed at the outdoor seats. The
restaurant is just north of Angel's Camp on
Highway 49.

Angels Camp Dog Travel Guide
Accommodations

Angels Camp

Best Western Cedar Inn & Suites
444 South Main Street
Angels Camp, CA 95222
209-736-4000
There is a $10 per day pet charge and dogs must
be over one year old. Pets are not to be left alone
in the room.

Parks

Angels Camp

Utica Park
Hwy 49
Angels Camp, CA
north of downtown
209-736-2187
Utica Park was built in 1954 on the site of the
Utica Mine after the ground had been leveled and
shafts filled to the 60 foot level. Today it is a great
park for having a picnic or watching the kids have
fun in the large playground area. The historic
Lightner Mine at this park operated from
1896-1915. It produced over $6 million dollars in
ore. The mine was filled, but you will still see
some of the equipment that was used above
ground. The park is located off Hwy 49, just north
of downtown Angels Camp.

Restaurants

Angels Camp

Dave's Diner
451 S Main St Highway 49
Angels Camp, CA 95222
209-736-8080
Dogs are allowed at the outdoor tables.

La Hacienda Restaurant
11 S. Main Street
Angels Camp, CA 95222
209-736-6711
Dogs are allowed at the outdoor seats on the
covered deck.

Arnold Dog Travel Guide
Accommodations

Arnold

Ebbetts Pass Lodge
1173 Highway 4, Box 2591
Arnold, CA 95223
209-795-1563
There is a $5 per day pet charge.

Parks

Arnold

Calaveras Big Trees State Park
Highway 4
Arnold, CA
209-795-2334
Just three species of redwood trees remain; the
dawn redwood in central China; the coast
redwood along the coast of northern California
and southern Oregon; and the Sierra redwoods
which grow at Calaveras Big Trees State Park

and other widely scattered groves along the western slope of the Sierra Nevada. These redwood trees have evolved from the Mesozoic Era, the time when dinosaurs roamed the Earth. Dogs are not allowed on the trails, but are allowed on the dirt fire roads. There are miles of fire roads at this park. They are used by hikers, bicyclists and equestrians. Dogs must be on leash. The state park is about a 35 minute drive from Angel's Camp on Highway 4.

Restaurants

Arnold

Giant Burger
846 Highway 4
Arnold, CA 95223
209-795-1594
Dogs are allowed at the outdoor tables.

Hungry Prospector
961 Highway 4
Arnold, CA 95223
209-795-2128
Dogs are allowed on the outdoor patio.

Pablito's of the Mother Lode
925 Highway 4 # J
Arnold, CA 95223
209-795-3303
Dogs are allowed at the outdoor seats.

Stores

Arnold

Sierra Nevada Adventure Company (SNAC)
2293 Highway 4
Arnold, CA 95223
209-795-9310
This store carries outdoor gear and clothing for kayaking, rock-climbing, hiking, cross-country skiing and more. They always encouraged dog owners to bring their pets into the store to try on dog packs, dog life vests, and more! It comes highly recommended from one of our readers and her Australian Shepherd.

Auburn Dog Travel Guide
Accommodations

Auburn

Best Western Golden Key

13450 Lincoln Way
Auburn, CA 95603
530-885-8611
There is a $15 one time pet charge. Dogs are allowed in certain pet rooms.

Holiday Inn
120 Grass Valley Highway
Auburn, CA 95603
530-887-8787
Amenities include room service, a heated pool, spa and fitness room. There is a $20 one time pet charge.

Travelodge
13490 Lincoln Way
Auburn, CA 95603
530-885-7025
There is a $10 per day pet fee.

Parks

Auburn

Auburn State Recreation Area
Highway 49 or Auburn-Foresthill Rd.
Auburn, CA
530-885-4527
Dogs on leash are allowed everywhere except at Lake Clementine. Located in the heart of the gold country, this recreation area covers over 35,000 acres along 40 miles of the North and Middle Forks of the American River. Major recreational uses include hiking, swimming, boating, fishing, camping, mountain biking, gold panning and off-highway motorcycle riding. One of the more popular trails is the Western States National Recreation Trail. It hosts the Tevis Cup Endurance Ride and Western States100 Endurance Run each summer. The park is located south of Interstate 80, stretching from Auburn to Colfax. The main access is from Auburn, either on Highway 49 or the Auburn-Foresthill Road.

Restaurants

Auburn

Awful Annie's
160 Sacramento St
Auburn, CA 95603
530-888-9857
This restaurant allows dogs at four of their tables. If you come during the breakfast or lunch rush, you might need to wait for one of the dog-friendly

tables. For breakfast they serve gourmet omelettes and for lunch they offer a variety of sandwiches, chili, soups, salads and more.

Bootleggers Tavern and Grill
210 Washington St
Auburn, CA 95603
530-889-2229
This restaurant is located in historic Auburn in the original City Hall which was built in 1870.
Leashed dogs are welcome at the outdoor tables.

Ikeda's Tasty Burgers
13500 Lincoln Way
Auburn, CA 95603
530-885-4243
Dogs are allowed at the outdoor tables at this popular restaurant.

La Bou
2150 Grass Valley Hwy
Auburn, CA 95603
530-823-2303
Dogs are allowed at the outdoor tables.

Lou La Bonte's
13460 Lincoln Way
Auburn, CA 95603
530-885-9193
They offer Continental and American cuisine.
Dogs are allowed at the outdoor tables.

Maidu Market and South Side Caffe
631 Auburn-Folsom Rd
Auburn, CA 95603
530-823-1717
This cafe allows dogs at the outdoor tables. They serve doughnuts, bagels and expresso for breakfast. For lunch they offer BBQ sandwiches, salads and soups.

Neighbor's Coffee Garden
799 Lincoln Way
Auburn, CA 95603
530-888-6490
Dogs are allowed at the outdoor tables.

Open Door Cafe
151 Sacramento Street
Auburn, CA 95603
530-887-9970
Dogs are allowed at the outdoor tables. This restaurant overlooks downtown Auburn.

Tio Pepe's
216 Washington Street
Auburn, CA 95603
530-888-6445

Dogs are allowed at the outdoor tables.

Wings Grill & Expresso Bar
13595 New Airport Road
Auburn, CA 95603
530-885-0428
They serve breakfast and lunch at this cafe. You can watch the airplanes take off and land while you and your pooch sit at the covered outdoor patio.

Cameron Park Dog Travel Guide
Accommodations

Cameron Park

Best Western Cameron Park Inn
3361 Coach Lane
Cameron Park, CA 95682
530-677-2203
Amenities include a complimentary continental breakfast, pool, and hairdryers in rooms. There is a $25 one time pet charge.

Vets and Kennels

Cameron Park

Mother Lode Pet Emergency Clinic
4050 Durock Rd
Cameron Park, CA 95682
Hwy 50 and Ponderosa Rd
530-676-9044
Monday - Thursday 6 pm to 8 am, Friday 6 pm to 8 am Monday.

Camino Dog Travel Guide
Attractions

Camino

Argyres Orchard
4220 N. Canyon Rd.
Camino, CA 95709
530-644-3862
Located in Apple Hill, this ranch is open mid-September through October. Leashed dogs are allowed outside. You can pick your own apples and grapes at this ranch.

Bolster's Hilltop Ranch
2000 Larsen Drive
Camino, CA 95709
between Hartwick Dr and Cable Rd.
530-644-2230

Located in Apple Hill, this ranch is open daily June through the beginning of December. Leashed dogs are allowed outside. This ranch offers u-pick blueberries from June through August including a Blueberry Festival in June (blueberry plants available), u-pick apples on the weekends from September to November, outdoor arts & crafts booths, BBQ, picnic area, pumpkins, Christmas trees and more.

Denver Dan's
4344 Bumblebee Ln.
Camino, CA 95709
near Hartwick Dr.
530-644-6881
Located in Apple Hill, this ranch is open during the fall season, September through mid-December. They are closed on Tuesdays and only open Friday, Saturday and Sunday from late November through December. Leashed dogs are allowed outside. This ranch offers a bake shop, candy & caramel apples, gift shop, picnic area and u-pick apples.

Grandpa's Cellar
2360 Cable Rd.
Camino, CA 95709
near Larsen Drive
530-644-2153
Located in Apple Hill, this ranch is open daily during the fall season, September through mid-December. Leashed dogs are allowed outside. The owners have an old black lab on the premises. This ranch offers a bake shop, country store, nature trail, and on the weekends only, an outdoor craft fair and BBQ.

Honey Bear Ranch
2826 Barkley Rd.
Camino, CA 95709
near Larsen Drive
530-644-3934
Located in Apple Hill, this ranch is open during the fall season, September through December. Open daily September through October, and weekends only November through mid-December). Leashed dogs are allowed outside and you need to clean up after them. This ranch offers a restaurant with outdoor dining, bake shop, fudge kitchen, general store with antiques & crafts, and a picnic area with outdoor arts & crafts booths and live music.

Jack Russell Brewing Company
2380 Larsen Drive
Camino, CA 95709
530-644-4722
You and your best friend are welcome at this

English farm-style brewery located near Placerville in the Sierra Foothills between Sacramento and Lake Tahoe. Adjacent to the brewery is a picnic area where you can enjoy a variety of hand-crafted beers. They also have homemade root beer. The founding mascot, a Jack Russell Terrier named Boomer, is on the beer label. The brewery is open on the weekends and during the summer they sometimes have live entertainment outside and English-style meat pies. Dogs are welcome outside including the picnic areas.

Kids, Inc.
3245 N. Canyon Rd.
Camino, CA 95709
near Hassler Rd.
530-622-0084
Located in Apple Hill, this ranch is open during the fall season. Open all week during September and October and open weekends only in November through mid-December. Leashed dogs are allowed outside. This ranch offers a bake shop, gift shop, antiques, grassy picnic area, farm animals, nature trail, family activities, apples, pumpkins and Christmas trees.

Mother Lode Orchards
4341 N. Canyon Rd.
Camino, CA 95709
near Larsen Drive
530-644-5101
Located in Apple Hill, this ranch is open during the fall season, September through December. Open weekends only in November through mid-December. Leashed dogs are allowed outside including at the picnic tables. This ranch offers over 30 varieties of fruit and vegetables, pumpkins and Christmas trees. The owner also has a dog on the premises.

O'Hallorans Apple Trail Ranch
2261 Cable Rd.
Camino, CA 95709

530-644-3389
Located in Apple Hill, this ranch is open during the fall season (September through mid-December). Leashed dogs are allowed outside. This ranch offers a fruit store, handmade crafts, nature trail, picnic area, u-pick pumpkin patch, and cut & choose Christmas trees.

Plubell's Family Orchard
1800 Larsen Dr.
Camino, CA 95709
near Cable Rd.
530-647-0613
Located in Apple Hill, this ranch is open during the fall season, September through mid-November. Leashed dogs are allowed outside. This ranch offers fresh produce, a grassy picnic area, nature walk, pumpkin patch and on weekends a BBQ, miniature horse & wagon rides and more.

Stone's Throw Vineyard & Winery
3541 North Canyon Rd.
Camino, CA 95709
530-622-5100
Leashed dogs are allowed at the picnic area. The owners also have their own dogs on the premises. Their wine tasting is open Thursday through Sunday year-round (except major holidays).

Summerfield Berry Farm
4455 Pony Express Trail
Camino, CA 95709
near Cable Rd.
530-647-2833
Located in Apple Hill, this ranch is open mid-June through mid-November on Fridays, Saturdays and Sundays. Leashed dogs are allowed in the u-pick fruit area and picnic area. You can pick fresh raspberries and blackberries.

Parks

Camino

Old Larsen Apple Tree Picnic Area
Larsen Drive
Camino, CA 95709
across from Larsen Apple Barn, 2461 Larsen Dr.

This is a large grassy picnic area located in the heart of Apple Hill. Dogs must be on leash. There are three acres with a waterfall and the oldest apple tree in El Dorado County. See our list of attractions for dog-friendly Apple Hill Orchards & Ranches in the area.

Restaurants

Camino

Mountain Mike's Pizza
3600 Carson Rd #C
Camino, CA 95709
Hwy 50
530-644-6000
Dogs are allowed at the outdoor tables.

Chinese Camp Dog Travel Guide
Parks

Chinese Camp

Red Hills Area Hiking
Red Hills Road
Chinese Camp, CA
916-985-4474
This 7,000 acres of public land has just over 17 miles of trails with various loops. Elevations vary between 750 and 1,750 feet. This is a popular area for hunting, hiking, horseback riding and wildflower viewing. Leashed dogs are welcome. Please clean up after your dog. There are no park fees. The land is located near Highways 49 and 120. From Sonora, take Highway 49 south 15 miles to Chinese Camp. Then drive south on Red Hills Road for .5 miles.

Colfax Dog Travel Guide
Parks

Colfax

Stevens Trail
North Canyon Way
Colfax, CA
916-985-4474
This 4.5 mile trail is a popular year-round hiking, mountain biking and horseback riding trail which follows the northwestern slope of the North Fork of the American River. The trail offers a gentle slope that is suitable for novice hikers. Along the trail you can enjoy great views of the river, pass by several mine shafts, and see the China Wall built by Chinese laborers during the Gold Rush era in the 1850s. Please stay away from the mines because they are extremely dangerous and unstable. In April and May there should be a nice wildflower display. Leashed dogs are welcome. Please clean up after your dog. To get there from Sacramento, head east on Highway 80 towards Colfax. Take the North Canyon Way exit. Take this road past the Colfax cemetery to the

trailhead. On weekends and in high use season, parking may be very limited.

Coloma Dog Travel Guide
Accommodations

Coloma

Golden Lotus Bed and Breakfast Inn
1006 Lotus Road
Coloma, CA 95613
530-621-4562
This pre-Victorian B&B, located in the historic town of Coloma, is surrounded by herb gardens. Dogs are allowed in one of their rooms. Dogs must be well-behaved and owners must agree to pay for any damages. There is a $20 per day additional pet fee.

Attractions

Coloma

Gold Country Carriages
Hwy 49
Coloma, CA
530-622-6111
Dogs and families are welcome on this horse and carriage ride located at Marshall Gold Discovery State Park in Coloma on Hwy 49 (see Attractions for more information about the park). They offer tours of historic Coloma. Dogs need to stay on the floor of the carriage, not on the seat.

Marshall Gold Discovery State Park
Hwy 49
Coloma, CA
530-622-3470
This is the place where James W. Marshall found some shining flecks of gold in the tailrace of a sawmill he was building for himself and John Sutter in 1848. This began the famous Gold Rush era. The park has a replica of the sawmill and a number of historic buildings. Gold Country Carriage operates frequently on Hwy 49 at this park and dogs are welcome to join their family on this horse and carriage ride (see Attractions). Dogs on leash are welcome at several trails near the river. They are allowed in the picnic areas, but not allowed in the hiking trails across the street from the river side. Throughout the year the park has many special events, and dogs are welcome at most of the outdoor events. The park is located in Coloma on Highway 49 between Placerville and Auburn. It is open year round from 8am to sunset. There is a minimal fee for parking and for dogs.

Venezio Winery & Vineyard
5821 Highway 49
Coloma, CA 95613
530-885-WINE
Leashed and well-behaved dogs are allowed in the picnic area. This vineyard is nestled in the lovely Coloma Valley, 3.5 miles from the dog-friendly Marshall Gold Discovery State Park. From Placerville, take Hwy 49 north. Go past the town of Coloma, and the winery will be on the right.

Parks

Coloma

Dave Moore Nature Area
Highway 49
Coloma, CA
916-985-4474
This nature area features a one mile loop and about half of the trail is wheelchair, walker and stroller accessible. It starts at the parking lot and goes down to the South Fork of the American River and back, passing through several types of habitat. Located in the heart of the historic Gold Rush area, the trail is lined with remnants from about 150 years ago when Chinese laborers channeled the creek water by hand with a pick and shovel to find gold. Leashed dogs are welcome. Please clean up after your dog. To get there from Sacramento, take Highway 50 east towards Placerville. In Shingle Springs, take the Ponderosa Road exit and go over the freeway bridge to the stop sign (located just north of Highway 50). Turn right onto North Shingles Road and go 3 miles. Turn left at the Y in the road onto Lotus Road. Continue for 5 miles heading north. At Highway 49 turn left and cross the bridge at the river. Continue for about 1 mile along Highway 49. Turn left at the cobblestone wall. There are no

park fees, but donations are accepted.

Restaurants

Coloma

Argonaut Cafe
Hwy 49
Coloma, CA

Thanks to one of our readers who writes:
"Located in the Marshall Gold Discovery State
Historic Park, The Argonaut serves up
sandwiches, sodas, candy, pie, ice cream, coffee
and more. Dogs are allowed in the outdoor dining
area of the porch which spans two sides of the
building."

Sutter Center Market
378 Highway 49
Coloma, CA 95613
530-626-0849
In addition to selling gifts and food items, this
market also has a deli where you can order
pastries, sandwiches, burritos, ice cream and
more. It is located near the dog-friendly Marshall
Gold Discovery State Park (see Parks). Dogs are
allowed at the outdoor picnic tables.

Columbia Dog Travel Guide
Accommodations

Columbia

Columbia Gem Motel
22131 Parrotts Ferry Rd
Columbia, CA 95310
by Columbia State Hist. Park
209-532-4508
This dog-friendly motel offers gracious, country
hospitality, comfort and privacy. The motel is set
on a sunny park-like acre beneath towering,

majestic pines, cedars and sequoias, which
provide a shady umbrella over their 6 cozy log
cabins and 4 motel rooms. For a little extra, they
can provide the perfect getaway with champagne
on ice, flowers, wine, cheese, crackers,
chocolates, or bubble bath waiting for you in your
room. They can also arrange breakfast in bed or
can help with any other ideas. The motel is
located within walking distance (about 1 mile)
from the popular dog-friendly Columbia State
Historic Park. The Gold Mine Winery/Micro-
Brewery is located about 1 block away from the
motel. The winery has a nice outdoor covered
patio and lawn area. They have free wine and
beer tasting and they also make pizza from
scratch, any way you like it. The management are
of the belief that people who travel with their "best
friends" are responsible pet owners and a
pleasure to have as guests at The Gem. Dog
owners are not penalized with an extra fee here.
Instead, management has a simple, common
sense pet regulation form they have each owner
read and sign. Dogs are not to be left unattended
in the rooms.

Accommodations - RV Parks and Campgrounds

Columbia

49er RV Ranch
23223 Italian Bar Road
Columbia, CA 95310
209-532-4978
There are no additional pet fees.

Attractions

Columbia

Columbia State Historic Park
Parrotts Ferry Rd.
Columbia, CA

123

209-532-0150

The popular Columbia State Historic Park represents a gold rush town of the 1850-1870 time period. In 1945 the State Legislature made this site a State Historic Park in order to preserve a typical Gold Rush town, an example of one of the most colorful eras in American history. The town's old Gold Rush-era business district has been preserved with many shops and restaurants. The proprietors of the shops are dressed in mid 1800s period clothing. Activities include viewing over a dozen historic structures, shopping, picnic facilities and a few hiking trails. One of the trails, The Karen Bakerville Smith Memorial Trail is a self-guided 1/2 mile loop trail which was dedicated to a teacher. The trail is located by the historic school building and there is a brochure describing the plants and surroundings. The park operates daily from 9am to 5 pm. They are closed on Thankgiving and Christmas days. Admission is free. Your leashed dog is welcome. It is located on Parrotts Ferry Road, between Hwy 4 and Hwy 49 (near Sonora).

Restaurants

Columbia

Columbia Frosty
22652 Parrotts Ferry Rd
Columbia, CA 95310
209-532-6773
Dogs are allowed at the tables outside.

The Lickskillet
11256 State Street
Columbia, CA 95310
209-536-9599
This nice restaurant is located in the Columbia State Historic Park and allows your dog to dine with you at the outdoor tables. The tables are on the lawn and some are in the shade. Thanks to one of our readers for recommending this

restaurant. She writes "..wanted to let you know about (this) extremely dog-friendly restaurant... We sat at a table on the lawn, in the shade, with a bowl of water for the dogs. And the food was wonderful - both of us were delighted with our dinners."

Downieville Dog Travel Guide
Accommodations

Downieville

Downieville Carriage House Inn
110 Commercial Street
Downieville, CA 95936
530-289-3573
This 9 room inn is located in historic downtown Downieville and is open year round. Well-behaved dogs are allowed. Dogs should be able to get along well with other guests, as this is a house. There is a $15 per day pet fee.

Downieville River Inn and Resort
121 River Street
Downieville, CA
530-289-3308
This pet-friendly inn, surrounded by Tahoe National Forest, is nestled in the historic town of Downieville. The inn is located on the North Yuba River, along Highway 49 and the Yuba-Donner Scenic Byway. They offer guest rooms and cottages, each with a private bath and porch or balcony. Fully equipped kitchens and suites are also available. Enjoy their English gardens, picnic areas with barbecue grills, wet/dry sauna, and heated swimming pool in season. The Downieville area offers year round outdoor activities including trout fishing, hiking, gold panning, cross country skiing, and snowshoeing. The entire inn is non-smoking. Well-behaved dogs of all sizes are welcome. There are no pet fees.

Accommodations - RV Parks and Campgrounds

Downieville

Rocky Rest Campground
Highway 49
Downieville, CA
530-288-3231
This 10 site campground is located in the Tahoe National Forest at a 2,000 foot elevation. Amenities include piped water and vault toilets. There is a $16 per site fee. The North Yuba trailhead is located at this campground. Pets must be leashed in the campsite and please clean up after your pets. The campground is located on Highway 49, 7.5 miles west of Downieville.

Parks

Downieville

North Yuba Trail
Highway 49
Downieville, CA
530-288-3231
This 7.5 mile moderate rated trail is located in the Tahoe National Forest. Pets must be either leashed or off-leash but under direct voice control. Please clean up after your pets. The trail is located on Highway 49, 7.5 miles west of Downieville at the Rocky Rest Campground.

Drytown Dog Travel Guide
Accommodations

Drytown

Old Well Motel
15947 State Highway 49
Drytown, CA 95699
209-245-6467
This motel is located near the Shenandoah Valley. There is a $5 per day additional pet fee.

Fair Play Dog Travel Guide
Attractions

Fair Play

Charles B. Mitchell Vineyards
8221 Stoney Creek Road
Fair Play, CA 95684
800-704-WINE
Leashed dogs are allowed in the picnic area. The owners have an older dog that resides on the premises. From E-16, take Fair Play Rd. east. Turn right on Stoney Creek Rd. The winery will be on the left.

Oakstone Winery
6440 Slug Gulch Rd.
Fair Play, CA 95684
530-620-5303
Well-behaved, leashed dogs are allowed in both of their picnic areas. From E-16, turn onto Fair Play Rd. Turn right on Slug Gulch Rd.

Perry Creek Vineyards
7400 Perry Creek Rd.
Fair Play, CA 95684
530-620-5175
Well-behaved, leashed dogs are allowed at the picnic area. Their tasting room opens to the spacious outdoor verandah picnic area. From E-16, turn onto Fair Play Rd. Turn left onto Perry Creek Rd. Winery will be on the left.

Foresthill Dog Travel Guide
Accommodations - RV Parks and Campgrounds

Foresthill

Big Reservoir/Morning Star Campground
Foresthill Divide Road
Foresthill, CA 95631

530-367-2129
This campground is located in the Tahoe National Forest and offers 100 sites at an elevation of 4,000 feet. Amenities include piped water and vault toilets. The Sugar Pine Trail is located nearby. Fees are $18 to $25 per site, depending on proximity to the waterfront. Pets must be leashed in the campground. Please clean up after your pets. To get there from Foresthill, go 18 miles northeast on Foresthill Divide Road.

French Meadows Reservoir Campground
Mosquito Ridge Road
Foresthill, CA 95631
530-367-2224
Located in the Tahoe National Forest, this 75 site campground is at an elevation of 5,300 feet. The campground is next to the French Meadows Reservoir. Camp amenities include piped water and flush/vault toilets. Pets are allowed but must be leashed in the campground. The campsite is located 36 miles east of Foresthill on Mosquito Ridge Road. Call to make a reservation.

Robinson Flat Campground
Foresthill Divide Road
Foresthill, CA 95631
530-367-2224
This campground is located at an elevation of 6,800 feet in the Tahoe National Forest, near the Little Bald Mountain Trail. The campground offer 14 sites (7 family sites and 7 equestrian sites) on a first-come, first-served basis. Amenities include well water and vault toilets. There is no fee. Pet must be on leash in the campground. Please clean up after your pets. To get there, go 28 miles from Foresthill on Foresthill Divide Road to Robinson Flat.

Robinson Flat Campground
Foresthill Divide Road
Foresthill, CA 95631
530-367-2224
This campground is located at an elevation of 6,800 feet in the Tahoe National Forest, near the Little Bald Mountain Trail. The campground offer 14 sites (7 family sites and 7 equestrian sites) on a first-come, first-served basis. Amenities include well water and vault toilets. There is no fee. Pet must be on leash in the campground. Please clean up after your pets. To get there, go 28 miles from Foresthill on Foresthill Divide Road to Robinson Flat.

Big Trees Loop
Mosquito Ridge Road
Foresthill, CA 95631
530-367-2224
This .5 mile easy trail is located in the Tahoe National Forest and is a popular interpretive trail. The trail is accessible when the road is open, generally from late May to early November. Pets on leash are allowed and please clean up after them. To get there from Foresthill, take Mosquito Ridge Road 24 miles to Road 16.

French Meadows Reservoir
Mosquito Ridge Road
Foresthill, CA 95631
530-367-2224
Activities at this reservoir include fishing, boating, swimming, picnicking, hiking, and viewing scenery. Dogs are allowed in the water. Pets must be either leashed or off-leash but under direct voice control. Please clean up after your pets. The reservoir is located in the Tahoe National Forest, 36 miles east of Foresthill on Mosquito Ridge Road.

Little Bald Mountain Trail
Foresthill Divide Road
Foresthill, CA 95631
530-367-2224
This trail is located in the Tahoe National Forest and is a 3.39 mile moderate rated trail. The trail is open from May to November, weather permitting. Pets must be either leashed or off-leash but under direct voice control. Please clean up after your pets. To get there, go 28 miles from Foresthill on Foresthill Divide Road to Robinson Flat and park in the day use area.

Sugar Pine Trail
Foresthill Divide Road
Foresthill, CA 95631
530-367-2224
This popular 3.5 mile easy trail goes around Sugar Pine Reservoir. Dogs are allowed on the trail and in the water on non-designated swim beaches. Pets must be either leashed or off-leash but under direct voice control. Please clean up after your pets. The primary season for this trail is usually from May to October. This trail is located in the Tahoe National Forest. To get there from Foresthill, go 18 miles northeast on Foresthill Divide Road.

Parks

Foresthill

Georgetown Dog Travel Guide
Accommodations

Georgetown

American River Bed and Breakfast Inn
Main and Orleans Streets
Georgetown, CA 95634
530-333-4499
They have certain pet rooms and you need to call in advance to make a reservation. All rooms are non-smoking. There is a refundable pet deposit.

Grass Valley Dog Travel Guide
Accommodations

Grass Valley

Bear River Retreat and Lodge
20010 Hwy 174
Grass Valley, CA
530-346-0078
According to one of our readers "Nestled on 13+ acres of pine and oak trees and various hiking trails, the lodge is a perfect doggie getaway."

Best Western Gold Country Inn
11972 Sutton Way
Grass Valley, CA 95945
530-273-1393
There is a $10 one time pet charge. Dogs cannot be left alone in the room and they need to be leashed when outside of the room.

Swan Levine House Bed and Breakfast
328 South Church Street
Grass Valley, CA 95945
916-272-1873
This renovated historic house was built in 1880. It was originally owned by a local merchant who made his fortune by selling mining equipment. He sold it to a doctor who converted the house into a hospital and it served as a community medical center until 1968. There are four rooms, each with a private bath. They have one room available for guests who bring a large dog. Dogs are not to be left alone in the room. There is a $15 per day pet charge. They are also kid-friendly. They do have a cat that resides in the house.

Attractions

Grass Valley

Empire Mine State Historic Park
10791 East Empire Street
Grass Valley, CA
530-273-8522
This park is home to one of the oldest, largest, deepest, longest, and richest gold mines in California. The park consists of over 800 acres and has eight miles of trails. Dogs on leash are allowed in the park and on the trails.

Restaurants

Grass Valley

Bubba's Bagels
11943 Nevada City Hwy
Grass Valley, CA 95945
530-272-8590
Dogs are allowed at the outdoor table.

Cousin Jack Pastries
100 S Auburn St
Grass Valley, CA 95945
Main Street
530-272-9230
Dogs are allowed at the covered outdoor tables. The restaurant is in downtown Grass Valley.

Grinders Restaurant
840 East Main Street
Grass Valley, CA 95945
530-477-8759
Dogs are allowed at the outdoor tables.

Jackson Dog Travel Guide
Accommodations

Jackson

Amador Motel
12408 Kennedy Flat Rd
Jackson, CA 95642
209-223-0970
This motel has a large backyard, not completely enclosed, where you can walk your dog. They allow all well-behaved dogs. There are no additional pet fees.

Jackson Gold Lodge
850 N. State Hwy 49
Jackson, CA 95642
N. of downtown Jackson
209-223-0486
This lodge has been dog-friendly for years. They allow dogs in the motel rooms and in the cottages. They have eight duplex cottages, each with a separate living room, kitchen, dining room, bedroom and patio. Amenities include a free continental breakfast. Dogs are an additional $10 per day. There are no designated smoking or non-smoking cottages.

Parks

Jackson

W.F. Detert Park
Hwy 49
Jackson, CA

This is a small but nice city park that allows leashed dogs. It has some picnic tables and a children's playground. It is located on Hwy 49, between the Jackson Gold Lodge and historic downtown Jackson.

Restaurants

Jackson

Caffe Tazza
214 N Main St
Jackson, CA 95642
209-223-4942
Dogs are allowed at the outdoor seats.

Mel & Faye's Drive In
205 N. State Hwy 49
Jackson, CA 95642
209-223-0853
This diner is open for breakfast, lunch and dinner. They have several outdoor covered picnic tables and benches where you and your pup can enjoy the American-style food. If it gets too chilly, they have an outdoor heater. The diner is located on Hwy 49, near historic downtown Jackson.

Jamestown Dog Travel Guide
Accommodations

Jamestown

Quality Inn
18730 SR 108
Jamestown, CA 95327
209-984-0315
There is a $10 per day pet fee.

Royal Hotel Bed and Breakfast
18239 Main Street
Jamestown, CA 95327
209-984-5271
Dogs are not allowed in the hotel, but are allowed in one of the private cottages. This hotel is located in historic Jamestown, near Yosemite National Park. There is a $10 per day pet charge.

The National Hotel
18183 Main Street

Jamestown, CA 95327
209-984-3446
Established in 1859, this is one of the oldest continuously operating hotels in California. Taking a day trip or going for a hike? Just ask for a picnic basket the day before and their chef will provide you with a meal to take with you and enjoy next to a cool Sierra Nevada stream or at one of the many picnic areas throughout the dog-friendly Stanislaus National Forest. There is a $10 per day pet charge. All rooms are non-smoking.

Attractions

Jamestown

Railtown 1897 State Historic Park
Highway 49
Jamestown, CA
209-984-3953
This park is home to one of America's last authentic, operating railroad roundhouses. Still a popular Hollywood location site, Railtown 1897 has been called "the most photographed railroad in the world." "Petticoat Junction," "The Wild, Wild West," "High Noon," "The Virginian," and "Unforgiven" were all filmed here. Movie crews also produced the railroad sequences in "Back to the Future Part III" at Railtown. Dogs on leash are allowed in the park, but not on the trains.

Restaurants

Jamestown

Pizza Plus
18251 Main St
Jamestown, CA 95327
209-984-3700
Dogs on leash are allowed at the outdoor seats.

Kyburz Dog Travel Guide
Accommodations

Kyburz

Kyburz Resort Motel
13666 Highway 50
Kyburz, CA 95720
530-293-3382
Nestled among the pines along 300 feet of the South Fork of the American River, this motel is located in the heart of the El Dorado National Forest. It is located about 30 minutes east of Placerville and about 15-20 minutes from Apple

Hill. Well-behaved dogs are allowed and they must be leashed when outside your room. There is a $10 per day pet fee.

Mount Aukum Dog Travel Guide
Attractions

Mount Aukum

Latcham Vineyards
2860 Omo Ranch Road
Mount Aukum, CA 95656
530-620-6642
Leashed dogs are allowed at the picnic tables. The winery is located on the north slope of a valley in Mt. Aukum. From E-16, take Omo Ranch Rd east. The winery will be on the right.

Murphys Dog Travel Guide
Restaurants

Murphys

Red Apple
4950 E Highway 4
Murphys, CA 95247
209-728-0414
Dogs may sit at the outdoor tables. There is also a dog walk in the apple orchard.

Nevada City Dog Travel Guide
Accommodations

Nevada City

The Outside Inn
575 E. Broad Street
Nevada City, CA 95959
530-265-2233
This inn is located in a quiet residential neighborhood two blocks from downtown Nevada City. This completely renovated 1940's era motor court features never smoked in rooms under tall pines. Children and pets are welcome. There is a $10 per night pet charge.

Accommodations - RV Parks and Campgrounds

Nevada City

Lodgepole Campground
off Yuba Gap
Nevada City, CA
916-386-5164

This 35 site campground is located in the Tahoe National Forest and is managed by PG&E. The campsite is located at an elevation of 5,800 feet. Pets must be leashed in the campground and please clean up after them. To get there from I-80, take the Yuba Gap exit for .4 miles. Go around Lake Valley Reservoir for 1.2 miles. Then take right fork 2.5 miles.

South Yuba Campground
North Bloomfield Road
Nevada City, CA
916-985-4474
This campground has 16 sites for tents or RVs. Camp amenities include picnic tables, fire grills, piped water, pit toilets and garbage collection. There are no RV hookups. The campground is open from April to mid-October. The cost per site is $5 per night with a 14 day maximum stay. Sites are available on a first-come, first-served basis. The South Yuba River Recreation Area is located about 10 miles northeast of Nevada City. From Nevada City, take Highway 49 north to North Bloomfield Road. Drive 10 miles to the South Yuba Recreation Area. From the one land bridge at Edwards Crossing, go about 1.5 miles on a dirt/gravel road to the campground and trailhead. Trailers and motorhomes should take Highway 49 and then turn right at the junction of Tyler Foote Road. At the intersection of Grizzly Hill Road turn right and proceed to North Bloomfield Road.

Attractions

Nevada City

Nevada City Horse & Carriage
downtown Nevada City
Nevada City, CA
530-265-9646
Well-behaved dogs are allowed to ride in this horse and carriage with their family.

Parks

Nevada City

Salmon Lakes Trail
Road 38
Nevada City, CA
530-265-4531
This 2 mile easy rated trail is located in the Tahoe National Park. It used by hikers, mountain bikers and equestrians. Pets must be leashed in the campground and please clean up after them. To get there from I-80 at Yuba Gap, go south for .3

miles and turn right toward Lodgepole Campground. After 1.1 miles, turn right on Road 19 (unpaved). After 2 miles turn left on Road 38. The trailhead is 2 miles ahead and .5 miles past Huysink Lake.

South Yuba Trail
North Bloomfield Road
Nevada City, CA
916-985-4474
This 12 mile trail is popular with hikers, runners, mountain bikers and horseback riders. The trail offers pine tree covered canyons, gentle slopes and open meadows. Along the trail you will see historic flumes and waterworks. Leashed dogs are welcome. Please clean up after your dog. The South Yuba River Recreation Area is located about 10 miles northeast of Nevada City. From Nevada City, take Highway 49 north to North Bloomfield Road. Drive 10 miles to the South Yuba Recreation Area. From the one lane bridge at Edwards Crossing, go about 1.5 miles on a dirt/gravel road to the campground and trailhead. Trailers and motorhomes should take Highway 49 and then turn right at the junction of Tyler Foote Road. At the intersection of Grizzly Hill Road turn right and proceed to North Bloomfield Road.

Tahoe National Forest
631 Coyote Street
Nevada City, CA 95959
530-265-4531
This national forest includes the Lake Tahoe Basin Management Area. Elevations range from 1,500 feet up to 9,400 feet. Please see our listings in the Gold Country and Sierra Nevada region for dog-friendly hikes and/or campgrounds.

Restaurants

Nevada City

Broad St Books and Expresso Bar
426 Broad St
Nevada City, CA 95959
530-265-4204
Dogs are not allowed on the patio, but there is one table near the back door. There is a water bowl for your dog next to this table.

The Top Dog
Broad Street Downtown
Nevada City, CA
530-265-8081
This Hot Dog Cart is usually in Downtown Nevada City on Broad Street. It is an easy place for you and your pup to get a quick bite to eat.

Pine Grove Dog Travel Guide
Attractions

Pine Grove

Indian Grinding Rock State Historic Park
14881 Pine Grove - Volcano Road
Pine Grove, CA 95665
209-296-7488
This park preserves a great outcropping of
marbleized limestone with 1185 mortar holes, the
largest collection of bedrock mortars anywhere in
North America. Visitors can find many
petroglyphs here. Dogs on leash are allowed at
the historic site, but not on any trails. The park is
located off Highway 88.

Restaurants

Pine Grove

88 Burgers
19845 State Highway 88
Pine Grove, CA 95665
209-296-7277
Dogs are allowed at the outdoor tables.

Placerville Dog Travel Guide
Accommodations

Placerville

Best Western Placerville Inn
6850 Green Leaf Dr.
Placerville, CA 95667
off Missouri Flat Rd.
530-622-9100
This motel overlooks the Sierra Foothills and
allows dogs in the first floor rooms. Amenities
include a heated pool and Jacuzzi. There is a
coffee shop next door if you want to order food to
go for the motel room. The motel is located within
a short drive to historic downtown Placerville.

Attractions

Placerville

Abel's Apple Acres
2345 Carson Rd.
Placerville, CA 95667
near Hassler Rd.
530-626-0138
Located in Apple Hill, this ranch is open daily,
September through Christmas Eve. Leashed dogs
are allowed outside. This ranch offers a bake
shop, fudge, homemade caramel, BBQ, fresh
apples, gift store, outdoor arts & crafts booths,
pony & horse rides, duck pond, picnic area, hay
maze & hay rides, and pumpkin patch.

Apple Creek Ranch
2979 Carson Rd.
Placerville, CA 95667
near North Canyon Rd.
530-644-5073
Located in Apple Hill, this ranch is open during
apple season, usually mid-September through
October. Leashed dogs are allowed outside. This
ranch offer fresh apples.

Boa Vista Orchards
2952 Carson Rd.
Placerville, CA 95667
near North Canyon Rd.
530-622-5522
This ranch is open year round (closed on
Christmas Day). Dogs are not allowed in the
store, but are allowed at the picnic tables. Dogs
must be leashed. At the tables, you and your
pooch can enjoy goodies from their bakery, like a
fresh apple pie with ice cream or try their BBQ
sandwiches on the weekends. They also have
outdoor arts and crafts booths during the fall, on
the weekends.

Boeger Winery
1709 Carson Road
Placerville, CA 95667
530-622-8094
Well-behaved leashed dogs are allowed at the
picnic tables at this winery. People can bring
some of the wine to the picnic tables to taste. The
winery is one of the oldest family owned and
operated wineries in the Sierra Foothills of
Northern California. They are open 10a.m.-5p.m.
daily.

Gold Hill Vineyard

5660 Vineyard Lane
Placerville, CA 95667
530-626-6522
Dogs are allowed at the picnic tables near the tasting room. They allow well-behaved and leashed dogs outside. From Hwy 50, take Cold Springs Rd. north (towards Coloma). Turn right on Vineyard Lane.

High Hill Ranch
2901 High Hill Rd.
Placerville, CA 95667
Carson Road
530-644-1973
Located in Apple Hill, this ranch is open daily during the fall season (September through December). Leashed dogs are allowed outside. They offer a bake shop (with lunch on the weekends), a cider mill, wine tasting, outdoor arts & crafts booths, a picnic area overlooking the Sierra Nevada mountains, trout fishing, pony rides (weekends only), a fudge shop and a farm shop including fresh apples and produce, apple butter, dried fruits, gift packs and more.

Hooverville Orchards
1100 Wallace Rd.
Placerville, CA 95667
off Coloma Rd.
530-622-2155
Open daily year-round, this orchard offers peaches, nectarines, plums, apricots, cherries, apples, avocados, pumpkins, vegetables and more. They also have a bake shop and a picnic area. Leashed dogs are allowed at the picnic area.

Lava Cap Winery
2221 Fruitridge Road
Placerville, CA 95667
530-621-0175
Well-behaved, leashed dogs are allowed at the tables on their deck. Relax on the deck with a picnic and savor the scenic view of their vineyard. They are located just 5 minutes from Hwy 50. From Placerville, exit Schnell School Rd. (at the exit, head north by turning left at stop sign), turn right onto Carson Rd, turn left on Union Ridge, then veer right on Hassler Rd, then left on Fruitridge Rd.

Placerville Downtown
Main Street & Hwy 49
Placerville, CA 95667
Hwy 50 and Hwy 49

This historic Gold Rush downtown has a large number of stores of all kinds, some of which may

allow your well-behaved dog to enter.

Sierra Vista Winery & Vineyard
4560 Cabernet Way
Placerville, CA 95667
530-622-7841
Leashed and well-behaved dogs are allowed in the picnic area. The picnic grounds offer a beautiful view of The Sierra Nevada mountains. From Pleasant Valley Road, turn right onto Leisure Lane. The winery is at the end of Leisure Lane.

Parks

Placerville

El Dorado Trail
Mosquito Rd.
Placerville, CA
just north of Hwy 50

This part of the El Dorado Trail is a nice paved path that is popular with runners and walkers. Leashed dogs are allowed. The trail was originally 2 miles each way for a total of 4 miles, but the trail has been expanded a few extra miles. Most of the path is wide enough that there is a dirt trail paralleling the paved trail. It is located near historic downtown Placerville. To get there from Hwy 50 heading east, exit Broadway and turn right. When Broadway ends, turn right onto Mosquito Rd and go back under the freeway. At the second street, turn left. If you go too far, you'll end up going back onto Hwy 50. The trail will be on the right. Park along the street.

Eldorado National Forest
100 Forni Road
Placerville, CA 95667
530-622-5061
This national forest covers over 590,000 acres of land which ranges in elevation from 1,000 feet in

the foothills to more than 10,000 feet along the Sierras. Please see our listings in the Gold Country and Sierra Nevada region for dog-friendly hikes and/or campgrounds.

Gold Bug Park
2635 Gold Bug Lane
Placerville, CA 95667
Hwy 50 and Bedford Ave
530-642-5207
Gold Bug Park is a 60 acre park that was once the home of many gold mines. Your leashed dog is allowed at the picnic areas and on the trails, but is not allowed into the mine.

Restaurants

Placerville

Chubby's Diner
3970 Missouri Flat Rd #H
Placerville, CA 95667
in KMART shopping center
530-642-7768
Dogs are allowed at the outdoor tables.

Creekside Cantina
451 Main Street #10
Placerville, CA 95667
530-626-7966
Dogs are allowed at the outdoor tables.

Dairy Depot
4601 Missouri Flat Rd
Placerville, CA 95667
near Pleasant Valley Rd
530-622-8548
Dogs are allowed at the outdoor tables.

Noah's Ark
535 Placerville Drive
Placerville, CA 95667
530-621-3663
This natural food market has outdoor tables where your well-behaved leashed dog is welcome. During the week they usually have pre-made vegan sandwiches and hot slices of organic veggie pizza. You will need to pick up your food inside and bring it to your outside table.

Pizza Factory
4570 Pleasant Valley Road
Placerville, CA 95667
530-644-6043
This restaurant serves a variety of pizzas, pasta and salad. Well-behaved leashed dogs are allowed at the outdoor tables.

Plaza Ritz Deli
3964 Missouri Flat Rd #E
Placerville, CA 95667
in KMART shopping center
530-642-9996
Dogs are allowed at the outdoor tables.

Straw Hat Pizza
3970 Missouri Flat Rd
Placerville, CA 95667
in KMART shopping center
530-626-8511
Dogs are allowed at the outdoor tables.

Sweetie Pie's
577 Main Street
Placerville, CA 95667
between Bedford & Clay
530-642-0128
Try the fresh cinnamon rolls at this restaurant. They also serve a delicious variety of food for breakfast and lunch. They are open 7 days a week from 6:30am to 4pm. They usually do not serve food outside during the winter. It is located on Main Street (between Bedford and Clay Streets), east of historic downtown Placerville.

Teriyaki Junction
1216 Broadway
Placerville, CA 95667
530-295-1413
This Japanese restaurant serves bento dishes, teriyaki, and sushi. There are 5-6 tables outside where you can enjoy lunch or dinner. The tables are also shared by Baskin Robbins. To get there from Hwy 50 heading east, take the Broadway exit and turn left. Then turn right into the shopping complex, near the McDonalds.

The Steak Out
1234 Broadway
Placerville, CA 95667
530-642-8217
This restaurant serves Greek cuisine, including broiled steak, chicken and lamb kabobs. Or try the homemade gourmet custom wrapps. The hours are from 11am until 9pm. To get there from Hwy 50 heading east, take the Broadway exit and turn left. Then turn right into the shopping complex.

Stores

Placerville

Act 1 Video & Music
1345 Broadway
Placerville, CA 95667
530-621-1919
Your leashed, well-behaved dog is allowed inside the store. Here you can rent your favorite video or browse through their selection of music CDs. The store is located across the street from the Mountain Democrat Newspaper building.

Plymouth Dog Travel Guide

Accommodations - RV Parks and Campgrounds

Plymouth

Far Horizons 49er Village
18265 Highway 49
Plymouth, CA 209-245-6981

This RV park is located in the wine and gold country of the Sierra Foothills and offers 329 shady RV sites. All sites have full hookups with water, sewer, 30 or 50 amp electricity and cable TV. Other amenities include two swimming pools, laundry, game room, and onsite deli and market. Well-behaved leashed dogs are welcome, up to three per site. There are no pet fees. Please clean up after your pet. The RV park is open all year.

Attractions

Plymouth

Montevina Wines
20680 Shenandoah School Road
Plymouth, CA 95669
1.5 miles from E-16
209-245-6942
Dogs are allowed at the outdoor tables in their patio. The hours are 11 - 4 daily.

Sobon Winery
14430 Shenandoah Rd
Plymouth, CA 95669
209-245-6554
Well-behaved leashed dogs are allowed at the picnic tables at this winery.

Restaurants

Plymouth

Cafe at the Park
18265 Hwy 49
Plymouth, CA 95669
in the 49er RV Park
209-245-6981
This cafe serves sandwiches, pastries, and ice cream. They are located at the entrance of the 49er RV Park in Plymouth. The dog-friendly outdoor seating is located behind the cafe. They are open weekdays from 7am to 8pm and weekends from 7am to 10pm. It is off Hwy 49, across the street from the Pokerville Market.

Gold Country Cafe
17830 State Highway 49
Plymouth, CA 95669
209-245-6218
Dogs are allowed at the outdoor tables.

Marlene and Glen's Diner
18726 Highway 49
Plymouth, CA 95669
209-245-5778
Dogs are allowed at the outdoor seats.

Pollock Pines Dog Travel Guide
Accommodations - RV Parks and
Campgrounds

Pollock Pines

Sly Park Campground
4771 Sly Park Road
Pollock Pines, CA 95726
530-644-2545
The wooded Sly Park Recreation Area offers 159 campsites at an elevation of 3,500 feet. Site amenities include a table, barbecue and fire ring. Camp amenities include water, vault and toilets. No hookups are available but there is a dump station at the park entrance. Pets on leash are allowed in the campground and on trails including the 8 to 9 mile trail which surround the lake. The campgrounds are open during the summer. Reservations are required.

Attractions

Pollock Pines

Harris Tree Farm
2640 Blair Road
Pollock Pines, CA 95709
530-644-2194
Harris Tree Farm features 30 acres of Christmas

trees and fruit orchard, plus a variety of fruits and home-made goodies. Come for a nature walk, picnic in the orchard, fruit pies or choose and cut your Christmas Tree. Your leashed dog is welcome here. They are open every year from August through December 24. During these months, the farm is open daily from 8:30am to 4-4:30pm. To get there, take Hwy 50 approximately 1 hour east of Sacramento to the town of Pollock Pines. Take the first Pollock Pines exit which is the Cedar Grove Exit and turn left on this street. At the Pony Express Trail Road turn right. Then turn left onto Blair Rd. Go approximately 1 mile and the Harris Tree Farm will be on the left.

Parks

Pollock Pines

Cedar Park Trail
Sly Park Road
Pollock Pines, CA
530-644-2349
This easy paved trail, set amongst pine and conifer trees, has two small paved loops which total 1.2 miles in length. The elevation ranges from about 3,640 to 3,700 feet. Pets must be leashed and please clean up after them. The trail is located in the Eldorado National Forest. From Highway 50 in Pollock Pines, take Sly Park Road south (away from the Safeway). Drive about 6 miles to the parking area and trailhead on the left side of the road. There is ample parking.

Sly Park/Jenkinson Lake
4771 Sly Park Road
Pollock Pines, CA
5-10 min. s. of Hwy 50
530-644-2545
This beautiful wooded recreation area is at an elevation of 3500 feet. There is an 8 mile loop trail that circles Jenkinson Lake. It is a popular park

for hiking, horseback riding, fishing and camping. Leashed dogs are allowed on the trails and in the campgrounds. The west side of the park (next to the campgrounds) offers wide fire road trails, while the east side has single track trails. Be sure to check your pup for ticks after walking here. The park is open from sunrise to sunset. It is located about 30 minutes from Placerville. To get there from Hwy 50, take the Sly Park Rd exit and turn right. Drive about 5-10 minutes and the park will be on the left.

Shingle Springs Dog Travel Guide
Restaurants

Shingle Springs

Caffeine Cuisine
4056 Mother Lode Dr
Shingle Springs, CA 95682
Hwy 50 and Ponderosa
530-676-2623
Dogs are allowed at the outdoor tables.

Stores

Shingle Springs

Lee's Feed and Western Store
4110 Mother Lode Dr
Shingle Springs, CA 95682
530-677-4891
Dogs are welcome in this pet supply and feed store. Store hours are 8:30am to 6pm Monday through Friday, 8:30am to 5pm on Saturday and Sunday.

Somerset Dog Travel Guide
Attractions

Somerset

Firefall Vineyards
5951 Mt. Aukum Road (E-16)
Somerset, CA 95684
530-626-5432
Located right off E-16, this tasting room has one picnic table located outside.

Sonora Dog Travel Guide
Accommodations

Sonora

Best Western Sonora Oaks

19551 Hess Avenue
Sonora, CA 95370
209-533-4400
There is a $10 per day pet charge. They are located within a short drive of the dog-friendly Columbia State Historic Park.

Sonora Aladdin Motor Inn
14260 Mono Way (Hwy 108)
Sonora, CA 95370
209-533-4971
This motel's rooms offer Southwest decor with king or queen sized beds, table & chairs, refrigerators, coffee makers, climate control, cable TV & HBO, and direct dial phones with free local & credit card calls. They also feature a guest laundry. Dogs are welcome with a $5 one time charge. The motel is about an hour and a half from Yosemite.

Parks

Sonora

Stanislaus National Forest
19777 Greenley Road
Sonora, CA 95370
209-532-3671
This national forest covers almost 900,000 acres of land which ranges in elevation from 1,200 to over 10,000 feet. Please see our listings in the Sierra Nevada Mountains region for dog-friendly hikes and campgrounds.

Restaurants

Sonora

Pine Tree Restaurant
19601 Hess Ave
Sonora, CA 95370
209-536-6065
Dogs are allowed at the outdoor tables.

Sutter Creek Dog Travel Guide
Attractions

Sutter Creek

Sutter Creek Wine Tasting
85 Main Street
Sutter Creek, CA 95685
209-267-5838
Dogs may sit with you at the outdoor picnic bench or the two small tables in the front while you

sample the wines from a local group of growers.

Restaurants

Sutter Creek

Paulette's Place
40 Hanford # C
Sutter Creek, CA 95685
209-267-0500
Dogs are allowed at the outdoor tables on the front patio.

Sutter Creek Coffee
20 Eureka Street
Sutter Creek, CA 95685
209-267-5550
Dogs are allowed on the patio seats in front. Dogs are not allowed at the tables on the porch.

Stores

Sutter Creek

Three Dog Bakery
16 Eureka St.
Sutter Creek, CA 95685
Hwy 49
209-267-1500
This dog cookie bakery is located in the historic town of Sutter Creek. Bring your dog in for a variety of goodies prepared and baked just for your best friend.

Tuttletown Dog Travel Guide
Attractions

Tuttletown

Mark Twain Cabin
Jackass Hill Rd.
Tuttletown, CA
Hwy 49

This replica of Mark Twain's cabin has the original chimney and fireplace. During 1864-1865, young Mark Twain was a guest of the Gillis Brothers. While he stayed at this cabin, he gathered material for The Jumping Frog of Calaveras County (this book brought him fame) and for Roughing It. The cabin is located near Sonora, approximately 1 mile northwest of Tuttletown off Hwy 49. There are several parking spots next to the cabin.

Volcano Dog Travel Guide
Accommodations

Volcano

The St. George Hotel
16104 Main Street
Volcano, CA 95689
209-296-4458
A well-behaved large dog is allowed in one of the bungalow rooms. The non-smoking pet-friendly room has hardwood floors, a queen bed, a private bath and garden views. Upon arrival, your pooch will receive treats and an extra blanket. There is a $20 per day pet charge.

Chapter 6

California Dog-Friendly Travel Guide
Sierra Nevada Mountains

Big Pine Dog Travel Guide

Accommodations

Big Pine

Big Pine Motel
370 S Main St
Big Pine, CA
760-938-2282
There is a $4 per day additional pet fee.

Bristlecone Motel
101 N. Main St.
Big Pine, CA
760-938-2067
According to one of our website readers "Neat, inexpensive rooms with kitchens or fridge and microwave. Barbecue and fish cleaning area. Easy day trip to the ancient Bristlecone Pine Forest, which is extremely dog friendly."

Accommodations - RV Parks and Campgrounds

Big Pine

Big Pine Creek Campground
Glacier Lodge Road
Big Pine, CA
760-873-2500
This 36 site campground is located in the Inyo National Forest at an elevation of 7,700 feet. Amenities include water and space for RVs. There are no hookups. For hiking, the trailheads for the Big Pine Canyon Trails are located here. The fee for a campsite is $13. The campground is open from about mid May to mid October. To make a reservation call 1-877-444-6777. Pets must be leashed while in the campground and please clean up after your pets. To get there from Highway 395, exit in Big Pine and go 11 miles west on Glacier Lodge Road.

Glacier Lodge RV Park
Glacier Lodge Road
Big Pine, CA
760-938-2837
This campground offers tent camping and some RV spaces with full hookups. Amenities include a general store and nearby hiking and fishing. Dogs are also allowed in the cabins for an extra $15 per pet per stay. The Big Pine Canyon trailheads are located here which offer miles of dog-friendly on or off-leash hiking trails. Pets must be leashed in

the campground and please clean up after them. The campground is open from April through October. To get there from Highway 395, exit in Big Pine and go 11 miles west on Glacier Lodge Road.

Parks

Big Pine

Big Pine Canyon Trails
Glacier Lodge Road
Big Pine, CA
760-873-2500
These trails start and an elevation of 7,800 feet and go up to 12,400 feet. There are about 15 miles of trails. The trails lead into the dog-friendly John Muir Wilderness. One of the closest lakes, Willow Lake, is a 4 mile hike from the trailhead. At the campgrounds pets must be on a 6 foot or less leash. While hiking on the trails, pets must be on leash or under voice command at all times. Dogs are also allowed in the lake. Please clean up after your pets. This trail is located in the Inyo National Forest. To get there from Highway 395, exit in Big Pine and go 11 miles west on Glacier Lodge Road.

John Muir Wilderness Trails
Glacier Lodge Road
Big Pine, CA
760-873-2500
The wilderness trails are located in the Inyo National Forest and can be accessed from many points, including the Big Pine Canyon Trails near Big Pine. See our listing for Big Pine Creek Canyon Trail. From these trailheads, there are about 9 miles of hiking trails and several campgrounds. To get there from Highway 395, exit in Big Pine and go 11 miles west on Glacier Lodge Road.

Bishop Dog Travel Guide

Accommodations

Bishop

Best Western Bishop Holiday Spa Lodge
1025 North Main Street
Bishop, CA 93514
760-873-3543
There are no extra pet charges. Dogs are allowed in certain rooms.

Comfort Inn
805 N. Main Street

Bishop, CA 93514
760-873-4284
The hotel has three non-smoking pet rooms.

Motel 6
1005 N Man Street
Bishop, CA
760-873-8426
There are no additional pet fees.

Rodeway Inn
150 E Elm Street
Bishop, CA
760-873-3564
There is a $5 per day pet fee. Dogs are allowed in certain rooms only.

Vagabond Inn
1030 N Main Street
Bishop, CA
760-873-6351
There is a $5 per day pet fee.

Accommodations - RV Parks and Campgrounds

Bishop

Four Jeffrey Campground
South Lake Road
Bishop, CA
760-873-2500
This 106 site campground is located in the Inyo National Forest at an elevation of 8,200 feet. Amenities include water, space for RVs and a dump station. There are no hookups. For hiking, the Bristlecone Pine Forest is located nearby and offers many dog-friendly trails. The fee for a campsite is $14. The campground is open from about mid April to mid October. To make a reservation call 1-877-444-6777. Pets must be leashed while in the campground and please clean up after your pets. To get there from Bishop, take Highway 168 west and continue for 14 miles. Then go south on South Lake Road. Go one mile.

Attractions

Bishop

Bristlecone Pine Forest
White Mountain Rd
Bishop, CA
760-873-2500
This forest, located in the Inyo National Forest, is home to the world's oldest known trees. They are the ancient bristlecone pines. Some of these trees were growing when the Egyptians built the pyramids over four thousand years ago. At the Schulman Grove Visitor's Center, there are picnic areas, restrooms, outdoor exhibits and two self-guided nature trails. You can also get information on hiking trails in the area from the visitor's center. Open daily from Memorial Day through October, weather permitting. July through September are usually the best months for hiking in the White Mountains. Dogs are allowed on leash. Driving time from Big Pine to Schulman Grove is approximately 45 minutes on paved roads. Take Highway 168 east 12 miles from Big Pine to White Mtn Road. Turn left and drive ten miles to the Schulman Grove Visitor Center. The Bristlecone Pines can be viewed from the parking area of the visitor center and along three nature trails.

Parks

Bishop

Hilton Lakes Trail
Rock Creek Canyon Rd.
Bishop, CA
760-873-2500
This trail is located in the Inyo National Forest. It starts at an elevation of 9,600 feet and goes up to 10,720 feet over 5.25 miles. From the trailhead you can hike to several lakes. At the campgrounds pets must be on a 6 foot or less leash. While hiking on the trails, pets must be on leash or under voice command at all times. Please clean up after your pets. To get there from Highway 395, exit at Tom's Place. Go up Rock Creek Canyon Road. The trail starts before the Rock Creek Pack Station on the road to Mosquito Flat.

Inyo National Forest
351 Pacu Lane, Suite 200
Bishop, CA 93514
760-873-2400
This national forest covers thousands of acres of land ranging in elevations up to 14,246 feet in the White Mountain Range which is located near Mt. Whitney. Please see our listings in the Gold Country and Sierra Nevada region for dog-friendly hikes and/or campgrounds.

Little Lakes Trail
Rock Creek Canyon Rd.
Bishop, CA
760-873-2500

This trail is located in the Inyo National Forest. It starts at an elevation of 10,300 feet and the first 1.5 miles of the trail goes up to 10,440 to Heart Lake. From there you can go several more miles up to elevations around 11,000 feet. At the campgrounds pets must be on a 6 foot or less leash. While hiking on the trails, pets must be on leash or under voice command at all times. Please clean up after your pets. To get there from Highway 395, exit at Tom's Place. Go up Rock Creek Canyon Road to the end, about 10 miles to the Mosquito Flat parking.

Vets and Kennels

Bishop

Bishop Veterinary Hospital
1650 N. Sierra Highway
Bishop, CA
760-873-5801
Weekdays 9 - noon, 2 - 5 pm. Saturday 9 - noon by appt. Emergency doctor on call 24 hours.

Bridgeport Dog Travel Guide
Accommodations

Bridgeport

Best Western Ruby Inn
333 Main Street
Bridgeport, CA 93517
760-931-7241
Dogs are allowed in certain pet rooms. There are no extra pet fees. Amenities include refrigerators and hairdryers in some rooms, an outdoor spa and BBQ area. This inn is located 20 miles from Bodie Ghost Town.

Attractions

Bridgeport

Bodie State Historic Park
State Route 270
Bridgeport, CA
760-647-6445
This park is a ghost town. It looks much the same today as it did 50 years ago. Bodie is now listed as one of the worlds 100 most endangered sites by the World Monuments Watch. A self guided brochure describing a brief history of each building is available at the park. Dogs are welcome but must be on a leash at all times. From Highway 395 seven miles south of

Bridgeport, take State Route 270. Go east 10 miles to the end of the pavement and continue 3 miles on an unsurfaced road to Bodie. The last 3 miles can at times be rough. Reduced speeds are necessary.

Camptonville Dog Travel Guide
Parks

Camptonville

Rebel Ridge Trail
Marysville Road
Camptonville, CA
530-288-3231
This 1.6 mile moderate rated trail is open all year. Pets must be either leashed or off-leash but under direct voice control. Please clean up after your pets. It is located in the Tahoe National Forest, on Marysville Road, .6 miles west of Highway 49.

Coleville Dog Travel Guide
Accommodations

Coleville

Andruss Motel
106964 Highway 395
Coleville, CA
530-495-2216
There are no additional pet fees.

Crowley Lake Dog Travel Guide
Accommodations - RV Parks and
Campgrounds

Crowley Lake

Crowley Lake Campground
Crowley Lake Drive
Crowley Lake, CA
760-873-2503
This campground is located in open high desert country at 7,000 feet and has 47 tent and RV sites available. Please note that there are no trees and the winds can be strong. The area overlooks Crowley Lake which is a popular site for fishing. The campground is usually open from late April until the end of October. Camp amenities include 4 pit toilets and pull through trailer spaces. There are no hookups. All sites are first-come, first-served. There are no fees but donations are appreciated. Dogs are allowed but please keep them under control. The closest convenience stores are located in Mammoth

Lakes, about 10 miles north of the campground or at a very small store in the Crowley Lake area. To get there, take Highway 395 to the Crowley Lake exit. Go west through the Crowley Lake community for about 2 miles. At Crowley Lake Drive turn north and go about 2 miles.

Dinkey Creek Dog Travel Guide
Accommodations - RV Parks and Campgrounds

Dinkey Creek

Dinkey Creek Campground
Dinkey Creek Road
Dinkey Creek, CA
559-297-0706
This campground is next to Dinkey Creek in the Sierra National Forest. The campground is on a large sandy flat above the river and shaded by cedar and pine trees. It is at an elevation of 5,400 feet. There are 128 tent and RV sites. RVs up to 35 feet are allowed and there are no hookups. Amenities include piped water, flush toilets, picnic tables and grills. There are several trails that start at this campground. Dogs are allowed at the campgrounds, on trails and in the water but only at non-designated swimming beaches. Pets must be leashed and please clean up after them. To make a reservation call 1-877-444-6777. To get there, take Hwy 168 east from Clovis towards Prather. Continue through Prather to Shaver Lake. Just before you reach Shaver Lake turn right on the Dinkey Creek Road. Travel 11.7 miles east to the Intersection of the Dinkey Creek Road and the McKinley Grove Road. Continue north on the Dinkey Creek Road for 3/10 of a mile to the Campground.

Graeagle Dog Travel Guide
Accommodations

Graeagle

Gray Eagle Lodge
5000 Gold Lake Rd.
Graeagle, CA 96103
800-635-8778
Stay in a rustic cabin at this mountain getaway located in the Sierra Mountains, about 1.5 hours north of Truckee. There are many hiking trails within a short walk from the cabins. There are over 40 alpine lakes nearby. There is a $20 per pet, per day, fee with a maximum of 2 pets per cabin. Guests are expected to follow guidelines provided by the lodge and will sign a pet policy

form upon arrival. Dogs up to 50 pounds are allowed.

Accommodations - RV Parks and Campgrounds

Graeagle

Lakes Basin Campground
County Road 519
Graeagle, CA
530-836-2575
This campground is located in the Plumas National Forest and offers 3 campsites. Amenities include water, vault toilets and trailer space. Located at this campground is the trailhead for the Grassy Lake Trail. In the campground dogs must be on leash. On the trails, dogs on leash or off-leash but under direct voice control are allowed. Reservations for the campsites can be made by calling 1-877-444-6777. The campground is located 9 miles southwest of Graeagle on County Road 519.

Parks

Graeagle

Grassy Lake Trail
County Road 519
Graeagle, CA
530-836-2575
This trail is located in the Plumas National Forest and is an easy one way .8 mile trail. This trail starts at an elevation of 6,320 feet and goes past Grassy Lake. It then crosses Gray Eagle Creek to join with the Long Lake Trail. If you continue on this trail, you can hike another 3 miles one way on a moderate rated trail. Long Lake Trail gradually climbs to Long Lake. Dogs on leash or off-leash but under direct voice control are allowed. Dogs are allowed on the trails and in the water. Please clean up after your pets. The trailhead is located in the Lakes Basin Campground. The campground is located 9 miles southwest of Graeagle on County Road 519.

Independence Dog Travel Guide
Accommodations

Independence

Independence Courthouse Motel
157 N Edwards Street
Independence, CA
760-878-2732

There is a $6 per day additional pet fee. All rooms are non-smoking.

Ray's Den Motel
405 N Edwards St
Independence, CA
760-878-2122
There is a $6 per day additional pet fee.

Wilder House Bed & Breakfast
325 Dusty Lane
Independence, CA
760-878-2119
There are no additional pet fees.

Accommodations - RV Parks and Campgrounds

Independence

Goodale Creek Campground
Aberdeen Cutoff Road
Independence, CA
760-872-5000
This campground is located at a 4,000 foot elevation on a volcanic flow, next to Goodale Creek. It offers great views of the Sierra Nevada Mountains. There are 62 tent and RV sites available. The campground is usually open from late April to the end of October. There are no fees, no hookups and no drinking water. All sites are on a first-come, first-served basis. Be aware of rattlesnakes in the area, especially during the summer months. The closest convenience stores are located in the towns of Independence and Big Pine. Dogs are allowed at the campground, but please keep them under control. To get there from Independence, go 16 miles north on Highway 395. Then take Aberdeen Cutoff Road west for 2 miles.

Parks

Independence

Manzanar National Historic Site
P.O. Box 426
Independence, CA 93526
760-878-2932
This site was one of ten camps where Japanese and Japanese American citizens were interned during World War II. It is located at the base of the Sierra Nevada mountains and has been identified as the best preserved camp. Dogs are allowed at the site, on the self-guided walking tour which takes about 1-2 hours, and on the 3.2 mile self-guided auto tour. A tour description and map is available at the camp entrance. Pets must be on leash and please clean up after them. The park is open all year and there is no parking fee. It is located off Highway 395, 12 miles north of Lone Pine and 5 miles south of Independence.

Johnsondale Dog Travel Guide
Accommodations - RV Parks and Campgrounds

Johnsondale

Redwood Meadow Campground
off Mountain Road 50
Johnsondale, CA
559-539-2607
This campground is located in the Sequoia National Forest at an elevation of 6,100 feet. It is across the road from the Trail of a Hundred Giants. The campground offers 15 tent and small RV sites. RVs up to 16 feet are allowed and there are no hookups. Vault toilets are located at the camp. Ideal camping is from May to October. Pets must be leashed and attended at all times. Please clean up after your pet. The campsite is located about 45 miles northwest of Kernville. From Kernville, take State Mountain Road 99 north to Johnsondale. Go west on 50 to the Western Divide Highway turnoff. Go 2 miles to the campground.

Parks

Johnsondale

Trail of a Hundred Giants
off Mountain Road 50
Johnsondale, CA
559-539-2607
This trail is located in the Giant National Sequoia Monument which is part of the Sequoia National Forest. The universally accessible trail meanders through over 125 giant sequoias in the Long Meadow Grove. The estimated age of the trees here are estimated between 500 and 1,500 years old. Pets must be leashed and attended at all times. Please clean up after your pet. The trail is located about 45 miles northwest of Kernville. From Kernville, take State Mountain Road 99 north to Johnsondale. Go west on 50 to the Western Divide Highway turnoff. Go 2 miles to the Redwood Meadow Campground. The trail is located across the road from the campground.

June Lake Dog Travel Guide

143

Accommodations - RV Parks and Campgrounds

June Lake

Silver Lake Resort
Route 3
June Lake, CA
760-648-7525
This resort offers an RV park with full hookups. All sites are situated side by side and have a paved patio slab and picnic table. Amenities include general store, cafe, showers, restrooms, laundry room and picnic area. Well-behaved leashed pets are allowed in the RV park. They need to be walked outside of the park and please clean up after your pet in the Sierra National Forest. The resort is open from the end of April to mid-October. They are located on the shore of Silver Lake.

Kernville Dog Travel Guide
Accommodations

Kernville

Falling Waters Rivers Resort
15729 Sierra Way
Kernville, CA 93238
760-376-2242
Located near Historic Kernville, this motel offers all non-smoking rooms. Pet rooms are available and there is an additional $10 per night pet fee. Dogs up to around 75 pounds are allowed.

Accommodations - RV Parks and Campgrounds

Weldon

Isabella Lake KOA
15627 Highway 178
Weldon, CA 93283
760-378-2001
Located near the dog-friendly Isabella Lake, this campground offers both tent sites and RV spaces. Well-behaved leashed dogs of all sizes are allowed. People need to clean up after their pets. There is no pet fee. Site amenities include a maximum length pull through of 40 feet and 30 amp service available. Other amenities include LP gas, an entrance gate, free modem dataport, snack bar and a seasonal swimming pool.

Parks

Lake Isabella

Lake Isabella
Highways 155 and 178
Lake Isabella, CA
661-868-7000
This lake is set at an elevation of over 2,500 feet and with a surface area of 11,200 acres it is Kern County's largest body of year round water. The lake is a popular spot for fishing and boating. Dogs are allowed at the lake and in the lake but must be on leash. Please clean up after your pets. There are nearby dog-friendly Sequoia National Forest trails within driving distance, including the Trail of a Hundred Giants. See our listing for this trail or call the Greenhorn Rangers District at 760-379-5646 for details.

Kirkwood Dog Travel Guide
Parks

Kirkwood

Meiss Lake Trail
Highway 88
Kirkwood, CA
530-622-5061
This 4 mile moderate rated trail is used by both hikers and equestrians. Bicycling is prohibited. Take the Pacific Crest Trail one mile to the ridge, which offers great views and a wildflower display around mid-summer. Hike another three miles to Meiss Lake. The trailhead is located on the north side of Highway 88, immediately west of the Carson Pass Information Center. There is a parking fee. Pets must be leashed and please clean up after them.

Lake Tahoe Dog Travel Guide
Accommodations

Hope Valley

Sorensen's Resort
14255 Highway 88
Hope Valley, CA 96120
530-694-2203
This secluded mountain resort is located in

beautiful Hope Valley which is about 30 minutes south of South Lake Tahoe. Dogs are allowed in several of the cabins. The dog-friendly cabins sleep from two up to four people. Each cabin has a wood-burning stove (for heat) and kitchen. The Hope Valley Cross Country Ski Rentals are located on the premises (see Attractions). Hiking is available during the summer on the trails of the Toiyable National Forest. There are also several nearby lakes. Cabin rates start at $85 per night and go up to about $450 for a large bedroom cabin. There are no additional pet fees.

South Lake Tahoe

Alder Inn
1072 Ski Run Blvd.
South Lake Tahoe, CA 96150
530-544-4485
This dog-friendly motel can schedule their local pet-sitter to watch your dog if you want to try your luck at the casinos. The sitter will take care of your pup in the motel room. There is a $12 per day pet fee.

Colony Inn at South Lake Tahoe
3794 Montreal Road
South Lake Tahoe, CA 96150
530-544-6481
The Colony Inn at South Lake Tahoe is located just 1.5 blocks from Harrah's and the other casinos and just down the street from Heavenly Ski Resort. Want to experience the beautiful outdoors? The Colony Inn's backyard is National Forest Land, featuring dog-friendly hiking, mountain biking, and peace and quiet. There is a $25 refundable pet deposit, and pets cannot be left unattended in the rooms.

Fireside Lodge
515 Emerald Bay Rd.
South Lake Tahoe, CA 96150
530-544-5515
This inn offers log cabin style suites. The rooms have a unique "Country Mountain" theme decor with crafted fireplaces, and custom woodwork. Each room offers a microwave, refrigerator and coffee-maker, private bath w/shower, cable TV and VCR with numerous free videos available in their Gathering Room. Full kitchen units are available as well as private 1 to 4 bedroom cabins, off the property. There is a $20 per day pet charge.

Inn at Heavenly B&B
1261 Ski Run Boulevard
South Lake Tahoe, CA 96150
530-544-4244
You and your dog are welcome at this log-cabin style bed and breakfast lodge. The property is all dog-friendly and dogs are allowed everywhere but their Gathering Room. They offer 14 individual rooms each with a private bath and shower. Room conveniences include refrigerators, microwaves and VCRs. Some rooms have a fireplace. Three to four bedroom cabins are also available. The lodge is located on a 2-acre wooded park complete with picnic areas, BBQs

and log swings. Continental breakfast is served and snacks are available throughout the day. One large dog is allowed per room and pet charges apply. Room rates range from the low to mid $100s per night. Call for cabin prices. The owners have friendly dogs on the premises. The lodge is located in South Lake Tahoe. There is a $20 per day pet fee per pet.

Sandor's Chateau Motel
1137 Emerald Bay Road
South Lake Tahoe, CA 96150
530-541-6312
This pet-friendly motel is located on the quiet end of South Lake Tahoe just as you come into town on Highway 50, away from the congestion and noise of the casinos. They are situated in a park-like setting just minutes from beautiful Lake Tahoe. There are no extra pet charges.

Super 8 Motel
3600 Lake Tahoe Blvd.
South Lake Tahoe, CA 96150
530-544-3476
This motel offers good size rooms and a nice front lawn where you can walk your dog or sit at the various tables. There is a restaurant on the premises with a few outdoor picnic tables. They sometimes serve food outside - I guess it depends on how many waiters/waitresses they have. At night, you can walk up to the bar window, place your order, and then sit outside at the picnic tables with your dog while you enjoy a beer or wine. The motel also has an outdoor pool and spa. Pets are allowed only on the first floor of this two story accommodation, so if you are looking for a non-smoking room, call ahead as they tend to fill up fast. It's located on Hwy 50, west of Ski Run Blvd. There is a $10 per day pet fee per pet.

Tahoe Vista

Rustic Cottages

7449 North Lake Blvd
Tahoe Vista, CA 96148
530-546-3523
There is a $10 per day pet fee.

Tahoma

Norfolk Woods Inn
6941 West Lake Blvd.
Tahoma, CA 96142
530-525-5000
This inn only allows dogs in the cabins...but your pup won't mind. They have wonderful cozy cottages with kitchens. They only have 4 cabins, so call ahead. Also note that the entire premises is smoke free. Located directly in front of this inn is the Tahoe bike trail where you and your pup can walk or run for several miles. The trail is mostly paved except for a small dirt path section. The inn is located approx. 8-9 miles south of Tahoe City on Hwy 89. There is a $10 per day additional pet fee per pet.

Tahoma Meadows Bed and Breakfast
6821 W. Lake Blvd.
Tahoma, CA 96141
530-525-1553
A well-behaved dog is allowed only if you let them know in advance that you are bringing your dog. Pets are allowed in one of their cabins, the

Mountain Hideaway (previously known as Dogwood). This cabin includes a Queen bed, a fireplace, claw foot soaking tub, private deck and an efficiency kitchen. There is an extra $25 one time pet charge per stay, plus a security deposit. Cabin rates start at $145 per night.

Zephyr Cove

Zephyr Cove Resort
460 Highway 50
Zephyr Cove, NV 89448
775-588-6644
Thanks to one of our readers for recommending this resort. Dogs are allowed in the cabins but not in the lodge or cabin number one. That still leaves a nice selection of cabins to choose from. There is a $10 per day pet fee. This resort is located near South Lake Tahoe on the Nevada side. Dogs are not allowed on the beach or at the outdoor seats at the restaurant.

Accommodations - RV Parks and Campgrounds

Lake Tahoe

Encore SuperPark Tahoe Valley
1175 Melba Drive
Lake Tahoe, CA 96150
877-717-8737
Located in South Lake Tahoe, this campground offers both tent sites and RV spaces. RV site amenities include full hookups with 30 or 50 amp service, cable and a picnic table. Other campground amenities include volleyball and tennis courts, seasonal heated outdoor pool, pool table, playground, video game center, general store, laundry facilities, modem hookup and even a dog run. Well-behaved leashed dogs are welcome. Please clean up after your pet. There is no pet fee.

South Lake Tahoe

Fall Leaf Campground
Fallen Leaf Lake Road
South Lake Tahoe, CA
530-543-2600
This campground is at a 6,377 foot elevation and is located in the Lake Tahoe Management Basin Unit of the National Forest. The camp offers 250 sites and 17 are available on a first-come, first-served basis. The maximum RV length allowed is 40 feet and there are no hookups. Amenities include water, flush toilets, fire rings, picnic tables and barbecues. There are miles of trails which begin at or near this campground. Pets on leash are allowed but not at the beach. Please clean up after your pets. The campground is open from Memorial Day weekend to the end of October. To get there from the intersections of Highways 89 and 50, take Highway 89 north about 2.5 to 3 miles. Then turn left on Fallen Leaf Lake Road. Access to the campgrounds is on a rough paved road. A regular passenger car will make it, but go slow. For reservations, call toll free at 1-877-444-6777.

Lake Tahoe South Shore KOA
760 North Highway 50
South Lake Tahoe, CA 96150
530-577-3693
This campground is located five miles from the lake and nine miles from the casinos. Located near Echo Creek, the camp is surrounded by pines and mountains. They offer both tent and RV sites. Maximum length for pull through sites is 60 feet. Sites have 30 amp service available. Other amenities include cable TV, LP gas, free modem dataport and a seasonal swimming pool. Well-behaved leashed dogs of all sizes are allowed. People need to clean up after their pets. There is a $3.50 pet fee per dog. They are open seasonally from April 1 through October 15.

Tahoe City

Meeks Bay Campground
Highway 89
Tahoe City, CA
530-543-2600
This campground is at a 6,225 foot elevation and is located in the Lake Tahoe Management Basin Unit of the National Forest. The camp offers 40 tent and RV sites. The maximum RV length allowed is 20 feet and there are no hookups. Amenities include water, flush toilets, fire rings, picnic tables and barbecues. Pets on leash are allowed but not at the beach. Please clean up

after your pets. The campground is open from Memorial Day weekend to the end of October. The camp is located on the west shore of Tahoe on Highway 89, about 10 miles south of Tahoe City. It is located near D.L. Bliss State Park. For reservations, call toll free at 1-877-444-6777.

Zephyr Cove

Zephyr Cove RV Park and Campground
460 Highway 50
Zephyr Cove, NV 89448
775-588-6644
This campground is located within minutes of South Lake Tahoe and Stateline. RV site amenities include full hookups, telephone lines and cable TV. RVs up to 40 feet can be accommodated. Tent sites are either drive-in or walk-in sites, some of which offer lake views. Well-behaved dogs on leash are allowed.

Accommodations - Vacation Home Rentals

Kings Beach

Tahoe Rental House
Call to Arrange.
Kings Beach, CA
510-665-8100
This four bedroom, three bathroom house in north Tahoe is available for weekend, weekday, and holiday rentals. Dogs are welcome. This house can sleep up to 12 people. There is a $15 per day pet charge and a one time cleaning fee of $125.00.

South Lake Tahoe

Accommodation Station
2516 Lake Tahoe Blvd.
South Lake Tahoe, CA 96150
S. of Hwy 50
530-542-5850
The Accommodation Station is a property management company that rents out vacation homes, cabins, and condos in the South Lake Tahoe area. Each unit is completely furnished and features a fully equipped kitchen and fireplace. There are also many parks and hikes in the area that allow dogs (see Lake Tahoe Parks). They have a few properties that currently allow pets, but are working on getting more owners to accommodate the dog-friendly demand. They do not charge guests for pets in a particular property, but do charge a fully refundable security deposit provided no damage occurs. To find out which

properties allow dogs, call 800-344-9364 or send an email to stay@tahoelodging.com. They will find out which rentals allow your pup.

Buckingham Properties Lake Tahoe
Call to Arrange
South Lake Tahoe, CA 96150
530-542-1114
This company offers vacation rentals on the South Shore of Lake Tahoe to Glenbrook, NV to Camp Richardson, CA. Many different types of rentals are available, some of which allow dogs.

Stonehenge Vacation Properties
Call to Arrange.
South Lake Tahoe, CA 96158
800-822-1460
This vacation rental company offers several elegant and unique dog-friendly vacation homes located around South Lake Tahoe.

Tahoe Keys Resort
599 Tahoe Keys Blvd
South Lake Tahoe, CA 96150
530-544-5397
They feature approximately 50 pet friendly cabins, condos and homes in South Lake Tahoe. All dogs receive treats upon check-in. A $25.00 pet fee is taken per reservation. There is also a $100.00 refundable security deposit upon check in.

Squaw Valley

Squaw Valley Chalet
1730 Navajo Ct
Squaw Valley, CA 96146
530-550-8600
With views of Squaw Valley's Mountains, this is a comfortable one bedroom home. Granite counters, a jetted tub, new big screen TV, large deck with B.B.Q. and a plush leather couch are just a few of the upgrades to make you feel at home. Dogs are welcomed with a squeaky toy,

dog cookies, clean dog towel, furniture sheet and more. Dogs stay Free!!!

Tahoe City

Tahoe Moon Properties
P.O. Box 7521
Tahoe City, CA 96145
530-581-2771
They have over 15 beautiful homes that allow well-behaved dogs. All of the houses are close to Tahoe City or ski areas. Bath and bed linens are provided. There are a few dog rules; no dogs on the furniture, dogs are not to be left alone in the house, you must clean up after your dog and pet owners are responsible for any damages. Rates start at $150 per night with a 2 night minimum. There is a $30 per dog charge.

Zephyr Cove

Lake Tahoe Lodging
P.O. Box 11489
Zephyr Cove, NV 89448
775-588-5253
Lake Tahoe Lodging has over 22 pet friendly vacation rentals in South Lake Tahoe. The properties range from 2 bedroom ski condos to 5 bedroom luxury lakefront estates. There is a $75.00 non-refundable pet security deposit. Also available is a homeopathic hourly pet sitting service through a local veterinarian.

Lake Village Resort
301 Highway 50
Zephyr Cove, NV 89448
775-589-6065
This vacation home rental company offers several pet-friendly condo rentals in Lake Tahoe. There is a $20 per day pet charge.

Attractions

Homewood

Mountain High Weddings
PO Box 294
Homewood, CA 96141
530-525-9320
Want to get married AND have your pooch with you to enjoy that special moment? Mountain High Weddings performs ceremonies on the North and West Shores of Lake Tahoe and they invite you to bring your dog. They have performed many ceremonies where rings were taken off the collars of special canine ring bearers. Couples have been married on skis on top of a mountain, under the full moon on the lake, or at a small intimate dinner party in the middle of a meadow. The weddings can be as traditional or unique as you desire. So if you are getting ready to tie the knot, now you can include your pooch in the wedding party.

Hope Valley

Hope Valley Cross Country Skis
14255 Hwy 88
Hope Valley, CA
east of Hwy 89
530-694-2203
Thirty minutes south of South Lake Tahoe is beautiful Hope Valley. The Hope Valley Cross Country Ski Center is located at the dog-friendly Sorensen's Resort (see Accommodations). Rent cross-country skis here (about $15-prices subject to change) and then take your pooch with you on the ungroomed trails in the Toiyabe National Forest. There are some advanced (uphill) trails next to the rental center. Beginners can take the skis and drive about a mile down the road to some easier trails. The Burnside Lake Trail is a flat, 14 mile cross-country loop trail around the lake. A smaller loop (about 4-5 miles) can be found at the Sawmill Trail. The rental center will be able to provide directions and/or maps.

Kirkwood

Kirkwood Cross Country Ski Center
Highway 88
Kirkwood, CA
209-258-7248
This ski resort allow dogs on two cross-country ski trails. They are the High Trail, located behind the Kirkwood Inn Restaurant, and the Inner Loop on the meadow. Adult passes are about $20 per day, children $6 per day and doggie passes are only $3 per day. Kirkwood is located about 45

minutes from South Lake Tahoe, on Hwy 88. The closest pet-friendly lodging to Kirkwood, that we know of, is in South Lake Tahoe. Thanks to one of our readers for recommending this attraction.

Olympic Valley

Ann Poole Weddings, Nature's Chapel
P.O. Box 3768
Olympic Valley, CA 96146
530-412-5436
This business offers Lake Tahoe and Bay Area Weddings. Make it a special day by bringing your dog along with you. Here is an excerpt from the Wedding Minister: "You are planning to marry the Love of Your Life... so naturally, you will bring your 'best friend' to your wedding, won't you? Dogs do great at weddings... they are excellent ring bearers or proudly stand up with you, with flowers around their collars. They seem to simply KNOW that this is a Special Day for you and that they have an important part in it." They have many Wedding locations to choose from. You can choose your own unique location or have your wedding in a wedding chapel, nestled in the woods, or at one of their favorite locations like on a cliff overlooking beautiful Lake Tahoe, surrounded by tall pine trees.

Squaw Valley Chapel
440 Squaw Peak Road
Olympic Valley, CA
530-525-4714
This chapel, supported by a local congregation of the United Church of Christ, welcomes persons of all faiths, and is very open to having your dog be part of the wedding ceremony. The chapel can seat up to 120 people and offers a piano and a CD and tape player sound system. They can also refer you to local florists, photographers and musicians if needed.

Squaw Valley USA-Gondola
1910 Squaw Valley Rd
Olympic Valley, CA 96146
off Hwy 89
530-583-5585
This is a summer only attraction. Dogs are allowed in the Gondola/Cable Car, but make sure your best friend is not claustrophobic. You can take the cable car from the parking lot (6,200 ft elevation) to High Camp (8,200 ft elevation). Once at the top, your well-behaved leashed pooch is welcome inside the lobby and the gift shop. Want some exercise? From High Camp, hike down the mountain along the ski path. Want a more strenuous hike? Try hiking up to High

Camp. Squaw Valley is located off Hwy 89 on the northwest shore of Lake Tahoe. Dogs are not allowed on the cable car on the 4th of July weekend because of the crowds and fireworks. Squaw Valley does have special events during the summer, like Full Moon Hikes and Stargazing at High Camp. Dogs are welcome at both events.

South Lake Tahoe

Tahoe Keys Boat Rentals
2435 Venice Drive E.
South Lake Tahoe, CA
Tahoe Keys Blvd.
530-544-8888
Rent a boat and cruise around on beautiful Lake Tahoe with your pup. Dogs are allowed as long as you clean up any 'accidents' your pup may do on the boat. Boat rentals can be seasonal, so please call ahead. It's located in Tahoe Keys. To get there from Hwy 89 north, take Hwy 50 east. Turn left onto Tahoe Keys Blvd and then right at Venice Drive East. Park at the end of Venice Drive and follow the signs to the rental office.

Tahoe Sport Fishing
900 Ski Run Boulevard
South Lake Tahoe, CA 96150
530-541-5448
This company offers sport fishing charters in the

morning or afternoon and your pooch can go with you. Travel from the south shore up to the north shore of Lake Tahoe and back. They have six fishing boats ranging from 30 to 45 foot boats. They will clean and bag the fish (trout) you catch. They can even suggest local restaurants that will cook your fresh catch for you. Call ahead to make a reservation. Rates for the morning charter are $80 per person and for the afternoon charter are $70 per person.

Tallac Historic Site
Highway 89
South Lake Tahoe, CA 96150

Three of Lake Tahoe's most luxurious playgrounds of the rich and famous were here on its south shore, including the Pope Estate. The Pope Estate is used as the interpretive center for the Tallac Historic Site; it features historic tours, exhibits, and living history programs. Dogs are allowed at the trails and outside of the historic buildings. The grounds are open year-round, though most of the buildings are open only during summer. From the intersection of highways 50 and 89 in South Lake Tahoe, travel 3.5 miles west on Highway 89. The entrance and parking areas are on the lake side of the highway.

Taylor Creek/Fallen Leaf-XCountry Ski
off Highway 89
South Lake Tahoe, CA

The Taylor Creek/Fallen Leaf area provides the newcomer to cross-country skiing an opportunity to enjoy winter adventure. Developed for the beginner, this well marked series of trails allows skiers to explore an area of forest with the knowledge that other people are near and there is no avalanche danger. The terrain is mostly flat and provides an excellent day tour for the whole family. The developed trails cover a large area and although heavily used, are not congested. The loop trail traverses through open meadows

and aspen groves. To get there, take Highway 89 north from South Lake Tahoe approximately 3-1/2 miles to the Taylor Creek Sno-Park. Snowmobiles are not allowed. You'll need to bring your own cross-country skis.

Stateline

Borges Sleigh and Carriage Rides
P.O. Box 5905
Stateline, NV 89449
775-588-2953
Take your pooch on a carriage or sleigh ride in Lake Tahoe. The carriage rides start in the casino area between Harveys and Horizon, and in front of Embassy Suites. The sleigh rides begin in the field next to Caesars Tahoe (on the corner of hwy 50 and Lake Parkway). The carriages and sleighs are pulled by their 2000 pound Blond Belgium horses or one of their rare American- Russian Baskhir Curlies which have been featured in Pasadena's Tournament of Rose Parade over the past few years. Carriage rides open noon until sunset daily, weather permitting. Prices are $15 per adult $7.50 per child under 11. Sleigh rides are given during the winter. Sleigh rides are open 10:00am to sunset (about 4:45pm). Sleigh rides are $15 per Adult $7.50 per child under 11.

Tahoe City

Blackwood Canyon Rd-XCountry Ski
off Highway 89
Tahoe City, CA

Picturesque scenery can be seen along this unmarked road winding through Blackwood Canyon. Follow the road to an obvious junction and stay to the right. This path will lead you to a beautiful meadow where snowmobiles are not allowed. For a longer, more strenuous outing, continue upward to Barker Pass. Snowmobiles are allowed on this part of the trail. Take Highway 89 three miles south of Tahoe City to Blackwood Canyon Road, across from Kaspian Picnic Area. Continue to the Blackwood Canyon Sno-Park. You'll need to bring your own cross-country skis.

Page Meadow-XCountry Ski & Snowshoeing
off Highway 89
Tahoe City, CA

Try this pleasant ski or snowshoeing trip through a meadow surrounded by a scenic forest. Here are directions from the Lake Tahoe Basin Management Unit: From Highway 89, two miles south of Tahoe City, turn on Fountain Ave. just north of William Kent Campground. Turn right on Pine Ave., left on Tahoe Park Heights Dr., right on Big Pine Dr. and left on Silvertip. Park along the street where the snowplowing ends. Parking is extremely limited. Ski down the road to the meadow. There are no designated trails. Snowmobiles are not allowed. You'll need to bring your own skis or snowshoes.

Reel Deal Sport Fishing & Lake Tours
P.O. Box 7724
Tahoe City, CA 96145
530-581-0924
This dog-friendly fishing charter runs year-round. After your fishing trip, they will clean the fish for you. They also offer lake tours during the summer months. Rates are $75 per person during the winter and $80 per person during the summer. Dogs are allowed on both the fishing tour and the lake tours.

Tahoe Cross Country Ski Area
Country Club Drive
Tahoe City, CA
near Hwy 28
530-583-5475
This is a winter only attraction. Tahoe Cross Country offers some of the best dog skiing in Lake Tahoe. It is a great place for dog lovers who want to enjoy cross country skiing with their pooch. They welcome dogs on 7.5 kilometers of trails (beginner and intermediate terrain). They also allow skijoring on their trails and offer skijoring equipment for sale (ask the store clerk to see the skijoring equipment). The dog trails are open on limited days (5.5 days a week, non-holiday). Bring your dog Monday through Friday 8:30am-5:00pm, and Sundays 2:00pm-5:00pm, non-holiday. Dog passes are $3.00 per dog per day, and season passes are $45.00 for the entire season. Prices are subject to change. Dogs are allowed on Special Green and Blue Trails and complimentary poop bags are provided.

Truckee River Raft Rentals
185 River Road
Tahoe City, CA 96145
530-581-0123
Your pooch is welcome to join you on a self-guided river rafting adventure. They just ask that your dog doesn't keep going in and out of the raft constantly because their nails can damage the raft. Enjoy a 2-3 hour leisurely, self guided, 5-mile float on the Truckee River from Tahoe City to the River Ranch Bar, Restaurant & Hotel. From there you can catch a free shuttle bus back to your car any time until 6 p.m. daily.

Parks

Glenbrook

Lake Tahoe State Park/Spooner Lake
Hwy 28
Glenbrook, NV
close to Hwy 50
775-831-0494
This hiking trail is known as the world famous "Flume Trail". This is one of the most beautiful places in the world to mountain bike. But as a hiker, you'll hardly notice the bicyclists because this trail is so long and a good portion of the path consists of nice wide fire trails. It starts at Spooner Lake and the entire loop of the Flume Trail is about 25 miles which can satisfy even the most avid hiker. For a shorter hike, try the trail that loops around Spooner Lake. For a longer 10-12 mile out and back hike, start at Spooner Lake and hike up to Marlette Lake. Although there is a rise in elevation, it's not a rock climbing path as most of this is a fire road trail. Even if you are used to hiking 10 miles, don't forget about the altitude which will make you tired quicker. Also, do not forget to bring enough water and food. To get to the start of the trail, from South Lake Tahoe, take Hwy 50 towards Nevada (north). Then turn left onto Hwy 28. Follow the signs to the Lake Tahoe State Park and Spooner Lake. Parking for Spooner Lake is on the right. There is a parking fee of approx. $5-7. This includes extra fee for the pup - but well worth it. From South Lake Tahoe, it's about a 25-30 minute drive to Spooner Lake. Dogs must be leashed in the park.

Kings Beach

Coon Street Beach
Coon Street
Kings Beach, CA

Located at the end of Coon Street, on the east side of Kings Beach is a small but popular dog beach. There are also picnic tables, BBQs and restrooms at this beach.

North Tahoe Regional Park
National Avenue
Kings Beach, CA
Donner Road

In the summer this park is used for hiking and during the winter, it's used by cross-country skiers. There are about 3-4 miles of wooded trails at this park. Want to go for a longer hike? There is a National Forest that borders up to this regional park and dogs are allowed on those trails as well. To get there, take Hwy 28 by Kings Beach to Gun Club Road (north). Turn left on Donner Road and then right on National Avenue. There is a large parking lot at the end. Dogs must be on a leash in the park.

Olympic Valley

Squaw Valley USA
1960 Squaw Valley Rd
Olympic Valley, CA 96146
off Hwy 89
530-583-6985

In the summer (non-snow season) you and your pup can hike on the trails at this ski resort. Both of you will feel very welcome at Squaw. You can take your dog into the lobby to purchase the tickets for the dog-friendly Cable Car ride and/or snacks. As for the trails, there are many miles of hiking trails. One of the main hikes is from High Camp to the main parking lot or visa versa. It's the trail designed for night skiing (follow the light posts). During the summer, Squaw Valley has several dog-friendly events like the Star Gazing and Full Moon Hikes where dogs are welcome. Dogs must be leashed at all times.

South Lake Tahoe

Cove East
Venice Drive East
South Lake Tahoe, CA
Tahoe Keys Blvd.

This short but nice path is located near the boat rentals and Tahoe Keys Resort. It's approximately 1-2 miles and will give your pup a chance to take care of business before hopping on board your rental boat. To get there from Hwy 89 north, take Hwy 50 east. Turn left onto Tahoe Keys Blvd and then right at Venice Drive East. Dogs must be leashed.

Desolation Wilderness
Fall Leaf Lake Road
South Lake Tahoe, CA
530-644-2349
This wilderness area is located in the Eldorado National Forest and has many access points. One of the trailheads is located at Fallen Leaf Lake. See our Fallen Leaf Lake listing in South Lake Tahoe for more details. Dogs need to be leashed and please clean up after them.

Eagle Falls
Hwy 89
South Lake Tahoe, CA

This beautiful moderate to strenuous hiking trail in the Desolation Wilderness starts at Hwy 89 and goes up to Eagle Lake. This trail is pretty popular because it's about a 1 mile hike from the road to the lake. If you want a longer hike, you can go another 4-5 miles where there are 3 other lakes. Dogs must be leashed. To get there from the intersection of Hwys 50 and 89, take Hwy 89 north and go approximately 8 miles. The Eagle Falls Picnic Area and parking are on the left. Day and Camping Wilderness Permits are required. Go here early because it is extremely popular and parking spots fill up fast. There is a minimal fee for parking. Dogs must be on leash on the trail.

Echo Lakes Trail
off Johnson Pass Road
South Lake Tahoe, CA

See a variety of alpine lakes on this moderate rated trail. Take Highway 50 to Echo Summit and turn onto Johnson Pass Road. Stay left and the road will lead you to the parking area by Lower Echo Lake. For a short hike, go to the far end of Upper Echo Lake. A longer hike leads you to one of the many lakes further down the trail. Day hikers, pick up your permit at the self serve area just to the left of the Echo Lake Chalet. Dogs should always be on leash.

Fallen Leaf Lake
Fallen Leaf Lake Rd off Hwy 89
South Lake Tahoe, CA

There are some nice walking trails on the north shore of Fallen Leaf Lake and the surrounding areas. To get there from the intersection of Hwys 89 and 50, take Hwy 89 north approximately 2.5 to 3 miles to Fallen Leaf Lake Rd. Turn left and in about 1/2 mile there will be parking on the right. The Fallen Leaf Lake Trail begins here. For a longer hike, there are two other options. For the first option, instead of taking the trailhead on the right, take the trail on the left side of Fallen Leaf Lake Rd. This trail is also known as the Tahoe Mountain Bike Trail. Option number two is to take Fallen Leaf Lake Rd further to the south side of Fallen Leaf Lake. Park at the Glen Alpine trailhead which offers about 3-4 miles of trails (parking is across from Lily Lake). There is also a trail here that heads off to the Desolation Wilderness which has miles and miles of trails. Dogs should be leashed.

Kiva Beach
Hwy 89
South Lake Tahoe, CA
530-573-2600
This small but lovely beach is a perfect place for your pup to take a dip in Lake Tahoe. Dogs must be on leash. To get there from the intersection of Hwys 89 and 50, take Hwy 89 north approx 2-3 miles to the entrance on your right. Follow the road and towards the end, bear left to the parking lot. Then follow the path to the beach.

Hwys 89 and 28 in Tahoe City. You can also join the path 1/2 - 1 mile out of town by heading north on Hwy 89 and then there are 1 or 2 parking areas on the left side which are adjacent to the path. Dogs must be on leash.

Tahoe City

Pebble Beach/Dog Beach
Hwy 89
Tahoe City, CA

This beach is not officially called "pebble beach" but it is an accurate description. No sand at this beach, but your water-loving dog won't mind. The water is crisp and clear and perfect for a little swimming. It's not a large area, but it is very popular with many dogs. There is also a paved bike trail that is parallel to the beach. There was no official name posted for this beach, but it's located about 1-2 miles south of Tahoe City on Hwy 89. From Tahoe City, the beach and parking will be on your left. Dogs should be on leash on the beach.

Truckee River Bike Path
Hwy 89
Tahoe City, CA

This paved path starts at Tahoe City and heads towards Squaw Valley, paralleling Highway 89. It's about 5 miles each way with spots for your water dog to take a dip in the Truckee River (just be careful of any quick moving currents.) To get there, the path starts near the intersection of

Pet Sitters

Zephyr Cove

Zephyr Feed & Boarding
396 Dorla Court - PO Box 10548
Zephyr Cove, NV 89448
775-588-3907
Zephyr Feed and Boarding offers daycare & overnight boarding while you are in the Lake Tahoe region. Doggie daycare is available by the hour or day. The kennel is climate controlled inside with full walls. They also have a veterinarian on call, an outside area for potty time, inside exercise runs and a large playroom.

Restaurants

Carnelian Bay

Old Post Office Coffee Shop
5245 North Lake Blvd
Carnelian Bay, CA
530-546-3205
This restaurant is open for breakfast and lunch. They welcome well-behaved dogs at their outdoor seats. Dogs need to be leashed while sitting at the table with you.

Homewood

Pisanos Pizza
5335 West Lake Blvd
Homewood, CA
530-525-6464
Enjoy pizza at one of the several outdoor tables.

The restaurant (formerly West Side Pizza) is located off Hwy 89 in Homewood (between Tahoe City and Tahoma on the west shore of Lake Tahoe.)

West Shore Cafe
5180 West Lake Blvd.
Homewood, CA 96145
530-525-5200
This restaurant comes highly recommended from one of our readers. They said the food was delicious and the place is very dog-friendly. They went there with several people and about 7 dogs. The outdoor dining area is located on a pier right next to beautiful Lake Tahoe. Take a look at their website for the lunch and dinner menu. The restaurant is open seven days a week during the summer, weather permitting, from about Memorial Day to Labor Day. Lunch is served from 11:30am to 3:00pm, Happy Hour is from 3:00pm-5:30pm, and Dinner is from 5:30pm-10:00pm.

Incline Village

Grog & Grist Market & Deli
800 Tahoe Blvd
Incline Village, NV 89451
775-831-1123
They have a few tables and some benches outside where your dog is welcome.

T's Rotisserie
901 Tahoe Blvd
Incline Village, NV 89451
775-831-2832
This restaurant serves rotisserie sandwiches and more. Your dog can sit with you at the outdoor tables.

Kings Beach

Brockway Bakery
8710 North Lake Blvd
Kings Beach, CA
530-546-2431
Grab one of the several outdoor tables at this bakery and enjoy. It's located on Hwy 28 in Kings Beach.

Olympic Valley

Thunder Ridge Cafe
150 Alpine Meadows Rd # 2
Olympic Valley, CA 96146
530-583-6896
Dogs are allowed at the outdoor tables.

South Lake Tahoe

Bountiful Cafe
717 Emerald Bay Rd
South Lake Tahoe, CA 96150
near 10th Street
530-542-4060
Leashed dogs are welcome to sit at the outdoor tables.

Carina's Cafe
3469 Lake Tahoe Blvd
South Lake Tahoe, CA 96150
530-541-3354
They are open for breakfast and lunch. Dogs are allowed at the outdoor tables. This cafe is located near the shoreline of Lake Tahoe.

Chris' Cafe
3140 Highway 50
South Lake Tahoe, CA 96150
530-577-5132
This cafe is located in Meyers which is off Highway 50, before you enter into South Lake Tahoe. Your dog is welcome at their outdoor picnic tables.

Colombo's Burgers A-Go-Go
841 US Hwy 89 Emerald Bay Rd
South Lake Tahoe, CA 96150
530-541-4646
Dogs are welcome at the outdoor tables.

Dixon's Restaurant & Brewery
675 Emerald Bay Rd
South Lake Tahoe, CA 96150
530-542-3389
Dogs are welcome at the outdoor tables.

Izzy's Burger Spa

2591 Highway 50
South Lake Tahoe, CA 96150
530-544-5030
Dogs are welcome at the outdoor tables.

J&J Pizza
2660 Lake Tahoe Blvd
South Lake Tahoe, CA 96150
near Sierra Blvd.
530-542-2780
They have a few outdoor tables on the sidewalk. The outdoor tables are seasonal.

Marie Callender's Restaurant
3599 Lake Tahoe Boulevard
South Lake Tahoe, CA 96150
near Ski Run Blvd.
530-544-5535
Dine with your pooch at the outdoor tables. The outside dining is seasonal.

Meyer's Downtown Cafe
3200 Highway 50
South Lake Tahoe, CA 96150
530-573-0228
This dog-friendly cafe is off Highway 50 in Meyers, before entering South Lake Tahoe.

Rude Brothers Bakery and Coffee House
3117 Harrison Ave #B
South Lake Tahoe, CA 96150
530-541-8195
Dogs are allowed at the outdoor tables.

Shoreline Cafe
3310 Lake Tahoe Blvd
South Lake Tahoe, CA 96150
530-541-7858
Dogs are allowed at the outdoor tables. They are open for breakfast and lunch. This cafe is located near the shoreline of Lake Tahoe.

Sno-Flake Drive In
966 Modesto Avenue
South Lake Tahoe, CA

This is a great place for a burger or chicken sandwich. You can walk up to the outside order window and then sit on the small patio and enjoy your lunch or dinner. To get there from the intersection of Hwys 50 and 89, take Hwy 50 south. It will be on your right at Modesto Ave.

Fast Eddies Texas Bar-B-Que
690 N Lake Blvd
Tahoe City, CA 96145
530-583-0950
Dogs are allowed at the outdoor tables.

Fiamma
521 North Lake Blvd
Tahoe City, CA
530-581-1416
This Italian restaurant has a few seats outside where dogs are welcome. Arrive early to get one of the tables.

Tahoe City

Black Bear Tavern
2255 West Lake Blvd.
Tahoe City, CA 96145
530-583-8626
Dogs are allowed at the outdoor tables at this upscale restaurant. The restaurant is located on Hwy 89, south of downtown Tahoe City.

Coyotes Mexican Grill
521 N Lake Blvd
Tahoe City, CA 96145
530-583-6653
Dogs are allowed at the outdoor tables.

Naughty Dawg Saloon & Grill
255 North Lake Blvd

Tahoe City, CA
530-581-3294
This is definitely a dog-friendly restaurant. They welcome your pup which is obvious from the dog dishes full of water on the patio. This is a very popular place for both local and vacationing dogs. Choose from a variety of foods on their menu (many of which have doggie names.). This is absolutely a place worth visiting either for lunch, dinner, or just a beer. It's located in Tahoe City on Hwy 28 which is on the northwest shore of Lake Tahoe.

Rosie's Cafe
571 North Lake Blvd
Tahoe City, CA
530-583-8504
Enjoy a delicious breakfast, lunch or dinner on the porch at this cafe. It's located in Tahoe City off Hwy 28 which is located on the northwest shore of Lake Tahoe.

Sierra Vista Lakefront Dining
700 N Lake Blvd
Tahoe City, CA 96145
530-583-0233
Dogs are allowed at the outdoor tables at this lakefront restaurant in the heart of Tahoe City. They have outside heaters if it gets a little too chilly. This restaurant offers a variety of dishes

including Chinese Stir Fry, Jambalaya, San Francisco Style Ciopinno and Chicken Cordon Bleu.

Syd's Bagelery & Expresso
550 N Lake Blvd
Tahoe City, CA 96145
530-583-2666
Your dog is welcome at the outdoor picnic tables.

Tahoe House Bakery and Gourmet Store
625 W Lake Blvd
Tahoe City, CA 96145
530-583-1377
They offer fresh baked breads, pastries, coffee drinks, cookies, European style tortes, deli lunches fully prepared meals to go with gourmet chesses, meats and more. Dogs are allowed at the outdoor tables.

Stores

Tahoe City

Bone Jour-Gift Store
521 North Lake Blvd.
Tahoe City, CA
530-581-2304
Dogs are welcome inside this specialty gift store for dogs, cats and people. They also have a selection of dog treats and toys. It is on the second story near Fiamma Restaurant. Bone Jour is located in Tahoe City on Hwy 28 which is on the northwest shore of Lake Tahoe.

Vets and Kennels

Carson City

Carson Tahoe Veterinary Hospital
3389 S. Carson Street
Carson City, NV
775-883-8238
Weekdays 7:30 am - 6 pm. Emergencies will be seen 24 hours with an additional $60 emergency fee.

South Lake Tahoe

Avalanche Natural Health Office for Pets and Kennel
964 Rubicon Trail
South Lake Tahoe, CA 96150
530-541-3551
This veterinary hospital specializes in alternative medicine. If you need some doggy day care, they also offer a kennel that is open all year, including Sundays. They are very flexible with all aspects of the boarding kennel including hours and accommodating special needs pets usually with no extra charge.

Lone Pine Dog Travel Guide
Accommodations

Lone Pine

Alabama Hills Inn
1920 South Main
Lone Pine, CA 93545
760-876-8700
There is a $5 per day pet fee. There is a large grass area near the hotel to walk your dog. The area around the hotel is where many Western films have been made.

Best Western Frontier Motel
1008 South Main Street
Lone Pine, CA 93545
760-876-5571
There are no extra pet charges. Mt. Whitney is about 13 miles from this motel.

Accommodations - RV Parks and Campgrounds

Lone Pine

Lone Pine Campground
Whitney Portal Road
Lone Pine, CA
760-876-6200
This 43 site campground is located in the Inyo National Forest at an elevation of 6,000 feet. Water is available at the site. There is a $12 fee per campsite. The campground is open from the end of April to mid October. To make a reservation call 1-877-444-6777. Pets must be leashed while in the campground. Please clean up after your pets. From Highway 395 take Whitney Portal Road.

Tuttle Creek Campground
off Horseshoe Meadows Road
Lone Pine, CA
760-876-6200
This campground is located at 5,120 feet and is shadowed by some of the most impressive peaks in the Sierra Nevada Mountain Range. The camp is located in an open desert setting with a view of Alabama Hills and Mt. Whitney. There are 85 tent and RV sites, but no hookups. Amenities include 9 pit toilets and picnic tables. All sites are based on a first-come, first-served basis. This campground is managed by the BLM (Bureau of Land Management). Pets on leash are allowed and please clean up after them. To get there go 3.5 miles west of Lone Pine on Whitney Portal Road. Then go 1.5 miles south on Horseshoe Meadows Road and follow the sign to the campsite.

Attractions

Lone Pine

Alabama Hills
Movie Road
Lone Pine, CA
760-876-6222
Located west of the town of Long Pine, there is an area called Alabama Hills which features unusual

rock formations. Since 1920 this area has been a favorite location for television and movie filmmakers. Over 250 movies, TV episodes and commercials have been filmed in this area. Movies like Gunga Din and Maverick were filmed here. A partial list of stars who have been filmed at Alabama Hills includes Hopalong Cassidy, Roy Rogers, Humphrey Bogard, Susan Hayward, Spencer Tracy, Natalie Wood, Clint Eastwood, Kirk Douglas, John Wayne, Steve McQueen, Shelly Winters, Luci and Desi Arnaz, Willie Nelson and Mel Gibson. You can take yourself and your pooch on a self-guided auto tour of this area. Go 2.5 miles west of Lone Pine and turn north at Movie Road. At the corner of Movie and Whitney Portal Roads, you will find the Movie Plaque which commemorates the many movies filmed in the nearby hills. Go north .25 miles to the Roy Rogers Movie Flats, an area were hundreds of westerns and other movies were filmed. Go north .25 miles and turn east to Lone Ranger Canyon. This spot is another popular filming area and was where some scenes of the Lone Ranger was filmed. Go 2.25 miles to the southern loop to find Moonscape Views. Turn south on Horseshoe Meadow Road and go 1 mile to Gunga Din Canyon. The classic 1939 movie used locations in the first canyon to the east for filming. Go south for 3 miles to the Tuttle Creek Campground. It used for camping and as a fishing spot. Go 2 miles southeast to view The Needles Formation. It is a sharp spine of rocks north of the housing area. Then take Tuttle Creek Canyon Road down the canyon and back to Lone Pine. Pets on leash are allowed to walk around the view points. Please clean up after your pets. For more information, stop by the InterAgency Visitor Center at the intersection of Highways 395 and 136 in Lone Pine. The center is open daily from 8am to 4:30pm.

Parks

Lone Pine

Mt. Whitney Trail
Whitney Portal Road
Lone Pine, CA
760-876-6200
Dogs are allowed on the first eight miles of the main Mt. Whitney Trail in the Inyo National Forest, but not on the last three miles of the trail leading to the summit which is located in Sequoia/Kings Canyon National Park. Dogs must be leashed on this trail and please clean up after them. The national forest advises that people should be aware of the high elevation affect on

dogs. There is no shade or cover available and the heat of the sun at higher elevations can be intense for pets. The trail is located 13 miles west of Lone Pine on Whitney Portal Road.

Long Barn Dog Travel Guide
Accommodations - RV Parks and Campgrounds

Long Barn

Fraser Flat Campground
Fraser Flat Road
Long Barn, CA
209-586-3234
At an elevation of 4,800 feet this campground offers forested sites on the South Fork of the Stanislaus River. There are 34 tent and RV sites with a maximum RV length of 22 feet. There are no hookups. Amenities include piped water, vault toilets, picnic tables and grills. All sites are on a first-come, first-served basis. Pets on leash are allowed and please clean up after them. This campground is located in the Stanislaus National Forest. To get there, drive 3 miles north of Highway 108 at Spring Gap turnoff (Fraser Flat Road).

Parks

Long Barn

Sugar Pine Railroad Grade Trail
Fraser Flat Road
Long Barn, CA
209-586-3234
This 3 mile easy rated trail parallels the South Fork of the Stanislaus River and overlays the historic Sugar Pine Railroad System. Pets on leash are allowed and please clean up after them. This trail is located in the Stanislaus National Forest. One access point to this trail is the Fraser Flat Campground. To get there, drive 3 miles north of Highway 108 at Spring Gap turnoff (Fraser Flat Road).

Mammoth Lakes Dog Travel Guide
Accommodations

Convict Lake

Convict Lake Resort

Convict Lake, CA
760-934-3800
There is a $15 per day pet fee. Cabins are not

designated as smoking or non-smoking.

Mammoth Lakes

Crystal Crag Lodge
P.O. Box 88
Mammoth Lakes, CA 93546
760-934-2436
This lodge offers cabins at 9,000 feet elevation on beautiful Lake Mary in the dog-friendly Inyo National Forest. Lake Mary is known as one of the best fishing spots in the Eastern Sierra, regularly producing trophy size trout. You will find a number of other lakes, most of the best hiking trailheads, Lake Mary Store, and some of the best scenery that the Eastern Sierra has to offer within walking distance of your cabin. The cabins, all non-smoking, have full kitchens and baths. Most cabins have living rooms with fireplaces. The lodge also offers 14-foot aluminum boats with or without a motor. Dogs are allowed on the boats as well. Please note that the lodge is only open during the summer season, from about late May to early October. Dogs are allowed for an additional $8 per day charge. Pets must never be left unattended in the cabins.

Motel 6
3372 Main St
Mammoth Lakes, CA 93546
760-934-6660
There are no additional pet fees.

Shilo Inn
2963 Main Street
Mammoth Lakes, CA 93546
760-934-4500
Your dog is welcome here. Each room in this motel is a mini-suite complete with microwaves, refrigerators and more. This motel is located across the street from the Visitors Center which has trails that border up to the Shady Rest Park where there are many hiking trails. If you are there in the winter, try some cross-country skiing with your pup. The cross country ski rental store is very close to this motel (see Attractions.) There is a $10 per day additional pet fee per pet.

Travelodge
54 Sierra Blvd.
Mammoth Lakes, CA 93546
760-934-8240
There are no additional pet fees.

Accommodationss

Mammoth Lakes

Edelweiss Lodge
1872 Old Mammoth Road
Mammoth Lakes, CA 93546
760-934-2445
Cabins on a 1 acre wooded site near hiking trails, lakes and streams. Dogs of all sizes are allowed. There is a $10 per day pet fee. All rooms are non-smoking.

Accommodations - RV Parks and Campgrounds

Mammoth Lakes

Lake George Campground
Lake George Road
Mammoth Lakes, CA
760-924-5500
This 16 site campground is located in the Inyo National Forest at an elevation of 9,000 feet. It is located near several trails. Amenities include water. There are no hookups. The fee for a campsite is $14. The campground is open from about the mid June to mid September. The sites are available on a first-come, first-served basis. Pets must be leashed while in the campground and please clean up after them. To get there from the intersection of Main Street and Hwy 203, take Lake Mary Road to the left. Go past Twin Lakes. You'll see a road that goes off to the left (Lake Mary Loop Rd.). Go past this road, you'll want the other end of the loop. When you come to another

road that also says Lake Mary Loop Rd, turn left. Then turn right onto Lake George Road and follow it to the campground.

Lake Mary Campground
Lake Mary Loop Road
Mammoth Lakes, CA
760-924-5500
This 48 site campground is located in the Inyo National Forest at an elevation of 8,900 feet. It is located near several trails. Amenities include water. There are no hookups. The fee for a campsite is $14. The campground is open from about the beginning of June to mid September. The sites are available on a first-come, first-served basis. Pets must be leashed while in the campground and please clean up after them. To get there from the intersection of Main Street and Hwy 203, take Lake Mary Road to the left. Pass Twin Lakes and then you'll come to Lake Mary. Turn left onto Lake Mary Loop Road.

New Shady Rest Campground
Sawmill Cutoff Road
Mammoth Lakes, CA
760-924-5500
This 94 site campground is located in the Inyo National Forest at an elevation of 7,800 feet. It is located near several trails. Amenities include water. There are no hookups. The fee for a campsite is $13. The campground is open from about mid May to the end of October. The sites are available on a first-come, first-served basis. Pets must be leashed while in the campground and please clean up after them. To make a reservation call 1-877-444-6777. To get there from the Mammoth Visitor's Center, take Hwy 203 towards town. The first street on your right will be Sawmill Cutoff Road. Turn right and Shady Rest Park is at the end of the road.

Reds Meadow Campground
off Highway 203
Mammoth Lakes, CA
760-924-5500
This 56 site campground is located in the Inyo National Forest at an elevation of 7,600 feet. It is near the dog-friendly Devil's Postpile National Monument and hiking trails including the John Muir Trail. Amenities include water. There are no hookups. The fee for a campsite is $15. The campground is open from about the mid June to mid September. The sites are available on a first-come, first-served basis. Pets must be leashed while in the campground and please clean up after them. From Highway 395, drive 10 miles west on Highway 203 to Minaret Summit. Then drive about 7 miles on a paved, narrow mountain

road.

Accommodations - Vacation Home Rentals

Mammoth Lakes

Villa De Los Pinos #3
3252 Chateau Rd
Mammoth Lakes, CA 93546
760-722-5369
This is a year-round vacation rental townhouse-style condominium in Mammoth Lakes. The amenities include two downstairs bedrooms, two bathrooms, a large living room, dining room, and kitchen. The condo is fronted by a large deck overlooking the development courtyard (where dogs are allowed off-leash), swimming pool, and Jacuzzi building. All dogs are welcome. The $25 per visit pet fee helps with the cleaning.

Attractions

Mammoth Lakes

Cross Country Skiing
Mammoth Visitor Center
Mammoth Lakes, CA
Hwy 203 (near Old Mammoth Rd)

Want to cross country ski with your pup? Follow this plan: Rent some skis and boots at the Ski Renter (760-934-6560) located next to the Shell Gas Station on Hwy 203 (by Old Mammoth Rd). Walk or drive the skis a block or two over to the Mammoth Visitor Center / Inyo National Forest. There are several trails that start at the Visitor Center. From there I've been told you can join up to Shady Rest Park which offers more miles of cross country skiing trails (beginner trails - not too steep.) And of course, take your dog with you since this is a dog-friendly National Forest. Just listen carefully and watch out for any snowmobilers. Dogs should be leashed.

Mammoth Mountain-Gondola
#1 Minaret Road
Mammoth Lakes, CA 93546
Hwy 203
760-934-0745
Want some awesome views of Mammoth Mountain and the surrounding areas? During the summer, you and your dog can hop on the Gondola (Cable Car) ride. You'll climb about 2,000 feet to the top of the mountain. Once there, you can enjoy a nice 1 1/2 - 2 hour hike down or take the Gondola back down the mountain. Dogs should be leashed.

Parks

Mammoth Lakes

Ansel Adams Wilderness
off Highway 203
Mammoth Lakes, CA
760-934-2289
The wilderness can be accessed at many points, including the John Muir Trail. See our listing for this trail under the city of Mammoth Lakes. There are miles of on or off-leash hiking opportunities.

Devil's Postpile National Monument
Minaret Rd.
Mammoth Lakes, CA
Mammoth Mtn Inn
760-934-2289
During the summer only, take a bus ride/shuttle to the Devil's Postpile National Monument with your pup. The shuttle is the only way to drive to this National Monument unless you have a camping permit or have a vehicle with 11 people or more. The shuttle begins at the Mammoth Mountain Inn off Hwy 203 and takes you and your dog on a scenic ride along the San Joaquin River to the National Monument. The travel time is about 45 minutes to Reds Meadow (past the Monument),

but there are 10 stops along the way to get out and stretch or hike. Once at the Monument, there is a short 1/2 mile walk. The Monument is a series of basalt columns, 40 to 60 feet high, that resembles a giant pipe organ. It was made by hot lava that cooled and cracked 900,000 years ago. The John Muir Trail crosses the monument, so for a longer hike, join up with nearby trails that are in the dog-friendly Inyo National Forest. Dogs should be on a leash.

John Muir Trail
off Highway 203
Mammoth Lakes, CA
760-934-2289
This trail crosses the dog-friendly Devil's Postpile National Monument. The John Muir Trail offers miles of hiking trails. Dogs must be on leash at the monument but can be off leash under direct voice control in the Inyo National Forest and Ansel Adams Wilderness. The trailhead is located near the ranger's station at the monument. To get there, you can drive directly to the monument and trailhead ONLY if you have a camping permit or a vehicle with 11 people or more. All day visitors must ride a shuttle bus from the Mammoth Mountain Ski Area at the end of Highway 203. Well-behaved leashed dogs are allowed on the bus. From Highway 395, drive 10 miles west on Highway 203 to Minaret Summit. Then drive 7 miles on a paved, narrow mountain road. Or take the shuttle bus at the end of Highway 203. The bus ride takes about 45 minutes to the monument with several stops along the way.

Lake George
Lake George Rd.
Mammoth Lakes, CA
Lake Mary Loop Rd.

At Lake George, you can find the trailheads for the Crystal Lake and Mammoth Crest trails. You'll be hiking among the beautiful pine trees and snow covered peaks. The trails start at the north side of Lake George. The hike to Crystal Lake is about a 3 mile round trip. If you want a longer hike, you'll have the option on your way to Crystal Lake. The Mammoth Crest trail is the trail that branches to the right. The Mammoth trail is about a 6 mile round trip and it's a more strenuous trail. To get there from the intersection of Main Street and Hwy 203, take Lake Mary Road to the left. Go past Twin Lakes. You'll see a road that goes off to the left (Lake Mary Loop Rd.). Go past this road, you'll want the other end of the loop. When you come to another road that also says Lake Mary Loop Rd, turn left. Then turn right onto Lake George Rd. Follow this road almost to the end and you should see signs for the Crystal Lake Trail. Dogs should be leashed.

Lake Mary
Lake Mary Loop Rd.
Mammoth Lakes, CA
Lake Mary Rd.

Here's another lake and hiking trail to enjoy up in the high country. Lake Mary is known as one of the best fishing spots in the Eastern Sierra, regularly producing trophy size trout. After your water dog is done playing in the lake, head to the southeast side of the lake to go for a hike on the Emerald Lake Trail. The trail starts at the Cold Water trailhead next to the Cold Water campgrounds. Take the trail to the right towards Emerald Lake and Sky Meadows. The trail to Emerald Lake is about 1 1/2 miles round trip (out and back). If you continue on to Sky Meadows, then your hike is about 4 miles round trip. To get there from the intersection of Main Street and Hwy 203, take Lake Mary Road to the left. Pass Twin Lakes and then you'll come to Lake Mary. Turn left onto Lake Mary Loop Road and the trailhead is located on the southeast side of the lake. Dogs should be on a leash.

Mammoth Mountain
Minaret Rd.
Mammoth Lakes, CA
by the Mammoth Mtn Inn (off Hwy 203)
760-934-2571
You can hike with your dog on "The" Mammoth Mountain in three ways. One way is to take the Gondola ride with your pup (summer only) up to the top of the mountain and then hike down. The second is to hike up the mountain from the parking lot by the Mammoth Mountain Inn and the Gondola. The third option is to start on the backside of the mountain and hike up and then of course down. For the third option, you can start at Twin Lakes (off Lake Mary Rd). The Dragon's Back Trail is on the west side of the lakes (by the

campgrounds). Dogs must be leashed.

Shady Rest Park and Trail
Sawmill Cutoff Rd.
Mammoth Lakes, CA
Hwy 203
760-934-8983
This park serves as a multi-use recreation park. During the winter it's popular with cross country skiers - yes dogs are allowed. In the summer, you can go for a hike on the 5-6 miles of single track and fire road trails. It's also used by 4x4 off road vehicles too, so just be aware. To get there from the Mammoth Visitor's Center, take Hwy 203 towards town. The first street on your right will be Sawmill Cutoff Road. Turn right and Shady Rest Park is at the end of the road. There are restrooms at this park which can come in handy for the humans before starting out on the trails. Dogs must be leashed.

Restaurants

Mammoth Lakes

Base Camp Cafe
3325 Main Street
Mammoth Lakes, CA
760-934-3900
Dogs are welcome at this cafe! They have a water

bowl outside for your pooch.

Giovanni's Pizza
437 Old Mammoth Rd
Mammoth Lakes, CA
760-934-7563
Dogs are allowed at the outdoor tables.

La Sierra's
3789 Main Street
Mammoth Lakes, CA
760-934-8083
Dogs are allowed at the outdoor tables.

Sierra's Best Coffee
452 Old Mammoth Rd
Mammoth Lakes, CA
760-934-7408
Dogs are welcome at the outdoor tables.

Susie's Subs
588 Old Mammoth Rd
Mammoth Lakes, CA
760-934-7033
Dogs are allowed at the outdoor tables.

Vets and Kennels

Mammoth Lakes

Alpen Veterinary Hospital
217 Sierra Manor Rd
Mammoth Lakes, CA
760-934-2291
Monday - Friday 9:30 am - 5:30 pm. Closed
Weekends. Vet available in Emergency other
hours.

High Country Veterinary Hospital
148 Mountain Blvd
Mammoth Lakes, CA
760-934-3775
Monday - Friday 9 am - 12 noon, 2 pm - 5 pm.
Closed weekends.

McGee Creek Dog Travel Guide
Accommodations - RV Parks and Campgrounds

McGee Creek

McGee Creek Campground
McGee Creek Road
McGee Creek, CA
760-873-2500
This 28 site campground is located in the Inyo

National Forest at an elevation of 7,600 feet. The
campsite is in an open area and adjacent to
McGee Creek. Amenities include water, flush
toilets and space for RVs. There are no hookups.
For hiking, the McGee Creek Trail is located
within a few miles from the campground. The fee
for a campsite is $15. The campground is open
from mid May to mid October. To make a
reservation call 1-877-444-6777. Pets must be
leashed while in the campground and please
clean up after your pets. To get there from
Highway 395, take the first exit after Crowley
Lake. Go 2 miles heading south on McGee Creek
Road to the campground.

Parks

McGee Creek

McGee Creek Trailhead
McGee Creek Road
McGee Creek, CA
760-873-2500
This trail is rated moderate to strenuous. It is
located in the Inyo National Forest. From the
trailhead you can hike to several lakes including
Steelhead Lake. Pets must either be leashed or
off-leash but under direct voice control. Please
clean up after your pets. To get there from
Highway 395, take the first exit after Crowley
Lake. Go 4 miles heading south on McGee Creek
Road to the trailhead.

Mono Lake Dog Travel Guide
Accommodations

Lee Vining

Inn at Lee Vining
45 2nd St
Lee Vining, CA
760-647-6300
There are no additional pet fees.

Murphey's Hotel
51493 Hwy 395
Lee Vining, CA
760-647-6316
There is a $5 per day additional pet fee. Dogs are
not to be left alone in rooms.

Accommodations - RV Parks and Campgrounds

Lee Vining

Glass Creek Campground
Highway 395
Lee Vining, CA
760-873-2408
This 50 site campground is located in the Inyo National Forest at an elevation of 7,600 feet. It is located near several trails. There are no hookups or water. The fee for a campsite is $14. The campground is open from about the end of April to the end of October. The sites are available on a first-come, first-served basis. Pets must be leashed while in the campground and please clean up after them. The campground is located between Lee Vining and Mammoth Lakes on Highway 395. It is at the intersection of the highway and the Crestview CalTrains Maintenance Station, about one mile north of the Crestview Rest Area.

Attractions

Lee Vining

Mono Basin National Forest Scenic Area
Hwy 395, 1/2 mile North of Lee Vining
Lee Vining, CA
760-647-3044
Mono is the westernmost basin of the Basin and Range province, which stretches across western North America between the Rocky Mountains and Sierra Nevada. In the heart of the Basin lies the majestic Mono Lake, a quiet inland sea nestled amidst the Sierra Mountains. Estimated between one million and three million years of age, Mono Lake is one of the oldest continuous lakes in North America. It is a "terminal" lake, which means that it has no outlet water flow. Thus fresh water flows in and can only leave through evaporation. For this reason the lake has a high content of salt. It is nearly three times saltier than the Pacific Ocean and 1,000 more alkaline than fresh water. A chemical twin of Mono Lake exists nowhere in the world; the closest kin would be found no closer than equatorial Africa. There are many trails here. The Lee Vining Creek Nature Trail is about 1 mile long and is located next to the Mono Basin National Forest Scenic Area Visitor Center. You can also get information about other hikes and trails at the visitor's center.

Onyx Dog Travel Guide
Accommodations - RV Parks and Campgrounds

Onyx

Walker Pass Campground
Highway 178
Onyx, CA
661-391-6000
This campground has 11 walk-in sites for Pacific Crest Trail hikers and two sites are available for vehicles. Drinking water is available from spring through fall. There are no hookups. Hitching racks and corrals are available for horses. There are no reservations or fees but donations are accepted. Dogs are allowed but need on leash while in the campground. To get there from Ridgecrest, go 27 miles west on Highway 178 to Walker Pass.

Parks

Onyx

Pacific Crest Trail-Owens Peak Segment
Highway 178
Onyx, CA
661-391-6000
The Owens Peak Segment of the Pacific Crest Trail is managed by the Bureau of Land Management. This section begins at Walker Pass in Kern County and goes 41 miles north to the Sequoia National Forest at Rockhouse Basin. Elevations on this portion range from 5,245 feet at Walker Pass to 7,900 feet on Bear Mountain. The trail offers great views of the surrounding mountains and valleys. Dogs are allowed on the Owen's Peak Segment of the Pacific Crest Trail. Trail conditions can change due to fires, storms and landslides. To confirm current conditions, contact the Bakersfield BLM Office at 661-391-6000. There are many trailheads, but one of the more popular staging areas is at Walker Pass. From Ridgecrest go 27 miles west on Highway 178 to Walker Pass.

Riverton Dog Travel Guide
Accommodations - RV Parks and Campgrounds

Riverton

Ice House Campground
Ice House Road
Riverton, CA
530-644-2349
This 83 site campground is located in the Eldorado National Forest at an elevation of 5,500 feet. It is located near the Ice House Bike Trail. There are no hookups or water. Camp amenities include restrooms, water, picnic tables, swimming, bicycling, hiking and more. Pets on

leash are allowed in the campground, on the trails and in the water. Please clean up after your pets. To make a reservation call 1-877-444-6777. To get there from Placerville, take Highway 50 east for 21 miles to Ice House Road turnoff. Turn left and go 11 miles north to the campground turnoff. Then go one mile to the campgrounds.

Wench Creek Campground
Ice House Road
Riverton, CA
530-644-2349
This campground is located in the Eldorado National Forest next to Union Valley Reservoir and offers 100 tent and RV campsites. There are no hookups. Camp amenities include restrooms, water, swimming, bicycling and hiking. Dogs are allowed in the campground, on the trails and in the water. Pets should be leashed and please clean up after them. To get there from Placerville, take Highway 50 east and go 21 miles to Riverton. Turn left on Ice House Road. Go about 19 miles north to the reservoir.

Parks

Riverton

Ice House Bike Trail
Ice House Road
Riverton, CA
530-644-2349
This 3.1 mile dirt trail winds along the ridge tops and shaded slopes, through old and new forest growths. The trail, located in the Eldorado National Forest at about 5,400 feet, is rated easy and offers great views of the Ice House Reservoir. Both hikers and mountain bikers use this trail. Dogs should be on leash and are allowed on the trail and in the water. To get there from Placerville, take Highway 50 east for 21 miles to Ice House Road turnoff. Turn left and go 11 miles north to the campground turnoff. Then go one mile to the campgrounds. The trail can be accessed from any of the Ice House Reservoir campgrounds or at the intersection of Road 12N06 and Ice House Road which is located about 200 yards north of the turnoff to Big Hill Lookout.

Union Valley Bike Trail
Ice House Road
Riverton, CA
530-644-2349
This 4.8 mile two-lane paved trail is located in the Eldorado National Forest. Elevations range from 4,860 to 5,160 feet. The trail connects all the

campgrounds on the east side of Union Valley Reservoir, from Jones Fork to Wench Creek Campgrounds. Parking is available at the campgrounds except for Lone Rock and Azalea Cove. Views and interpretive signs complement this high country trail. Dogs should be on leash and are allowed on the trail and in the water. To get there from Placerville, take Highway 50 east and go 21 miles to Riverton. Turn left on Ice House Road. Go about 19 miles north to the reservoir.

Sequoia National Park Dog Travel Guide
Accommodations

Three Rivers

Best Western Holiday Lodge
40105 Sierra Dr
Three Rivers, CA 93271
559-561-4119
There are no additional pet fees.

Woodlake

Wickyup Bed and Breakfast Cottage
22702 Avenue 344
Woodlake, CA 93286
559-564-8898
Dogs are allowed in the Calico Room Cottage. It offers bunk beds, a half-bath, and a discrete, enclosed outdoor shower. The cottage is located in the garden and has a private entrance.

Accommodations - RV Parks and Campgrounds

Three Rivers

Sequoia and Kings Canyon National Park Campgrounds
47050 General Highway
Three Rivers, CA 93271
559-565-3341
This park offers many campgrounds which range in elevation from 2,100 feet to 7,500 feet. The Lodgepole, Dorst, Grant Grove and Atwell Mill campgrounds are located near giant sequoia groves. The Lodgepole campground, located at 6,700 foot elevation, is one of the largest camps and offers 250 sites. Tent and RV camping is available, with a maximum RV length of 35 feet. Amenities at this campground include a laundromat, deli, market, gift shop, pay showers, flush toilets and more. Some of the campgrounds are open all year. Pets must be leashed and

attended at all times. Please clean up after your pet. Dogs are not allowed on any trails or hikes in this park, but see our listings in the towns of Johnsondale for details about nearby dog-friendly hiking, sightseeing and additional camping in the Sequoia National Forest.

Parks

Three Rivers

Sequoia and Kings Canyon National Park
47050 General Highway
Three Rivers, CA 93271
559-565-3341
This national park does not really have much to see or do if you bring your pooch, except for driving through a giant redwood forest in your car and staying overnight at the campgrounds. However, located to the west and south of this national park is the dog-friendly Giant National Sequoia Monument. There you will be able to find dog-friendly hiking, sightseeing and camping. See our listings in the towns of Johnsondale and Hume for more details. Pets must be leashed and attended at all times. Please clean up after your pet.

Shaver Lake Dog Travel Guide
Accommodations - RV Parks and
Campgrounds

Shaver Lake

Camp Edison at Shaver Lake
42696 Tollhouse Road
Shaver Lake, CA 93664
559-841-3134
This campground is located at Shaver Lake in the Sierra National Forest and is managed by Southern California Edison. There are 252 campsites with electricity and free cable TV. Amenities include picnic tables, restroom with heated showers, laundromats, marina and general store. Dogs are allowed at the campgrounds, on trails and in the water but only at non-designated swimming beaches. Pets must be leashed and please clean up after them. There is a $4 per night per pet fee. To make a reservation call 559-841-3134.

Dorabelle Campground
Dorabella Street
Shaver Lake, CA
559-297-0706
This campground is next to Shaver Lake in the

Sierra National Forest. Some of the sites have lake views and all of the sites have shade from dense pines trees. The camp is at an elevation of 5,500 feet. There are 68 tent and RV sites. RVs up to 40 feet are allowed and there are no hookups. Amenities include water, vault toilets, picnic tables and grills. Be sure to bring some mosquito repellant. There are several trails here that provide access around the lake. Dogs are allowed at the campgrounds, on trails and in the water but only at non-designated swimming beaches. Pets must be leashed and please clean up after them. To make a reservation call 1-877-444-6777. To get there, take Hwy 168 east from Clovis to Shaver Lake. In Shaver Lake turn right on Dorabella St. (Just after the 76 gas station). Travel 5/10 of a mile to Dorbelle Campground.

Tom's Place Dog Travel Guide
Accommodations - RV Parks and
Campgrounds

Tom's Place

East Fork Campground
Rock Creek Canyon Road
Tom's Place, CA
760-873-2500
This 133 site campground is located in the Inyo National Forest at an elevation of 9,000 feet. Amenities include water, flush toilet, picnic tables and space for RVs. There are no hookups. For hiking, there are several trailheads nearby including the Hilton Lakes and Little Lakes Valley trails. The fee for a campsite is $15. The campground is open from about the end of May to the end of September. To make a reservation call 1-877-444-6777. Pets must be leashed while in the campground and please clean up after them. To get there from Bishop, take Highway 395 north for about 30 miles. Take the Tom's Place exit and go 4 miles on Rock Creek Canyon Road.

Truckee Dog Travel Guide
Accommodations

Truckee

The Inn at Truckee
11506 Deerfield Drive
Truckee, CA 96161
530-587-8888
The Inn at Truckee specializes in relaxed accommodations and fun filled days for Truckee Tahoe Visitors. North Lake Tahoe resorts are

located within a few minutes of this inn's doorstep. There is a $11 per day pet charge.

Accommodations - RV Parks and Campgrounds

Truckee

Lakeside Campground
off Highway 89
Truckee, CA
530-587-3558
This 30 site campground is located in the Tahoe National Forest at an elevation of 5,741 feet. Camp amenities include vault toilets. There is no water. Sites are $12 per night. The campground is located next to the reservoir and activities include fishing and swimming. Pets must be leashed in the campground. To get there from I-80, take Highway 89 North to Prosser Reservoir. To make a reservation call 1-877-444-6777.

Accommodations - Vacation Home Rentals

Truckee

Andrea's Grinnin Bear Cabin
Call to Arrange.
Truckee, CA
530-582-8703
Located on a quiet cul-de-sac on a pine tree lot, this spacious 3 bedroom home is available for rent to people with pets. Nearby there are dog walks, hikes and places to explore. The Truckee river, Mardis Creek, Donner Lake and beach, Boca, Stampede and Prosser Reservoirs are all less than 15 minutes away.

Fore Paw Cottage
14906 Davos Drive
Truckee, CA 96161
530-587-4082
A cottage in a peaceful setting with fantastic views of Tahoe Donner golf course. Sleeps 6 comfortably with two queen beds, one king bed plus a bunk bed and a pull out queen bed. There is a maximum of two dogs, which always stay free. There is skiing at any of six major downhill ski areas located within 15 minutes.

Parks

Truckee

Commemorative Overland Emigrant Trail
Alder Creek Road

Truckee, CA
530-587-3558
This 15 mile moderate rated trail is located in the Tahoe National Forest. While the trail is open from May to November, it is most heavily used in the spring. The trail is popular with both hikers and mountain bikers. Pets must be either leashed or off-leash but under direct voice control. To get there from Interstate 80, take the Highway 89 North exit and go 2.3 miles to Alder Creek Road. Turn left and go 3 miles. The trail starts on the south side of the road.

Donner Memorial State Park
Highway 80
Truckee, CA
530-582-7892
While dogs are not allowed at the China Cove Beach Area and the nature trail behind the museum, they are allowed on the rest of the trails at this park. Dogs are also allowed in the lake. Pets must be on leash at all times and please clean up after them. The park has campgrounds but they are undergoing renovation from 2003 to 2004. It is located off Highway 80 in Truckee.

Glacier Meadow Loop Trail
Castle Peak
Truckee, CA
530-587-3558
This .5 mile easy loop trail is located in the Tahoe National Forest and is used for hiking only. It is a very popular trail from June to October. Pets must be either leashed or off-leash but under direct voice control. To get there from I-80, exit Castle Peak, on the south side of I-80, turn left. The trailhead is on the east side of the parking lot.

Sand Ridge Lake Trail
Castle Peak
Truckee, CA
530-587-3558
This 6 miles one way moderate rated trail is located in the Tahoe National Forest. From June to October, it is heavily used for hiking and horseback riding. Pets must be either leashed or off-leash but under direct voice control. To get there from I-80, exit Castle Peak, on the south side of I-80, turn left. The trailhead is on the east side of the parking lot.

Summit Lake Trail
Castle Peak
Truckee, CA
530-587-3558
This 2 mile easy rate trail is located in the Tahoe National Forest and is popular for hiking, mountain biking and horseback riding. The trail is

most frequently used from June to October. Pets must be either leashed or off-leash but under direct voice control. To get there from Interstate 80, exit Castle Peak, on the south side of I-80, turn left. The trailhead is on the east side of the parking lot.

Restaurants

Truckee

Earthly Delights
10087 W River St
Truckee, CA 95603
530-587-7793
This deli cafe allows dogs at their outdoor tables. They also offer freshly baked breads and pastries.

Twin Bridges Dog Travel Guide
Parks

Twin Bridges

Bryan Meadows Trail
Bryan Road
Twin Bridges, CA
530-644-2545
This 4 mile moderate rated trail passes through stands of lodgepole pine and mountain hemlock. From the parking area, hike one mile up Sayles Canyon Trail along the creek to the junction of Bryan Meadows Trail. The trail continues east for about three miles. The elevation ranges from about 7,200 to 8,400 feet. Pets must be leashed and please clean up after them. This trail is located in the Eldorado National Forest. From Highway 50 go about 48 miles east of Placerville. Turn onto the Sierra-At-Tahoe Road and go 2 miles. Turn right onto Bryan Road (17E13). Go another 2.5 miles to the parking area where the trailhead is located.

Pyramid Creek Loop Trail
Highway 50
Twin Bridges, CA
530-644-2545
This 1.7 mile trail is rated moderate to strenuous. The elevation ranges from 6,120 to 6,400 feet. At the trailhead, begin your hike by heading east and then north up to Pyramid Creek. Turn right (east) at the sign and follow the trail along the creek. The trail offers great views of the American River Canyon, Lover's Leap, Horsetail Falls and other geological interests. Follow the trail north, then loop back south on the old trail bed down to the

granite slabs and return to Highway 50. Pets must be leashed and please clean up after them. This trail is located in the Eldorado National Forest. The trailhead is located on the north side of Highway 50 at Twin Bridges, about .5 miles east of Strawberry.

Yosemite Dog Travel Guide
Accommodations

Coulterville

Yosemite Gold Country Motel
10407 Highway 49
Coulterville, CA 95311
209-878-3400
All rooms are completely furnished with a heater and air conditioner, color TV, telephones, bathroom with tub-shower and free coffee. Your dog is more than welcome here, but he or she must stay on a leash when outside and should use their Doggie Park when going to the bathroom. Also, they require that you do not leave your dog outside unattended. This motel is located about hour from Yosemite Valley (40 min. to the main gate and 20 min. to the valley). There are no additional pet fees.

Fish Camp

Apple Tree Inn at Yosemite
1110 Highway 41
Fish Camp, CA 93623
559-683-5111
This 54 unit inn is nestled among acres of trees. There is dog-friendly hiking right from the property on fire roads in the Sierra National Forest (on Jackson/Big Sandy Road which is also the road to the Yosemite Trails Pack Station). Pets must be leashed on the inn's property and in the forest. The next property over from the inn is the Tenaya Lodge which doesn't allow dogs, but has several cafes with food to go. The inn is located two miles from the southern entrance to Yosemite National Park (about 45 minutes to Yosemite Valley). There is a $50 one time pet charge.

Narrow Gauge Inn
48571 Highway 41
Fish Camp, CA 93623
559-683-7720
This inn is located amidst pine trees in the Sierra Mountains. They are located about four miles from the southern entrance to Yosemite National Park (about 45 minutes to Yosemite Valley). There are some trails nearby in the dog-friendly

Sierra National Forest near Bass Lake. All rooms are non-smoking. Dogs are allowed in the main level rooms and there is a $25 one time per stay pet fee. Children are also welcome.

Groveland

Historic Groveland Hotel
18767 Main Street
Groveland, CA 95321
209-962-4000
Your dog or cat is welcome at this 1849 historic inn. Country Inns Magazine rated the Groveland Hotel as one of the Top 10 Inns in the United States. The inn is located 23 miles from Yosemite's main gate. Their restaurant can pack a gourmet picnic basket for your day trip to Yosemite. Make your reservations early as they book up quickly. This inn is located about an hour from Yosemite Valley. There are no additional pet fees. All rooms are non-smoking.

Sunset Inn
33569 Hardin Flat Rd.
Groveland, CA 95321
209-962-4360
This inn offers three cabins near Yosemite National Park. The cabins are located on two acres and are surrounded by a dog-friendly National Forest at a 4500 foot elevation. All cabins are non-smoking and include kitchens and private bathrooms. Children are also welcome. The Sunset Inn is located just 2 miles from the west entrance to Yosemite, one mile from Highway 120. There is a $10 per day pet charge and a $150 refundable pet deposit.

Yosemite Westgate Motel
7633 Hwy 120
Groveland, CA 95321
209-962-5281
This motel has one pet room available and it is a non-smoking room. There is a $10 per night pet fee. The motel is located about 40 minutes from

Yosemite Valley.

Mariposa

Best Western Yosemite Way Station
4999 S. Highway 140
Mariposa, CA 95338
209-966-7545
There is a $5 per day pet charge. The oldest courthouse in California is located just 7 blocks from this inn. If you take Highway 140, this motel is located about 50 minutes from Yosemite Valley.

The Mariposa Lodge
5052 Hwy 140
Mariposa, CA 95338
209-966-3607
Thanks to one of our readers for recommending this hotel. Here is what they said about it: "We stayed here after a clogged 4 hour drive from San Jose, CA. Mia at the front desk was courteous and friendly -- not what you always get when you are traveling with a 90 pound dog (black lab). The room was large, new and very nice. Lovely pool and jacuzzi. A little sitting area under a patch of trees with benches. It was very warm and Mia recommended a restaurant where we could sit outside and take our dog. Castillos on 5th Street. Our extra nice waitress brought him water and us an excellent Mexican dinner. Couldn't have been nicer. All in all Mariposa and the hotel was an A+ experience." If you take Highway 140, this motel is located about 50 minutes from Yosemite Valley (45 min. to the main gate and about 10 min. to the valley). Pets are an additional $10 per pet per night.

Oakhurst

Best Western Yosemite Gateway Inn
40530 Highway 41
Oakhurst, CA 93644
559-683-2378
This inn is located in the mountain town of Oakhurst. Amenities include laundry services, an indoor and outdoor pool and more. There are no additional pet fees, but pets must not be left alone in the room. Yosemite Valley is about a one hour drive from this inn.

Pine Rose Inn Bed and Breakfast
41703 Road 222
Oakhurst, CA 93644
559-642-2800
The inn is located 13 miles from the south gate of Yosemite National Park, 2 miles from Bass Lake and surrounded by the Sierra National Forest. The entire inn is non-smoking, except for outside. There is a $10 per day pet charge. Dogs and other pets are welcome.

Accommodations - RV Parks and Campgrounds

Bass Lake

Lupine/Cedar Bluff Campground
off Road 222
Bass Lake, CA
559-877-2218
This campground is next to Bass Lake in the Sierra National Forest. It is at an elevation of 3,400 feet and offers shade from dense pine, oak and cedar frees. There are 113 campsites for tent and RV camping. RVs up to 40 feet are allowed and there are no hookups. Camp amenities include piped water, flush toilets, picnic tables and grills. The campground is open all year. A .5 mile trail called The Way of the Mono Trail, is located near this campground. Dogs are allowed at the campgrounds, on trails and in the water but only at non-designated swimming beaches. Pets must be leashed and please clean up after them. To make a reservation call 1-877-444-6777. To get there, Take Hwy 41 north from Fresno; continue thru Oakhurst to Road 222. Turn right on Road 222, travel east 3 miles and turn right (Road 222), continue for 3/10 of a mile bear right again. Travel 3.5 miles around the south side of the Lake to Lupine Cedar Campground. Check in at the Bass Lake Campground office before heading to your campsite. The office is located at the west end of the lake near Recreation Point.

Groveland

Yosemite Pines RV Resort
20450 Old Highway 120
Groveland, CA 95321
209-962-7690
This 30 acre RV park offers sites with both full and partial hookups as well as tent sites. Well-behaved dogs on a 10 foot or less leash are allowed. There is no pet fee. Please clean up after your pets.

Yosemite National Park

Yosemite National Park Campgrounds
PO Box 577
Yosemite National Park, CA 95389
209-372-0200
There are 10 dog-friendly campgrounds to choose from at this national park. Pets are allowed in all campgrounds except Camp 4, Tamarack Flat, Porcupine Flat, all walk-in sites and all group campsites. Most of the campgrounds allow both tents and RVs up to 40 feet, but there are no RV hookups. Generators can be used sparingly only between 7am and 7pm. Some of the campgrounds are open all year but all are open during the summer. Reservations should be made well in advance, especially during the summer season. While this national park does not allow dogs on most of the trails, there are still about 6-7 miles of both paved and unpaved trails that allow dogs. See our Yosemite National Park listing for more details. Dogs must be on a 6 foot or less leash and attended at all times. People must also clean up after their pets.

Accommodations - Vacation Home Rentals

Yosemite National Park

The Redwoods In Yosemite
PO Box 2085; Wawona Station
Yosemite National Park, CA 95389
209-375-6666
Dog-friendly vacation rentals inside Yosemite National Park offer year-round vacation rentals that range in size from one to six bedrooms. Some of the rentals allow pets, but not all, so please specify your need for a pet unit when you make your reservation. There is a $10/night pet fee (per pet). Please abide by Yosemite's pet regulations, which require that pets be leashed at all times and are not permitted on many Park

trails (a couple of exceptions are paved paths in the Valley Floor and a couple of short trails in the south Yosemite area). The rentals are located approximately 10 minutes inside the southern entrance of Yosemite National Park and offer 120 privately owned vacation rentals.

Attractions

Fish Camp

Yosemite Mountain Sugar Pine Railroad
56001 Highway 41
Fish Camp, CA 93623
559-683-7273
Hop aboard a four mile railroad excursion with your pooch and enjoy a narrative ride through the Sierra National Forest. One of their steam engines is the heaviest operating narrow gauge Shay locomotive in use today. Well-behaved leashed dogs are welcome. The railroad is located near Yosemite Park's south gate on Highway 41.

Yosemite National Park

Yosemite National Park
PO Box 577
Yosemite National Park, CA 95389
209-372-0200
This 750,000 acre park is one of the most popular national parks in the country. Yosemite's geology is world famous for its granite cliffs, tall waterfalls and giant sequoia groves. As with most national parks, pets have limited access within the park. Pets are not allowed on unpaved or poorly paved trails, in wilderness areas including hiking trails, in park lodging (except for some campgrounds) and on shuttle buses. However, there are still several nice areas to walk with your pooch and you will be able to see the majority of sights and points of interest that most visitors see. Dogs are allowed in developed areas and on fully paved trails, include Yosemite Valley which offers about 2 miles of paved trails. From these trails you can view El Capitan, Half Dome and Yosemite Falls. You can also take the .5 mile paved trail right up to the base of Bridalveil Fall which is a 620 foot year round waterfall. The best time to view this waterfall is in the spring or early summer. The water thunders down and almost creates a nice rain at the base. Water-loving dogs will be sure to like this attraction. In general dogs are not allowed on unpaved trails, but this park does make the following exceptions. Dogs are allowed on the Meadow Loop and Four Mile fire roads in

Wawona. They are also allowed on the Carlon Road and on the Old Big Oak Flat Road between Hodgdon Meadow and Hazel Green Creek. Dogs must be on a 6 foot or less leash and attended at all times. People must also clean up after their pets. For a detailed map of Yosemite, visit their web site at http: //www.nps.gov/yose/pphtml/maps.html. The green dots show the paved trails. There are four main entrances to the park and all four lead to the Yosemite Valley. The park entrance fees are as follows: $20 per vehicle, $40 annual pass or $10 per individual on foot. The pass is good for 7 days. Prices are subject to change. Yosemite Valley is open year round and may be reached via Highway 41 from Fresno, Highway 140 from Merced, Highway 120 from Manteca and in late spring through late fall via the Tioga Road (Highway 120 East) from Lee Vining. From November through March, all park roads are subject to snow chain control (including 4x4s) or temporary closure at any time due to hazardous winter driving conditions. For updated 24 hour road and weather conditions call (209) 372-0200.

Parks

Bass Lake

The Way of the Mono Trail
off Road 222
Bass Lake, CA
559-877-2218
On this .5 mile trail you can see authentic Mono Indian grinding holes, plus you will get some great views of Bass Lake. The trail is located next to Bass Lake in the Sierra National Forest. Stop at the Yosemite/Sierra Visitors Bureau at 41969 Highway 41 in Oakhurst for the trail location. The office is open 7 days a week from 8:30am to 5pm.

Oakhurst

Shadow of the Giants Trail
off Sky Ranch Road
Oakhurst, CA
559-297-0706
This one mile each way self-guided trail is located in the Nelder Grove Giant Sequoia Preservation Area. Along the trail you will see some of the best giant sequoia trees in the state. Pets on leash are allowed and please clean up after them. The trail is located in the Nelder Grove Giant Sequoia Preservation Area of the Sierra National Forest. To get there from Oakhurst, go about 5 miles north on Highway 41. Turn right (east) onto Sky Ranch Road. Along Sky Ranch Road you will find Nelder Grove.

Sierra National Forest
1600 Tollhouse Road
Clovis, CA 93612
Trails near Oakhurst
559-297-0706
The dog-friendly Sierra National Forest, just south of Yosemite, consists of 1.3 million acres. Your leashed dog is allowed in this forest and on over 1,000 miles of trails. Just make sure you stay within the Sierra National Forest and do not accidentally cross over to the bordering National Parks which don't allow dogs on hiking trails. The Sierra National Forest trails offer gentle meadows, pristine lakes and streams, and rugged passes in the forest's five wilderness areas. A Wilderness Visitor Permit is required if you plan on hiking into one of the five wilderness areas. In the Sierra National Forest, one of the more popular trails is the Lewis Creek National Recreation Trail. This 3.7 mile hike makes a great day hike as it offers scenic views of waterfalls like the Corlieu and Red Rock Falls. The trail gains 880 feet in elevation from south to north. There are three trailheads along the Lewis Creek Trail. From Oakhurst, take Highway 41 north towards Yosemite National Park. The southernmost trailhead, located 7 miles from Oakhurst, is about 0.5 mile off the highway along the Cedar Valley Road. The middle trailhead is about 3 miles further along Highway 41, at a large turnout just beyond the snow chain station. The northernmost trailhead is just off Highway 41 along the Sugar Pine Road, 500 feet past the bridge on the south side of the road.

Round-Up BBQ
18745 Back Street
Groveland, CA 95321
209-962-0806
Dogs are allowed at the outdoor tables.

Oakhurst

Pizza Factory
40120 Highway 41 #B
Oakhurst, CA 93644
559-683-2700
Well-behaved dogs may sit at the outside tables.

Subway
40278 Road 425a
Oakhurst, CA 93644
559-683-3066
Dogs are allowed at the outdoor tables.

Vets and Kennels

Oakhurst

Hoof and Paw Veterinary Hospital
41149 Highway 41
Oakhurst, CA 93644
559-683-3313

Oakhurst Veterinary Hospital
40799 Highway 41
Oakhurst, CA 93644
559-683-2135

Restaurants

Groveland

Chapter 7

California Dog-Friendly Travel Guide
Central Coast

Avila Beach Dog Travel Guide
Beaches

Avila Beach

Avila Beach
off Avila Beach Drive
Avila Beach, CA
805-595-5400
This beach is about a 1/2 mile long. Dogs are not allowed between 10am and 5pm and must be leashed.

Olde Port Beach
off Avila Beach Drive
Avila Beach, CA
805-595-5400
This beach is about a 1/4 mile long. Dogs are not allowed between 10am and 5pm and must be leashed.

Big Sur Dog Travel Guide
Accommodations - RV Parks and Campgrounds

Big Sur

Big Sur Campground and Cabins
Highway 1
Big Sur, CA
831-667-2322
This tent and RV campground is set amongst redwood trees along the Big Sur River. For RVs there are full hookups and some pull through sites. Camp amenities include a general store, playground, basketball court and more. Well-behaved leashed dogs of all sizes are allowed in the tent and RV sites but not in the cabins. Pets must be attended at all times. People need to clean up after their pets. They are located about 5 miles from the dog-friendly Pfieffer Beach and 2.5 miles from Big Sur Station. The campground is open all year.

Fernwood at Big Sur
Highway 1
Big Sur, CA
831-667-2422
Dogs are allowed at the campgrounds but not in the motel. RVs are permitted and there are hookups are available.

Ventana Big Sur Campground
Highway 1
Big Sur, CA
831-667-2712
This campground is nestled among trees and along a stream. RVs up to 22 feet are permitted but there are no hookups and generators cannot be used at any time. The campground is usually open from April through mid-October. Dogs are allowed but should be kept quiet and on a leash at all times. There is a maximum of 2 pets per campsite.

Ventana Campground
Hwy One
Big Sur, CA
831-667-2712
This 40 acre campground, located in a redwood tree lined canyon, offers 80 camp sites nestled among the trees and along the edge of the stream. RV's are limited to 22 feet and there are no hookups. Well-behaved quiet leashed dogs of all sizes are allowed, maximum of two dogs per site. People need to clean up after their pets. There is a $5 per night pet fee per dog. The campground is open from mid-March through mid-October.

Accommodations - Vacation Home Rentals

Big Sur

Big Sur Vacation Retreat
off Highway One
Big Sur, CA
831-624-5339 Ext 13
Rent this vacation rental by the week or longer. The home is situated on ten acres and at an elevation of 1,700 feet which is usually above the coastal fog and winds. Well-behaved dogs are welcome. No children under 10 years old allowed without the prior consent of the owner. This rental is usually available between June and mid-October. Rates are about $2300 per week. The home is located about 45 minutes south of Carmel.

Beaches

Big Sur

Pfieffer Beach
Sycamore Road
Big Sur, CA
805-968-6640
Dogs on leash are allowed at this day use beach which is located in the Los Padres National Forest. The beach is located in Big Sur, south of

the Big Sur Ranger Station. From Big Sur, start heading south on Highway 1 and look carefully for Sycamore Road. Take Sycamore Road just over 2 miles to the beach. There is a $5 entrance fee per car.

Parks

Big Sur

Los Padres National Forest
Big Sur Station #1
Big Sur, CA 93920
831-385-5434
While dogs are not allowed in the state park in Big Sur, they are welcome in the adjacent Los Padres National Forest. Dogs should be on leash. One of the most popular trails is the Pine Ridge Trail. This trail is miles long and goes through the Los Padres National Forest to the dog-friendly Ventana Wilderness. To get there, take Highway 1 south, about 25-30 miles south of Carmel. Park at the Big Sur Station for a minimal fee. From the Big Sur Station in Big Sur, you can head out onto the Pine Ridge Trail. The Los Padres National Forest actually stretches over 200 miles from the Carmel Valley all the way down to Los Angeles County. For maps and more information about the trails, contact the Monterey Ranger District at 831-385-5434 or at the Forest Headquarters in Goleta at 805-968-6640.

Carmel Dog Travel Guide
Accommodations

Carmel

Carmel Country Inn
P.O. Box 3756
Carmel, CA 93921
831-625-3263
This dog-friendly bed and breakfast has 12 rooms and allows dogs in several of these rooms. It's close to many downtown outdoor dog-friendly restaurants (see Restaurants). A 20-25 minute walk will take you to the dog-friendly Carmel City Beach. There is a $20 per night per pet charge.

Carmel Tradewinds Inn
Mission St & 3rd Ave.
Carmel, CA 93921
831-624-2776
This motel allows dogs in several of their rooms. They are a non-smoking inn. It's located about 3-4 blocks north of Ocean Ave and close to many outdoor dog-friendly restaurants in downtown

Carmel. A 20-25 minute walk will take you to the dog-friendly Carmel City beach. There is a $25 per day pet charge. Dogs are not allowed on the bed.

Casa De Carmel
Monte Verde & Ocean Ave
Carmel, CA
831-624-2429
There is an additional fee of $20 per day for 1 pet, and $30 a day for 2 pets.

Coachman's Inn
San Carlos St. & 7th
Carmel, CA 93921
831-624-6421
Located in downtown, this motel allows dogs. It's close to many downtown outdoor dog-friendly restaurants (see Restaurants). A 20-25 minute walk will take you to the Carmel City beach which allows dogs. There is a $15 per day additional pet fee.

Cypress Inn
Lincoln & 7th
Carmel, CA 93921
831-624-3871
This hotel is located within walking distance to many dog-friendly outdoor restaurants in the quaint town of Carmel and walking distance to the

Carmel City Beach. This is definitely a pet-friendly hotel. Here is an excerpt from the Cypress Inn's web page "Co-owned by actress and animal rights activist Doris Day, the Cypress Inn welcomes pets with open arms -- a policy which draws a high percentage of repeat guests. It's not unusual to see people strolling in and out of the lobby with dogs of all sizes. Upon arrival, animals are greeted with dog biscuits, and other pet pamperings." Room rates are about $125 - $375 per night. If you have more than 2 people per room (including a child or baby), you will be required to stay in their deluxe room which runs approximately $375 per night. There is a $25 per day pet charge.

Hofsas House Hotel
San Carlos Street
Carmel, CA 93921
831-624-2745
There is a $15 per day additional pet fee. The hotel is located between 3rd Ave and 4th Ave in Carmel. Thanks to one of our readers for recommending this hotel.

Lincoln Green Inn
PO Box 2747
Carmel, CA
831-624-7738
These cottages are owned and booked through the dog-friendly Vagabond's House Inn in Carmel. One big difference between the two accommodations is that the Vagabond's House does not allow children, whereas the Lincoln Green does allow children. The Lincoln Green is located very close to a beach. All cottages are non-smoking and there is a $20 per day pet fee.

Sunset House
Camino Real and Ocean Ave
Carmel, CA 93923
831-624-4884
There is a $20 one time pet fee. Thanks to one of our readers who writes "Great B&B, breakfast

brought to your room every morning."

The Forest Lodge Cottages
Ocean Ave. and Torres St. (P.O. Box 1316)
Carmel, CA 93921
831-624-7055
These cottages are surrounded by oak and pine trees among a large garden area. They are conveniently located within walking distance to many dog-friendly restaurants and the dog-friendly Carmel City Beach. There is a $10 one time additional pet fee.

Vagabond's House Inn B&B
P.O. Box 2747
Carmel, CA 93921
831-624-7738
This dog-friendly bed and breakfast is located in downtown and has 11 rooms. It's close to many downtown outdoor dog-friendly restaurants. A 20-25 minute walk will take you to the dog-friendly Carmel City beach. Children 12 years and older are allowed at this B&B inn.

Wayside Inn
Mission St & 7th Ave.
Carmel, CA 93921
831-624-5336
This motel allows dogs in several of their rooms and is close to many downtown outdoor dog-friendly restaurants. A 20-25 minute walk will take you to the dog-friendly Carmel City beach. Pets are welcome at no extra charge. Dogs up to about 75 pounds are allowed.

downtown Carmel or at one of the dog-friendly beaches. Rates with seasonal changes are from $139 to $319 per night. Dogs are an extra $10 per day and up to two dogs per room. There is no charge for childen under 16. The lodge is located in Carmel Valley. From Carmel, head south on Hwy 1. Turn left on Carmel Valley Rd., drive about 11-12 miles and the lodge will be located at Ford Rd.

Carmel Valley

Best Western Carmel Mission Inn
3665 Rio Rd.
Carmel Valley, CA 93921
831-624-1841
Located in Carmel Valley off Hwy 1, this inn is a few blocks from The Crossroads Shopping Center which has several outdoor dog-friendly restaurants and a pet store. The Garland Ranch Park is located within a 10-15 minute drive. There is also a $35 one time pet fee.

Los Laureles Lodge
313 West Carmel Valley Road
Carmel Valley, CA 93924
831-659-2233
There is a $20 per day pet fee. Dogs may not be left in the room unattended. This large ranch lodge sits on 10 acres in rural Carmel Valley, about 10 minutes from the Carmel seaside and near world class golf, hiking, wineries and everything else Carmel has to offer. Nearby Garland Ranch is available for hiking.

Carmel Valley Lodge
Carmel Valley Rd
Carmel Valley, CA 93924
831-659-2261
Your dog will feel welcome at this country retreat. Pet amenities include heart-shaped, organic homemade dog biscuits and a pawtographed picture of Lucky the Lodge Dog. Dogs must be on leash, but for your convenience, there are doggy-hitches at the front door of every unit that has a patio or deck and at the pool. There are 31 units which range from standard rooms to two bedroom cottages. A great community park is located across the street and several restaurants with outdoor seating are within a 5 minute walk. Drive about 15 minutes from the lodge and you'll be in

Accommodations - RV Parks and Campgrounds

Carmel

Carmel by the River RV Park
27680 Schulte Road
Carmel, CA

831-624-9329

This RV park is located right next to the river. Amenities include hookups, basketball court, recreation room and dog walk area. Per Monterey County's Ordinance, maximum length per stay from April through September is 14 days and from October through March is 8 weeks. Well-behaved quiet dogs of all sizes are allowed, up to a maximum of three pets. Pets must be kept on a short leash and never left unattended in the campsite or in your RV. People need to clean up after their pets. There is no pet fee. The owners have dogs that usually stay at the office. The RV park is open all year.

Attractions

Carmel

Carmel Village Shopping Area
Ocean Ave
Carmel, CA
between Mission & Casanova St.

This shopping expedition is more of a window shopping adventure, however there are some dog-friendly stores throughout this popular and quaint village. Just ask a store clerk before entering into a store with your pooch. We do know that the Galerie Blue Dog (Blue Dog Gallery) located at 6th Ave. and Lincoln St. is dog-friendly. There are also many dog-friendly restaurants throughout the village (see Restaurants).

Carmel Walks-Walking Tours
Lincoln and Ocean Streets
Carmel, CA
courtyard of The Pine Inn
831-642-2700
Discover the special charms and secrets of Carmel on this two hour guided walking tour. Walk through award-winning gardens, by enchanting fairytale cottages and learn the homes, haunts, and history of famous artists, writers, and movie stars. Your leashed dog is welcome to join you. Tours are offered every Saturday at 10am and 2pm. Tuesday thru Friday, the tours are at 10am. The cost is $20 per person and dogs get the tour for free. Prices are subject to change. Reservations are required.

Seventeen Mile Drive
Seventeen Mile Drive
Carmel, CA

This toll road costs $8 and allows you to access a

very scenic section of coastline, walking trails and beaches. Dogs are allowed all along 17 mile drive on leash.

Carmel Valley

Crossroads Shopping Center
Cabrillo Hwy (Hwy 1)
Carmel Valley, CA
near Carmel Valley Rd.

This is an outdoor shopping mall with many dog-friendly outdoor restaurants and a pet store. While your dog cannot go into the shops, he or she is more than welcome inside the pet store.

Quail Lodge Golf Club
8205 Valley Greens Drive
Carmel Valley, CA 93922
831-624-2888
Well-behaved, leashed dogs are welcome at this 18-hole championship golf course. Dogs must be leashed and either in your golf cart or tied to your pull cart. The course is open to members, resort guests (dogs are allowed at the hotel) and non-resort guests.

Beaches

Carmel

Carmel City Beach
Ocean Avenue
Carmel, CA
At end of Ocean Ave.
831-624-9423
This beach is within walking distance (about 7 blocks) from the quaint village of Carmel. There are a couple of hotels and several restaurants that are within walking distance of the beach. Your pooch is allowed to run off-leash as long as he or she is under voice control. To get there, take the Ocean Avenue exit from Hwy 1 and

follow Ocean Ave to the end.

Carmel River State Beach
Carmelo Street
Carmel, CA
831-624-9423
This beach is just south of Carmel. It has approximately a mile of beach and leashes are required. It's located on Carmelo Street.

Garrapata State Park
Highway 1
Carmel, CA
831-649-2836
There are two miles of beach front at this park. Dogs are allowed but must be on a 6 foot or less leash and people need to clean up after their pets. The beach is on Highway 1, about 6 1/2 miles south of Rio Road in Carmel. It is about 18 miles north of Big Sur.

Parks

Carmel Valley

Garland Ranch Regional Park
Carmel Valley Rd.
Carmel Valley, CA
831-659-4488
This dog-friendly 4,500 acre regional park offers

approx. 5-6 miles of dirt single-track and fire road trails. The trail offers a variety of landscapes, with elevations ranging from 200 to 2000 feet. If you are looking for some exercise in addition to the beaches, this is the spot. Dogs must be on leash. The park is located 8.6 miles east of Highway 1 on Carmel Valley Road.

Restaurants

Carmel

Casanova Restaurant
Mission & 5th
Carmel, CA
831-625-0501
This dog-friendly restaurant has several outdoor tables in the front with heaters. It's located in downtown near several hotels and within a 20-25 minute walk to the dog-friendly beach.

Forge in the Forest
5th and Junipero, SW Corner
Carmel, CA 93921
831-624-2233
Dogs are allowed to dine in this elegantly designed outdoor patio. Dogs are only allowed at certain tables on the upper patio.

Le Coq D'Or
Mission between 4th & 5th
Carmel, CA
831-626-9319
Your well-behaved dog is welcome on their heated outdoor patio. This is a European country restaurant that serves an innovative menu of German and French specialties. Your pooch will feel welcome here.

Carmel Valley

Cafe Stravaganza
241 The Crossroads
Carmel Valley, CA
Crossroads Shopping Center
831-625-3733
Located in the Crossroads Shopping Center in Carmel Valley, this restaurant offers dog-friendly outdoor dining. A pet store is nearby.

Nico Restaurant
San Carlos & Ocean Ave
Carmel, CA
831-624-6545
Dogs are allowed at the outdoor tables.

PortaBella
Ocean Ave
Carmel, CA
between Lincoln & Monte Verde
831-624-4395
Dogs... come here to be treated first class. Your waiter will bring your pup water in a champagne bucket. They have several outdoor tables with heaters. It's located in downtown near several hotels and within a 20-25 minute walk to the beach.

Carmen's Place
211 The Crossroads
Carmel Valley, CA
Crossroads Shopping Center
831-625-3030
This restaurant offers a delicious breakfast. Lunch is also served here. It's located in the Crossroads Shopping Center in Carmel Valley. A pet store is nearby.

Oak Deli
24 W Carmel Valley Rd
Carmel Valley, CA 93924
Carmel Valley Village
831-659-3416
Dogs are allowed at the outdoor tables.

Plaza Linda
9 Del Fino Pl
Carmel Valley, CA 93924
831-659-4229
This "dog-friendly" restaurant has a sign out front
that says so. Sit on the front patio.

Sole Mio Caffe Trattoria
3 Del Fino Pl
Carmel Valley, CA 93924
Carmel Valley Village
831-659-9119
Dogs are allowed at the outdoor tables.

The Corkscrew Cafe
55 W Carmel Valley Rd
Carmel Valley, CA 93924
831-659-8888
Their daily menu reflects the use of fresh herbs
and seasonal produce from their large gardens,
paired with local fish and meats. Dogs are
allowed at the outdoor tables.

Stores

Carmel

Blue Dog Gallery
6th Ave. and Lincoln St.
Carmel, CA
831-626-4444
First created in 1984, Blue Dog is based on the
mythical "loup garou," a French-Cajun ghost dog,
and Tiffany, Rodrique's own pooch who had
passed away a few years prior to the notoriety.
Blue Dog represents a dog who is between
heaven and earth. Ask about the story behind
Blue Dog when you visit this gallery. The painter,
Rodrique, is an internationally acclaimed painter.
Blue Dog will probably look familiar to you
because Absolut Vodka and other companies
have used it for their marketing campaigns. This
gallery usually has some cookies and treats for
visiting pooches. Thanks to one of our readers
who writes: "A most wonderful place, I called
asking for information after Rodrigue did a picture
for Neiman Marcus . . . the lady with whom I
spoke sent us information plus dog biscuits for
our corgi.."

Yellow Dog Gallery
Dolores & 5th Ave
Carmel, CA 93923
831-624-3238
This contemporary art gallery has a large number
of dog works and allows your dog to visit with
you.

Vets and Kennels

Monterey

Monterey Peninsula - Salinas Emergency Vet
2 Harris Court Suite A1
Monterey, CA
Ryan Ranch and Hwy 68
831-373-7374
Monday - Thursday 5:30 pm to 8 am. Friday 5:30 pm to Monday 8 am.

Gorda Dog Travel Guide
Accommodations - RV Parks and Campgrounds

Gorda

Kirk Creek Campground
Highway 1
Gorda, CA
831-385-5434
Located in the Los Padres National Forest, this campground is situated on an open bluff 100 feet above sea level and offers great views of the ocean and coastline. The beach is reached by hiking down from the campgrounds. The Kirk Creek trailhead is also located at the campground and leads to the Vicente Flat Trail which offers miles of hiking trails. Dogs are allowed in the campgrounds, on the hiking trails, and on the beach but must be leashed. Be aware that there are large amounts of poison oak on the trails. RVs up to 30 feet are permitted but there are no hookups. The campground is located about 25 miles south of Big Sur.

Plaskett Creek Campground
Highway 1
Gorda, CA
831-385-5434
Located in the Los Padres National Forest, this

campground is nestled among large Monterey Pine trees. The campsites are within walking distance of the dog-friendly Sand Dollar Beach. Dogs must be leashed in the campgrounds and on the beach. RVs are permitted in the campgrounds but there are no hookups. The campground is about 5 miles south of the Kirk Creek and about 30 miles south of Big Sur.

Beaches

Gorda

Kirk Creek Beach and Trailhead
Highway 1
Gorda, CA
831-385-5434
Both the Kirk Creek Beach and hiking trails allow dogs. Pets must be leashed. You can park next to the Kirk Creek Campground and either hike down to the beach or start hiking at the Kirk Creek Trailhead which leads to the Vicente Flat Trail where you can hike for miles with your dog. The beach and trailhead is part of the Los Padres National Forest and is located about 25 miles south of Big Sur.

Sand Dollar Beach
Highway 1
Gorda, CA
805-434-1996
Walk down a path to one of the longest sandy beaches on the Big Sur Coast. This national forest managed beach is popular for surfing, fishing and walking. Dogs must be on leash and people need to clean up after their pets. There is a minimal day use fee. The dog-friendly Plaskett Creek Campground is within walking distance. This beach is part of the Los Padres National Forest and is located about 5 miles south of the Kirk Creek and about 30 miles south of Big Sur.

Willow Creek Beach
Highway 1
Gorda, CA
831-385-5434
Dogs on leash are allowed at this day use beach and picnic area. The beach is part of the Los Padres National Forest and is located about 35 miles south of Big Sur.

Hollister Dog Travel Guide
Accommodations - RV Parks and Campgrounds

Hollister

Casa de Fruita RV's Orchard Resort
10031 Pacheco Pass Highway
Hollister, CA 95023
408-842-9316
This RV park is located at a popular roadside orchard resort which features a fruit stand, store, 24 hour restaurant, zoo, rock shop, gold panning, children's train ride, children's playground and picnic areas. Amenities at the RV park include full hookups, pull through sites, shady areas, TV hookups and tent sites. Well-behaved leashed dogs are allowed. There is a $3 per night pet fee per pet. Please clean up after your pets. The resort is located on Highway 152/Pacheco Pass, two miles east of the Highway 156 junction.

King City Dog Travel Guide
Accommodations - RV Parks and Campgrounds

King City

San Lorenzo Regional Park
1160 Broadway
King City, CA 93930
831-385-5964
This campground is located in the dog-friendly San Lorenzo Park where leashed dogs are allowed on the hiking trails. Tent sites on grass and shaded RV spaces with full hookups are available. RVs up to 50 feet can be accommodated. Camp amenities include laundry facilities, putting green, internet access kiosk, restrooms and showers. Well-behaved leashed dogs of all sizes are allowed in the campground, maximum of two dogs per site. Pets must be attended at all times. People need to clean up after their pets. There is a $2 per night pet fee per dog. The campground is open all year.

Parks

King City

San Lorenzo Campground and RV Park
1160 Broadway
King City, CA 93930
831-385-5964
This park is located in the foothills of the Santa Lucia Mountains and along the Salinas River. Amenities include a walking trail along the river, picnic areas, playgrounds, volleyball courts, softball areas and camping. Dogs are allowed but must be leashed. Please clean up after your pets.

Lompoc Dog Travel Guide
Accommodations

Lompoc

Days Inn - Vandenberg Village
3955 Apollo Way
Lompoc, CA 93436
805-733-5000
There is a $250 refundable deposit and a $20 one time pet fee. Dogs may not be left alone in the rooms.

Motel 6
1521 North H Street
Lompoc, CA 93436
805-735-7631
There are no additional pet fees.

Quality Inn & Suites
1621 N. H Street
Lompoc, CA 93436
805-735-8555
There is a $25 one time pet fee.

Parks

Lompoc

La Purisima Mission State Historic Park
2295 Purisima Road
Lompoc, CA
805-733-3713
This mission was founded in 1787 and is one of the most completely resorted Spanish missions in California. While dogs are not allowed in the buildings, they are allowed on the grounds and on miles of trails. Pets must be on a 6 foot or less leash and please clean up after them. The park is located about 2 miles northeast of Lompoc.

Monterey Dog Travel Guide
Accommodations

Marina

Motel 6
100 Reservation Rd
Marina, CA 93933
831-384-1000
There are no additional pet fees.

Monterey

Bay Park Hotel

1425 Munras Ave
Monterey, CA
831-649-1020
There is a $10 per day pet fee. Pets may not be
left alone in the room.

Best Western Monterey Beach Hotel
2600 Sand Dunes Drive
Monterey, CA 93940
831-394-3321
This beachfront hotel allows dogs. Dogs stay in
the first floor rooms on the garden side (not facing
the beach). They originally just allowed small
dogs, but now they allow all dogs that are well-
behaved and well-trained. While there are no
restaurants within an easy walking distance, the
sandy beach is right at the hotel. Dogs are
allowed on the beaches that stretch from this
hotel down to Fisherman's Wharf - about 2 miles.
If you want a longer walk, once at Fisherman's
Wharf, continue on the paved Monterey
Recreation Trail. The hotel is located off Hwy 1 at
the Del Rey Oaks exit. There is a $25 one time
fee for pets.

Best Western Victorian Inn
487 Foam Street
Monterey, CA 93940
831-373-8000
This inn is a few blocks from the beautiful dog-
friendly Monterey Recreation Trail that parallels
the ocean. The inn has nice spacious rooms with
fireplaces and of course it has a great location for
ocean lovers and their water dogs. There is a
$100 refundable pet deposit and a one time $35
pet cleaning charge for the room. Thanks to one
of our readers who writes: "...He received upon
arriving to our room the "pooch package" of treats
overflowing in a bowl, and his own bottle of water
for walks along the surf. "

El Adobe Inn
936 Munras Ave.
Monterey, CA 93940
831-372-5409
This inn is located on Munras Ave. about 1/2 mile
east of Hwy 1. There is a $10 per day additional
pet fee.

Hyatt Resort
1 Old Golf Course Rd
Monterey, CA
831-372-1234
There is a $50 one time pet fee for each dog.
Dogs must be on leash and certain areas of the
hotel are off limits to pets. The front desk will
explain the restrictions upon check in.

Monterey Fireside Lodge
1131 10th Street
Monterey, CA 93940
831-373-4172
All 24 rooms have gas fireplaces. There is an
additional $20/day pet charge.

Motel 6
2124 N Fremont St
Monterey, CA 93940
831-646-8585
One well-behaved pet is permitted per room. Pets are not to be left alone in the room. There are no additional pet fees.

Pacific Grove

Andril Fireplace Cottages
569 Asilomar Blvd
Pacific Grove, CA
831-375-0994
There is an additional fee of $14 per day for a pet. Well-behaved dogs are allowed.

Lighthouse Lodge and Suites
1249 Lighthouse Ave
Pacific Grove, CA
831-655-2111
There are no additional pet fees.

Attractions

Monterey

Monterey Bay Whale Watch Boat Tours
Fisherman's Wharf
Monterey, CA
at Sam's Fishing Fleet
831-375-4658
Monterey Bay Whale Watch offers year-round whale watching trips to observe whales and dolphins in Monterey Bay. Tours are 3 - 6 hours. Well-behaved dogs on leash are allowed. The tours are located at Sam's Fishing Fleet on Fisherman's Wharf in Monterey.

Old Fisherman's Wharf
Del Monte & Washington
Monterey, CA
831-373-0600
Old Fisherman's Wharf in Monterey contains many outdoor ordering fish markets and cafes, boat tours (some of which allow dogs) and an observation deck where you can view sea lions and other animals.

Sea Life Tours
90 Fishermans Wharf
Monterey, CA 93940
831-372-7150
This boat allows leashed dogs on its 45 minute tours of the Monterey bay where you can view sea lions and sometimes whales and other sea life.

Beaches

Monterey

Monterey Recreation Trail
various (see comments)
Monterey, CA
Hwy 1

Take a walk on the Monterey Recreation Trail and experience the beautiful scenery that makes Monterey so famous. This paved trail extends for miles, starting at Fisherman's Wharf and ending in the city of Pacific Grove. Dogs must be leashed. Along the path there are a few small beaches that allow dogs such as the one south of Fisherman's Wharf and another beach behind Ghiradelli Ice Cream on Cannery Row. Along the path you'll find a few more outdoor places to eat near Cannery Row and by the Monterey Bay

Aquarium. Look at the Restaurants section for more info.

Monterey State Beach
various (see comments)
Monterey, CA
Hwy 1
831-649-2836
Take your water loving and beach loving dog to this awesome beach in Monterey. There are various starting points, but it basically stretches from Hwy 1 and the Del Rey Oaks Exit down to Fisherman's Wharf. Various beaches make up this 2 mile (each way) stretch of beach, but leashed dogs are allowed on all of them . If you want to extend your walk, you can continue on the paved Monterey Recreation Trail which goes all the way to Pacific Grove. There are a few smaller dog-friendly beaches along the paved trail.

Pacific Grove

Asilomar State Beach
Along Sunset Drive
Pacific Grove, CA
Pico
831-372-4076
Dogs are permitted on leash on the beach and the scenic walking trails. If you walk south along

the beach and go across the stream that leads into the ocean, you can take your dog off-leash, but he or she must be under strict voice control and within your sight at all times.

Parks

Monterey

El Estero Park
Camino El Estero & Fremont St
Monterey, CA 93940
831-646-3860
This is a city park with a lake, trails around the lake, a children's play area and many places to walk your dog. It's located on the east side of town.

Jacks Peak County Park
25020 Jacks Peak Park Road
Monterey, CA 93940
831-755-4895
This wooded park offers great views of the Monterey Bay area. You and your dog can enjoy almost 8.5 miles of hiking trails which wind through forests to ridge top vistas. Park amenities include picnic areas and restrooms. There is a $2 vehicle entrance fee during the week and a $3 fee on weekends and holidays. Dogs need to be leashed and please clean up after them.

Restaurants

Monterey

Archie's Hamburgers & Breakfast
125 Ocean View Blvd.
Monterey, CA
(by Monterey Bay Aquarium)
831-375-6939
Enjoy a hamburger or chicken sandwich for lunch and dinner or come early and have some breakfast at this restaurant that overlooks the ocean. The Monterey Recreation Trail is directly across the street.

Captain's Gig Restaurant
6 Fishermans Wharf #1
Monterey, CA 93940
831-373-5559
This restaurant has outdoor seating on Fisherman's Wharf in Monterey.

El Palomar Mexican Restaurant
724 Abrego St
Monterey, CA 93940
831-372-1032
Dogs are allowed at the outdoor tables.

Ghiradelli Ice Cream
616 Cannery Row

Monterey, CA
on Cannery Row
831-373-0997
Come here for some of the best tasting ice cream. While there, you have a choice of outdoor seating. They have nice patio seating shaded by a large tree or ocean view seating that is covered. Afterwards you and your pup can enjoy the small beach below (dogs on leash only).

Lighthouse Bistro
401 Lighthouse Ave
Monterey, CA 93940
831-649-0320
This restaurant has a large number of outdoor seats and heaters.

London Bridge Pub & Restaurant
Municipal Wharf
Monterey, CA
(north of Fisherman's Wharf)
831-655-2879
Enjoy tasty English food at this British Pub located on the Municipal Wharf between Fisherman's Wharf and the Monterey Beaches. They serve lunch outside and possibly dinner depending how cold it gets at night.

Mi Casita Taqueria
638 Wave St
Monterey, CA 93940
831-655-4419
This restaurant has a few outdoor tables and heaters. Dogs are welcome at these tables.

Monterey Bay Pie Company
481 Alvarado St
Monterey, CA 93940
831-656-9743
Monterey Bay Pie Company is in Old Monterey. Dogs are allowed at the outdoor tables.

Morgan's Coffee Shop
498 Washington St

Monterey, CA 93940
831-373-5601
Morgan's Coffee Shop has a large number of outdoor seats in the Old Monterey area.

Peter B's Brewery & Restaurant
2 Portola Plaza
Monterey, CA 93940
Doubletree Hotel
831-649-4511
This restaurant is located in the Doubletree Hotel just east of Fisherman's Wharf and near the Monterey State Historic Park. They do not always offer the outdoor dining so call ahead. If they are serving outside you can order a good lunch and great beer.

Pino's Italian Cafe & Ice Cream
211 Alvarado St
Monterey, CA
(east of Fisherman's Wharf)
831-649-1930
This Italian cafe & ice cream/gelato shop has a few outdoor seats and is located between Fisherman's Wharf and the Doubletree Hotel near the Monterey State Historic Park.

Shnarley's Pizza
685 Cannery Row #100
Monterey, CA 93940
831-373-8463
This pizza place has outdoor seats and heaters for you and your dog.

Tarpy's Road House
2999 Monterey Salinas Hwy #1
Monterey, CA 93940
831-647-1444
This 1800's looking complex is an interesting atmosphere for dining with your dog. There is a courtyard with a large number of outdoor tables. The restaurant is about 5 miles out of town on the Salinas highway.

Trailside Cafe
550 Wave Street
Monterey, CA
near Cannery Row
831-649-8600
Thanks to one of our readers for recommending this dog-friendly restaurant: "A terrific restaurant we found for breakfast during our morning walks is the Trailside Cafe. I know you request an address, but i don't have a specific one, except to say it is on the Monterey Rail Trail (Monterey Recreation Trail). ...my pooch loved the ocean view of the trail, but most importantly the special biscuit treats he recieved from the waitstaff when we ordered our wonderful breakfasts. the food is marvelous and staff very good... the patio has a breathtaking view of the pacific. Remember,,,, TRAILSIDE CAFE...on the rail trail in Monterey, only 2 blocks from the Victorian Inn."

Turtle Bay Taqueria
431 Tyler St
Monterey, CA 93940
831-333-1500
Turtle Bay Taqueria is in Old Monterey. It has a few outdoor tables for dining with your pup.

Whole Foods Market
800 Del Monte Center

Monterey, CA 93940
831-333-1600
This natural food supermarket offers natural and organic foods. Order some food from their deli and bring it to an outdoor table where your well-behaved leashed dog is welcome.

Pacific Grove

Bagel Bakery
1132 Forest Ave
Pacific Grove, CA 93950
831-649-6272
Dogs are allowed at the outdoor tables.

First Awakenings
125 Ocean View Blvd #105
Pacific Grove, CA 93950
831-372-1125
Dogs are allowed at the outdoor tables.

Seventeenth Street Grill
617 Lighthouse Ave
Pacific Grove, CA 93950
831-373-5474
Dogs are allowed at the outdoor tables.

Tinnery at the Beach
631 Ocean View Blvd
Pacific Grove, CA 93950
831-646-1040
This restaurant is at Lovers Point Park, at the western end of the Monterey/Pacific Grove Recreation Trail.

Toasties Cafe
702 Lighthouse Ave
Pacific Grove, CA 93950
831-373-7543
Toasties Cafe has a large number of outdoor tables for you and your dog.

Seaside

Bagel Bakery
2160 California Ave
Seaside, CA
831-392-1581
Dogs are allowed at the outdoor tables.

Jamba Juice
2160 California Ave
Seaside, CA
831-583-9696
Dogs are allowed at the outdoor tables.

Stores

Pacific Grove

Best Friends Pet Wash
167 Central Ave # A
Pacific Grove, CA 93950
831-375-2477
After a day at the beach with your pup you may
want to wash the sand away here at a self serve
pet wash.

Vets and Kennels

Monterey

Monterey Peninsula - Salinas Emergency Vet
2 Harris Court Suite A1
Monterey, CA
Ryan Ranch and Hwy 68
831-373-7374
Monday - Thursday 5:30 pm to 8 am. Friday 5:30
pm to Monday 8 am.

Newbury Park Dog Travel Guide
Restaurants

Newbury Park

Baja Fresh Mexican Grill
1015 Broadbeck Dr.
Newbury Park, CA
805-376-0808
This Mexican restaurant is open for lunch and
dinner. They use fresh ingredients and making
their salsa and beans daily. Some of the items on
their menu include Enchiladas, Burritos, Tacos
Salads, Quesadillas, Nachos, Chicken, Steak and
more. Well-behaved leashed dogs are allowed at
the outdoor tables.

Salinas Dog Travel Guide
Accommodations - RV Parks and
Campgrounds

Salinas

Laguna Seca Campground and RV Park
1025 Monterey Highway 68
Salinas, CA 93908
831-755-4895
The popular Laguna Seca raceway is the
highlight of this park. The park also offers a rifle
range and an OHV and Off-Highway Motocross
Track. Dogs are not permitted on any of the
tracks including the OHV area. Dogs on leash are
allowed at the RV and tent campgrounds. RV
sites are paved and offer hookups with up to 30
amp service. Tent sites are dirt pads with
showers, telephones and a playground within
walking distance. Camping fees are subject to
change depending on events that are being held
at the raceway. Call ahead for rates and
reservations.

Parks

Salinas

Toro County Park
501 Monterey-Salinas Highway 68
Salinas, CA 93908
831-755-4895
This 4,756 acre park offers over 20 miles of hiking, biking and horseback riding trails. Other park amenities include playgrounds, picnic sites, volleyball courts and an equestrian staging area. There is a $3 vehicle entrance fee during the week and a $5 fee on weekends and holidays. This park is located 6 miles from downtown Salinas and 13 miles from the Monterey Peninsula. Dogs need to be leashed and please clean up after them.

San Luis Obispo Dog Travel Guide
Accommodations

Arroyo Grande

Best Western Casa Grande Inn
850 Oak Park Road
Arroyo Grande, CA 93420
805-481-7398
Dogs up to 75 pounds are okay. There is a $25 refundable pet deposit required.

Atascadero

Motel 6
9400 El Camino Real
Atascadero, CA 93422
805-466-6701
There are no additional pet fees.

Cambria

Cambria Pines Lodge
2905 Burton Drive
Cambria, CA 93428
805-927-4200
This lodge is a 125 room retreat with accommodations ranging from rustic cabins to fireplace suites. It is nestled among 25 acres of Monterey Pines with forested paths and flower gardens. There is a $25 one time pet charge.

Cambria Shores Inn
6276 Moonstone Beach Dr.
Cambria, CA 93428
805-927-8644
This motel offers a beautiful ocean view from just about every room. You and your pup can enjoy ocean views, coastal walks (along the bluff, not on the beach) and pacific sunsets. Amenities include an in-room continental breakfast delivered to your door, in-room refrigerators and more. Dogs over 18 months old are allowed and there is a $10 per day pet charge.

Fogcatcher Inn
6400 Moonstone Beach Drive
Cambria, CA 93428
805-927-1400
There is a $25 per day additional pet fee. Two pet rooms are available. Thanks to one of our readers for recommending this place.

Cayucos

Cayucos Beach Inn
333 South Ocean Avenue
Cayucos, CA 93430
805-995-2828
There is a $10 one time pet fee. All rooms in the inn are non-smoking. Family pets are welcome. The inn even has a dog walk and dog wash area. Thanks to one of our readers for this recommendation.

Cypress Tree Motel
125 S. Ocean Avenue
Cayucos, CA 93430
805-995-3917
This pet-friendly 12-unit motel is located within walking distance to everything in town. Amenities include a garden area with lawn furniture and a barbecue. There is a $10 one time pet charge.

Dolphin Inn
399 S Ocean Ave
Cayucos, CA 93430
805-995-3810
There is a $10 per day pet charge.

Shoreline Inn
1 North Ocean Avenue
Cayucos, CA 93430
805-995-3681
This dog-friendly motel is located on the beach (dogs are not allowed on this State Beach). Dogs are allowed in the first floor rooms which have direct access to a patio area. There is a $10 per day charge for dogs.

Morro Bay

Adventure Inn On The Sea
1150 Embarcadero
Morro Bay, CA 93442
805-772-5607
Amenities include a continental breakfast served poolside each morning and an onsite gourmet restaurant serving lunch and dinner. There is a $10 per day pet charge.

Days Inn
1095 Main Street
Morro Bay, CA 93442
805-772-2711
There is an $11 per day pet fee.

Pleasant Inn Motel
235 Harbor Street

Morro Bay, CA 93442
805-772-8521
This motel, family owned and operated, is just one block east of the beautiful Morro Bay waterfront and one block west of old downtown. All rooms are non-smoking. Dogs and cats are welcome for an extra $5 per day.

Pismo Beach

Motel 6
860 4th St
Pismo Beach, CA 93449
805-773-2665
There are no additional pet fees.

Oxford Suites
651 Five Cities Drive
Pismo Beach, CA 93449
805-773-3773
This motel is located within a short drive of the dog-friendly Pismo State Beach. Amenities include a year-round pool & spa, complimentary full breakfast buffet, an evening reception with beverages & light hor d'oeuvres. Room amenities for the guest suites include a work table, sofa, microwave oven, refrigerator, TV/VCR, and wheelchair accessibility. There is a $10 per day pet charge. Dogs must never be left unattended in the room, even if they are in a crate.

Sandcastle Inn
100 Stimson Avenue
Pismo Beach, CA 93449
805-773-2422
This inn has one non-smoking pet room. There is a $10 per day pet charge.

Sea Gypsy Motel
1020 Cypress Street
Pismo Beach, CA 93449
805-773-1801
This motel is located on the beach and they allow

dogs of any size. There is a $15 per day pet charge.

San Luis Obispo

Best Western Royal Oak
214 Madonna Rd.
San Luis Obispo, CA 93405
805-544-4410
This motel is located near Cal Poly. Amenities include a heated pool and jacuzzi, complimentary continental breakfast, guest laundry, wheelchair accessible rooms and more. There is a $10 per day pet charge.

Motel 6 - South
1625 Calle Joaquin
San Luis Obispo, CA 93401
805-541-6992
One pet is permitted per room.

Sands Suites & Motel
1930 Monterey Street
San Luis Obispo, CA 93401
805-544-0500
This motel is close to Cal Poly. Amenities include a heated pool and spa, free continental breakfast, self serve laundry facilities and wheelchair accessibility. There is a $10 one time pet fee.

Vagabond Inn
210 Madonna Rd.
San Luis Obispo, CA 93405
805-544-4710
This motel is located near Cal Poly. Amenities include a heated pool and whirlpool, complimentary continental breakfast, dry cleaning/laundry service and more. There is a $5 per day pet charge.

San Simeon

Best Western Cavalier Oceanfront Resort
9415 Hearst Drive
San Simeon, CA 93452
805-927-4688
This dog-friendly motel is located next to the beach. Thanks to one of our readers, who has a 95 pound German Shepherd, for recommending this place. The motel sits on a bluff overlooking the ocean. Walk down one of the paths and you'll be on the beach. Amenities include beach access, two pools & a spa, room service, guest laundry facilities and a fitness center. All rooms feature a refrigerator, hair dryer, honor bar, remote cable TV with video cassette player, phone voice mail, and computer port. Some of the rooms offer ocean views with a wet bar, wood-burning fireplace and private patio. If you want to sit outside, there are firepits, surrounded by chairs which overlook the ocean. The firepits are lit at sunset and left burning through the night for those folks that want to enjoy the fire, the sound of the ocean and the distant light from the Piedras Blancas Lighthouse. There are no additional pet fees. All rooms are non-smoking.

Motel 6
9070 Castillo Dr
San Simeon, CA 93452
805-927-8691
A large well-behaved dog is okay. Dogs may not be left alone in the room.

Silver Surf Motel
9390 Castillo Drive
San Simeon, CA 93452
805-927-4661
This coastal motel is situated around a courtyard in a park like setting. There are beautiful flower gardens, majestic pine trees, and scenic ocean views. Some rooms offer private balconies, fireplaces or ocean views. Amenities include an indoor pool & spa, and guest laundry facility. There is a $10 per day pet charge.

Accommodations - RV Parks and Campgrounds

Arroyo Grande

Lake Lopez Recreation Area Campground
6820 Lopez Drive
Arroyo Grande, CA 93420
805-788-2381
This campground has 354 campsites which

overlook the lake or are nestled among oak trees. Full hookups are available at some of the sites. This lake is popular for fishing, camping, boating, sailing, water skiing, canoeing, bird-watching and miles of hiking trails ranging from easy to strenuous. The marina allows dogs on their boat rentals for an extra $10 fee. Other amenities at the marina include a laundromat, grocery store and tackle shop. Dogs must be leashed at all times and people need to clean up after their pets. Reservations for the campsites are accepted.

Bradley

Lake San Antonio Campground
2610 San Antonio Road
Bradley, CA
805-472-2311
The south shore of Lake San Antonio offers three camping areas with over 500 campsites and a picnic area. They have full hookups for RVs. The north shore provides shoreline camping and full hookup sites. The majority of campsites are available on a first-come, first-served basis, but there are a limited amount of individual and group reservation sites. Up to two dogs are allowed per campsite. Dogs are also allowed on miles of hiking trails and in the water. Pets need to be leashed and please clean up after them. There is a $2 per night pet fee.

Oceano

Pacific Dunes RV Resort
1025 Silver Spur Place
Oceano, CA 93445
888-908-7787
Walk to the dog-friendly sand dunes and beach from this campground. Well-behaved leashed dogs are welcome in the tent sites and RV spaces. Please clean up after your pet. There is no pet fee. The RV pull through or back-in sites offer full hookups including 50 amp service, water, electric, sewer hookups, cable TV and a picnic table. Other campground amenities include a volleyball court, pool table, basketball courts, horseback riding, barbecue facilities, bicycle and walking paths, general store, laundry facilities, lighted streets, restrooms/showers, modem hookup and a clubhouse.

Paso Robles

Lake Nacimiento Campgrounds
Lake Nacimiento Drive

Paso Robles, CA
805-238-3256
This campground offers over 400 campsites and RV sites have both full or partial hook ups. Dogs are allowed around and in the lake. Be careful about letting your dog get too far into the water, as there are many boats on the lake. Pets must be on leash and attended at all times. There is a $5 per day charge for dogs. The lake is located west of Hwy 101, seventeen miles north of Paso Robles. Take the 24th Street (G-14 West) exit in Paso Robles and proceed west on G-14 to the lake.

Lake Nacimiento Resort RV and Campgrounds
10625 Nacimiento Lake Drive
Paso Robles, CA
805-238-3256
Dogs are allowed in the campgrounds, but not in the lodge. RVs are permitted and the resort offers full hookups. Dogs can swim in the lake, but be very careful of boats, as this is a popular lake for water-skiing. Proof of your dog's rabies vaccination is required.

Pismo Beach

Pismo Coast Village RV Park
165 South Dolliver Street
Pismo Beach, CA 93449
805-773-1811
This 26 acre RV park is located right on the dog-friendly Pismo State Beach. There are 400 full hookup sites each with satellite TV. RVs up to 40 feet can be accommodated. Park amenities include a general store, arcade, laundromat, guest modem access in lobby, heated pool, bicycle rentals and miniature golf course. The maximum stay is 29 consecutive nights. Well-behaved leashed dogs of all sizes are allowed, up to a maximum of three pets. People need to clean up after their pets. There is no pet fee. The campground is open all year.

San Luis Obispo

El Chorro Regional Park Campground
Highway 1
San Luis Obispo, CA
805-781-5930
This campground offers 62 campsites for tent or RV camping. Some of the RV spaces are pull through sites and can accommodate RVs up to 40 feet . Most of the sites offer full hookups with electricity, water and sewer. All sites are available on a first-come, first-served basis. Use t he self-registration envelopes upon arrival. There are

several hiking trails to choose from at this park, from hiking on meadows to walking along a creek. Dogs must be leashed at all times on the trails and in the campground. Please clean up after your pets. There is a dog park located in this regional park where your pooch can run leash free. To get to the park from Highway 101, head south and then take the Santa Rosa St. exit. Turn left on Santa Rosa which will turn into Highway 1 after Highland Drive. Continue about 5 miles and the park will be on your left, across from Cuesta College.

Santa Margarita

Santa Margarita KOA
4765 Santa Margarita Lake Road
Santa Margarita, CA 93453
805-438-5618
This campground is located near Santa Margarita Lake Regional Park which has miles of dog-friendly trails. Up to two dogs are allowed at each tent site, RV site and cabin. Pets cannot be left alone in the cabins. Well-behaved leashed dogs of all sizes are allowed. People need to clean up after their pets. There is no pet fee. Site amenities include a maximum length pull through of 35 feet and 30 amp service available. Other amenities include LP gas, an entrance gate and a seasonal swimming pool. They are open all year.

Santa Margarita Lake Regional Park Camping
off Pozo Road
Santa Margarita, CA
805-781-5930
Primitive boat-in sites are available at this park. This lake is popular for fishing, boating and hiking. Swimming is not allowed at the lake because it is a reservoir which is used for city drinking water. There is a seasonal swimming pool at the park. Hiking can be enjoyed at this park which offers miles of trails, ranging from easy to strenuous. Dogs must be leashed at all times and people need to clean up after their pets.

Attractions

Arroyo Grande

Lake Lopez Boat Rentals
6820 Lopez Drive
Arroyo Grande, CA 93420
805-489-1006
Rent a motor boat or pontoon boat on Lake Lopez and take your dog along with you. Boat rentals

start at about $35 for 2 hours and there is a $10 one time per rental pet fee. The rentals are available year-round.

Cambria

Cambria Historic Downtown
1880-2580 Main Street
Cambria, CA 93428
Burton and Bridge Streets

Cambria was settled in the early 1860s. In the 1880s it was the second largest town in the county, with an active center of shipping, mining, dairy farming, logging, and ranching. The isolation of Cambria occurred in 1894, when railroad lines were extended into San Luis Obispo from the south, resulting in the decline of coastal shipping. The town's main industry today is tourism. Cambria's Historic Downtown includes 22 historic sites which can be viewed on a self-guided walking tour with your dog. A list of the historic sites can be found at their website (http://new.cambria-online.com/historic/index.asp). There are a few outdoor cafes in downtown Cambria where you and your pup can grab some lunch or dinner.

Paso Robles

Le Cuvier Winery
9750 Adelaida Road
Paso Robles, CA 93446
805-238-5706
Dogs on leash are allowed at this winery in Paso Robles wine country. Its hours are 11 am to 5 pm daily.

San Luis Obispo

San Luis Obispo Botanical Garden
Post Office Box 4957
San Luis Obispo, CA 93403
805-546-3501
This dog-friendly botanical garden is devoted to the display and study of the plants and ecosystems of the five Mediterranean-climate zones of the world: parts of California, Chile, Australia, South Africa and the countries surrounding the Mediterranean Sea. Dogs on leash are allowed. Please pick up after them. The garden is located on Highway 1 in El Chorro Regional Park, between San Luis Obispo and Morro Bay. The garden is open during daylight hours and admission is free. On the weekends, there is a dog fee for entering the regional park. There is also an off leash area for your dog to run, just up the street from the garden.

Beaches

Oceano

Oceano Dunes State Vehicular Recreation Area
Highway 1
Oceano, CA
805-473-7220
This 3,600 acre off road area offers 5 1/2 miles of beach which is open for vehicle use. Pets on leash are allowed too. Swimming, surfing, horseback riding and bird watching are all popular activities at the beach. The park is located three miles south of Pismo Beach off Highway 1.

Paso Robles

Lake Nacimento Resort Day Use Area
10625 Nacimiento Lake Drive
Paso Robles, CA
805-238-3256
In addition to the campgrounds and RV area, this resort also offers day use of the lake. Dogs can swim in the water, but be very careful of boats, as this is a popular lake for water-skiing. Day use fees vary by season and location, but in general rates are about $5 to $8 per person. Senior discounts are available. Dogs are an extra $5 per day. Proof of your dog's rabies vaccination is required.

Pismo Beach

Pismo State Beach
Grand Ave.
Pismo Beach, CA
Hwy 1
805-489-2684

Leashed dogs are allowed on this state beach. This beach is popular for walking, sunbathing, swimming and the annual winter migration of millions of monarch butterflies (the park has the largest over-wintering colony of monarch butterflies in the U.S.). To get there from Hwy 101, exit 4th Street and head south. In about a mile, turn right onto Grand Ave. You can park along the road.

San Simeon

Coastal Access
off Hearst Drive
San Simeon, CA 93452

There is parking just north of the Best Western Hotel, next to the "Coastal Access" sign. Dogs must be on leash.

Parks

Arroyo Grande

Lake Lopez Recreation Area
6820 Lopez Drive
Arroyo Grande, CA 93420
805-781-5930
This lake has 22 miles of shoreline and is a popular place for fishing, camping, boating, sailing, water skiing, canoeing, birdwatching and hiking. There are miles of hiking trails, ranging from easy to strenuous. The marina allows dogs on their boat rentals for an extra $10 fee. Dogs must be leashed at all times and people need to clean up after their pets.

Atascadero

Heilmann Regional Park
Cortez Avenue
Atascadero, CA
805-781-5930
This park offers hiking trails, tennis courts and a disc golf course. The Blue Oak trail is 1.3 miles and is an easy multi-use trail. The Jim Green trail is 1.7 miles multi-use trail that is rated moderate. Dogs must be leashed at all times and people need to clean up after their pets.

Bradley

Lake San Antonio
2610 San Antonio Road
Bradley, CA 93426
805-472-2311
This park offers a variety of activities including boating, swimming, fishing and miles of hiking trails. Dogs are allowed on the trails and in the water. This park also offers dog-friendly campgrounds. Pets need to be leashed and please clean up after them. There is a $6 day use fee per vehicle.

Paso Robles

Lake Nacimiento
Lake Nacimiento Drive
Paso Robles, CA
805-238-3256
There are approximately 170 miles of tree lined shoreline at this lake. This is a popular lake for boating and fishing. It is the only lake in California that is stocked with White Bass fish. There is also a good population of largemouth and smallmouth bass. The lake offers over 400 campsites and RV sites have both full or partial hook ups. Dogs are allowed around and in the lake. They must be on leash and attended at all times. There is a $5 per day charge for dogs. The lake is located west of Hwy 101, seventeen miles north of Paso Robles. Take the 24th Street (G-14 West) exit in Paso Robles and proceed west on G-14 to the lake.

San Luis Obispo

El Chorro Regional Park and Dog Park
Hwy 1
San Luis Obispo, CA
near Cuesta College
805-781-5930
This regional park offers hiking trails, a botanical garden, volleyball courts, softball fields, campground and a designated off-leash dog park. The hiking trails offer scenic views on Eagle Rock and a cool creek walk along Dairy Creek. The Eagle Rock trail is about .7 miles and is rated strenuous. There are two other trails including Dairy Creek that are about 1 to 2 miles long and rated easy. Dogs must be on leash at all times, except in the dog park. To get to the park from Highway 101, head south and then take the Santa Rosa St. exit. Turn left on Santa Rosa which will turn into Highway 1 after Highland Drive. Continue about 5 miles and the park will be on your left, across from Cuesta College.

Santa Margarita

Santa Margarita Lake Regional Park
off Pozo Road
Santa Margarita, CA
805-781-5930
This lake is popular for fishing, boating and hiking. Swimming is not allowed at the lake because it is a reservoir which is used for city drinking water. There is a seasonal swimming pool at the park. Hiking can be enjoyed at this park which offers miles of trails, ranging from easy to strenuous. Dogs must be leashed at all times and people need to clean up after their pets.

Restaurants

Arroyo Grande

Baja Fresh Mexican Grill
929 Rancho Pkwy
Arroyo Grande, CA
805-474-8900
This Mexican restaurant is open for lunch and dinner. They use fresh ingredients and making their salsa and beans daily. Some of the items on their menu include Enchiladas, Burritos, Tacos Salads, Quesadillas, Nachos, Chicken, Steak and more. Well-behaved leashed dogs are allowed at the outdoor tables.

Branch Street Deli
203 E. Branch St

Arroyo Grande, CA 93420
805-489-9099
This deli allows well-behaved dogs at the outdoor tables.

Old Village Grill
101 E. Branch St
Arroyo Grande, CA 93420
805-489-4915
This restaurant has several outdoor dog-friendly tables.

Cambria

Cambria Courtyard Deli
604 Main Street
Cambria, CA 93428
805-927-3833
Dogs are welcome in the outdoor garden patio. Located in the village of Cambria, this deli offers a variety of cold and hot sandwiches, salads, soups, smoothies and fresh squeezed juices. Try one of the sandwiches like the Mother Nature Veggie, Italian Sub, Big Sur Tuna Avocado, Chicken, Roast Beef or Black Bean Veggie Burger. They are open 7 days a week. Monday through Thursday and on Sunday, they are open from 10:30 to 4pm. On Friday and Saturday they are open from 10:30am to 6pm. Well-behaved leashed dogs are welcome at the outdoor tables.

Mustache Pete's
4090 Burton Drive
Cambria, CA 93428
805-927-8589
Dogs are allowed at the outdoor eating area, which has heaters and a roof. They have been known to bring a bowl of water for the pup as well.

Paso Robles

Chubby Chandler's Pizza
1304 Railroad St.
Paso Robles, CA 93446
805-239-2141
You and your pup can order some pizza from the outdoor window and then enjoy it at one of their outdoor picnic tables.

Good Ol' Burgers
1145 24th Street
Paso Robles, CA 93446
805-238-0655
Dogs are allowed at the outdoor tables on the grass and at the side of the building. Your pup will help you enjoy the burgers or the delicious steak sandwich. There is also a little tree house next to the tables for kids to enjoy.

San Luis Obispo

Baja Fresh Mexican Grill
1085 Higuera Street
San Luis Obispo, CA
805-544-5450
This Mexican restaurant is open for lunch and dinner. They use fresh ingredients and making their salsa and beans daily. Some of the items on their menu include Enchiladas, Burritos, Tacos Salads, Quesadillas, Nachos, Chicken, Steak and more. Well-behaved leashed dogs are allowed at the outdoor tables.

Firestone Bar & Grill
1001 Higuera St
San Luis Obispo, CA 93401
805-783-1001
Located in downtown San Luis Obispo, this restaurant serves American food and Firestone beer like the Double Barrel Ale and Windsor Pale Ale. If it gets a little chilly outside, there are outdoor heaters. Leashed dogs are allowed to accompany their people at the outdoor tables.

Mo's Smokehouse
970 Higuera Street
San Luis Obispo, CA
805-544-6193
This authentic hickory-smoked barbecue restaurant serves pork, chicken, turkey and beef. They also have a variety of side orders including onion rings, fires, coleslaw and potato salad. Well-behaved leashed dogs are allowed at the sidewalk tables.

Pizza Solo
891 Higuera Street
San Luis Obispo, CA
805-544-8786
This restaurant serves gourmet pizzas plus a variety of salads and sandwiches including several chicken and vegetarian sandwiches. Well-behaved leashed dogs are allowed at the

courtyard tables.

San Simeon

San Simeon Restaurant
9520 Castillo Dr.
San Simeon, CA 93452
805-927-4604
Dogs are allowed at the outdoor tables at this restaurant.

Stores

Cambria

Reigning Cats and Dogs
816 Main Street, Suite B
Cambria, CA 93428
805-927-0857
Located on the Central Coast of California, near San Luis Obispo, this store specializes in gifts, collectibles, and unique pet gifts and merchandise for both common and uncommon dog breeds. They are usually open seven days a week.

Vets and Kennels

Arroyo Grande

Central Coast Pet Emergency Clinic
1558 W Branch St
Arroyo Grande, CA 93420
Hwy 101 and Oak Park Blvd
805-489-6573
Monday - Friday 6 pm to 8 am, 24 hours on weekends.

Santa Barbara Dog Travel Guide
Accommodations

Carpinteria

Motel 6
4200 Via Real
Carpinteria, CA 93013
805-684-6921
There are no additional pet fees.

Motel 6 - South
5550 Carpinteria Ave
Carpinteria, CA 93013
805-684-8602
Dogs must never be left unattended in rooms.

Goleta

Motel 6
5897 Calle Real
Goleta, CA 93117
805-964-3696
There are no additional pet fees.

Santa Barbara

Casa Del Mar Hotel
18 Bath Street
Santa Barbara, CA 93101
805-963-4418
This popular Mediterranean-style inn is within walking distance of several restaurants, shops and parks. Amenities include a relaxing courtyard Jacuzzi and sun deck surrounded by lush gardens year round. All rooms are non-smoking and equipped with a writing desk and chair or table, telephone, color TV with remote control, and private bathroom. There is a 2 or 3 night minimum stay on the weekends. Pets are welcome. They allow up to two pets per room and there is a $10 per pet charge. Pets must never be left alone or unattended, especially in the rooms. Children under 12 are free and there is no charge for a crib. State Street, a popular shopping area, is within walking distance.

There is a $10 per day pet fee. Dogs up to 50 pounds are permitted.

Fess Parker's Doubletree Resort
633 E. Cabrillo Boulevard
Santa Barbara, CA 93103
805-564-4333
This beautiful 24 acre ocean front Spanish-style tropical resort allows your best friend in the elegant rooms. This especially pet-friendly resort includes special amenities for your best friend like a gourmet pet welcome gift at check-in and an in-room pet service menu available- this includes ground sirloin (for dogs) and seared ahi tuna (for cats). Their spa even offers pet treatments such as massages. Other hotel amenities for people include a fitness room, 24 hour room service, coin laundry, a walking path around the resort, a heated outdoor pool (dogs are not allowed in the pool area) and more. Room amenities include private patios or balconies, hairdryers, newspapers, private stocked refrigerator, modem lines and more. Room rates range from approximately $179 to $270 and up per night. There is no additional pet charge. This resort is within walking distance of several restaurants, shops and parks.

Motel 6 - Beach
443 Corona Del Mar
Santa Barbara, CA 93103
805-564-1392
There are no additional pet fees.

Motel 6 - State
3505 State St
Santa Barbara, CA 93105
805-687-5400
There are no additional pet fees.

San Ysidro Ranch
900 San Ysidro Lane
Santa Barbara, CA 93108
805-969-5046
This is an especially dog-friendly upscale resort located in Santa Barbara. They offer many dog amenities including a Privileged Pet Program doggie turn down and several miles of trails and exercise areas. Pet Massage Service is available. Choose from the Slow & Gentle Massage or the Authentic Reiki massage for your dog. Dogs are allowed in the freestanding cottages and prices start around $600 and up per night. There is a $100 per pet non-refundable cleaning fee.

Montecito Del Mar
316 W Montecito St
Santa Barbara, CA 93101
805-962-2006

Secret Garden Inn & Cottages
1908 Bath Street
Santa Barbara, CA 93101
805-687-2300
Dogs are allowed in the cabins only. There is a $50 refundable pet deposit.

Attractions

Goleta

Chumash Painted Cave State Historic Park
Painted Caves Road
Goleta, CA
805-733-3713
The drawings in this cave are from Chumash Native Americans and coastal fishermen that date back to the 1600s. Dogs are allowed but need to be leashed. Please clean up after your pets. The cave is located in a steep canyon above Santa Barbara. The site is located three miles south of the San Marcos Pass. To get there, take Highway 154 out of Santa Barbara and turn right on Painted Caves Road. The cave is on the left, about two miles up a steep narrow road. There is parking for only one or two vehicles. Trailers and RVs are not advised.

Santa Barbara

State Street Shopping Area
100-700 State Street
Santa Barbara, CA 93101
between Cabrillo & Carrillo
805-963-2202
In downtown Santa Barbara there are several popular shopping areas. One shopping area is on State Street. Two dog-friendly stores, Big Dog Sportswear and The Territory Ahead, allows dogs inside the store. Another area, an outdoor mall adjacent to State Street, is called the Paseo Nuevo Shopping Center. Here there are several outdoor retail kiosks. State Street shopping is

between the 100 and 700 block of State Street between Cabrillo Boulevard and Carrillo Street. Paseo Nuevo is around the 700 block of State Street, between Ortega Street and Canon Perdido Street.

TJ Paws Pet Wash
2601 De La Vina Street
Santa Barbara, CA 93101
Constance
805-687-8772
This self-serve pet wash can come in very handy after your pup has played around on some dirt trails or in the ocean and sand. Dogs can ruff it during the day and come back to the hotel nice and clean. At TJ Paws, you'll wash and groom your pet yourself, using their supplies and equipment. The staff at TJs will be there if any assistance is required.

Beaches

Goleta

Goleta Beach County Park
5990 Sandspit Road
Goleta, CA 93101
off Hwy 217
805-568-2460
Leashed dogs are allowed at this county beach.

The beach and park are about 1/2 mile long. There are picnic tables and a children's playground at the park. It's located near the Santa Barbara Municipal Airport in Goleta, just north of Santa Barbara. To get there, take Hwy 101 to Hwy 217 and head west. Before you reach UC Santa Barbara, there will be an exit for Goleta Beach.

Santa Barbara

Arroyo Burro Beach County Park
2981 Cliff Drive
Santa Barbara, CA 93101
near Las Positas Rd (Hwy 225)
805-967-1300
Leashed dogs are allowed at this county beach and park. The beach is about 1/2 mile long and it is adjacent to a palm-lined grassy area with picnic tables. To get to the beach from Hwy 101, exit Las Positas Rd/Hwy 225. Head south (towards the ocean). When the street ends, turn right onto Cliff Drive. The beach will be on the left.

Arroyo Burro Off-Leash Beach
Cliff Drive
Santa Barbara, CA

While dogs are not allowed off-leash at the Arroyo Burro Beach County Park (both the beach and grass area), they are allowed to run leash free on the adjacent beach. The dog beach starts east of the slough at Arroyo Burro and stretches almost to the stairs at Mesa Lane. To get to the off-leash area, walk your leashed dog from the parking lot to the beach, turn left and cross the slough. At this point you can remove your dog's leash.

Rincon Park and Beach
Bates Road
Santa Barbara, CA
Hwy 101

This beach is at Rincon Point which has some of the best surfing waves in the world. In the winter, it is very popular with surfers. In the summer, it is a popular swimming beach. Year-round, leashed dogs are welcome. The beach is about 1/2-1 mile long. Next to the parking lot there are picnic tables, phones and restrooms. The beach is in Santa Barbara County, about 15-20 minutes south of Santa Barbara. To get there from Santa Barbara, take Hwy 101 south and go past Carpinteria. Take the Bates Rd exit towards the ocean. When the road ends, turn right into the Rincon Park and Beach parking lot.

Parks

San Ysidro

Manning Park
Manning Park
San Ysidro, CA
One mile north of 101
805-969-0201
The park is open 8 am to Sunset. Dogs on leash are allowed throughout the city park.

Santa Barbara

Beach Walkway
Cabrillo Blvd.
Santa Barbara, CA 93101
between Milpas & Castillo St.

We couldn't find the official name of this paved path (it might be part of Chase Palm Park), so we are labeling it the "Beach Walkway". This path parallels the beach. While dogs are not allowed on this beach, they can walk along the paved path which has grass and lots of palm trees. There are also many public restrooms along the path. The path is about 1.5 miles long each way.

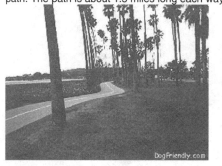

Chase Palm Park
323 E. Cabrillo Boulevard
Santa Barbara, CA 93101
Garden Street & Calle Cesar Chavez
805-564-5433
This beautiful waterfront city park opened in May 1998. It is about a mile long and has many sections including a carousel, plaza, pavilion, shipwreck playground, the wilds, fountain gateway and casa las palmas. It is on Cabrillo Blvd. between Garden Street and Calle Cesar Chavez Street.

Plaza Del Mar
129 Castillo Street
Santa Barbara, CA 93101
Cabrillo Street

This city park is about 4 blocks long and is close to several hotels and restaurants. The park is home to the Old Spanish Days Carriage Museum. While dogs are not allowed inside the museum, you can see many of the carriages from the outside.

Shoreline Park
1200 Shoreline Drive
Santa Barbara, CA 93101
northwest of Leadbetter Beach

This 1/2 mile paved path winds along the headlands and provides scenic overlooks of Santa Barbara and the ocean. It is located northwest of Leadbetter Beach and Santa Barbara City College.

Restaurants

Carpinteria

Tony's Italian Dinners and BBQ Ribs
699 Linden Ave
Carpinteria, CA 93013
805-684-3413
Dogs must be on leash while on the premises.
Dogs are allowed at the outdoor tables.

Goleta

Baja Fresh Mexican Grill
7127 Hollister Ave.
Goleta, CA
805-685-9988
This Mexican restaurant is open for lunch and
dinner. They use fresh ingredients and making
their salsa and beans daily. Some of the items on
their menu include Enchiladas, Burritos, Tacos
Salads, Quesadillas, Nachos, Chicken, Steak and
more. Well-behaved leashed dogs are allowed at
the outdoor tables.

Quizno's Subs
5723 Calle Real
Goleta, CA 93117

805-683-3122
Dogs are allowed at the outdoor tables.

Sonny's Fish Market
5722 Calle Real
Goleta, CA 93117
805-964-1440
Dogs are allowed at the outdoor tables.

Montecito

Tutti's Restaurant
1209 Coast Village Road
Montecito, CA
805-969-5809
Well-behaved leashed dogs are allowed at the
outdoor tables.

Santa Barbara

Baja Fresh Mexican Grill
3851 State Street
Santa Barbara, CA
805-687-9966
This Mexican restaurant is open for lunch and
dinner. They use fresh ingredients and making
their salsa and beans daily. Some of the items on
their menu include Enchiladas, Burritos, Tacos
Salads, Quesadillas, Nachos, Chicken, Steak and
more. Well-behaved leashed dogs are allowed at
the outdoor tables.

Dargan's Irish Pub
18 E. Ortega Street
Santa Barbara, CA
805-568-0702
Dogs are allowed on the outdoor patio. The pub
serves food and drinks. It's hours are 4 pm to 2
am Monday to Friday and 11:30 am to 2 am on
Saturday and Sunday.

Italian and Greek Deli
636 State Street
Santa Barbara, CA
805-962-6815
Dogs are allowed at the outdoor tables.

Jeannine's Bakery and Cafe
3607 State St
Santa Barbara, CA 93105
805-687-8701
Dogs are allowed at the outdoor tables.

Montecito Wine Bistro
1280 Coast Village Rd
Santa Barbara, CA 93108
805-969-3784

Dogs are allowed at the outdoor tables.

Summerland

The Summerland Beach Cafe
2294 Lillie Ave
Summerland, CA
805-969-1019
This restaurant comes highly recommended from one of our readers who says "It is just south of Montecito and Santa Barbara proper. The cafe was recommended by some locals and it is great. The restaurant is situated in an old house and seating extends to a wide porch around the front and side. We sat on the porch with at least 3 other pet families. They brought Willow a water bowl and 2 bones. Lucky dog."

Stores

Santa Barbara

Big Dog Sportswear Store
6 E. Yanonali Street
Santa Barbara, CA 93101
State Street
805-963-8728
This factory outlet store allows dogs inside. Big Dogs Sportswear is a Santa Barbara-based company and produces high quality, reasonably priced activewear and accessories for men, women, and children of all ages. No clothes for the pup, but the human clothes have the cool "Big Dog" logo. The store is located at the corner of State Street and Yanonali Street, across from the Amtrak station.

The Territory Ahead Store
515 State Street
Santa Barbara, CA 93101
between Haley & Cota Streets
805-962-5558 x181
The Territory Ahead was founded in 1988 and set out to create a new kind of clothing catalog that offered personality through special fabrics, distinguishing details, and easy, wearable designs. All the men's and women's clothing, as well as many of the accessory and gift items are designed in-house, to offer a collection of merchandise that can't be found anywhere else. The Territory Ahead allows well-behaved dogs inside their flagship store on State Street.

Three Dog Bakery
727 State Street
Santa Barbara, CA 93110
805-962-8220
Take your dog to this dog cookie bakery for some mouth-watering treats. The goodies will look good enough for you to eat, but remember, they are for your pup.

Vets and Kennels

Santa Barbara

CARE Hospital
301 E. Haley St.
Santa Barbara, CA 93101
805-899-2273
This 24 hour veterinary has a state-of-the-art veterinary center which offers advanced medical and surgical procedures for pets. They have a veterinarian on the premises at all times and a surgeon on call for emergency surgeries.

Pacific Emergency Pet Hospital
2963 State Street
Santa Barbara, CA 93105
805-682-5120
Monday - Friday 6 pm to 8 am, 24 hours on weekends.

Santa Maria Dog Travel Guide
Accommodations

Santa Maria

Best Western Big America
1725 North Broadway
Santa Maria, CA 93454
805-922-5200
Thanks to one of our readers for recommending this hotel. Here is what they had to say about it: "We stayed here with our Lab last month and were very pleased. There was no extra charge for our dog and it was one of the nicest rooms we have ever stayed in. The room rates are very reasonable. It's just outside the wine tasting trail for those who want a day of picnics and wine tasting." Dogs are not to be left alone in the rooms.

Motel 6
2040 N Preisker Lane
Santa Maria, CA 93454
805-928-8111
There are no additional pet fees.

Santa Nella Dog Travel Guide
Accommodations

Santa Nella

Holiday Inn Express
28976 W. Plaza Drive
Santa Nella, CA 95322
209-826-8282
There are no additional pet fees.

Motel 6
12733 S Hwy 33

Santa Nella, CA 95322
209-826-6644
There are no additional pet fees.

Ramada Inn
13070 S Hwy 33
Santa Nella, CA
209-826-4444
There is a $10 per night additional pet fee.

Solvang Dog Travel Guide
Accommodations

Buellton

Motel 6
333 McMurray Rd
Buellton, CA 93427
805-688-7797
Dogs are not to be left alone in the room.

Rodeway Inn
630 Ave of Flags
Buellton, CA 93427
805-688-0022
This motel (formerly Econo Lodge) is located about 4 miles from the village of Solvang. Amenities include cable TV and movies. Handicap accessible rooms are available. There is a $25 one time pet charge.

Solvang

Royal Copenhagen Inn
1579 Mission Drive
Solvang, CA 93463
800-624-6604
This inn is located in the heart of the Solvang village. Walk to dog-friendly restaurants, stores and parks. Well-behaved dogs are allowed. There is no pet fee.

Accommodations - RV Parks and Campgrounds

Buellton

Flying Flags RV Park and Campground
180 Avenue of the Flags
Buellton, CA 93427
805-688-3716
There are no additional pet fees.

Attractions

Santa Ynez

LinCourt Vineyards
343 North Refugio Rd
Santa Ynez, CA 93460
805-688-8381
Dogs are allowed at the outdoor picnic tables.

Solvang

Buttonwood Farm Winery
1500 Alamo Pintado Rd
Solvang, CA 93463
805-688-3032

Solvang Horsedrawn Streetcars
P.O. Box 531

Solvang, CA 93464
805-686-0022
When this streetcar is not too crowed, your well-behaved dog is welcome. They offer a twenty minute guided tour of the beautiful Danish village of Solvang. The tour costs less than $5 per person. Prices are subject to change. The tour starts on Copenhagen Drive, opposite the Blue Windmill.

Solvang Village
1500-2000 Mission Drive
Solvang, CA 93463
800-468-6765
As the Solvang Visitor's Bureau states, "Visiting Danes have described Solvang as 'more like Denmark than Denmark' - a remarkable tribute to the town's passion for Danish architecture, cuisine and customs." Solvang is a quaint shopping village and a great place to walk with your dog. Several stores along Mission Drive are dog-friendly like The Book Loft and Lemo's Feed & Pet Supply (please always verify that stores are dog-friendly by asking the clerk before entering). There are also many dog-friendly restaurants in town including bakeries that have mouth watering goodies. Sunset Magazine recently voted Solvang as one of the '10 Most Beautiful Small Towns' in the Western United States.

Parks

Santa Ynez

Santa Ynez Recreation Area
Paradise Road
Santa Ynez, CA
805-967-3481
Dogs on leash are allowed on the nature trails and hikes. There are miles of trails at this park. Other activities include swimming and fishing. This recreation area is actually part of the Los Padres National Forest. From Highway l0l at west

end of Santa Barbara, turn north on Highway 154 (San Marcos Pass Road) for about10- 12 miles, then go east on Paradise Road to the Santa Ynez Recreation Area.

Solvang

Hans Christian Anderson Park
Atterdag Road
Solvang, CA 93463
3 blocks n. of Mission Dr.

You and your leashed pup can enjoy a 1.3 mile round trip hike along meadows lined with majestic oak trees. This park's 50 acres also has picnic facilities, a playground for kids and tennis courts. It is open daily from 8 a.m. to dusk. The park is located within walking distance of the village. It on Atterdag Road, just 3 blocks north of Mission Drive and the village of Solvang.

Solvang Park
Mission Drive
Solvang, CA 93463
corner of First Street

This small city park is located in the middle of the Solvang village. It is a nice spot to rest after walking around town. It is located on Mission Drive at the corner of First Street.

Nojoqui Falls Park
Alisal Road
Solvang, CA 93463
7 m. south of Solvang

Nojoqui Falls is a 160+ foot waterfall which towers over the park grounds. It is best viewed after a rainy period. You and your leashed pup can view the waterfall by embarking on an easy 10 minute hike through a wooded canyon. This park also has a sports playing field, playgrounds for kids, and a picnic area. The park is open every day from dawn to dusk. It is located on Alisal Road, just 7 miles south of Solvang on a country road.

Restaurants

Los Olivos

Los Olivos Cafe
2879 Grand Ave
Los Olivos, CA 93441
805-688-7265
Dogs are allowed at the outdoor tables.

Solvang

Bit O'Denmark
473 Alisal Rd.
Solvang, CA 93463
805-688-5426
This restaurant allows 1 dog per table (maybe 2, depending on how many other dogs are there).

They are open from 9:30am until 9pm.

El Rancho Coffee Cafe
1680 Mission Drive
Solvang, CA 93463
805-686-9770
Dogs are also welcome in the attached
bookstore, the Book Loft. Dogs are allowed at the
outdoor tables.

Giovanni's Italian Restaurant
1988 Old Mission Drive
Solvang, CA 93463
805-688-1888
This pizza place is located about one mile outside
of the village. To get there, head east on Mission
Drive/Hwy 246 and it will be on the left. They are
open from 11am until 9:30pm. On Friday and
Saturday, they are open until 10:30pm.

Greenhouse Cafe
487 Atterdag Road
Solvang, CA 93463
805-688-8408
Dogs are allowed on the side patios only, not the
front patio.

Heidelberg Inn Restaurant
1618 Copenhagen Drive
Solvang, CA 93463
805-688-6213
Dogs are allowed at the outdoor tables.

Manny's Mexican Restaurant
444 Atterdag Road
Solvang, CA 93463
805-688-3743
Dogs are allowed at the outdoor tables.

McConnell's Ice Cream
1588 Mission Drive
Solvang, CA 93463
805-688-9880
They are open daily from 11am until 9pm.

New Danish Inn
1547 Mission Dr
Solvang, CA 93463
805-688-4311
Dogs are allowed at the outdoor tables.

Olsen's Danish Village Bakery
1529 Mission Drive
Solvang, CA 93463
805-688-6314
The bakery is open from 7:30am until 6pm.

River Grill at The Alisal
150 Alisal Rd
Solvang, CA 93463
805-688-7784
The River Grille has a nice outdoor patio for you and your well-behaved pup to watch the golf course. But beware of stray golf balls.

Subway
1641 Mission Dr
Solvang, CA 93463
805-688-7650
Dogs are allowed at the outdoor tables.

Panino
475 First Street
Solvang, CA 93463
805-688-0608
One well-behaved dog is okay at the outdoor tables.

Sushi Q's Japanese Restaurant
443 2nd Street
Solvang, CA 93463
805-693-0437
Dogs are allowed at the outdoor tables.

The Belgian Cafe
1671 Copenhagen Drive
Solvang, CA 93463
805-688-6630
They only have 1 table outside, so come early. Many people with dogs sit at this outdoor table. The table seats up to 4-5 people. The hours are from 7am until 3pm.

The Big Bopper
1510 Mission Drive
Solvang, CA 93463
805-688-6018
You and your pup can order food from the outside window. They are open from 11am until 8:30pm.

The Touch
475 First Street
Solvang, CA 93463
near Mission Drive.
805-686-0222
This dog-friendly restaurant serves American style breakfast and lunch. They serve Chinese food for dinner. The owner of this restaurant is a dog lover and has several dogs.

The Little Mermaid
1546 Mission Drive
Solvang, CA 93463
805-688-6141
They serve breakfast, lunch and dinner. The hours are from 7:30am until 9pm. The name was derived from the The Little Mermaid, which is a life-size statue of a mermaid sitting on a rock in the harbor in Denmark. It considered to be a symbol of Denmark, and several smaller copies exist around the globe, including Solvang.

Tower Pizza
436 Alisal Rd, Units C + D
Solvang, CA 93463
805-688-3036
Dogs are allowed at the outdoor tables.

Viking Garden Restaurant
446C Alisal Rd
Solvang, CA 93463
805-688-1250
Dogs are allowed at the outdoor tables.

What's Brew'n
1564 Copenhagen Dr
Solvang, CA 93463
805-688-1558
Dogs are allowed at the outdoor tables.

Stores

Solvang

Big Dog
485 Alisal Rd #D1-2
Solvang, CA 93463
805-693-0899
Your well-behaved, leashed dog may shop with
you at this Big Dog shop.

Book Loft
1680 Mission Drive
Solvang, CA 93463
805-688-6010
Your leashed, well-behaved dog can browse this
bookstore with you and sit with you at the outdoor
seats of the attached Kaffe Hus.

Lemo's Feed and Pet Supply
1511 Mission Dr
Solvang, CA 93463
805-693-8180
This feed and pet store in Solvang has some nice
treats for your dog, as well as regular dog
supplies.

Vets and Kennels

Buellton

Valley Pet Emergency Clinic
914 W Highway 246
Buellton, CA 93427
805-688-2334
Monday - Friday 8 am - 5:30 pm, Saturday 8 am -
5 pm, Closed Sunday.

Ventura - Oxnard Dog Travel Guide
Accommodations

Camarillo

Motel 6
1641 E Daily Dr
Camarillo, CA 93010
805-388-3467
Dogs may not be left alone in rooms.

Oxnard

Casa Sirena Hotel and Resort
3605 Peninsula Rd
Oxnard, CA 93035
805-985-6311
There is a $50 one time pet fee. There is an on-
site tennis court and an exercise room. Some
rooms have views of the Channel Islands Harbor.

Radisson Hotel Oxnard
600 E. Esplanade Drive
Oxnard, CA 93030
805-485-9666
There is a $50 one time pet fee. Dogs up to 50
pounds are allowed.

Residence Inn by Marriott
2101 West Vineyard Avenue

Oxnard, CA 93030
805-278-2200
Every room in this motel is a suite with a separate living area, kitchen and bedroom. Amenities include an outdoor pool, tennis court, exercise room, self service laundry and dinner delivery service from local restaurants. Room rates start at around $100. There is a non-refundable $100 pet deposit and $6 per day pet charge. They allow pets up to about 75 pounds.

Vagabond Inn
1245 N. Oxnard Blvd.
Oxnard, CA 93030
805-983-0251
Amenities at this motel include a free continental breakfast and weekday newspaper. They also have an on-site coffee shop, which might be helpful in getting food to go for the room. Pets are an additional $5 per day.

Ventura

Best Western Inn of Ventura
708 E. Thompson Blvd.
Ventura, CA 93001
805-648-3101
Amenities at this motel include an outdoor pool & hot tub, and a free continental breakfast. There is a $25 per day pet charge up to a maximum of $50

per visit.

La Quinta Inn Ventura
5818 Valentine Road
Ventura, CA
805-658-6200
Dogs of all sizes are allowed at the hotel.

Motel 6
2145 E Harbor Blvd
Ventura, CA 93001
805-643-5100
There are no additional pet fees.

Vagabond Inn
756 E. Thompson Blvd.
Ventura, CA 93001
805-648-5371
Amenities at this motel include a free continental breakfast, weekday newspaper, and heated jacuzzi. They also have an on-site coffee shop, which might be helpful in getting food to go for the room. There is a $10 per day pet fee. Dogs are allowed in a few of the non-smoking rooms.

Attractions

Oxnard

Hopper Boat Rentals

218

3600 Harbor Blvd # 368
Oxnard, CA 93035
Channel Islands Blvd.
805-382-1100
This boat rental company, located at Fisherman's Wharf in Oxnard, allows well-behaved dogs on their motor skiff boats. You and your pup can cruise the Channel Islands Harbor between the hours of 10am until dusk. The boat rentals are $45 per hour. Prices are subject to change.

Santa Barbara

Santa Barbara Botanical Garden
1212 Mission Canyon Road
Santa Barbara, CA 93101
1 mi. fr the Old Mission
805-682-4726
This beautiful botanical garden is located on 65 acres in historic Mission Canyon and they allow dogs in the garden and on the trails. This garden features over 1,000 species of rare and indigenous California plants. There are five and a half miles of scenic trails that take you through meadows and canyons, across historic Mission Dam, and along ridge-tops that offer sweeping views of the California Islands. The garden is about a 15-20 minute drive from downtown Santa Barbara.

Ventura

Albinger Archaeological Museum
113 East Main Street
Ventura, CA 93001
805-648-5823
Well-behaved dogs are allowed. This museum was once the home to five different cultures spanning 3,500 years of history. Learn about the Chumash Indians, Chinese immigrants and others who resided on the site, as well as the archaeological digs uncovered in 1974. The museum is on the National Register of Historic Places. It is open Wednesday through Sunday.

Ventura Harbor Village
1559 Spinnaker Drive
Ventura, CA 93001
Olivas Park Drive
805-644-0169
This nice seaside shopping village allows your leashed dog. While dogs are not allowed inside the stores, there are several outdoor dog-friendly restaurants (see Restaurants). During the summer weekends, the village usually has outdoor art exhibits and concerts where your pup is welcome.

Beaches

Oxnard

Hollywood Beach
various addresses
Oxnard, CA

This beach is located on the west side of the Channel Islands Harbor. The beach is 4 miles southwest of Oxnard. Dogs must be on leash and owners must clean up after their pets. Thanks to one of our readers for recommending this beach.

Oxnard Shores Beach

Harbor Blvd.
Oxnard, CA

This beach stretches for miles. If you enter at 5th Street and go north, there are no houses and very few people. Dogs must be on leash and owners must clean up after their pets. Thanks to one of our readers for recommending this beach.

Silverstrand Beach
various addresses
Oxnard, CA

This beach is located between the Channel Islands Harbor and the U.S. Naval Construction Battalion Center. The beach is 4 miles southwest of Oxnard. Dogs must be on leash and owners must clean up after their pets. Thanks to one of our readers for recommending this beach.

Parks

Ojai

Cozy Dell Trail
Highway 33
Ojai, CA

This trail offers great panoramic views of the Ojai Valley. It is about a 4 mile round trip trail and can take a couple of hours to walk. It is rated an easy to moderate trail. The trail might be a little overgrown during certain times of the year. This trail is located in the Los Padres National Forest. To get there, take Highway 33 north and go about 3.3 miles north of Ojai. The trail begins near the Friends Ranch Packing House. Park on the left side of the highway. Dogs need to be leashed.

Oxnard

Orchard Park
Geranium Place
Oxnard, CA
Camelot Way

This small city park has tennis courts and a nice playground for kids. It is located on the corner of Geranium Place and Camelot Way. Dogs must be on leash.

Ventura

Grant Park
Brakey Road
Ventura, CA 93001

The park has a few hiking trails and the Padre Serra Cross. There are some great views of the Ventura Harbor from this park. It is located about 1/2 mile north of Hwy 101, near California Street. Dogs must be on leash.

Restaurants

Camarillo

Baja Fresh Mexican Grill
1855 Daily Drive
Camarillo, CA
805-383-6884
This Mexican restaurant is open for lunch and dinner. They use fresh ingredients and making their salsa and beans daily. Some of the items on their menu include Enchiladas, Burritos, Tacos Salads, Quesadillas, Nachos, Chicken, Steak and more. Well-behaved leashed dogs are allowed at the outdoor tables.

Oak View

Avanti!
710 Ventura Avenue
Oak View, CA 93022
805-649-9001
This Italian restaurant specializes in wood-fired pizza and fresh pasta. The outdoor tables are close to the parking lot, but dogs are allowed at the outdoor tables.

Oak Pit Restaurant
820 Ventura Ave
Oak View, CA 93022
805-649-9903
Dogs are allowed at the outdoor tables.

Ojai

Antonio's Breakfast Coffee
106 S Montgomery St
Ojai, CA 93023
805-646-6353
Dogs are allowed at the outdoor tables.

Calypsos Bar & Grill
139 E Ojai Ave
Ojai, CA 93023
805-640-8001
Dogs on leash are allowed at the outdoor tables.

Deer Lodge Tavern
2261 Maricopa Hwy
Ojai, CA 93023
805-646-4256
Dogs are allowed at the outdoor tables.

Jim & Rob's Fresh Grill
535 E Ojai Ave
Ojai, CA 93023
805-640-1301
Dogs are allowed at the outdoor tables.

Pisacali
585 El Roblar
Ojai, CA 93023
805-640-3726
Dogs are allowed at the outdoor tables.

Rainbow Bridge Natural Store and Deli
211 E Matilija St
Ojai, CA 93023
805-646-6623
Dogs are allowed at the outdoor tables.

Tottenham Court
242 E. Ojai Avenue

Ojai, CA 93023
805-646-2339
Dogs are allowed at the outdoor tables in the garden patio. Lunches and teas are served at this tea room.

Oxnard

Baja Fresh Mexican Grill
2350 Vineyard Ave
Oxnard, CA
805-988-7878
This Mexican restaurant is open for lunch and dinner. They use fresh ingredients and making their salsa and beans daily. Some of the items on their menu include Enchiladas, Burritos, Tacos Salads, Quesadillas, Nachos, Chicken, Steak and more. Well-behaved leashed dogs are allowed at the outdoor tables.

Buon Appetito
2721 Victoria Ave
Oxnard, CA 93035
Channel Islands Blvd.
805-984-8437
This restaurant allow dogs at their perimeter tables. It is located on Fisherman's Wharf.

Port Hueneme

Chinese Dumpling House
575 W. Channel Islands Blvd.
Port Hueneme, CA 93041
805-985-4849
This restaurant is open from 11am until 9pm.

Manhattan Bagel
585 W Channel Islands Blvd.
Port Hueneme, CA 93041
805-984-3550
This bagel store is open for breakfast and lunch. They have several outdoor seats where you and your pup can enjoy some bagels and cream cheese.

Salsa Mexican Grill
575 W. Channel Islands Blvd.
Port Hueneme, CA 93041
805-382-0061
This restaurant serves lunch and dinner.

Ventura

Baja Fresh Mexican Grill
4726-2 Telephone Road
Ventura, CA
805-650-3535
This Mexican restaurant is open for lunch and dinner. They use fresh ingredients and making their salsa and beans daily. Some of the items on their menu include Enchiladas, Burritos, Tacos Salads, Quesadillas, Nachos, Chicken, Steak and more. Well-behaved leashed dogs are allowed at the outdoor tables.

Pelican Bay Cafe
1575 Spinnaker Dr.
Ventura, CA 93001
805-658-2228
This cafe is located in the dog-friendly Ventura Harbor Village. The cafe used to be called Lorenzoni's.

Spinnaker Seafood
1583 Spinnaker Dr.
Ventura, CA 93001
805-658-6220
This seafood restaurant is located in the dog-friendly Ventura Harbor Village.

Tony's Pizzeria

186 E Thompson Blvd
Ventura, CA 93001
805-643-8425
They welcome all dogs on a leash in the outdoor patio. People just tie their dogs right to the tables and enjoy the pizza. No dogs allowed inside but you can order from the side window. They are located one block from the beach.

Vets and Kennels

Ventura

Pet Emergency Clinic
2301 S Victoria Ave
Ventura, CA 93003
Hwy 101
805-642-8562
Monday - Friday 6 pm to 8 am, 24 hours on weekends.

Watsonville Dog Travel Guide
Accommodations

Watsonville

Best Western Inn
740 Freedom Boulevard
Watsonville, CA 95076
831-724-3367
There is a $5 per day pet charge.

Red Roof Inn
1620 West Beach Street
Watsonville, CA 95076
831-740-4520
There are no additional pet fees.

Accommodations - RV Parks and Campgrounds

Watsonville

Santa Cruz/Monterey Bay KOA
1186 San Andreas Road
Watsonville, CA 95076
831-722-0551
This 20 acre campground offers both tent and RV sites. Well-behaved leashed dogs of all sizes are allowed in the campgrounds and RV spaces, but not in the lodge or cabins. People need to clean up after their pets. There is no pet fee. The camp is located within a short drive of the dog-friendly Manresa State Beach. Site amenities include a maximum pull through length of 50 feet and 50 amp service available. Other amenities include an available pavilion/meeting room, entrance gate, LP gas, free modem dataport, swimming pool, and hot tub/sauna. They are open all year.

Parks

Watsonville

Mount Madonna

Watsonville, CA
408-842-2341
This 3,219 acre park is dominated by a redwood forest. The park offers redwood and oak forests as well as meadows. Visitors may choose from 118 drive-in and walk-in first-come, first-served campsites spread throughout four campgrounds. Each site comes equipped with a barbecue pit, food locker and picnic table. Showers (for a small fee) are also available, as well as 17 partial hook-up RV sites. Hikers have access to an extensive 20 mile trail system. Park visitors may learn about areas where Ohlone Indians hunted and harvested. A one mile self-guided nature trail winds around the ruins of cattle baron Henry Miller's summer home. White fallow deer, descendants of a pair donated by William Randolph Hearst in 1932, can be viewed in an enclosed pen. The park is located on Highway 152 (Hecker Pass Highway), ten miles west of Gilroy.

Royal Oaks Park

537 Maher Road
Watsonville, CA 95076
831-755-4895

This 122 acre park offers miles of hiking trails, a playground, picnic areas, basketball, volleyball and tennis courts. There is a $3 vehicle entrance fee during the week and a $5 fee on weekends and holidays. Dogs need to be leashed and please clean up after them.

Chapter 8

California Dog-Friendly Travel Guide
Central Valley

Bakersfield Dog Travel Guide
Accommodations

Bakersfield

Best Western Crystal Palace Inn & Suites
2620 Buck Owens Blvd.
Bakersfield, CA 93308
661-327-9651
There is a $10 per day pet charge. Dogs are
allowed in certain pet rooms.

Best Western Hill House
700 Truxton Avenue
Bakersfield, CA 93301
661-327-4064
They offer spacious guest rooms with a well-lit
workspace, refrigerator in all rooms, free cable
television, free locals and more. There is a $10
per day pet charge.

Doubletree Hotel
3100 Camino Del Rio Ct
Bakersfield, CA
661-323-7111
There is a $15 per day additional pet fee.

La Quinta Inn Bakersfield
3232 Riverside Drive
Bakersfield, CA
661-325-7400
Dogs of all sizes are allowed at the hotel.

Motel 6
1350 Easton Dr
Bakersfield, CA 93309
661-327-1686
Pets are not to be left alone in the room.

Days Hotel and Golf
4500 Buck Owens Blvd
Bakersfield, CA 93308
661-324-5555
There is a $20 one time pet fee.

Motel 6
8223 E Brundage Lane
Bakersfield, CA 93307
661-366-7231
There are no additional pet fees.

Motel 6
5241 Olive Tree Ct
Bakersfield, CA 93308
661-392-9700
Large dogs are allowed if they are well-behaved.

Rio Bravo Resort
11200 Lake Ming Rd
Bakersfield, CA
661-872-5000
There is a $50 refundable pet deposit.

Ramada Inn
830 Wible Rd
Bakersfield, CA
661-831-1922
There is a $5 per day pet fee.

Super 8
901 Real Rd
Bakersfield, CA 93309
661-322-1012
There is a $10 refundable deposit for pets.

Residence Inn
4241 Chester Lane
Bakersfield, CA 93309
661-321-9800
$40 one time fee for a studio room, more for a larger room. There is also a $6 per day pet fee.

Accommodations - RV Parks and Campgrounds

Bakersfield

Orange Grove RV Park
1452 South Edison Road
Bakersfield, CA 93307
661-366-4662
This RV park is on a 40 acre orange grove, about
eight miles east of Highway 99. Site amenities
include pull through sites and 50 amp full utility
hookups. Other amenities include a rig and car
wash, a children's playground, oranges available
from December through March, a swimming pool,
laundry facilities, propane, TV/group meeting
room and a country store. Well-behaved leashed
dogs are welcome. They have a special pet walk
area and there are no pet fees. Please clean up
after your pet.

Shafter

Bakersfield KOA
5101 E Lerdo Highway
Shafter, CA 93263
661-399-3107
RV spaces and grassy tent sites are available at
this campground. RV site amenities include a
maximum length pull through of 70 feet and 50
amp service. Other campground amenities
include a seasonal swimming pool, modem
dataport, LP gas. Gas stations and 24 hour
restaurants are within walking distance. Well-
behaved leashed dogs of all sizes are allowed in
the tent and RV sites, but not in the cabins.
People need to clean up after their pets. There is
no pet fee. The campground is open all year.

Parks

Bakersfield

Beach Park
Oak Street and Rosedale Hwy
Bakersfield, CA
Hwy 99 and Rosedale Hwy

This city park is a good park to take your dog
while in Bakersfield. The Kern River Parkway
paved exercise trail passes through here and
there are picnic tables and open areas. Dogs
must be on leash in the park and on the Kern
River Parkway trail.

Hart Park
Harrell Highway
Bakersfield, CA
Near Lake Ming
661-868-7000
Hart Park is 8 miles northeast of Bakersfield on
Alfred Harrell Highway. It is on 370 acres along
the Kern River. There are hiking trails and fishing.
Pets are allowed but must always be on leash.

Kern River County Park
Lake Ming Road
Bakersfield, CA
661-868-7000
This park consists of over 1,000 acres and
includes a river, a lake, campgrounds and picnic
areas. Hills surround the lake, and the Greenhorn
Mountains stretch along the eastern horizon.
Please note that Kern River currents are very
strong at times and can be extremely dangerous.
Do not leave children or dogs unattended at the
river. The park is located about10 miles northeast
of Bakersfield, off the Alfred Harrell Highway on
the Lake Ming Road exit. Dogs must be on leash.

Kern River Parkway
Oak Street and Rosedale Hwy
Bakersfield, CA
Hwy 99 and Rosedale Hwy

The Kern River Parkway trail is a paved biking, walking and running trail along the Kern River. It can be entered at many points, including Beach Park at the address listed here. The trail is about 12 miles long. Dogs on leash are permitted.

The Bluffs - Panorama Park
Panorama Drive
Bakersfield, CA

This walking and jogging trail overlooks the oil wells in the valley below. It stretches a number of miles from Bakersfield along Panorama Drive towards Lake Ming and Hart Park. There is also an exercise trail. Dogs on leash are permitted.

Restaurants

Bakersfield

Baja Fresh Mexican Grill
9660 Hageman Rd.
Bakersfield, CA
661-587-8700
This Mexican restaurant is open for lunch and dinner. They use fresh ingredients and making their salsa and beans daily. Some of the items on their menu include Enchiladas, Burritos, Tacos Salads, Quesadillas, Nachos, Chicken, Steak and more. Well-behaved leashed dogs are allowed at the outdoor tables.

Baja Fresh Mexican Grill
9000 Ming Ave.
Bakersfield, CA
661-665-2252
This Mexican restaurant is open for lunch and dinner. They use fresh ingredients and making their salsa and beans daily. Some of the items on their menu include Enchiladas, Burritos, Tacos Salads, Quesadillas, Nachos, Chicken, Steak and more. Well-behaved leashed dogs are allowed at the outdoor tables.

Black Angus
3601 Rosedale Highway
Bakersfield, CA 93308
at Hwy 99
661-324-0814
Dogs are allowed at the outdoor tables.

Cafe Med
4809 Stockdale Hwy
Bakersfield, CA 93309
661-834-4433
Dogs are allowed at the outdoor tables.

Cottage Sandwich Shoppe
1032 Truxtun Ave
Bakersfield, CA 93301
near Convention Center
661-322-4149
Well-behaved dogs are allowed at the outdoor tables.

Filling Station
1830 24th Street
Bakersfield, CA 93301
661-323-5120
This is a drive-thru and walk-thru coffee and tea outlet. During spring and summer they have outdoor seats as well.

Jamba Juice
5180 Stockdale Hwy #AB
Bakersfield, CA 93309
661-322-6722
Dogs are allowed at the outdoor tables.

Krispy Kreme Doughnuts
5300 Stockdale Hwy
Bakersfield, CA 93309
661-336-0705
Dogs are allowed at the outdoor tables.

Los Hermanos
3501 Union Ave
Bakersfield, CA 93305
661-328-1678
Dogs are allowed at the outdoor tables.

Los Hermanos
8200 Stockdale Hwy #N
Bakersfield, CA 93311
661-835-7294
Dogs are allowed at the outdoor tables.

Pizza Market
5482 California Ave
Bakersfield, CA 93309
661-861-1500
Dogs are allowed at the outdoor tables.

Mimi's Cafe
4025 California Ave
Bakersfield, CA 93309
661-326-1722
Dogs are allowed at the outdoor tables.

Plumberry's
13001 Stockdale Hwy
Bakersfield, CA 93312
661-589-8889
Dogs are allowed at the outdoor tables. They
have outdoor tables only in the spring and
summer months.

Patio Mexican Grill
13001 Stockdale Hwy
Bakersfield, CA 93312
at Allen
661-587-6280
Dogs are allowed at the outdoor tables.

Rosemary's Family Creamery
2733 F Street
Bakersfield, CA 93301
661-395-0555
Dogs are allowed at the outdoor tables. They
have outdoor tables in the spring and summer
months only.

Dogs are allowed at the outdoor tables.

Sequoia Sandwich Company
1231 18th Street
Bakersfield, CA 93301
661-323-2500
Dogs are allowed at the outdoor tables.

Sonic Drive In
1402 23rd Street
Bakersfield, CA 93301
661-324-9100
Dogs are allowed at the outdoor tables.

Sonic Drive-In
13015 Stockdale Hwy
Bakersfield, CA 93312
661-587-9400
Dogs are allowed at the outdoor tables.

Sub Station
5464 California Ave
Bakersfield, CA 93309
at Stockdale
661-323-2400
Dogs are allowed at the outdoor tables.

Subway
8346 East Brundage Lane
Bakersfield, CA 93307
661-366-3300

Tapas Mexican Restaurant
1800 Chester Ave
Bakersfield, CA 93301
north of Traxton
661-631-8540
Dogs are allowed at the outdoor tables.

The Gourmet Shoppe
4801 Stockdale Hwy
Bakersfield, CA 93309
661-834-5522
Dogs are allowed at the outdoor tables.

Village Grill
2809 F Street
Bakersfield, CA 93301
661-325-1219
Dogs are allowed at the outdoor tables in the
courtyard.

Stores

Bakersfield

Barnes and Noble Bookstore
4001 California Ave
Bakersfield, CA 93309
661-631-2575
Well-behaved and leashed or carried dogs are allowed to accompany you into the Barnes and Noble off Highway 99 at California Avenue in Bakersfield.

Vets and Kennels

Bakersfield

Kern Animal Emergency Clinic
4300 Easton Dr #1
Bakersfield, CA 93309
661-322-6019
Monday - Friday 5:30 pm to 8 am, Noon Saturday to 8 am Monday.

Berry Creek Dog Travel Guide
Accommodations

Berry Creek

Lake Oroville Bed and Breakfast
240 Sunday Drive
Berry Creek, CA 95916
530-589-0700
Dogs are welcome, but should be okay around other dogs. The owner has dogs and cats on the premises. There is a $10 per day pet fee. Children are also welcome.

Parks

Berry Creek

Bald Mountain Trail
Road #57
Berry Creek, CA
530-534-6500
This trail is located in the Plumas National Forest and is a short one way .5 mile hike through the forest to impressive rock formations. The elevation ranges from 3100 feet to 3270 feet. Big Bald Rock provides great views of Oroville Lake and the Sacramento Valley. The trail is usually open for hiking from February to December, weather permitting. Dogs on leash or off-leash but under direct voice control are allowed. Please clean up after your pets. To get there from Oroville, take Highway 162 east. Drive for about 17-18 miles and turn right onto Bald Rock Road. Drive for about 5.8 on the gravel road. Then turn left at the Big Bald Rock turn-off and go .1 miles.

Brownsville Dog Travel Guide
Parks

Brownsville

Lakeshore Trail
off La Porte Road
Brownsville, CA 530-534-6500

This trail is located in the Plumas National Forest and is an easy but long 13.5 mile hike around the Little Grass Valley Reservoir. The trail is at a 5,100 foot elevation and is heavily used by hikers. In some areas the trail becomes a walk along the beach. Dogs on leash are allowed on the trail and in the water. The trail is usually open for hiking from early June to early September, weather permitting. Please clean up after your pets. To get there from Oroville, take Highway 162 east. Drive for about 7 miles and then turn right onto Forbestown Road (Challenge Cut-Off). Drive 16.6 miles and then turn left on La Porte Road. Go

27.4 miles and then make a right at Road #57 (South Fork Rec Area).

Buttonwillow Dog Travel Guide
Accommodations

Buttonwillow

Motel 6
20638 Tracy Ave
Buttonwillow, CA 93206
661-764-5153
There are no additional pet fees.

Super 8
20681 Tracy Ave
Buttonwillow, CA 93206
661-764-5117
There are no additional pet fees.

Chowchilla Dog Travel Guide
Accommodations

Chowchilla

Days Inn
Hwy 99 & Robertson Blvd
Chowchilla, CA
559-665-4821
There is a $5 per day additional pet fee.

Clear Lake Dog Travel Guide
Accommodations - RV Parks and Campgrounds

Clearlake Oaks

Island RV Park
12840 Island Drive
Clearlake Oaks, CA 95423
707-998-3940
Located on a small island in Clear Lake, this RV park offers 30 full hookup sites and 4 tent sites. Amenities include laundry facilities, boat ramps and docks and hot showers. Well-behaved leashed dogs are allowed. Please clean up after them. The RV park is located .25 miles off State Route 20 on Island Drive. You will cross a bridge to get to the island. They do not accept credit cards.

Kelseyville

Clear Lake State Park Campgrounds
Soda Bay Road

Kelseyville, CA
707-279-4293
This park offers 149 campsites for RV or tent camping. There are no hookups. Amenities include picnic tables, restrooms, showers and grills. While dogs are not allowed on the trails or the swimming beaches at this park, they are allowed in the campgrounds and in the water at non-designated swim areas. One of the non-designated swim beaches is located between campgrounds 57 and 58. Pets must be on leash and please clean up after them. The park is located is 3.5 miles northeast of Kelseyville.

Parks

Kelseyville

Clear Lake State Park
Soda Bay Road
Kelseyville, CA
707-279-4293
While dogs are not allowed on the trails or the swimming beaches at this park, they are allowed in the campgrounds and in the water at non-designated swim areas. One of the non-designated swim beaches is located between campgrounds 57 and 58. Pets must be on leash and please clean up after them. The park is located is 3.5 miles northeast of Kelseyville.

Coalinga Dog Travel Guide
Accommodations

Coalinga

Motel 6
25008 W Dorris Ave
Coalinga, CA 93210
559-935-1536
There are no additional pet fees.

Pleasant Valley Inn
25278 W Doris St
Coalinga, CA
559-935-2063
There is a $5 per day additional pet fee.

Davis Dog Travel Guide
Accommodations

Davis

Best Western University Lodge
123 B Street

Davis, CA 95616
530-756-7890
There is no additional pet charge.

Econo Lodge
221 D Street
Davis, CA 95616
530-756-1040
There are no additional pet fees.

Howard Johnson Hotel
4100 Chiles Road
Davis, CA 95616
530-792-0800
Dogs of all sizes are welcome. There is a $10 per day pet fee. They have one non-smoking pet room, but cannot guarantee it will be available.

Motel 6
4835 Chiles Rd.
Davis, CA 95616
530-753-3777
There are no additional pet fees.

University Inn Bed and Breakfast
340 A Street
Davis, CA 95616
530-756-8648
All rooms are non-smoking. There are no pet fees. Children are also allowed.

University Park Inn & Suites
1111 Richards Blvd.
Davis, CA 95616
530-756-0910
Located within walking distance of downtown Davis. They have one pet room available and there is a $10 per night pet charge.

Davis

Cemetery Dog Run Park
Poleline Rd at East 8th
Davis, CA

Dogs are allowed on the east side of the cemetery over the small hill. Here three sides are fenced but the other side is open but not to heavy traffic. All other off-leash parks in Davis are entirely open and not fenced. Your dog should be well-behaved and reliably able to come when called to use this off leash park.

Community Park
1405 F Street
Davis, CA
14th Street

Dogs on leash are permitted in this and most parks in Davis. The park is 28 acres in size.

Restaurants

Davis

Ben & Jerry's
500 1st St #9
Davis, CA
530-756-5964
This Ben & Jerry's Ice Cream is at the Davis Common in Downtown. Dogs are allowed at the outdoor tables.

Bruegger's Bagels
206 F Street
Davis, CA
530-753-6770
This bagel shop is in downtown Davis. Dogs are allowed at the outdoor tables.

Chico's Tecate Grill
425 2nd Street
Davis, CA
530-750-2252
This Mexican restaurant is located in downtown Davis. Dogs are allowed at the outdoor tables.

Jamba Juice
500 1st Street #3
Davis, CA
530-757-8499
This Juice Bar is located at the Davis Common in downtown. Dogs are allowed at the outdoor tables.

Mishka's
514 2nd Street
Davis, CA
530-759-0811
Dogs are allowed at the outdoor tables.

Redrum
978 Olive Drive
Davis, CA 95616
Richards Blvd.
530-756-2142
This burger place is a local favorite in this college town (the original name was Murder Burger and the new name is Redrum Burger). They serve

regular hamburgers and ostrich burgers, chicken sandwiches, shakes and more. You can order with your pup from the outside window. Then enjoy the food at the covered seating next to the building or under a large shade tree in the back. To get there from Sacramento, take Hwy 80 south and exit Richards Blvd. Turn right onto Richards Blvd. Then turn left onto Olive Drive.

Steve's Place Pizza, Pasta & Grill
314 F Street
Davis, CA
530-758-2800
Steve's Place has a nice outdoor seating area for you and your leashed dog.

Subway
4748 Chiles Rd
Davis, CA 95616
530-753-2141
Dogs are allowed at the outdoor tables.

Stores

Davis

The Cultured Canine
231 G Street #3
Davis, CA 95616
530-753-3470

Well-behaved dogs are allowed inside this gift store.

Delano Dog Travel Guide
Accommodations

Delano

Shilo Inn
2231 Girard Street
Delano, CA 93215
661-725-7551
Your pet is welcome. Amenities include complimentary continental breakfast, in-room iron, ironing board & hair dryer, guest laundromat, seasonal outdoor pool & spa. Conveniently located between Fresno & Bakersfield off Highway 99.

Dixon Dog Travel Guide
Accommodations

Dixon

Super 8
2500 Plaza Court
Dixon, CA 95620
707-678-3399
There is a $10 per day additional pet fee.

Dunnigan Dog Travel Guide
Accommodations

Dunnigan

Best Western Country
3930 County Rd. 89
Dunnigan, CA 95937
530-724-3471
Amenities include a free continental breakfast and a refrigerator in each room. There are no extra pet fees.

Fresno Dog Travel Guide
Accommodations

Fresno

Best Western Garden Court
2141 N Parkway Dr
Fresno, CA 93705
559-237-1881
Pets are welcome at this Best Western. Most rooms face a one acre courtyard. There is a $10 per day pet charge. To get there from Hwy 99 south, take the Motel Drive exit towards Clinton Ave. Turn right onto Clinton Ave and then left onto North Parkway Drive. The motel will be on the right.

Best Western Parkside Inn
1415 West Olive Avenue
Fresno, CA 93728
559-237-2086
There is a $10 per day pet charge. Large dogs are okay if they are well-behaved and leashed.

Days Inn-Parkway
1101 N Parkway Dr
Fresno, CA 93728
559-268-6211
This motel has a playground for the kids. They also have 2 two bedroom suites available. Room rates include a free breakfast. To get there from Hwy 99 south, take the Olive Ave exit. Turn right onto Olive Ave and then left onto North Parkway Drive. The motel will be on the right. There is a $5 per day additional pet fee.

Econo Lodge
445 N Parkway Dr
Fresno, CA
559-485-5019
A large well-behaved dog is okay. There is a $10 refundable pet deposit.

Holiday Inn Express and Suites
5046 N. Barcus Rd
Fresno, CA 93722
559-277-5700
There is a $20 one time pet fee per visit.

Knights Inn
3093 N Parkway Dr
Fresno, CA 93722
559-275-7766
This motel shares a lobby with the Travelodge. To get there from Hwy 99 south, take the Shields Ave exit. Then turn right onto N Parkway Drive. There is a $7 per day additional pet fee.

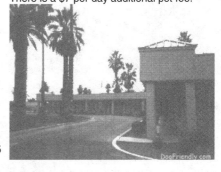

Motel 6
4245 N Blackstone Ave
Fresno, CA 93726
559-221-0800
There are no additional pet fees.

Motel 6

4080 N Blackstone Ave
Fresno, CA 93726
559-222-2431
Dogs must always be attended.

Ramada Limited
1804 W Olive Ave
Fresno, CA 93728
559-442-1082
There is a MacDonald's restaurant next door to this motel (previously a National 9 Inn). To get there from Hwy 99 south, take the Olive Ave exit. The motel will be on the right. There is a $10 per day additional pet fee.

Travelodge
3093 N Parkway Dr
Fresno, CA 93722
559-276-7745
This motel shares a lobby with the Knights Inn. There is a $10 per day pet charge. To get there from Hwy 99 south, take the Shields Ave exit. Then turn right onto N Parkway Drive.

Red Roof Inn - Hwy 99
5021 N Barcus Avenue
Fresno, CA 93722
559-276-1910
There is a $20 one time pet fee per visit.

Red Roof Inn - North
6730 Blackstone
Fresno, CA 93710
559-431-3557
If paying by cash there is a $25 refundable pet deposit.

Residence Inn by Marriott
5322 N. Diana Avenue
Fresno, CA 93710
559-222-8900
Every room at this inn is a suite. Amenities include an outdoor pool, exercise room, room service, complimentary breakfast, self-service laundry facilities and more. Room amenities include full kitchens, refrigerators, data ports, work desk with lamp and more. There is a one time non-refundable $50 pet charge and a $5 per day additional pet fee.

Parks

Fresno

Kearny Park
7160 W. Kearney Blvd
Fresno, CA 93706
7 miles W. of Fresno
559-441-0862
This park consists of over 220 green acres with a variety of trees and plants. The park features several playgrounds, picnic tables, soccer fields, and the Kearny Mansion Museum. The Kearney Mansion was the home of M. Theo Kearney. It was constructed in the early 1900s. Kearny was a key Fresno land developer and agricultural leader. He was known as the "Raisin King of California" and formed the California Raisin Growers' Association. When he passed away in 1906, he donated his entire 5000 acre estate to

the University of California. Thus 220 acres were developed into Kearny Park. Dogs on leash are allowed at the park, but not in the museum. The park is located about 7 miles west of Fresno off Kearny Road.

Roeding Park
W. Olive Avenue
Fresno, CA
Hwy 99
559-498-1551
This large city park has public tennis courts, an exercise course, BBQ and picnic areas, and playgrounds. Leashed dogs are allowed. There is a minimal fee for parking. The park entrance is on W. Olive Avenue by Hwy 99.

Woodward Park
E. Audubon Drive
Fresno, CA
N. Friant Road

Leashed dogs are allowed at this regional park. There are over 280 acres for you and your pup to explore. This park has some small hills, lakes and streams. It is located on the north side of Fresno, near Hwy 41. Take Hwy 41, exit N. Friant Rd to the right. Turn left onto Audubon and the park will be on the right.

Woodward Park Dog Park
E. Audubon Drive
Fresno, CA

Thanks to one of our readers who writes "Woodward Park now has a wonderful, enclosed area built specifically for dogs to play off-leash. It is located inside the park area and contains toys, water bowls and plastic bags."

Restaurants

Fresno

Baja Fresh Mexican Grill
7675 N. Blackstone
Fresno, CA
559-431-8811
This Mexican restaurant is open for lunch and dinner. They use fresh ingredients and making their salsa and beans daily. Some of the items on their menu include Enchiladas, Burritos, Tacos Salads, Quesadillas, Nachos, Chicken, Steak and more. Well-behaved leashed dogs are allowed at the outdoor tables.

City Cafe
5048 N Blackstone Ave
Fresno, CA 93710
W. Shaw Avenue
559-224-4399
This popular cafe serves sandwiches, salads, coffee and pastries. They are open for breakfast, lunch and dinner from 6:30am until midnight 7 days a week. They have many seats outside where your dog is welcome to join you. The cafe is located on Blackstone Avenue near Shaw Avenue.

Red Pepper Cafe
2426 Ventura Street
Fresno, CA 93721
N Street
559-485-5677
This Mexican restaurant has nice patio seating
with tropical shade umbrellas and outdoor heaters
for when it gets too chilly.

Revue News
620 E. Olive Avenue
Fresno, CA 93710
N. Echo Avenue
559-499-1844
This news stand also serves coffee and pastries.
They are open from 8am-10pm and allow dogs at
the outdoor tables. It is located on Olive Avenue
between N. Blackstone Avenue and N. Palm
Avenue.

Subway
3071 W. Shaw Ave #107
Fresno, CA 93711
559-225-6900
Dogs are allowed at the outdoor tables.

TGI Fridays
1077 E. Herndon Avenue
Fresno, CA 93710
559-435-8443
This casual dining restaurant chain allows well-
behaved leashed dogs at the outdoor tables.
Thanks to one of our readers for recommending
this restaurant.

Whole Foods Market
650 West Shaw Avenue
Fresno, CA 93711
559-241-0300
This natural food supermarket offers natural and
organic foods. Order some food from their deli
and bring it to an outdoor table where your well-
behaved leashed dog is welcome.

Vets and Kennels

Fresno

Veterinary Emergency Services
1639 N Fresno St
Fresno, CA 93703
E McKinley Ave
559-486-0520
Open 24 hours.

Gorman Dog Travel Guide
Accommodations

Gorman

Econo Lodge

49713 Gorman Post Rd
Gorman, CA 93243
661-248-6411
There is a $10 per day pet fee.

Kettleman City Dog Travel Guide
Accommodations

Kettleman City

Super 8
33415 Powers Drive
Kettleman City, CA 93239
559-386-9530
There is a $40 refundable pet deposit and a $10 per day additional pet fee.

Lathrop Dog Travel Guide
Accommodations

Lathrop

Days Inn
14750 South Harlan Rd
Lathrop, CA 95330
209-982-1959
There is a $10 per day pet fee.

Lebec Dog Travel Guide
Parks

Lebec

Fort Tejon State Historical Park
Interstate 5
Lebec, CA
661-248-6692
Fort Tejon State Historical Park is a nice stop on the Grapevine about 77 miles north of LA. Dogs on leash can roam the grounds, the historical cabins and the small museum.

Lincoln Dog Travel Guide
Parks

Lincoln

Lincoln Dog Park
Third Street
Lincoln, CA
916-624-6808
The amenities at this dog park include 2.5 fenced acres for dogs to run off-leash, potable water, handicap accessible, parking, and limited seating. The park is open from dawn to dusk and is closed

Wednesdays until 12pm. To get there, take Highway 65 (City of Lincoln) to Third Street. Go west on Third Street 1.8 miles to Santa Clara (just past the big oak tree).

Los Banos Dog Travel Guide
Accommodations

Los Banos

Days Inn
2169 East Pacheco Blvd
Los Banos, CA 93635
209-826-9690
There is a $5 per day pet fee.

Sunstar Inn
839 W. Pacheco Blvd
Los Banos, CA
209-826-3805
There is a $10 per day additional pet fee.

Lost Hills Dog Travel Guide
Accommodations

Lost Hills

Days Inn
14684 Aloma St
Lost Hills, CA
661-797-2371
There are no additional pet fees.

Motel 6
14685 Warren St
Lost Hills, CA 93249
661-797-2346
A well-behaved large dog is ok.

Accommodations - RV Parks and Campgrounds

Lost Hills

Lost Hills KOA
I-5 and Highway 46
Lost Hills, CA 93249
661-797-2719
RV spaces and grassy tent sites are available at this campground. RV site amenities include 50 amp service. Other camp amenities include a large seasonal swimming pool, playground, phone hookups, LP gas and showers. Gas stations and 24 hour restaurants are within walking distance. Well-behaved leashed dogs of

all sizes are allowed. People need to clean up after their pets. There is no pet fee. The campground is open all year.

Madera Dog Travel Guide
Accommodations

Madera

Best Western Madera Valley Inn
317 North G Street
Madera, CA 93637
559-673-5164
There is a $30 one time pet charge. If you are paying with cash, there is a $100 refundable deposit. Pets must not be left alone in rooms.

Days Inn
25327 Ave 16
Madera, CA 93637
559-674-8817
There is a $5 per day pet fee.

Super 8
1855 W. Cleveland Ave
Madera, CA 93637
559-661-1131
There is a $5 per day additional pet fee.

Merced Dog Travel Guide
Accommodations

Merced

Best Western Sequoia Inn
1213 V Street
Merced, CA 95340
209-723-3711
There is an additional $15 pet charge per stay.

Motel 6
1410 V St
Merced, CA 95340
209-384-2131
There are no additional pet fees.

Super 8
1983 E. Childs Ave
Merced, CA 95340
209-384-1303
There is a $5 per day additional pet fee.

Travelodge
1260 Yosemite Park Way
Merced, CA
209-722-6225

There is a $10 per day additional pet fee.

Vagabond Inn
1215 R Street
Merced, CA 95340
209-722-2737
There are no additional pet fees.

Modesto Dog Travel Guide
Accommodations

Modesto

Best Western Town House Lodge
909 16th Street
Modesto, CA 95354
209-524-7261
There is a $25 refundable pet deposit required.

Red Lion Hotel
1612 Sisk Rd
Modesto, CA 95359
209-521-1612
There are no additional pet fees.

Vagabond Inn
2025 W Orangeburg Ave
Modesto, CA 95350
209-577-8008
A well-behaved large dog is okay.

Restaurants

Modesto

Baja Fresh Mexican Grill
3801 Pelandale Ave
Modesto, CA
209-545-4111
This Mexican restaurant is open for lunch and dinner. They use fresh ingredients and making their salsa and beans daily. Some of the items on their menu include Enchiladas, Burritos, Tacos Salads, Quesadillas, Nachos, Chicken, Steak and more. Well-behaved leashed dogs are allowed at the outdoor tables.

Baja Fresh Mexican Grill
801 Oakdale Road Ste
Modesto, CA
209-238-0222
This Mexican restaurant is open for lunch and dinner. They use fresh ingredients and making their salsa and beans daily. Some of the items on their menu include Enchiladas, Burritos, Tacos Salads, Quesadillas, Nachos, Chicken, Steak and

more. Well-behaved leashed dogs are allowed at the outdoor tables.

Vets and Kennels

Modesto

Veterinary Medical Clinic
1800 Prescott Rd
Modesto, CA 95350
209-527-8844
Monday - Thursday 6 pm - 8 am. Friday 6 pm - Monday 8 am. 24 hours holidays.

New Cuyama Dog Travel Guide
Accommodations - RV Parks and Campgrounds

New Cuyama

Selby Campgrounds
Soda Lake Road
New Cuyama, CA
661-391-6000
Primitive camping is available at this campground which is located at the base of the Caliente Mountains and near the dog-friendly Caliente Mountain Access Trail. There are 5 picnic tables and 4 fire pits, but no shade trees. There is no garbage pickup service, electricity or drinking water. Leave vehicles along the edge of the road, do not drive to your chosen campsite. Be aware of rattlesnakes in the area. Dogs on leash are allowed. Please clean up after your dog. The campground is located off Highway 166, about 14 miles west of New Cuyama, on Soda Lake Road. There will be signs.

Parks

New Cuyama

Caliente Mountain Access Trail
Highway 166
New Cuyama, CA
661-391-6000
This trail is popular with hikers and mountain bikers. It is also used by hunters who take the trail to get access to adjacent public lands. This open space has a nice display of wildflowers in the Spring. The trailhead is located about 14 miles west of New Cuyama. The trail starts on the north side of the highway after crossing a bridge over the Cuyama River. Dogs are allowed on the trail.

Oroville Dog Travel Guide
Accommodations

Oroville

Days Inn
1745 Feather River Blvd
Oroville, CA 95965
530-533-3297
One large dog per room is okay. There is a $7 per day pet fee.

Motel 6
505 Montgomery St
Oroville, CA 95965
530-534-7653
One large dog is permitted per room. Dogs may never be left unattended.

Travelodge
580 Oroville Dam Blvd
Oroville, CA 95965
530-533-7070
There is a $40 refundable pet deposit.

Porterville Dog Travel Guide
Accommodations

Porterville

Motel 6
935 W Morton Ave
Porterville, CA 93257
559-781-7600
There are no additional pet fees.

Parks

Porterville

Sequoia National Forest
900 West Grand Avenue
Porterville, CA 93257
559-784-1500
This national forest covers hundreds of thousands of acres of land which ranges in elevation from 1,000 to 12,000 feet. Please see our listings in the Sierra Nevada Mountains region for dog-friendly hikes and campgrounds.

Sacramento Dog Travel Guide
Accommodations

Folsom

Lake Natoma Inn
702 Gold Lake Drive
Folsom, CA 95630
916-351-1500
This inn offers 120 guest rooms and 12 Lakeview Suites nestled in a wooded natural environment overlooking Lake Natoma. Enjoy over 20 miles of beautiful bike and dog-friendly walking trails along the American river. This inn is also located next to Historic Folsom. There is a $45 one time per stay pet fee and a $15 per day pet charge per pet.

Residence Inn by Marriott
2779 Prospect Park Drive
Rancho Cordova, CA 95670
916-851-1550
This hotel offers 90 spacious suites. Amenities include an indoor pool and an exercise room, a complimentary breakfast and more. There is a $50 pet fee and a $10 per day pet charge.

Residence Inn
2555 Iron Point Road
Folsom, CA 95630
916-983-7289
This extended-stay inn offers a complimentary continental breakfast and an indoor pool. There is a $100 one time per stay pet charge and a $10 per day pet fee.

North Highlands

Motel 6
4600 Watt Ave
North Highlands, CA 95660
916-973-8637
A large, well-behaved dog is okay. Dogs may not be left unattended in a room.

Rancho Cordova

Inns of America
12249 Folsom Blvd
Rancho Cordova, CA 95670
916-351-1213
This motel offers a complimentary continental breakfast. To get there from Sacramento, take Hwy 5 and exit Hazel Ave. Turn right onto Hazel. Then turn right onto Folsom Blvd. The hotel will be on the right. There is a $5 per day additional pet fee.

Roseville

Best Western Roseville Inn
220 Harding Blvd.
Roseville, CA 95678
916-782-4434
They have a pet building at this inn. There is a $10 pet charge.

Oxford Suites
130 N Sunrise Ave
Roseville, CA 95661
916-784-2222
This inn features a health club, self-service laundry, heated pool and spa, and video rentals. Each room has a separate living area, 2 phones, 2 TVs, a microwave, refrigerator and more. To get there from Hwy 80, exit Douglas Blvd. and head east. Then turn left on N Sunrise Ave. There is a $15 one time pet fee.

Canterbury Inn Hotel
1900 Canterbury Rd
Sacramento, CA 95815
916-927-0927
This inn is located about a 5-10 minute drive from Old Sacramento. Guest laundry services are available. To get there from Hwy 160, take the Leisure Lane ramp towards Canterbury Rd. Turn right onto Canterbury Rd. There is a $5 per day additional pet fee.

Sacramento

Candlewood Suites
555 Howe Ave.
Sacramento, CA 95825
916-646-1212
This hotel offers studio and one bedroom suites fully equipped with kitchens, oversized work areas and more. Amenities include a fitness center and spa. There is a $75 pet charge.

Motel 6
1254 Halyard Dr
Sacramento, CA 95691
916-372-3624
There are no additional pet fees.

Ramada Inn
2600 Auburn Blvd
Sacramento, CA 95821
916-487-7600
This inn offers complimentary continental breakfast, an exercise room and an outdoor pool. There is a $100 refundable pet deposit. To get there from Business Route 80, exit Fulton Ave and head south. Then turn left onto Auburn Blvd.

Residence Inn by Marriott
1530 Howe Ave
Sacramento, CA 95825
916-920-9111
This inn offers a complimentary continental breakfast, self service laundry facilities and a complimentary newspaper. Each guest room is a two room suite which includes hair dryers, ironing boards and data ports on phones. Fireplaces are available in some rooms. This Residence Inn charges a one-time $100 pet cleaning fee for the room. The inn is located about 1/2 mile from Howe Dog Park (see Parks). To get there from Hwy 80, exit Arden Way and head east. Turn right on Howe Ave. It is located on Howe Ave, between Arden Way and Hallmark Drive.

Sheraton Grand Sacramento Hotel
1230 J Street
Sacramento, CA 95814
916-447-1700
Dogs up to 85 pounds are allowed. Dogs may not be taken into the bar or restaurant areas. There are no additional pet fees.

Attractions

Folsom

Old Towne Folsom
Sutter St & Riley St
Folsom, CA

This few block area of Folsom represents the historic mid 1800's gold rush days. There are shops, restaurants, and places to explore. Some of the restaurants will allow your well-behaved, leashed dog at their outdoor tables.

Residence Inn by Marriott - South Natomas
2410 West El Camino Avenue
Sacramento, CA 95833
916-649-1300
This hotel offers 126 spacious suites. Amenities include an outdoor pool and an exercise room, a complimentary breakfast and more. Dinner delivery service is available from local restaurants. There is a $50 pet fee and a $6 per day pet charge.

Rancho Cordova

Nimbus Fish Hatchery
2001 Nimbus Rd
Rancho Cordova, CA 95670
near Highway 50 and Hazel

916-358-2884
There is a free self-guided tour of the fish hatchery, where salmon eggs are hatched every year. Your well-behaved dog may accompany you leashed. The hours are daily 9 am - 3 pm.

Sacramento

Capitol Park-Self-Guided Walk
10th and L Streets
Sacramento, CA
916-324-0333
At this park, you can enjoy the historic nostalgia of California's State Capitol. The Capitol Building has been the home of the California Legislature since 1869. While dogs are not allowed inside the Capitol Building, you can walk up to it and around it on the 40 acres known as Capitol Park. This park is home to a variety of different trees from around the world. There is a self-guided tour that explains the origin of the trees and plants. Squirrels are also in abundance here, so be sure to hold on to the leash if your pup likes those little creatures. Capitol Park is located in downtown Sacramento at 10th and L Streets.

Old Sacramento Historic Area
between I and L Streets
Sacramento, CA 95814
near Hwy 5 & Sacramento River

916-442-7644
Old Sacramento is a state historic park located in downtown Sacramento, next to the Sacramento River. This National Registered Landmark covers 28 acres and includes a variety of shops and restaurants (see Restaurants). Take the self-guided audio tour of Old Sacramento and learn about life in the 1860's. There are nine audio stations ($.50 per station) placed throughout Old Sacramento. The California State Railroad Museum is also located here. Dogs aren't allowed inside the museum, but there are several locomotives outside. You and your pup can investigate these large trains outside of the museum. Dogs are allowed on the horse and carriage rides located throughout town. Top Hand Ranch Carriage Rides will be more than happy to take you and your well-behaved pup on their carriages. (see Attractions). Old Sacramento is located in downtown Sacramento, between I and L Streets, and Hwy 5 and the Sacramento River. Parking garages are located at 3rd and J Streets or at Capitol Mall and Front Streets. There is a minimal fee for parking.

Top Hand Ranch Carriage Rides
Old Sacramento
Sacramento, CA 95814
J Street & 2nd Street
916-655-3444
Top Hand Ranch offers horse and carriage rides in Old Sacramento and around the State Capitol. Your pooch is welcome in the carriage. Prices are subject to change, but when we checked it cost $10 for a 15 minute ride or $30 for a 35 minute ride around Old Sacramento. If you want to tour Sacramento in style, take the horse and carriage from Old Sacramento to the State Capitol Building and back. This ride lasts about 50 minutes and costs $50. The carriage rides are available daily in Old Sacramento. The carriages are located in several spots, but the main location is at the Old Supreme Court building near J and 2nd Streets. Old Sacramento is located in downtown

Sacramento, between I and L Streets, and Hwy 5 and the Sacramento River. Parking garages are located at 3rd and J Streets or at Capitol Mall and Front Streets. There is a minimal fee for parking.

botanical garden is accessed from Antelope Rd and Rosswood. Dogs must be on leash at all times.

Parks

Carmichael

Carmichael Park and Dog Park
Fair Oaks Blvd & Grant Ave
Carmichael, CA
Grant Ave
916-485-5322
This is a one acre off leash dog park. It is located in Carmichael Park which can be accessed from Fair Oaks Blvd in Carmichael. The rest of the park is nice for picnics and other activities. Dogs must be leashed when not inside the dog park.

Citrus Heights

Rusch Community Park and Gardens
Antelope Road & Auburn Blvd
Citrus Heights, CA
Auburn Blvd

This is a nice city park with walkways, bridges and views plus a botanical garden to explore. The

Folsom

Folsom Lake State Recreation Area
various (see comments)
Folsom, CA
916-988-0205
This popular lake and recreation area is located in the Sierra Foothills. The Folsom Lake State Rec Area is approximately 18,000 acres, of which, 45% is land. Leashed dogs are allowed almost everywhere in this park except on the main beaches (there will be signs posted). But there are many other non-main beaches all around Folsom Lake where your dog is welcome. There are about 80 miles of dog-friendly trails in this park. This park is also adjacent to the American River Parkway, a 32 mile paved and dirt path, which stretches from Folsom Lake to downtown Sacramento. Folsom Lake has various entry points and can be reached via Hwy 80 or Hwy 50. It is located about 25 miles east of Sacramento. From Hwy 80, exit Douglas Blvd in Roseville and head east. From Hwy 50, exit Folsom Blvd. and head north. There is a minimal day use fee.

North Highlands

Gibson Ranch Park
Elverta Rd West of Watt Ave
North Highlands, CA
Watt Ave
916-875-6961
This park allows dogs on leash. There are a lot of dirt walking or jogging trails which must be shared with horses as this is predominantly an equestrian park. There is a lake in the center with picnic areas and fishing available.

Orangevale

Orangevale Community Park
Oak Ave & Filbert Ave
Orangevale, CA
916-988-4373
Dogs must be on leash at this city park.

Roseville

Maidu Park
Rocky Ridge Rd & Maidu Dr
Roseville, CA
916-774-5969
Dogs must be on leash in this new 152 acre park in Roseville.

Marco Dog Park
1800 Sierra Gardens Drive
Roseville, CA
Douglas Blvd.
916-774-5950
RDOG (Roseville Dog Owners Group) helped to establish this 2 acre dog park which is Roseville's first off-leash dog park. This park was named Marco Dog Park in memory of a Roseville Police Department canine named Marco who was killed in the line of duty. The park has a large grassy area with a few trees and doggie fire hydrants. It is closed on Wednesdays from dawn until 3:30pm for weekly maintenance. Like other dog parks, it may also be closed some days during the winter due to mud. To get there from Hwy 80, exit Douglas Blvd. heading east. Go about 1/2 mile and turn left on Sierra Gardens Drive. Marco Dog Park will be on the right.

Sacramento

American River Parkway
various (see comments)
Sacramento, CA
916-875-6672
The American River Parkway is a very popular recreation trail for locals and visitors. There are over 32 miles of paved and dirt paths that stretch

from Folsom Lake in the Sierra Foothills to Old Sacramento in downtown Sacramento. It is enjoyed by hikers, wildlife viewers, boaters, equestrians and bicyclists. And of course, by dogs. Dogs must be on leash. There are various starting points, like the Folsom Lake State Recreation Area in Folsom or just north of downtown Sacramento. To start just north of downtown, take Hwy 5 north of downtown and exit Richards Blvd. Turn left onto Richards Blvd. Then turn right on Jibboom Street. Take Jibboom St to the parking lot.

Howe Dog Park
2201 Cottage Way
Sacramento, CA 95825
Howe Ave
916-927-3802
Howe Dog Park is completely fenced and located in Howe Park. It has grass and several trees. To get there, take Business Route 80 and exit El Camino Ave. Head east on El Camino Ave. Turn right on Howe Ave. Howe Park will be on the left. Turn left onto Cottage Way and park in the lot. From the parking lot, the dog park is located to the right of the tennis courts.

Bannon Creek Dog Park
Bannon Creek Drive near West El Camino
Sacramento, CA
West El Camino
916-264-5200
This off leash dog park is in Bannon Creek Park. Its hours are 5am to 10 pm daily. The park is 0.6 acres in size.

Partner Park Dog Park
5699 South Land Park Drive
Sacramento, CA
916-264-5200
This dog park is located behind the Bell Cooledge Community Center. The park is 2.5 acres and its hours are 5 am to 10 pm daily. There are lights at the park.

Granite Park Dog Park
Ramona Avenue near Power Inn Rd
Sacramento, CA
916-264-5200
This dog park is in Granite Regional Park. Its hours are 5 am to 10 pm daily. It is 2 acres in size.

Restaurants

Carmichael

Bella Bru Coffee Co
5038 Fair Oaks Blvd
Carmichael, CA 95608
near Arden Way
916-485-2883
They allow dogs at their outdoor tables and may even have dog cookies for your pup.

Citrus Heights

Krispy Kreme Doughnuts
7901 Greenback Lane
Citrus Heights, CA
Sunrise
916-721-3667
Dogs are allowed at the outdoor tables.

Elk Grove

Baja Fresh Mexican Grill
7419 Laguna Blvd. Ste 220
Elk Grove, CA
916-691-2252
This Mexican restaurant is open for lunch and

dinner. They use fresh ingredients and making their salsa and beans daily. Some of the items on their menu include Enchiladas, Burritos, Tacos Salads, Quesadillas, Nachos, Chicken, Steak and more. Well-behaved leashed dogs are allowed at the outdoor tables.

Fair Oaks

Steve's Place Pizza
11711 Fair Oaks Blvd
Fair Oaks, CA 95628
Madison Ave
916-961-1800
Dogs are allowed at the outdoor tables.

Folsom

Baja Fresh Mexican Grill
1870 Prairie City Rd.
Folsom, CA
916-985-2112
This Mexican restaurant is open for lunch and dinner. They use fresh ingredients and making their salsa and beans daily. Some of the items on their menu include Enchiladas, Burritos, Tacos Salads, Quesadillas, Nachos, Chicken, Steak and more. Well-behaved leashed dogs are allowed at the outdoor tables.

Bella Bru Coffee
1115 E Bidwell St #126
Folsom, CA
916-983-4003
Dogs are allowed at the outdoor tables.

Chevy's Fresh Mex
705 Gold Lake Dr #200
Folsom, CA 95630
Old Towne Folsom
916-985-4696
Dogs are allowed at the outdoor tables.

Coffee Republic
6610 Folsom Auburn Rd
Folsom, CA 95630
Old Towne Folsom
916-987-8001
Dogs are allowed at the outdoor tables.

Lanza's Restaurant
718 Sutter St #200
Folsom, CA 95630
Old Towne Folsom
916-353-0273
Dogs are allowed in the outdoor seats in the back only, not on the front deck.

Pizzeria Classico
702 Sutter St
Folsom, CA 95630
Old Towne Folsom
916-351-1430
Outdoor seating is available during the summer months only.

Snook's Candies and Ice Cream
702 Sutter St #G
Folsom, CA 95630
Old Towne Folsom
916-985-0620
Dogs are allowed at the outdoor tables.

Yager's Tap House and Grille
727 Traders Lane
Folsom, CA 95630
Old Towne Folsom
916-985-4677
Dogs are allowed at the outdoor tables.

Granite Bay

La Bou
4110 Douglas Blvd
Granite Bay, CA 95746
Sierra College Blvd
916-791-2142

Dogs are allowed at the outdoor tables.

Rancho Cordova

The Cellar Cafe
12401 Folsom Blvd
Rancho Cordova, CA 95742
Hazel Ave
916-985-0202
Enjoy lunch or dinner at this cafe. It is located in the Nimbus Winery Center. To get there from Sacramento, take Hwy 5 east and exit Hazel Ave. Turn right on Hazel and then left on Folsom Blvd. The cafe is on the left.

Rocklin

Baja Fresh Mexican Grill
2210 Sunset Blvd.
Rocklin, CA
916-772-1600
This Mexican restaurant is open for lunch and dinner. They use fresh ingredients and making their salsa and beans daily. Some of the items on their menu include Enchiladas, Burritos, Tacos Salads, Quesadillas, Nachos, Chicken, Steak and more. Well-behaved leashed dogs are allowed at the outdoor tables.

Jasper's Giant Hamburgers
4820 Granite Dr
Rocklin, CA 95677
Rocklin Rd - Sierra Meadows Plaza
916-624-9055
Dogs are allowed at the outdoor tables.

Redrum Burger
5070 Rocklin Rd
Rocklin, CA 95677
at Sierra College
916-624-4040
Dogs are allowed at the outdoor tables.

Roseville

Baja Fresh Mexican Grill
1850 Douglas Blvd
Roseville, CA
916-773-2252
This Mexican restaurant is open for lunch and dinner. They use fresh ingredients and making their salsa and beans daily. Some of the items on their menu include Enchiladas, Burritos, Tacos Salads, Quesadillas, Nachos, Chicken, Steak and more. Well-behaved leashed dogs are allowed at the outdoor tables.

Baja Mexican Grille
1850 Douglas Blvd #512
Roseville, CA 95661
916-773-2252
Dogs are allowed at the outdoor tables.

Dos Coyotes Border Cafe
2030 Douglas Blvd #4
Roseville, CA 95661
Eureka
916-772-0775
Dogs are allowed at the outdoor tables.

Quizno's Classic Subs
1228 Galleria Blvd #130
Roseville, CA 95678
916-787-1940
Dogs are allowed at the outdoor tables.

Togo's Eatery
1825 Douglas Blvd
Roseville, CA 95661
Sierra Gardens Drive
916-782-4546
This is a fast food sandwich place. It is within walking distance of Marco Dog Park (see Sacramento Parks). To get there, take Hwy 80 and exit Douglas Blvd. east (towards Folsom). Turn left at the third street which is Sierra Gardens Drive. Then make a left turn into the parking lot. Dogs are allowed at the outdoor tables.

Sacramento

Annabelle's Pizza-Pasta
200 J Street
Sacramento, CA 94086
2rd Street
916-448-6239
Located in Old Sacramento, this restaurant allows dogs at the outdoor seating area in the back of the restaurant. There you will find several picnic tables.

Baja Fresh Mexican Grill
2100 Arden Way
Sacramento, CA
916-564-2252
This Mexican restaurant is open for lunch and dinner. They use fresh ingredients and making their salsa and beans daily. Some of the items on their menu include Enchiladas, Burritos, Tacos Salads, Quesadillas, Nachos, Chicken, Steak and more. Well-behaved leashed dogs are allowed at the outdoor tables.

Baja Fresh Mexican Grill
2600 Gateway Oaks Dr.
Sacramento, CA
916-920-5201
This Mexican restaurant is open for lunch and

dinner. They use fresh ingredients and making their salsa and beans daily. Some of the items on their menu include Enchiladas, Burritos, Tacos Salads, Quesadillas, Nachos, Chicken, Steak and more. Well-behaved leashed dogs are allowed at the outdoor tables.

Danielle's Creperie
3535 B Fair Oaks Blvd
Sacramento, CA 95864
Watt Ave
916-972-1911
The outdoor tables here are seasonal. Well-behaved dogs on leash are permitted at the outdoor tables.

Krispy Kreme Doughnuts
3409 Arden Way
Sacramento, CA
916-485-3006
Dogs are allowed at the outdoor tables.

La Bou
5420 Madison Ave
Sacramento, CA 95841
Garfield
916-349-1002
They gave our pup a dog cookie at the drive-thru. Dogs are allowed at the outdoor tables.

La Bou
10395 Rockingham Dr
Sacramento, CA 95827
at Mather Field Rd and Highway 50
916-369-7824
Dogs are allowed at the outdoor tables.

Metro Expresso
1030 K St
Sacramento, CA 95814
Downtown
916-444-8129
Dogs are allowed at the outdoor tables.

Original Pete's
2001 J Street
Sacramento, CA
916-442-6770
Thanks to one of our readers for recommending this restaurant. Well-behaved leashed dogs are allowed at the outdoor tables.

The Bread Store
1716 J Street
Sacramento, CA
916-557-1600
This sandwich shoppe allows dogs at the outdoor patio. The patio is covered.

Tony Roma's
1441 Howe Ave
Sacramento, CA 95825
Hallmark Drive
916-922-8787
This restaurant is one of the Tony Roma's U.S. chain of restaurants. It is famous for its BBQ ribs. They also serve chicken, steak, seafood and delicious desserts. You and your pup are welcome at the outdoor seats located in the front of the restaurant. To get there from Hwy 160, exit Arden Way heading east. Then turn right onto Howe Ave.

Whole Foods Market

4315 Arden Way
Sacramento, CA 95864
916-488-2800
This natural food supermarket offers natural and organic foods. Order some food from their deli and bring it to an outdoor table where your well-behaved leashed dog is welcome.

Stores

Sacramento

Home Depot
3611 Truxel Rd
Sacramento, CA 95834
916-928-0722
Your well-behaved leashed dog is allowed inside this store.

My Best Friend's Barkery
1050 Front Street #120
Sacramento, CA 95814
In Old Sacramento
916-448-3436
Your dog will be drooling over the freshly baked treats here. They are welcome to sniff around the store and pick out their favorite goodies. This store is located in Old Sacramento in the Public Market area which is next to the train tracks and along the waterfront (next to Bike Sacramento). After a trip to the bakery, wander around dog-friendly Old Sacramento or take a horse and carriage ride with your pooch.

Transportation Systems

Sacramento

RT (Rapid Transit)
Regional
Sacramento, CA
916-321-2877
Small dogs in carriers are allowed on the buses and light rail. The carrier must fit on the person's lap.

Vets and Kennels

Carmichael

Kenar Pet Resort
3633 Garfield Ave
Carmichael, CA 95608
near Whitney Ave
916-487-5221

Monday - Saturday 7 am - 6 pm, Sunday 3 pm - 6 pm pickup with extra day fee.

Fair Oaks

Greenback Pet Resort
8311 Greenback Lane
Fair Oaks, CA 95628
Overhill Rd
916-726-3400
This kennel is attached to a veterinary clinic. The kennel hours are Monday - Friday 8am to 6 pm, Saturday 8am - 5pm, Sunday 10am - 5pm.

Greenback Veterinary Hospital
8311 Greenback Lane
Fair Oaks, CA 95628
Overhill Rd
916-725-1541
There is also an on site kennel - Greenback Pet Resort. This is a 24 hour emergency veterinarian.

pool, propane, club/meeting rooms, satellite TV, restrooms, showers and handicapped access. Well-behaved leashed dogs of all sizes are allowed. People need to clean up after their pets. There is no pet fee. The campground is open all year.

Mission Farms RV Park & Campground
400 San Juan Hollister Rd.
San Juan Bautista, CA
831-623-4456
Thanks to one of our readers for recommending this campground. The camp sites are $28 per night and there is a $2 pet fee.

Roseville

Pet Emergency Center
1100 Atlantic St
Roseville, CA 95678
Hwy 80
916-632-9111
The vet is open 24 hours for emergencies.

Sacramento

Emergency Animal Clinic
9700 Business Park Dr #404
Sacramento, CA 95827
Hwy 50 and Bradshaw
916-362-3146
Monday - Saturday 9 am - 6 pm, Emergencies handled 24 hours.

Sacramento Emergency Vet Clinic
2201 El Camino Ave
Sacramento, CA 95821
Howe Ave
916-922-3425
Monday - Friday 6 pm to 8 am, 24 hours on the weekend.

San Juan Bautista Dog Travel Guide
Accommodations - RV Parks and Campgrounds

San Juan Bautista

Betabel RV Park
9664 Betabel Road
San Juan Bautista, CA 95045
831-623-2202
Located about 5 miles south of Gilroy, this RV park is set in the quiet countryside. RV sites offer full hookups with 30 or 50 amp service. Other amenities include a mini mart, seasonally heated

Selma Dog Travel Guide
Accommodations

Selma

Best Western Selma Inn
2799 Floral Avenue
Selma, CA 93622
559-891-0300
There is a $20 one time pet charge. Dogs are allowed in certain pet rooms.

Stockton Dog Travel Guide
Accommodations

Stockton

La Quinta Inn Stockton
2710 West March Lane
Stockton, CA
209-952-7800
Dogs of all sizes are allowed at the hotel.

Motel 6 - Southeast
1625 French Camp Turnpike Rd
Stockton, CA 95206
209-467-3600
There are no additional pet fees.

Motel 6 - West
817 Navy Drive
Stockton, CA 95206
209-946-0923
Dogs must be attended at all times.

Residence Inn - Stockton
March Lane & Brookside
Stockton, CA 95219
209-472-9800
There is a $60 one time pet fee and a $10 per day additional pet fee. Dogs are not allowed in the

lobby.

Travelodge
1707 Fremont St
Stockton, CA
209-466-7777
There is a $25 refundable pet deposit.

Motel 6
3810 Tracy Blvd
Tracy, CA 95376
209-836-4900
There are no additional pet fees.

Baja Fresh Mexican Grill
5350 Pacific Ave
Stockton, CA
209-477-5024
This Mexican restaurant is open for lunch and dinner. They use fresh ingredients and making their salsa and beans daily. Some of the items on their menu include Enchiladas, Burritos, Tacos Salads, Quesadillas, Nachos, Chicken, Steak and more. Well-behaved leashed dogs are allowed at the outdoor tables.

Baja Fresh Mexican Grill
1855 W. 11th Street
Tracy, CA
209-834-2252
This Mexican restaurant is open for lunch and dinner. They use fresh ingredients and making their salsa and beans daily. Some of the items on their menu include Enchiladas, Burritos, Tacos Salads, Quesadillas, Nachos, Chicken, Steak and more. Well-behaved leashed dogs are allowed at the outdoor tables.

Associated Veterinary Emergency Hospital
3008 E Hammer Lane #115
Stockton, CA 95212
209-952-8387
Monday - Friday 6 pm to 8 am, 24 hours on

weekends.

Letts Lake Complex Campground
Forest Road #17N02
Stonyford, CA
530-934-3316
This campground is located in the Mendocino National Forest and is next to a 35 acre lake. Water-based activities include non-motorized boating, trout fishing and swimming. There are 22 campsites and camp amenities include toilets, fire rings, water and trailer space. The access road and camps are suitable for 16 to 20 foot camping trailers. The campground is at an elevation of 4,500 feet and is closed in the winter. There is a $8 per day campsite fee. Prices are subject to change. Dogs on leash are allowed at the campground, on trails and in the water at non-designated swimming areas only. The camp is located 19 miles west of Stonyford.

Best Western Town and Country
1051 N Blackstone Ave
Tulare, CA 93274
559-688-7537
Dogs may not be left alone in the rooms.

Days Inn
1183 N Blackstone St
Tulare, CA 93274
559-686-0985
There is a $5 per day pet fee.

Howard Johnson Express Inn
1050 E Rankin Ave
Tulare, CA 93274
559-688-6671
There is a $6 per day pet fee.

Motel 6
1111 N Blackstone Dr
Tulare, CA 93274
559-686-6374
There are no additional pet fees.

Turlock Dog Travel Guide
Accommodations

Turlock

Best Western Orchard Inn
5025 N Golden State Blvd
Turlock, CA 95380
209-667-2827
There is a $25 one time pet fee per visit.

Motel 6
250 S Walnut Ave
Turlock, CA 95380
209-667-4100
A large well-behaved dog is okay.

Vacaville Dog Travel Guide
Accommodations

Vacaville

Residence Inn
360 Orange Dr
Vacaville, CA 95687
707-469-0300
There is a $100 one time pet fee and a $10 per
day additional pet fee.

Super 8 Motel - Vacaville
101 Allison Court
Vacaville, CA 95688
707-449-8884
$10/stay for up to 3 dogs in one room. FREE 8-
minute long distance call each night. FREE
continental breakfast. Coffee maker, night light,
clock/radio, safe in each room. Seasonal outdoor
pool. On-site guest laundry. Kids 12 & under stay
free. I-80, Monte Vista Exit to Allison Drive, then
Allison Court. Motel is behind Wendy's.

Restaurants

Vacaville

Baja Fresh Mexican Grill
150 Nut Tree Parkway
Vacaville, CA
707-446-6736
This Mexican restaurant is open for lunch and
dinner. They use fresh ingredients and making
their salsa and beans daily. Some of the items on
their menu include Enchiladas, Burritos, Tacos
Salads, Quesadillas, Nachos, Chicken, Steak and
more. Well-behaved leashed dogs are allowed at
the outdoor tables.

Visalia Dog Travel Guide
Accommodations

Visalia

Holiday Inn
9000 W. Airport Drive
Visalia, CA 93277
559-651-5000
There is a $25 one time pet fee.

Super 8
4801 W Noble Ave
Visalia, CA 93277
559-627-2885
A large well-behaved dog is okay. Sequoia
National Park is 50 miles away.

Parks

Visalia

Sunset Park
Monte Verde and Liserdra
Visalia, CA
559-713-4300
Thanks to one of our readers who writes "It is a
well kept park with plenty of friendly people and
dogs."

Westley Dog Travel Guide
Accommodations

Westley

Days Inn
7144 McCracken Rd
Westley, CA 95387
209-894-5500
There is a $10 per day additional pet fee.

Econo Lodge
7100 McCracken Rd
Westley, CA 95387
209-894-3900
There is a $10 per day pet fee.

Super 8
7115 McCracken Rd
Westley, CA 95387
209-894-3888
There is a $5 per day additional pet fee.

Williams Dog Travel Guide
Accommodations

Williams

Comfort Inn
400 C St
Williams, CA 95987
530-473-2381
There is a $5 per day pet fee.

Motel 6
455 4th Street
Williams, CA 95987
530-473-5337
A large well-behaved dog is okay.

Parks

Williams

Milk Ranch Loop

Williams, CA

This trail is 9.5 miles long and is rated moderate. Located in the Mendocino National Forest at an elevation of 5,200 feet, this trail is one of the most popular loops on Snow Mountain. The route offers dense red fir forests, meadows and a barren peak. The Milk Ranch meadow is private property, but the landowner allows horse and foot travelers to pass through on the trail. They just request that no camps be set up within the posted portion of the meadow. Pets are allowed on the trail. They must be leashed in the campground, but are allowed off-leash under voice control on the trail. Please clean up after your pets. The loop can be started at the Summit Springs Trailhead in the Mendocino National Forest. From Stonyford, take the M10 Road west for about 18 miles. Then take a Forest Service Road to the Summit Springs Trailhead.

Willows Dog Travel Guide

Accommodations

Willows

Best Western Gold Pheasant Inn
249 North Humboldt Avenue
Willows, CA 95988
530-934-4603
There is a $10 per day pet charge. Guests are responsible for any damage caused by pets.

Days Inn
475 N Humboldt Ave

Willows, CA 95988
530-934-4444
There is a $5 per day additional pet fee.

Super 8
457 Humboldt Ave
Willows, CA 95988
530-934-2871
There is a $20 refundable pet deposit.

Parks

Willows

Mendocino National Forest
825 North Humboldt Avenue
Willows, CA 95988
530-934-3316
This dog-friendly forest straddles the eastern spur of the Coastal Mountain Range in northwestern California, just a three hour drive north of San Francisco and Sacramento. The Forest is approximately 65 miles long and 35 miles across, consisting of one million acres of mountains and canyons which offer a variety of recreational opportunities including camping, hiking, backpacking, boating, fishing, hunting, nature study, photography, and off highway vehicle travel. This is the only one of California's 18 National Forests not crossed by a paved road or highway. Elevations in the forest range from 750 feet up to 8092 feet, with an average elevation of 4,000 feet. One popular area is the Lake Red Bluff Recreation Area which is located east of the city of Red Bluff in the Sacramento Valley. This area includes the Lake Red Bluff Trail (1.5 mi.), which is accessible and paved. The trail travels along the Sacramento River and through a wildlife/riparian viewing area. Popular activities at the lake include boating, water skiing, swimming, camping and fishing. The facilities include accessible restrooms with showers, a boat ramp and campground. Dogs should be leashed. For maps and more information on trails throughout this national forest, please contact the forest office in Willows.

Woodland Dog Travel Guide

Accommodations

Woodland

Motel 6
1564 Main Street
Woodland, CA 95776
530-666-6777

There are no additional pet fees.

Sacramento - Days Inn
1524 East Main Street
Woodland, CA 95776
530-666-3800
There is a $10 per day pet fee.

Yuba City Dog Travel Guide
Accommodations

Yuba City

Comfort Inn
730 Palora Ave
Yuba City, CA 95991
530-674-1592
There is a $10 per day pet fee.

Days Inn
700 N Palora Ave
Yuba City, CA 95991
530-674-1711
There is a $7 per day pet fee.

Chapter 9

California Dog-Friendly Travel Guide Los Angeles

Agoura Hills Dog Travel Guide
Attractions

Agoura Hills

Paramount Ranch
Cornell Road
Agoura Hills, CA
805-370-2301
Part of the Santa Monica National Recreation Area, Paramount Ranch is a Western Town movie set that has been used in hundreds of televisions shows and movies. Most recently the set was used to film the television show, Dr. Quinn, Medicine Woman from 1991 to 1998. You and your leashed pooch can walk around the set and explore the Western Town. Just remember the town is a movie set only so walk carefully on the boardwalks and do not lean or climb on the buildings. There are also a few trails located in this 700 acre park. The Coyote Canyon Trail is an easy .5 mile round trip which follows a small chaparral-covered canyon and climbs to a small knoll overlooking the valley. It is located on the west side of the Western Town. The Medea Creek Trail is an easy .75 mile round trip which loops through the streamside and oak woodlands. From this trail you an reach the Overlook Trail which is another .5 mile one way moderate climb. The Medea Creek Trail starts at the southern end of the parking area. To get to the park take the Ventura Freeway/101 to the Kanan exit and head south for .75 miles. Turn left onto Cornell Way and continue south for 2.5 miles to the main entrances on the right side.

Parks

Agoura Hills

Peter Strauss Ranch
Mulholland Highway
Agoura Hills, CA
805-370-2301
The Peter Strauss Trail is an easy .6 mile round trip trail which traverses through chaparral and oak trees. Dogs are allowed on the trail but must be leashed and people need to clean up after their pets. From the Ventura Freeway/101, take the Kanan exit and head south for 2.8 miles to Troutdale Rd. Turn left onto Troutdale Rd and then left on Mulholland Highway. This park is part of the Santa Monica Recreation Area.

Rocky Oaks Park
Mulholland Highway
Agoura Hills, CA
805-370-2301
This park offers an open grassland area with oak groves and small rock outcroppings. There are four trails ranging from 100 yards to just over one mile and are rated easy to moderate. Dogs are allowed on the trails but must be leashed and people need to clean up after their pets. To get there take the Ventura Freeway/101 to Kanan Road. Head south on Kanan and then turn right on Mulholland Highway. Then make a right into the parking lot. This park is part of the Santa Monica Recreation Area.

Restaurants

Agoura Hills

Adobe Cantina
29100 Agoura Rd
Agoura Hills, CA 91301
818-991-3474
Dogs are allowed at a couple of the outdoor perimeter tables at this Mexican restaurant.

Agua Dulce Dog Travel Guide
Parks

Agua Dulce

Vasquez Rocks Natural Area Park
10700 W. Escondido Canyon Rd.
Agua Dulce, CA 91350
661-268-0840
This 745 acre park is located in the high desert and offers unique geological rock formations. The park features a history trail tour of the Tatavian Indians and Spanish settlers. Dogs must be on leash and please clean up after them.

Arcadia Dog Travel Guide
Accommodations

Arcadia

Motel 6
225 Colorado Pl
Arcadia, CA 91007
626-446-2660
There are no additional pet fees.

Residence Inn - Arcadia
321 E. Huntington Dr/Gateway

Arcadia, CA 91006
626-446-6500
There is a $250 refundable deposit for pets.
There is a $50 one time pet fee and a $6 per day
additional pet fee.

Parks

Arcadia

Angeles National Forest
701 N Santa Anita Ave
Arcadia, CA 91006
626-574-1613
This national forest covers over 650,000 acres
and is known as the backyard playground to the
metropolitan area of Los Angeles. Elevations
range from 1,200 to 10,064 feet. Please see our
listings in this region for dog-friendly hikes and/or
campgrounds.

Beverly Hills Dog Travel Guide
Accommodations

Beverly Hills

Loews Beverly Hills Hotel
1224 S. Beverwil Drive
Beverly Hills, CA 90035
310-277-2800
All well-behaved dogs of any size are welcome.
This upscale hotel offers their "Loews Loves
Pets" program which includes room service for
pets, special pet treats, local dog walking routes,
and a list of nearby pet-friendly places to visit.
There are no pet fees.

Attractions

Beverly Hills

Beverly Hills Rodeo Drive Shopping District
Rodeo Drive
Beverly Hills, CA 90210

Rodeo Drive, located in Beverly Hills, is one of
the most prestigious and expensive shopping
streets in the world. This is the street where the
movie "Pretty Woman" starring Julia Roberts was
filmed. Some actors and actresses shop along
this street. Dogs are welcome to window shop
with you. Tiffany & Company is one store we
know of which allows dogs inside, at least
pooches up to about 50 pounds. Just off of Rodeo
Drive is Beverly Drive which is host to many dog-

friendly stores such as Anthropologie, Banana
Republic, Crate and Barrel, The Gap, Pottery
Barn, and Williams-Sonoma. All of these stores
allow well-behaved leashed dogs. Find more
details about these stores, including addresses,
under our Stores section. When you visit this
shopping district, please note that it is often very
crowded and it can be tough to find a parking
spot.

Hollywood Star's Homes
Self-Guided Walking Tour
Beverly Hills, CA

Want to check out the Star's homes in Beverly
Hills with your dog? How about a self-guided
walking tour of the Star's homes? All you need is
a map and a good starting point. Maps can be
purchased at many of the tourist shops on
Hollywood Blvd. A good place to begin is at the
Will Rogers Memorial Park in Beverly Hills
(between Sunset Blvd, Beverly Dr and Canon
Drive). It's a small park but still a good place for
both of you to stretch your legs before beginning
the walk. You can certainly plot out your own tour,
but we have a few samples tours that will help
you get started. TOUR 1 (approx 1 mile): From
the park and Canon Street, turn left (heading
west) onto Sunset Blvd. Turn right on Roxbury.
Cross Benedict Canyon Rd and the road
becomes Hartford Way. Take Hartford Way back
to the park. TOUR 2 (approx 3 miles): From the
park, head north on Beverly Drive and cross
Sunset Blvd. Turn right on Rexford Drive. Turn
right on Lomitas Ave and then left onto Crescent
Drive. Make a right at Elevado Ave, walk for
about 5 blocks and turn right onto Bedford Dr.
Then turn left on Lomitas Ave, right on Whittier Dr
and left on Greeway. Then turn right on Sunset
Blvd and head back to the park.

Parks

Beverly Hills

Roxbury Park
471 S. Roxbury Dr.
Beverly Hills, CA 90210
310-285-2537
This city park offers gently rolling green hills and shady areas. The park has large children's playgrounds, tennis courts and other sports courts. Dogs are allowed but must be on a 6 foot or less leash and people are required to clean up after their pets.

Restaurants

Beverly Hills

Baja Fresh Mexican Grill
475 N. Beverly Drive
Beverly Hills, CA
310-858-6690
This Mexican restaurant is open for lunch and dinner. They use fresh ingredients and making their salsa and beans daily. Some of the items on their menu include Enchiladas, Burritos, Tacos Salads, Quesadillas, Nachos, Chicken, Steak and more. Well-behaved leashed dogs are allowed at the outdoor tables.

Stores

Beverly Hills

Anthropologie
320 North Beverly Dr.
Beverly Hills, CA
310-385-7390
Thanks to one of our readers who writes "They have always been especially lovely when Hector and I go in!"

Banana Republic
357 N Beverly Drive
Beverly Hills, CA 90210
310-858-7900
This apparel store offers both mens and womens clothing as well as home collection, shoes, accessories and more. Well-behaved leashed dogs are allowed in the store.

Crate and Barrel

438 N. Beverly Drive
Beverly Hills, CA 90210
310-247-1700
Home furnishings are the focus of this store. Well-behaved leashed dogs are allowed in the store.

Pottery Barn
300 N Beverly Drive
Beverly Hills, CA 90210
310-860-9506
This store offers stylish and quality home furnishings. Well-behaved leashed dogs are allowed in the store.

The Gap
420 N Beverly Drive
Beverly Hills, CA 90210
310-274-0461
This store offers clothing for men, women and children. Well-behaved leashed dogs are allowed in the store.

Tiffany & Co.
210 N Rodeo Drive
Beverly Hills, CA 90210
310-273-8880
This store offers a selection of jewelry, gifts and accessories. Well-behaved leashed dogs up to about 50 pounds are allowed in this store.

Williams Sonoma
339 N. Beverly Drive
Beverly Hills, CA 90210
310-274-9127
This store offers cookware, cutlery, electronics, food and more. Well-behaved leashed dogs are allowed in the store.

Burbank Dog Travel Guide
Accommodations

Burbank

Hilton Burbank
2500 Hollywood Way
Burbank, CA 91505
800-840-6450
This hotel is located across from the Burbank Airport. It offers 24 hour room service, two on-site fitness centers, pools, spas and saunas. There is a $25 non-refundable pet fee.

Attractions

Burbank

Los Angeles Equestrian Center
480 Riverside Drive
Burbank, CA 91506
818-840-9066
This is a nice diversion for those pups that enjoy being around horses. Southern California's largest Equestrian Center has a covered arena where many top-rated horse shows are held throughout the year. Your dog is welcome to watch the horse shows if he or she doesn't bark and distract the horses. To see their upcoming events list, check out the official website at http://www.la-equestriancenter.com or call 818-840-9066. When there are no shows, you can still walk around on the grounds. There is a horse trail to the right of the main entrance where you can walk your dog. Or if you want to do some shopping, your dog is welcome in 1 of the 2 equestrian stores (which also has some dog treats and toys). The dog-friendly store is called Dominion Saddlery and is located behind the store that is next to the parking lot. They even have water bowls in the store for your pup.

Restaurants

Burbank

Baja Fresh Mexican Grill
877 N. San Fernando Blvd.
Burbank, CA
818-841-4649
This Mexican restaurant is open for lunch and dinner. They use fresh ingredients and making their salsa and beans daily. Some of the items on their menu include Enchiladas, Burritos, Tacos Salads, Quesadillas, Nachos, Chicken, Steak and more. Well-behaved leashed dogs are allowed at the outdoor tables.

La Bamba
2600 North Glenoaks Blvd.
Burbank, CA

818-846-3358
This Caribbean restaurant allows dogs at the outdoor tables.

The Riverside Cafe
1221 Riverside Dr
Burbank, CA
818-563-3567
This British style bistro allows dogs at its outdoor seats. It is closed Mondays. The restaurant is open for lunch and dinner on Tuesday through Friday, and for brunch, lunch and dinner on weekends. According to a reader dogs get their own bowl of water and maybe a dog bone.

Calabasas Dog Travel Guide
Parks

Calabasas

Ahmanson Ranch Park
26135 Mureau Road
Calabasas, CA
818-878-4225
This park is part of the Santa Monica Mountains Conservancy and allows leashed dogs on the trails. Please clean up after your pets. No hunting is allowed in the park. In the past, some movies have been filmed at this ranch, including Gone With The Wind. The easiest access to the trails is at the north end of Las Virgenes Road. In early 2004 there are plans to having a parking area at the end of Victory Blvd. in Woodland Hills.

Calabasas Bark Park
Las Virgines Road
Calabasas, CA
s. of Agoura Rd.

Thanks to one of our readers for recommending this dog park. It is located on Las Virgines Road, south of the Agoura Road and Las Virgines Road intersection.

Restaurants

Calabasas

Baja Fresh Mexican Grill
23697 Calabasas Parkway
Calabasas, CA
818-591-2262
This Mexican restaurant is open for lunch and dinner. They use fresh ingredients and making their salsa and beans daily. Some of the items on their menu include Enchiladas, Burritos, Tacos

Salads, Quesadillas, Nachos, Chicken, Steak and more. Well-behaved leashed dogs are allowed at the outdoor tables.

Canyon Country Dog Travel Guide
Restaurants

Canyon Country

Telly's Diner
27125 Sierra Hwy
Canyon Country, CA 91351
661-250-0444
Thanks to one of our readers who writes: "Traditional diner fare and Greek dishes. Breakfast, lunch, dinner."

Culver City Dog Travel Guide
Accommodations

Culver City

Four Points by Sheraton
5990 Green Valley Circle
Culver City, CA 90230
310-641-7740
There is a $25 one time pet fee. Dogs are allowed only on the first floor.

Restaurants

Culver City

Baja Fresh Mexican Grill
10768 Venice Blvd
Culver City, CA
310-280-0644
This Mexican restaurant is open for lunch and dinner. They use fresh ingredients and making their salsa and beans daily. Some of the items on their menu include Enchiladas, Burritos, Tacos Salads, Quesadillas, Nachos, Chicken, Steak and more. Well-behaved leashed dogs are allowed at the outdoor tables.

Vets and Kennels

Culver City

Affordable Emergency Clinic
5558 Sepulveda Blvd
Culver City, CA 90230
Jefferson Blvd
310-397-4883
9:30 am - 12 midnight 7 days a week

El Monte Dog Travel Guide
Vets and Kennels

El Monte

Emergency Pet Clinic
3254 Santa Anita Ave
El Monte, CA 91733
Hwy 10
626-579-4550
Monday - Friday 6 pm to 8 am, Noon Saturday to 8 am Monday.

El Segundo Dog Travel Guide
Parks

El Segundo

El Segundo Recreation Park
Grande Ave at Eucalyptus Dr
El Segundo, CA

This park allows dogs during all hours that the park is open, but they must be on leash at all times. Please clean up after your dogs, so the city continues to allow their presence. This park is bounded by the following streets: North by E. Pine St, South by Grande Ave, West by Eucalyptus Dr. and East by Penn St. Thanks to one of our readers for recommending this park.

Encino Dog Travel Guide
Attractions

Encino

Los Encinos State Historic Park
16756 Moorpark Street
Encino, CA 91436
by Balboa & Ventura Blvds.
818-784-4849
This park covers 5 acres and includes several historic buildings. The park contains exhibits on early California ranch life. The springs at this site attracted Native Americans for centuries. The spot later became a stagecoach stopover and a Basque sheepherder's home before construction of the rancho buildings. While dogs are not allowed inside the buildings, they are allowed to walk (leashed) on the grounds. The park is closed on Monday and Tuesday. The rest of the week, the park is open from 10am-5pm.

Oak and head north. Then turn right on Victory and the park will be on the right.

Parks

Encino

Beilenson Park Lake Balboa
6300 Balboa Blvd
Encino, CA 91316
Victory Blvd.
818-756-9743
This park consists of large grass fields, sports fields and a nice lake. There is an approximate 1 mile walk around the lake perimeter. You and your leashed pup are welcome to explore this 70+ acre park. To get there, take the Balboa Blvd exit from Hwy 101. Head north on Balboa.

Sepulveda Basin Dog Park
17550 Victory Blvd.
Encino, CA
at White Oak Road

This is a nice large 5 acre off-leash dog park with separate sections for big dogs and little dogs. Features include parking for 100 cars, an on-leash picnic area and public phones. The park is open daily - sunrise to sunset (except on Fridays, 11am to sunset) It adjacent to Balboa Park in Encino. Park heading south on Victory, just past White Oak. To get there from Hwy 101, exit White

Restaurants

Encino

Baja Fresh Mexican Grill
16542 Ventura Blvd
Encino, CA
818-907-9998
This Mexican restaurant is open for lunch and dinner. They use fresh ingredients and making their salsa and beans daily. Some of the items on their menu include Enchiladas, Burritos, Tacos Salads, Quesadillas, Nachos, Chicken, Steak and more. Well-behaved leashed dogs are allowed at the outdoor tables.

Cha Cha Cha
17499 Ventura Boulevard
Encino, CA 91316
818-789-3600
They have one outdoor table and your pooch is welcome. This restaurant serves contemporary Caribbean and California cuisine.

More Than Waffles
17200 Ventura Blvd.
Encino, CA
818-789-5937
Dogs are allowed at the outdoor tables. This restaurant is open for breakfast, lunch and dinner. In addition to their huge selection of breakfast favorites like Belgian Waffles, omelettes and pancakes, this restaurant also offers a great selection of foods for lunch and dinner.

Rubio's Restaurant
17200 Ventura Blvd
Encino, CA 91316
between Balboa & Louise
818-784-1497

This popular chain serves a variety of Mexican food like tacos, burritos and more.

Glendale Dog Travel Guide
Accommodations

Glendale

Vagabond Inn
120 W. Colorado Street
Glendale, CA 91204
Brand Ave.
818-240-1700
This motel is located near Universal Studios. Amenities include a complimentary breakfast and during the week, a free USA Today newspaper. There is a $10 per day pet fee.

Restaurants

Glendale

Whole Foods Market
826 North Glendale Avenue
Glendale, CA 91206
818-240-9350
This natural food supermarket offers natural and organic foods. Order some food from their deli and bring it to an outdoor table where your well-

behaved leashed dog is welcome.

Vets and Kennels

Glendale

Animal Emergency Clinic
831 Milford St
Glendale, CA 91203
near I-5 and 134
818-247-3973
Mon - Tues 8 am - 7 pm. Wed - Fri 8 am - 6 pm, Sat 8 am - 12 noon, Closed Sunday.

Granada Hills Dog Travel Guide
Parks

Granada Hills

O'Melveny Park
Orozco Street
Granada Hills, CA
near Balboa Blvd.

This 600+ acre park has a nice variety of single track and fire road hiking trails. The park is popular with bird watchers, mountain bikers, hikers and leashed dogs. The best way to get there is from Hwy 118. Take the Balboa Blvd. exit and head north. Go about 1.5 to 2 miles and turn left onto Orozco. Take this road to the park.

Vets and Kennels

Granada Hills

Affordable Animal Emergency Clinic
16907 San Fernando Mission
Granada Hills, CA 91344
Balboa Blvd
818-363-8143
Monday - Friday 6 pm - Midnight for

appointments, Midnight to 8 am for emergencies. Saturday 1:30 pm - Monday 8 am. You must call ahead during emergency hours after midnight.

Harbor City Dog Travel Guide
Accommodations

Harbor City

Motel 6
820 W Sepulveda Blvd
Harbor City, CA 90710
310-549-9560
There are no additional pet fees.

Irwindale Dog Travel Guide
Parks

Irwindale

Santa Fe Dam Recreation Area
15501 E. Arrow Highway
Irwindale, CA 91706
626-334-1065
This 836 acre park has a 70 acre lake which popular for sailing and fishing. The lake is stocked with bass, trout and catfish. Other park amenities include picnic areas and hiking and biking trails. Dogs are allowed on the hiking trails, but not in the lake. Pets must be leashed and people need to clean up after their pet.

Restaurants

Irwindale

Picasso's Cafe
6070 N. Irwindale Ave.
Irwindale, CA 91706
626-969-6100
The owners of this restaurant are very dog-friendly. This restaurant was one of the sponsors in the spcaLA's 1999 Petelethon. Your pup is welcome to dine with you at the outdoor tables. They serve a full breakfast and lunch. Also enjoy some great dessert from their bakery. The hours are Monday through Friday from 7am-2:30pm. To get there from the 210 Freeway, exit Irwindale and head south. Turn right at Gateway Business and Picasso's is on the corner.

La Crescenta Dog Travel Guide
Restaurants

La Crescenta

Baja Fresh Mexican Grill
2637 Foothill Blvd
La Crescenta, CA
818-541-0568
This Mexican restaurant is open for lunch and dinner. They use fresh ingredients and making their salsa and beans daily. Some of the items on their menu include Enchiladas, Burritos, Tacos Salads, Quesadillas, Nachos, Chicken, Steak and more. Well-behaved leashed dogs are allowed at the outdoor tables.

Lakeview Terrace Dog Travel Guide
Parks

Lakeview Terrace

Hansen Dam
11770 Foothill Blvd.
Lakeview Terrace, CA
Hwy 210
818-756-8190
This 1,437-acre basin has lots of hills and grassy meadows. There are several large picnic areas and firepits, and a children's play area. There wasn't much water in the lake but your leashed pup will have lots of land to roam. To get there, take Hwy 210 and exit Foothill Blvd south. The park will be on your left.

Long Beach Dog Travel Guide
Accommodations

Long Beach

Guesthouse International
5325 East Pacific Coast Highway
Long Beach, CA 90804
562-597-1341
There is a $10 one time pet fee.

Holiday Inn
2640 Lakewood Blvd
Long Beach, CA 90815
562-597-4401
Dogs are not allowed in the main tower. There is a $25 one time additional pet fee.

Beaches

Long Beach

Haute Dogs on the Beach
on the beach
Long Beach, CA
562-570-3100
Once a month, during the spring and summer months, a certain section of the beach is open to dogs. Between 300 to 450 dogs come to play leash free in the shore each time. The special once a month event is organized by a private citizen and his website is http: //www.hautedogs.org/. Take a look at his website for dates and times.

Long Beach Dog Beach Zone
between Roycroft and Argonne Avenues
Long Beach, CA 20803

This is a new three acre off-leash dog beach zone during specified hours daily. This is the only off leash beach that we are aware of in Los Angeles County and one of the few in Southern California. The hours vary by season and are 6 - 9 am & 6 - 8 pm during the summer from Memorial Day to Labor Day. During the rest of the year the hours are 6 - 9 am & 4 - 6 pm. Dogs are not permitted on the beach at any other time other than the scheduled hours. Dogs must be under visual and voice control of the owners. You can check with the website http://www.hautedogs.org for updates and additional rules about the Long Beach Dog Beach Zone.

Parks

Long Beach

Recreation Park Dog Park
7th St & Federation Dr
Long Beach, CA
562-570-3100
Licensed dogs over four months are allowed to run leash-free in this area by the casting pond. As usual with all dog parks, owners are responsible for their dogs and must supervise them at all times. The Recreation Park Dog Park is located

off 7th Street and Federation Drive behind the Casting Pond. It is open daily until 10 p.m. Thanks to one of our readers for recommending this park.

Restaurants

Long Beach

Baja Fresh Mexican Grill
5028 E. Second St
Long Beach, CA
562-434-0466
This Mexican restaurant is open for lunch and dinner. They use fresh ingredients and making their salsa and beans daily. Some of the items on their menu include Enchiladas, Burritos, Tacos Salads, Quesadillas, Nachos, Chicken, Steak and more. Well-behaved leashed dogs are allowed at the outdoor tables.

Wild Oats Natural Marketplace
6550 E. Pacific Coast Highway
Long Beach, CA 90803
562-598-8687
This full service natural food market offers both natural and organic food. You can get food from the deli and bring it to an outdoor table where your well-behaved leashed dog is welcome.

Vets and Kennels

Long Beach

Evening Pet Clinic
6803 Cherry Ave
Long Beach, CA 90805
Hwy 91
562-422-1223
Mon - Fri 8 am - 9 pm with certain lunch and dinner breaks, Sat - Sun 12 - 6 pm.

Los Angeles Dog Travel Guide
Accommodations

Los Angeles

Beverly Laurel Hotel
8018 Beverly Blvd
Los Angeles, CA 90048
323-651-2441
There is a $10 per day pet fee. Up to two pets per room are allowed. Thanks to one of our readers who wrote "Our large German Shepherd was welcome."

Four Points by Sheraton - LAX

9750 Airport Blvd
Los Angeles, CA 90045
310-645-4600
There is a $50 refundable deposit and a $10 per day pet fee. Dogs must be on a leash at all times on the premises.

Holiday Inn - Downtown

750 Garland Ave @ 8th St.
Los Angeles, CA 90017
213-628-9900
There is a $15 per day pet fee. A well-behaved large dog is okay.

Hotel Sofitel

8555 Beverly Blvd
Los Angeles, CA 90052
310-278-5444
This upscale hotel is located next to West Hollywood and Beverly Hills. You and your dog will feel most welcome at this hotel. Since parking is limited in this area, your car will be valet parked. They open the car doors not only for you, but for your dog too. You can feel comfortable registering at the front desk with your pup at your side and then taking the elevator to the room that awaits you. There is a restaurant at this hotel that has outdoor dining where your dog is also welcome. Room rates run about $150-250 per night, but your dog will be treated first class.

Le Meridien Hotel

465 South La Cienega Blvd.
Los Angeles, CA 90048
Burton Way
310-247-0400
Dogs up to 50 pounds are allowed. This luxury class hotel is located in one of the most prestigious areas in Los Angeles. They welcome both business and leisure travelers, as well as your dog of any size. Room rates at this first class hotel start at the low $300s per night. They

sometimes offer special weekend rates. There is an additional $100 pet fee for the first night and an additional $25 for each additional day.

Los Angeles Airport Marriott Hotel

5885 W. Century Blvd.
Los Angeles, CA 90045
(.5 miles E of LAX airport)
310-641-5700
Dogs are allowed on the ground floor only of this 18 story hotel, so be sure to call ahead and reserve a room. They have 24-hour room service. The hotel is located approximately a 1/2 mile from the Los Angeles Airport. Parking is $9 per day and valet parking is $11 per day. It's located on Century Blvd between Sepulveda & Aviation Blvds.

Travelodge Hotel at LAX

5547 W. Century Blvd.
Los Angeles, CA 90045
(1 mile E of LAX airport)
310-649-4000
This inn offers free parking, a feature not found with many of the L.A./West Hollywood hotels. They welcome pets here at this 2 story inn which has interior/exterior corridors, a gift shop and heated pool. It is located about one mile east of the Los Angeles Airport. There is a $10 per day additional pet fee per pet.

Vagabond Inn
3101 S. Figueroa St.
Los Angeles, CA 90007
213-746-1531
This motel is located just 2 blocks from the University of Southern California (USC) and 2 miles from the LA Convention Center. It features an outdoor swimming pool, cable television, air conditioning and many more amenities. There is a $10 per day pet fee.

Attractions

Los Angeles

Century City Shopping Center
10250 Santa Monica Blvd
Los Angeles, CA 93309
310-277-3898
This dog-friendly outdoor shopping center, located just one mile from Rodeo Drive in Beverly Hills, is popular with many Hollywood actors and actresses. Your well-behaved dog is allowed inside many of the stores. For a list of dog-friendly stores, please look at our stores category. Your dog is also welcome to join you at the outdoor cafe tables in the food court area.

Griffith Observatory
2800 East Observatory Road
Los Angeles, CA 90027
(In Griffith Park)
323-664-1181
Please note: The Observatory will close in January 2002 and re-open to the public in late 2004. This observatory has been a major Los Angeles landmark since 1935. Star-gazing dogs are not allowed inside the Observatory, but you are allowed to walk to the roof (on the outside stairs) and get some great views of the Los Angeles basin and the Hollywood sign. Located across the parking lot from the Observatory is the

Griffith Park snack shop and the Mt. Hollywood Trail (about 6 miles of dog-friendly trails). To get to there, take Hwy 5 to the Los Feliz Blvd exit and head west. Turn right on Hillhurst or Vermont Ave (they merge later). Go past the Bird Sanctuary and Greek Theater. Stay on Vermont Ave and you'll come to the Griffith Observatory.

Griffith Park Southern Railroad
4400 Crystal Springs Drive
Los Angeles, CA
Los Feliz Blvd.
323-664-6788
Does your pup want to try a train ride? This small train ride (serving the public since 1948) is popular with kids, but your dog will love it too. The seating area is kind of small and larger dogs will need to sit or stand on the floor by your feet. But don't worry, it's a pretty short ride which goes about 1 mile in distance. It'll give your pup a chance to decide if he/she is made for the rails. It's located in Griffith Park which also has several nice hikes that of course allow dogs. Hungry? There is a small snack stand located nearby with many picnic tables. While you eat lunch, you can watch the kids ride the rental ponies. Griffith Park is pretty large, so to find the train ride, take Los Feliz Blvd (near Hwy 5) to Crystal Springs Drive/Griffith Park Drive. Head north on Crystal Springs and the train ride will be on your right.

Hollywood Walk of Fame

6100-6900 Hollywood Blvd.
Los Angeles, CA
323-469-8311
Want to see the star that was dedicated to your favorite actor or actress? Then come to the famous Hollywood Walk of Fame on Hollywood Blvd. You'll find about 10-15 blocks of Hollywood stars placed in the sidewalks of Hollywood Blvd. Don't forget to look at the famous Footprints located at the Mann's Chinese Theatre on Hollywood Blvd between Orange Drive and Orchid Ave. Want to see an actor or actress receive their honorary Star? This takes place throughout the year in front of the Hollywood Galaxy General Cinemas on Hollywood Blvd. It may be too crowded for your pup to stand directly in front of the Cinemas, but you can see plenty from across the street. Just make sure your dog is comfortable with crowds yelling and cheering as this will happen when the actor/actress arrives. Our pup was able to see Nicolas Cage receive his Hollywood Star. To find out the schedule of when the next actor/actress will receive their star, look at the Hollywood Chamber of Commerce website at http://www.hollywoodcoc.org or call 323-469-8311. To get to the Hollywood Walk of Fame, take Hwy 101 North past Sunset Blvd. Take the next exit which is Hollywood Blvd and turn left (west). The Hollywood Stars are located on 6100-6900 Hollywood Blvd. between Gower Street and Sycamore Avenue.

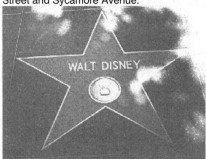

Travel Town Museum

5200 Zoo Drive
Los Angeles, CA
In Griffith Park
323-662-5874
Dogs are allowed on leash throughout the Travel Town Museum in Griffith Park in LA. Here you can see many trains, cars and lots more. Your well-behaved dog is also allowed on the miniature train ride.

Parks

Los Angeles

Griffith Park

Los Feliz Blvd.
Los Angeles, CA
Hwy 5

This is the park that allows dogs on their small trains (see Attractions), has the Griffith Observatory, the famous Hollywood sign and plenty of hiking trails. The Mt. Hollywood Trail is about a 6 mile round trip and can get very hot in the summer season, so head out early or later in the evening during those hot days. There is also a more shaded trail that begins by the Bird Sanctuary. Be careful not to go into the Sanctuary because dogs are not allowed there. Instead go to the trail to the left of the Sanctuary entrance. That trail should go around the perimeter of the Bird Sanctuary. For more trail info, pick up a map at one of the Ranger stations (main Ranger's station is at Crystal Springs/Griffith Park Drive near Los Feliz Blvd). To get to there, take Hwy 5 to the Los Feliz Blvd exit and head west. Turn right on Hillhurst or Vermont Ave (they merge later). The trail by the Bird Sanctuary will be on the right, past the Greek Theater. To get to the Mt. Hollywood Trail, continue until you come to the Griffith Observatory. Park here and the trail is across the parking lot from the Observatory (near the outdoor cafe). Please note that no one is allowed to actually hike to the famous Hollywood sign - it is very well guarded. But from some of the trails in this park, you can get a long distance view of the sign. Dogs must be leashed in the park.

Griffith Park Dog Park

North 200 Drive
Los Angeles, CA
323-913-7390
This dog park is located 1/2 mile west of the 134

Fwy.

Laurel Canyon Park
8260 Mulholland Dr.
Los Angeles, CA 90046

This nice dog park is located in the hills of Studio City. It is completely fenced with water and even a hot dog stand. The on-leash hours are 10am-3pm and off-leash hours are 6am to10am and 3pm to dusk. To get there, take Laurel Canyon Blvd and go west on Mulholland Blvd. Go about a 1/4 mile and turn left. There is a parking lot below.

Runyon Canyon Park
Mulholland Hwy
Los Angeles, CA 90046
Desmond Street

From this popular hiking trail you can see views of Hollywood, the Wilshire District, and the skyscrapers of downtown L.A. This park has mostly off-leash and some on-leash hiking trails. The top of the trail is located off Mulholland Hwy (about 2 miles east of Laurel Canyon Blvd) at Desmond Street in the Hollywood Hills. The bottom part of the trail is located at the end of Fuller Ave. Parking is available on the street. The trailhead might be kind of tricky to find from Fuller, but you'll probably see other people going to or coming from the trail.

Silverlake Dog Park
2000 West Silverlake Blvd.
Los Angeles, CA
South part of the reservoir

This is one of the best dog parks in the Los Angeles area and it usually averages 30-40 dogs. It is located at approximately 2000 West Silverlake Blvd. It's on the south side of the reservoir in Silverlake, which is between Hollywood and downtown L.A. between Sunset Blvd. and the 5 Freeway. The easiest way to get there is to take the 101 Freeway to Silverlake Blvd. and go east. Be careful about street parking because they ticket in some areas. Thanks to one of our readers for recommending this dog park.

Restaurants

Los Angeles

Baja Fresh Mexican Grill
7919 Sunset Blvd.
Los Angeles, CA
323-436-3844
This Mexican restaurant is open for lunch and dinner. They use fresh ingredients and making their salsa and beans daily. Some of the items on their menu include Enchiladas, Burritos, Tacos Salads, Quesadillas, Nachos, Chicken, Steak and more. Well-behaved leashed dogs are allowed at the outdoor tables.

Baja Fresh Mexican Grill
5757 Wilshire Blvd.
Los Angeles, CA
323-549-9080
This Mexican restaurant is open for lunch and dinner. They use fresh ingredients and making their salsa and beans daily. Some of the items on their menu include Enchiladas, Burritos, Tacos Salads, Quesadillas, Nachos, Chicken, Steak and

more. Well-behaved leashed dogs are allowed at the outdoor tables.

Fred's 62
1854 N Vermont Ave
Los Angeles, CA 90027
323-667-0062
Dogs are allowed at the outdoor tables.

Griffith Park snack stand
Vermont Ave
Los Angeles, CA
(Griffith Observatory)

This is a basic snack stand but what makes it nice is the fact that it's in Griffith Park between the Griffith Observatory and the Mt. Hollywood Trail. Your pup can't go in the Observatory, but can walk up the outside stairs to the roof and check out the view of Los Angeles. At the Mt. Hollywood Trail, there is a 6 mile round trip dog-friendly trail. Load up on snacks and water at this stand. To get to there, take Hwy 5 to the Los Feliz Blvd exit and head west. Turn right on Hillhurst or Vermont Ave (they merge later). Go past the Bird Sanctuary and Greek Theater. Stay on Vermont Ave and you'll come to the Griffith Observatory and snack shop parking.

Hollywood Blvd restaurants
Hollywood Blvd.
Los Angeles, CA
various

While you are looking at the Stars on the Hollywood Walk of Fame at Hollywood Blvd., you can take a lunch or snack break at one of the many outdoor cafes that line this popular street. Many of them only have a few tables, but you should be able to find one.

Home
1760 Hillhurst Avenue
Los Angeles, CA 90027
323-669-0211
This American restaurant is open for breakfast, lunch and dinner. They welcome dogs at their outdoor tables. Dogs should be on leash. Thanks to one of our readers for recommending this restaurant.

In-N-Out Burgers
7009 Sunset Blvd.
Los Angeles, CA 90028
Orange Drive
800-786-1000
We decided to mention this specific In-N-Out Burgers because it's very close to the Hollywood Blvd. Walk of Fame. It's a few blocks south of Hollywood Blvd (Walk of Fame). Head south on Orange Drive which is near the Mann's Chinese Theatre. The In-N-Out is near the corner of Sunset Blvd. and Orange. Dogs are allowed at the outdoor tables.

Johnny Rockets
1000 N. La Cienga Blvd.
Los Angeles, CA
(between 3rd & Beverly Blvd.)
310-657-6073

Johnny Rockets is a popular chain that serves hamburgers, fries and malts with a traditional 1950's style. Dogs are allowed at the outdoor tables.

Mel's Drive-In
8585 Sunset Blvd.
Los Angeles, CA
La Cienga Blvd.
310-854-7200
This 24 hour West Hollywood restaurant serves you and your pup breakfast, lunch or dinner outside.

Tail O The Pup
329 N. San Vicente Blvd.
Los Angeles, CA
Beverly Blvd.
310-652-4517
This food stand serves a fast-food type of breakfast and then for lunch they serve hamburgers and hot dogs. Order with your pup at the "Hot Dog" window and then sit at one of their several outdoor tables.

The Back Door Bakery
1710 Silver Lake Blvd
Los Angeles, CA 90026
323-662-7927
This restaurant is two blocks from the Silver Lake Dog Park, so it gets a regular group of 4 legged customers at the outdoor tables. They have dog biscuits for the dogs. The hours are 7:30 am to 7 pm Tuesday through Sunday.

The Pig, Memphis-Style BBQ
612 N. La Brea Ave
Los Angeles, CA 90036
323-935-1116
This restaurant is very dog friendly. There are a lot of doggy regulars at the "Pig". Closed Mondays. Open from 11 am to at least 10 pm other days. Dogs are welcome to dine with you at the outdoor tables.

Whole Foods Market
11737 San Vicente Blvd.
Los Angeles, CA 90049
310-826-4433
This natural food supermarket offers natural and organic foods. Order some food from their deli and bring it to an outdoor table where your well-behaved leashed dog is welcome.

Whole Foods Market
6350 West 3rd Street
Los Angeles, CA 90036
323-964-6800
This natural food supermarket offers natural and organic foods. Order some food from their deli and bring it to an outdoor table where your well-behaved leashed dog is welcome.

Whole Foods Market
7871 West Santa Monica Blvd.
Los Angeles, CA 90046
323-848-4200
This natural food supermarket offers natural and

organic foods. Order some food from their deli and bring it to an outdoor table where your well-behaved leashed dog is welcome.

Whole Foods Market
11666 National Boulevard
Los Angeles, CA 90064
310-996-8840
This natural food supermarket offers natural and organic foods. Order some food from their deli and bring it to an outdoor table where your well-behaved leashed dog is welcome. The market is located at the corner of National and Barrington.

Whole Foods Market
1050 S. Gayley
Los Angeles, CA 90024
310-824-0858
This natural food supermarket offers natural and organic foods. Order some food from their deli and bring it to an outdoor table where your well-behaved leashed dog is welcome.

Stores

Los Angeles

Brentano's Books
Century City Shopping Center
Los Angeles, CA 93309
310-785-0204
Your well-behaved leashed dog is allowed inside this store.

Foot Locker
Century City Shopping Center
Los Angeles, CA 93309
310-556-1498
Your well-behaved leashed dog is allowed inside this store.

Gap
Century City Shopping Center
Los Angeles, CA 93309
310-556-1080
Your well-behaved leashed dog is allowed inside this store.

Illiterature
452 S La Brea Ave
Los Angeles, CA 90036
323-937-3505
Dogs are allowed but they must be leashed.

Laura Ashley
Century City Shopping Center
Los Angeles, CA 93309

310-553-0807
Your well-behaved leashed dog is allowed inside this store.

Origins
Century City Shopping Center
Los Angeles, CA 93309
310-772-0272
Your well-behaved leashed dog is allowed inside this store.

Pottery Barn
Century City Shopping Center
Los Angeles, CA 93309
310-552-0170
Your well-behaved leashed dog is allowed inside this store.

Restoration Hardware
Century City Shopping Center
Los Angeles, CA 93309
310-551-4995
Your well-behaved leashed dog is allowed inside this store.

Rocket Video
726 N La Brea Ave
Los Angeles, CA 90038
323-965-1100
Well-behaved leashed dogs are welcome in this store which is Los Angeles' premier independent video store.

Vets and Kennels

Los Angeles

Animal Emergency Clinic
1736 S Sepulveda Blvd #A
Los Angeles, CA 90025
Santa Monica Blvd
310-473-1561
Monday - Friday 6 pm - 8 am. 24 hours weekends and holidays.

Eagle Rock Emergency Pet Clinic
4252 Eagle Rock Blvd
Los Angeles, CA 90065
near Occidental College
323-254-7382
Monday - Friday 6 pm - 8 am. Saturday 12 noon - Monday 8 am.

Malibu Dog Travel Guide
Accommodations - RV Parks and Campgrounds

Malibu

Leo Carrillo State Park Campground
Highway 1
Malibu, CA
818-880-0350
The campgrounds offer tent and RV camping near the beach. The campsites are located on the inland side of Highway 1. You can walk to the beach along a road that goes underneath the highway. Dogs on leash are allowed in the campgrounds and on a certain section of the beach. Please clean up after you pets. The campground is located on Highway 1, about 30 miles northwest of Santa Monica.

Beaches

Malibu

Leo Carrillo State Beach
Hwy 1
Malibu, CA
30 miles n. of Santa Monica
818-880-0350
This beach is one of the very few dog-friendly beaches in the Los Angeles area. In a press release dated November 27, 2002, the California State Parks clarified the rules for dogs at Leo Carrillo State Beach. We thank the State Parks for this clear announcement of the regulations. Dogs are allowed on a maximum 6 foot leash when accompanied by a person capable of controlling the dog on all beach WEST (up coast) of lifeguard tower 3 at Leo Carrillo State Park, Staircase Beach, County Line Beach, and all Beaches within Point Mugu State Park. Dogs are NOT allowed EAST of lifeguard tower 3 at Leo Carrillo State Beach at any time. And please note that dogs are not allowed in the tide pools at Leo Carrillo. There should be signs posted. A small general store is located on the mountain side of the freeway. Here you can grab some snacks and other items. The park is located on Hwy 1, approximately 30 miles northwest of Santa Monica. We ask that all dog people closely obey these regulations so that the beach continues to be dog-friendly.

Parks

Malibu

Circle X Ranch
Yerba Buena Road
Malibu, CA
805-370-2301
There are both easy and strenuous trails at this park. The Backbone Trail is a strenuous 3 mile round trip hike which starts at an elevation of 2,050 feet. This trail offers views on the Conejo and San Fernando Valleys and the Pacific Coast. This trail continues to Point Mugu State Park but dogs are not allowed on those trails. The Grotto Trail is a 3.5 mile round trip trail rated moderate to strenuous. The trail is all downhill from the starting point which means you will be hiking uphill when you return. The Canyon View Trail is almost 2 miles and is rated easy to moderate. There are many access points to this trail, but one is located .3 miles east of the Ranger Station on Yerba Buena Road. Dogs are allowed but must be leashed and people need to clean up after their pets. To get there go about 5.4 miles north on Yerba Buena Road from Highway 1. This park is part of the Santa Monica Recreation Area.

Escondido Canyon Park
Winding Way
Malibu, CA
805-370-2301
The Escondido Falls trail is a little over 4 miles long. The trailhead is reached by a one mile walk up the road from the parking lot. The trail will cross the creek several times before opening up to grassland. You will see the waterfall about one mile from the trailhead. Hiking, horseback riding, and mountain bicycling are popular activities at the park. Dogs on a 6 foot or less leash are allowed and people need to clean up after their pets. The park is located in Malibu, about one

mile from the Pacific Coast Highway on Winding Way. This park is part of the Santa Monica Recreation Area.

Solstice Canyon Park
Corral Canyon Road
Malibu, CA
805-370-2301
This park is a wooded, narrow coastal canyon which offers five trails, ranging from easy to moderate hikes. One of the trails is called the Solstice Canyon Trail. This is an easy 2.1 mile round trip walk which passes by the Keller House which is believed to be the oldest existing stone building in Malibu. Dogs are allowed on the trails but must be leashed and people need to clean up after their pets. To get there from the Pacific Coast Highway 1, go through Malibu and turn inland onto Corral Canyon Road. In about .25 miles the entrance will be on your left at a hairpin curve in the road. This park is part of the Santa Monica Recreation Area.

Manhattan Beach Dog Travel Guide
Accommodations

Manhattan Beach

Residence Inn by Marriott
1700 N Sepulveda Blvd
Manhattan Beach, CA 90266
Manhattan Beach Blvd.
310-546-7627
Every room at this inn is a suite with a living room, kitchen and bedroom. Amenities include an outdoor pool, complimentary continental breakfast, self service laundry facilities, and dinner delivery service from local restaurants. Room rates start at $125 and up. There is a $75 one time pet charge and an additional $8 per day for pets. If you reserve one of the penthouses, then there is a $100 one time pet charge.

Restaurants

Manhattan Beach

Johnny Rockets
1550 Rosecrans Ave.
Manhattan Beach, CA 90266
310-536-9464
Dogs are allowed at the outdoor tables at this Johnny Rockets.

Marina Del Rey Dog Travel Guide
Restaurants

Marina Del Rey

Baja Fresh Mexican Grill
13424 Maxella Avenue
Marina Del Rey, CA
310-578-2252
This Mexican restaurant is open for lunch and dinner. They use fresh ingredients and making their salsa and beans daily. Some of the items on their menu include Enchiladas, Burritos, Tacos Salads, Quesadillas, Nachos, Chicken, Steak and more. Well-behaved leashed dogs are allowed at the outdoor tables.

Newhall Dog Travel Guide
Parks

Newhall

Placerita Canyon Nature Center
19152 Placerita Canyon Road
Newhall, CA 91321
661-259-7721
This 350 acre nature park is one of the first places where gold was discovered in California. An early frontier cabin called Walker's Cabin is located at this park. Hiking trails are accessible for wheelchairs and strollers. The paved trail is

about .3 miles. Dogs must be on leash and please clean up after them.

William S. Hart Regional Park
24151 N. San Fernando Road
Newhall, CA 91321
661-259-0855
This 265 acre ranch was donated to the public by William S. Hart, also known as "Two Gun Bill". He was a popular cowboy actor during the silent film era. The park includes a western art museum and barnyard animals including wild buffalo. Dogs are allowed at the park and on trails, but not inside any buildings. Pets must be leashed and please clean up after them.

North Hollywood Dog Travel Guide
Restaurants

North Hollywood

Chez Nous
10550 Riverside Drive
North Hollywood, CA
Cahueriga Blvd.
818-760-0288
Enjoy lunch dining and table service at this restaurant located in North Hollywood. Dogs are allowed at the outdoor tables.

Northridge Dog Travel Guide
Restaurants

Northridge

Whole Foods Market
19340 Rinaldi
Northridge, CA 91326
818-363-3933
This natural food supermarket offers natural and organic foods. Order some food from their deli and bring it to an outdoor table where your well-

behaved leashed dog is welcome.

Stores

Northridge

REI
18605 Devonshire St
Northridge, CA
818-831-5555
This clothing and outdoor adventure store allows well-behaved, leashed dogs to accompany shoppers.

Norwalk Dog Travel Guide
Accommodations

Norwalk

Motel 6
10646 E Rosecrans Ave
Norwalk, CA 90650
562-864-2567
There are no additional pet fees.

Vets and Kennels

Norwalk

Crossroads Animal Emergency Hospital
11057 Rosecrans Ave
Norwalk, CA 90650
Hwy 605
562-863-2522
Monday - Thursday 6 pm to 8 am, Friday 6 pm to 8 am Monday.

Pacific Palisades Dog Travel Guide
Attractions

Pacific Palisades

Will Rogers State Hist. Park
1501 Will Rogers State Park Rd.
Pacific Palisades, CA
Sunset Blvd.
310-454-8212
This park was Will Roger's personal home and ranch. Mr. Rogers was famous for his horse and rope tricks. He performed on Broadway and then moved on to Hollywood to star in many movies. The ranch was made into a state historic park in 1944 after the death of Mrs. Rogers and it reflects Will Rogers avid horsemanship. On the ranch there is a large polo field, which is the only

outdoor polo field in Los Angeles county and the only field that is regulation size. The polo field has been featured in many movies and TV shows. The ranch buildings and grounds have been maintained to show how the Rogers' family lived back in the late 1920s and 1930s. Today, the grounds are also a working ranch with a variety of western equestrian activities. Leashed dogs are allowed on the property, in the horse barn, and on the Inspiration Point Trail. They are not allowed inside the ranch house. Dogs, along with people and children, should not touch the horses. The ranch staff enforces the leash law and will fine violators $82. The entrance fee to the park is $6 per car and $1 per dog.

Parks

Pacific Palisades

Temescal Canyon Park
15601 Sunset Blvd.
Pacific Palisades, CA
805-370-2301
There are several trails at this park. Dogs are allowed but must be on a 6 foot or less leash and people need to clean up after their pets. The Sunset Trail is almost a half mile trail that begins at the lower parking lot by Sunset Blvd. It parallels Temescal Creek. The Temescal Loop Trail is about a four and a half mile hike up a canyon. Some areas area steep. If you go about 1.2 miles from the trailhead, you will reach the Temescal waterfall which is seasonal. The park is located at the intersection of Temescal Canyon Road and Sunset Blvd. This park is part of the Santa Monica Recreation Area.

Pasadena Dog Travel Guide
Attractions

Pasadena

Frisbee Golf Course
Oak Grove Drive
Pasadena, CA
in Hahamongna Watershed Park

This disc golf course in Pasadena is the world's first disc golf course. It is an extremely popular course, with over 100 golfers playing daily during the week and twice that on the weekends. If you are a beginner, this might not be the right course for you, but you can watch some of the pros at work. Disc golf is similar to golf with clubs and balls, but the main difference is the equipment. Discs are shot into elevated baskets/holes. Your dog is allowed to go with you on this course, just watch out for flying discs. Dogs must be leashed and poop bags/scoopers are necessary. During the summer months, there can be rattlesnakes, so make sure your dog stays leashed. You'll also want to keep your pup away from the ground squirrels (they can potentially be rabid). This course is located in Hahamongna Watershed Park (formerly Oak Grove Park). If you don't have any discs, you can purchase them online at http://www.gottagogottathrow.com. The prices range from $8-12. Directions to the course are on their website. The park is off Hwy 210 near Altadena.

Old Town Pasadena
100W-100E Colorado Blvd.
Pasadena, CA 91106

Old Town Pasadena is Pasadena's premier shopping and dining district. This area is a nice place to walk around with your pup. While dogs are not allowed inside the stores (with the exception of the Three Dog Bakery), they can sit at one of the many dog-friendly outdoor cafes and dine with you (see Restaurants). A major portion of the popular annual Rose Parade takes place on this part of Colorado Boulevard. The shopping area is the 100 West to 100 East blocks of Colorado Blvd., and between Marengo & Pasadena Avenues.

Parks

Pasadena

Eaton Canyon Nature Center
1750 N. Altadena Drive
Pasadena, CA 91107
626-398-5420
This 184 acre nature park is located at the base of Mt. Wilson. There are five miles of nature and hiking trails plus an equestrian trail. Dogs must be on leash and please clean up after them.

Hahamongna Watershed
Oak Grove Drive
Pasadena, CA
near Hwy 210

The Hahamongna Watershed Park (formerly Oak Grove Park) allows leashed dogs on the trails and on the world's first disc golf course. During the summer months, there can be rattlesnakes here, so make sure your dog stays leashed. You'll also want to keep your pup away from the ground squirrels. Some squirrels in this mountain range have been known to carry rabies. Aside from being a very popular disc golf course, this park is also very popular with bird watchers. To get there from Hwy 210, take the Berkshire Ave. exit and head east. Turn left onto Oak Grove Drive and the park will be on the right. To get to one of the trails, follow the signs to the disc golf course. After going downhill, turn right and the trail begins.

Restaurants

Pasadena

All India Cafe
39 S Fair Oaks Ave
Pasadena, CA 91105
626-440-0309
Dogs are allowed at the outdoor tables.

Baja Fresh Mexican Grill
899 E. Del Mar
Pasadena, CA
626-792-0446
This Mexican restaurant is open for lunch and dinner. They use fresh ingredients and making their salsa and beans daily. Some of the items on their menu include Enchiladas, Burritos, Tacos Salads, Quesadillas, Nachos, Chicken, Steak and more. Well-behaved leashed dogs are allowed at the outdoor tables.

Barney's Ltd
93 W. Colorado Blvd.
Pasadena, CA 91105
in Old Town Pasadena
626-577-2739
This restaurant has good chili, salads, sandwiches and a large selection of beers. Your pup is welcome to join you at the outdoor tables.

Crocodile Cafe
88 W. Colorado Blvd.
Pasadena, CA 91105
in Old Town Pasadena
626-568-9310
You are welcome to dine with your dog at the outdoor tables.

Gaucho Grill
121 W. Colorado Blvd.
Pasadena, CA 91105
in Old Town Pasadena
626-683-3580
This restaurant allows dogs to dine with you at their outdoor tables.

Jake's Diner & Billiards
38 W. Colorado Blvd.
Pasadena, CA 91105
in Old Town Pasadena
626-568-1602
Come here for some English-style meat pies, burgers or just a beer. Dogs are welcome to join their people and the restaurant staff will even bring out some water for your pup.

Trattoria Farfalla
43 E. Colorado Blvd.
Pasadena, CA 91105
in Old Town Pasadena
626-564-8696
The outdoor tables are pretty close together, but your dog is welcome to join you for lunch or dinner.

Wok n Roll
55 E. Colorado Blvd.
Pasadena, CA 91105
in Old Town Pasadena
626-304-1000
Not only does this restaurant allow your dog, they will also bring him or her water. Dogs are allowed at the outdoor tables.

Stores

Pasadena

Saks Fifth Avenue
35 N De Lacey Ave
Pasadena, CA 91103
626-396-7100
Leashed, well - behaved dogs are allowed in the store.

Three Dog Bakery
24 Smith Alley A
Pasadena, CA 91106
in One Colorado
626-440-0443
Your pup is invited inside this dog bakery store which is located in Old Town Pasadena. Here he or she can choose from a variety of special dog cookies and pastries. The goodies look yummy enough for people to eat, but remember they are for dogs, not for humans. After your pup has indulged in the treats, both of you can dine at one of the many dog-friendly outdoor restaurants located within walking distance (see Restaurants).

Vets and Kennels

Pasadena

Animal Emergency Clinic
2121 E Foothill Blvd
Pasadena, CA 91107
Lola Ave
626-564-0704
Monday - Friday 6 pm - 8 am. Saturday 12 noon - Monday 8 am.

Pico Rivera Dog Travel Guide

Accommodations

Pico Rivera

Days Inn - Pico Rivera
6540 S. Rosemead Blvd
Pico Rivera, CA 90660
562-942-1003
There is a $15 per day pet fee.

Piru Dog Travel Guide
Accommodations - RV Parks and Campgrounds

Piru

Lake Piru Marina
4780 Piru Canyon Road
Piru, CA 93040
805-521-1231
While dogs are not allowed in the water at Lake Piru, they are allowed on a boat on the water. This marina rents pontoon boats starting at $65 for 4 hours. Well-behaved dogs are allowed on the boats.

Olive Grove Campground
4780 Piru Canyon Road
Piru, CA 93040
805-521-1500
Located at Lake Piru, this campground allows well-behaved leashed dogs in the developed campgrounds, but not in the water. However, dogs are allowed on a boat on the water. The Marina rents pontoon boats and dogs are allowed on the rentals. Campsite amenities including laundry facilities, showers, water, picnic areas and dumping stations. Five of the RV sites have hookups. There is a $2 per day pet fee. Please clean up after your pets.

Porter Ranch Dog Travel Guide
Restaurants

Porter Ranch

Baja Fresh Mexican Grill
19701 Rinaldi St.
Porter Ranch, CA
818-831-3100
This Mexican restaurant is open for lunch and dinner. They use fresh ingredients and making their salsa and beans daily. Some of the items on their menu include Enchiladas, Burritos, Tacos Salads, Quesadillas, Nachos, Chicken, Steak and more. Well-behaved leashed dogs are allowed at

the outdoor tables.

Redondo Beach Dog Travel Guide
Parks

Redondo Beach

Redondo Beach Dog Park
Flagler Lane
Redondo Beach, CA
at 190th St.
310-378-8555
This dog park is located next to Dominguez Park. Local dogs and vacationing dogs are welcome at the dog park. There is a separate section for small dogs and big dogs. It is completely fenced and has pooper scooper bags available.

fourth of the land in Los Angeles County. We have selected a couple of trails near San Fernando Valley ranging from 2.5 to 3 miles. Dogs are allowed on leash or leash free but under voice control. Both of the trails are single-track, foot trails. The first trail is called Gold Creek Trail. It is about 2.5 miles long. The second trail is called Oaks Springs Trail and it is about 3 miles long. To get there from Hwy 215, take the Foothill Blvd. exit and head north towards the mountains. Turn left onto Little Tujunga Canyon Rd. You will see the Little Tujunga Forest Station on the left. After you pass the station, continue on Little Tujunga Canyon Rd. Go about 1-1.5 miles and then turn right onto Gold Creek Rd. Go about 1 mile and on the right you will see the trailhead for Oak Springs Trail. If you continue to the end of Gold Creek Rd, you will see the trailhead for Gold Creek Trail. There should be parking along the road.

Restaurants

Redondo Beach

Whole Foods Market
405 N. Pacific Coast Hwy.
Redondo Beach, CA 90277
310-376-6931
This natural food supermarket offers natural and organic foods. Order some food from their deli and bring it to an outdoor table where your well-behaved leashed dog is welcome.

San Fernando Dog Travel Guide
Parks

San Fernando

Angeles National Forest
Little Tujunga Canyon Rd.
San Fernando, CA
near Hwy 210
626-574-1613
This forest is over 690,000 acres and covers one-

Santa Fe Springs Dog Travel Guide
Accommodations

Santa Fe Springs

Motel 6
13412 Excelsior Dr
Santa Fe Springs, CA 90670
562-921-0596
There are no additional pet fees.

Santa Monica Dog Travel Guide
Accommodations

Santa Monica

Le Merigot Beach Hotel and Spa
1740 Ocean Avenue
Santa Monica, CA
310-395-9700
The hotel provides pet dishes and toys upon arrival. There is a $35 one time pet fee. There is

also a $150 refundable pet deposit.

Loews Santa Monica Beach Hotel
1700 Ocean Avenue
Santa Monica, CA 90401
310-458-6700
All well-behaved dogs of any size are welcome. This upscale hotel offers their "Loews Loves Pets" program which includes special pet treats, local dog walking routes, and a list of nearby pet-friendly places to visit. There are no pet fees.

Parks

Santa Monica

Memorial Park
1401 Olympic Blvd
Santa Monica, CA
310-450-1121
There is an off-leash dog run located in this park.

Restaurants

Santa Monica

Baja Fresh Mexican Grill
720 Wilshire Blvd.
Santa Monica, CA
310-393-9313
This Mexican restaurant is open for lunch and dinner. They use fresh ingredients and making their salsa and beans daily. Some of the items on their menu include Enchiladas, Burritos, Tacos Salads, Quesadillas, Nachos, Chicken, Steak and more. Well-behaved leashed dogs are allowed at the outdoor tables.

Stores

Santa Monica

Barnes and Noble Bookstore
1201 3rd Street
Santa Monica, CA 90401
310-260-9110
Your well-behaved leashed dog is allowed inside this store. One of our readers writes "They (dogs) are totally welcome there!"

Sherman Oaks Dog Travel Guide
Parks

Sherman Oaks

Van Nuys/Sherman Oaks Park
14201 Huston St
Sherman Oaks, CA 91423
between Van Nuys & Hazeltine
818-783-5121
This park has an approximate 1.5 mile walking and jogging path that winds through and around the sports fields. There are also many picnic tables near the Recreation Center. To get there from Hwy 101, take the Van Nuys exit and head north.

Restaurants

Sherman Oaks

Baja Fresh Mexican Grill
14622 Ventura Blvd.
Sherman Oaks, CA
818-789-0602
This Mexican restaurant is open for lunch and dinner. They use fresh ingredients and making their salsa and beans daily. Some of the items on their menu include Enchiladas, Burritos, Tacos Salads, Quesadillas, Nachos, Chicken, Steak and more. Well-behaved leashed dogs are allowed at the outdoor tables.

Solleys Deli
4578 Van Nuys Blvd
Sherman Oaks, CA 91403
between Ventura & Hwy 101
818-905-5774
This deli is located several blocks from the Van Nuys/Sherman Oaks Park.

Whole Foods Market
12905 Riverside Drive
Sherman Oaks, CA 91423
818-762-5548
This natural food supermarket offers natural and organic foods. Order some food from their deli and bring it to an outdoor table where your well-behaved leashed dog is welcome.

Whole Foods Market
4520 Sepulveda Boulevard
Sherman Oaks, CA 91403
818-382-3700
This natural food supermarket offers natural and organic foods. Order some food from their deli and bring it to an outdoor table where your well-behaved leashed dog is welcome.

Vets and Kennels

Sherman Oaks

Emergency Animal Clinic
14302 Ventura Blvd
Sherman Oaks, CA 91423
near Van Nuys Blvd
818-788-7860
24 hours everyday.

Simi Valley Dog Travel Guide
Restaurants

Simi Valley

Baja Fresh Mexican Grill
2679 Tapo Cyn Rd
Simi Valley, CA
805-581-6001
This Mexican restaurant is open for lunch and dinner. They use fresh ingredients and making their salsa and beans daily. Some of the items on

their menu include Enchiladas, Burritos, Tacos Salads, Quesadillas, Nachos, Chicken, Steak and more. Well-behaved leashed dogs are allowed at the outdoor tables.

South El Monte Dog Travel Guide
Parks

South El Monte

Whittier Narrows Nature Center
1000 N. Durfee Ave.
South El Monte, CA 91733
626-575-5523
This park has over 200 acres of natural woodland and includes four lakes which offer a winter sanctuary for migrating waterfowl. Dogs are allowed on the trails, but not in the water. Pets must be leashed and please clean up after them.

Studio City Dog Travel Guide
Restaurants

Studio City

Gaucho Grill
12050 Ventura Blvd.
Studio City, CA 91604
Laurel Canyon Blvd.
818-508-1030
This Argentinean restaurant is located on the second floor of a strip mall in Studio City. The outdoor seats are pretty popular during the lunch and dinner rush hours, so try to come a little early to ensure a seat.

Louise's Trattoria
12050 Ventura Blvd.
Studio City, CA 91604
Laurel Canyon Blvd.
818-762-2662
This Italian restaurant is located on the second

floor of a strip mall in Studio City. The outdoor seats are pretty popular during the lunch and dinner rush hours, so try to come a little early to ensure a seat.

Stores

Studio City

Maxwell Dog
12332 Ventura Blvd
Studio City, CA 91604
818-505-8411
Dogs are welcome at this specialty gift store for pets. You will find toys, dog beds, accessories, healthy food and treats and more. Store hours are 10am to 6pm Monday through Saturday and noon to 5pm on Sunday.

Vets and Kennels

Studio City

Animal Emergency Center
11740 Ventura Blvd
Studio City, CA 91604
818-760-3882
Monday - Friday 6 pm to 8 am, Saturday 2 pm - Monday 8 am.

Sun Valley Dog Travel Guide
Restaurants

Sun Valley

Big Jim's
8950 Laurel Canyon Blvd
Sun Valley, CA 91352
818-768-0213
Thanks to one of our readers who writes:
"Outdoor patio is shady with plants and a fountain. Steaks, Mexican, Sunday Champagne

Brunch."

Sylmar Dog Travel Guide
Accommodations

Sylmar

Motel 6
12775 Encinitas Ave
Sylmar, CA 91342
818-362-9491
There are no additional pet fees.

Thousand Oaks Dog Travel Guide
Accommodations

Thousand Oaks

Motel 6
1516 Newbury Rd
Thousand Oaks, CA 91320
805-499-0711
One pet per room is permitted.

Thousand Oaks Inn
75 W. Thousand Oaks Blvd.
Thousand Oaks, CA 91360
next to Hwy 101
805-497-3701
This motel allows both dogs and cats. They have a $75 non-refundable pet deposit.

Parks

Thousand Oaks

Wildwood Regional Park
Ave. De Los Arboles
Thousand Oaks, CA
near Wildwood School

This park has hiking trails that run along a

beautiful hill and streams (the streams have water at certain times of the year). It makes for a great morning hike in the summer. Leashed dogs are allowed on the trails. There are also picnic tables at the park. During the winter (rainy season), the trails are subject to flash flooding. To get there from the 101 freeway, take the Lynn Road exit and head north. Turn left onto Avenida de los Arboles. Go until you reach Wildwood School. Park there and take the trail to the left of the parking lot. It will take you to a large wooden "Fort". Go past or through the fort to the trails. Thanks to one of our readers for recommending this park.

805-495-3211
The Meat Locker tempts barbecue lovers with their large outdoor barbecue. Dogs are allowed at the outdoor tables.

Restaurants

Thousand Oaks

Baja Fresh Mexican Grill
595 N Moorpark Rd
Thousand Oaks, CA
805-778-0877
This Mexican restaurant is open for lunch and dinner. They use fresh ingredients and making their salsa and beans daily. Some of the items on their menu include Enchiladas, Burritos, Tacos Salads, Quesadillas, Nachos, Chicken, Steak and more. Well-behaved leashed dogs are allowed at the outdoor tables.

Noah's New York Bagels
33 N Moorpark Rd
Thousand Oaks, CA 91360
N. of Hwy 101
805-379-6767
Your pup can join you for breakfast or lunch at this Noah's Bagels.

Thousand Oaks Meat Locker
2684 E Thousand Oaks Blvd
Thousand Oaks, CA
between Erbes & Hampshire

Whole Foods Market
451 Avenida de los Arboles
Thousand Oaks, CA 91360
805-492-5340
This natural food supermarket offers natural and organic foods. Order some food from their deli and bring it to an outdoor table where your well-behaved leashed dog is welcome.

Vets and Kennels

Thousand Oaks

Pet Emergency Clinic
2967 N Moorpark Rd
Thousand Oaks, CA 91360
south of Olsen Rd
805-492-2436
Monday - Friday 6 pm to 8 am, 24 hours on weekends.

Toluca Lake Dog Travel Guide
Restaurants

Toluca Lake

Baja Fresh Mexican Grill
10760 Riverside Drive
Toluca Lake, CA
818-762-7326
This Mexican restaurant is open for lunch and dinner. They use fresh ingredients and making their salsa and beans daily. Some of the items on their menu include Enchiladas, Burritos, Tacos Salads, Quesadillas, Nachos, Chicken, Steak and more. Well-behaved leashed dogs are allowed at the outdoor tables.

Torrance Dog Travel Guide
Accommodations

Torrance

Residence Inn - Torrance
3701 Torrance Blvd
Torrance, CA 90503
310-543-4566
There is a $40 one time pet fee and a $8 per day additional pet fee. There is also a $4 per day fee for each additional pet.

Restaurants

Torrance

Whole Foods Market
2655 Pacific Coast Highway
Torrance, CA 90505
310-257-8700
This natural food supermarket offers natural and organic foods. Order some food from their deli and bring it to an outdoor table where your well-behaved leashed dog is welcome.

Universal City Dog Travel Guide
Accommodations

Universal City

Sheraton Universal Hotel
333 Universal Hollywood Drive
Universal City, CA 91608
818-980-1212
Dogs up to 80 pounds are allowed. There are no additional pet fees.

Attractions

Universal City

Universal Studios Kennel
Hollywood Frwy (Hwy 101)
Universal City, CA
Lankershim Blvd.
818-508-9600
This isn't really an attraction for your pup, but will allow humans to spend several hours in the world's largest film and TV studio. Universal Studios has a day kennel located at the main entrance. There is no full time attendant, but the kennels are locked. Simply stop at one of the information booths and ask for assistance. There is no fee for this service. At Universal Studios, you can learn how movies are made, visit set and sound stages, and enjoy a variety of special effect rides.

Valencia Dog Travel Guide
Restaurants

Valencia

BJ's Restaurant and Brewhouse
24320 Town Center Dr
Valencia, CA 91355
661-288-1299
Thanks to a reader for recommending this restaurant. Dogs are allowed at the perimeter tables. Enjoy deep dish pizza, chicken, ribs and more. Plus choose from a wide variety of hand-crafted beers.

Baja Fresh Mexican Grill
23630 W. Valencia Blvd.
Valencia, CA
661-254-6060
This Mexican restaurant is open for lunch and dinner. They use fresh ingredients and making their salsa and beans daily. Some of the items on their menu include Enchiladas, Burritos, Tacos Salads, Quesadillas, Nachos, Chicken, Steak and more. Well-behaved leashed dogs are allowed at the outdoor tables.

Cabo Cabana
25710 The Old Road
Valencia, CA
661-222-7022
Thanks to one of our readers who recommended this restaurant. The restaurant serves Mexican food.

Venice Dog Travel Guide
Parks

Venice

Westminster Dog Park
1234 Pacific Ave
Venice, CA 90291
310-392-5566
Thanks to one of our readers who writes: "Spacious (half a block in size), clean (mulched) dog run in dog-friendly Venice. Only five minutes walk from Hydrant Cafe."

Restaurants

Venice

Baja Fresh Mexican Grill
245 Main Street
Venice, CA
310-392-3452
This Mexican restaurant is open for lunch and dinner. They use fresh ingredients and making their salsa and beans daily. Some of the items on their menu include Enchiladas, Burritos, Tacos Salads, Quesadillas, Nachos, Chicken, Steak and more. Well-behaved leashed dogs are allowed at the outdoor tables.

West Covina Dog Travel Guide
Accommodations

West Covina

Hampton Inn
3145 E. Garvey Ave
West Covina, CA 91791
626-967-5800
There are no additional pet fees.

West Hills Dog Travel Guide
Restaurants

West Hills

Baja Fresh Mexican Grill
22815 Victory Blvd. Ste C
West Hills, CA
818-704-4267
This Mexican restaurant is open for lunch and dinner. They use fresh ingredients and making their salsa and beans daily. Some of the items on their menu include Enchiladas, Burritos, Tacos Salads, Quesadillas, Nachos, Chicken, Steak and more. Well-behaved leashed dogs are allowed at the outdoor tables.

West Hollywood Dog Travel Guide
Restaurants

West Hollywood

Basix Cafe
8333 Santa Monica Blvd.
West Hollywood, CA 90069
323-848-2460
This cafe offers flavor-infused, health-conscious cuisine using the freshest ingredients. Here you can enjoy specialties like fresh-baked breads, pastas, sandwiches, wood-fired pizzas. They also serve breakfast including items like eggs and omelettes, pancakes and more. Well-behaved leashed dogs are allowed at the outdoor tables. Thanks to one of our readers for recommending this dog-friendly cafe.

Marix West Hollywood
1108 N. Flores Street
West Hollywood, CA
323-656-8800
This Tex-Mex restaurant allows well-behaved leashed dogs at their outdoor tables. They are open 11am to 11pm seven days a week.

Stores

West Hollywood

Video West
805 Larrabee Street
West Hollywood, CA
310-659-5762
Very dog friendly video store. Dogs always welcome and usually they have dog biscuits. The owner is a dog lover and is active in dog rescue. The store is open 10am-midnight, 7 days a week.

Westlake Village Dog Travel Guide
Restaurants

Westlake Village

Baja Fresh Mexican Grill
30861 Thousand Oaks Blvd.
Westlake Village, CA
818-889-1347
This Mexican restaurant is open for lunch and dinner. They use fresh ingredients and making their salsa and beans daily. Some of the items on their menu include Enchiladas, Burritos, Tacos Salads, Quesadillas, Nachos, Chicken, Steak and more. Well-behaved leashed dogs are allowed at the outdoor tables.

Westwood Dog Travel Guide
Restaurants

Westwood

Native Foods
1110 1/2 Gayley Avenue
Westwood, CA 90025
310-209-1055
This restaurants serves organic vegetarian food. Dogs are allowed at the outdoor tables.

Whittier Dog Travel Guide
Restaurants

Whittier

Baja Fresh Mexican Grill
13582 Whittier Blvd
Whittier, CA
562-464-5900
This Mexican restaurant is open for lunch and dinner. They use fresh ingredients and making their salsa and beans daily. Some of the items on their menu include Enchiladas, Burritos, Tacos Salads, Quesadillas, Nachos, Chicken, Steak and more. Well-behaved leashed dogs are allowed at the outdoor tables.

Woodland Hills Dog Travel Guide
Accommodations

Woodland Hills

Vagabond Inn
20157 Ventura Blvd.
Woodland Hills, CA 91364
Winnetka Ave.
818-347-8080
Amenities at this motel include a heated pool and a free breakfast. An adjacent coffee shop is open 24 hours a day, which might be helpful for getting food to go. There is a $5 per day pet fee.

Restaurants

Woodland Hills

Baja Fresh Mexican Grill
19960 Ventura Blvd.
Woodland Hills, CA
818-888-3976
This Mexican restaurant is open for lunch and dinner. They use fresh ingredients and making their salsa and beans daily. Some of the items on their menu include Enchiladas, Burritos, Tacos Salads, Quesadillas, Nachos, Chicken, Steak and more. Well-behaved leashed dogs are allowed at the outdoor tables.

Baja Fresh Mexican Grill
5780 Canoga Avenue
Woodland Hills, CA
818-347-9033
This Mexican restaurant is open for lunch and dinner. They use fresh ingredients and making their salsa and beans daily. Some of the items on their menu include Enchiladas, Burritos, Tacos Salads, Quesadillas, Nachos, Chicken, Steak and more. Well-behaved leashed dogs are allowed at the outdoor tables.

La Fontana di Trevi
21733 Ventura Blvd
Woodland Hills, CA 91364
818-888-0206
There is a covered outdoor seating area for you and your pup.

My Brother's BBQ
21150 Ventura Blvd
Woodland Hills, CA 91364
between Domencio & Serrania
818-348-2020
The barbecue smoke coming from this restaurant will attract any BBQ lover. They have several outdoor tables where your pup can join you for lunch or dinner.

Pickwick's Pub
21010 Ventura Blvd
Woodland Hills, CA 91364
between Canoga & Serrania
818-340-9673
Dogs are allowed at the outdoor tables.

Whole Foods Market
21347 Ventura Blvd.

Woodland Hills, CA 91364
818-610-0000
This natural food supermarket offers natural and
organic foods. Order some food from their deli
and bring it to an outdoor table where your well-
behaved leashed dog is welcome.

Chapter 10

California Dog-Friendly Travel Guide
Orange County

Aliso Viejo Dog Travel Guide
Restaurants

Aliso Viejo

JACKShrimp
26705 Aliso Creek Rd.
Aliso Viejo, CA 92656
949-448-0085
Cajun food and shrimp are the focus here at JACKShrimp. Enjoy the Spiced Shrimp Caesar Salad, Mardi Gras Pasta, Jammin Jambalaya or Butterfly Shrimp Sandwich. Dogs are allowed at the outdoor tables.

Anaheim Dog Travel Guide
Accommodations

Anaheim

Anaheim Marriott
700 W. Convention Way
Anaheim, CA 92802
714-750-8000
This hotel is located within walking distance of Disneyland. Pets are allowed only on the first floor and they allow pets of all sizes. No deposit or fee, just be a responsible owner and pay for any damages. Room service is available. If you go to Disneyland, there are day kennels at the entrance of the Disneyland amusement park. Thanks to one of our readers for recommending this hotel.

Econolodge at the Park
1126 West Katella Ave
Anaheim, CA
714-533-4505
There is a $10 daily pet fee.

Embassy Suites Hotel
3100 E. Frontera Ave
Anaheim, CA
714-632-1221
There is a $50 one time pet fee per visit.

Hawthorn Suites
1752 S. Clementine
Anaheim, CA
714-635-5000
There is a $150 one time pet fee.

Motel 6
1440 N State College
Anaheim, CA 92806
714-956-9690
One well-behaved pet permitted in a room. Pets are not to be left alone in the room.

Quality Hotel Maingate
616 W Convention Way
Anaheim, CA 92802
Harbor Blvd.
714-750-3131
This hotel is located about two blocks from Disneyland. The hotel offers room service, self service laundry facilities and more. Rooms start at the low $100s and up. Parking is $8 per night. There is a $10 per night per pet and a non-refundable pet cleaning fee of $25.00. If you go to Disneyland for the day, please don't leave your dog in the room. Instead, take him or her to the Disneyland Kennel which offers friendly day boarding for your dog. (see Attractions).

Residence Inn by Marriott
1700 S. Clementine Street
Anaheim, CA 92802
714-533-3555
There is a $40 one time pet fee and a $10 per day pet charge.

Staybridge Suites
1845 S. Manchester Ave
Anaheim, CA 92802
714-748-7700
There is a $75 one time pet fee. This hotel is near Disneyland in Anaheim.

Accommodations - RV Parks and Campgrounds

Anaheim

Canyon RV Park at Featherly
24001 Santa Ana Canyon Road
Anaheim, CA 92802
714-637-0210
This RV park is situated on the Santa Ana River surrounded by mature cottonwood and sycamore trees. They have 140 RV hookup sites. Other amenities include a playground and bike trails. This park is about 14 miles from Disneyland. Well-behaved leashed dogs are welcome for an

additional $1 per day. Please clean up after your pets. The RV park is open all year.

Attractions

Anaheim

Disneyland Kennel
1313 Harbor Blvd
Anaheim, CA
In Disneyland Park
714-781-4565
Disneyland is really more of an attraction for people, but we thought we would mention it because of their kennel. The great folks at Disneyland offer a day kennel for your pup while the rest of the family enjoys the theme park. There is a full time attendant at the kennels and the kennel hours are the same as the park hours. The cost is $10 for the whole day and you can come and walk your dog or just say hi as many times as you want. Just be sure to get your hand stamped for in/out park privileges. The cast members (Disneyland employees) suggest that you might want to bring a favorite blanket for your pup to lay on if he or she is used to that. The kennel is located to the right of the main Disneyland entrance/ticket booths. Please note the following special information: When driving to Disneyland, follow the signs to the main parking lot. At the parking garage toll booth, tell the attendant that you have a dog and would like to use the RV/Oversize parking lot so you can be within closer walking distance to the kennels. From this parking lot, you can either walk to the main entrance of Disneyland (about 10-15 minutes) or take the parking lot tram from the parking lot to the entrance. Dogs are allowed on the parking lot tram, just make sure they are in the middle of the seat so they won't fall out during the ride. Once you arrive at Disneyland, make sure you walk your dog straight to the kennels. Dogs are not allowed in Downtown Disney and the security guards will remind you of this. If you are approached by a guard, just ask where the kennels are and they will point you in the right direction.

Parks

Anaheim

Santa Ana River Path
E. La Palma Ave.
Anaheim, CA

This path stretches for about 20 miles each way. The trail parallels the Santa Ana River. In most spots, there are two sets of trails, one for bikes and one for horses. Dogs are allowed on either trail (paved and dirt). Parking is available at the Yorba Regional Park which is located on E. La Palma Avenue between the Imperial Hwy (Hwy 90) and S. Weir Canyon Rd. There is a minimal fee for parking.

Yorba Regional Park
E. La Palma Ave.
Anaheim, CA
Imperial Hwy (Hwy 90)
714-970-1460
This regional park has 175 acres with several streams and four lakes. There are also over 400 picnic tables and over 200 BBQ stoves. If you want an longer walk or jog, the park is adjacent to the twenty mile long Santa Ana River Bike Path and Trail. The park is located on E. La Palma Avenue between the Imperial Hwy (Hwy 90) and S. Weir Canyon Rd. There is a minimal fee for parking.

Restaurants

Anaheim

Subway Sandwiches

514 N Euclid Street
Anaheim, CA 92801
I-5
714-535-3444
Dogs are allowed at the outdoor tables.

Anaheim Hills Dog Travel Guide
Restaurants

Anaheim Hills

Baja Fresh Mexican Grill
5781 E. Santa Ana Canyon Rd.
Anaheim Hills, CA
714-685-9386
This Mexican restaurant is open for lunch and dinner. They use fresh ingredients and making their salsa and beans daily. Some of the items on their menu include Enchiladas, Burritos, Tacos Salads, Quesadillas, Nachos, Chicken, Steak and more. Well-behaved leashed dogs are allowed at the outdoor tables.

Brea Dog Travel Guide
Restaurants

Brea

Baja Fresh Mexican Grill
2445 Imperial Hwy. Suite H
Brea, CA
714-671-9992
This Mexican restaurant is open for lunch and dinner. They use fresh ingredients and making their salsa and beans daily. Some of the items on their menu include Enchiladas, Burritos, Tacos Salads, Quesadillas, Nachos, Chicken, Steak and more. Well-behaved leashed dogs are allowed at the outdoor tables.

Schlotzsky's Deli
2500 E. Imperial Hwy #196
Brea, CA 92821
714-256-1100
Dogs are allowed at the outdoor tables.

Seattle's Best Coffee
2435 E. Imperial Hwy #A
Brea, CA 92821
714-257-9188
Dogs are allowed at the outdoor tables.

Buena Park Dog Travel Guide
Accommodations

Buena Park

Motel 6
7051 Valley View
Buena Park, CA 90620
714-522-1200
Large dogs are allowed only if they are well-behaved.

Restaurants

Buena Park

Baja Fresh Mexican Grill
7855 La Palma Blvd.
Buena Park, CA
714-521-9500
This Mexican restaurant is open for lunch and dinner. They use fresh ingredients and making their salsa and beans daily. Some of the items on their menu include Enchiladas, Burritos, Tacos Salads, Quesadillas, Nachos, Chicken, Steak and more. Well-behaved leashed dogs are allowed at the outdoor tables.

Capistrano Beach Dog Travel Guide
Accommodations

Capistrano Beach

Seaside Inn
34862 Pacific Coast Hwy.
Capistrano Beach, CA
949-496-1399
There is a $25 one time pet fee.

Corona Del Mar Dog Travel Guide
Beaches

Corona Del Mar

Corona Del Mar State Beach
Iris Street and Ocean Blvd.
Corona Del Mar, CA
949-644-3151
This is a popular beach for swimming, surfing and diving. The sandy beach is about a half mile long. Dogs are allowed on this beach during certain hours. They are allowed before 9am and after 5pm, year round. Pets must be on a 6 foot or less leash. Tickets will be issued if your dog is off leash.

Restaurants

Corona Del Mar

Baja Fresh Mexican Grill
3050 E. Coast Hwy
Corona Del Mar, CA
949-760-8000
This Mexican restaurant is open for lunch and dinner. They use fresh ingredients and making their salsa and beans daily. Some of the items on their menu include Enchiladas, Burritos, Tacos Salads, Quesadillas, Nachos, Chicken, Steak and more. Well-behaved leashed dogs are allowed at the outdoor tables.

Caffe Panini
2333 E Pacific Coast Hwy
Corona Del Mar, CA 92625
MacArthur Blvd.
949-675-8101
Come here for breakfast, lunch and on some nights, dinner. They have several outdoor tables where you can dine with your pup. They are open Sunday through Wednesday from 6am until 3pm and on Thursday through Saturday from 6am until 10pm. This restaurant is also located within walking distance of the Three Dog Bakery (see Attractions).

714-241-8800
There is a $60 one time pet fee and a $10 per day additional pet charge. Every room at this inn is a suite with a bedroom area, living room and kitchen. Rooms start at the low $100s and up. A few cafes are located next door and have no outdoor seating, but you can take food back to the room. The Bark Park dog park is located nearby. (see Parks.)

Vagabond Inn
3205 Harbor Blvd
Costa Mesa, CA 92626
Gisler Ave & Hwy 405
714-557-8360
This motel offers a complimentary continental breakfast. The Bark Park dog park is located nearby. There is a $5 per day pet fee.

Costa Mesa Dog Travel Guide
Accommodations

Costa Mesa

La Quinta Inn Costa Mesa
1515 South Coast Drive
Costa Mesa, CA
714-957-5841
Dogs up to 75 pounds are allowed at the hotel.

Residence Inn by Marriott
881 Baker St
Costa Mesa, CA 92802
Hwy 73

Parks

Costa Mesa

Bark Park Dog Park
Arlington Dr
Costa Mesa, CA
Junipero Dr
714-754-5252
Located in TeWinkle Park, this two acre dog park is fully fenced. It is open from 7am until dusk

every day except for Tuesday, which is clean-up day. The park is located near the Orange County Fairgrounds on Arlington Drive, between Junipero Drive and Newport Blvd.

Talbert Nature Preserve
Victoria Street
Costa Mesa, CA
949-923-2250
This 180 acre park offers hiking trails. Dogs on a 6 foot or less leash are allowed and please clean up after them.

Restaurants

Costa Mesa

Baja Fresh Mexican Grill
3030 Harbor Blvd
Costa Mesa, CA
949-675-2252
This Mexican restaurant is open for lunch and dinner. They use fresh ingredients and making their salsa and beans daily. Some of the items on their menu include Enchiladas, Burritos, Tacos Salads, Quesadillas, Nachos, Chicken, Steak and more. Well-behaved leashed dogs are allowed at the outdoor tables.

Bamboo Terrace
1773 Newport Blvd
Costa Mesa, CA 92627
949-645-5550
Dogs are allowed at the outdoor tables.

Golden Truffle
1767 Newport Blvd
Costa Mesa, CA 92627
949-645-9858
Dogs are allowed at the outdoor tables.

Gustaf Anders
3851 Bear Street

Costa Mesa, CA
South Coast Plaza Village
714-668-1737
Gustaf Anders was called a "knockout" in a major Los Angeles Times Magazine review and it has been named among the top 50 restaurants in the nation by Conde Nast Traveler. They have a wonderful lunch and dinner menu which include items such as Roasted Chicken with Balsamic Vinegar, Lamb Fricassee, Beef Lindstrom, Swedish Pancakes and much more. All of this and they allow your best friend to dine with you at the outdoor tables. The restaurant owner, Gustaf, is a dog lover and owner.

Mother's Market & Kitchen
225 East 17th Street
Costa Mesa, CA 92627
949-631-4741
This natural food market offers natural and organic food plus a kitchen where you can order a smoothie, sandwiches and more. Well-behaved leashed dogs are allowed at their outdoor tables.

Side Street Cafe
1799 Newport Blvd #A105
Costa Mesa, CA 92627
949-650-1986
Dogs are allowed at the outdoor tables.

Cypress Dog Travel Guide
Accommodations

Cypress

Woodfin Suite Hotel
5905 Corporate Ave
Cypress, CA 90630
714-828-4000
All rooms are non-smoking. All well-behaved dogs are welcome. Every room is a suite with wetbars or full kitchens. Hotel amenities include a pool, exercise facility, complimentary video movies, and a complimentary hot breakfast buffet. There is a $5 per day pet fee and you will need to sign a pet waiver.

Dana Point Dog Travel Guide
Accommodations

Dana Point

Marriott's Laguna Cliffs Resort
25135 Park Lantern
Dana Point, CA 92629
949-661-5000

Thanks to one of our readers for recommending this hotel. This Marriott allows dogs of all sizes. Directly in front of the hotel, there is a big open park which overlooks the ocean. Hotel amenities include a pool and tennis courts. Room amenities include hairdryers, iron and ironing boards and more. Room service is also available. Rooms rates start at about $120 and up. There is a $75 non-refundable fee for pets. The hotel is located on Park Lantern, just west of Hwy 1.

Restaurants

Dana Point

Yama Teppan House
24961 Dana Point Harbor Dr.
Dana Point, CA 92629
Golden Lantern
949-240-6610
The restaurant serves dinner on Sunday through Thursday from 5pm-10pm and Friday through Saturday from 5pm-11pm. They have outside heaters just in case the weather is a little cool. To get there from Hwy 5, take the Camino Las Ramblas Exit.

Fountain Valley Dog Travel Guide
Accommodations

Fountain Valley

Residence Inn
9930 Slater Ave
Fountain Valley, CA 92626
714-965-8000
There is a $100 one time fee for pets and a $10 per day additional pet fee.

Restaurants

Fountain Valley

Sammy's Woodfired Pizza
18315 Brookhurst St
Fountain Valley, CA 92708
714-593-5800
Dogs are allowed at the outdoor tables.

Fullerton Dog Travel Guide
Accommodations

Fullerton

Marriott - Fullerton
2701 East Nutwood Ave
Fullerton, CA 92831
714-738-7800
There is a $100 pet deposit, of this $75 is refundable. The hotel is near Cal State Fullerton University.

Garden Grove Dog Travel Guide
Vets and Kennels

Garden Grove

Orange County Emergency Pet Hospital
12750 Garden Grove Blvd
Garden Grove, CA 92843
near Hwy 22
714-537-3032
Monday - Friday 6pm to 8am, Noon Saturday to 8 am Monday.

Huntington Beach Dog Travel Guide
Accommodations - RV Parks and Campgrounds

Huntington Beach

Bolsa Chica State Beach Campground
Pacific Coast Highway
Huntington Beach, CA
714-377-5691
This campground offers RV sites with hookups. Most RVs can be accommodated, just let them know when making a reservation if your RV is over 25 feet. Pets on leash are allowed and please clean up after them. While dogs are not allowed on this state beach, they are allowed on several miles of paved trails that follow the coast. Dogs are also allowed at the adjacent Huntington Dog Beach. The campground is located on the Pacific Coast Highway between Golden West to Warner Avenue.

Beaches

Huntington Beach

Huntington Dog Beach
Pacific Coast Hwy (Hwy 1)
Huntington Beach, CA 92647
Golden West St
714-536-5486
This beautiful beach is about a mile long and allows dogs from dawn to dusk. Dogs must be on leash and owners must pick up after them. They are permitted off leash ONLY in the water and must be under control at all times. Dogs are only allowed on the beach between Golden West Street and Seapoint Ave. Please adhere to these rules as there are only a couple of dog-friendly beaches left in the entire Los Angeles area. The beach is located off the Pacific Coast Hwy (Hwy 1) at Golden West Street. Please remember to pick up after your dog... the city wanted to prohibit dogs in 1997 because of the dog waste left on the beach. But thanks to The Preservation Society of Huntington Dog Beach (http://www.dogbeach.org), it continues to be dog-friendly. City ordinances require owners to pick up after their dogs.

Parks

Huntington Beach

Huntington Beach Dog Park
Edwards Street
Huntington Beach, CA
Inlet Drive
949-536-5672
This dog park has a small dog run for pups under 25 pounds and a separate dog run for the larger pooches. It's been open since 1995 and donations are always welcome. They have a coin meter at the entrance. The money is used to keep the park maintained and for doggie waste bags. If you want to go for a walk with your leashed pup afterwards, there many walking trails at the adjacent Huntington Central Park.

Huntington Central Park
Golden West Street
Huntington Beach, CA
between Ellis & Slater Aves.
949-960-8847
This city park is over 350 acres with six miles of trails. There are expansive lawns, lots of trees and two lakes. Huntington Lake is by Inlet Drive between Golden West and Edwards Streets and next to Alice's Breakfast in the Park Restaurant. Talbert Lake is off Golden West near Slater Ave and Gothard St. The Huntington Dog Park is located within this park.

Restaurants

Huntington Beach

Alice's Breakfast in the Park
Huntington Central Park
Huntington Beach, CA
Inlet Drive
714-848-0690
Dine at one of the several picnic tables at this restaurant which is located next to the Huntington Lake in Huntington Central Park. There are lots of

ducks and other birds around, so your pup will be entertained. Try one of the delicious breakfast items like the fresh baked cinnamon rolls, pancakes, or omelets. For lunch, they have hamburgers and sandwiches. Breakfast and lunch are served all day. They are open daily from 7am until 1:30pm. It's located in Huntington Central Park, where Inlet Drive and Central Park Dr (Varsity Dr) meet.

El Ranchito
318 Main Street
Huntington Beach, CA 92648
714-960-9696
Dogs are allowed at the outdoor tables.

Ibiza Bistro
209 Main Street
Huntington Beach, CA
714-536-7887
Dogs are allowed at the outdoor tables.

Momo's Margarita and Taco Bar
211 Main Street
Huntington Beach, CA 92648
714-960-5282
Dogs are allowed at the outdoor tables.

Taste of France
7304 Center Ave
Huntington Beach, CA 92647
714-895-5305
Dogs are allowed at the outdoor tables.

The Chicken Company
9017 Adams Ave
Huntington Beach, CA 92646
714-963-0500
Dogs are allowed at the outdoor tables.

The Park Bench Cafe
17732 Golden West Dr
Huntington Beach, CA
between Slater & Talbert

714-842-0775
This is THE most dog-friendly restaurant we have found yet. Your dog will absolutely feel welcome here. They even have a separate Doggie Dining Area. And if these tables are full (which they normally are), the nice folks will try to accommodate you and your pooch at the perimeter tables of the other seating area which is next to the dog dining area. Dogs also have their own special menu. It's actually on the people's menu, but includes items like Hot Diggity Dog (hot dog a la carte), Bow Wow Chow (skinless chicken), Annabelle's Treat (chopped bacon bits) and Doggie Kibble (dog kibble for dogs that don't eat table food). For those especially pampered pups, order the Chili Paws (single scoop of Vanilla ice cream) for dessert. This restaurant can arrange special events like Poochie Parties for your dog and a minimum of six of his or her best friends. The party menu has a mouth-watering array of foods for dogs. They do ask that your dog stay off the tables and chairs. But with all the other canine amenities, pooches don't get upset about that rule. The people food here is quite tasty too. They serve a full breakfast ranging from omelets to pancakes and Belgium waffles. Lunch includes a variety of hamburgers and sandwiches. This cafe is located in Huntington Central Park at 17732 Golden West Drive between Slater Dr and Talbert Ave. Hours are Tuesday through Friday from 8am-2pm, Saturday and Sunday from 8am-3pm, and closed on Mondays. Come and enjoy the food and atmosphere.

Irvine Dog Travel Guide
Accommodations

Irvine

La Quinta Inn East Irvine
14972 Sand Canyon Avenue
Irvine, CA

949-551-0909
Dogs up to 50 pounds are allowed at the hotel.

Residence Inn - Irvine
10 Morgan
Irvine, CA 92618
949-380-3000
There is a $40 one time pet fee and a $6 per day pet fee.

Irvine

Central Bark
6405 Oak Canyon
Irvine, CA
949-724-7740
Thanks to one of our readers who writes: "Irvine's dog park is open daily from 6:30 am to 9 pm, closed Wednesdays." The dog park is located next to the shelter.

Restaurants

Irvine

Baja Fresh Mexican Grill
13248 Jamboree Rd
Irvine, CA
714-508-7777
Dogs are allowed at the outdoor seats.

Baja Fresh Mexican Grill
13248 Jamboree Rd.
Irvine, CA
714-508-7777
This Mexican restaurant is open for lunch and dinner. They use fresh ingredients and making their salsa and beans daily. Some of the items on their menu include Enchiladas, Burritos, Tacos Salads, Quesadillas, Nachos, Chicken, Steak and more. Well-behaved leashed dogs are allowed at the outdoor tables.

Britta's Cafe
4237 Campus Drive B-165
Irvine, CA 92612
949-509-1211
According to one of our readers: "Upscale restaurant with informal touch of elegance. Flower's on the table, candles at night." Dogs are allowed on the outdoor patio.

Corner Bakery Cafe
13786 Jamboree Rd

Irvine, CA
714-734-8270
Dogs are allowed at the outdoor seats.

Mother's Market & Kitchen
2963 Michelson Drive
Irvine, CA 92612

This natural food market offers natural and organic food plus a kitchen where you can order a smoothie, sandwiches and more. Well-behaved leashed dogs are allowed at their outdoor tables.

La Mirada Dog Travel Guide
Accommodations

La Mirada

Residence Inn - La Mirada
14419 Firestone Blvd
La Mirada, CA 90638
714-523-2800
There is a $75 one time pet fee and a $6 per day additional pet fee.

La Palma Dog Travel Guide
Accommodations

La Palma

La Quinta Inn La Palma/Theme Park Area
3 Centerpointe Drive
La Palma, CA
714-670-1400
Dogs of all sizes are allowed at the hotel.

Laguna Beach Dog Travel Guide
Accommodations

Laguna Beach

Carriage House Bed and Breakfast
1322 Catalina Street
Laguna Beach, CA 92651
949-494-8945
The Carriage House, a country style bed & breakfast, was built in the early 1920's and is a designated landmark. They are located one mile south of downtown Laguna Beach in a quiet neighborhood. Well-mannered, flea protected, friendly dogs over 18 months old are allowed at an extra charge of $10 per pet per night. Please cover the beds with your own blanket, or ask for a sheet, if your dog sleeps on the bed. Towels are provided upon request for your pet. Never leave

your pet unattended, unless they are "crated" and you'll need to leave a cell phone or number where you can be reached. Owners are responsible for any damages caused by pets. There is also a resident dog & cat on the property. Dogs must always be leashed in Laguna, even on the beach. There is a dog park for off-leash exercise in Laguna Canyon (closed on Wednesday's year round). During the summer, dogs are allowed on the beach from June 1-September 16 before 8 a.m. and after 6 p.m. only.

Casa Laguna Inn
2510 S. Coast Hwy
Laguna Beach, CA 92651
949-494-2996
This lovely Spanish-style bed and breakfast is on a nicely landscape hillside with panoramic views of the ocean. It was voted Orange County's Best B&B four years in a row. The rooms are decorated with a blend of antique and contemporary furnishings. There are 15 guest rooms plus several guest suites and cottages. While in Laguna Beach, browse the variety of specialty shops or dine at one of the dog-friendly restaurants. Interested in a stroll on the beach? Main Beach (certain dog hours) is a short drive from the inn. There is a $10 per day additional pet fee.

Parks

Laguna Beach

Laguna Beach Dog Park
Laguna Canyon Rd
Laguna Beach, CA
near El Toro Rd

This dog park, known by the locals as Bark Park, is open six days a week and closed on Wednesdays for clean-up. The park is open from dawn to dusk.

Beaches

Laguna Beach

Main Beach
Pacific Hwy (Hwy 1)
Laguna Beach, CA
Broadway/Laguna Canyon Rd
949-497-3311
Dogs are allowed on this beach between 6pm and 8am, June 1 to September 16. The rest of the year, they are allowed on the beach from dawn until dusk. Dogs must be on a leash at all times.

Restaurants

Laguna Beach

Food Village
211-217 Broadway St
Laguna Beach, CA
Pacific Coast Hwy (Hwy 1)

The Food Village consists of several different restaurants like Gina's Pizza, El Pollo Loco and more. All of these restaurants share the same 8-10 tables. Just order food inside and grab one of the tables outside. It's located on Broadway St at Pacific Coast Hwy.

Laguna Hills Dog Travel Guide
Restaurants

Laguna Hills

Baja Fresh Mexican Grill
26548 Moulton Park Way
Laguna Hills, CA
949-360-4222
This Mexican restaurant is open for lunch and dinner. They use fresh ingredients and making their salsa and beans daily. Some of the items on their menu include Enchiladas, Burritos, Tacos Salads, Quesadillas, Nachos, Chicken, Steak and more. Well-behaved leashed dogs are allowed at the outdoor tables.

Laguna Niguel Dog Travel Guide
Parks

Laguna Niguel

Laguna Niguel Pooch Park
Golden Latern
Laguna Niguel, CA
fire station 49

This fully enclosed dog park is located in the city of Laguna Niguel, which is between Laguna Beach and Dana Point. The park is operated by the City of Laguna Niguel's Parks and Recreation Department. It is located on Golden Latern, next to fire station 49. From the Pacific Coast Highway in Dana Point, go up Goldern Latern about 2 miles. Thanks to one of our readers for this information.

Mission Viejo Dog Travel Guide
Parks

Mission Viejo

Holy Jim Historic Trail
Trabuco Canyon Road
Mission Viejo, CA
909-736-1811
This trail is part of the Cleveland National Forest. It is about a 4.5 mile hike on a combination of fire roads and single track trails. You can see a small waterfall on this trail which is best viewed in early spring. This trail is used by both hikers and mountain bikers. Pets on leash are allowed and please clean up after them. To get there from Highway 5, exit El Toro Road and head north (away from the coast). Take Live Oak Canyon Road to the right, then turn left onto Trabuco Canyon Road.

Restaurants

Mission Viejo

Baja Fresh Mexican Grill
27620 Marguerite Pkwy Ste C
Mission Viejo, CA
949-347-9033
This Mexican restaurant is open for lunch and dinner. They use fresh ingredients and making their salsa and beans daily. Some of the items on their menu include Enchiladas, Burritos, Tacos Salads, Quesadillas, Nachos, Chicken, Steak and more. Well-behaved leashed dogs are allowed at the outdoor tables.

Vets and Kennels

Mission Viejo

Animal Urgent Care Clinic
28085 Hillcrest
Mission Viejo, CA 92692
Marguerite Pkwy
949-364-6228
Monday - Friday 6pm to 8am, Noon Saturday to 8 am Monday.

Newport Beach Dog Travel Guide
Accommodations - RV Parks and Campgrounds

Newport Beach

Newport Dunes Waterfront Resort
1131 Back Bay Drive
Newport Beach, CA 92660

949-729-3863
This RV resort offers 394 RV sites with hookups. Amenities include a playground, fitness center, bike trail, laundry facilities, general store, onsite cafe and pet walk. Up to two well-behaved dogs per site are allowed but must be leashed, never left unattended, kept inside your RV at night and not allowed at the beach or in the water.

Attractions

Newport Beach

Fashion Island Mall
1133 Newport Center Dr
Newport Beach, CA
near Hwy 1 & San Joaquin Hills Rd
800-495-4753
Fashion Island Mall is known as Southern California's premier open-air shopping center. And they allow dogs. Some of the stores allow your well-behaved dog inside. Please always ask the store clerk before bringing your dog inside, just in case policies have changed. For a list of dog-friendly stores, please look at our stores category. You can also shop at the numerous outdoor retail kiosks located throughout the mall. Work up an appetite after walking around? Try dining at the fast food court located upstairs which has many outdoor seats complete with heaters.

Fun Zone Boat Tours
6000 Edgewater Place
Newport Beach, CA 92661
end of Palm St
949-673-0240
The people here are very dog-friendly and welcome your pup on several of their boat tours. The narrated trips range in length from 45 to 90 minutes and can include a harbor, sea lion and Lido Island tour. The prices range from $6.00 to $9.00 and less for children. Prices are subject to

change. Boat tours depart every half hour seven days a week. They do have a summer and winter schedule, so please call ahead for the hours. Whale watching tours are also available from January through March. (see Attractions). The Fun Zone Boat Co. is located at the end of Palm Street next to the Ferris Wheel.

Fun Zone Boat-Whale Watching Tours
600 Edgewater Place
Newport Beach, CA
end of Palm St
949-673-0240
These nice folks allow dogs on their whale watching boat tours. The tour guide has a golden retriever that rides with him. He asks that your dog be friendly around other dogs and remain leashed while on the boat. He might also limit the number of dogs on the tour depending on how all the pups get along with each other. The whale watching tours are seasonal and last from January through the end of March. Tours are $12 per person for 2 hours. The boat departs for the tour twice per day, so please call ahead for hours. Fun Zone Boat Co. is located off Balboa Blvd. in Balboa (near Newport Beach). It's next to the Balboa Fun Zone and Ferris Wheel.

Marina Water Sports-Boat Rentals
600 E Bay Ave

307

Newport Beach, CA 92661
Washington Ave
949-673-3372
Want to drive your own rental boat on Newport Bay? This company allows dogs on their pontoon boats. These are flat bottom boats usually with canopies on top which are great for dogs. Rental rates start at $45-50 per hour. They are located on Bay Ave next to the Balboa Fun Zone/Ferris Wheel near Washington Ave and Palm St.

Beaches

Newport Beach

Newport and Balboa Beaches
Balboa Blvd.
Newport Beach, CA
949-644-3211
There are several smaller beaches which run along Balboa Blvd. Dogs are only allowed before 9am and after 5pm, year round. Pets must be on a 6 foot or less leash and people are required to clean up after their pets. Tickets will be issued if your dog is off leash. The beaches are located along Balboa Blvd and ample parking is located near the Balboa and Newport Piers.

Parks

Newport Beach

Upper Newport Bay Regional Park
University Dr & Irvine Ave
Newport Beach, CA
949-640-1751
This regional park borders the Newport Back Bay and consists of approximately 140 acres of open space. This coastal wetland is renowned as one of the finest bird watching sites in North America. During winter migration, there can be tens of thousands of birds at one time. It is also home to six rare or endangered bird species. The park has

a 2-3 mile one-way paved path that is used by walkers, joggers and bicyclists. Additional dirt trails run along the hills. You can park at a variety of points along the road, but many people park at Irvine Ave and University Dr. Dogs must be leashed in the park.

Restaurants

Newport Beach

Baja Fresh Mexican Grill
1324 Bison Avenue
Newport Beach, CA
949-759-0010
This Mexican restaurant is open for lunch and dinner. They use fresh ingredients and making their salsa and beans daily. Some of the items on their menu include Enchiladas, Burritos, Tacos Salads, Quesadillas, Nachos, Chicken, Steak and more. Well-behaved leashed dogs are allowed at the outdoor tables.

Charlie's Chili
102 McFadden Place
Newport Beach, CA 92663
949-675-7991
Charlie's Chili is next to the Newport Beach Pier. Dogs are welcome at the outdoor tables. The restaurant is closed Mondays.

Francoli
1133 Newport Center Dr
Newport Beach, CA 92660
in Fashion Island Mall
949-721-1289
This restaurant is located in the dog-friendly Fashion Island Mall. It is located next to Macy's. They serve salads, sandwiches, pasta and more.

Park Avenue Cafe
501 Park Avenue
Newport Beach, CA
949-673-3830
Dogs are allowed at the outdoor tables. Thanks to one of our readers for recommending this cafe.

Stores

Newport Beach

Anthropologie
Fashion Island Mall
Newport Beach, CA
949-720-9946
Your well-behaved leashed dog is allowed inside this store.

Barnes and Noble
Fashion Island Mall
Newport Beach, CA
949-759-0982
Your well-behaved leashed dog is allowed inside this store.

Bebe
Fashion Island Mall
Newport Beach, CA
949-640-2429
Your well-behaved leashed dog is allowed inside this store.

Bloomingdale's
Fashion Island Mall
Newport Beach, CA
949-729-6600
Your well-behaved leashed dog is allowed inside this store.

Georgiou
Fashion Island Mall
Newport Beach, CA

949-760-2558
Your well-behaved leashed dog is allowed inside this store. They told us on the phone that "We always welcome dogs!".

Neiman Marcus
601 Newport Center Drive
Newport Beach, CA 92660
Fashion Island Shopping Center
949-759-1900
This famous department store, which sells everything from clothing to home furnishings, allows your well-behaved leashed dog to shop with you. It is located in Fashion Island Shopping Center, which is very dog-friendly.

Pottery Barn
Fashion Island Mall
Newport Beach, CA
949-644-2406
Your well-behaved leashed dog is allowed inside this store.

Restoration Hardware
Fashion Island Mall
Newport Beach, CA
949-760-9232
Your well-behaved leashed dog is allowed inside this store.

Robinsons-May
Fashion Island Mall
Newport Beach, CA
949-644-2800
Your well-behaved leashed dog is allowed inside this store.

Sharper Image
Fashion Island Mall
Newport Beach, CA
949-640-8800
Your well-behaved leashed dog is allowed inside this store.

St. Croix
Fashion Island Mall
Newport Beach, CA
949-760-8191
Your well-behaved leashed dog is allowed inside this store.

The Limited
Fashion Island Mall
Newport Beach, CA
949-720-9891
Your well-behaved leashed dog is allowed inside this store.

Three Dog Bakery
924 Avacado
Newport Beach, CA 92660
Hwy 1 (near MacArthur Blvd)
949-760-3647
Bring your pup here for a real treat. This is a bakery specifically for canines. They have a variety of baked goodies ranging from cookies to cakes for your dog. Come into the store and let your dog drool over the selections.

Victoria's Secret
Fashion Island Mall
Newport Beach, CA
949-721-9606
Your well-behaved leashed dog is allowed inside this store.

Orange Dog Travel Guide
Accommodations

Orange

Motel 6
2920 W Chapman Ave
Orange, CA 92868
714-634-2441
There are no additional pet fees.

Residence Inn - Orange
3101 W. Chapman Avenue
Orange, CA 92868
714-976-7700
There is a $100 one time pet fee and a $10 per day additional pet fee.

Parks

Orange

Irvine Regional Park
1 Irvine Park Rd

Orange, CA 92862
Santiago Canyon
714-633-8074
Located in the foothills, this is California's oldest regional park. With over 470 acres, this park has a variety of Oak and Sycamore groves, streams, a pond, a paved trail, picnic tables and BBQs. There are also several historical sites and plaques located throughout the park. Maps are available from the park ranger at the main entrance. Because this park is also a wilderness area with mountain lions, park rules state that minors must be under adult supervision at all times. Dogs must be leashed. There is a minimal parking fee.

Peters Canyon Regional Park
Canyon View Ave
Orange, CA
between Newport & Jamboree Rd
714-538-4400
This park has over 350 acres of coastal sage scrub, woodlands, a freshwater marsh, and a 55 acre reservoir. They have a variety of dirt paths and trails (approx. 2-3 miles) which are frequented by hikers, mountain bikers, equestrians and of course, leashed dogs. All trails are closed for three days following rainfall. To get there from Hwy 5 or Hwy 405, take the Jamboree Road exit north. Then turn left at Canyon View Ave. Proceed 1/4 mile to the park entrance and parking lot. Maps should be available at a stand near the parking lot.

Restaurants

Orange

Byblos Mediterranean Cafe
129 W Chapman Ave
Orange, CA 92866
Old Town Orange
714-538-7180
Dogs are allowed at the outdoor tables.

Krispy Kreme Doughnuts
330 The City Dr S
Orange, CA 92868
714-769-4330
Dogs are allowed at the outdoor tables.

Two's Company
22 Plaza Square
Orange, CA 92866
Old Town Orange
714-771-7633
Dogs are allowed at the outdoor tables.

Stores

Orange

Barnes and Noble Bookstore
791 S Main Street
Orange, CA 92868
714-558-0028
Well-behaved, leashed dogs may accompany shoppers in the bookstore or at the outdoor tables at the coffee shop.

San Clemente Dog Travel Guide
Accommodations

San Clemente

Holiday Inn
111 S. Ave. De Estrella
San Clemente, CA 92672
949-361-3000
There is a $10 per day pet fee.

Restaurants

San Clemente

Baja Fresh Mexican Grill
979 Avenida Pico
San Clemente, CA
949-361-4667
This Mexican restaurant is open for lunch and dinner. They use fresh ingredients and making their salsa and beans daily. Some of the items on their menu include Enchiladas, Burritos, Tacos Salads, Quesadillas, Nachos, Chicken, Steak and more. Well-behaved leashed dogs are allowed at the outdoor tables.

San Juan Capistrano Dog Travel Guide
Stores

San Juan Capistrano

Dakota's Place
31761 Camino Capistrano
San Juan Capistrano, CA 92675
949-661-3647
Dogs are welcome in this store which offers fine gifts and collectibles for pets and their people. Dakota the dog will usually greet people at the door.

Santa Ana Dog Travel Guide
Accommodations

Santa Ana

Motel 6
1623 E First Street
Santa Ana, CA 92701
714-558-0500
Dogs must be on leash on the premises.

Red Roof Inn
2600 N Main Street
Santa Ana, CA 92705
714-542-0311
There is a $10 one time pet fee.

Stores

Santa Ana

REI
1411 Village Way
Santa Ana, CA
McFadden Place
714-543-4142
This clothing and outdoor adventure store allows
well-behaved, leashed dogs to accompany
shoppers.

Trabuco Canyon Dog Travel Guide
Parks

Trabuco Canyon

O'Neill Regional Park
30892 Trabuco Canyon Road
Trabuco Canyon, CA 92678
949-923-2260
This heavily wooded park offers hiking trails.
Dogs on a 6 foot or less leash are allowed and
please clean up after them.

Tustin Dog Travel Guide
Restaurants

Tustin

Whole Foods Market
14945 Holt Ave.
Tustin, CA 92780
714-731-3400
This natural food supermarket offers natural and
organic foods. Order some food from their deli
and bring it to an outdoor table where your well-
behaved leashed dog is welcome.

Chapter 11

California Dog-Friendly Travel Guide
Inland Empire

Arrowbear Dog Travel Guide
Accommodations - RV Parks and Campgrounds

Arrowbear

Crab Flats Campground
off Green Valley Road
Arrowbear, CA
909-337-2444
This San Bernardino National Forest campground is located at an elevation of 6,200 feet. It is a popular campsite and off-highway vehicle staging area. Off-road and hiking trails are located near this campground. Tent and small RV sites are available, with a maximum RV length of 15 feet. Sites are available on a first-come, first-served basis. Pets on leash are allowed and please clean up after them. To get there take 330 north and go through Running Springs and Arrowbear to Green Valley Road. Turn left and go about 4 miles to the Crab Flats Campground sign at Forestry (dirt road). Turn left and go about 4.5 miles.

Green Valley Campground
Green Valley Lake Road
Arrowbear, CA
909-337-2444
This 36 site campground is located in the San Bernardino National Forest. RVs up to 22 feet are allowed and there are no hookups. The lake offers fishing, swimming and boating. Trails are located nearby. Pets on leash are allowed and please clean up after them. To make a reservation, call 1-877-444-6777. To get there, take Highway 330 north. Go through Running Springs and Arrowbear to Green Valley Lake Road. Turn left and go about 6 miles to the campground.

Parks

Arrowbear

Crab Creek Trail
off Green Valley Road
Arrowbear, CA
909-337-2444
This 2.5 mile moderate rated trail is located in the San Bernardino National Forest. On the trail, you may have to cross Deep Creek. Do not attempt to cross the creek when the water is high as it is too dangerous. Pets are allowed but must be on a 6

foot or less leash. Please clean up after them. The trailhead is located at Forest Road 3N34, west of the Crab Flats Campground. To get there take 330 north and go through Running Springs and Arrowbear to Green Valley Road. Turn left and go about 4 miles to the Crab Flats Campground sign at Forestry (dirt road). Turn left and go about 4.5 miles.

Crabflats Trail
off Green Valley Road
Arrowbear, CA
909-337-2444
This 1.3 mile long moderate rated trail is located in the San Bernardino National Forest. The trail descends and joins up with the Pacific Crest Trail west of the Holocomb Crossing Trail Camp. Pets are allowed but must be on a 6 foot or less leash. Please clean up after them. The trailhead is located at Forest Road 3N34, west of the Crab Flats Campground. To get there take 330 north and go through Running Springs and Arrowbear to Green Valley Road. Turn left and go about 4 miles to the Crab Flats Campground sign at Forestry (dirt road). Turn left and go about 4.5 miles.

Pacific Coast National Scenic Trail
off Green Valley Road
Arrowbear, CA
909-337-2444
The 40 mile one way moderate rated trail is located in the San Bernardino National Forest. Pets are allowed but must be on a 6 foot or less leash. Please clean up after them. One entry point to this trail is at Forest Road 3N16, which is near the Crab Flats Campground. To get there take 330 north and go through Running Springs and Arrowbear to Green Valley Road. Turn left and go about 4 miles to the Crab Flats Campground sign at Forestry (dirt road). Turn left and go about 4.5 miles.

Banning Dog Travel Guide
Accommodations

Banning

Super 8
1690 W. Ramsey St
Banning, CA 92220
909-849-6887
There is a $5 per day additional pet fee.

Travelodge
1700 W. Ramsey Street
Banning, CA 92220

909-849-1000
A well-behaved large dog is allowed. There is a $5 per day pet charge.

Beaumont Dog Travel Guide
Accommodations

Beaumont

Best Western El Rancho Motor Inn
480 East 5th Street
Beaumont, CA 92223
909-845-2176
There is a $16 per day pet charge. Dogs are allowed in certain pet rooms.

Big Bear City Dog Travel Guide
Accommodations

Big Bear City

Cienaga Creek Ranch
P.O. Box 2773
Big Bear City, CA 92314
909-584-1147
There is a $10 per day pet fee. Pets may not be left unattended in the cottages. According to a reader "4 cozy, clean and comfortable cottages on 40 acres adjoining BLM land. Very relaxed, run by nice people. Plenty of leash-free hiking right from your door."

Vets and Kennels

Big Bear City

Bear City Animal Hospital
214 Big Bear Blvd W
Big Bear City, CA 92314
909-585-7808
Monday - Friday 7:30 am - 6 pm. Closed Weekends.

VCA Lakeside Animal Hospital
42160 N Shore Dr
Big Bear City, CA 92314
909-866-2021
Monday - Saturday 8 am - 6 pm. Sunday 9 am - 5 pm.

Big Bear Lake Dog Travel Guide
Accommodations

Big Bear Lake

Big Bear Frontier
40472 Big Bear Blvd
Big Bear Lake, CA 92315
909-866-5888
The Big Bear Frontier is a group of cabins and motel rooms nestled in a beautiful mountain setting. The Big Bear Frontier is located on Big Bear Lake. It is located in easy walking distance to Big Bear Village. Amenities include pool, jacuzzi, gym and more. There is a $15 per night pet fee. Pets may not be left unattended and must be kept on a leash when out of the room.

Eagle's Nest Lodge
41675 Big Bear Blvd.
Big Bear Lake, CA 92315
909-866-6465
There are 5 cabins and only 1 allows dogs, but it is a pretty nice cabin. It's called the Sierra Madre and includes a kitchen, fireplace and separate bedroom. You can order breakfast delivered to the room for an additional $10 per person.

Grey Squirrel Resort
39372 Big Bear Blvd
Big Bear Lake, CA 92315
909-866-4335
This dog-friendly resort has cabins that accommodate from 1-2 people up to 20 people. They have a heated pool, indoor spa, basketball and horseshoes. Some of the cabins have fireplaces and kitchens. All units have VCRs and microwaves. There is a $10 per day additional pet fee.

Holiday Inn
42200 Moonridge Rd
Big Bear Lake, CA 92315
909-866-6666
There is a $15 per day pet fee. Dogs may not be left alone in the room.

Mtn. Resort Adventure Hostel
PO Box 1951
Big Bear Lake, CA
909-866-8900
According to the people at the Hostel "Rent beds or private rooms in our cozy hostel overlooking Big Bear Lake. Fenced grass yard for dogs to play in. All dogs welcome as long as they are friendly with our dogs."

Shore Acres Lodge
40090 Lakeview Drive
Big Bear Lake, CA 92315
909-866-8200
This resort has 11 cabins and is next to Big Bear Lake and has its own private boat dock. Other amenities include BBQs, volleyball, a children's playground, pool and spa.

Timber Haven Lodge
877 Tulip Lane
Big Bear Lake, CA

909-866-7207
Dogs are not allowed to remain unattended in the cabins. There is a $10 per day additional pet fee.

Timberline Lodge
39921 Big Bear Blvd.
Big Bear Lake, CA 92315
909-866-4141
The "Pets Welcome" sign at the main entrance will let you know your pup is more than welcome here. Some of the 13 cabins have fireplaces and full kitchens. There is also a playground for kids. There is a $10 per day additional pet fee per pet.

Wildwood Resort
40210 Big Bear Blvd.
Big Bear Lake, CA 92315
909-878-2178
This cabin resort has about 15 cabins of various sizes. Most rooms have fireplaces and all cabins have private picnic benches and BBQs. There is also a pool & spa and if your pup is well-behaved, he or she can be tied to the rails on the inside of the pool area. It's a close drive to town and to some of the parks and attractions. Not too many restaurants within walking distance, but there is a local service that delivers food - check with the front desk. This is a nice place to relax and unwind. There is a $10 per day additional pet fee. There are no designed smoking or non-smoking cabins.

Accommodations - RV Parks and Campgrounds

Big Bear Lake

Holcomb Valley Campground
Van Dusen Canyon Road
Big Bear Lake, CA
909-866-3437
This tent and RV campground is located in the historic Holcomb Valley about a mile from the Belleville Ghost Town. See our listing under Big Bear Lake for more information about the ghost town. There is no water and no hookups at the campsite. Camp amenities include toilets. The sites are on a first-come, first-served basis. Pets are allowed but must be leashed and cannot be left unattended. Watch out for rattlesnakes, especially during the warm summer months. The campground is located in the San Bernardino National Forest. To get there from the northeast corner of Big Bear Lake, take Highway 38 east and turn left onto Van Dusen Canyon Road. Once on this road, you will travel about 4 to 5 miles on a dirt road. The campground will be on the left.

Holloway's RV Park
398 Edgemoor Road
Big Bear Lake, CA 92315
909-866-5706
This RV park offers large level sites with a nice view of Big Bear Lake. RV sites offer full hookups, tables, barbecues. and TV cable. Park amenities include a small convenience store, restrooms, showers, laundry room, playground with horseshoes, basketball and boat rentals. Dogs are allowed at the campgrounds and on the boat rentals. Pets must be leashed and please clean up after them.

Pineknot Campground
Bristlecone
Big Bear Lake, CA
909-866-3437
This 52 site campground is part of the San Bernardino National Forest. It is located at an elevation of 7,000 feet. There are both tent and RV spaces with a maximum RV length of 45 feet. Amenities include water, flush toilets and picnic areas. Pets must be on leash and cannot be left unattended. Please clean up after your pets. The campground is on Bristlecone near Summit Blvd. Call to make a reservation.

Serrano Campground

4533 North Shore Drive
Big Bear Lake, CA
909-866-3437
This campground, located within steps of Big Bear Lake, offers tent and RV sites with full hookups. Well-behaved leashed dogs are welcome. Dogs are allowed at the campground, on the trails and in the lake. Pets cannot be left alone in the campground. Please clean up after your pet. To make a reservation, call 1-877-444-6777. The camp is located 4.5 miles east of the dam on the north side of the lake.

Accommodations - Vacation Home Rentals

Big Bear Lake

Mountain Lodging Unlimited
41135 Big Bear Blvd
Big Bear Lake, CA 92315
909-866-5500
Dogs are allowed in some of the vacation rentals, cabins, and motels. They will tell you which rentals allow dogs.

Attractions

Big Bear Lake

Belleville Ghost Town
Holcomb Valley Road
Big Bear Lake, CA

Belleville Ghost Town, located in Holcomb Valley, is one of the old Southern California ghost towns. To get there, you'll take a dirt road, but it is rated a 2 wheel drive road meaning you don't necessarily need a 4WD. At the ghost town, you'll find the old saloon, mining equipment, hanging tree, mines, graves and foundations. This ghost town is located within a National Forest which means you and your pup are welcome to walk or hike on almost any of the trails (the Pacific Crest Trail is the exception). To get there from the northeast corner of Big Bear Lake, take Hwy 38 east and turn left onto Van Dusen Canyon Road. Once on this road, you'll travel about 4-5 miles on a dirt road. When the road ends (there is a campground to the left), turn right on Holcomb Valley Road. The ghost town of Belleville will be approx. less than 1 mile on the right. Go during the late spring through fall when there is no snow.

Big Bear Bikes/Snowshoes
41810 Big Bear Blvd.
Big Bear Lake, CA
Summit Rd. (by KFC)
909-866-2224
Rent some snowshoes and go for a snowy mountain hike with your best friend. Big Bear Bikes rents snowshoes and cross-country skis. After picking up the snow gear ($10-15) and the National Forest Adventure Pass for parking ($5), head over to the forest trail off Mill Creek Rd (by the Alpine Slides). Prices are subject to change. The rental shop will be able to provide directions and/or maps. Once at the trail, you'll be able to go snowshoeing for miles.

Big Bear Marina
500 Paine Road
Big Bear Lake, CA 92315
909-866-3218
At Big Bear Marina you can rent fishing boats for a fishing trip on the lake. Dogs are only allowed on the fishing boats, not the other types of boats rented here.

Holloway's Marina
398 Edgemoor Road
Big Bear Lake, CA 92315
909-866-5706
Here you and your pup can rent a covered pontoon boat or a fishing boat for a morning, afternoon, or day on the lake.

Pine Knot Landing-Boat Rentals
439 Pine Knot Road
Big Bear Lake, CA 92315
Big Bear Blvd.
909-866-2628
Rent a boat with your pup in beautiful Big Bear Lake. You'll drive your own gas powered pontoon boat which goes up to 15 miles per hour. These are nice boats which have a covering and a good amount of room for your dog to walk around.

Remember to bring along some water. If you've never driven a boat, don't worry. The people working there say if you know how to drive a car, you'll be fine. Rent a boat by the hour or day. The rate for 3 hours is about $100. Prices are subject to change. This boat rental company is at Pine Knot Landing which is located at the end of Pine Knot Road near Hwy 18 (Big Bear Blvd.)

Pleasure Point Landing
603 Landlock Landing Rd
Big Bear Lake, CA 92315
909-866-2455
You can rent boats here for boating on Big Bear Lake.

Parks

Big Bear Lake

Alpine Pedal Path
Hwy 38
Big Bear Lake, CA
Stanfield Cutoff

This path is mostly paved and is about a 4-5 mile round trip. Throughout most of the path, there are various access points to the lake and various beaches. The beginning of the path is located off of the Stanfield Cutoff (bridge over Big Bear Lake, close to the village). For easier access, (going away from the village), take the Stanfield Cutoff to the other side of the lake and turn left onto Hwy 38. In about 1/4 - 1/2 mile, parking will be on the left.

Big Bear Lake beaches
Hwy 38
Big Bear Lake, CA
Stanfield Cutoff

There are various beaches along the lake on Hwy 38. You can get to any of the beaches via the Alpine Pedal Path. To get there, (going away from the village), take the Stanfield Cutoff to the other side of the lake and turn left onto Hwy 38. In about 1/4 - 1/2 mile, parking will be on the left.

Pine Knot Trail
Tulip Lane
Big Bear Lake, CA
Hwy 18
909-866-3437

This hiking trail is about 3 miles each way and is rated moderate to difficult. To get there from the village, head west on Hwy 18 and turn left onto Tulip Lane. The trail begins by the Alpine Glen Picnic Area. Remember, to park here, you'll need a Forest Day Pass. Check with your hotel or some of the stores in the village for info on where to purchase this pass.

Grout Bay Trail
Hwy 38
Big Bear Lake, CA
909-866-3437
This hiking trail is about 3-5 miles each way and is rated easy to moderate. To get there from the village, head west on Hwy 18. Take Hwy 38 to the right, towards the northwest corner of the lake. The trail begins by the Grout Bay Picnic Area.

Woodland Trail / Nature Walk
Hwy 38
Big Bear Lake, CA
by the Stanfield Cutoff
909-866-3437
This is a nature trail with about 20 informational stops. Pick up one of the maps and follow the self-guided 1.5 mile nature walk. This is rated as an easy loop. To get there, (going away from the village), take the Stanfield Cutoff to the other side of the lake and turn left onto Hwy 38. In about 1/2 mile, parking will be on the right.

Restaurants

Big Bear Lake

Alpine High Country Cafe
41546 Big Bear Blvd
Big Bear Lake, CA
909-866-1959
They have one outdoor table.

Belotti's Bakery & Pizza
41248 Big Bear Blvd
Big Bear Lake, CA 92315
909-866-9686
Come here for some fresh baked pastries and other goodies. For lunch, they serve pizza and a few other Italian dishes.

Big Bear Mountain Brewery
40260 Big Bear Blvd
Big Bear Lake, CA
at Red Hawk Golf Course
909-866-2337
Dogs are allowed at the outdoor tables.

Blue Whale Lakeside Restaurant
350 Alden Rd
Big Bear Lake, CA
909-866-5771

Dogs are allowed at the outdoor tables.

Main Street Cafe
40736 Village Drive
Big Bear Lake, CA
909-866-8020
Dogs are allowed at the outdoor tables.

Pine Knot Coffee House and Bakery
959 Pine Knot
Big Bear Lake, CA 92315
Hwy 18
909-866-3537
This is a nice spot for breakfast, lunch or dinner. On the weekends and sometimes during the weekdays, there is live entertainment. If you sit at the tables on the front porch, you'll easily be able to hear the music. You and your pup have a choice of tables on the front porch or on the side patio.

Village Pizza
40568 Village Dr
Big Bear Lake, CA 92315
near the village
909-866-8505
This pizza place is within walking distance to Big Bear Village.

Claremont Dog Travel Guide

Travel Guide - Please always call ahead to make sure an establishment is still dog-friendly.

Accommodations

Claremont

Ramada Inn
840 South Indian Hill Blvd
Claremont, CA 91711
909-621-4831
There are no additional pet fees.

Parks

Claremont

Pooch Park
College Ave
Claremont, CA
near Arrow Hwy

This park has lots of grass and trees and a ravine for the dogs to climb up and down. There is a 3 foot fence around the park. The Pooch Park is near the colleges. Take the I-10 to Monte Vista and go north to Arrow Highway. Go west on Arrow Hwy to College Ave. Go north on College Ave. 1 block until you see park sign on the east side. Thanks to one of our readers for recommending this dog park.

Restaurants

Claremont

Aruffo's Italian Cuisine
126 Yale Ave
Claremont, CA 91711
909-624-9624
Dogs are allowed at the outdoor tables.

Heroes Bar and Grill
131 Yale Avenue
Claremont, CA 91711
909-621-6712
Dogs are allowed at the outdoor tables.

Some Crust Bakery
119 Yale Avenue
Claremont, CA 91711
909-621-9772
Dogs are allowed at the outdoor tables.

Village Grill
148 Yale Ave
Claremont, CA 91711
909-626-8813
Dogs are allowed at the outdoor tables.

Colton Dog Travel Guide
Accommodations

Colton

Days Inn
2830 Iowa Ave
Colton, CA
909-788-9900
A well-behaved large dog is okay. There is a $5 per day additional pet fee.

Corona Dog Travel Guide
Accommodations

Corona

Motel 6
200 N Lincoln Ave
Corona, CA 92882
909-735-6408
There are no additional pet fees.

Parks

Corona

Butterfield Park Dog Park
1886 Butterfield Drive
Corona, CA
909-736-2241
This .8 acre fenced off-leash dog area is located in Butterfield Park. The dog park is well-shaded with benches, a picnic table and a doggie drinking fountain. From the 91 Freeway, take the Maple Street exit and go north. Maple will dead end at Smith Street. Go left on Smith Street about .5 miles to Butterfield Drive. Then turn left to Butterfield Park just across the street from the airport. Thanks to one of our readers for recommending this dog park.

Diamond Bar Dog Travel Guide
Vets and Kennels

Diamond Bar

East Valley Emergency Pet Clinic
938 N Diamond Bar Blvd
Diamond Bar, CA 91765
909-861-5737
Monday - Friday 6 pm to 8 am, Saturday 12 noon to 8 am Monday.

Fawnskin Dog Travel Guide

Accommodations

Fawnskin

Quail Cove
P.O. Box 117
Fawnskin, CA 92333
800-595-2683
This lodge offers rustic and cozy cabins in a quiet wooded surrounding on Big Bear Lake. They are located within walking distance to several restaurants, markets, marinas and some of the hiking trails and fishing spots. Pets are always welcome. There is a $10 per day pet charge. Never leave your pet unattended in the cabin.

Accommodations - RV Parks and Campgrounds

Fawnskin

Hanna Flat Campground
Rim of the World Drive
Fawnskin, CA
909-337-2444
This 88 site campground is located in the San Bernardino National Forest at an elevation of 7,000 feet. RVs up to 40 feet are allowed and there are no hookups. Amenities include picnic tables, fire rings, paved parking, flush toilets and trash dumpster. The Hanna Flat Trailhead is located at this camp. Pets on leash are allowed and please clean up after them. To make a reservation, call 1-877-444-6777. To get there take Highway 18 to Big Bear Lake Dam. Go straight, do not cross over the dam. Highway 18 becomes Highway 38. Go the Fawnskin Fire Station and turn left onto the Rim of the World Drive. Go about 2.5 miles on a dirt road to the campsite.

Parks

Fawnskin

Hanna Flat Trail
Rim of the World Drive
Fawnskin, CA
909-337-2444
This 9 mile round trip moderate rated trail is located in the San Bernardino National Forest. Pets on leash are allowed and please clean up after them. This trail is closed every year from November 1 to April 1 due to the bald eagle wintering habitat. To get there take Highway 18 to Big Bear Lake Dam. Go straight, do not cross over the dam. Highway 18 becomes Highway 38. Go the Fawnskin Fire Station and turn left onto the Rim of the World Drive. Go about 2.5 miles on a dirt road to the campsite and trailhead.

Grand Terrace Dog Travel Guide
Vets and Kennels

Grand Terrace

Animal Emergency Clinic
12022 La Crosse Ave
Grand Terrace, CA 92313
215 and Barton Rd
909-783-1300
Monday - Friday 6 pm to 8 am, 24 hours on weekends and holidays.

Hemet Dog Travel Guide
Accommodations

Hemet

Super 8
3510 W. Florida
Hemet, CA 92545
909-658-2281
There is a $5 per day additional pet fee.

Hesperia Dog Travel Guide
Accommodations

Hesperia

Days Suites
14865 Bear Valley Rd
Hesperia, CA 92345
760-948-0600
There is a $7 per day pet fee.

Idyllwild Dog Travel Guide
Accommodations

Idyllwild

Silver Pines Lodge
25955 Cedar St
Idyllwild, CA 92549
909-659-4335
This lodge sits on 1 1/2 acres of wooded pine forest overlooking Strawberry Creek. The lodge is approximately 2 blocks from the main village of Idyllwild where there are many eateries and shops. Each cabin is individually decorated and has its own unique features. Most rooms have

fireplaces and about half have kitchens. Every room has its own refrigerator, bathroom, color cable TV and complimentary coffee. Dogs are welcome in all of the cabins, except the Foley Cabin. There is a $10 one time pet charge. They also ask that you please abide by the following pet rules. Never leave pets alone in the room. Pets should not go on the beds or furniture. Keep your dog leashed when on the property. Clean up after your pooch. Please wipe off your pets paws if it's snowy, rainy or muddy outside (they provide dog towels).

Tahquitz Inn
25840 Highway 243
Idyllwild, CA 92549
909-659-4554
This inn is located in the heart of scenic Idyllwild and allows all well-behaved dogs. They offer one and two bedroom suites with a separate bedroom, kitchen and porches. The inn has also been a location for several Hollywood film shoots. All of their rooms accommodate dogs. There is a $10 per day pet charge, but mention DogFriendly.com when making your reservation, and your pet stays for only $5 per night!

Attractions

Idyllwild

Annual Plein Air Festival
North Circle Drive
Idyllwild, CA
866-439-5278
Idyllwild is rated as one of the 100 Best Small Art Towns in America. Once a year there is a festival, usually held on a Saturday in the beginning of September, where artists create original works of art in the streets of the Idyllwild. Leashed dogs are welcome to accompany you at this outdoor event. For more details, please contact the Art Alliance of Idyllwild at 866-439-5278.

Parks

Idyllwild

Humber Park
Fern Valley Road
Idyllwild, CA
909-659-2117
The Devil's Slide Trail begins at this park. It is rated as a moderately difficult trail. The trail goes for about 6 miles and there is about a 3,000 foot elevation gain. Day passes are required. To get

there, take Highway 243 to North Circle Drive. Turn right onto South Circle Drive, and then left to Fern Valley Road. Follow the signs to Humber Park.

Idyllwild Park Nature Center
Highway 243
Idyllwild, CA
909-659-3850
This park offers 5 1/2 miles of hiking trails. Most of the trails are rated as easy, with the exception of one steep trail. Dogs are allowed, but need to be leashed. Your dog will also need to have a current rabies identification tag. The day use fees are $2 per person, $2 per dog and $1 per child. The park is located on Highway 243, about one mile northwest of Idyllwild.

Restaurants

Idyllwild

Arriba Mexican Restaurant
25980 Highway 243
Idyllwild, CA
909-659-4960
They are open for breakfast, lunch and dinner. Well-behaved,leashed dogs are allowed at the outdoor tables.

Cafe Aroma
North Circle Drive
Idyllwild, CA 92549
909-659-5212
This cafe is open daily and serves breakfast, lunch and dinner. Items on the menu include salads, soups, pizza, pasta, and more. Well-behaved,leashed dogs are allowed at the outdoor tables.

Jo Ans Restaurant and Bar
25070 N. Village Center Drive
Idyllwild, CA 92549
909-659-0295
Well-behaved, leashed dogs are allowed at the outdoor tables.

Oma's European Restaurant
54241 Ridgeview Drive
Idyllwild, CA
909-659-2979
This restaurant offers European cuisine in a scenic setting. They are open for breakfast and lunch. Well-behaved,leashed dogs are allowed at the outdoor tables.

La Verne Dog Travel Guide
Restaurants

La Verne

Aoki Japanese Restaurant
2307 D Street
La Verne, CA 91750
909-593-2239
Dogs are allowed at the outdoor tables.

Cafe Allegro
2124 3rd Street
La Verne, CA 91750
909-593-0788
Dogs are allowed at the outdoor tables.

Casa Garcia's Grill
2112 Bonita Ave
La Verne, CA 91750
909-593-9092
Dogs are allowed at the outdoor tables.

Phoenix Garden
2232 D Street #101
La Verne, CA 91750
909-392-2244
Dogs are allowed at the outdoor tables.

Lake Arrowhead Dog Travel Guide
Accommodations

Lake Arrowhead

Arrowhead Saddleback Inn
PO Box 1890
Lake Arrowhead, CA 92352
at the entrance to Lake Arrowhead Village
800-858-3334
This historic inn was originally constructed in 1917 as the Raven Hotel. It is now totally restored and a historical landmark. The inn is located at the entrance of the Lake Arrowhead Village. Dogs are allowed in some of the cottages. The cottages feature stone fireplaces, double whirlpool baths, heated towel racks and refrigerators. There is an $8 per day pet fee. Dog owners also need to sign a pet agreement.

Arrowhead Tree Top Lodge
27992 Rainbow Drive
Lake Arrowhead, CA 92352
909-337-2311
This inn is nestled among the tall pines on four acres of heavily forested grounds. You and your pup can enjoy a stroll on their private nature trail or find a spot at Deep Creek to sit, relax and watch the squirrels and birds. Amenities include microwaves in each of the rustic alpine rooms. It is located within walking distance of the Lake Arrowhead Village. There is an $8 per day pet fee.

Gray Squirrel Inn
326 State Hwy 173
Lake Arrowhead, CA 92352
909-336-3602
This inn is near Lake Arrowhead and has ten guest rooms. Room amenities include mini-refrigerators and coffee makers. Dogs are welcome in some of the rooms. There are no additional pet fees.

Prophet's Paradise B&B
26845 Modoc Lane
Lake Arrowhead, CA 92352
909-336-1969
This bed and breakfast has five stories which cascade down its alpine hillside. This provides guests with privacy and intimate decks. All rooms have private baths. Amenities include a gym, a pool room, ping-pong, and darts, a horseshoe pit and a nearby hiking trail. Room rates start at $100 per night and include a gourmet breakfast. Your well-behaved dog is welcome. The owners also have pets. There are no additional pet fees.

Accommodations - RV Parks and Campgrounds

Lake Arrowhead

North Shore Campground
Torrey Road
Lake Arrowhead, CA
909-337-2444
This 27 site campground is located in the San Bernardino National Forest. RVs up to 22 feet are allowed and there are no hookups. The trailhead for the North Shore National Recreation Trail is located at this campground. Pets on leash are allowed and please clean up after them. To make

a reservation, call 1-877-444-6777. The camp is located near the north shore of Lake Arrowhead, about two miles northeast of the village. To get there from the Lake Arrowhead Marina, go east on Torrey Road. At the first left, take the dirt road to Forest Road 2N25 to the trailhead.

Attractions

Lake Arrowhead

Lake Arrowhead Village
28200 Highway 189
Lake Arrowhead, CA 92352
Hwy 173
909-337-2533
This outdoor shopping resort features unique specialty and factory outlet stores. While dogs are not allowed in the stores (with the exception of the Big Dogs store), it is a nice place to walk with your pup. During the summer there are usually outdoor events next to the lake. Dogs must be leashed and you must clean up after your dog.

Parks

Lake Arrowhead

Indian Rock Trail
Highway 173
Lake Arrowhead, CA
909-337-2444
This .5 mile easy walk is located in the San Bernardino National Forest. The trail takes you to large stone slabs that were used by the Serrano Indians to grind acorns into flour. Pets on leash are allowed and please clean up after them. To get there take Highway 173 north to the Rock Camp Station.

North Shore National Recreation Trail
Torrey Road
Lake Arrowhead, CA

909-337-2444

This 1.7 mile moderate rated trail is located in the San Bernardino National Forest. The trail descends to Little Bear Creek and then goes to Forest Road 2N26Y. Pets on leash are allowed and please clean up after them. To get there from the Lake Arrowhead Marina, go east on Torrey Road. At the first left, take the dirt road to Forest Road 2N25 to the trailhead.

Stores

Lake Arrowhead

Big Dogs Sportswear
28200 Hwy 189
Lake Arrowhead, CA 92352
Hwy 173
909-336-1998
This retail store sells sportswear for people and allows well-behaved dogs inside. It is located in the Lake Arrowhead Village.

Lakeview Dog Travel Guide
Accommodations - RV Parks and Campgrounds

Lakeview

Lake Perris Campgrounds
off Cajalco Expressway
Lakeview, CA
909-657-0676
This campground offers 434 campsites including two RV areas with full hookups. While dogs are not allowed in the lake or within 100 feet of the water, they are allowed on miles of trails including the bike trail that loops around the lake. Pets must be leashed and please clean up after them. The campground is located 11 miles south of Riverside. From Interstate 215 exit at Cajalco Expressway and head east. Call to make reservations.

Parks

Lakeview

Lake Perris State Recreation Area
off Cajalco Expressway
Lakeview, CA
909-657-0676
While dogs are not allowed in the lake or within 100 feet of the water, they are allowed on miles of trails including the bike trail that loops around the lake. Pets must be leashed and please clean up after them. Pets are also allowed in the campgrounds. The park is located 11 miles south of Riverside via Highway 60 or Interstate 215.

Montclair Dog Travel Guide
Stores

Montclair

Barnes and Noble Bookstore
9041 Central Avenue
Montclair, CA 91763
909-621-5553
Well-behaved and leashed or carried dogs are allowed in this Barnes and Noble bookstore located off Highway 10 at Central Ave.

Vets and Kennels

Montclair

Emergency Pet Clinic of Pomona
8980 Benson Ave
Montclair, CA 91763
W D Street
909-981-1051
Monday - Friday 6 pm to 8 am, Noon Saturday to 8 am Monday.

Moreno Valley Dog Travel Guide
Accommodations

Moreno Valley

Econo Lodge
24412 Sunnymead Blvd
Moreno Valley, CA 92553
909-247-6699
There is a $50 refundable pet deposit and a $5 per day pet fee.

Norco Dog Travel Guide

Restaurants

Norco

Rubio's Baja Grill
110 Hidden Valley Pkwy
Norco, CA 92860
909-898-3591
Dogs are allowed at the outdoor tables.

Ontario Dog Travel Guide
Accommodations

Ontario

Country Suites by Carlson
231 N. Vineyard Ave.
Ontario, CA 91764
909-937-6000
This motel offers studio rooms, and one to two bedroom suites. Amenities include a heated pool, whirlpool, complimentary breakfast & evening beverages, and coin operated laundry facilities. Management suggests that large dogs stay in the one bedroom units and up. The studio rooms are okay for small and medium size dogs. There is a $10 per day pet charge.

Holiday Inn
3400 Shelby Street
Ontario, CA 91764
909-466-9600
Amenities include a heated pool, spa, exercise room, sauna, billiards, ping pong tables, video games and basketball courts. Rooms include refrigerators with free juices and bottled water, microwave ovens with free popcorn, hair dryers, and iron/ironing boards. There is a $50 pet deposit and $25 is refundable.

Marriott - Ontario Airport
2200 E. Holt Blvd
Ontario, CA 91761
909-975-5000
There is a $250 refundable pet deposit. There is also a $50 one time pet fee per visit.

Motel 6
1560 E Fourth St
Ontario, CA 91764
909-984-2424
A large well-behaved, well maintained dog is okay.

Red Roof Inn
1818 E Holt Blvd.
Ontario, CA 91761
909-988-8466
Amenities include a heated pool, sauna and whirlpool. There are no additional pet fees.

Parks

Ontario

Cucamonga-Guasti Park
800 N. Archibald Ave.
Ontario, CA 91764
at Highland Avenue

909-945-4321
This regional park allows leashed dogs. There is a nice path that winds along the lake which is a popular fishing spot. There is a minimal day use fee.

Restaurants

Ontario

Baja Fresh Mexican Grill
929 N. Milliken Ave Ste C
Ontario, CA
909-484-6200
This Mexican restaurant is open for lunch and dinner. They use fresh ingredients and making their salsa and beans daily. Some of the items on their menu include Enchiladas, Burritos, Tacos Salads, Quesadillas, Nachos, Chicken, Steak and more. Well-behaved leashed dogs are allowed at the outdoor tables.

Casa Corona
401 N. Euclid Ave
Ontario, CA 91762
909-986-5200
Dogs are allowed at the outdoor tables.

In-N-Out Burger
1891 E. G Street
Ontario, CA 91764
Vineyard Ave.
800-786-1000
This In-N-Out Burger has an outside window where you can place an order with your pup.

Joey's Pizza
790 N. Archibald Ave.
Ontario, CA 91764
909-944-6701
Pizza, salads, lasagna and more are served at this restaurant which has dog-friendly outdoor seating. It is located next to Cucamonga Regional Park (see Parks).

Perris Dog Travel Guide
Parks

Perris

Harford Springs Reserve
Gavilan Road
Perris, CA
909-684-7032
This 325 acre park offer hiking and equestrian trails. The park is located about 7 miles west of Perris, 2 miles south of Cajalco Road on Gavilan Road. Dogs must be leashed and please clean up after them.

Pomona Dog Travel Guide
Accommodations

Pomona

Sheraton Suites Fairplex
601 West McKinley Avenue
Pomona, CA 91768
909-622-2220
Dogs of all sizes are allowed. There is a $50 one time pet fee.

Shilo Inn
3200 Temple Ave
Pomona, CA 91768
909-598-0073
Amenities include a complimentary breakfast buffet, outdoor pool & spa, guest laundromat, fitness center and fresh fruit, popcorn & coffee. Rooms include microwaves, refrigerators, hair dryers, iron/ironing boards and more. There is a $10 per day additional pet fee.

Accommodations - RV Parks and Campgrounds

Pomona

Los Angeles/Fairplex KOA
2200 North White Avenue
Pomona, CA 91768
909-593-8915
Located about 30 miles from Disneyland and next to the Fairplex, this 12 acre campground offers both tent and RV spaces. RV site amenities include a maximum length pull through of 70 feet, 50 amp service and telephone service. Other campground amenities include a free modem dataport, snack bar, swimming pool, hot tub/sauna and pavilion/meeting room available. Well-behaved leashed dogs of all sizes are allowed for short term stays. For a one month stay or longer, they have certain size and breed restrictions. People need to clean up after their pets. There is no pet fee. The campground is open all year.

Parks

Pomona

Ganesha Park
McKinley Ave
Pomona, CA 91768
at White Ave

It is not a large park, but is a nice place to walk with your dog. The park also has several playground and picnic areas. Dogs must be leashed.

Redlands Dog Travel Guide
Parks

Redlands

Prospect Park
Cajon Street
Redlands, CA
at Highland Avenue
909-798-7572
Prospect Park is a 11.4 acre natural park with trails and picnic facilities. Dogs on leash are allowed.

Rialto Dog Travel Guide

Accommodations

Rialto

Best Western Empire Inn
475 W Valley Blvd
Rialto, CA 92376
909-877-0690
There is an additional $5 per day pet fee.

Rimforest Dog Travel Guide
Accommodations - RV Parks and Campgrounds

Rimforest

Dogwood Campground
Highway 18
Rimforest, CA
909-337-2444
This 93 site campground is located in the San
Bernardino National Forest. RVs up to 22 feet are
allowed and there are no hookups. Pets on leash
are allowed and please clean up after them. To
make a reservation, call 1-877-444-6777. To get
there go 20 miles northeast of San Bernardino on
Highway 18. The camp is located less than mile
from Rimforest and 3 miles from Lake Arrowhead.

Riverside Dog Travel Guide
Accommodations

Riverside

Best Western of Riverside
10518 Magnolia Avenue
Riverside, CA 92505
909-359-0770
There is a $10 per day pet charge and a $100
refundable pet deposit. Large dogs are okay if
they are well-behaved and leashed.

Motel 6 - East
1260 University Ave
Riverside, CA 92507
909-784-2131
Pets are not to be left unattended in rooms.

Attractions

Riverside

Citrus State Historic Park
Van Buren Blvd.
Riverside, CA 92516

at Dufferin Ave.
909-780-6222
This 400-acre historic park recognizes the
importance of the citrus industry in southern
California. In the early 1900s, "Citrus was King"
and there was a "second Gold Rush" which
brought potential citrus barons to California. The
park, which is reminiscent of a 1900s city park,
has demonstration groves, an interpretive
structure and picnic areas. Today it is also a
working citrus grove and continues to produce
high-quality fruits. Dogs are not allowed in the
buildings, but are welcome to walk leashed on the
grounds, including several trails around the
groves. The park is located in Riverside, one mile
east of Highway 91. It at the corner of Van Buren
Blvd. and Dufferin Ave.

Parks

Riverside

Box Springs Mountain Reserve
Pigeon Pass Road
Riverside, CA
909-684-7032
This 1,155 acre park offers hiking and equestrian
trails. The park is located 5 miles east of
Riverside off Highway 60 and Pigeon Pass Road.
Dogs must be leashed and please clean up after
them.

Hidden Valley Wildlife
Arlington Avenue
Riverside, CA
909-785-6362
Dogs on leash are allowed at this wildlife reserve.
It is a popular spot for birdwatching and walking.
There is a minimal fee for day use. This reserve is
part of the Santa Ana River Regional Park. To get
there from the 91 Fwy, go east to the city of
Riverside. Exit on La Sierra Ave. and turn left
(north). La Sierra dead-ends into Arlington. Bear

left at the signal. Drive past the hills until you come to the sign that says "Hidden Valley." Take the first dirt road to the right.

Mount Rubidoux Park
Mt. Rubidoux Drive
Riverside, CA
9th Avenue

This park is the highest point in downtown Riverside. It is a popular hiking trail which offers a spectacular 360 degree view of Riverside. Dogs on leash are allowed on the trails. To get there from downtown Riverside, take Mission Inn Avenue northeast (towards the Santa Ana River). Turn left (west) onto Redwood Street. Continue straight to stay on Redwood (otherwise you will go onto University Ave). Turn right on 9th Street and follow it to the park.

Rancho Jurupa Park
Crestmore Road
Riverside, CA
off Mission Inn/Buena Vista
909-684-7032
This 350 acre park is part of the Santa Ana Regional Park and has more than 10 miles of hiking and equestrian trails. There are also horseshoe pits and picnic areas. To get there from downtown Riverside, take Mission Inn Ave

northwest (towards the Santa Ana River). Go over the river and turn left at Crestmore Road. Follow this road to the park entrance. There is a minimal fee for parking and for dogs. Dogs must be leashed.

Riverside Off-Leash Area
Mission Inn Ave
Riverside, CA
near the Santa Ana River
909-715-3440
This dog park is located near the river. It is also near Mt. Rubidoux Park, which is a good place for hiking before or after your visit to the dog park. To get to the dog park, take the 91 freeway to Mission Inn St. and go west through downtown Riverside past Market St. The park is on the south side just after you cross a large bridge but before you get to the riverbed. Thanks to one of our readers for recommending this dog park.

Restaurants

Riverside

Antonious Pizza
3737 Main Street
Riverside, CA 92504
909-682-9100
This pizza place, which has dog-friendly outdoor

seating, is located in downtown Riverside.

Rowland Heights Dog Travel Guide
Parks

Rowland Heights

Schabarum Regional Park
17250 E. Colima Road
Rowland Heights, CA 91748
626-854-5560
This 640 acre wilderness park offers open space, picturesque canyons and rolling hills. Popular activities at the park including hiking, biking and horseback riding. Park amenities include an 18 station fitness trail, picnic areas, equestrian center, playgrounds and sports fields. There is a parking fee on weekends, holidays and during special events. Dogs are allowed at the park and on the hiking trails. Pets must be leashed and people need to clean up after their pet.

San Bernardino Dog Travel Guide
Accommodations

San Bernardino

Motel 6
111 Redlands Blvd
San Bernardino, CA 92408
909-825-6666
Well-behaved large dogs are okay.

Parks

San Bernardino

San Bernardino National Forest
1824 S. Commercenter Circle
San Bernardino, CA 92408
909-382-2600
This national forest covers over 600,000 acres of land which ranges in elevation from 2,000 to 11,502 feet. Please see our listings in this region for dog-friendly hikes and/or campgrounds.

Wildwood Dog Park
536 E. 40th St
San Bernardino, CA 92404

Thanks to one of our readers who writes: "We have 3.5 acres divided into 2 large areas & 1 smaller area just for little and older dogs. The larger areas are rotated to help reduce wear & tear on the turf. Amenities include: Fencing, Benches, Handicapped Access, Lighting, Parking, Poop Bags, Restrooms, Shelter, Trash Cans, Water Available. Current Shots & License Required. We are also Double-Gated for Safety."

Restaurants

San Bernardino

Baja Fresh Mexican Grill
745 E. Hospitality Lane Ste C
San Bernardino, CA
909-890-1854
This Mexican restaurant is open for lunch and dinner. They use fresh ingredients and making their salsa and beans daily. Some of the items on their menu include Enchiladas, Burritos, Tacos Salads, Quesadillas, Nachos, Chicken, Steak and more. Well-behaved leashed dogs are allowed at the outdoor tables.

San Dimas Dog Travel Guide
Accommodations - RV Parks and Campgrounds

San Dimas

East Shore RV Park
1440 Camper View Road
San Dimas, CA 91773
909-599-8355
This family RV park offers over 500 full hookup paved sites including some pull through sites. Site amenities include a grassy area, view sites, and full hookups with 20, 30 or 50 amp service. Park amenities include picnic areas, children's playground, laundry room, swimming pool, general store and market, video rentals, basketballs and volleyballs, email station, restrooms and 24 hour check-in. Well-behaved dogs are allowed in the RV park, but not in the tenting area. Pets must be leashed and please clean up after them. There is a $2 per day pet fee.

This RV park is open year-round.

Parks

San Dimas

Frank Bonelli Park
120 Via Verde Road
San Dimas, CA 91773
909-599-8411
This 1,980 acre park has a 250 acre lake for swimming, water skiing, wind surfing, sailing and fishing. The lake is stocked with trout, bluegill, catfish, and largemouth bass. Park amenities include hiking trails, playgrounds and food stands. There is a parking fee on weekends, holidays and during special events. Dogs are allowed at the park and on the hiking trails, but not in the water or at the beach area. Pets must be leashed and people need to clean up after their pet.

San Dimas Canyon Nature Center
1628 N. Sycamore Canyon Road
San Dimas, CA 91773
909-599-7512
This 1,000 plus acre park offers a variety of nature trails. There is a minimal parking fee. Dogs are allowed on the trails, but must be leashed. Please clean up after your dog.

Restaurants

San Dimas

Roady's Restaurant
160 W. Bonita Ave
San Dimas, CA 91773
909-592-0980
Dogs are allowed at the outdoor tables.

Sky Forest Dog Travel Guide
Attractions

Sky Forest

Children's Forest
Keller Peak Road
Sky Forest, CA
Hwy 18 E. of Running Springs
909-338-5156
In 1993, San Bernardino National Forest set aside a 3,400-acre site within the forest to create the first Children's Forest in the United States. Forty children and teenagers from around the country were selected and brought to work with key Forest Service staff and other experts to design a trail and interpretive exhibits that teach young people about the Forest. Dogs are not allowed on the guided tour, but you and your pooch can take a self-guided tour on the 1/2 mile paved interpretive trail. Children's Forest is located off Highway 18 at Keller Peak Road, east of Running Springs in the San Bernardino Mountains.

Temecula Dog Travel Guide
Accommodations

Temecula

Comfort Inn
27338 Jefferson Ave.
Temecula, CA 92590
909-296-3788
There is a $20 per night pet charge.

Motel 6
41900 Moreno Rd
Temecula, CA 92590
909-676-6383
One well-behaved dog per room is allowed.

Accommodations - RV Parks and Campgrounds

Temecula

Lake Skinner Campground
Rancho California Road
Temecula, CA
909-926-1541
This campground offers tent and RV sites with full
hookups. The campground is located in a 6,040
acre park which features a lake, hiking trails and
equestrian trails. Dogs are allowed on the trails
and in the campgrounds, but not in the lake or
within 50 feet of the lake. Dogs must be on a 6
foot or less leash and please clean up after them.
To get there, take Highway 15 to Rancho
California Road and go north 10 miles.

Pechanga RV Resort
45000 Pala Road
Temecula, CA 92592
909-587-0484
This RV resort is located at the Pechanga Casino
in Temecula.

Vail Lake Wine Country RV Resort
38000 Hwy 79 S
Temecula, CA 92592
909-303-0174
This RV resort is located in the country, about 15
minutes from Interstate 15. There are several
hiking trails throughout the RV park where you
can walk with your dog.

Attractions

Temecula

Filsinger Vineyards and Winery
39050 De Portola Rd
Temecula, CA 92592
909-302-6363
Dogs are allowed at the outdoor picnic tables.

Keyways Vineyard and Winery
37338 De Portola Rd
Temecula, CA 92592
909-302-7888
Dogs are allowed at the outdoor picnic tables.

Maurice Car'rie Winery
34225 Rancho California Rd
Temecula, CA 92591
909-676-1711
Dogs are allowed at the outdoor picnic area.
There are usually several outdoor arts and crafts
vendors at the winery.

Wilson Creek Winery
35960 Rancho California Rd
Temecula, CA 92591
909-699-9463
Dogs are allowed at the outdoor picnic tables.

Old Town Temecula
Front Street
Temecula, CA
Rancho California Rd

Old Town Temecula is a quaint historic area with wooden sidewalks where you and your leashed dog can walk. There are shops and some restaurants with outdoor seating.

Parks

Temecula

Duck Pond
Rancho California and Ynez Rd
Temecula, CA
Old Town
909-836-3285
Dogs on leash are allowed in the park. Owners must pick up after their dog.

Van Roekel Winery
34567 Rancho California Rd
Temecula, CA 92591
909-699-6961
Dogs are allowed at the picnic area.

Lake Skinner Recreation Area
Rancho California Road
Temecula, CA
909-926-1541
This 6,040 acre park features a lake, hiking trails, equestrian trails and camping. Dogs are allowed on the trails and in the campgrounds, but not in the lake or within 50 feet of the lake. Dogs must be on a 6 foot or less leash and please clean up after them. To get there, take Highway 15 to Rancho California Road and go north 10 miles. There is a minimal fee for day use of the park.

Sam Hicks Park
Old Town Temecula
Temecula, CA
909-836-3285
Dogs are allowed on leash. Owners must pick up after their pets.

Restaurants

Temecula

Aloha Joe's
27497 Ynez Rd
Temecula, CA 92591
909-506-9889
Dogs are allowed at the outdoor tables.

Baja Fresh Mexican Grill
40688 Winchester Rd
Temecula, CA
909-719-1570
This Mexican restaurant is open for lunch and dinner. They use fresh ingredients and making their salsa and beans daily. Some of the items on their menu include Enchiladas, Burritos, Tacos Salads, Quesadillas, Nachos, Chicken, Steak and more. Well-behaved leashed dogs are allowed at the outdoor tables.

Mad Madeline's Grill
28495 Front Street
Temecula, CA 92590
Old Town Center
909-699-3776
Dogs are allowed at the outdoor tables.

Marie Callender's
29363 Rancho California Rd
Temecula, CA 92591
909-699-9339
Dogs are allowed at the outdoor tables.

Scarcella's Italian Grille
27525 Ynez Rd
Temecula, CA 92591
909-676-5450
Dogs are allowed at the outdoor tables.

Temecula Pizza Company
44535 Bedford Ct # D
Temecula, CA 92592
909-694-9463
Dogs are allowed at the outdoor tables.

The Grape Arbor
28464 Front Street
Temecula, CA
909-694-0292
The Grape Arbor has wine and beer tasting in Old Town Temecula.

Vets and Kennels

Temecula

Emergency Pet Clinic
27443 Jefferson Ave
Temecula, CA 92590
Winchester Rd
909-695-5044
Monday - Friday 6 pm to 8 am, 24 hours on weekends.

Victorville Dog Travel Guide
Accommodations

Victorville

Howard Johnson Express Inn
16868 Stoddard Wells Rd.
Victorville, CA 92392
760-243-7700
Dogs of all sizes are welcome. There is a $10 per day pet fee per pet.

Ramada Inn
15494 Palmdale Road
Victorville, CA 92392
760-245-6565
There is a $25 one time pet fee.

Red Roof Inn
13409 Mariposa Rd
Victorville, CA 92392
760-241-1577
There is a $10 one time pet fee.

Accommodations - RV Parks and Campgrounds

Victorville

Victorville/Inland Empire KOA
16530 Stoddard Wells Road
Victorville, CA 92392
760-245-6867
This campground offers large shaded sites in the high desert. RV spaces and tent sites are available. RV site amenities include a maximum pull through length of 75 feet and 30 amp service. Other camp amenities include a seasonal swimming pool, free modem dataport, LP gas and pavilion/meeting room. Well-behaved leashed dogs of all sizes are allowed for short term stays. For a one month stay or longer, they have certain size and breed restrictions. People need to clean up after their pets. There is no pet fee. The campground is open all year.

Chapter 12

California Dog-Friendly Travel Guide
San Diego

There is a $10 one time pet fee.

Bonsall Dog Travel Guide
Restaurants

Bonsall

Sazio Italian Restorante
5256 S. Mission Rd
Bonsall, CA 92003
760-758-9855
Dogs are allowed at the outdoor tables.

Cardiff Dog Travel Guide
Accommodations - RV Parks and Campgrounds

Cardiff

San Elijo State Beach Campground
Old Highway 101
Cardiff, CA
760-753-5091
This campground offers RV sites with limited hookups. RVs up to 26 feet can use the hookup sites and RVs up to 35 feet are allowed. They offer both inland and ocean view spaces. While dogs are not allowed at this beach, you can walk to the dog-friendly Cardiff State Beach. The beach is about 1 mile south of Cardiff.

Beaches

Cardiff

Cardiff State Beach
Old Highway 101
Cardiff, CA
760-753-5091
This is a gently sloping sandy beach with warm water. Popular activities include swimming, surfing and beachcombing. Dogs on leash are allowed and please clean up after your pets. The beach is located on Old Highway 101, one mile south of Cardiff.

Carlsbad Dog Travel Guide
Accommodations

Carlsbad

Inns of America
751 Raintree
Carlsbad, CA
760-931-1185

Motel 6
1006 Carlsbad Village Dr
Carlsbad, CA 92008
760-434-7135
Large dogs must be well-behaved. Pets are not to be left alone in the room.

Motel 6
750 Raintree Dr
Carlsbad, CA 92009
760-431-0745
Large well-behaved dogs are ok.

Residence Inn - Carlsbad
2000 Faraday Ave
Carlsbad, CA 92008
760-431-9999
There is a $150 one time pet fee and a $10 per day additional pet fee.

Attractions

Carlsbad

Carlsbad Village
Carlsbad Village Drive
Carlsbad, CA
Carlsbad Blvd

Carlsbad Village has a number of shops and restaurants that are dog-friendly. Its about 4 blocks long and 2 blocks wide.

Restaurants

Carlsbad

Boar Cross'n Bar and Grill
390 Grand Ave
Carlsbad, CA 92008
760-729-2989
This is a bar that requires human visitors to be 21. However, dogs don't have to be this old and they are welcome on the patio in the back. Dogs are allowed at the outdoor tables.

Cafe Elysa
3076 Carlsbad Blvd
Carlsbad, CA 92008
760-434-4100
Dogs are allowed at the outdoor tables.

Don's Country Kitchen
2885 Roosevelt Street

Carlsbad, CA 92008
760-729-2274
Dogs are allowed at the outdoor tables.

Grand Deli
595 Grand Ave
Carlsbad, CA 92008
760-729-4015
Dogs are allowed at the outdoor tables.

Greek Corner Cafe
2939 Carlsbad Blvd
Carlsbad, CA 92008
760-720-9961
Dogs are allowed at the outdoor tables.

Pizza Port
571 Carlsbad Village Dr
Carlsbad, CA 92008
760-720-7007
This pizza house and brewery has heaters
outside for their visitors with dogs.

Spirito's Restaurant and Pizzeria
300 Carlsbad Village Dr #208
Carlsbad, CA 92008
760-720-1132
Dogs are allowed at the outdoor tables.

Village Grille
2833 State Street
Carlsbad, CA 92008
760-729-3601
Here you can order food from an outside window
with your pup. Dogs are allowed at the outdoor
tables.

Vinaka Cafe
300 Carlsbad Village Dr #211
Carlsbad, CA 92008
760-720-7890
Dogs are allowed at the outdoor tables.

Chula Vista Dog Travel Guide
Accommodations

Chula Vista

La Quinta Inn San Diego - Chula Vista
150 Bonita Road
Chula Vista, CA
619-691-1211
Dogs of all sizes are allowed at the hotel.

Motel 6
745 E Street
Chula Vista, CA 91910

619-422-4200
A well-behaved large dog is okay. Dogs must be
attended at all times.

Vagabond Inn
230 Broadway St.
Chula Vista, CA 91910
619-422-8305
This motel is located within several miles of
downtown San Diego. Amenities include two
swimming pools, continental breakfast, cable
television and more hotel amenities. Pets are an
additional $10 per day.

Coronado Dog Travel Guide
Accommodations

Coronado

Crown City Inn
520 Orange Ave
Coronado, CA 92118
619-435-3116
This inn is located in beautiful Coronado which is
across the harbor from downtown San Diego.
Walk to several outdoor restaurants or to the
Coronado Centennial Park. Room service is
available. Pet charges are $8 per day for a
designated pet room and $25 per day for a non-
designated pet room. They have non-smoking
rooms available. Pets must never be left
unattended in the room.

Loews Coronado Bay Resort
4000 Coronado Bay Road
Coronado, CA 92118
619-424-4000
All well-behaved dogs of any size are welcome.
This upscale hotel offers their "Loews Loves
Pets" program which includes special pet treats,
local dog walking routes, and a list of nearby pet-
friendly places to visit. There are no pet fees.

Beaches

Coronado

North Beach Dog Run
Ocean Blvd.
Coronado, CA
Ocean Drive

This dog beach is located in the city of Coronado
at the end of Ocean Blvd next to the U.S. Naval
Station entrance. Park on the street and walk
along the Naval Station fence until you reach the
ocean and then bear right. There will be signs
posted for the North Beach Dog Run.

Parks

Coronado

Bayshore Bikeway
Silver Strand Blvd.
Coronado, CA
(Glorietta Bay Park)

If you are in Coronado and really want to stretch
your legs, you can go for a run or walk on the
Bayshore Bikeway. The path is about 6 miles long
each way. It starts by the Glorietta Bay Park and
continues south along Silver Strand Blvd. There's
not too much shade along this path, so your pup
might not want to go on a hot day. Dogs need to
be leashed.

Centennial & Tidelands Parks
Orange Ave and First St.
Coronado, CA

We have combined these two parks because
there is a scenic 1/2 - 1 mile path between them.
Both of these parks provide nice photo
opportunities of downtown San Diego and the
San Diego Bay. Dogs must be leashed.

Restaurants

Coronado

Cafe 1134
1134 Orange Ave
Coronado, CA
619-437-1134
Cafe 1134 offers coffee and a full bistro menu.
Dogs are allowed at the outdoor tables.

PrimaVera Pastry Caffe
956 Orange Ave
Coronado, CA
619-435-4191
Come to this bakery and deli for breakfast, lunch
or dinner. Dogs are allowed at the outdoor tables.

Rhinoceros Cafe and Grill
1166 Orange Ave
Coronado, CA
619-435-2121
The folks we spoke with here said they are very
dog-friendly. For lunch and dinner, they serve
steaks, ribs, chicken and pasta dishes seven
days a week. Breakfast is served on the
weekends. Dogs are welcome at the outdoor
tables.

Del Mar Dog Travel Guide
Accommodations

Del Mar

Best Western Stratford Inn
710 Camino del Mar
Del Mar, CA 92014
858-755-1501
There is a $50 one time pet fee. Dogs up to 50
pounds are allowed.

Les Artistes Hotel
944 Camino Del Mar
Del Mar, CA 92014
858-755-4646
There is a $50 refundable deposit and a one time
$20 pet fee. Well-behaved dogs are ok at the
hotel.

Beaches

Del Mar

Del Mar Beach
Seventeenth Street
Del Mar, CA
858-755-1556
Dogs are allowed on the beach as follows. South
of 17th Street, dogs are allowed on a 6 foot leash
year-round. Between 17th Street and 29th Street,
dogs are allowed on a 6 foot leash from October
through May (from June through September, dogs
are not allowed at all). Between 29th Street and
northern city limits, dogs are allowed without a
leash, but must be under voice control from
October through May (from June through
September, dogs must be on a 6 foot leash).
Owners must clean up after their dogs.

Rivermouth Beach

Highway 101
Del Mar, CA
south of Border Avenue

This beach allows voice controlled dogs to run leash free from September 15 through June 15 (no specified hours). Leashes are required during mid-summer tourist season from mid June to mid Sept. Fans of this beach are trying to convince the Del Mar City council to extend the leash-free period to year round. The beach is located on Highway 101 just south of Border Avenue at the north end of the City of Del Mar. Thanks to one of our readers for recommending this beach.

Restaurants

Del Mar

Del Mar French Pastry Cafe
1140 Camino Del Mar
Del Mar, CA 92014
858-481-8622
Dogs are allowed at the outdoor tables.

En Fuego Cantina & Grill
1342 Camino del Mar
Del Mar, CA 92014
858-792-6551
Enjoy dining with your dog at the tables in the nicely designed patio. Thanks to one of our readers for recommending this restaurant.

Pacifica Breeze Hotel
1555 Camino Del Mar #209
Del Mar, CA 92014
858-509-9147
Dogs are allowed at the outdoor tables.

Stratford Court Cafe
1307 Stratford Court
Del Mar, CA
858-792-7433
Thanks to one of our readers who writes: "This is THE dog-friendly restaurant in Del Mar. All seating outdoor and you and your dog can order at a walk-up counter. They even offer home-made dog biscuits and have a stack of water bowls. Only a few minutes drive from the off-leash Rivermouth beach, so there are always lots of dogs. Breakfast and lunch only - California cuisine."

Stores

Del Mar

Dexter's Deli
1229 Camino Del Mar
Del Mar, CA 92014
858-792-3707
Specializing in natural food diets, fresh baked treats and cakes and a selection of dog and cat toys and gifts.

Descanso Dog Travel Guide
Accommodations - RV Parks and Campgrounds

Descanso

Cuyamaca Ranch State Park
12551 Highway 79
Descanso, CA 92016
760-765-0755
Five cabins are available at Paso Picacho campground. The log cabins are 12 feet by 12 feet with a deck. Each cabin has bunk beds that sleep four (no mattresses, you must bring your own bedding.) Amenities at each cabin include a picnic table, fire ring, barbecue and room for a small tent. Restrooms with pay showers and water are located near each site. The fee is $15 per night. There is an eight person maximum per site. You may bring your own padlock if you wish to lock the cabin during your stay. Dogs are allowed in the cabin but must not be left unattended. Dogs are allowed on two of the paved fire road trails in this park. This park is located about 10 miles from the town of Julian.

Parks

Descanso

Cuyamaca Ranch State Park
12551 Highway 79
Descanso, CA 92016
760-765-0755
Leashed dogs are allowed on the paved Cuyamaca Peak Fire Road and the Los Caballos/Stonewall Mine Road trails. Bicycles and horseback riders are also allowed on these trails. Dogs are not allowed on any other trails in the park. The Cuyamaca Peak Fire Road is approximately 3.5 miles and goes all the way to the top of the park. The Cuyamaca Peak Fire Road begins at Hwy 79 about 1/4 mi south of the Paso Picacho Campground (the road is also accessible from the campground).

El Cajon Dog Travel Guide

Travel Guide - Please always call ahead to make sure an establishment is still dog-friendly.

Accommodations

El Cajon

Motel 6
550 Montrose Court
El Cajon, CA 92020
619-588-6100
There are no additional pet fees.

Encinitas Dog Travel Guide
Parks

Encinitas

Encinitas Park
D Street
Encinitas, CA

Thanks to one of our readers who recommends the following two dog parks in Encinitas Park. Encinitas Viewpoint Park, on "D" Street at Cornish Drive, off-leash dogs permitted 6:00-7:30 AM and 4:00-6:00 PM on MWF only. Other days of the week, dogs must on-leash. Orpheus Park, on Orpheus Avenue at Union Street, off-leash dogs permitted 6:00-7:30 AM and 4:00-6:00 PM on MWF only. Other days of the week, dogs must on-leash.

Restaurants

Encinitas

Baja Fresh Mexican Grill
194 El Camino Real Blvd
Encinitas, CA
760-633-2262
This Mexican restaurant is open for lunch and dinner. They use fresh ingredients and making their salsa and beans daily. Some of the items on their menu include Enchiladas, Burritos, Tacos Salads, Quesadillas, Nachos, Chicken, Steak and more. Well-behaved leashed dogs are allowed at the outdoor tables.

Escondido Dog Travel Guide
Accommodations

Escondido

Castle Creek Inn Resort
29850 Circle R Way
Escondido, CA 92026
760-751-8800

There are no additional pet fees.

Palm Tree Lodge
425 W Mission Ave
Escondido, CA 92025
760-745-7613
There is a $10 per day pet fee.

Attractions

Escondido

Orfila Vineyards
13455 San Pasqual Rd
Escondido, CA 92025
760-738-6500
Open Daily from 10 am - 6 pm most of the year. They close at 5 pm in the winter. Dogs are allowed in the outdoor areas.

Parks

Escondido

Mayflower Dog Park
3420 Valley Center Road
Escondido, CA
East End of Town

Mayflower Dog Park is a 1.5 acre fenced area for off-leash dog play.

Restaurants

Escondido

Baja Fresh Mexican Grill
890 W Valley Parkway
Escondido, CA
760-480-9997
This Mexican restaurant is open for lunch and dinner. They use fresh ingredients and making their salsa and beans daily. Some of the items on their menu include Enchiladas, Burritos, Tacos Salads, Quesadillas, Nachos, Chicken, Steak and more. Well-behaved leashed dogs are allowed at the outdoor tables.

Vets and Kennels

Escondido

Veterinary Urgent Care
2525 S Centre City Pkwy
Escondido, CA 92025

W Citracado
760-738-9600
Monday - Friday 6 pm to 8 am, Friday 6pm - Monday 8 am.

Fallbrook Dog Travel Guide
Restaurants

Fallbrook

Firehouse Broiler
1019 S. Main Ave
Fallbrook, CA 92028
760-728-8008
Dogs are allowed at the outdoor tables.

Greek Style Chicken
904 S. Main Ave
Fallbrook, CA 92028
760-723-8050
Dogs are allowed at the outdoor tables.

Me and Charlies Bakery and Coffee
945 S. Main Ave
Fallbrook, CA 92028
760-728-1491
Dogs are allowed at the outdoor tables.

Guatay Dog Travel Guide
Stores

Guatay

Tryyn Wooden Spoon Gallery
27540 Old Hwy 80
Guatay, CA
619-473-9030
Located on the road from I-8 to Julian, this shop has crafted spoons, wine, jewelry, and other items. Your well-behaved, potty trained dog is allowed inside on leash.

Julian Dog Travel Guide
Accommodations

Julian

Apple Tree Inn
4360 Highway 78
Julian, CA 92070
800-410-8683
This is a small country motel located near the historic gold mining town of Julian. Families are always welcome. There is a $10 per day pet charge and a $50 refundable pet deposit.

Accommodations - RV Parks and Campgrounds

Julian

Lake Cuyamaca
15027 Highway 79
Julian, CA 92036
877-581-9904
This campground has 40 RV sites with hookups and 14 tent sites located next a popular fishing lake. There is a 3.5 mile trail surrounding the lake. Dogs on leash are welcome both in the campground and on the trail, but they are not allowed in the water. People need to clean up after their pets. The campground does not take reservations, so all the sites are available on a first-come, first-served basis.

Pinezanita Trailer Ranch and Campground
4446 Highway 79
Julian, CA 92036
760-765-0429
They have a fishing pond, stocked with blue gill and catfish. You can find fishing tackle and bait in the Campground Registration Office. Dogs are not allowed in the cabins, but they are welcome to stay with you at your RV, trailer, or campsite. There is a $2 per day pet charge. Pets must be on a 6 foot or shorter leash at all times. Noisy pets are cause for eviction. Carry plastic bags or a pooper scooper and pick up after your pet.

Accommodations - Vacation Home Rentals

Julian

Flat Top Mountain Retreat
Call to Arrange.
Julian, CA
800-810-1170
Secluded mountain vacation home on eight acres. Located 1 1/2 miles north of the old gold mining town of Julian. This home has panoramic views of the mountain countryside to the ocean. It is fully furnished, with a wood burning stove, TV, VCR, and fully equipped kitchen. There are three bedrooms, sleeping 8 people, and 3 decks for viewing the peaceful surroundings and wildlife including deer, and wild turkey birds. Rates range from $170 to $220 per night and there is a 9% lodging tax added. Minimum stay is two nights.

Pine Haven Cabin Rental
Call to Arrange.
Julian, CA
760-726-9888

Enjoy this dog-friendly mountain getaway on 1.25 acres. The entire lot is securely fenced, offering your pet the freedom to run off-leash. The cabin has one bedroom plus a small loft upstairs, a bathroom with a tiled walk-in shower (no tub), and a fully equipped kitchen. The cabin sleeps 2 people. Other amenities include air conditioning, stereo system, VCR with hit movie library, karaoke machine, back patio with a picnic table, Weber grill and more. The cabin is off a small private lane, so you will have lots of privacy. Located in the Pine Hills area of Julian (about one hour east of San Diego), the cabin is only 4 miles from historic downtown Julian. No smoking allowed. Cabin rental rates range from $160 to $180 per night. There is a $30 pet fee. For reservations call Teresa at 760-726-9888 or email to pinehavencabin@sbcglobal.net.

Attractions

Julian

Country Carriages
Washington and Main St
Julian, CA
760-765-1471
Reservations are recommended on the weekends. Your dog is welcome. The carriage rides go a mile out of town and back. The driver points out historic sites on the way.

Julian Historical Walking Tour
Main Street
Julian, CA
760-765-1857
You and your pooch can take a self-guided tour of Julian's historical buildings which highlight history from the Gold Rush era to the 1920s. Follow the tour through Main, Second, Third, B, C, and Washington Streets. A map is available at the Julian Chamber of Commerce located on Main and Washington Streets inside the Town Hall.

Restaurants

Julian

Apple Alley Bakery
2122 Main Street
Julian, CA 92036
760-765-2532
Dogs are allowed at the outdoor tables in the year-round patio. The bakery is open for breakfast and lunch, seven days a week. They offer apple pies made from fresh apples, pastries, cookies and more.

Margarita's
2018 Main Street
Julian, CA 92036
760-765-3980
This restaurant serves Mexican and American food and is open for breakfast, lunch and dinner. Dogs are allowed at the outdoor tables. The tables are usually out in late spring through summer.

The Bailey Wood Pit Barbecue
Main and A Streets
Julian, CA 92036
760-765-3757
Dogs are allowed at the outdoor tables. Tables are seasonal.

La Jolla Dog Travel Guide
Accommodations

La Jolla

Andrea Villa Inn
2402 Torrey Pines Rd
La Jolla, CA 92037
858-459-3311
Nestled in the heart of beautiful La Jolla, this inn is conveniently located near cosmopolitan shopping and dining experiences. The beaches of La Jolla Shores are within easy walking distance. There is a $25 one time pet charge.

La Jolla Village Lodge
1141 Silverado Street
La Jolla, CA 92037
858-551-2001
There is a $20 one time pet fee. Thanks to a reader for recommending this hotel.

Residence Inn by Marriott
8901 Gilman Dr.
La Jolla, CA 92037
Exit La Jolla Village Dr.
858-587-1770
Every room is a suite that includes a bedroom area, living room, and kitchen. This inn is located about 3-4 miles north of downtown La Jolla. There is a $50 one time pet fee and a $10 per day pet fee.

then park or turn right onto Coast Blvd. Parking is limited around the village area.

Beaches

La Jolla

La Jolla Shores Beach
Camino Del Oro
La Jolla, CA
Vallecitos Ct
619-221-8900
Leashed dogs are allowed on this beach and the adjacent Kellogg Park from 6pm to 9am. The beach is about 1/2 mile long. To get there, take Hwy 5 to the La Jolla Village Drive exit heading west. Turn left onto Torrey Pines Rd. Then turn right onto La Jolla Shores Drive. Go 4-5 blocks and turn left onto Vallecitos. Go straight until you reach the beach and Kellogg Park.

Point La Jolla Beaches
Coast Blvd.
La Jolla, CA
near Prospect & Ivanhoe
619-221-8900
Leashed dogs are allowed on this beach and the walkway (paved and dirt trails) from 6pm to 9am. The beaches and walkway are at least a 1/2 mile long and might continue further. To get there, exit La Jolla Village Drive West from Hwy 5. Turn left onto Torrey Pines Rd. Turn right on Prospect and

Restaurants

La Jolla

Elijah's
8861 Villa La Jolla Drive
La Jolla, CA
858-455-1461
Dogs are allowed at the outdoor tables.

Girard Gourmet
7837 Girard Ave
La Jolla, CA
858-454-3321
This cafe and bakery serves gourmet deli food and baked goods. They have several outdoor tables.

Putnam's Restaurant & Bar
910 Prospect St
La Jolla, CA
858-454-2181
Located in the Grand Colonial Inn, Putnam's serves breakfast, lunch, dinner and Sunday brunch. They offer contemporary world cuisine by an award-winning chef. Dogs are allowed at the outdoor tables.

Whole Foods Market
8825 Villa La Jolla Drive
La Jolla, CA 92037
858-642-6700
This natural food supermarket offers natural and organic foods. Order some food from their deli and bring it to an outdoor table where your well-behaved leashed dog is welcome. The market is located at the corner of Villa La Jolla and Nobel Drive.

Stores

La Jolla

Restoration Hardware
4405 La Jolla Village Drive
La Jolla, CA
858-784-0575
Your well-behaved leashed dog is allowed inside this store.

La Mesa Dog Travel Guide
Accommodations

La Mesa

Motel 6
7621 Alvarado Rd
La Mesa, CA 91941
619-464-7151
There are no additional pet fees.

Parks

La Mesa

Harry Griffen Park
9550 Milden Street
La Mesa, CA
619-667-1307

Thanks to one of our readers who writes: "A leash-free dog area - very nice area of the park and no restrictions on dog size."

Lake San Marcos Dog Travel Guide
Accommodations

Lake San Marcos

Quails Inn Hotel
1025 La Bonita Drive
Lake San Marcos, CA 92069
760-744-0120
There is a $10 per day pet fee. This resort has a number of golf packages available.

National City Dog Travel Guide
Accommodations

National City

Super 8
425 Roosevelt Ave
National City, CA 91950
619-474-8811
There is a $15 per day additional pet fee.

Ocean Beach Dog Travel Guide
Beaches

Ocean Beach

Dog Beach
Point Loma Blvd.
Ocean Beach, CA
619-221-8900
Dogs are allowed to run off leash at this beach anytime during the day. This is a very popular dog beach which attracts lots and lots of dogs on warm days. To get there, take Hwy 8 West until it ends and then it becomes Sunset Cliffs Blvd. Then make a right turn onto Point Loma Blvd and follow the signs to Ocean Beach's Dog Beach.

There is a $50 refundable deposit for pets.

Ocean Beach
Point Loma Blvd.
Ocean Beach, CA
619-221-8900
Leashed dogs are allowed on this beach from
6pm to 9am. The beach is about 1/2 mile long. To
get there, take Hwy 8 West until it ends and then
it becomes Sunset Cliffs Blvd. Then make a right
turn onto Point Loma Blvd and follow the signs to
Ocean Beach Park. A separate beach called Dog
Beach is at the north end of this beach which
allows dogs to run off-leash.

Parks

Ocean Beach

Dusty Rhodes Dog Park
Sunset Cliffs Blvd.
Ocean Beach, CA
619-236-5555
This dog park is located in Dusty Rhodes
Neighborhood Park. The park is on Sunset Cliffs
Blvd. between Nimitz and West Point Loma.

Oceanside Dog Travel Guide
Accommodations

Oceanside

Motel 6
3708 Plaza Dr
Oceanside, CA 92056
760-941-1011
There are no additional pet fees.

Ramada Limited
1140 Mission Ave
Oceanside, CA
760-967-4100

Restaurants

Oceanside

Daphne's Greek Cafe
409 Mission Avenue
Oceanside, CA 92054
760-967-6679
Dogs are allowed at the outdoor tables.

Ol Smoky
608 Mission Ave
Oceanside, CA 92054
760-439-4763
Dogs are allowed at the outdoor tables.

Rice Garden
401 Mission Ave #B110
Oceanside, CA 92054
760-721-4330
Dogs are allowed at the outdoor tables.

Palomar Mountain Dog Travel Guide
Attractions

Palomar Mountain

Palomar Observatory
County Road S-6
Palomar Mountain, CA 92060
760-742-2100
The observatory is located within the Cleveland
National Forest on Palomar Mountain at an
elevation of 5000 feet. Dogs on leash may
accompany you on the self-guided tour and on
the grounds including the gallery to view the 200
inch telescope. To reach Palomar exit Interstate
15 at Highway 76 east. Take S-6 to the left in 25
miles up the mountain to Palomar. The hours are
9 am - 4 pm daily except Christmas and
Christmas eve. The gift shop is only open on
weekends except in July and August.

Parks

Palomar Mountain

Observatory National Recreational Trail
Observatory Campground
Palomar Mountain, CA
760-788-0250
This trail is located in the dog-friendly Cleveland
National Forest. The 2. 2 mile trail offers a

pleasant hike to the Palomar Observatory site. It meanders through pine and oak woodlands and offers some great views of the Mendenhall and French Valleys. There is a 200 foot elevation gain, with a starting elevation of 4800 feet. Dogs are allowed on leash. From San Diego, drive north on I-15 to Highway 76 (Oceanside-Pala exit) Head east on Hwy 76 to S6 and drive north toward Palomar Mountain. Follow S6 to Observatory Campground. Trailhead parking is near the amphitheater inside the campground (follow the signs). The trailhead is adjacent to the amphitheater. Vehicles must display a Forest Adventure Pass. The pass can be purchased from local vendors and from the Forest Service Offices. Call (760) 788-0250 for a list of forest offices.

Pine Valley Dog Travel Guide
Accommodations - RV Parks and Campgrounds

Pine Valley

Laguna Campground
Sunrise Highway
Pine Valley, CA
619-445-6235
This 104 site campground is located in the Cleveland National Forest. It is located at an elevation of 5,600 feet and offers both tent and RV sites. RVs up to 40 feet are allowed and there are no hookups. Flush toilets are at this campground. There is a $13 fee per site. To make a reservations, call 1-877-444-6777. Pets on leash are allowed and please clean up after them. To get there, take Interstate 8 to the Sunrise Highway exit. Go about 13 miles to the campground.

Parks

Pine Valley

Big Laguna Trail
Sunrise Highway
Pine Valley, CA
619-445-6235
This 6.7 mile easy rated trail is located in the Cleveland National Forest. The trail elevation changes from 5,400 to 5,960 feet. It is a popular trail for hiking, horseback riding and mountain biking. The trail is open year round except during winter storms. Pets on leash are allowed and please clean up after them. To reach the upper end, take Sunrise Highway from I-8 (near Pine

Valley) and drive north 13.5 miles to just past the second cattle guard on the highway. Vehicles should park on either side of the highway on the paved turnouts. The access to the Big Laguna trail is via the Nobel Canyon trail that departs the western turnout and is marked by a small sign. Follow the Nobel Canyon trail about 100 yards to reach the Big Laguna trail junction. The other end of the Big Laguna trail makes a junction with the Pacific Crest Trail about .25 miles northeast of the Laguna Station (the Forest Service fire station).

Rancho Bernardo Dog Travel Guide
Restaurants

Rancho Bernardo

Baja Fresh Mexican Grill
11980-11976 Bernardo Plaza Dr.
Rancho Bernardo, CA
858-592-7788
This Mexican restaurant is open for lunch and dinner. They use fresh ingredients and making their salsa and beans daily. Some of the items on their menu include Enchiladas, Burritos, Tacos Salads, Quesadillas, Nachos, Chicken, Steak and more. Well-behaved leashed dogs are allowed at the outdoor tables.

Rancho Santa Fe Dog Travel Guide
Accommodations

Rancho Santa Fe

Rancho Valencia Resort
5921 Valencia Circle
Rancho Santa Fe, CA 92067
858-756-1123
This upscale golf and tennis resort allows well-behaved dogs of all sizes. There is a $25 per day pet fee.

San Diego Dog Travel Guide
Accommodations

San Diego

Best Western Lamplighter Inn & Suites
6474 El Cajon Blvd
San Diego, CA 92115
800-545-0778
This motel is located in the suburbs of San Diego. If you are visiting someone from San Diego State University, this motel is nearby. It's also about 7-8 miles from the dog-friendly Mission Trails

Regional Park. There is a $10 per day pet charge.

Harborview Inn & Suites
550 West Grape St
San Diego, CA
619-233-7799
There is a $15 per day pet fee.

Holiday Inn on the Bay
1355 N Harbor Dr
San Diego, CA 92101
619-232-3861
This Holiday Inn has a 5 and 14 story building which overlooks the harbor. Across the street from the hotel is a harborside walkway. There is a $100 pet deposit ($75 refundable and $25 non-refundable).

Homestead Suites
7444 Mission Valley Rd
San Diego, CA
619-299-2292
There is a $75 one time pet fee per visit.

La Quinta Inn San Diego - Rancho Penasquitos
10185 Paseo Montril
San Diego, CA
858-484-8800
Dogs up to 50 pounds are allowed at the hotel.

Marriott San Diego Marina
333 West Harbor Drive
San Diego, CA 92101
619-234-1500
This hotel is right next to the the San Diego Harbor. If you want to stretch your legs, there is also a nice walkway that goes about a mile along the harborside. There are no pet charges.

Motel 6 - North
5592 Clairemont Mesa Blvd
San Diego, CA 92117
858-268-9758
There are no additional pet fees.

Ocean Villa Inn
5142 West Point Loma Blvd.
San Diego, CA 92107
619-224-3481
There is a $100 per deposit for up to 2 pets. Of this $25 is non-refundable and $75 is refundable. There is an additional charge for more than 2 pets.

Pacific Inn Hotel & Suites
1655 Pacific Hwy
San Diego, CA
619-232-6391
There is a $10 per day additional pet fee.

Premier Inn
2484 Hotel Circle Place
San Diego, CA
619-291-8252
There is no pet fee.

Premier Inn
3333 Channel Way
San Diego, CA 92110
619-223-9500
There is no pet fee.

Red Lion Hanalei Hotel

2270 Hotel Circle North
San Diego, CA 92108
619-297-1101
This hotel is located in the heart of Mission Valley. Dogs under 50 pounds are allowed. There is a $50 refundable pet deposit.

Residence Inn
11002 Rancho Carmel Dr
San Diego, CA 92128
858-673-1900
There is a $150 one time pet fee and a $10 per day additional pet fee.

Residence Inn
5995 Pacific Mesa Court
San Diego, CA 92121
858-552-9100
There is a $150 one time pet fee and a $10 per day additional pet fee.

Residence Inn - Downtown
1747 Pacific Highway
San Diego, CA 92101
619-338-8200
There is a $100 one time pet fee and a $10 per day additional pet fee.

Residence Inn by Marriott
5400 Kearny Mesa Rd
San Diego, CA 92111
858-278-2100
This suite style inn is located north of San Diego. Dinner delivery service is available from local restaurants. Limit two pets per room. They charge a $100 non-refundable pet fee and $7 per day pet charge. Dogs up to 65 pounds are allowed.

San Diego Marriott - Mission Valley
8757 Rio San Diego Dr
San Diego, CA 92108
619-692-3800
This hotel is about 3-4 miles from Old Town State Historic Park and approximately 5-6 miles from the Mission Trails Regional Park. Room service is available. There is a $200 pet deposit ($150 is refundable and $50 is non-refundable.)

San Diego Marriott Suites
701 A Street
San Diego, CA 92101
619-696-9800
There is a $50 one time pet fee per visit.

Sheraton San Diego Hotel and Marina
1380 Harbor Island Drive
San Diego, CA 92101
619-291-2900
Dogs up to 80 pounds are allowed. There are no additional pet fees. Only one dog is permitted per room.

Sheraton Suites San Diego
701 A. Street
San Diego, CA 92101
619-696-9800
Dogs of all sizes are allowed. There is a $100 one time pet fee per stay. There is a $50 refundable deposit per stay for pets.

Staybridge Suites
6639 Mira Mesa Blvd
San Diego, CA 92121
800-238-8000
There is a $75 one time pet fee.

Vagabond Inn-Mission Bay
4540 Mission Bay Dr.
San Diego, CA 92109
858-274-7888
This motel is located within several miles of the Old Town Historic State Park and SeaWorld. It is also close to the popular Dog Beach in Ocean Beach. The motel features an outdoor swimming pool, cable television, guest laundry service and more hotel amenities. There is an additional pet charge of $10 per day.

858-581-4200
This RV park is located on Mission Bay, across the water from Sea World. RV sites have full hookups and some offer beach front, bay view or primitive locations. Amenities include boat slips, a boat launch, store with a market, game room and a laundry room. Dogs are allowed in certain areas. They must be leashed and please clean up after them. There is a $3 per day pet fee.

Accommodations - Vacation Home Rentals

San Diego

Vagabond Inn-Point Loma
1325 Scott St.
San Diego, CA 92106
619-224-3371
This motel is located less than five miles from downtown San Diego and Sea World. It is close to the popular Dog Beach in Ocean Beach. The motel features an outdoor swimming pool, family unit rooms, cable television and more hotel amenities. Dogs up to about 70-75 pounds are allowed and there is an additional $10 per day pet fee.

The Hohe House
4905 Dixie Drive
San Diego, CA 92109
858-273-0324
The Hohe House is a non-smoking, 2 bedroom/2 bath vacation rental in the Pacific Beach neighborhood and offers an ocean view. It is located close to beaches, restaurants and shopping. The house sleeps 6 (1 King, 2 Doubles, and a queen sleeper sofa) and is fully furnished with all linens provided. Amenities include beach chairs, beach towels, boogie boards, umbrellas, coolers and bicycles. There is a 4 night minimum during the low season, $200 nightly, (Mid-Sept to Mid-June), and rates vary for low to high season, from $1275 to $1875 weekly. An additional 10.5% hotel room tax applies and rates are subject to change. A $350 refundable, security deposit is required to reserve a week's stay and balance is due 30 days prior to arrival. There is a $10 per night pet fee. Well-behaved dogs over 18 months and under 80 pounds are welcome. They will gladly email the entire pet policy to you.

Attractions

San Diego

W San Diego
421 West B. Street
San Diego, CA 92101
619-231-8220
Dogs up to 80 pounds are allowed. There is a $100 non-refundable cleaning fee for pets. There is a $25 per night pet fee.

Accommodations - RV Parks and Campgrounds

San Diego

Campland on the Bay
2211 Pacific Beach Drive
San Diego, CA

Cinderella Carriage Rides

San Diego, CA
619-239-8080
You and your dog can enjoy a carriage ride throughout downtown San Diego. The horse and carriages are located in the Gaslamp Quarter at 5th and F Streets, or call ahead and get a carriage to pick you up from your downtown hotel. The rides are from 6pm-11pm. Rates start at $15 for about a 10 minute ride and go up to $95 for 60 minutes. Prices are subject to change. The carriages hold 3-4 people plus a dog. They accept cash or credit card.

Family Kayak Adventure Center
4217 Swift Avenue
San Diego, CA 92104
619-282-3520
This company offers guided kayaking adventure tours to people of all ages and abilities. For beginners they offer paddles on flat water in stable tandem kayaks that hold one to four people. All equipment and instruction is provided for an enjoyable first outing. Well-behaved dogs are also welcome. There is even a "Dog Paddles" tour which is an evening tour on Mission Bay that includes quality time on the water and on Fiesta Island's leash free area.

Old Town State Historic Park
San Diego Ave & Twiggs St
San Diego, CA
619-220-5422
Old Town demonstrates life in the Mexican and early American periods of 1821 to 1872 (including 5 original adobe buildings). There are shops, several outdoor cafes and live music. Since pups are not allowed inside the buildings, you can shop at the many outdoor retail kiosks throughout the town. There are several food concessions where you can order the food and then take it to an outdoor table. After walking around, relax with your best friend by listening to a variety of live music. If your dog wants to see more trees and green grass, take a quick drive over to Presidio Park which is close to Old Town (see Parks).

SeaWorld of California-Kennels
1720 South Shore Rd.
San Diego, CA 92109
in Mission Bay
619-226-3901
This may not be your dog's idea of an attraction, but it is nice to know that SeaWorld has day kennels at the main entrance of their Adventure Park. The kennels are attended at all times and you can visit your dog throughout the day when you need a break from the attractions. The day boarding is open the same hours as the park and cost only $5 for the whole day. Kennels range in size from small to large. Thanks to one of our San Diego readers for telling us about this.

Seaforth Boat Rentals
333 W Harbor Dr
San Diego, CA 92101
Marriott Marina-Gate 1
619-239-BOAT
Rent a sail or power boat from this shop located between Seaport Village and the Marriott San Diego Marina Hotel. You'll find much to see in the San Diego Bay, but remember you'll also be sharing the space with fishing boats and some Navy ships like aircraft carriers. Prices start at $25/hr for a 14' sail boat (up to 30' available) and $65/hr for a 17' power boat (up to 27' available). They say dogs are allowed as long as you clean up after them. Prices are subject to change.

Beaches

San Diego

Fiesta Island
Fiesta Island Road
San Diego, CA
Mission Bay Drive
619-221-8900
On this island, dogs are allowed to run off-leash anywhere outside the fenced areas, anytime during the day. It is mostly sand which is perfect for those beach loving hounds. You might, however, want to stay on the north end of the island. The south end was used as the city's sludge area (mud and sediment, and possibly smelly) processing facility. The island is often used to launch jet-skis and motorboats. There is a one-way road that goes around the island and there are no fences, so please make sure your dog stays away from the road. About half way around the island, there is a completely fenced area on the beach. Please note that the fully enclosed area is not a dog park. The city of San Diego informed us that is supposed to be locked and is not intended to be used as a dog park even though there may occasionally be dogs running in this off-limits area.

Parks

San Diego

Balboa Park
El Prado St
San Diego, CA
Hwy 163
619-235-1121
Balboa Park is a 1200 acre urban cultural park located just east of downtown. Dogs must be leashed and under control of the owner at all times, including on the trails and in the canyons. The park is known for its brilliant displays of seasonal flowers, an award-winning rose garden, shady groves of trees, and meandering paths. Many of Balboa Park's museums are magnificent Spanish Colonial Revival buildings, originally constructed for the 1915-1916 Panama-California Exposition. If you are interested in the architecture, you and your pup can take an outdoor walking tour around the various buildings. Work up an appetite after walking around? There is a concession stand called In the Park. It has many outdoor seats and is located at the corner of Village Place and Old Globe Way. For a map of the park, stop by the Visitors Center on El Prado St near Hwy 163. There is also an unfenced dog run on the west side of the park by El Prado and Balboa Drive.

Balboa Park Dog Run
Balboa Dr
San Diego, CA
El Prado St
619-235-1100
The dog-friendly Balboa Park has set aside a portion of land for an off leash dog run. It's not fenced, so make sure your pup listens to voice commands. It is located between Balboa Drive and Hwy 163.

Park.

Cleveland National Forest
10845 Rancho Bernardo Rd., Suite 200
San Diego, CA 92127
858-673-6180
This national forest covers 460,000 acres and offers 356 miles of trails. Please see our listings in this region for dog-friendly hikes and/or campgrounds.

Mission Bay Park
Mission Bay Drive
San Diego, CA
Clairemont Dr & Hwy 5
619-221-8900
Leashed dogs are allowed in this park from 6pm to 9am. There are over 20 miles of beaches that make up this park (including Fiesta Island). If you come during the above mentioned hours, there is also a nice path that meanders through the grass and trees.

Mission Beach & Promenade
Mission Blvd.
San Diego, CA
Mission Bay Drive
619-221-8900
Leashed dogs are allowed on this beach and promenade walkway from 6pm to 9am. It is about 3 miles long and located west of Mission Bay

Mission Trails Regional Park
1 Father Junipero Serra Trail
San Diego, CA 92119
Mission Gorge Rd
619-668-3275
This 6,000 acre regional park has a nice variety of trails ranging from an easy 1 mile loop to a strenuous 5 mile hike with elevation gains of up to 1150 feet. Dogs are allowed, but must be leashed at all times. Don't forget to bring enough water since it can get pretty warm here year-round. The park is located off Mission Gorge Rd at the corners of Father Junipero Serra Trail and Echo Dell Rd. It is located about 8-9 northeast of downtown San Diego. Maps are available at the Visitor and Interpretive Center on Father Junipero Serra Trail.

Presidio Park
Jackson St
San Diego, CA
by Old Town
619-235-1100
This is a nice park for your pup to stretch his or her legs before or after you visit Old Town State Historic Park which is located about 2-3 blocks away. Dogs must be leashed in the park.

Tecolote Canyon Natural Park
Tecolote Road
San Diego, CA
Hwy 5
619-581-9952
This is a very nice natural park with over 6 miles (12 round trip) of walking, running or mountain biking trails. There are nine entry points into the park, but we recommend you start at the Visitors and Nature Center where you can pick up a trail map from the ranger. If you start at the Nature Center, most of the trail (first five miles) is relatively flat. It gets steeper in the last mile and there could be some creek crossings. From the Nature Center, follow the path which will take you past a golf course. At the end of the golf course, you'll need to take Snead Ave which will join up with the rest of the path. There might be a few more street crossings, but the majority of the walk is on the dirt trail. With the all the natural surroundings it seems like it is far from the city, but it's located only 6-7 miles from downtown. To get there, take Tecolote Road until it ends. Dogs must be on leash in the park.

Restaurants

San Diego

Baja Fresh Mexican Grill
3369 Rosecrans
San Diego, CA
619-222-3399
This Mexican restaurant is open for lunch and dinner. They use fresh ingredients and making their salsa and beans daily. Some of the items on their menu include Enchiladas, Burritos, Tacos Salads, Quesadillas, Nachos, Chicken, Steak and more. Well-behaved leashed dogs are allowed at the outdoor tables.

Baja Fresh Mexican Grill
120 W. Washington St.
San Diego, CA
619-497-1000
This Mexican restaurant, located in the Hillcrest area, is open for lunch and dinner. They use fresh ingredients and making their salsa and beans daily. Some of the items on their menu include Enchiladas, Burritos, Tacos Salads, Quesadillas, Nachos, Chicken, Steak and more. Well-behaved leashed dogs are allowed at the outdoor tables.

Baja Fresh Mexican Grill
9015 Mira Mesa Blvd
San Diego, CA
858-577-0590
This Mexican restaurant is open for lunch and dinner. They use fresh ingredients and making their salsa and beans daily. Some of the items on their menu include Enchiladas, Burritos, Tacos Salads, Quesadillas, Nachos, Chicken, Steak and more. Well-behaved leashed dogs are allowed at the outdoor tables.

Baja Fresh Mexican Grill
3737 Murphy Cyn Rd
San Diego, CA
858-277-5700
This Mexican restaurant is open for lunch and dinner. They use fresh ingredients and making their salsa and beans daily. Some of the items on their menu include Enchiladas, Burritos, Tacos Salads, Quesadillas, Nachos, Chicken, Steak and more. Well-behaved leashed dogs are allowed at the outdoor tables.

Baja Fresh Mexican Grill
845 Camino De La Reina
San Diego, CA
619-295-1122
This Mexican restaurant is open for lunch and dinner. They use fresh ingredients and making their salsa and beans daily. Some of the items on their menu include Enchiladas, Burritos, Tacos Salads, Quesadillas, Nachos, Chicken, Steak and more. Well-behaved leashed dogs are allowed at

the outdoor tables.

Boardwalk Bistro
3704 Mission Blvd
San Diego, CA 92109
858-488-9484
This cafe is located near Mission Bay. Well-behaved, leashed dogs are allowed at the outdoor tables.

Champagne French Bakery Cafe
12955 El Camino Real
San Diego, CA 92130
858-792-2222
Located in the Del Mar Highlands Town Center, this restaurant allows well-behaved leashed dogs at the outdoor tables. Thanks to one of our readers for recommending this cafe.

City Delicatessen
535 University Ave
San Diego, CA 92103
619-295-2747
This restaurant is located in the Hillcrest area and serves a variety of sandwiches. Well-behaved, leashed dogs are allowed at the outdoor tables.

Gulf Coast Grill
4130 Park Blvd
San Diego, CA 92103
619-295-2244
Gulf Coast Grill serves lunch and dinner daily. The specialty is southern and southwestern cuisine. Dogs may dine with you on the outside patio.

Hard Rock Cafe
801 4th Ave
San Diego, CA
(downtown)
619-615-7625
This is one of the Hard Rock Cafe chain locations. They have 2-3 outdoor tables for dining. The menu offers a variety of burgers, chicken, desserts and more.

Kemo Sabe
3958 Fifth Ave.
San Diego, CA 92103
619-220-6802
Located in the Hillcrest area, this restaurant serves food that is influenced by Asian and New Mexican cuisines. They have about 6 outdoor tables and you will need to sign up on a waiting list if all tables are taken. Well-behaved, leashed dogs are allowed at the outside tables.

Rubio's Baja Grill
901 4th Ave
San Diego, CA
(downtown)
619-231-7731
Rubio's prides themselves on their fish tacos, but they also have a variety of other food like tacos, burritos, and even healthy low fat items. They are a large chain located throughout Southern California. Dogs are allowed at the outdoor tables.

Saffron
3731 India Street
San Diego, CA 92013
619-574-0177
This Thai restaurant allows well-behaved leashed dogs at their outdoor seating area.

Sally's Restaurant & Bar
1 Market Place
San Diego, CA
(by Seaport Village)
619-687-6080
Dogs are welcome at the tables that are next to the lawn. Dogs need to sit or lay on the grass, which is next to your table. This popular seafood restaurant usually draws a crowd at the outdoor tables, so call ahead so that they can hold a table near the grass. There are nice views of the marina and San Diego Bay from the patio. Sally's is located between Seaport Village and the

Marriott San Diego Marina Hotel. The restaurant is open for lunch and dinner.

Seven 17 Restaurant
717 4th Ave
San Diego, CA
(downtown)
619-232-4440
The restaurant allows well-behaved dogs at their outside tables. They are open 7 days a week for dinner.

Terra
3900 Block of Vermont
San Diego, CA 92103
619-293-7088
This restaurant comes highly recommended from one of our readers who says "It has dog food from The Original Paw Pleasers on the menu and lets you bring your dogs to eat with you at their outdoor dining area... Sometimes they have pet parties too." They are located in the Hillcrest area of San Diego.

The Alamo
2502 San Diego Ave
San Diego, CA 92110
619-296-1112
This Mexican restaurant serves some tasty dishes and is located next to Old Town State

Historic Park. Dogs are allowed at the outdoor tables.

The Boardwalk
3704 Mission Blvd
San Diego, CA 92109
858-488-9484
Well-behaved leashed dogs are allowed at the outdoor seating area.

Trattoria Fantastica
1735 India Street
San Diego, CA 92101
619-234-1735
Dogs are allowed at the tables on the front patio.

Whole Foods Market
711 University Avenue
San Diego, CA 92103
619-294-2800
This natural food supermarket offers natural and organic foods. Order some food from their deli and bring it to an outdoor table where your well-behaved leashed dog is welcome.

Stores

San Diego

Neiman Marcus
7027 Friars Road
San Diego, CA 92108
Fashion Valley Center
619-692-9100
This famous department store, which sells everything from clothing to home furnishings, allows your well-behaved leashed dog to shop with you. It is located in Fashion Valley Center.

The Original Paw Pleasers Bakery
1220 Cleveland Ave
San Diego, CA 92103
Vermont

619-293-PAWS

Has your dog every dreamed of going to a bakery where the fresh baked cookies and cakes are made just for canines? Your pup will be sure to drool over the specialty goodies like Tail Waggin' Treats, Bark-La-Va, Carob Brownies, Birthday Cakes and more. The cakes look perfect enough for human consumption, but they are actually for dogs. You'll be able to tell from the sign, "Pets Welcome, Owners Optional", that your pooch is more than welcome to peruse and drool over the treats. And if your pup is thirsty, these nice folks will provide a bowl of water. Also, make sure your pet tries the dog and cat yogurt bar with soft-serve frozen yogurt and a toppings bar that includes freeze-dried liver. The yogurt bar is available weekends in May & June and open daily in July & August. When in San Diego, be sure to stop by. If you don't have time, you can order via phone at 888-670-PAWS.

Transportation Systems

San Diego

Metropolitan Transit System
Regional
San Diego, CA
619-233-3004
Small dogs in enclosed carriers are allowed on the buses and light rail. You must be able to transport your dog and the carrier by yourself, and you need to hold the carrier on your lap. Noise or odor may give cause for refusal to transport the animal.

Vets and Kennels

San Diego

Animal ER of San Diego
5610 Kearny Mesa Rd
San Diego, CA 92111

Hwy 52
858-569-0600
Monday - Friday 6 pm to 8 am, 24 hours on weekends.

Animal Emergency Clinic
13240 Evening Creek Dr S
San Diego, CA 92128
858-748-7387
24 hours everyday.

Emergency Animal Clinic
2317 Hotel Cir S # A
San Diego, CA 92108
619-299-2400
Monday - Friday 6 pm to 8 am, 24 hours on weekends.

San Marcos Dog Travel Guide
Restaurants

San Marcos

Mocha Marketplace
1080 W. San Marcos Blvd #176
San Marcos, CA
760-744-2112
Dogs are allowed at the outdoor tables.

Old California Mining Company
1020 W. San Marcos Blvd #118
San Marcos, CA 92069
760-761-4900
Dogs are allowed at the outdoor tables.

Tony Roma's
1020 W San Marcos Blvd #124
San Marcos, CA 92069
760-736-4343
Dogs are allowed at the outdoor tables.

San Ysidro Dog Travel Guide
Accommodations

San Ysidro

Motel 6 - Border
160 E Calie Primera
San Ysidro, CA 92173
619-690-6663
This hotel is very close to the Mexican border in San Diego.

Santa Ysabel Dog Travel Guide

Accommodations - RV Parks and Campgrounds

Santa Ysabel

Lake Henshaw Resort
26439 Highway 76
Santa Ysabel, CA
760-782-3487
Lake Henshaw Resort, located at a lake which rests at the foot of the Palomar Mountains, offers camping and RV hookups. There are 15 sites with full RV hook-ups and 85 mobile home park sites. Children and pets are welcome. Lake Henshaw is a great place for fishermen of all levels. This resort is located off Highway 76, north of Julian.

Vista Dog Travel Guide
Accommodations

Vista

La Quinta Inn Vista
630 Sycamore Avenue
Vista, CA
760-727-8180
Dogs up to 75 pounds are allowed at the hotel.

Attractions

Vista

Antique Gas and Steam Engine Museum
2040 North Santa Fe Avenue
Vista, CA 92083
760-941-1791
Well-behaved dogs are allowed at the museum. Unique from many other museums, this one is a working collection. Ninety-five percent of the collections on display are operational. The Museum depicts life in the early 1900's through exhibits, ongoing restoration projects and live demonstrations. The museum also has a blacksmith and wheelwright shop, farmhouse with a parlor, sawmill, gristmill, and more. It is located on 40 acres of rolling farm land in Guajome Regional Park in San Diego County.

Restaurants

Vista

Baja Fresh Mexican Grill
620 Hacienda Dr.
Vista, CA

760-643-0110
This Mexican restaurant is open for lunch and dinner. They use fresh ingredients and making their salsa and beans daily. Some of the items on their menu include Enchiladas, Burritos, Tacos Salads, Quesadillas, Nachos, Chicken, Steak and more. Well-behaved leashed dogs are allowed at the outdoor tables.

Vets and Kennels

Vista

A Coastal Emergency Animal Hospital
1900 Hacienda Dr
Vista, CA 92083
760-630-6343
Monday - Friday 5 pm to 8 am, Friday 5 pm - Monday 8 am.

Warner Springs Dog Travel Guide
Parks

Warner Springs

Barker Spur Trail
Forest Road 9S07
Warner Springs, CA
760-788-0250
This 3.4 mile moderate rated trail is located in the Cleveland National Forest. The trail elevation changes from 4,000 to 5,100 feet. It is open from early spring through late fall. Pets on leash are allowed and please clean up after them. To get there, take Highway 79 south toward Warner Springs. At about 2 miles southeast of Sunshine Summit take Forest Road 9S07 west. In about 7 miles the trailhead sign will be found on the left side of the road. Parking is in the wide area along the road. (Vehicles must display a Forest Adventure Pass.)

Chapter 13

California Dog-Friendly Travel Guide
The Desert Regions

Baker Dog Travel Guide
Accommodations - RV Parks and Campgrounds

Baker

Mohave National Preserve Campgrounds
72157 Baker Road
Baker, CA 92309
760-255-8800
This park offers two family campgrounds, the Mid Hills Campground and Hole-in-the-Wall Campground. Elevations range from 4,400 feet to 5,600 feet. The campgrounds offer tent camping and one camp offers spaces for RVs. There are no hookups. The campsites are usually booked during deer hunting season. Spaces are available on a first-come, first-served basis. Pets are allowed but should be leashed. Please clean up after your pet. Contact the park for campground locations and more details.

Parks

Baker

Mohave National Preserve
72157 Baker Road
Baker, CA 92309
760-255-8800
Located in the heart of the Mohave Desert, this 1.6 million acre park offers rose-colored sand dunes, volcanic cinder cones and Joshua tree forests. The park offers hundreds of miles of dirt roads to explore the land in your own 4 wheel drive vehicle. There are many hiking opportunities including the Teutonia Peak Hike. This trail lets you explore a dense Joshua tree forest on the way to a peak on Cima Dome. The 4 mile roundtrip trail is located 10.5 miles south of I-15 on Cima Road. Dogs are allowed on trails and in the campgrounds. They must be leashed except dogs that are being used for hunting. Please clean up after your pet. For more park details and information, including maps, visit the Baker Desert Information Center in Baker. They are open all year from 9am to 5pm.

Barstow Dog Travel Guide
Accommodations

Barstow

Days Inn
1590 Coolwater Lane
Barstow, CA 92311
760-256-1737
There is a $10 per day pet fee.

Econo Lodge
1230 E. Main Street
Barstow, CA 92311
760-256-2133
One large well-behaved dog is permitted per room. There is a $5 per day pet fee.

Holiday Inn Express
1861 W. Main St.
Barstow, CA 92311
760-256-1300
This 3 story motel, located along Historic Route 66, offers rooms with microwaves, refrigerators, iron/ironing boards, hair dryers and data ports. There is $20 refundable pet deposit.

Motel 6
150 N Tucca Ave
Barstow, CA 92311
760-256-1752
There are no additional pet fees.

Ramada Inn
1511 E Main Street
Barstow, CA 92311
760-256-5673
There is a $20 one time pet fee per visit.

Super 8 Motel
170 Coolwater Lane
Barstow, CA 92311
760-256-8443
There is a $5 per day pet charge.

Accommodations - RV Parks and Campgrounds

Yermo

Barstow/Calico KOA
35250 Outer Highway 15 North
Yermo, CA 92398
760-254-2311
This campground is located in a desert setting and is about 3.5 miles from the dog-friendly Calico Ghost Town. RV spaces and tent sites are available. RV site amenities include a maximum pull through length of 70 feet and 50 amp service. Other camp amenities include a seasonal swimming pool, free modem dataport, LP gas, snack bar, pavilion/meeting room and dog

walking area. Well-behaved leashed dogs of all sizes are allowed. People need to clean up after their pets. There is no pet fee. The campground is open all year.

Attractions

Barstow

Calico Early Man Site
Minneola Road
Barstow, CA
760-252-6000
In 1942 amateur archaeologists discovered what they believed to be primitive stone tools at this site. Archaeologists have classified the site as a possible stone tool workshop, quarry and camp site for early nomadic hunters and gatherers. It is estimated that the soil at this site may date back to over 200,000 years. The site is open on Wednesday from 12:30pm to 4:30pm and Thursday through Sunday from 9am to 4:30pm. Guided tours are available on Wednesday at 1:30pm and 3:30pm, and on Thursday through Sunday at 9:30am, 11:30am, 1:30pm and 3:30pm. There is a $5 fee per person and less for children and seniors. Well-behaved leashed dogs are allowed. Please clean up after your dog.

Route 66 Mother Road Museum
681 North First Ave
Barstow, CA
760-255-1890
The museum offers a collection of historic photographs and artifacts related to Route 66 and the Mojave Desert Communities. Displays include the development of the U.S. Route 66 from early pioneer trails and railroads to automotive history, businesses and sites. Well-behaved, leashed dogs are welcome. The museum is open Friday through Sunday from 11am-4pm. Admission is free. The museum is located in the historic Casa del Desierto Harvey House.

Yermo

Calico Ghost Town
PO Box 638
Yermo, CA 92398
760-254-2122
Dogs are allowed at this old ghost town but not inside the restaurants. Founded in March 1881, it grew to a population of 1,200 with 22 saloons and more than 500 mines. Calico became one of the richest mining towns in California, producing $86 million in silver, $45 million in borax and gold.

After 1907, when silver prices dropped and borax mining moved to Death Valley, Calico became a ghost town. Today, Calico is one of the few remaining original mining towns of the western United States. It was preserved by Walter Knott (founder of Knott's Berry Farm and a relative of the owner of Calico's Silver King mine). Mr. Knott donated Calico Ghost Town to the County of San Bernardino in 1966, and it remains alive and well as a 480-acre County Regional Park. Live events like gunfights and living history reenactments are common at the park. Take a self-guided town tour or go for a hike on one of their trails. You and your pooch can also take a guided walking tour (Mon-Fri) with Calico's historian who will examine the history of the miners, the famous 20-mule team and a U.S. Postal Mail dog named Dorsey. The park also offer many festivals throughout the year. Camping and RV hookups are available here. The park is located 8 miles north of Barstow and 3 miles east of Interstate 15.

Restaurants

Barstow

Baja Fresh Mexican Grill
2854 Lenwood Rd
Barstow, CA
760-253-2505
This Mexican restaurant is open for lunch and dinner. They use fresh ingredients and making their salsa and beans daily. Some of the items on their menu include Enchiladas, Burritos, Tacos Salads, Quesadillas, Nachos, Chicken, Steak and more. Well-behaved leashed dogs are allowed at the outdoor tables.

Blythe Dog Travel Guide
Accommodations

Blythe

Best Western Sahara Motel
825 W. Hobson Way
Blythe, CA 92225
760-922-7105
Pets are allowed with no restrictions and there are no pet fees. Amenities include a free continental breakfast, pool, spa, and microwave and VCRs in some rooms.

Holiday Inn Express
600 W. Donion St
Blythe, CA 92225
760-921-2300

There is a $10 per day pet fee.

Borrego Springs Dog Travel Guide Accommodations

Borrego Springs

Borrego Valley Inn
405 Palm Canyon Drive
Borrego Springs, CA 92004
760-767-0311
Built in 1998, the Borrego Valley Inn is a 15 room Inn situated on 10 acres of property that borders the Anza-Borrego Desert State Park. Surrounded by mountain peaks that range from 4,000 to 7,000 feet, the inn's natural desert landscaping blends perfectly with the surrounding environment. All of the rooms are decorated in Southwestern/Mexican decor and have private patios and walk-in showers. Breakfast is included with your room. There is lots of room for your pet to roam here. You can even take your dog for some exercise at the back of the property where there's a walking trail that leads up to the mountain's ledge. There is a one time $25 pet fee per dog per stay.

Parks

Borrego Springs

Anza-Borrego Desert State Park
Highway 78
Borrego Springs, CA
760-767-5311
Dogs are not allowed on any trails. They are allowed in day use areas and on over 500 miles of dirt roads. The roads can be used by cars but there is usually not too much traffic. Pets must be leashed and please clean up after them. The park is located about a 2 hour drive from San Diego, Riverside and Palm Springs off Highways S22 and 78.

Death Valley Dog Travel Guide Accommodations

Death Valley

Stovepipe Wells Village Motel
Highway 190
Death Valley, CA 92328
760-786-2387
All of the 83 guest rooms are non-smoking and air conditioned. There are no phones in the rooms.

The main building has a restaurant, saloon, gift shops and swimming pool. They are located in the Death Valley National Park. There is no pet fee.

Panamint Springs

Panamint Springs Resort
Highway 190
Panamint Springs, CA
775-482-7680
There is a $5 per day additional pet fee. The resort is located on Highway 190, 48 miles east of Lone Pine and 31 miles west of Stovepipe Wells.

Accommodations - RV Parks and Campgrounds

Death Valley

Death Valley National Park Campgrounds
Highway 190
Death Valley, CA 92328
760-786-3200
There are 10 campgrounds to choose from at this park, ranging from 196 feet below sea level to 8,200 feet above sea level. The Emigrant campground, located at 2,100 feet, offers tent camping only. This free campground offers 10 sites with water, tables and flush toilets. The Furnace Creek campground, located at 196 feet below sea level has 136 sites with water, tables, fireplaces, flush toilets and a dump station. Winter rates are $16 per night and less for the summertime. There are no hookups and some campgrounds do not allow generators. The Stovepipe Wells RV Campground is managed by the Stovepipe Wells Resort and offers 14 sites with full hookups but no tables or fireplaces. See our listing in Death Valley for more information about this RV park. About half of the campgrounds are open all year. Pets must be leashed and attended at all times. Please clean up after your pets. Dogs are not allowed on any trails in Death Valley National Park, but they can walk along roads. Pets are allowed up to a few hundred yards from the paved and dirt roads.

Stovepipe Wells Village Campgrounds and RV Park
Highway 190
Death Valley, CA 92328
760-786-2387
In addition to the motel, this establishment also offers a campground and RV park with full hookups. The main building has a restaurant, saloon, gift shops and swimming pool. They are

located in the Death Valley Nationa Park. Well-behaved leashed dogs are allowed.

Attractions

Death Valley

Death Valley National Park
Highway 190
Death Valley, CA
760-786-2331
Death Valley is one of the hottest places on Earth, with summer temperatures averaging well over 100 degrees Fahrenheit. It is also the lowest point on the Western Hemisphere at 282 feet below sea level. Average rainfall here sets yet another record. With an average of only 1.96 inches per year, this valley is the driest place in North America. Because of the high summer heat, the best time to visit the park is during the winter. Even though dogs are not allowed on any trails, you will still be able to see the majority of the sights and attractions from your car. There are several scenic drives that are popular with all visitors, with or without dogs. Dante's View is a 52 mile round trip drive that takes about 2 hours or longer. Some parts of the road are graded dirt roads and no trailers or RVs are allowed. On this drive you will view scenic mudstone hills which are made of 7 to 9 million year old lakebed sediments. You will also get a great view from the top of Dantes View. Another scenic drive is called Badwater. It is located about 18 miles from the Visitor Center and can take about 1.5 to 2 hours or longer. On this drive you will view the Devil's Golf Course where there are almost pure table salt crystals from an ancient lake. You will also drive to Badwater which is the lowest point in the Western Hemisphere at 282 feet below sea level. Dogs are allowed at view points which are about 200 yards or less from roads or parking lots. Pets must be leashed and attended at all times. Please clean up after your pets. While dogs are not allowed on any trails in the park, they can walk along roads. Pets are allowed up to a few hundred yards from the paved and dirt roads. Stop at the Furnance Creek Visitor Center to pick up a brochure and more information. The visitor center is located on Highway 190, north of the lowest point.

El Centro Dog Travel Guide
Attractions

El Centro

Tumco Historic Townsite
Ogilby Road
El Centro, CA
760-337-4400
Located in the mountains east of El Centro, is an abandoned gold mine town called Tumco. Today a few buildings and mine shafts remain. The mine shafts have very steep drop offs and are dangerous, so make sure you and your pooch stay clear of them. Also be aware of rattlesnakes in the area. It is best to visit during the fall, winter or spring months when it is not too hot. The remote site is managed by the Bureau of Land Management. Dogs must be on leash and please clean up after your dogs. To get there from Highway 8, east of El Centro, take Highway S34 North.

Joshua Tree National Park Dog Travel Guide
Accommodations

Twentynine Palms

Best Western Garden Inn & Suites
71487 Twentynine Palms Highway
Twentynine Palms, CA 92277
760-367-9141
There is a $10 per day pet charge and a $100 refundable pet deposit.

Yucca Valley

Super 8
57096 29 Palms Hwy
Yucca Valley, CA 92284
760-228-1773
There is a $20 refundable pet deposit and a $5 per day pet fee. The hotel is 10 miles from Joshua Tree National Park.

Accommodations - RV Parks and Campgrounds

Twentynine Palms

29 Palms RV Resort
4949 Desert Knoll
Twentynine Palms, CA 92277
760-367-3320
This RV resort is located less than 10 minutes from the Joshua Tree National Park visitor center. RV sites include full hookups and shade trees. They can accommodate large motorhomes and trailers. Park amenities include a recreation hall, fitness room, tennis courts, shuffle board, heated indoor pool, laundry, showers and restrooms. You

can stay for a day, a week or all winter. Pets on leash are welcome. There is no pet fee, just clean up after your dog.

Joshua Tree National Park Campgrounds
74485 National Park Drive
Twentynine Palms, CA 92277
760-367-5500
There are nine campgrounds at this park which range from 3,000 foot to 4,500 foot elevations. Many have no fees and offer pit toilets. Only a few of the campgrounds offer water and flush toilets. There are no hookups and generators are not allowed between the hours of 10pm and 6am.

Parks

Twentynine Palms

Joshua Tree National Park
74485 National Park Drive
Twentynine Palms, CA 92277
760-367-5500
Dogs are not allowed on the trails, cannot be left unattended, and must be on leash. However, they are allowed on dirt and paved roads including the Geology Tour Road. This is actually a driving tour, but you'll be able to see the park's most fascinating landscapes from this road. It is an 18 mile tour with 16 stops. The park recommends taking about 2 hours for the round trip. At stop #9, about 5 miles out, there is room to turnaround if you do not want to complete the whole tour.

Lancaster Dog Travel Guide
Accommodations

Lancaster

Best Western Antelope Valley Inn
44055 North Sierra Highway
Lancaster, CA 93534
661-948-4651
There is a $35 one time pet charge.

Mojave Dog Travel Guide
Accommodations

Mojave

Econo Lodge
2145 SR 58
Mojave, CA 93501
661-824-2463
There is a $5 per day pet fee.

Motel 6
16958 Hwy 58
Mojave, CA 93501
661-824-4571
There are no additional pet fees.

Needles Dog Travel Guide
Accommodations

Needles

Days Inn and Suites
1215 Hospitality Lane
Needles, CA 92363
760-326-5836
There are no additional pet fees.

Econo Lodge
1910 N. Needles Hwy
Needles, CA 92363
760-326-3881
There is a $5 per day pet fee.

Motel 6
1420 J St
Needles, CA 92363
760-326-3399
A well-behaved large dog is allowed. The motel is located 26 miles from the Laughlin Casinos.

Super 8
1102 E Broadway
Needles, CA 92363
760-326-4501
There is a $5 per day additional pet fee.

Travelers Inn
1195 3rd Street Hill
Needles, CA 92363
760-326-4900
There are no additional pet fees.

Accommodations - RV Parks and Campgrounds

Needles

Moabi Regional Park Campground
Park Moabi Road
Needles, CA
760-326-3831
This park has a campground with 35 RV sites with full hookups and unlimited tent sites. The sites are situated in the main section of the park and along 2.5 miles of shoreline. The park is

located on the banks of the Colorado River and is popular for camping, fishing, boating, swimming and water skiing. Dogs can go into the water but they strongly advise against it because there are so many fast boats in the water. Dogs must be leashed and please clean up after them. This park is located 11 miles southeast of Needles on Interstate 40.

Needles KOA
5400 National Old Trails Highway
Needles, CA 92363
760-326-4207
Located in the desert on historic Route 66, this campground offers tent and RV spaces. Dogs are allowed in the cabins too. RV site amenities include a maximum length pull through of 75 feet and 50 amp service. Other campground amenities include a seasonal swimming pool, seasonal deli open November through April, snack bar, modem dataport, and LP gas. Well-behaved leashed dogs of all sizes are allowed. People need to clean up after their pets. There is no pet fee. The campground is open all year.

Olancha Dog Travel Guide
Accommodations

Olancha

Ranch Motel
2051 S Highway 395
Olancha, CA
760-764-2387
There are no additional pet fees.

Palm Springs Dog Travel Guide
Accommodations

East Palm Canyon

Motel 6
595 E Palm Canyon Dr
East Palm Canyon, CA 92264
760-325-6129
One large dog is allowed as long as it is well-behaved.

Indio

Holiday Inn Express
84-096 Indio Springs Pkwy
Indio, CA 92201
760-342-6344
There is a $50 refundable deposit if you pay with cash.

Palm Shadow Inn
80-761 Highway 111
Indio, CA 92201
760-347-3476
A well-behaved large dog is okay. Nestled among date palm groves, there are eighteen guest rooms which overlook nearly three acres of lawns, flowers and citrus trees. There is a $5 per day pet charge.

Quality Inn
43505 Monroe Street
Indio, CA 92201
760-347-4044
There are no additional pet fees.

Royal Plaza Inn
82347 Hwy 111
Indio, CA 92201
760-347-0911
This motel offers a laundry room, whirlpool and room refrigerators. There is a $10 per day additional pet fee.

North Palm Springs

Motel 6
63950 20th Ave
North Palm Springs, CA 92258
760-251-1425
There are no additional pet fees.

Palm Desert

Comfort Suites
39-585 Washington St
Palm Desert, CA 92211
760-360-3337
There is a $25 refundable pet deposit.

Motel 6
78100 Varner Rd

Palm Desert, CA 92211
760-345-0550
There are no additional pet fees.

The Inn at Deep Canyon
74470 Abronia Trail
Palm Desert, CA 92260
760-346-8061
This hotel features a palm garden, pool and fully-equipped kitchenettes. They have pet-friendly rooms available. There is a $10 per day additional pet fee.

Palm Springs

7 Springs Inn and Suites
950 N. Indian Canyon Dr.
Palm Springs, CA 92262
760-320-9110
7 Springs Inn and Suites offers a variety of accommodations in the heart of Palm Springs. Enjoy fully furnished suites with Kitchens, free daily Continental Breakfast, Heated Pool, Jacuzzi, BBQ area, Remote control T.V., direct dial telephones, free parking. Close to area shopping, restaurants, casinos, golf, tennis, and indian canyons. Pets are welcome for a $15 per night fee. Pets cannot be left unattended and must be kept on a leash when out of the room.

Caliente Tropics Resort
411 E. Palm Canyon Drive
Palm Springs, CA 92264
760-327-1391
This Polynesian style resort motor hotel is entirely non-smoking and pet-friendly. The pet rooms are on the first floor, near the end of each building. There is a $20 per night pet fee for the first pet and $10 per night for each additional pet.

Casa Cody Country Inn
175 S. Cahuilla Rd.
Palm Springs, CA 92262

760-320-9346
This is a quaint romantic historic inn that was founded in the 1920s. The founder, Harriet Cody, was a cousin of Buffalo Bill. The inn is nestled against the mountains and has adobe buildings. The rooms have fireplaces, kitchens and private patios. There is a $10 per day pet charge.

Hilton Palm Springs Resort
400 E. Tahquitz Canyon Way
Palm Springs, CA 92262
760-320-6868
This 13-acre resort is about a block from the Palm Canyon Drive Shopping Area. It is an ideal location if you want to be within walking distance of the many key local attractions like sidewalk cafes, shops and more. All rooms have balconies or patios and refrigerators. There is a required pet deposit.

La Serena Villas
339 South Belardo Road
Palm Springs, CA 92262
760-325-3216
These dog-friendly villas cater to those who prefer a relaxing, secluded hideaway in Palm Springs. Built in the 1930's, the villas are nestled in the foothills of the San Jacinto Mountains. Palm Springs Village is within walking distance. Your pet is welcome. There is a $10 per day pet

charge. Pets must be on leash and please pick up after your dog.

Orchid Tree Inn
261 South Belardo Road
Palm Springs, CA 92262
760-325-2791
This inn has two pet rooms. Dogs must be attended at all times and leashed when outside the room. There is a $250 refundable pet deposit.

Palm Springs Riviera Resort
1600 North Indian Canyon Drive
Palm Springs, CA 92262
760-327-8311
This 24 acre full service resort with 476 guest rooms allows well-behaved dogs of all sizes. Each room features oversized beds, individually controlled central air conditioning and heating units, small refrigerators, irons and ironing boards and multi-line phones with dataports. Amenities at the resort include an 18-hole putting course, nine tennis courts, a volleyball and basketball court and a workout room. They are located one mile from Palm Canyon Drive. There is a $20 per day pet fee and a $200 refundable pet deposit.

Porto Romantico
596 W. Via Escuela
Palm Springs, CA 92262
760-323-4944
This dog-friendly guest cottage is located in the Little Tuscany section of Old Palm Springs. Amenities include a king bed, down comforter, custom furniture, original artwork, kitchenette, two person whirlpool tub, climate control and a view of the San Jacinto Mountains. There is a continental breakfast each morning. Porto Romantico is a mile and a half from downtown Palm Springs in a quiet area. Read or lounge by the pool. Porto Romantico is entirely non-smoking. There is no additional pet fee but there is a $50 refundable pet deposit. The owners of this B&B also have a dog on the premises.

San Marino Hotel
225 West Baristo Road
Palm Springs, CA 92262
800-676-1214
The hotel, a favorite of writers and artists, is the closest lodging to the Palm Springs historic shopping area. Dogs are allowed, but not in the poolside rooms. There is a $10 per day pet charge.

Super 8 Lodge - Palm Springs
1900 N. Palm Canyon Drive
Palm Springs, CA 92262
760-322-3757
$10/stay for up to 3 dogs in one room. FREE 8-minute long distance call each night. FREE continental breakfast. Coffee maker, refrigerator, night light, clock/radio, safe in each room. Outdoor pool. On-site guest laundry. Kids 12 & under stay free. Off I-10, from West take Hwy 111 (N. Palm Canyon Drive); from East take Indian Avenue. Next to Billy Reed's restaurant.

Rancho Mirage

Motel 6
69-570 Hwy 111
Rancho Mirage, CA 92270
760-324-8475
One large dog is allowed per room

Accommodations - RV Parks and Campgrounds

Indio

Indian Wells RV Resort
47-340 Jefferson Street
Indio, CA 92201
800-789-0895
This RV resort offers many amenities such as three swimming pools, two spas, shuffleboard courts, basketball courts, pavilion with gas grills, billiards, horseshoes, fitness area, library, modem hookup, putting green, laundry facility, computer center and even a dog run. Site amenities include full hook-ups with 50 amp service, electric, water, sewer, paved pad and patio, and phone service for stays of 30 days or longer. Well-behaved leashed dogs are welcome. Please clean up after your pet. There is no pet fee. The RV park is located about 20 minutes from Palm Springs.

Attractions

Indio

Oasis Date Gardens
59111 Hwy 111
Indio, CA
800-827-8017
You and your dog are welcome to walk through the date gardens at Oasis. They also have picnic tables outside where you can enjoy the dates and a variety of date products. Dogs must be leashed.

Palm Springs

Palm Canyon Drive/Star Walk
Palm Canyon Drive
Palm Springs, CA

Take a stroll down historic Palm Canyon Drive (between Tahquitz and Ramon) with your dog. The street is lined with beautiful palm trees and all kinds of restaurants and specialty shops including the Cold Nose, Warm Heart store (see Attractions). If you want to see some stars, Hollywood-style stars, this is the place to be. The Palm Springs Walk of Stars is dedicated to honoring many Hollywood celebrities that have come to Palm Springs. Come see if your favorite actor or actress has a dedicated star in the sidewalk of Palm Canyon Drive. If you want to watch a celebrity receive his/her star, look at the Star Walk website (http: //www.palmsprings.com/stars/) or call 760-322-1563 for a current list of upcoming star dedications (date, time and address included.)

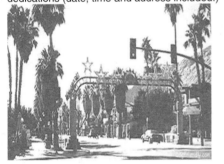

Parks

Indio

Lake Cahuilla Recreation Area
Avenue 58
Indio, CA
(Riverside County Park)
760-564-4712
Come here to sit by the lake, walk around it or on one of the many trails at this 710 acre park. There are also 50 campsites at the park. The park is located in Indio, 4 miles southeast of La Quinta. To get there, take Interstate 10 to Washington St., south on Washington 3 miles to Highway 111, east on 111, 2 miles to Jefferson Street, south on Jefferson, 3 miles to Avenue 54, east on Avenue 54 one mile to Madison Street, south on Madison 2 miles to Avenue 58, west on Avenue 58 one

mile to the park. There is a day use fee. Dogs must be leashed.

Palm Desert

Magnesia Park
Palm Desert Comm. Park
Palm Desert, CA
760-347-3484
Enjoy walking through this shaded park or having lunch at one of the many picnic tables. It's located in the city of Palm Desert at Magnesia Falls Drive and Portola Avenue. Dogs must be leashed.

Palm Springs

Lykken Trail
Ramon Road
Palm Springs, CA

When you begin this hike, there is a choice of two trails (one is pretty steep) which eventually join together up the mountain. The hike is a total of 6 miles round trip and includes a 1,000 foot elevation gain. This trail provides excellent views. It is located at the west end of Ramon Road. Dogs must be leashed.

Palm Springs Dog Park
222 Civic Dr North
Palm Springs, CA 92262
(behind City Hall)
760-322-8362
This fenced dog park is complete with green grass, trees, and fire hydrants. The dog park is on 1.6 acres. It's located at 222 Civic Drive North behind City Hall.

Restaurants

Palm Desert

Native Foods
73-890 El Paseo
Palm Desert, CA 92260
760-836-9396
This restaurants serves organic vegetarian food. Dogs are allowed at the outdoor tables.

Palm Springs

Cafe Totonaca
555 S. Sunrise Way
Palm Springs, CA
760-323-9487
Located in the RX Natural Health Food Market,

this cafe serves vegan and vegetarian food. For breakfast choose from their omelets, French toast, whole grain pancakes, oatmeal or bagels. For lunch and dinner they offer vegetarian, tofu and cheese sandwiches, veggie burgers, salads, and daily specials including a quesadilla plate, burrito plate, pasta dishes, dairy free fruit smoothies and more. Well-behaved leashed dogs are allowed at the outdoor tables. The tables are nicely shaded with patio umbrellas.

Del Rio's Fresh Mexican Grill
155 S. Palm Canyon Drive
Palm Springs, CA
760-320-9100
This Mexican restaurant offers a wide variety of food including soups, salads, quesadillas, enchiladas, burritos, fajitas, vegetarian dishes and more. Well-behaved leashed dogs are allowed at the outdoor tables.

Del Rio's Taqueria Grill
125 E. Tahquitz Canyon Way
Palm Springs, CA
760-778-5391
This Mexican restaurant offers a wide variety of food including soups, salads, quesadillas, enchiladas, burritos, fajitas, vegetarian dishes and more. Well-behaved leashed dogs are allowed at the outdoor tables.

Hair of the Dog English Pub
238 N Palm Canyon Dr
Palm Springs, CA
760-323-9890
This English Pub has a couple of outdoor tables which are pretty close together, but your dog is welcome.

Jamba Juice
111 S. Palm Canyon Drive
Palm Springs, CA
760-327-3151
This fruit bar offers a variety of smoothies and

fruit juices. Well-behaved leashed dogs are allowed at the outdoor tables.

Native Foods
1775 E. Palm Canyon Drive
Palm Springs, CA 92264
760-416-0070
This restaurant serves organic vegetarian dishes. Dogs are welcome at the outdoor seats. The hours are 11:30 am to 9:30 pm except Sunday when the restaurant is closed.

New York Pizza Delivery
260 N. Palm Canyon Drive
Palm Springs, CA
760-778-6973
This pizza restaurant allows well-behaved leashed dogs at their outdoor tables.

Palm Springs Creamery
125 E. Tahquitz Canyon Wy
Palm Springs, CA
760-778-1855
Need to satisfy that sweet tooth? Try some of this ice cream.

Peabody's Coffee Bar
134 S Palm Canyon Dr
Palm Springs, CA 92262
760-322-1877
Bring yourself and your dog for breakfast, lunch or dinner at this restaurant and coffee bar.

Penguin's Frozen Yogurt
333 N. Palm Canyon Drive
Palm Springs, CA
760-327-6455
Come here for a frozen yogurt dessert. Well-behaved leashed dogs are allowed at the outdoor tables.

Pomme Frite
256 S. Palm Canyon Drive
Palm Springs, CA
760-778-3727
This bistro features Belgian and French food. They are open six days a week for dinner and both lunch and dinner is served on the weekends. The restaurant is closed on Tuesdays. Well-behaved leashed dogs are allowed at the outdoor tables.

Rainbow Cactus Cafe
212 S. Indian Canyon Drive
Palm Springs, CA
760-325-3868
Well-behaved leashed dogs are allowed at the outdoor tables.

Shermans Deli and Bakery
401 E Tahquitz Canyon Way
Palm Springs, CA 92262
760-325-1199
Enjoy bagels and bakery treats or choose from their selection of hot or cold sandwiches.

Spencer's Restaurant
701 West Baristo Road
Palm Springs, CA 92262
760-327-3446
This restaurant features California Continental Cuisine. Well-behaved leashed dogs are allowed at the outdoor tables. The restaurant is located four blocks west of Palm Canyon Drive on Baristo. Thanks to one of our readers for recommending this restaurant.

Starbucks
682 S. Palm Canyon Drive
Palm Springs, CA
760-323-8023
This coffee shop allows well-behaved leashed dogs at their outdoor tables.

Togo's Eatery
255 S. Palm Canyon Drive
Palm Springs, CA
760-322-3727
This sandwich shop offers a variety of salads and hot or cold sandwiches. Well-behaved leashed dogs are allowed at the outdoor tables.

Stores

Palm Springs

Cold Nose, Warm Heart-Gift Store
187 S. Palm Canyon Drive
Palm Springs, CA 92262
760-327-7747
Enjoy browsing inside this specialty gift store with your pup. (The previous name of the store was "Dog Gone It.") They have all kinds of gifts for dog lovers. And your dog is welcome on leash in the store. This store is located at the main shopping area (Palm Canyon Drive) in downtown Palm Springs. They are open daily from 10am until 6pm.

Vets and Kennels

Thousand Palms

Animal Emergency Clinic
72374 Ramon Rd
Thousand Palms, CA 92276
I-10
760-343-3438
Monday - Friday 5 pm to 8 am, Saturday noon - Monday 8 am.

Palmdale Dog Travel Guide
Accommodations

Palmdale

Residence Inn
514 West Avenue P
Palmdale, CA 93551
661-947-4105
There is a $100 one time pet fee and a $10 per day additional pet fee.

Restaurants

Palmdale

Baja Fresh Mexican Grill
39332 10th St. W.
Palmdale, CA
661-947-1682
This Mexican restaurant is open for lunch and dinner. They use fresh ingredients and making their salsa and beans daily. Some of the items on their menu include Enchiladas, Burritos, Tacos Salads, Quesadillas, Nachos, Chicken, Steak and more. Well-behaved leashed dogs are allowed at the outdoor tables.

Vets and Kennels

Lancaster

Animal Emergency Clinic
1055 W Avenue M #101
Lancaster, CA 93534
Hwy 14
661-723-3959
Monday - Friday 6 pm to 8 am, Saturday noon - Monday 8 am.

Pearblossom Dog Travel Guide
Accommodations - RV Parks and Campgrounds

Pearblossom

South Fork Campground
Valyermo Road
Pearblossom, CA
661-296-9710
This 21 site campground is located in the Angeles National Forest an elevation of 4,500 feet. There are both tent and small RV sites. RVs up to 16 feet are allowed. Amenities include vault toilets. There are many hiking trails nearby including one which leads to the dog-friendly Devil's Punchbowl County Park. Pets on leash are allowed and please clean up after them. From Highway 138 in Pearblossom, turn south on Longview Road. Turn right on Avenue W which then becomes Valyermo Road. Go past the Forest Service Raner Station. About .25 miles after you cross the bridge, turn right and go about 2 miles to the campground.

Parks

Pearblossom

Devil's Punchbowl Nature Center
28000 Devil's Punchbowl Road
Pearblossom, CA 93553
661-944-2743
This 1,310 acre nature park offers unusual rock formations and is just one mile away from the famous San Andreas fault. The park elevation starts at 4,200 feet and climbs up to 6,500 feet. There are miles of trails rated easy to strenuous. The visitor center is open daily from 9am to 4pm. There is no charge for parking. Dogs must be on leash and please clean up after them.

Rancho Mirage Dog Travel Guide
Restaurants

Rancho Mirage

Baja Fresh Mexican Grill
71-800 Highway 111, Ste A-116
Rancho Mirage, CA
760-674-9380
This Mexican restaurant is open for lunch and dinner. They use fresh ingredients and making their salsa and beans daily. Some of the items on their menu include Enchiladas, Burritos, Tacos Salads, Quesadillas, Nachos, Chicken, Steak and more. Well-behaved leashed dogs are allowed at the outdoor tables.

Ridgecrest Dog Travel Guide
Accommodations

Ridgecrest

Motel 6
535 S China Lake Blvd
Ridgecrest, CA 93555
760-375-6866
There are no additional pet fees.

Tehachapi Dog Travel Guide
Accommodations

Tehachapi

Best Western Mountain Inn
416 West Tehachapi Boulevard
Tehachapi, CA 93561
661-822-5591
There are no extra pet charges.

Travelodge
500 Steuber Rd
Tehachapi, CA 93581
661-823-8000
There is a $7 per day pet fee.

Parks

Tehachapi

Tehachapi Mountain Park
Highway 58
Tehachapi, CA
661-868-7000
This 5,000 acre park offers views of the Tehachapi Mountains, the dividing line between the San Joaquin Valley and the Los Angeles Basin. The Nuooah Nature Trail is an interesting

interpretative 1/4 mile trail. The park is located between Bakersfield and Mojave. It is 8 miles southwest of the town of Tehachapi and is on the southern side of Hwy. 58. Dogs must be on leash.

Chapter 14

Nevada Dog-Friendly Travel Guide

Battle Mountain Dog Travel Guide
Accommodations

Battle Mountain

Comfort Inn
521 E. Front Street
Battle Mountain, NV 89820
775-635-5880
There is a $100 refundable pet deposit.

Beatty Dog Travel Guide
Accommodations

Beatty

Motel 6 - Death Valley
700 E. Highway 95 N
Beatty, NV 89003
775-553-9090
This motel is located just east of Death Valley
National Park. It is also near the Rhyolite Ghost
Town. There are no pet fees.

Attractions

Beatty

Rhyolite Ghost Town
off Highway 374
Beatty, NV
760-786-3200
In 1904 two prospectors found quartz all over a
hill which was "full of free gold". Soon the rush
was on and camps were set up in the area
including the townsite called Rhyolite. The name
was derived from the silica-rich volcanic rock in
the area. The most prominent mine in the area
was the Montgomery Shoshone mine which
prompted everyone to move to Rhyolite. This
boomtown once had a 3 story building, a stock
exchange, board of trade, red light district, hotels,
stores, a school for 250 children, an ice plant, two
electric plants, foundries, machine shops and a
miner's union hospital. Today you can see several
remnants of Rhyolite. The 3 story building still has
some walls standing and so does an old jail. A
privately owned train depot was restored and so
was the Bottle House. The Bottle House was
made out of whiskey bottles by a miner. This
house was restored in 1925 by Paramount
Pictures. Rhyolite is located 35 miles from the
Furnace Creek Visitor Center in Death Valley

National Park. Drive towards Beatty, Nevada.
Before you reach Beatty, take a paved road north
(left) from Highway 374. It will take you right into
the ghost town. Pets are allowed but must be
leashed. Please clean up after your pet.
Remember to watch out for rattlesnakes.

Carson City Dog Travel Guide
Accommodations

Carson City

Best Value Motel
2731 S Carson St
Carson City, NV
775-882-2007
There is a $30 refundable pet deposit.

Super 8 Motel
2829 S. Carson Street
Carson City, NV
775-883-7800
There is a $6 per day pet fee.

Parks

Carson City

Toiyabe National Forest
Hwy 395
Carson City, NV
S. Stewart St.

There are several dog-friendly hiking trails on the
national forest land in Carson City. These are
desert-like trails, so only go with your dog when
the weather is cooler. If it's hot, the sand may
burn your pup's paws. Visit the Carson Ranger
Station for maps and trail information about the
Toiyable National Forest. The station is located
on Hwy 395, near S. Stewart Street. Dogs should
be leashed.

Washoe Lake State Park
4855 East Lake Blvd.
Carson City, NV 89704
775-687-4319
This park is frequently used for bird watching, hiking, horseback riding, picnicking, windsurfing, water skiing, jet skiing, fishing and during certain times of the year, hunting. There are many trails at this park for hikers, mountain bikers, and equestrians. Pets must be leashed at all times, except at the Wetlands during hunting season. The park is located off U.S. 395, 10 miles north of Carson City and 15 miles south of Reno.

Restaurants

Carson City

Comma Coffee
312 S. Carson Street
Carson City, NV 775-883-2662

This cafe serves breakfast and lunch, as well as fruit smoothies, juices, cappuccinos, lattes, mochas and more. Dogs are welcome at the outdoor patio tables.

Mom and Pop's Diner
224 S. Carson St.
Carson City, NV 89701
775-884-4411
This restaurant serves breakfast, lunch and dinner. Dogs are allowed at the outdoor tables.

Quiznos
3228 N. Carson Street
Carson City, NV
775-882-7849
This restaurant serves a variety of sandwiches. Dogs are allowed at the outdoor tables.

Schlotzsky's Deli
1410 East Williams St.

Carson City, NV
775-882-5777
They have a few tables outside. Dogs are allowed at the outdoor tables.

Vets and Kennels

Carson City

Carson Tahoe Veterinary Hospital
3389 S. Carson Street
Carson City, NV
775-883-8238
Weekdays 7:30 am - 6 pm. Emergencies will be seen 24 hours with an additional $60 emergency fee.

Elko Dog Travel Guide
Accommodations

Elko

Best Western Gold Country Inn
2050 Idaho Street
Elko, NV 89801
775-738-8421
There is a $15 one time pet fee.

Comfort Inn
2970 Idaho St
Elko, NV 89801
775-777-8762
There is a $10 per day pet fee.

High Desert Inn
3015 Idaho Street
Elko, NV 89801
775-738-8425
There is a $15 one time pet charge.

Motel 6
3021 Idaho Street
Elko, NV 89801
775-738-4337
There are no additional pet fees.

Red Lion Casino
2065 Idaho Street
Elko, NV
775-738-2111
There is a $15 one time pet fee.

Shilo Inn
2401 Mountain City Highway
Elko, NV 89801
775-738-5522

There is a $10 per day pet charge.

Accommodations - RV Parks and Campgrounds

Elko

Double Dice RV Park
3730 Idaho Street
Elko, NV 89801
775-738-5642
This RV park offers 140 full hookup sites which come with water, sewer, 30 or 50amp electric, instant phone and 43 channel TV hookups. They have 75 sites which are pull through sites and can accommodate rigs as long as 65 feet. Park amenities include a game room, laundry room, free email/web center and showers. Tent sites are also available. Well-behaved leashed dogs are welcome. Please clean up after your pets. There is a $1 per night pet fee.

Ely Dog Travel Guide
Accommodations

Ely

Best Western Main Motel
1101 Aultman
Ely, NV 89301
775-289-4529
There is a $20 one time pet fee.

Best Western Park Vue
930 Aultman
Ely, NV 89301
775-289-4497
There is a $20 one time pet fee.

Ramada Inn Copper Queen Casino
805 Great Basin Blvd
Ely, NV 89301
775-289-4884
There are no additional pet fees.

Accommodations - RV Parks and Campgrounds

Ely

Ely KOA
HC 10, Box 10800
Ely, NV 89301
775-289-3413
This campground offers cabins, shaded RV sites and grassy tent sites. RV site amenities include

hookups with 50 amp service, cable TV and a maximum length pull through of 85 feet. Other amenities include a seasonal swimming pool, playground, food mart, LP gas and modem dataport. Well-behaved leashed dogs are allowed at the tent sites, RV sites and in the cabins. Please clean up after your pets. There are no pet fees unless you stay in a cabin and then there is a refundable pet security deposit. The park is open all year. They are located about 3 miles south of Ely on Highway 50/6.

Fallon Dog Travel Guide
Accommodations

Fallon

Super 8
855 W. Williams Ave
Fallon, NV 89406
775-423-6031
There is a $5 per day additional pet fee.

Fernley Dog Travel Guide
Accommodations

Fernley

Best Western Fernley Inn
1405 E Newlands Dr
Fernley, NV 89408
775-575-6776
There is a $7 per day addition pet fee.

Gerlach Dog Travel Guide
Accommodations

Gerlach

Soldier Meadows Guest Ranch and Lodge
Soldier Meadows Rd
Gerlach, NV 89412
530-233-4881
Dating back to 1865 when it was known as Camp McGarry, this historic cattle ranch lies in the Black Rock Desert about three hours north of Reno. Soldier Meadows is a family owned working cattle ranch with over 500,000 acres of public and private land to enjoy. It is one of the largest and remotest guest ranches in the nation. There are no phones, faxes, or computers here. Horseback riders can work with the cowboys, take trail rides to track wild mustangs and other wildlife, or ride out to the natural hot springs for a soak. Or you may chose to go mule deer hunting, fishing,

hiking, mountain biking or 4-wheeling. The lodge offers 10 guest rooms, and one suite with a private bathroom and kitchenette. The main lodge has a common living room with a large fireplace. Pets are not allowed in the kitchen area. There is a $20 one time pet charge.

Lake Tahoe Dog Travel Guide
Please see Lake Tahoe, California for Listings

Las Vegas Dog Travel Guide
Accommodations

Boulder City

Super 8
704 Nevada Hwy
Boulder City, NV 89005
702-294-8888
There is a $10 per day pet fee.

Henderson

Residence Inn
2190 Olympic Road
Henderson, NV 89014
702-434-2700
There is a $50 one time pet fee and a $10 per day pet fee. One dog is allowed per room and dogs up to 65 pounds are allowed.

Las Vegas

Best Western Nellis
5330 East Craig Street
Las Vegas, NV 89115
702-643-6111
This motel is located away from the busy downtown area, but within minutes from the Las Vegas Strip. Amenities include an outdoor pool, a playground, laundry/valet services and complimentary continental breakfast on the weekends. There is a $10 per day pet charge.

Best Western Parkview
921 Las Vegas Blvd North
Las Vegas, NV 89101
702-385-1213
This motel is located within a 15 minute drive from the Las Vegas Strip. Amenities include an outdoor pool and a guest laundry. There is a $8 per day pet charge.

Comfort Inn
910 E. Cheyenne Rd.
Las Vegas, NV 89030
702-399-1500
This motel is located about three miles from the Las Vegas Strip. Amenities at this motel include a heated outdoor pool & hot tub, gift shop, free continental breakfast and wheelchair accessibility. There is a $5 per day pet charge.

Hampton Inn
7100 Cascade Valley Court
Las Vegas, NV 89128
702-360-5700
There is a $25 one time pet fee.

Hawthorn Suites-The Strip
5051 Duke Ellington Way
Las Vegas, NV 89119
702-739-7000
This suites hotel has no size restrictions for dogs as long as they are well-behaved (no barking, potty trained, etc.). There is a $125 pet deposit and $25 of it is non-refundable. Hotel amenities include a guest laundry, outdoor pool, exercise room and more.

Holiday Inn Express-The Lakes
8669 W. Sahara Avenue
Las Vegas, NV 89117
702-256-3766
Dogs are welcome at this inn. There is a $20 one time pet charge. Amenities include guest laundry facilities. They are located about 6.5 miles from downtown Las Vegas.

La Quinta Inn Las Vegas - Nellis
4288 N. Nellis Rd.
Las Vegas, NV
702-632-0229
Dogs of all sizes are allowed at the hotel.

La Quinta Inn Las Vegas - Tropicana
4975 South Valley View
Las Vegas, NV
702-798-7736
Dogs of all sizes are allowed at the hotel.

La Quinta Suites Las Vegas - West/Lakes
9570 W. Sahara
Las Vegas, NV
702-243-0356
Dogs of all sizes are allowed at the hotel.

Motel 6 - Boulder Hwy
4125 Boulder Hwy
Las Vegas, NV 89121
702-457-8051
There is a $10 per day additional pet fee.

Motel 6 - Tropicana
195 E. Tropicana Ave
Las Vegas, NV 89109
702-798-0728
Pets may not be left unattended in rooms at any time.

Residence Inn - Hughes Center
370 Hughes Center Drive
Las Vegas, NV 89109
702-650-0040
There is a $50 one time pet fee and a $10 per day pet charge.

Rodeway Inn & Suites
167 E. Tropicana Ave
Las Vegas, NV 89109
702-795-3311
There is a $100 refundable pet deposit.

Mount Charleston

Mount Charleston Lodge and Cabins
HCR 38 Box 325
Mount Charleston, NV 702-872-5408
800-955-1314
The lodge sits at over 7,700 feet above sea level and about 35 miles from the Las Vegas Strip. There are several dog-friendly trails nearby for hikers. Dogs are welcome for an additional $10 per day pet charge.

Accommodations - RV Parks and Campgrounds

Las Vegas

Las Vegas International RV Resort
6900 East Russell Road
Las Vegas, NV
702-547-5777
This RV park is located just east of Boulder Highway, away from the freeway and airport noise. They are located two minutes away from the largest shopping complex in Las Vegas. The shopping center includes a Super Wal-Mart, Costco, Target, Galleria mall with many restaurants and a Petco. Amenities at the RV park include full hookups with 30 and 50 amp

service, 24 hour video security at the entrance, direct dial phones at all sites, restrooms, pool, spa, business center, laundry facilities, clubhouse with a big screen TV, pool table, library, fitness area and more. Well-behaved leashed dogs are welcome. Please clean up after your pets. The park is located about 10-15 minutes from the Las Vegas Strip.

Las Vegas KOA at Circus Circus
500 Circus Circus Drive
Las Vegas, NV 89109
800-562-7270
This RV park is located right on the Las Vegas Strip, next to Circus Circus. There are 400 full hookup sites, a heated pool, Jacuzzi, video arcade, full service convenience store and dog run. Well-behaved leashed dogs are allowed. Please clean up after your pets. There is no pet fee. If you are coming from the south on I-15, exit Sahara Avenue traveling east (to the right). Go to the first stop light (Las Vegas Blvd.) and turn right. Go to the first stop light (Circus Circus Drive) and turn right. The entrance will be on the right.

Attractions

Blue Diamond

Bonnie Springs Old Nevada
1 Gunfighter Lane
Blue Diamond, NV 89004
702-875-4191
Visit a replica of an 1880's mining town near Las Vegas. While dogs are not allowed on the miniature train ride, in the restaurant or in the zoo, there are still other activities you can do with your best friend. Watch a gunfight in the street and check out all the historic replica buildings. Well-behaved, leashed dogs are welcome.

Las Vegas

Historic Spring Mountain Ranch
State Route 159
Las Vegas, NV 89004
15 miles W of Las Vegas
702-875-4141
Previous owners of this historic ranch include Chester Lauck of the comedy team "Lum & Abner," German actress Vera Krupp, and millionaire Howard Hughes. Guided tours through the Ranch House and other historic ranch buildings are available on weekends and holidays. The visitor center is open Monday

through Friday and on holidays. Dogs on leash are allowed on the grounds, but not inside the buildings. Other amenities at this park include a tree-shaded picnic area and scenic hiking trails.

Las Vegas Strip Walking Tour
3300-3900 Las Vegas Blvd.
Las Vegas, NV

Since dogs are not allowed inside the buildings or attractions on the Vegas strip, we have put together an outdoor self-guided walking tour that you can take with your pooch. It is kid-friendly too! While you can take the tour any time of day, probably the best time is late afternoon or early evening because of the special effects and light shows at some of the points of interest. All places mentioned can be viewed from the sidewalk. Start the walk at the Treasure Island Hotel at 3300 South Las Vegas Blvd. In the front of this hotel you can view two battle ships duke it out. Every 90 minutes, each evening at Buccaneer Bay, musket and cannon fire are exchanged in a pyrotechnic battle between the pirate ship Hispaniola and the British frigate H.M.S. Britannia. This is a popular attraction and it can become very crowded on the sidewalk. Next stop is the Volcano in front of the Mirage Hotel at 3400 South Las Vegas Blvd. From dusk to midnight, every 15 minutes, flames shoot into the sky, spewing smoke and fire 100 feet above the water, transforming a tranquil waterfall into streams of molten lava. For a little musical entertainment, walk over to the Musical Fountains at the Bellagio Hotel at 3600 South Las Vegas Blvd. Here you will find spectacular fountains that fill a 1/4 mile long lake in front of the hotel. Every evening there is a water show that is timed to music. The show takes place every 15 minutes. For some interesting architecture, walk over to the Eiffel Tower at the Paris Hotel at 3655 South Las Vegas Blvd. While your pooch cannot go into the Paris Hotel or the tower, you can view this half size Paris replica from the street. You can also visit the Statue of Liberty right in Las Vegas. Walk over to the New York, New York Hotel at 3790 South Las Vegas Blvd. Again, your pooch cannot go inside this hotel, but you can view the replica from the street. The last stop is the Luxor Hotel at 3900 South Las Vegas Blvd. From the sidewalk you will see the large pyramid with hotel rooms inside and a large sphinx in the front of the hotel. Please note that some of the attractions might be closed during certain times of the year or during bad weather, especially when it is windy.

Old Las Vegas Mormon Fort
500 E Washington Ave
Las Vegas, NV 89101
702-486-3511
This park includes a remnant of the original adobe fort which housed the first permanent non-native Mormon missionary settlers in the Las Vegas Valley. They successfully diverted water from the Las Vegas Creek in 1855 for farming. There are future plans to re-create many more historic features at this park. The park is open all year and allows leashed dogs on the outside grounds.

Parks

Boulder City

Lake Mead National Recreation Area
Lakeshore Rd/166
Boulder City, NV 89005
702-293-8907
This recreation area covers 1.5 million acres. The west side of the park is about 25 miles from downtown Las Vegas. We didn't see any designated trails, but leashed dogs are allowed on many of the trails and at the lake. To get there from Las Vegas, take Hwy 146 east to Lakeshore Rd./166. Lakeshore Rd. is the scenic drive along Lake Mead.

Las Vegas

Desert Breeze County Park
8425 W. Spring Mtn. Road
Las Vegas, NV
Durango Drive

This county park has picnic tables, sports fields, a bike/walking path and a dog park. It is located approximately 5 miles east of downtown Las Vegas and the Strip. From Flamingo Road/589 in downtown, head west and pass Hwy 15. Turn right on Durango Drive. Then turn right onto Spring Mountain Road and the park will be on the corner. Dogs must be leashed, except for in the dog park.

Desert Breeze Dog Run
8425 W. Spring Mtn. Road
Las Vegas, NV
Durango Drive

This dog park/run is fully enclosed. Thanks to one of our readers who recommended this park. She also suggested that we remind people that they shouldn't bring their puppies to the dog park until they have had all their shots. Young puppies can be very susceptible to parvo. The park is located approximately 5 miles east of downtown Las

Vegas and the Strip. From Flamingo Road/589 in downtown, head west and pass Hwy 15. Turn right on Durango Drive. Then turn right onto Spring Mountain Road. The dog park is located off Spring Mountain Rd., between the Community Center and Desert Breeze County Park.

Dog Fancier's Park
5800 E. Flamingo Rd.
Las Vegas, NV
702-455-8200
Dog Fancier's Park is a 12 acre park that allows canine enthusiasts to train their dogs off leash. Owner's must still have control over their dogs and may be cited if their dogs (while off leash) interfere with other animals training at the park. This dog park has benches, poop bags and water taps.

Lorenzi Park
3333 W. Washington Ave.
Las Vegas, NV
702-229-6297
This park is about a mile west of downtown Las Vegas. Leashed dogs are allowed. Lorenzi Park features tennis courts, playgrounds, picnic tables and a five acre lake.

Red Rock Canyon National Area
Charleston Blvd/159

Las Vegas, NV
702-363-1921
Located just 20-25 minutes west of downtown Las Vegas is the beautiful Red Rock Canyon National Conservation Area. This preserve has over 60,000 acres and includes unique geological formations. There is a popular 13 mile one-way scenic loop road that winds around the park, providing sightseeing, vistas and overlooks. Many of the hiking trails begin off this road. Leashed dogs are allowed on most of the trails. Some of the trails they are not allowed on are more like rock climbing expeditions than hiking trails. There are a variety of hiking trails ranging from easy to difficult. The visitor center is open daily and should have trail maps. On the trails, be aware of extreme heat or cold. Also watch out for flash floods, especially near creeks and streams. According to the BLM (Bureau of Land Management), violent downpours can cause flash flooding in areas untouched by rain. Do not cross low places when water is running through a stream. The park entrance fee is $5 per vehicle and $5 per dog. To get there from downtown Las Vegas, take Charleston Blvd./159 and head west.

Shadow Rock Dog Run
2650 Los Feliz on Sunrise Mountain
Las Vegas, NV
702-455-8200
This is a 1.5 acre dog park with benches, poop bags and water taps.

Sunset Park Dog Run
2601 E. Sunset Rd
Las Vegas, NV
702-455-8200
Located in Sunset Park, this dog park offers about 1.5 acres of land for your pooch to play. The dog park has benches, poop bags and water taps.

Mount Charleston

Spring Mountain National Recreation Area
Echo Road
Mount Charleston, NV
702-515-5404
This 316,000 acre park, part of the Toiyabe
National Forest, is located about 35 miles
northwest of Las Vegas. Mt. Charleston is located
in this dog-friendly park and has many hiking
trails. Temperatures here can average 25 to 30
degrees cooler than in Las Vegas. The Mary Jane
Falls trail, located on Mt. Charleston, is one of the
more popular trails. The trail passes a seasonal
waterfall and several small caves. The trail is
about 2.4 miles and starts at about 7840 foot
elevation. To reach the trailhead, take State
Route 157, travel 2 miles west of the ranger
station to Echo Road. After traveling .35 mile,
take the left fork off Echo Road and continue up
until the road ends. Dogs must be on leash.

Restaurants

Henderson

Baja Fresh Mexican Grill
675 Mall Ring Circle
Henderson, NV
702-450-6551
This Mexican restaurant is open for lunch and
dinner. They use fresh ingredients and making
their salsa and beans daily. Some of the items on
their menu include Enchiladas, Burritos, Tacos
Salads, Quesadillas, Nachos, Chicken, Steak and
more. Well-behaved leashed dogs are allowed at
the outdoor tables.

Manhattan Bagel
1500 N. Green Valley Parkway
Henderson, NV
702-260-9511
Dogs are allowed at the outdoor tables.

Wild Oats Natural Marketplace
517 North Stephanie St.
Henderson, NV 89014
702-458-9427
This full service natural food market offers both
natural and organic food. You can get food from
the deli and bring it to an outdoor table where
your well-behaved leashed dog is welcome.

Las Vegas

Baja Fresh Mexican Grill
1380 E Flamingo Rd
Las Vegas, NV

702-699-8920
Dogs are allowed at the outdoor tables.

Baja Fresh Mexican Grill
8780 W Charleston Blvd # 100
Las Vegas, NV
702-948-4043
Dogs are allowed at the outdoor tables.

Baja Fresh Mexican Grill
7501 W Lake Mead Blvd # 100
Las Vegas, NV
702-838-4100
Dogs are allowed at the outdoor tables.

Baja Fresh Mexican Grill
9310 S Eastern Ave
Las Vegas, NV
702-563-2800
Dogs on leash are allowed at the outdoor tables.

Baja Fresh Mexican Grill
7930 W. Tropical Pkwy.
Las Vegas, NV
702-307-2345
This Mexican restaurant is open for lunch and
dinner. They use fresh ingredients and making
their salsa and beans daily. Some of the items on
their menu include Enchiladas, Burritos, Tacos
Salads, Quesadillas, Nachos, Chicken, Steak and
more. Well-behaved leashed dogs are allowed at
the outdoor tables.

Baja Fresh Mexican Grill
4760 W. Sahara Blvd.
Las Vegas, NV
702-878-7772
This Mexican restaurant is open for lunch and
dinner. They use fresh ingredients and making
their salsa and beans daily. Some of the items on
their menu include Enchiladas, Burritos, Tacos
Salads, Quesadillas, Nachos, Chicken, Steak and
more. Well-behaved leashed dogs are allowed at
the outdoor tables.

Baja Fresh Mexican Grill
4190 S. Rainbow Blvd.
Las Vegas, NV
702-876-4193
This Mexican restaurant is open for lunch and
dinner. They use fresh ingredients and making
their salsa and beans daily. Some of the items on
their menu include Enchiladas, Burritos, Tacos
Salads, Quesadillas, Nachos, Chicken, Steak and
more. Well-behaved leashed dogs are allowed at
the outdoor tables.

Baja Fresh Mexican Grill

4343 N. Rancho Rd.
Las Vegas, NV
702-396-2553
This Mexican restaurant is open for lunch and dinner. They use fresh ingredients and making their salsa and beans daily. Some of the items on their menu include Enchiladas, Burritos, Tacos Salads, Quesadillas, Nachos, Chicken, Steak and more. Well-behaved leashed dogs are allowed at the outdoor tables.

Baja Fresh Mexican Grill
3385 Russell Rd
Las Vegas, NV
702-212-6800
This Mexican restaurant is open for lunch and dinner. They use fresh ingredients and making their salsa and beans daily. Some of the items on their menu include Enchiladas, Burritos, Tacos Salads, Quesadillas, Nachos, Chicken, Steak and more. Well-behaved leashed dogs are allowed at the outdoor tables.

Einstein Brothers Bagels
9031 W. Sahara Ave
Las Vegas, NV
702-254-0919
Dogs are allowed at the outdoor tables.

In-N-Out Burger
2900 W. Sahara Ave.
Las Vegas, NV
800-786-1000
This fast food restaurant serves great hamburgers and fries.

Java Joint
23 N Nellis Blvd
Las Vegas, NV
702-459-8166
Dogs are allowed at the outdoor tables.

Joey's Only Seafood Restaurants
114 Durango Drive

Las Vegas, NV 89129
702-242-2888
This restaurant serves seafood appetizers, soups, salads, main dishes and more. Dogs are allowed at the outdoor tables.

Leo's Deli
4055 S. Maryland Parkway
Las Vegas, NV
702-733-7827
Dogs are allowed at the outdoor tables. The deli, located in the Target shopping center, is named after the owner's dog, Leo.

McCormick & Schmick's
335 Hughes Center Drive
Las Vegas, NV 89109
702-836-9000
This seafood restaurant allows well-behaved leashed dogs at their outdoor tables.

Mountain Ham Deli
920 S Rampart Blvd
Las Vegas, NV
702-933-4262
Dogs are allowed at the outdoor tables.

Mountain Springs Saloon
Highway 160
Las Vegas, NV
702-875-4266
Dogs are welcome at the outdoor dining area. This bar has a limited food menu and serves a variety of beer. The bar has live music Friday and Saturday nights. They are located near the Mountain Springs Summit, about 15-20 minutes west of downtown Las Vegas.

Starbucks
395 Hughes Center Drive
Las Vegas, NV 89109
702-369-5537
This coffee shop allows well-behaved leashed dogs at their outdoor tables.

Whole Foods Market
8855 West Charleston Blvd.
Las Vegas, NV 89117
702-254-8655
This natural food supermarket offers natural and organic foods. Order some food from their deli and bring it to an outdoor table where your well-behaved leashed dog is welcome.

Wild Oats Natural Marketplace
7250 W. Lake Mead Blvd
Las Vegas, NV 89128
702-942-1500
This full service natural food market offers both natural and organic food. You can get food from the deli and bring it to an outdoor table where your well-behaved leashed dog is welcome.

Wild Sage Cafe
600 E Warm Springs Rd
Las Vegas, NV
702-944-7243
Dogs are allowed at the outdoor tables.

Stores

Las Vegas

Harley-Davidson Store
2605 S. Eastern Avenue
Las Vegas, NV 89109
702-431-8500
Well-behaved, leashed dogs are allowed inside this store, which is the world's largest Harley dealership. Whether you own a Harley or just wish you could own one, stop by the store and take a look around. This is a popular place for locals and tourists. The store is located about 15 minutes north of downtown Las Vegas.

Vets and Kennels

Las Vegas

A-V.I.P. Kennel
6808 La Cienega
Las Vegas, NV
s. of McCarran Airport
702-361-8900
This kennel offers day boarding and long-term boarding. They have indoor/outdoor kennel runs and a grass exercise yard. The indoor facilities are climate controlled. The day boarding runs about $14 per day for a large dog (possibly less for a small dog). They are open Monday through

Saturday from 8am-5pm and Sunday from 10am-2pm. There are no specific drop off or pick up times. However, you might want to call ahead and make a reservation just in case. The kennel is located about 5 minutes from the Strip, and the airport and their slogan is "Where Your Pets Are Treated Like Family".

Animal Emergency Service
1914 E Sahara Ave
Las Vegas, NV 89104
near Eastern Ave
702-457-8050
Monday - Friday 6 pm to 8 am, Saturday noon - Monday 8 am.

The Animal Inn Kennels
3460 W Oquendo Road
Las Vegas, NV 89118
702-736-0036
Full service boarding kennel. Well established in Las Vegas for over 40 years. Conveniently located right off of I-15. Daycare, overnight and long term boarders welcome. $14 - $18 standard daily rate. Discounts for 2 or more dogs boarding together. Weekly and monthly discounts available. Large individual indoor/outdoor climate controlled runs. Special diets or medications administered at no extra charge. 1/2 acre tree lined grass play yard. Office hours are Mon - Fri 8 am - 6 pm, Sat - Sun 8 am - 5 pm. Please call 702-736-0036 to make a reservation.

Laughlin Dog Travel Guide
Accommodations

Bullhead City

Best Western Inn
1126 Highway 95
Bullhead City, AZ
928-754-3000
This hotel is in Bullhead City, Arizona. This is across the river from Laughlin, NV. There is a $10 per day pet fee.

Laughlin

Pioneer Hotel and Gambling Hall
2200 S. Casino Drive
Laughlin, NV 89029
702-298-2442
This hotel allows dogs of all sizes. However, there are only ten pet rooms and these are all smoking rooms. We normally do not include smoking room only pet rooms but since the selection of pet

friendly lodging in Laughlin is so limited we have listed this one.

Accommodations - RV Parks and Campgrounds

Laughlin

Don Laughlin's Riverside RV Resort
1650 S. Casino Drive
Laughlin, NV 89029
800-227-3849
This RV park, located across the street from the Riverside Resort Hotel, offers 740 full hookup RV sites. Amenities include laundry facilities, showers, and 24 hour security. Well-behaved leashed dogs are allowed. Please clean up after your pets. There is no pet fee.

Lovelock Dog Travel Guide
Accommodations

Lovelock

Ramada Inn Sturgeon's Casino
1420 Cornell Ave
Lovelock, NV 89419
775-273-2971
There is a $100 refundable pet deposit.

Mesquite Dog Travel Guide
Accommodations - RV Parks and Campgrounds

Mesquite

Virgin River RV Park
100 Pioneer Blvd.
Mesquite, NV 89027
800-346-7721
This RV park is located behind the Virgin River Hotel and Casino. They offer full hookups, showers and laundry facilities. Well-behaved leashed dogs are allowed. Please clean up after your pets. There is no pet fee. The park is open all year.

Overton Dog Travel Guide
Accommodations

Overton

Best Western North Shore Inn
520 N. Moapa Valley Blvd
Overton, NV 89040

702-397-6000
There is a $50 refundable pet deposit. The hotel is 10 miles from Lake Mead.

Parks

Overton

Valley of Fire State Park
off Interstate 15, exit 75
Overton, NV 89040
702-397-2088
This park derives its name from red sandstone formations, formed from great shifting sand dunes during the age of dinosaurs, 150 million years ago. Ancient trees are represented throughout the park by areas of petrified wood. There is also a 3,000 year-old Indian petroglyph. Popular activities include camping, hiking, picnicking and photography. Sites of special interest are the Atlatl Rock, the Arch Rock, the Beehives, Elephant Rock, Seven Sisters, and more. There are many intriguing hikes available. Please inquire at the visitor center for suggestions on day hikes of varying length and terrain. The visitor's center is open daily, 8:30am to 4:30pm. The park is open all year. Pets are welcome, but they must be kept on a leash of not more than six feet in length. They are not allowed in the visitor center. The park is located six miles from Lake Mead and 55 miles northeast of Las Vegas via Interstate 15 and on exit 75.

Reno Dog Travel Guide
Accommodations

Reno

Days Inn
701 E 7th
Reno, NV 89512
775-786-4070
There is a $10 per day pet fee.

Holiday Inn
1000 E. 6th St.
Reno, NV 89512
775-786-5151
This hotel is located only 4 blocks from Reno's famous gaming strip and within walking distance to the Reno Livestock & Events Center. Amenities include a heated pool and gift shop. There is a $10 per day pet charge.

Motel 6 - Livestock Center
866 N. Wells Ave
Reno, NV 89512
775-786-9852
This hotel is near the Livestock Events Center in Reno.

Motel 6 - Virginia/Plumb
1901 S. Virginia St
Reno, NV 89502
775-827-0255
There are no additional pet fees.

Motel 6 - West
1400 Stardust Street
Reno, NV 89503
775-747-7390
Pets may not be left alone in the rooms.

Residence Inn by Marriott
9845 Gateway Drive
Reno, NV 89511
775-853-8800
Every room is a suite with a bedroom area, living room area and kitchen. Amenities include room service, self service laundry facilities, complimentary continental breakfast, an outdoor pool and exercise room. Rooms include hairdryers and iron/ironing boards. There is a one time non-refundable $80 pet charge and an additional $6 per day for pets.

Rodeway Inn
2050 Market Street
Reno, NV 89502
775-786-2500
This hotel (previously Travelodge) is about a mile from the Reno gambling strip. Amenities include a complimentary continental breakfast, heated outdoor pool, kitchenettes in some rooms, and wheelchair accessible rooms. There is a $10 per day pet charge.

Truckee River Lodge
501 W. 1st Street
Reno, NV 89503
775-786-8888
There is a $10 per day pet fee. All rooms in the hotel are non-smoking. There is a park across the street.

Vagabond Inn
3131 S. Virginia St.
Reno, NV 89502
775-825-7134
This motel is located less than a couple miles from the downtown casinos and the Convention Center. Amenities include a swimming pool, 24 hour cable television, air conditioning, and more. There is a $10 per day pet fee.

Sparks

Motel 6 - Airport/Sparks
2405 Victorian Ave
Sparks, NV 89431
775-358-1080
There are no additional pet fees.

Accommodations - RV Parks and Campgrounds

Reno

Bonanza Terrace RV Park
4800 Stoltz Road
Reno, NV 89506
775-329-9624
This RV park is located in a quiet spot two miles north of downtown Reno off Highway 395. The Bonanza Casino is across the street from the RV park. RV sites include a gravel parking pad, up to 50 amp electric, water, sewer and phone line. RVs up to 40 feet are welcome. Well-behaved leashed pets accompanied by their owner are welcome. There is a $1 per night pet fee. Please clean up after your pet.

Reno KOA
2500 East 2nd Street
Reno, NV 89595
775-789-2147
This campground, located at the Reno Hilton, offers RV sites with 50 amp service and a maximum length pull through of 65 feet. Amenities include direct access to the Reno Hilton's heated pool and health club, meeting room, snack bar, LP gas and modem dataport. Well-behaved leashed dogs are welcome. Please clean up after your pets. There is no pet fee. The park is open all year. From the junction of Interstate 80 and Highway 395 (Exit 15), go south 1 mile on Highway 395 to Glendale Avenue. The

KOA is located at the Reno Hilton.

Reno RV Park
735 Mill Street
Reno, NV 89502
775-323-3381
This RV park is located about 4 blocks from the casinos. They offer full hookups, restrooms, showers, 24 hour security, electric gates, propane available, recreation area, picnic area and more. Well-behaved leashed dogs are welcome. Please clean up after your pets. There is no pet fee.

Parks

Reno

Donnelly Park
Mayberry Drive
Reno, NV
at McCarran Blvd.

This is a small, but nice park to walk around with your dog. It is across the street from Scraps Dog Bakery and Walden's Coffee. Dogs must be leashed.

Rancho San Rafael Park
Hillside Drive
Reno, NV
N. Sierra St.

Dogs are allowed in the undeveloped areas of this park. Leashed dogs are allowed on a hiking and walking path which crosses over McCarren Blvd. It is a dirt trail which narrows to a single track trail once you cross over McCarren Blvd. Just be careful when crossing over McCarren - the speed limit is about 45-50mph. To get there from Hwy 80, exit Keystone Ave. Head north on Keystone. Turn right onto Coleman Drive. Take Coleman until it almost ends and turn right into the park. Park near the Coleman intersection and the trailhead will be nearby. Dogs must be leashed.

Sutcliffe

Pyramid Lake
Hwy 445
Sutcliffe, NV
775-574-1000
Pyramid Lake is located in an Indian reservation, but visitors to the lake are welcomed guests of the Pyramid Lake Tribe of the Paiute Indians. Your leashed dog is also welcome. The lake is a beautiful contrast to the desert sandstone mountains which surround it. It is about 15 miles long by 11 miles wide, and among interesting rock formations. Pyramid Lake is Nevada's largest natural lake. It is popular for fishing and photography. The north end of the lake is off-limits to visitors because it is a sacred area to the Paiutes. There is a beach area near the ranger's station in Sutcliffe. Be careful when wading into the water, as there are some ledges which drop off into deeper water. Also, do not wade in the water at the south end of the lake because the dirt acts like quick sand. The lake is about 35-40 minutes north of Reno, off Hwy 445.

Restaurants

Reno

Archie's Grill
2195 N. Virginia St.
Reno, NV 89503
775-322-9595
This restaurant serves breakfast, lunch and dinner. Your dog is allowed at the outdoor tables.

Baja Fresh Mexican Grill
5140 Kietzke Ln.
Reno, NV
775-826-8900
This Mexican restaurant is open for lunch and dinner. They use fresh ingredients and making their salsa and beans daily. Some of the items on their menu include Enchiladas, Burritos, Tacos Salads, Quesadillas, Nachos, Chicken, Steak and more. Well-behaved leashed dogs are allowed at the outdoor tables.

Chevy's Fresh Mex Restaurant
4955 S. Virginia Street
Reno, NV
775-829-8008
Dogs are allowed at the outdoor tables.

Java Jungle
246 W. 1st Street
Reno, NV 89509
775-329-4484
Java Jungle was voted "Best Espresso and Cappuccino of Reno" in the Reno Gazette-Journal reader surveys. The wide variety of their customers include lawyers and judges on their way to the Washoe County Courthouse as well as joggers and dog walkers. It is located in downtown Reno, near the Truckee River. Dogs are welcome at the outdoor tables.

My Favorite Muffin & Bagel Cafe
340 California Ave.
Reno, NV 89509
775-333-1025
This cafe was voted Reno's Best Bagels. As the name of the cafe implies, they serve bagels and muffins. Your dog is allowed at the outdoor tables.

Peg's Glorified Ham & Eggs
425 S. Sierra St.
Reno, NV 89501
775-329-2600
This restaurant is located in downtown and has a few outdoor tables. Your dog is allowed at the outdoor tables.

Quiznos
4965 S. Virginia Street
Reno, NV
775-828-5252
They serve a variety of sandwiches. Dogs are allowed at the outdoor tables.

Romanos Macaroni Grill
5505 S. Virginia St.
Reno, NV
775-448-9994
Well-behaved, leashed dogs are allowed at some of the perimeter tables.

Sage Creek Grill and Taproom
5851 South Virginia Street
Reno, NV
775-829-4600
Well-behaved dogs are allowed at the outdoor tables, but must be leashed. The restaurant is open for lunch and dinner.

Schlotzsky's Deli
10590 N McCarran Blvd.
Reno, NV
775-746-8284
Dogs are allowed at the outdoor tables.

Schlotzsky's Deli
8030 S. Virginia Street
Reno, NV
775-852-3354
Dogs are allowed at the outdoor tables. Please remember to keep your dog leashed.

Walden's Coffee Co.
3940 Mayberry Drive
Reno, NV 89509
775-787-3307
Your dog is welcome at the outdoor tables at coffee house. They have a variety of pastries and snacks available. The Scraps Dog Bakery is in the same shopping center (see Attractions.)

Wild Oats Natural Marketplace
5695 S. Virginia St.
Reno, NV 89502
775-829-8666
This full service natural food market offers both natural and organic food. You can get food from the deli and bring it to an outdoor table where your well-behaved leashed dog is welcome. Outdoor seating is seasonal.

Sparks

Rapscallions' Roadhouse Grill
1250 Disc Drive
Sparks, NV
775-626-7066
Dogs are allowed at one of their perimeter tables.

Stores

Reno

Harley Davidson of Reno
2295 Market Street
Reno, NV 89502
775-329-2913
Well-behaved leashed dogs are allowed in this store. In addition to the motorcycles, they also sell collectibles, riding gear and accessories.

Scraps Dog Bakery
3890 Mayberry Drive
Reno, NV 89509
775-787-3647
Your dog is welcome inside this bakery which sells cookies and goodies for your pup. They also have a general store which sells other doggie items.

Vets and Kennels

Reno

Animal Emergency Center
6427 S Virginia St
Reno, NV 89511
Hwy 395 and Del Monte Lane
775-851-3600
Monday - Friday 6 pm to 8 am, Saturday noon - Monday 8 am.

Tonopah Dog Travel Guide
Accommodations

Tonopah

Best Western Hi-Desert Inn
320 Main Street
Tonopah, NV 89049
775-482-3511
Pets may not be left unattended in the room. There are no pet fees.

Virginia City Dog Travel Guide
Accommodations - RV Parks and Campgrounds

Virginia City

Virginia City RV Park
Carson and F Streets
Virginia City, NV
775-847-0999
Located just two blocks from downtown Virginia City, this park offers 50 RV sites with full hookups. Amenities include phone equipped spaces, showers, swimming pool, tennis courts park access, onsite market and deli, video rentals, laundry facility, slot machines and tent camping. Well-behaved leashed dogs are allowed. Please clean up after your pets. Reservations are accepted for busy periods. The park is open all year.

Attractions

Virginia City

Virginia & Truckee Railroad Co.
565 S. K Street
Virginia City, NV 89440
775-847-0380
You and your dog can ride back in time on this steam train. The train takes you on a leisurely 35 minute round trip to the historic station in the city of Gold Hill. Passengers can get off the train at

Gold Hill, visit the historic old town and then board the next train. The conductor gives a narration of the many historic sites you will view from the train. Your dog is welcome to join you on either the open air railcar or the enclosed railcar. Trains operate everyday from May through October. The round trip fare is about $5 for adults and about $3 for children. Prices are subject to change. Tickets can be purchased at the railcar on C Street or next to the train depot near Washington and F Streets. The train ride is located in Virginia City, about 30-40 minutes south of Reno.

Virginia City
Hwy 341
Virginia City, NV 89440
775-847-0311
This small town was built in the late 1800s and was a booming mining town. The restored Old Western town now has a variety of shops with wooden walkways. Dogs are allowed to window shop with you. Dogs are also welcome to ride the Virginia & Truckee Steam Train with you. Virginia City is located about 30-40 minutes south of Reno.

Restaurants

Virginia City

Angel Station Deli
204 South C Street
Virginia City, NV

This deli serves a variety of sandwiches, wrapps and salads. Dogs are allowed at the outdoor tables. They usually have a dog bowl of water for visiting pooches.

Firehouse BBQ
204 South C Street
Virginia City, NV 89440
775-847-4774
You and your pup will be tempted to stop here for lunch or dinner after you smell the delicious BBQ. This restaurant is located on the main street in historic Virginia City. Dogs are allowed at the outdoor tables.

Stores

Virginia City

Bogie's Beer Collectibles
182 South C
Virginia City, NV 89440
Hwy 341
775-847-9300
Bogie's Beer Collectibles is a small retail store in historic Virginia City. They sell beer collectibles, brew bags and other fun collectible items. The owner is a dog lover and allows your dog inside the store. They even have a sign outside that says "Kids, Dogs & Cats Welcome in Bogie's. Please Tie Horses & Mules Outside."

Wendover Dog Travel Guide
Accommodations

Wendover

Super 8
Wendover Blvd (I-80 Exit 410)
Wendover, NV 89883
775-664-2888
There is a $7.50 per day pet fee. Take exit 410 off of I-80 and turn right on Wendover Blvd.

Accommodations - RV Parks and Campgrounds

Wendover

Wendover KOA
651 North Camper Drive
Wendover, NV 89883
775-664-3221
This campground offers both RV and tent sites. RV site amenities include hookups with 50 amp service, cable TV and a maximum length pull through of 80 feet. Other amenities include a swimming pool, meeting room, LP gas, modem dataport and snack bar. Well-behaved leashed dogs are allowed. Please clean up after your pets. There is no pet fee. They are open all year. To get there from Interstate 80, take the West Wendover Exit 410 to Wendover Blvd. Turn right and go .25 miles to Camper Drive and turn left.

Winnemucca Dog Travel Guide
Accommodations

Winnemucca

Best Western Gold Country Inn
921 West Winnemucca Boulevard
Winnemucca, NV 89445

775-623-6999
There is a $10 one time pet charge.

Best Western Holiday Motel
670 W. Winnemucca Blvd
Winnemucca, NV 89445
775-623-3684
There are no additional pet fees.

Days Inn
511 W. Winnemucca Blvd
Winnemucca, NV 89445
775-623-3661
There is a $10 per day pet fee.

Holiday Inn Express
1987 W. Winnemucca Blvd
Winnemucca, NV 89445
775-625-3100
There is a $50 pet deposit and $10 of the deposit is non-refundable.

Motel 6
1600 Winnemucca Blvd
Winnemucca, NV 89445
775-623-1180
Pets may not be left unattended in rooms at any time.

Red Lion Inn & Casino
741 West Winnemucca Boulevard
Winnemucca, NV 89445
775-623-2565
There is a $20 refundable pet deposit. They have a 24 hour restaurant on the premises.

Santa Fe Motel
1620 W. Winnemucca Blvd
Winnemucca, NV 89419
775-623-1119
There are no additional pet fees.

Super 8
1157 Winnemucca Blvd
Winnemucca, NV 89445
775-625-1818
There is a $5 per day pet fee.

Accommodations - RV Parks and Campgrounds

Winnemucca

Model T RV Park
1130 West Winnemucca Blvd.
Winnemucca, NV
775-623-2588

This RV park is located in town within walking distance to many services. Amenities include full hookup sites, laundry facilities, seasonal pool, restrooms and showers. Well-behaved leashed pets are allowed. There is no pet fee, just please clean up after your pet. The RV park is part of the Model T Casino and Winnemucca Quality Inn. To get there, take Interstate 80 to Exit 176. Then drive east on Winnemucca Blvd. for three minutes.

Chapter 15

Arizona Dog-Friendly Travel Guide

Benson Dog Travel Guide
Accommodations

Benson

Motel 6
637 S. Whetstone Commerce Dr
Benson, AZ 85602
520-586-0066
There are no additional pet fees.

Bisbee Dog Travel Guide
Accommodations - Vacation Home Rentals

Bisbee

Sleepy Dog Guest House
212A Opera Drive
Bisbee, AZ 85603
520-432-3057
There is a one bedroom and two bedroom guest house overlooking Bisbee. No credit cards, smoking outside only. There are no additional pet fees.

Camp Verde Dog Travel Guide
Accommodations

Camp Verde

Comfort Inn
340 N Industrial Dr
Camp Verde, AZ 86322-4692
928-567-9000
There is a $15 pet fee.

Casa Grande Dog Travel Guide
Accommodations

Casa Grande

Holiday Inn
777 N Pinal Ave
Casa Grande, AZ 85222
520-426-3500
There are no additional pet fees.

Chambers Dog Travel Guide
Accommodations

Chambers

Best Western Chieftain Inn
Hwy 40 and Chambers
Chambers, AZ 86502
928-688-2754
There is a $10 per day pet fee.

Eagar Dog Travel Guide
Accommodations

Eagar

Best Western Sunrise Inn
128 N Main Street
Eagar, AZ 85925
928-333-2540
There is a $25 refundable pet deposit if you are paying with cash.

Ehrenberg Dog Travel Guide
Accommodations

Ehrenberg

Flying J Motel
I-10, Exit 1
Ehrenberg, AZ 85334
928-923-9711
This hotel has a couple of pet rooms. There is a $10 refundable pet deposit.

Flagstaff Dog Travel Guide
Accommodations

Flagstaff

Comfort Inn I-17 & I40
2355 S Beulah Blvd.
Flagstaff, AZ 86001
928-774-2225
There is a $5 per day pet fee.

Days Inn - Highway 66
1000 West Business 40
Flagstaff, AZ 86001
928-774-5221
There is a $10 per day pet fee.

Holiday Inn
2320 E Lucky Lane
Flagstaff, AZ 86004
928-714-1000
There is a $25 one time pet fee per visit.

Howard Johnson Inn
3300 E. Rt. 66

Flagstaff, AZ 86004
800-437-7137
Dogs of all sizes are welcome. There is a $7 one time pet fee.

La Quinta Inn & Suites Flagstaff
2015 South Beulah Blvd.
Flagstaff, AZ
928-556-8666
Dogs of all sizes are allowed at the hotel.

Motel 6
2010 E Butler Ave
Flagstaff, AZ 86004
928-774-1801
One large well-behaved dog is okay.

Ramada Suites Limited
2755 Woodland Village Blvd
Flagstaff, AZ 86001
928-773-1111
There is a $10 per day pet fee.

Red Roof Inn
2520 E Lucky Ln
Flagstaff, AZ 86004
928-779-5121
There is a $20 refundable deposit for pets. Large dogs ok, if well-behaved.

Sleep Inn
2765 S. Woodlands Village Blvd.
Flagstaff, AZ 86001
928-556-3000
There is a $50 non-refundable deposit.

Woodlands Village

Motel 6
2745 S. Woodlands Village
Woodlands Village, AZ 86001
928-779-3757
There are no pet fees. Just let them know that you have a pet when you check in.

Gila Bend Dog Travel Guide
Accommodations

Gila Bend

Best Western Space Age Lodge
401 E Pima
Gila Bend, AZ 85337
928-683-2273
There are no pet fees. You just need to sign a pet agreement.

Glendale Dog Travel Guide
Parks

Glendale

Saguaro Ranch Dog Park
63rd Avenue
Glendale, AZ

This fully fenced dog park has a large grassy area with trees, fire hydrants, benches and even a doggie drinking fountain. The park is located at 63rd Avenue and Mountain View Road. The off-leash area is just north of the west parking lot and just south of the softball complex. Thanks to one of our readers for recommending this dog park!

Globe Dog Travel Guide
Accommodations

Globe

Comfort Inn at Round Mountain Park
1515 South St.
Globe, AZ 85501
928-425-7575
There is a $20 per night pet fee.

Grand Canyon Dog Travel Guide
Accommodations

Grand Canyon

Rodeway Inn-Red Feather Lodge
Highway 64
Grand Canyon, AZ 86023
928-638-2414
This motel is located just one mile south of the south entrance to the Grand Canyon National Park. Pets are welcome, but they must not be left unattended in the room. There is a $50 refundable pet deposit and a $10 pet fee per night per pet.

Williams

Highlander Motel
533 W. Bill Williams Avenue
Williams, AZ 86046
928-635-2541
There is a $5/day pet charge. Room prices are in the $50 range. This motel is about 1 hour from the Grand Canyon.

Holiday Inn

950 N. Grand Canyon Blvd
Williams, AZ 86046
928-635-4114
There are no additional pet fees.

Motel 6 - Grand Canyon
831 W Rt 66
Williams, AZ 86046
520-635-9000
There are no additional pet fees.

Motel 6 Park Inn
710 W. Bill Williams Avenue
Williams, AZ 86046
928-635-4464
This motel is about 1 hour from the Grand
Canyon. There are no additional pet fees.

Quality Inn - Mountain Ranch Resort
6701 E. Mountain Ranch Road
Williams, AZ 86046
928-635-2693
Amenities include tennis courts, a heated pool
and whirlpool (closed during the winter). There is
a one time $20 charge for pets. Room prices
range from $50-100. This motel is about 1 hour
from the Grand Canyon.

Attractions

Grand Canyon

Grand Canyon National Park
Hwy 64
Grand Canyon, AZ 86023
928-638-7888
The Grand Canyon, located in the northwest
corner of Arizona, is considered to be one of the
most impressive natural splendors in the world. It
is 277 miles long, 18 miles wide, and at its
deepest point, is 6000 vertical feet (more than 1
mile) from rim to river. The Grand Canyon has
several entrance areas, but the most popular is
the South Rim. Dogs are not allowed on any trails
below the rim, but leashed dogs are allowed on
the paved rim trail. This dog-friendly trail is about
2.7 miles each way and offers excellent views of
the Grand Canyon. Remember that the elevation
at the rim is 7,000 feet, so you or your pup may
need to rest more often than usual. Also, the
weather can be very hot during the summer and
can be snowing during the winter, so plan
accordingly. And be sure you or your pup do not
get too close to the edge! Feel like taking a tour?
Well-behaved dogs are allowed on the Geology
Walk. This is a one hour park ranger guided tour
and consists of a leisurely walk along a 3/4 mile

paved rim trail. They discuss how the Grand
Canyon was created and more. The tour departs
at 11am daily (weather permitting) from the
Yavapai Observation Station. The Grand Canyon
park entrance fee is currently $20.00 per private
vehicle, payable upon entry to the park.
Admission is for 7 days, includes both South and
North Rims, and covers the entrance fee only.

Williams

Historic Route 66 Driving Tour
Bill Williams Avenue
Williams, AZ

Route 66 was the main route between Los
Angeles and Chicago during the 1920's through
the 1960's. It was completely paved in 1938. This
historic route symbolizes the American adventure
and romance of the open road. Begin your self-
guided driving tour on Bill Williams Avenue in
Williams. This portion of Route 66 is considered
"America's Main Street," where you will find gas
stations, restaurants, shops and motels that have
served travelers since the 1920's. Then head east
on Old 66 to the I-40 interchange. Continue east
on I-40 for 6 miles. Take the Pittman Valley exit
and left left, pass over I-40, and turn right onto
historic Route 66. This portion of the road was
originally paved in 1939. Stop and park at the
Oak Hill Snowplay Area. You and your pooch can
take a 2 mile round trip hike to the Keyhole Sink
petroglyphs. After your walk, continue driving and
you will come to a community called Parks.
Located here is a country store that has been in
operation since about 1910. At this point you can
turn around and head back to Williams via I-40.
Directions and descriptions are from the USDA
Forest Service in Williams, Arizona.

Parks

Williams

Kaibab National Forest
800 South 6th Street
Williams, AZ 86046
928-635-8200
Dogs on leash are allowed on many trails
throughout this national forest. Hiking trails range
greatly in difficulty, from eash to very difficult. A
couple of the more popular trails are the Keyhole
Sink Trail and the Bill Williams Mountain Trail.
The Keyhole Sink Trails is an easy trail that is 2
miles round trip. Walk through a ponderosa pine
forest until you reach a box canyon. At the

canyon, you will find petroglyphs (prehistoric sketches on the rock), that are about 1,000 years old. The message suggests that the area was an important hunting ground. To get there from Williams, take I-40 east to the Pitman Valley Exit (#171). Turn left and cross over the Interstate. Proceed east on Historic Route 66 for about 2 miles to the Oak Hill Snowplay Area. The trail begins on the north side of the road. Park in the lot provided. The Bill Williams Mountain Trail is rated moderate and is about 4 miles long. The trailhead starts at 7,000 feet. To get there, go west from downtown Williams on Bill Williams Avenue about one mile; turn left at Clover Hill and proceed along the frontage road to the turnoff to Williams Ranger District office. Follow the signs to the trailhead.

Restaurants

Grand Canyon

Grand Canyon Snack Bars
Grand Canyon National Park
Grand Canyon, AZ

Dogs are permitted at the outdoor benches at park operated snack bars located at the South Rim area. Please note that these snack bars typically have benches only and not tables. There were no other restaurants we found at the Grand Canyon that had outdoor tables. The closest outdoor dining we found was in Williams, Arizona.

Williams

Cruiser's Cafe
233 West Route 66
Williams, AZ
928-635-2445
This cafe is located on Old Route 66 in historic downtown Williams. The cafe is located in a renovated gas station and displays hundreds of Route 66 memorabilia items. Dogs are allowed at the outdoor tables.

Grand Canyon Coffee Cafe
125 West Route 66
Williams, AZ
928-635-1255
There is one outdoor table. Dogs are allowed at the outdoor table.

Smash Hit Subs and Pizza
5235 North Highway 64
Williams, AZ

928-635-1487
There are a few benches and tables outside. This restaurant also serve bakery items. Dogs are allowed at the outdoor tables.

Subway Sandwiches
1050 North Grand Canyon Blvd.
Williams, AZ
928-635-0955
Dogs are allowed at the outdoor table.

The Route 66 Place
417 East Route 66
Williams, AZ
928-635-0266
Dogs are allowed at the outdoor tables. This cafe is named after the Old Route 66, which was the main route between Los Angeles and Chicago during the 1920's through the 1960's.

Heber Dog Travel Guide
Accommodations

Heber

Best Western Sawmill Inn
1877 Hwy 260
Heber, AZ 85928
928-535-5053
There is a $5 per day pet fee.

Holbrook Dog Travel Guide
Accommodations

Holbrook

Best Western Adobe Inn
615 W Hopi Dr
Holbrook, AZ 86025
928-524-3948
There is a $25 refundable pet deposit.

Best Western Arizonian Inn
2508 Navajo Blvd
Holbrook, AZ 86025
928-524-2611
There is a $30 refundable pet deposit.

Comfort Inn
2602 E. Navajo Blvd.
Holbrook, AZ 86025
928-524-6131
There is no pet fee. A credit card will be required.

Holiday Inn Express
1308 E Navajo Blvd

Holbrook, AZ 86025
928-524-1466
There is a $10 per day additional pet fee.

Motel 6
2514 Navajo Blvd
Holbrook, AZ 86025
928-524-6101
There are no additional pet fees.

Kingman Dog Travel Guide
Accommodations

Kingman

Best Western A Wayfarer's Inn
2815 East Andy Devine
Kingman, AZ 86401
928-753-6271
There is a $25 refundable pet deposit. Nice clean rooms.

Best Western King's Inn
2930 East Andy Devine
Kingman, AZ 86401
928-753-6101
There are no additional pet fees.

Days Inn East
3381 E Andy Devine
Kingman, AZ
928-757-7337
There is a $10 per day additional pet fee.

Motel 6
3351 E Andy Devine Ave
Kingman, AZ 86401
928-757-7151
There are no additional pet fees.

Quality Inn
1400 E. Andy Devine Ave.
Kingman, AZ 86401
928-753-4747
There is a one time pet fee of $10.

Super 8 Motel
3401 E. Andy Devine
Kingman, AZ 86401
928-757-4808
There is a $10 per day pet charge.

Lake Havasu City Dog Travel Guide
Accommodations

Lake Havasu City

Best Western Lake Place Inn
31 Wings Loop
Lake Havasu City, AZ 86403
928-855-2146
There is a $10 per day pet fee.

Holiday Inn
245 London Bridge Rd
Lake Havasu City, AZ 86403
928-855-2379
There is a $10 per day additional pet fee.

Island Inn Hotel
1300 W McCulloch Blvd
Lake Havasu City, AZ 86403
928-680-0606
There is a $10 per day pet charge.

Motel 6
111 London Bridge Rd
Lake Havasu City, AZ 86403
928-855-3200
Dogs may not be left alone in the room.

Page - Lake Powell Dog Travel Guide
Accommodations

Page

Best Western Arizonainn
716 Rimview Drive
Page, AZ 86040
928-645-2466
There is a $10 per day pet fee. This hotel is near Lake Powell on the Arizona and Utah border.

Best Western Weston Inn & Suites
207 N Lake Powell Blvd
Page, AZ 86040
928-645-2451
There is a $10 per day pet fee. This hotel is near Lake Powell.

Motel 6
637 S. Lake Powell Blvd
Page, AZ 86040
928-645-5888
There are no additional pet fees.

Quality Inn
287 N. Lake Powell Blvd.
Page, AZ 86040
928-645-8851
There is no fee for pets. Pets are allowed on the first floor only.

Wahweap Lodge and Marina
2.5 miles SE of US 89 at Lake Powell
Page, AZ
928-645-2433
This lodge is next to beautiful Lake Powell. There are boat rentals here for you and your pup. There are no additional pet fees.

Attractions

Page

Lake Powell - Glen Canyon Recreation Area

Page, AZ
435-684-7400
Beautiful Lake Powell is called America's Natural Playground and is home to the world's largest natural bridge (standing 290 feet high), the Rainbow Bridge National Monument. The Wahweap Lodge, located in Page, rents powerboats for sight-seeing on the lake. Rent and drive your own boat, and your dog is welcome to join you. If you rent a boat, there is a one half mile trail to the Rainbow Bridge from the Rainbow Bridge courtesy dock. Also at Lake Powell near Bullfrog, there is a 3 mile round-trip hiking trail called Pedestal Alley. For boat rentals, the Wahweap Lodge is located 2.5 miles SE of US 89 at Lake Powell. The best time to visit the lake is during the fall season when temperatures are mild.

Parker Dog Travel Guide
Accommodations

Parker

Motel 6
604 California
Parker, AZ 85344
928-669-2133
There are no additional pet fees.

Petrified Forest National Park Dog Travel Guide
Attractions

Petrified Forest National Park

Petrified Forest National Park
Entrances on Hwy 40 and Hwy 180
Petrified Forest National Park, AZ
928-524-6228
The Petrified Forest is located in northeastern

Arizona and features one of the world's largest and most colorful concentrations of petrified wood. Also included in the park's 93,533 acres are the multi-hued badlands of the Painted Desert, archeological sites and displays of 225 million year old fossils. Your leashed dog is welcome on all of the paved trails and scenic overlooks. Take a walk on the self-guided Giant Logs trail or view ancient petroglyphs from an overlook. The entrance fee is $10 per private vehicle.

Phoenix Dog Travel Guide
Accommodations

Phoenix

Comfort Inn
5050 N. Black Canyon Highway
Phoenix, AZ 85017
602-242-8011
There is a $25 pet deposit if the room is paid for in cash. If the room is paid for by credit card there is no fee.

Comfort Inn
255 North Kyrene Blvd
Phoenix, AZ 85226
480-705-8882
There is no pet fee.

Comfort Suites
8473 West Paradise Ln.
Phoenix, AZ 85382
623-334-3993
There is a $50 pet deposit.

Crowne Plaza
2532 W. Peoria Ave
Phoenix, AZ 85029
602-943-2341
Exit I-17 at Peoria Ave.

Embassy Suites Hotel - Thomas Rd
2333 E Thomas Rd
Phoenix, AZ 85016
602-957-1910
There is a $15 per day pet fee.

Hampton Inn
8101 N Black Canyon Hwy
Phoenix, AZ 85021
602-864-6233
There is a $25 one time fee for pets.

Hilton Suites
10 E Thomas Road

Phoenix, AZ 85012
602-222-1111
There are no additional pet fees.

Holiday Inn - West
1500 N 51st Ave
Phoenix, AZ 85043
602-484-9009
There is a $25 one time pet fee.

Holiday Inn Express
3401 E University Dr
Phoenix, AZ 85034
602-453-9900
There are no additional pet fees

Holiday Inn Express Hotel & Suites
15221 S. 50th St
Phoenix, AZ 85044
480-785-8500
There is a $5 per day additional pet fee.

Holiday Inn Select - Airport
4300 E. Washington St
Phoenix, AZ 85034
602-273-7778
There is a $25 refundable pet deposit.

Howard Johnson Inn
124 S 24th St.
Phoenix, AZ 35034
602-220-0044
Dogs up to 60 pounds are allowed. There is a $20 one time pet fee.

La Quinta Inn Phoenix AP North
4727 E. Thomas Rd.
Phoenix, AZ
602-956-6500
Dogs up to 50 pounds are allowed at the hotel.

La Quinta Inn Phoenix North
2510 West Greenway
Phoenix, AZ
602-993-0800
Dogs of all sizes are allowed at the hotel.

La Quinta Inn Phoenix Thomas Road
2725 N Black Canyon Highway
Phoenix, AZ
602-258-6271
Dogs up to 75 pounds are allowed at the hotel.

Lexington Hotel at City Square
100 W Clarendon Ave
Phoenix, AZ 85013
602-279-9811
There is a $100 refundable deposit required for

dogs.

Motel 6
2330 W Bell Rd
Phoenix, AZ 85023
602-993-2353
Pets may never be left alone in the room.

Motel 6
4130 N Black Canyon Hwy
Phoenix, AZ 85017
602-277-5501
Pets may not be left unattended in the room and must be on a leash when outside the room. The hotel is at the Indian School exit on I-17.

Motel 6
8152 N. Black Canyon Hwy
Phoenix, AZ 85051
602-995-7592
The hotel is at the Northern Ave exit on I-17.

Motel 6
5315 E Van Buren Street
Phoenix, AZ 85008
602-267-8555
Pets may not be left alone in the room.

Premier Inn
10402 N Black Canyon Hwy
Phoenix, AZ 85051
602-943-2371
There are no additional pet fees. Pets are not allowed in deluxe rooms.

Quality Hotel & Resort
3600 N 2nd Ave
Phoenix, AZ 85013
602-248-0222
There is a one time non-refundable fee of $25.

Quality Inn South Mountain
5121 E. La Puente Ave.
Phoenix, AZ 85044
480-893-3900
Pets may not be left alone. There is a $50 pet fee of which $25 is refundable.

Quality Suites
3101 N. 32nd St
Phoenix, AZ 85018
602-956-4900
There is a $10 per day pet fee.

Red Lion Metrocenter
12027 N 28th Dr
Phoenix, AZ 85029
602-866-7000

There are no additional pet fees.

Red Roof Inn
5215 W Willetta
Phoenix, AZ 85043
602-233-8004
Dogs under about 80 pounds are allowed. There are no additional pet fees.

Residence Inn
8242 N Black Canyon Hwy
Phoenix, AZ 85051
602-864-1900
There is a $50 non-refundable pet fee.

Sheraton Crescent Hotel
2620 West Dunlap Avenue
Phoenix, AZ 85021
602-943-8200
Dogs up to 80 pounds are allowed. There is no additional pet fee.

Sheraton Wild Horse Pass Resort and Spa
Gila River Indian Community
Phoenix, AZ
602-225-0100
Dogs up to 55 pounds are allowed. All rooms are non-smoking. There are no pet fees.

Sleep Inn
6347 E. Southern Ave.
Phoenix, AZ 85206
480-807-7760
There is a $25 pet deposit. Pets may not be left alone.

Sleep Inn North
18235 N. 27th Ave.
Phoenix, AZ 85053
602-504-1200
There is a $25 pet deposit.

Sleep Inn Sky Harbor Airport
2621 S 47th Pl
Phoenix, AZ 85034
480-967-7100
There is a $25 one time pet fee.

Studio 6
8405 North 27th Avenue
Phoenix, AZ 85053
602-843-1151
There is a $10 per day additional pet fee. Exit Union Hills Drive west from I-17.

Townplace Suites
9425-B N Black Canyon Hwy
Phoenix, AZ 85021

602-943-9510
There is a one-time $100 pet fee.

Accommodations - Vacation Home Rentals

Phoenix

South Mountain Village Pet Friendly Vacation Apartment
113 E. La Mirada Drive
Phoenix, AZ 85042
602-243-3452
Located in the foothills of South Mountain Park. 1 bedroom, 1 bath apartment, completely furnished, including dishes, utensils, cookware, linens and much more for a self-catering vacation. Pets have free range of completely fenced 1/8 acre gated yard. Pool, spa, laundry, off-street parking for one automobile. Horse riding stables, golf, hiking trials nearby. Rates are seasonal, starting at $300 per week and $975 per month for 2 adults and 1 pet (fees apply for additional guests/pets). Tax and cleaning fees are extra.

Attractions

Phoenix

Biltmore Fashion Park
2502 E. Camelback Rd.
Phoenix, AZ 85016
602-955-8400
Well-behaved leashed dogs are welcome at this outdoor shopping mall and most of the stores are pet-friendly. This mall even has a list of pet-friendly stores on their website. Some of the stores that allow dogs include Macy's, Sak's Fifth Avenue, Restoration Hardware, Pottery Barn, Godiva Chocolatier, The Sharper Image, Williams-Sonoma, Three Dog Bakery, and Baily, Banks & Biddle. Many of the outdoor restaurant also allow dogs. Please check our restaurant section for listings.

Deer Valley Rock Art Center
3711 West Deer Valley Rd.
Phoenix, AZ
623-582-8007
Run by Arizona State University, this 47 acre attraction offers a self-guided walking tour to an archeological site where you can view petroglyphs with your pooch. The Hedgpeth Hills site has over 1,500 petroglyphs on almost 600 boulders. Researchers believe the petroglyphs are 200 to 2,000 years old. Dogs are not allowed inside the building, but can accompany you on

the self-guided trail. A map of the trail is included with admission. Pets must be leashed and please clean up after your pet.

Pioneer Living History Village
3901 West Pioneer Road
Phoenix, AZ 85086
623-465-1052
This living history museum offers over 90 acres of an old 1800's village with original buildings and historically accurate reproductions. You will find costumed interpreters, cowboys, lawmen, Victorian ladies plus a working blacksmith shop and more. There are also "shootouts" that start daily at 11:30am. Well-behaved leashed dogs are welcome. The village is located 30 minutes north of Phoenix. This attraction is open year-round, but the best time is during the winter when it's not too hot for your dog to walk around. Winter hours are from mid-September through the end of May.

Parks

Phoenix

Camelback Mountain
Cholla Lane
Phoenix, AZ
602-262-6862
This park offers sheer red sandstone cliffs and strenuous hiking trails. There are some easier trails which allow for a close-up view around Camelback's base. The easy trails and one of the strenuous trails begin off of Echo Canyon Parkway near McDonald Drive. Parking is very limited at the trailheads. Pets must be leashed and please clean up after them.

North Mountain Area
7th Street
Phoenix, AZ
602-262-6862
North Mountain is over 2,100 feet and offers panoramic views of Phoenix. There are a variety of trails rated easy to difficult. The trailheads for two of the easy to moderate trails are located at the north end of Mountain View Park at 7th Avenue and Cheryl Drive. The North Mountain National Trail is rated moderate to difficult hiking and the trailhead is located at the Maricopa picnic area off 7th Street (not 7th Avenue). Parking is available. Pets must be leashed and please clean up after them.

Papago Park
Galvin Parkway
Phoenix, AZ

602-262-6862
This park offers sandstone buttes and mostly easy hikes with little elevation gain. One of the trails is called the Hole-In-The-Rock Trail which is a short trail that leads to a popular landmark with some good views. Parking is available. Pets must be leashed and please clean up after them.

Pecos Park Dog Park
48th Street
Phoenix, AZ
602-262-6862
This dog park is scheduled to open in the fall of 2003. It will be located in Pecos Park which is at 48th Street and Pecos Parkway.

PetsMart Dog Park
21st Avenue
Phoenix, AZ
602-262-6971
This fully fenced dog park has over 2.5 grassy acres. Amenities include a water fountain and two watering stations for dogs, benches, bag dispensers and garbage cans. This off-leash park is located in Washington Park on 21st Avenue north of Maryland (between Bethany Home and Glendale roads).

Reach 11 Recreation Area
Cave Creek Road
Phoenix, AZ
602-262-6862
This 1,500 acre park is about 7 miles long and less than 1/2 mile wide. The park runs along the north side of the Central Arizona Project canal. There are about 18 miles of multi-use trails to enjoy. In general the trails are flat and easy. The trails run the length of the recreation area from Cave Creek Road east to Scottsdale Road. Access points include Cave Creek Road, Tatum Blvd., Scottsdale Road and 56th Street. Pets must be leashed and please clean up after them.

South Mountain Park
10919 S. Central Avenue
Phoenix, AZ 85040
602-534-6324
At 16,000 acres, this park is the largest municipal park in the world. It is popular for hiking, biking and horseback riding. There are over 58 miles of trails rated easy to difficult. Many of the trails start off of or near Central Avenue or San Juan Road. Pets must be leashed and please clean up after them.

Squaw Peak/Dreamy Draw Area
Squaw Peak Drive
Phoenix, AZ

602-262-6862
Squaw Peak is 2,608 feet high and is one of the best known peaks in Phoenix. The summit trail is rated moderate to difficult hiking and is one of the most popular trails. There are also several easy trails. Some of the trails begin off Squaw Peak Drive. Parking is available. Pets must be leashed and please clean up after them.

Restaurants

Phoenix

Aunt Chilada's
7330 N. Dreamy Draw Drive
Phoenix, AZ 85020
602-944-1286
This Southwestern restaurant offers a variety of food including quesadillas, soup, salads, tacos, enchiladas, fajitas, and burritos. Well-behaved leashed dogs are allowed at the outdoor tables.

Baja Fresh Mexican Grill
1615 E Camelback Rd Ste F
Phoenix, AZ
602-263-0110
This Mexican restaurant chain offers a variety of items on their menu including burritos, tacos, salads, quesadillas, fajitas, and enchiladas. Well-behaved leashed dogs are allowed at the outdoor tables.

Baja Fresh Mexican Grill
10810 N. Tatum Blvd, Ste 108
Phoenix, AZ
602-569-8600
This Mexican restaurant chain offers a variety of items on their menu including burritos, tacos, salads, quesadillas, fajitas, and enchiladas. Well-behaved leashed dogs are allowed at the outdoor tables.

Baja Fresh Mexican Grill
430 East Bell Rd.
Phoenix, AZ
602-843-6770
This Mexican restaurant chain offers a variety of items on their menu including burritos, tacos, salads, quesadillas, fajitas, and enchiladas. Well-behaved leashed dogs are allowed at the outdoor tables.

Baja Fresh Mexican Grill
3923 E. Thomas Rd. Ste B-5
Phoenix, AZ
602-914-9000
This Mexican restaurant chain offers a variety of

items on their menu including burritos, tacos, salads, quesadillas, fajitas, and enchiladas. Well-behaved leashed dogs are allowed at the outdoor tables.

Baja Fresh Mexican Grill
50 N. Central Ave
Phoenix, AZ
602-256-9200
This Mexican restaurant chain offers a variety of items on their menu including burritos, tacos, salads, quesadillas, fajitas, and enchiladas. Well-behaved leashed dogs are allowed at the outdoor tables.

Bamboo Club
2596 E. Camelback Rd.
Phoenix, AZ 85016
602-955-1288
This restaurant offers Pacific Rim food, including Thailand, Korean, Vietnam, and Chinese. Well-behaved leashed dogs are allowed at the outdoor tables. This restaurant is located in the dog-friendly Biltmore Fashion Park.

Christopher's Fermier Brasserie
2584 E. Camelback Rd.
Phoenix, AZ
602-522-2344
This restaurant offers a combination French and American cuisine. Some of their specialty items include house-smoked salmon, and lightly smoked truffle-cured sirloin. Well-behaved leashed dogs are allowed at the outdoor tables. This restaurant is located in the dog-friendly Biltmore Fashion Park.

Coffee Plantation
2468 E. Camelback Rd.
Phoenix, AZ 85016
602-553-0203
This is a tropical coffeehouse and bean store. They offer coffee, espresso, iced drinks, fresh Artisan Breads, Baguettes, specialty bread loaves and more. Well-behaved leashed dogs are allowed at the outdoor tables. This restaurant is located in the dog-friendly Biltmore Fashion Park.

Duck and Decanter
1651 East Camelback Road
Phoenix, AZ 85016
602-274-5429
This restaurant offers a variety of sandwiches, salads, and soups. Some of their Signature Sandwiches include The Duckling with smoked duck, The Pocket with your choice of meat, and Where's the Beef which is their veggie sandwich. Well-behaved leashed dogs are allowed at the

outdoor tables. The restaurant is located to the east of Albertson's, behind Copenhagen Furniture.

Haagen-Dazs
2454 E. Camelback Rd.
Phoenix, AZ 85016
602-508-8053
This popular ice cream shop offers a variety of ice creams, sorbet, frozen yogurt, sundaes, banana split, specialty shakes, espresso, and ice cream cakes. Well-behaved leashed dogs are allowed at the outdoor tables. This restaurant is located in the dog-friendly Biltmore Fashion Park.

Juice Works
10895 North Tatum Boulevard
Phoenix, AZ
480-922-5337
This juice bar serves fresh fruit smoothies and juices. Well-behaved leashed dogs are allowed at the outdoor tables.

Rubio's Fresh Mexican Grill
4340 E. Indian School Rd., Ste. 1
Phoenix, AZ 85018
602-508-1732
This Mexican restaurant chain serves items like chargrilled steak and chicken burritos, tacos, quesadillas, seafood including lobster, shrimp, Mahi-Mahi, and their famous fish taco. Well-behaved leashed dogs are allowed at the outdoor tables.

Rubio's Fresh Mexican Grill
4747 East Bell Road #17
Phoenix, AZ 85032
602-867-1454
This Mexican restaurant chain serves items like char-grilled steak and chicken burritos, tacos, quesadillas, seafood including lobster, shrimp, Mahi-Mahi, and their famous fish taco. Well-behaved leashed dogs are allowed at the outdoor tables.

Sam's Cafe
2566 E. Camelback Rd.
Phoenix, AZ 85016
602-954-7100
This restaurant specializes in Southwestern cuisine and welcomes dogs to their outdoor patio. Their entrees include the Fire Grilled Tuna, Desert Fire Pasta, Blackened Salmon Caesar, Grilled Vegetable Paella and the classic Southwest steak. Well-behaved leashed dogs are welcome at the outdoor tables. This restaurant is located in the dog-friendly Biltmore Fashion Park.

The Capital Grille
2502 E. Camelback Rd.
Phoenix, AZ 85016
602-952-8900
This steak house offers dry aged steaks, North Atlantic lobsters and fresh seafood. Well-behaved leashed dogs are allowed at the outdoor tables. This restaurant is located in the dog-friendly Biltmore Fashion Park.

The Farm at South Mountain
6106 South 32nd Street
Phoenix, AZ
602-276-6360
This restaurant specializes in organic and natural foods. All seating is outdoors, either in their patio under pecan trees or at picnic tables. An organic garden is on the premises and they often use ingredients from it. They serve sandwiches, salads, and baked goods. Well-behaved leashed dogs are allowed at the outdoor tables. The restaurant is open daily weather permitting from 8am to 3pm, except they are closed on Mondays.

Vintage Market
2442 B East Camelback Rd.
Phoenix, AZ 85016
602-955-4444
This cafe also has a wine bar and gourmet gift shop. They are open for dinner. Well-behaved leashed dogs are allowed at the outdoor tables. This restaurant is located in the dog-friendly Biltmore Fashion Park.

Wild Oats Natural Marketplace
3933 E. Camelback Rd.
Phoenix, AZ
602-954-0584
This natural food market has a deli with outdoor seats. Well-behaved leashed dogs are allowed at the outdoor tables.

Phoenix Area Dog Travel Guide
Accommodations

Carefree

Boulders Resort
34631 N Tom Darlington Rd
Carefree, AZ 85377
480-488-9009
There is a one-time $100 dog fee.

Chandler

Red Roof Inn

7400 W Boston St
Chandler, AZ 85226
480-857-4969
There are no additional pet fees.

Sheraton San Marcos Golf Resort and Conference Center
One San Marcos Place
Chandler, AZ 85224
480-812-0900
Dogs up to 80 pounds are allowed. Larger dogs are put in rooms that are closer to the walking areas. There is a $100 refundable deposit for dogs.

Windmill Inn of Chandler
3535 W Chandler Blvd
Chandler, AZ 85226
480-812-9600
There is no additional pet fee. There is a special pet section of the hotel.

Goodyear

Best Western Goodyear Inn
55 N Litchfield Rd
Goodyear, AZ 85338
623-932-3210
There is a $10 per day pet fee.

Hampton Inn and Suites
2000 N Litchfield Rd
Goodyear, AZ 85338
623-536-1313
There are no additional pet fees.

Holiday Inn Express
1313 Litchfield Rd
Goodyear, AZ 85338
623-535-1313
Exit I-10 at Litchfield Rd.

Mesa

Arizona Golf Resort
425 S Power Road
Mesa, AZ 85206
480-832-3202
There are no additional pet charges.

Best Western Mesa Inn
1625 E Main St
Mesa, AZ 85203
480-964-8000
There is a $5 per day additional pet fee.

Holiday Inn Hotel and Suites
1600 S Country Club
Mesa, AZ 85210
480-964-7000
There is a $20 one time pet fee.

Homestead Village
1920 W Isabella
Mesa, AZ 85202
480-752-2266
There is a $75 one time pet fee.

Motel 6
336 W Hampton Ave
Mesa, AZ 85210
480-844-8899
One large well-behaved dog is okay.

Motel 6
630 W Main Street
Mesa, AZ 85201
480-969-8111
There are no additional pet fees.

Motel 6
1511 S. Country Club Dr
Mesa, AZ 85210
480-834-0066
One well-behaved pet is allowed per room.

Residence Inn
941 W Grove Ave
Mesa, AZ 85210
480-610-0100
There is a $50 one time pet fee and $10 each day.

Sleep Inn
6347 E Southern Ave
Mesa, AZ 85206
480-807-7760
There is a one-time $25 fee for pets.

Paradise Valley

Hermosa Inn
5532 N Palo Cristi Rd
Paradise Valley, AZ 85253
602-955-8614
There is a $50 refundable pet deposit.

Scottsdale

Hampton Inn Oldtown
4415 N Civic Center Plaza
Scottsdale, AZ 85251

480-941-9400
There is a one-time $50 pet fee.

Homestead Village
3560 N Marshall Way
Scottsdale, AZ 85251
480-994-0297
There is a $75 one time pet fee.

Inn at the Citadel
8700 E Pinnacle Peak Rd
Scottsdale, AZ 85255
480-585-6133
This B&B is located in an adobe-like complex of stores and next to the foothills of Pinnacle Peak. There are no additional pet fees.

La Quinta Inn & Suites Scottsdale
8888 East Shea Blvd.
Scottsdale, AZ
480-614-5300
Dogs of all sizes are allowed at the hotel.

Motel 6
6848 E Camelback Rd
Scottsdale, AZ 85251
480-946-2280
Pets must be attended at all times.

Pima Inn and Suites
7330 N Pima Rd
Scottsdale, AZ 85258
480-948-3800
There is a $10 one time pet fee. Dogs are not allowed in the lobby.

Residence Inn
6040 N Scottsdale Rd
Scottsdale, AZ 85253
480-948-8666
There is a $50 one time pet fee plus $6 per day pet fee.

Sleep Inn
16630 N. Scottsdale Rd
Scottsdale, AZ 85254
480-998-9211
This hotel has 107 rooms which have either 2 double beds or one King bed. They offer a deluxe continental breakfast, outdoor heated pool, spa, and fitness room. They accept all types of pets and charge a $10 per day fee for the first 5 days of your stay. No deposits are required.

Tempe

Holiday Inn - Tempe

915 E. Apache Blvd
Tempe, AZ 85281
480-968-3451
One well-behaved large dog is okay.

La Quinta Inn Phoenix Sky Harbor Tempe
911 South 48th Street
Tempe, AZ
480-967-4465
Dogs of all sizes are allowed at the hotel.

Motel 6
1720 S. Priest Drive
Tempe, AZ 85281
480-968-4401
There are no additional pet fees.

Motel 6
1612 N Scottsdale Rd/Rural Rd
Tempe, AZ 85281
480-945-9506
Pets may not be left alone in the room.

Quality
1375 E. University Dr.
Tempe, AZ 85251
480-774-2500
There is no pet fee. A credit card will be required.

Studio 6
4909 South Wendler Dr.
Tempe, AZ 85282
602-414-4470
There is a $10 per day or $30 per week pet fee.

Restaurants

Scottsdale

Baja Fresh Mexican Grill
4032 N. Scottsdale Rd, Ste 1
Scottsdale, AZ
480-429-8270
This Mexican restaurant chain offers a variety of items on their menu including burritos, tacos, salads, quesadillas, fajitas, and enchiladas. Well-behaved leashed dogs are allowed at the outdoor tables.

Rubio's Fresh Mexican Grill
15704 N. Pima Rd., #C8 & 9
Scottsdale, AZ 85260
480-348-0195
This Mexican restaurant chain serves items like chargrilled steak and chicken burritos, tacos, quesadillas, seafood including lobster, shrimp, Mahi-Mahi, and their famous fish taco. Well-

behaved leashed dogs are allowed at the outdoor tables.

Rubio's Fresh Mexican Grill
32415 N. Scottsdale Road, Ste. C
Scottsdale, AZ 85262
480-575-7280
This Mexican restaurant chain serves items like chargrilled steak and chicken burritos, tacos, quesadillas, seafood including lobster, shrimp, Mahi-Mahi, and their famous fish taco. Well-behaved leashed dogs are allowed at the outdoor tables.

Tempe

Baja Fresh Mexican Grill
414 W. University Drive
Tempe, AZ
480-446-3116
This Mexican restaurant chain offers a variety of items on their menu including burritos, tacos, salads, quesadillas, fajitas, and enchiladas. Well-behaved leashed dogs are allowed at the outdoor tables.

Rubio's Fresh Mexican Grill
1712 East Guadalupe Rd., Ste. 109
Tempe, AZ 85283
480-897-3884
This Mexican restaurant chain serves items like char-grilled steak and chicken burritos, tacos, quesadillas, seafood including lobster, shrimp, Mahi-Mahi, and their famous fish taco. Well-behaved leashed dogs are allowed at the outdoor tables.

Pinetop Dog Travel Guide
Accommodations

Pinetop

Best Western Inn of Pinetop
404 S. White Mountain Blvd
Pinetop, AZ 85935
928-367-6667
There is a $10 per day pet fee.

Prescott Dog Travel Guide
Accommodations

Prescott

Comfort Inn
1290 White Spar Rd.
Prescott, AZ 86303

928-778-5770
There is no pet fee in a smoking room. There is a $10 pet fee in a non-smoking room. There are walking trails nearby.

Lynx Creek Farm Bed and Breakfast
SR69 and Onyx Rd
Prescott, AZ 86302
928-778-9573
There is an additional $10 per day pet fee. Pets may not be left in the room unattended.

Super 8 Motel - Prescott
1105 E. Sheldon Street
Prescott, AZ 86301
928-776-1282
$10/stay for up to 3 dogs in one room. FREE 8-minute long distance call each night. FREE continental breakfast. Coffee maker, night light, clock/radio, safe in each room. Seasonal outdoor pool. On-site guest laundry. Kids 12 & under stay free. On Sheldon St (BR 89), West of intersection of US 89 & AZ 69.

Prescott Valley

Days Inn
7875 E AZ 69
Prescott Valley, AZ 86314
928-772-8600
There is a $50 refundable pet deposit.

Safford Dog Travel Guide
Accommodations

Safford

Best Western Desert Inn
1391 Thatcher Blvd
Safford, AZ 85546
928-428-0521
There is a $6 per day pet fee.

Sedona Dog Travel Guide
Accommodations

Sedona

Best Western Inn of Sedona
1200 Hwy 89A
Sedona, AZ 86336
928-282-3072
There is a $10 per day pet fee.

Matterhorn Motor Lodge

230 Apple Ave
Sedona, AZ 86336
928-282-7176
This inn is located in the center of uptown Sedona.

Oak Creek Terrace Resort
4548 N. Hwy. 89A
Sedona, AZ 86336
928-282-3562
Relax by the creek or in one of the jacuzzi rooms. Dogs welcome with a $35 non-refundable pet fee. Amenities include in-room fireplaces, barbecue and picnic areas, air conditioning and cable TV.

Quail Ridge Resort
120 Canyon Circle Dr
Sedona, AZ 86351
928-284-9327
There is a $10 per day pet fee.

Sky Ranch Lodge
Airport Rd
Sedona, AZ 86339
928-282-6400
There is a $10.00 per day pet fee, dogs up to 75 pounds ok.

Attractions

Sedona

Red Rock Country - Coconino National Forest
various
Sedona, AZ 86004
928-527-3600
This park offers a colorful collection of buttes, pinnacles, mesas, canyons and red rock vistas. Over the years, this area has served as the setting of many western novels and movies and has been the subject of uncounted paintings, photographs and other works of art. Your leashed dog is allowed on the scenic Red Rock Country hiking trails with you.

Show Low Dog Travel Guide
Accommodations

Show Low

Best Western Paint Pony Lodge
581 W Deuce of Clubs
Show Low, AZ 85901
928-537-5773
There is a $15 refundable pet deposit.

Motel 6
1941 E Duece of Clubs
Show Low, AZ 85901
928-537-7694
There are no additional pet fees.

Sleep Inn
1751 W. Deuce of Clubs
Show Low, AZ 85901
928-532-7323
There is a $25 per day pet fee.

Sierra Vista Dog Travel Guide
Accommodations

Sierra Vista

Best Western Mission Inn
3460 E Fry Blvd
Sierra Vista, AZ 85635
520-458-8500
There is a $5 per day additional pet fee.

Motel 6
1551 E Fry Blvd
Sierra Vista, AZ 85635
520-459-5035
There are no additional pet fees.

Super 8 Motel - Sierra Vista
100 Fab Avenue
Sierra Vista, AZ 85635
520-459-5380
$10/stay for up to 3 dogs in one room. FREE 8-minute long distance call each night. FREE continental breakfast. Coffee maker, refrigerator, night light, clock/radio, safe in each room. Seasonal outdoor pool. On-site guest laundry. Kids 12 & under stay free. I-10, Exit 302, straight on Buffalo Soldier Trail, 30 miles, through light to Fry Blvd.; Left 1 block.

Tombstone Dog Travel Guide
Accommodations

Tombstone

Best Western Lookout Lodge
Highway 80 West
Tombstone, AZ 85638
520-457-2223
This is Tombstone's newest motel. Amenities include a pool. It is located within a short drive to historic Tombstone. There is a $5 per day pet charge.

Travel Guide - Please always call ahead to make sure an establishment is still dog-friendly.

Trail Rider's Inn
13 N. 7th Street
Tombstone, AZ 85638
520-457-3573
You and your pup can walk to the historic
Tombstone district from this inn. They offer large,
clean, quiet rooms and cable TV. There is a $5
per day pet fee.

Attractions

Tombstone

1880 Historic Tombstone
70 miles from Tucson
Tombstone, AZ
800-457-3423
This historic Western town is one of the most
famous and glamorized mining towns in America.
Prospector Ed Schieffelin was told he would only
find his tombstone in the San Pedro Valley. He
named his first silver claim Tombstone, and it
later became the name of the town. The town is
situated on a mesa at an elevation of 4,540 feet.
While the area became notorious for saloons,
gambling houses and the O.K. Corral shootout, in
the 1880s Tombstone had become the most
cultivated city in the West. Surviving the Great
Depression and relocation of the County Seat to
Bisbee, in the 1930s Tombstone became known
as "The Town Too Tough To Die." You an your
leashed dog are welcome to take a step back in
time and walk along the wooden sidewalks and
dirt streets. Here is a side note about the town:
dogs are not allowed inside the O.K. Corral shootout area. This historic town is a must visit when
you go to Arizona!

Old Tombstone Stagecoach Tours
Allen Street (between 4th and 5th Streets)
Tombstone, AZ
520-457-3018
You and your pooch are welcome to hop on the
stagecoach and tour the old town of Tombstone.
They offer horse drawn tours daily. Prices run
about $10 for a 10-15 minute tour.

WF Trading Company
418 Allen St
Tombstone, AZ 85638
520-457-3664
Located in the heart of historic Tombstone, this
retail store allows your well-behaved leashed dog
inside the store. They sell gift items, jewelry,
clothing and more.

Restaurants

Tombstone

O.K. Cafe
220 E. Allen Street
Tombstone, AZ 85638
520-457-3980
Come here for breakfast and lunch. Dogs are
allowed at the outdoor tables.

Tucson Dog Travel Guide
Accommodations

Tucson

Best Western Executive Inn
333 West Drachman Street
Tucson, AZ 85705
520-791-7551
There is a $15 one time pet fee per visit.

Clarion Hotel & Suites Santa Rita
88 E. Broadway Blvd.
Tucson, AZ 85701
520-622-4000
There is a $50 pet deposit of which $25 is non-
refundable.

Comfort Suites
6935 S. Tucson Blvd.
Tucson, AZ 85706-
520-295-4400
There is a non-refundable pet deposit of $50.

Comfort Suites at Tucson Mall
515 W. Automall Dr.
Tucson, AZ 85705
520-888-6676
There is a one time pet fee of $10.

Doubletree Guest Suites
6555 E Speedway Blvd
Tucson, AZ 85710
520-721-7100
There is a $25 per visit pet fee.

Hawthorn Suites Ltd
7007 E Tanque Verde Rd
Tucson, AZ 85715
520-298-2300
There is a $25 pet fee per visit.

Loews Ventana Canyon Resort
7000 North Resort Drive
Tucson, AZ 85750
520-299-2020

All well-behaved dogs of any size are welcome. This upscale hotel offers their "Loews Loves Pets" program which includes special pet treats, local dog walking routes, and a list of nearby pet-friendly places to visit. There are no pet fees.

Motel 6 - 22nd Street
1222 S Frwy
Tucson, AZ 85713
520-624-2516
A clean well-behaved large dog is okay. Exit 22nd Street from I-10 and go west. There are no additional pet fees.

Motel 6 - Airport
1031 E Benson Hwy
Tucson, AZ 85713
520-628-1264
There are no additional pet fees.

Motel 6 - Benson Hwy N
755 E Benson Hwy
Tucson, AZ 85713
520-622-4614
There are no additional pet fees.

Motel 6 - Congess St
960 S. Freeway
Tucson, AZ 85745
520-628-1339
Exit I-10 at exit 258, take the frontage road south. There are no additional pet fees.

Motel 6 - North
4630 W Ina Rd
Tucson, AZ 85741
520-744-9300
Take Ina Rd exit off of I-10. There are no additional pet fees.

Red Roof Inn Tucson North
4940 W Ina Rd
Tucson, AZ 85743
520-744-8199
There are no additional pet fees. Dogs up to 80 pounds are allowed. Pets must never be left alone in the rooms.

Residence Inn by Marriott
6477 E Speedway Blvd
Tucson, AZ 85710
520-721-0991
There is a $50 one time pet fee per visit.

Sheraton Tucson Hotel and Suites
5151 East Grant Road
Tucson, AZ
520-323-6262

Dogs up to 80 pounds are allowed. There is a $25 per night additional pet fee. Dogs may not be left in the room by themselves.

Studio 6
4950 S. Outlet Center Dr
Tucson, AZ 85706
520-746-0030
There is a $10 per day or $50 per week additional pet fee.

Westward Look Resort
245 East Ina Road
Tucson, AZ 85704
520-297-1151
This resort comes highly recommended from one of our readers. They said it was the most pet-friendly resort around and they can't say enough good things about it. This former 1912 guest ranch, now a desert resort hideaway, is nestled in the foothills of Tucson's picturesque Santa Catalina Mountains. It offers guests a Southwestern experience on 80 desert acres. They have walking trails at the resort, tennis, swimming pools and much more. Special room rates can be as low as $69 during certain times and seasons. There is a $50 one time additional pet fee.

Windmill Inn at St Philip's Plaza
4250 N Campbell Ave
Tucson, AZ 85718
520-577-0007
There are no additional pet fees.

Attractions

Tucson

Old Tucson Studios
201 S. Kinney Road
Tucson, AZ 85735
520-883-0100
Well-behaved, leashed dogs are welcome at this outdoor studio which offers "Hollywood" stunt shows, re-enacted gunfights and more. See locations in this Old West town where popular Wild West films were shot. There are also many shops in the town that offer authentic western wear, gifts, books and collectibles. Well-behaved leashed dogs are also allowed inside the stores.

Pima Air and Space Museum
6000 East Valencia Road
Tucson, AZ 85706
520-574-0462
Dogs are allowed at the outdoor exhibits at this

air museum. This museum has over 250 aircraft on display on 80 acres. Please make sure your pooch does not lift a leg on the aircraft. Have him or her take care of business before entering the museum.

Parks

Tucson

Christopher Columbus Park Dog Run
600 N. Silverbell Rd.
Tucson, AZ
520-791-4873
There is almost 15,000 square feet of enclosed space for your pooch to run leash-free. About 5,500 square feet has grass. Other doggie amenities include doggie bags, water, trees, and more.

Rillito River Trail
La Cholla Blvd
Tucson, AZ
520-877-6000
This popular paved trail stretches for miles, offering plenty of opportunity for your pooch to stretch his or her legs. Just be careful to go early in the morning or early evening if it is a hot day, as the paved path and the adjacent desert sand can become too hot for paws. A popular section of the trail is located between La Cholla Blvd. and Campbell Avenue, along the Rillito River. There is parking and restrooms available near La Cholla Boulevard.

Restaurants

Tucson

El Charro Cafe
311 North Court Avenue
Tucson, AZ
520-622-1922
Well-behaved dogs are allowed at the outdoor tables. Choose from a selection of fajitas, tamales, chalupas, enchiladas, salads and more.

Famous Sam's Restaurant and Bar
8058 North Oracle Rd
Tucson, AZ
520-531-9464
Dogs are allowed at the outdoor tables, but need to enter through the patio gate. Have a server open the gate for you.

Li'l Abner's Steakhouse

8501 North Silverbell Rd
Tucson, AZ
520-744-2800
Dogs are allowed at the outdoor tables.

Mama's Famous Pizza and Heros
7965 North Oracle Rd
Tucson, AZ
520-297-3993
Enjoy pizza or sandwiches at this restaurant. Dogs are allowed at the outdoor tables.

Ric's Cafe
5605 East River Rd
Tucson, AZ 85750
520-577-7272
Dogs are allowed at the outdoor tables.

Schlotzsky's Deli
6301 East Broadway Blvd.
Tucson, AZ 85710
520-722-1100
Dogs are allowed at the outdoor tables. Choose from a variety of hot and cold sandwiches, salads and more.

Schlotzsky's Deli
5121 East Grant Rd
Tucson, AZ 85712
520-325-5185
Dogs are allowed at the outdoor tables. Choose from a variety of hot and cold sandwiches, salads and more.

Schlotzsky's Deli
3270 East Valencia
Tucson, AZ 85706
520-741-2333
Dogs are allowed at the outdoor tables. Choose from a variety of hot and cold sandwiches, salads and more.

Wickenburg Dog Travel Guide
Accommodations

Wickenburg

Best Western Rancho Grande
293 E Wickenburg Way
Wickenburg, AZ 85390
928-684-5445
There are no additional pet fees.

Wilcox Dog Travel Guide
Accommodations

Wilcox

Best Western Plaza Inn
1100 W Rex Allen Dr
Wilcox, AZ 85643
520-384-3556
There is an $8 per day additional pet fee.

Motel 6
921 N Bisbee Ave
Wilcox, AZ 85643
520-384-2201
From I-10, take Rex Allen Dr East, then north on Bisbee.

Winslow Dog Travel Guide
Accommodations

Winslow

Days Inn
2035 W. Hwy 66
Winslow, AZ 86047
928-289-1010
There is a $20 refundable pet deposit.

Econo Lodge
I40 & Exit 253 North Park Dr
Winslow, AZ 86047
928-289-4687
There is a $5 per day additional pet fee.

Holiday Inn Express
816 Transcon Lane
Winslow, AZ 86047
928-289-2960
There is a $10 per day additional pet fee.

Attractions

Winslow

Homolovi Ruins State Park
State Route 87
Winslow, AZ
928-289-4106
This site is Arizona's first archaeological state park. Homolovi, a Hopi word meaning 'place of the little hills,' consists of four major pueblo sites thought to have been occupied between A.D. 1200 and 1425 by ancestors of today's Hopi Indians. Homolovi sites I and II are accessible to visitors. Your leashed dog is welcome to view the sites with you. Just stay on the trail because there are rattlesnakes in the area. The park is located five miles northeast of Winslow on State Route 87. Tale I-40 to Exit 257, then go 1.3 miles north on Highway 87.

Yuma Dog Travel Guide
Accommodations

Yuma

Comfort Inn
1691 S. Riley Ave.
Yuma, AZ 85365
928-782-1200
There is a pet fee of $5 per day.

Holiday Inn Express
3181 S. 4th Ave
Yuma, AZ 85364
928-344-1420
There are no additional pet fees.

Motel 6 - Downtown
1640 S Arizona Ave
Yuma, AZ
928-782-6561
There are no additional pet fees.

Motel 6 - East
1445 E 16th St
Yuma, AZ 85365
928-782-9521
There are no additional pet fees.

Chapter 16

Oregon Dog-Friendly Travel Guide

Albany Dog Travel Guide
Accommodations

Albany

La Quinta Inn & Suites Albany
251 Airport Road SE
Albany, OR
541-928-0921
Dogs of all sizes are allowed at the hotel.

Ashland Dog Travel Guide
Accommodations

Ashland

Best Western Bard's Inn
132 N Main Street
Ashland, OR 97520
541-482-0049
There is a $15 per day additional pet fee. All rooms are non-smoking. Pets may not be left alone in the rooms.

Best Western Windsor Inn
2520 Ashland St
Ashland, OR 97520
541-488-2330
There is a $10 per day additional pet fee.

La Quinta Inn & Suites Ashland
434 S. Valley View Road
Ashland, OR
541-482-6932
Dogs of all sizes are allowed at the hotel.

Astoria Dog Travel Guide
Accommodations

Astoria

Red Lion Inn
400 Industry St
Astoria, OR 97103
503-325-7373
There is a $10 per day pet fee.

Baker City Dog Travel Guide
Accommodations

Baker City

Quality Inn
810 Campbell St.
Baker City, OR 97814
541-523-2242
There is a pet fee of $5 per day.

Bandon Dog Travel Guide
Accommodations

Bandon

Best Western Inn at Face Rock
3225 Beach Loop Rd
Bandon, OR 97411
541-347-9441
There is a $15 one time pet fee.

Driftwood Motel
460 Hwy 101
Bandon, OR 97411
541-347-9022
There is a $10 per day pet fee.

Sunset Motel
1755 Beach Loop Rd
Bandon, OR 97411
541-347-2453
There is a $10 per day pet charge. All rooms are non-smoking.

Beaches

Bandon

Bullards Beach State Park
Highway 101
Bandon, OR
541-347-2209
Enjoy a walk along the beach at this park. Picnic tables, restrooms, hiking and campgrounds are available at the park. There is a minimal day use fees. Leashed dogs are allowed on the beach. Dogs are also allowed on hiking trails and campgrounds. They must be on a six foot or less leash at all times and people are required to clean up after their pets. On beaches located outside of Oregon State Park boundaries, dogs might be allowed off-leash and under direct voice control, please look for signs or postings. This park is located off U.S. Highway 101, 2 miles north of Bandon.

Seven Devils State Recreation Site
Highway 101
Bandon, OR
800-551-6949

Enjoy several miles of beach at this park. Picnic tables are available at this park. There are no day use fees. Dogs are allowed on the beach. They must be on a six foot or less leash at all times and people are required to clean up after their pets. On beaches located outside of Oregon State Park boundaries, dogs might be allowed off-leash and under direct voice control, please look for signs or postings. This park is located off U.S. Highway 101, 10 miles north of Bandon.

Bend Dog Travel Guide
Accommodations

Bend

Best Western Inn and Suites
721 NE 3rd St
Bend, OR 97701
541-382-1515
There is a $5 per day additional pet fee.

Entrada Lodge
19221 Century Dr
Bend, OR 97702
541-382-4080
There is a $5 per day pet fee. Pets may not be left alone in the room.

Holiday Inn Express Hotel
20615 Grandview Drive
Bend, OR 97701
541-317-8500
There is a $5 per day pet fee.

Motel 6
201 NE Third St
Bend, OR 97701
541-382-8282
There are no additional pet fees.

Red Lion Inn North
1415 NE 3rd St
Bend, OR 97701
541-382-7011
There are no additional pet fees.

Sleep Inn
600 NE Bellvue
Bend, OR 97701
541-330-0050
There is a one time fee of $8. Pets may not be left alone in the room.

The Riverhouse Resort
3075 N Hwy 97
Bend, OR 97701

541-389-3111
You need to sign a pet policy.

Redmond

Motel 6
2247 S Hwy 97
Redmond, OR 97756
541-923-2100
There are no additional pet fees.

Sunriver

Sunray Vacation Rentals
P.O. Box 4518
Sunriver, OR 97707
800-531-1130
They have over 200 homes and condos for rent in Sunriver (about 20 miles from Bend, OR) and most of the rentals allow pets.

Brookings Dog Travel Guide
Beaches

Brookings

Harris Beach State Park
Highway 101
Brookings, OR
541-469-2021
The park offers sandy beaches for beachcombing, whale watching, and sunset viewing. Picnic tables, restrooms (including an ADA restroom) and shaded campsites are available at this park. There is a minimal day use fee. Leashed dogs are allowed on the beach. Dogs are also allowed at the campgrounds. They must be on a six foot or less leash at all times and people are required to clean up after their pets. On beaches located outside of Oregon State Park boundaries, dogs might be allowed off-leash and under direct voice control, please look for signs or postings. This park is located off U.S. Highway 101, just north of Brookings.

McVay Rock State Recreation Site
Highway 101
Brookings, OR
800-551-6949
This beach is a popular spot for clamming, whale watching and walking. Picnic tables and restrooms are available at this park. There are no day use fees. Dogs are allowed on the beach. They must be on a six foot or less leash at all times and people are required to clean up after their pets. On beaches located outside of Oregon

State Park boundaries, dogs might be allowed off-leash and under direct voice control, please look for signs or postings. This park is located off U.S. Highway 101, just south of Brookings.

Samuel H. Boardman State Scenic Corridor
Highway 101
Brookings, OR
800-551-6949
Steep coastline at this 12 mile long corridor is interrupted by small sandy beaches. Picnic tables, restrooms (including an ADA restroom), and a hiking trail are available at this park. There are no day use fees. Leashed dogs are allowed on the beach. Dogs are also allowed on the hiking trail. They must be on a six foot or less leash at all times and people are required to clean up after their pets. On beaches located outside of Oregon State Park boundaries, dogs might be allowed off-leash and under direct voice control, please look for signs or postings. This park is located off U.S. Highway 101, 4 miles north of Brookings.

Cannon Beach Dog Travel Guide
Accommodations

Cannon Beach

Best Western Cannon Beach
3215 S. Hemlock
Cannon Beach, OR 97110
503-436-9085
There is a $10 per day pet fee. A maximum of two pets per room is allowed.

Surfsand Resort
148 W. Gower
Cannon Beach, OR 97110
503-436-2274
This resort offers views of Haystack Rock and the Pacific Ocean from oceanfront and ocean-view rooms. The Surfsand is a nice vacation spot for families and couples. The hotel caters to four-legged family members and they host an annual "For Fun" Dog Show. The resort is entirely non-smoking and it is located near a dog-friendly restaurant called The Local Scoop. There is a $12 per day pet fee.

The Haystack Resort
3361 S. Hemlock
Cannon Beach, OR 97110
503-436-1577
Every room and suite at the Haystack Resort offers complete ocean views. Your pet is always welcome. They are located near a dog-friendly restaurant called "The Local Scoop. There is a

$10 per day additional pet fee.

Beaches

Cannon Beach

Arcadia Beach State Recreation Site
Highway 101
Cannon Beach, OR
800-551-6949
This sandy ocean beach is just a few feet from where you can park your car. Picnic tables and restrooms are available at this park. There are no day use fees. Dogs are allowed on the beach. They must be on a six foot or less leash at all times and people are required to clean up after their pets. On beaches located outside of Oregon State Park boundaries, dogs might be allowed off-leash and under direct voice control, please look for signs or postings. This park is located off U.S. Highway 101, 3 miles south of Cannon Beach.

Ecola State Park
Highway 101
Cannon Beach, OR
503-436-2844
According to the Oregon State Parks Division, this park is one of the most photographed locations in Oregon. To reach the beach, you will need to walk down a trail. Restrooms, hiking and primitive campgrounds are available at this park. There is a $3 day use fee. Leashed dogs are allowed on the beach. Dogs are also allowed on hiking trails and campgrounds. They must be on a six foot or less leash at all times and people are required to clean up after their pets. On beaches located outside of Oregon State Park boundaries, dogs might be allowed off-leash and under direct voice control, please look for signs or postings. This park is located off U.S. Highway 101, 2 miles north of Cannon Beach.

Hug Point State Recreation Site
Highway 101
Cannon Beach, OR
800-551-6949
According to the Oregon State Parks Division, people used to travel via stagecoach along this beach before the highway was built. Today you can walk along the originial trail which was carved into the point by stagecoaches. The trail is located north of the parking area. Visitors can also explore two caves around the point, but be aware of high tide. Some people have become stranded at high tide when exploring the point! This beach is easily accessible from the parking area. Picnic tables and restrooms are available at

this park. There are no day use fees. Dogs are allowed on the beach. They must be on a six foot or less leash at all times and people are required to clean up after their pets. On beaches located outside of Oregon State Park boundaries, dogs might be allowed off-leash and under direct voice control, please look for signs or postings. This park is located off U.S. Highway 101, 5 miles south of Cannon Beach.

Tolovana Beach State Recreation Site
Highway 101
Cannon Beach, OR
800-551-6949
Indian Beach is popular with surfers. There is a short walk down to the beach. Picnic tables are available at this park. There are no day fees. Dogs are allowed on the beach. They must be on a six foot or less leash at all times and people are required to clean up after their pets. On beaches located outside of Oregon State Park boundaries, dogs might be allowed off-leash and under direct voice control, please look for signs or postings. This park is located off U.S. Highway 101, 1 mile south of Cannon Beach.

Cave Junction Dog Travel Guide
Accommodations

Cave Junction

Junction Inn
406 Redwood Hwy
Cave Junction, OR
541-592-3106
There is a $5 per day additional pet fee. They normally put dogs in smoking rooms, but will make exceptions.

Coos Bay Dog Travel Guide
Accommodations

Coos Bay

Motel 6
1445 Bayshore Dr
Coos Bay, OR 97420
541-267-7171
There are no pet fees. A large dog is okay if it is well-behaved.

Beaches

Coos Bay

Sunset Bay State Park
Highway 101
Coos Bay, OR
541-888-4902
This park offers sandy beaches protected by towering sea cliffs. The campgrounds located at the park are within a short walk to the beach. You will also find a network of hiking trails here and in two adjacent parks. Picnic tables and restrooms (including an ADA restroom) are available at this park. There is a minimal day use fee. Leashed dogs are allowed on the beach. Dogs are also allowed on hiking trails and campgrounds. They must be on a six foot or less leash at all times and people are required to clean up after their pets. On beaches located outside of Oregon State Park boundaries, dogs might be allowed off-leash and under direct voice control, please look for signs or postings. This park is located off U.S. Highway 101, 12 miles southwest of Coos Bay.

Cottage Grove Dog Travel Guide
Accommodations

Cottage Grove

Best Western - The Village Green
725 Row River Rd.
Cottage Grove, OR 97424
541-942-2491
The hotel is at exit 174 on I-5.

Comfort Inn
845 Gateway Blvd.
Cottage Grove, OR 97424
541-942-9747
There is a $10 pet deposit.

Holiday Inn Express
1601 Gateway Blvd
Cottage Grove, OR 97424
541-942-1000
There is a $10 per day pet fee.

Depoe Bay Dog Travel Guide
Beaches

Depoe Bay

Fogarty Creek State Recreation Area
Highway 101
Depoe Bay, OR
800-551-6949
This beach and park offer some of the best birdwatching and tidepooling. Picnic tables and hiking are available at this park. There is a $3 day

use fees. Leashed dogs are allowed on the beach. Dogs are also allowed on hiking trails. They must be on a six foot or less leash at all times and people are required to clean up after their pets. On beaches located outside of Oregon State Park boundaries, dogs might be allowed off-leash and under direct voice control, please look for signs or postings. This park is located off U.S. Highway 101, 2 miles north of Depoe Bay.

Eugene Dog Travel Guide
Accommodations

Eugene

Best Western Greentree Inn
1759 Franklin Blvd
Eugene, OR 97403
541-485-2727
There is a $25.00 refundable pet deposit.

Best Western New Oregon Motel
1655 Franklin Blvd
Eugene, OR 97403
541-683-3669
There are no additional pet fees.

Eugene Hilton
66 East 6th Avenue
Eugene, OR 97401
541-342-2000
There is a $25 one time pet fee.

La Quinta Inn & Suites Eugene
155 Day Island Rd.
Eugene, OR
541-344-8335
Dogs of all sizes are allowed at the hotel.

Motel 6
3690 Glenwood Dr
Eugene, OR 97403
541-687-2395
There are no additional pet fees.

Quality Inn & Suites
2121 Franklin Blvd
Eugene, OR 97403
541-342-1243
There is no pet fee.

Ramada Inn
225 Coburg Rd
Eugene, OR 97401
541-342-5181
There is a $15 one time pet fee.

The Valley River Inn
1000 Valley River Way
Eugene, OR 97401
541-687-0123
There are no additional pet fees.

Florence Dog Travel Guide
Beaches

Florence

Carl G. Washburne Memorial State Park
Highway 101
Florence, OR
541-547-3416
This park offers five miles of sandy beach. Picnic tables, restrooms, hiking and campgrounds are available at this park. There is a day use fee. Leashed dogs are allowed on the beach. Dogs are also allowed on hiking trails and campgrounds. They must be on a six foot or less leash at all times and people are required to clean up after their pets. On beaches located outside of Oregon State Park boundaries, dogs might be allowed off-leash and under direct voice control, please look for signs or postings. This park is located off U.S. Highway 101, 14 miles north of Florence.

Heceta Head Lighthouse State Scenic Viewpoint
Highway 101
Florence, OR
800-551-6949
Go for a walk above the beach or explore the natural caves and tidepools along the beach. This is a great spot for whale watching. According to the Oregon State Parks Division, the lighthouse located on the west side of 1,000-foot-high Heceta Head (205 feet above ocean) is one of the most photographed on the Oregon coast. Picnic tables, restrooms and hiking are available at this park. There is a $3 day use fee. Leashed dogs are allowed on the beach. Dogs are also allowed on hiking trails. They must be on a six foot or less leash at all times and people are required to clean up after their pets. On beaches located outside of Oregon State Park boundaries, dogs might be allowed off-leash and under direct voice control, please look for signs or postings. This park is located off U.S. Highway 101, 13 miles north of Florence.

Gold Beach Dog Travel Guide
Accommodations

Gold Beach

Econo Lodge
29171 Eltensburg Ave
Gold Beach, OR 97444
541-247-6606
There is a $5 one time pet fee.

Jot's Resort
94360 Wedderburn Loop
Gold Beach, OR 97491
541-247-6676
There is a $10 per day pet fee. Pets are allowed in the deluxe rooms overlooking the river.

Beaches

Gold Beach

Pistol River State Scenic Viewpoint
Highway 101
Gold Beach, OR
800-551-6949
This beach is popular for ocean windsurfing. There has even been windsurfing national championships held at this beach. Picnic tables and restrooms are available here. There are no day use fees. Dogs are allowed on the beach. They must be on a six foot or less leash at all times and people are required to clean up after their pets. On beaches located outside of Oregon State Park boundaries, dogs might be allowed off-leash and under direct voice control, please look for signs or postings. This park is located off U.S. Highway 101, 11 miles south of Gold Beach.

Grants Pass Dog Travel Guide
Accommodations

Grants Pass

Best Western Grants Pass Inn
111 NE Agness Ave
Grants Pass, OR 97526
541-476-1117
There is a $5 per day additional pet fee.

Comfort Inn
1889 NE 6th St
Grants Pass, OR 97526
541-479-8301
There is a $100 pet deposit.

Holiday Inn Express
105 NE Agness Ave
Grants Pass, OR 97526
541-471-6144
There is a $5 per day additional pet fee.

La Quinta Inn & Suites Grants Pass
243 NE Morgan Lane
Grants Pass, OR
541-472-1808
Dogs of all sizes are allowed at the hotel.

Motel 6
1800 Northeast 7th St
Grants Pass, OR 97526
541-474-1331
There are no additional pet fees.

Harbor Dog Travel Guide
Accommodations

Harbor

Best Western Beachfront Inn
16008 Boat Basin Rd
Harbor, OR 97415
541-469-7779
There is a $5 per day pet fee. You need to tell the hotel that you are bringing a dog when you make a reservation. There are a limited number of pet rooms.

Hillsboro Dog Travel Guide
Accommodations

Hillsboro

Best Western Cavanaughs Hillsboro Hotel
3500 NE Cornell Rd
Hillsboro, OR 97124
503-648-3500
There is a $5 per day additional pet fee. A maximum to 2 pets per room are allowed.

Hines Dog Travel Guide
Accommodations

Hines

Comfort Inn
504 N Hwy 20
Hines, OR 97738
541-573-3370
There is a $50 pet deposit if paid with cash. If using a credit card there is no fee.

Hood River Dog Travel Guide
Accommodations

Hood River

Best Western Hood River Inn
1108 E. Marina Way
Hood River, OR 97031
541-386-2200
There is a $12 per day additional pet fee.

Columbia Gorge
4000 Westcliff Dr
Hood River, OR 97031
541-386-5566
There is a $25 pet charge.

Vagabond Lodge
4070 Westcliff Dr
Hood River, OR 97031
541-386-2992
There are no additional pet fees.

King City Dog Travel Guide
Accommodations

King City

Best Western Northwind Inn & Suites
16105 SW Pacific Hwy
King City, OR 97224
503-431-2100
There is a $20 one time pet fee.

Klamath Falls Dog Travel Guide
Accommodations

Klamath Falls

Best Western Klamath Inn
4061 South Sixth Street
Klamath Falls, OR 97603
541-882-1200
There are no additional pet fees.

Cimarron Motor Inn
3060 S Sixth St
Klamath Falls, OR 97603
541-882-4601
There is a $5 one time fee for pets.

CrystalWood Lodge
38625 Westside Road
Klamath Falls, OR 97601
541-381-2322
Located in the Southern Oregon Cascades, this
lodge welcomes all well-behaved dogs. There is
no pet fee.

Motel 6
5136 S 6th St
Klamath Falls, OR 97603
541-884-2110
There are no additional pet fees.

Quality Inn
100 Main St.
Klamath Falls, OR 97601
541-882-4666
There are no pet fees, but a credit card will be
required.

Red Lion Inn
3612 S 6th St
Klamath Falls, OR 97603
541-882-8864
There are no additional pet fees. Pet owners must
sign a pet waiver form.

Shilo Suites Hotel
2500 Almond St
Klamath Falls, OR 95601
541-885-7980
There is a $10 per day pet fee.

LaGrande Dog Travel Guide
Accommodations

LaGrande

Howard Johnson Inn
2612 Island Avenue
LaGrande, OR 97850
541-963-7195
Dogs of all sizes are welcome. There is a $10 per
day pet fee.

Lincoln City Dog Travel Guide
Accommodations

Lincoln City

Ester Lee Motel
3803 S.W. HWY. 101
Lincoln City, OR 97367
541 996 3606
Pets are welcome in the cottages but not the
motel. There is a $7 per day additional pet fee.
Some of the cottages are non-smoking.

Looking Glass Inn
861 SW 51st Street
Lincoln City, OR 97367
541-996-3996

The inn overlooks Siletz Bay and the Pacific Ocean. Suites with kitchens, gas fireplaces and great views. Great low beach access. There are a maximum of 2 dogs per room. Dogs may not be left alone in the room unless they are in a crate. Each dog is $10 per night.

Looking Glass Inn
861 SW 51st Street
Lincoln City, OR 97367
541-996-3996
They provide a basket of dog supplies when you check in. There is a $10 per day additional pet fee.

Beaches

Lincoln City

D River State Recreation Site
Highway 101
Lincoln City, OR
800-551-6949
This beach, located right off the highway, is a popular and typically windy beach. According to the Oregon State Parks Division, this park is home to a pair of the world's largest kite festivals every spring and fall which gives Lincoln City the name Kite Capital of the World. Restrooms are available at the park. Dogs are allowed on the beach. They must be on a six foot or less leash at all times and people are required to clean up after their pets. On beaches located outside of Oregon State Park boundaries, dogs might be allowed off-leash and under direct voice control, please look for signs or postings. This park is located off U.S. Highway 101 in Lincoln City.

Roads End State Recreation Site
Highway 101
Lincoln City, OR
800-551-6949
There is a short trail here that leads down to the beach. Picnic tables are available at this park. There are no day use fees. Dogs are allowed on the beach. They must be on a six foot or less leash at all times and people are required to clean up after their pets. On beaches located outside of Oregon State Park boundaries, dogs might be allowed off-leash and under direct voice control, please look for signs or postings. This park is located off U.S. Highway 101, 1 mile north of Lincoln City.

Madras Dog Travel Guide
Accommodations

Madras

Best Western Rama Inn
12 SW 4th Street
Madras, OR 97741
541-475-6141
There is a $10 one time pet fee.

Manzanita Dog Travel Guide
Beaches

Manzanita

Nehalem Bay State Park
Highway 101
Manzanita, OR
503-368-5154
The beach can be reached by a short walk over the dunes. This park is a popular place for fishing and crabbing. Picnic tables, restrooms (including an ADA restroom), hiking and camping are available at this park. There is a $3 day use fee. Leashed dogs are allowed on the beach. Dogs are also allowed on hiking trails and campgrounds. They must be on a six foot or less leash at all times and people are required to clean up after their pets. On beaches located outside of Oregon State Park boundaries, dogs might be allowed off-leash and under direct voice control, please look for signs or postings. This park is located off U.S. Highway 101, 3 miles south of Manzanita Junction.

Oswald West State Park
Highway 101
Manzanita, OR
800-551-6949
The beach is located just a quarter of a mile from the parking areas. It is a popular beach that is frequented by windsurfers and boogie boarders. Picnic tables, restrooms, hiking, and campgrounds are available at this park. There are no day use fees. Leashed dogs are allowed on the beach. Dogs are also allowed on hiking trails and campgrounds. They must be on a six foot or less leash at all times and people are required to clean up after their pets. On beaches located outside of Oregon State Park boundaries, dogs might be allowed off-leash and under direct voice control, please look for signs or postings. This park is located off U.S. Highway 101, 10 miles south of Cannon Beach.

Medford Dog Travel Guide
Accommodations

Medford

Best Western
1154 E Barnett Rd
Medford, OR 97504
541-779-5085
There is a $10 per day pet charge.

Doubletree Hotel
200 N Riverside
Medford, OR 97501
541-779-5811
There are no additional pet fees.

Motel 6
2400 Biddle Rd
Medford, OR 97504
541-779-0550
There are no additional pet fees.

Motel 6
950 Alba Dr
Medford, OR 97504
541-773-4290
One pet is allowed per room.

Reston Hotel
2300 Crater Lake Hwy
Medford, OR 97504
541-779-3141
There is a $20 one time pet fee.

Mount Hood Dog Travel Guide
Accommodations

Mount Hood

Cooper Spur Mountain Resort
10755 Cooper Spur Rd
Mount Hood, OR 97041
541-352-6692
There are designated pet rooms. There is a $20 one time per stay additional pet fee.

Neskowin Dog Travel Guide
Beaches

Neskowin

Neskowin Beach State Recreation Site
Highway 101
Neskowin, OR
800-551-6949
Not really any facilities (picnic tables, etc.) here, but a good place to enjoy the beach. Dogs are allowed on the beach. They must be on a six foot or less leash at all times and people are required to clean up after their pets. On beaches located outside of Oregon State Park boundaries, dogs might be allowed off-leash and under direct voice control, please look for signs or postings. This park is located off U.S. Highway 101 in Neskowin.

Newport Dog Travel Guide
Accommodations

Newport

Best Western
3019 North Coast Hwy
Newport, OR 97365
541-265-9411
There is a $10 one time pet fee.

Hallmark Resort
744 SW Elizabeth St
Newport, OR 97365
541-265-2600
There is a $5 per day pet fee, Dogs are allowed on the first floor only.

La Quinta Inn & Suites Newport
45 SE 32nd
Newport, OR
541-867-7727
Dogs up to 75 pounds are allowed at the hotel.

Shilo Oceanfront Resort
536 SW Elizabeth St
Newport, OR 97365
541-265-7701
There is a $10 per day pet fee.

Beaches

Newport

Agate Beach State Recreation Site
Highway 101
Newport, OR
800-551-6949
This beach is popular with surfers. Walk through a tunnel to get to the beach. According to the Oregon State Parks Division, many years ago Newport farmers led cattle westward through the tunnel to the ocean salt. Picnic tables and restrooms are available at this park. There is no day use fees. Dogs are allowed on the beach. They must be on a six foot or less leash at all times and people are required to clean up after their pets. On beaches located outside of Oregon

State Park boundaries, dogs might be allowed off-leash and under direct voice control, please look for signs or postings. This park is located off U.S. Highway 101, 1 mile north of Newport.

Beverly Beach State Park
Highway 101
Newport, OR
541-265-9278
To get to the beach, there is a walkway underneath the highway that leads to the ocean. Picnic tables, restrooms (including an ADA restroom), a walking trail and campgrounds are available at this park. There is a day use fee. Leashed dogs are allowed on the beach. Dogs are also allowed on the walking trail and campgrounds. They must be on a six foot or less leash at all times and people are required to clean up after their pets. On beaches located outside of Oregon State Park boundaries, dogs might be allowed off-leash and under direct voice control, please look for signs or postings. This park is located off U.S. Highway 101, 7 miles north of Newport.

Devils Punch Bowl State Natural Area
Highway 101
Newport, OR
800-551-6949
This is a popular beach for surfing. Picnic tables, restrooms and hiking are available at this park. There are no day use fees. Leashed dogs are allowed on the beach. Dogs are also allowed on hiking trails. They must be on a six foot or less leash at all times and people are required to clean up after their pets. On beaches located outside of Oregon State Park boundaries, dogs might be allowed off-leash and under direct voice control, please look for signs or postings. This park is located off U.S. Highway 101, 8 miles north of Newport.

South Beach State Park
Highway 101
Newport, OR
541-867-4715
This beach offers many recreational opportunities like beachcombing, fishing, windsurfing and crabbing. Picnic tables, restrooms (including an ADA restroom), hiking (including an ADA hiking trail), and campgrounds are available at this park. There is a day use fee. Leashed dogs are allowed on the beach. Dogs are also allowed on hiking trails and campgrounds. They must be on a six foot or less leash at all times and people are required to clean up after their pets. On beaches located outside of Oregon State Park boundaries, dogs might be allowed off-leash and under direct

voice control, please look for signs or postings. This park is located off U.S. Highway 101, 2 miles south of Newport.

Ontario Dog Travel Guide
Accommodations

Ontario

Best Western Inn & Suites
251 Goodfellow Street
Ontario, OR 97914
541-889-2600
There is a $50 refundable pet deposit.

Motel 6
275 NE 12th St
Ontario, OR 97914
541-889-6617
There are no pet fees. A well-behaved large dog is okay.

Pacific City Dog Travel Guide
Beaches

Pacific City

Bob Straub State Park
Highway 101
Pacific City, OR
800-551-6949
This is a nice stretch of beach to walk along. Picnic tables and restrooms (including an ADA restroom) are available at this park. There are no day use fees. Dogs are allowed on the beach. They must be on a six foot or less leash at all times and people are required to clean up after their pets. On beaches located outside of Oregon State Park boundaries, dogs might be allowed off-leash and under direct voice control, please look for signs or postings. This park is located off U.S. Highway 101 in Pacific City.

Cape Kiwanda State Natural Area
Highway 101
Pacific City, OR
800-551-6949
This beach and park is a good spot for marine mammal watching, hang gliding and kite flying. Picnic tables are available at this park. There are no day use fees. Dogs are allowed on the beach. They must be on a six foot or less leash at all times and people are required to clean up after their pets. On beaches located outside of Oregon State Park boundaries, dogs might be allowed off-leash and under direct voice control, please look

for signs or postings. This park is located off U.S. Highway 101, 1 mile north of Pacific City.

Pendleton Dog Travel Guide
Accommodations

Pendleton

Best Western Pendleton Inn
400 SE Nye Ave
Pendleton, OR 97801
541-276-2135
There is a $10 per day pet fee.

Holiday Inn Express
600 SE Nye Ave
Pendleton, OR 97801
541-966-6520
There is a $10 one time pet fee.

Motel 6
325 SE Nye Ave
Pendleton, OR 97801
541-276-3160
There are no additional pet fees. Pets must be attended at all times.

Port Orford Dog Travel Guide
Beaches

Port Orford

Cape Blanco State Park
Highway 101
Port Orford, OR
541-332-6774
Take a stroll on the beach or hike on over eight miles of trails which offer spectacular ocean vistas. Picnic tables, restrooms, hiking and campgrounds are available at this park. There is a minimal day use fee. Leashed dogs are allowed on the beach. Dogs are also allowed on hiking trails and campgrounds. They must be on a six foot or less leash at all times and people are required to clean up after their pets. On beaches located outside of Oregon State Park boundaries, dogs might be allowed off-leash and under direct voice control, please look for signs or postings. This park is located off U.S. Highway 101, 9 miles north of Port Orford.

Humbug Mountain State Park
Highway 101
Port Orford, OR
541-332-6774
This beach is frequented by windsurfers and

scuba divers. A popular activity at this park is hiking to the top of Humbug Mountain (elevation 1,756 feet) . Picnic tables, restrooms, hiking and campgrounds are available at this park. There is a minimal day use fee. Leashed dogs are allowed on the beach. Dogs are also allowed on hiking trails and campgrounds. They must be on a six foot or less leash at all times and people are required to clean up after their pets. On beaches located outside of Oregon State Park boundaries, dogs might be allowed off-leash and under direct voice control, please look for signs or postings. This park is located off U.S. Highway 101, 6 miles south of Port Orford.

Portland Dog Travel Guide
Accommodations

Portland

5th Avenue Suites
506 S.W. Washington
Portland, OR 97204
503-222-0001
Well-behaved dogs of all sizes are welcome at this pet-friendly hotel. The luxury boutique hotel offers both rooms and suites. Hotel amenities include complimentary evening wine service, and a 24 hour on-site fitness room. There are no pet fees, just sign a pet liability form.

Best Western Inn at the Meadows
1215 N Hayden Meadows Dr
Portland, OR 97217
503-286-9600
There is a $21.80 one time pet fee.

Comfort Inn
8855 SW Citizen Dr.
Portland, OR 97070`
503-682-9000
There is a pet fee of $10 per day.

Days Inn
9930 N Whitaker Rd
Portland, OR 97217
503-289-1800
There is a $15 one time pet fee.

Hotel Lucia
400 SW Broadway
Portland, OR 97205
503-228-7221
There is a $100 refundable pet deposit.

Hotel Vintage Plaza
422 SW Broadway

Portland, OR 97205
503-228-1212
Well-behaved dogs of all sizes are welcome at this pet-friendly hotel. The luxury boutique hotel offers both rooms and suites. Hotel amenities include complimentary evening wine service, complimentary high-speed Internet access in all guest rooms, 24 hour room service and an on-site fitness room. There are no pet fees, just sign a pet liability form.

Howard Johnson Hotel
7101 NE 82nd Ave.
Portland, OR 97220
503-255-6722
Dogs of all sizes are welcome. There is a $15 per day pet fee.

La Quinta Inn & Suites Portland Northwest
4319 NW Yeon
Portland, OR
503-497-9044
Dogs of all sizes are allowed at the hotel.

La Quinta Inn Portland - Lloyd
431 NE Multnomah
Portland, OR
503-233-7933
Dogs up to 75 pounds are allowed at the hotel.

Mallory Hotel
729 SW 15th
Portland, OR 97205
503-223-6311
There is a $10 one time fee for pets.

Motel 6
3104 SE Powell Blvd
Portland, OR 97202
503-238-0600
There are no pet fees. Pets must never be left alone in rooms.

Quality Inn Portland Airport
8247 NE Sandy Blvd.
Portland, OR 97220
503-256-4111
There is a pet fee of $15 per day.

Sheraton Portland Airport Hotel
8235 NE Airport Way
Portland, OR 97220
503-281-2500
Dogs of all sizes are allowed. There is a $25 one time per stay pet fee.

Sleep Inn
2261 NE 181st Ave.

Portland, OR 97230
503-618-8400
There is a pet fee of $10 per day, to a maximum of $50.

Staybridge Suites
11936 NE Glenn Widing Drive
Portland, OR 97220
503-262-8888
There is a $25 one time pet fee plus a pet fee of $10 per day.

Attractions

Portland

Portland Saturday Market
108 West Burnside
Portland, OR
503-222-6072
This is the largest outdoor arts and crafts market in continuous operation in the United States. It is also one of Portland's top tourist attractions. You will find over 350 artisans, live music and lots of food vendors. There are also many pet-related booths that sell anything from dog cookies, bandanas, and dog beds to waterproof fleece-lined dog coats. Well-behaved leashed dogs are allowed. This market is open Saturdays from 10am to 5pm and on Sundays from 11am to 4:30pm. The market is located between Front Avenue and SW 1st Avenue under the Burnside Bridge.

Portland Walking Tours
SW Broadway and Yamhill
Portland, OR 97205
503-774-4522
Take an award-winning guided outdoor walking tour of Portland. Their most popular tour is called The Best of Portland. This 2 to 2.5 hour morning tour features an overview of Portland including history, architecture, artwork, and more. The tour goes through downtown Portland, the Cultural District, Historic Yamhill and along the riverfront. Tours are held rain or shine on Friday, Saturday and Sunday at 10:30am and 3pm, from April through November. The cost is $15 per person and free for dogs and young children. At the beginning of the tour, the guide will ask if everyone is okay with dogs. If there is anyone in your tour that is uncomfortable around dogs, you might have to keep your pooch away from that person by staying on the other side of the group. The overwhelming majority of people on these tours are okay with dogs. All tours leave from the Pioneer Courthouse Square. Please note that

they strongly recommend reservations, even a week or two in advance.

The Grotto

NE 85th and Sandy Blvd.
Portland, OR 97294
503-254-7371
This is a 62 acre Catholic Shrine and botanical garden. While dogs are not allowed on the upper level, they are allowed outdoors on the first level, both in the plaza and in the botanical garden. The Grotto holds special events throughout the year, including a Blessing of the Animals each July. Well-behaved leashed dogs are allowed. The main public entrance to the Grotto is located on Sandy Blvd (Hwy 30) at Northeast 85th Avenue. It is near the junction of the I-205 and I-84 freeways just minutes from downtown Portland.

Parks

Portland

Chimney Dog Park

9360 N. Columbia Blvd
Portland, OR
503-823-7529
This entire 16-acre park is designated as an off-leash area. The park has meadows and trails but is not fenced and no water is available. The park is open year-round and is located next to the City Archives Building.

East Delta Park Off-Leash Area

N. Union Court
Portland, OR
503-823-7529
This 5 acre off-leash fenced field has trees and benches, but no water. It is open during the dry season only, from May through October. Dogs are allowed off-leash, but not on the sports fields. The park is located off exit 307 on I-5 across from the East Delta Sports Complex.

Gabriel Park and Off-Leash Area

SW 45 Ave and Vermont
Portland, OR
503-823-7529
This popular regional park offers trails, a natural area and picnic tables. Dogs are not allowed on the playgrounds, sports fields, tennis courts, or in the wetlands and creeks. They are allowed in the rest of the park but must be leashed, except for the designated off-leash area. There is a 1.5 acre fenced dog park that has trees, picnic tables and water. The dog park is only open during the dry season, from May through October.

Portland Rose Gardens

various locations
Portland, OR
503-823-7529
There are three main rose gardens in Portland. The International Rose Test Garden in Washington Park is one of the world's most famous rose gardens. It is a popular tourist site with great views and more than 8,000 roses. Ladd's Addition Rose Garden, located at SE 16th and Harrison, displays over 3,000 roses. The Peninsula Park Rose Garden, located at N. Ainsworth between Kerby and Albina, offers more than 8,800 fragrant roses. Dogs may accompany you to all of the rose gardens, but pets must be leashed and you are required to clean up after your dog.

Powell Butte Nature Park

SE 162nd Avenue and Powell Blvd
Portland, OR 97230
503-823-7529
This 592 acre park is an extinct volcano and is Portland's second largest park. There are over 9 miles of hiking trails which are popular with mountain bicyclists, horseback riders, and hikers. Dogs must be leashed and people must clean up after their dogs.

Tom McCall Waterfront Park

Naito Parkway
Portland, OR
503-823-7529
This waterfront park follows the Willamette River, between SW Clay and NW Glisan. The park offers walking and bicycling trails. Dogs are allowed but must be leashed and people need to clean up after their pets.

Washington Park

SW Park Place
Portland, OR 97210
503-823-7529
This 129 acre park offers hiking trails and a popular rose garden. Dogs must be leashed and people must clean up after their dogs.

West Delta Park Off-Leash Area

N. Expo Road & Broadacre
Portland, OR
503-823-7529
This 3 acre field is not fenced and there is no water available. It is open year-round but the ground gets soggy after heavy rains. Dogs are allowed off-leash. The park is located off exit 306B on I-5 next to the entrance to Portland International Raceway (PIR).

Restaurants

Portland

Baja Fresh Mexican Grill
1121 W. Burnside St.
Portland, OR
503-595-2252
This Mexican restaurant chain offers a variety of items on their menu including burritos, tacos, salads, quesadillas, fajitas, and enchiladas. Well-behaved leashed dogs are allowed at the outdoor tables.

Baja Fresh Mexican Grill
1505 NE 40th Ave
Portland, OR
503-331-1000
This Mexican restaurant chain offers a variety of items on their menu including burritos, tacos, salads, quesadillas, fajitas, and enchiladas. Well-behaved leashed dogs are allowed at the outdoor tables.

Bibo Juice
1445 NE Weidler St.
Portland, OR
503-288-5932
This juice bar offers a variety of smoothies and fruit juices. They also have nutritional supplements that can be added to the drinks. Well-behaved leashed dogs are allowed at the outdoor tables.

Dogs Dig Vegetarian Deli
212 NW Davis, Old Town Area
Portland, OR
503-223-3362
This small deli has a few outdoor tables. Well-behaved leashed dogs are allowed at the outdoor tables.

Garbonzo's
6341 S.W. Capitol Highway
Portland, OR 97201
503-293-7335
This Middle Eastern fast food restaurant has patio dining. Well-behaved leashed dogs are allowed at the outdoor tables.

Jake's Famous Crawfish
401 SW 12th Ave.
Portland, OR
at Stark St
503-226-1419
This seafood restaurant is part of the McCormick & Schmick's chain. Well-behaved leashed dogs

are allowed at the outdoor tables.

Lucky Labrador Brewing Co.
915 SE Hawthorne Blvd.
Portland, OR
503-236-3555
This dog-friendly brew pub has a labrador retriever as their mascot and on their beer labels. At the outside seating area, your pooch can relax at your feet while you unwind with some beer or food. The pub offers a nice variety of food including veggie and meat sandwiches, bentos (chicken or veggies over rice), soup and more. Of course, if you love beer, you will also have to try their ales like the Black Lab Stout, the Dog Day India Pale Ale or the Top Dog Extra Special Pale Ale. And if you visit during the month of October, don't miss their Dogtoberfest usually held on a Saturday. They celebrate the pub's anniversary on this day. The highlight of the day is the dog wash, which helps to raise money for dog-related causes or dog organizations. For treats, humans can try a special Dogtoberfest ale and doggies can get dog cookies and biscuits. The pub might even have a band for musical entertainment as well. Please keep pets leashed.

Lucky Labrador Public House
7675 SW Capitol Highway
Portland, OR
503-244-2537
This restaurant is a spin-off from the original Lucky Labrador Brewing Co. Dogs are welcome at the outdoor tables. The restaurant serves pizza, salads, and draught ale direct from their brewery in southeast Portland. They are located on Capitol Highway, near 31st Street. Please keep pets leashed.

McCormick and Schmick's Harborside Restaurant
309 SW Montgomery
Portland, OR
503-220-1865
This seafood restaurant is located in the RiverPlace Marina. Well-behaved leashed dogs are allowed at the outdoor tables.

Rubio's Fresh Mexican Grill
1307 NE 102nd Avenue
Portland, OR 97220
503-258-8340
This Mexican restaurant chain serves items like char-grilled steak and chicken burritos, tacos, quesadillas, seafood including lobster, shrimp, Mahi-Mahi, and their famous fish taco. Well-behaved leashed dogs are allowed at the outdoor tables.

The Divine Cafe
9th and SW Alder Street
Portland, OR
503-314-9606
This outdoor food vendor offers vegan and organic foods. There are a few outdoor seats. Well-behaved leashed dogs are allowed at the outdoor tables.

Vita Cafe
3024 NE Alberta
Portland, OR
503-335-8233
This natural food restaurant specializes in vegan dishes, but they also offer meat too. Organic foods and ingredients are used whenever possible. Well-behaved leashed dogs are allowed at the outdoor tables.

Wild Oats Natural Marketplace
3535 15th Ave.
Portland, OR
503-288-3414
This natural food market has a deli with outdoor seats. Well-behaved leashed dogs are allowed at the outdoor tables. They are located on 15th Avenue at Fremont.

Wild Oats Natural Marketplace
6344 SW Capitol Highway
Portland, OR
503-244-3110
This natural food market has a deli with a couple of outdoor seats. Well-behaved leashed dogs are allowed at the outdoor tables. The deli is located in the Hillsdale Shopping Center.

Wild Oats Natural Marketplace
2825 East Burnside Street
Portland, OR
503-232-6601
This natural food market has a deli with outdoor seats. Well-behaved leashed dogs are allowed at the outdoor tables.

Portland Area Dog Travel Guide
Accommodations

Gresham

Hawthorn Inn & Suites
2323 NE 181st Ave
Gresham, OR 97230
503-492-4000
There is a $10 per stay pet fee.

Lake Oswego

Crowne Plaza
14811 Kruse Oaks Dr
Lake Oswego, OR 97035
503-624-8400
There is a $10 per day pet fee.

Tigard

Motel 6
17950 SW McEwan Rd
Tigard, OR 97224
503-620-2066
There are no additional pet fees. Pets must not be left alone in rooms.

Tualatin

Sweetbrier Inn
7125 SW Nyberg
Tualatin, OR 97062
503-692-5800
There is a $25 refundable pet deposit for standard rooms, $50 for suites.

Wilsonville

Holiday Inn Select
25425 SW 95th Ave
Wilsonville, OR 97070
503-570-8500
There is a $10 per day pet fee.

Reedsport Dog Travel Guide
Accommodations

Reedsport

Economy Inn
1593 Highway Ave 101
Reedsport, OR 97467
541-271-3671
There is a $5 per day pet fee.

Rice Hill Dog Travel Guide
Accommodations

Rice Hill

Best Western Rice Hill Inn
621 John Long Rd
Rice Hill, OR 97462
541-849-2500

There is a $10 one time pet fee.

Rockaway Beach Dog Travel Guide
Beaches

Rockaway Beach

Manhattan Beach State Recreation Site
Highway 101
Rockaway Beach, OR
800-551-6949
The beach is a short walk from the parking area.
Picnic tables are available at this park. There are
no day use fees. Dogs are allowed on the beach.
They must be on a six foot or less leash at all
times and people are required to clean up after
their pets. On beaches located outside of Oregon
State Park boundaries, dogs might be allowed off-
leash and under direct voice control, please look
for signs or postings. This park is located off U.S.
Highway 101, 2 miles north of Rockaway Beach.

Roseburg Dog Travel Guide
Accommodations

Roseburg

Best Western Douglas Inn
511 SE Stephens
Roseburg, OR 97470
541-673-6625
There is a $6 per day additional pet fee.

Comfort Inn
1539 Mullholland Dr.
Roseburg, OR 97470
541-957-1100
There is a pet fee of $10 per day. All rooms are
non-smoking.

Holiday Inn Express
375 Harvard Blvd
Roseburg, OR 97470
541-673-7517
There is a $5 per day pet fee. Pets are allowed in
the first floor rooms only.

Motel 6
3100 NW Aviation
Roseburg, OR 97470
541-464-8000
There are no additional pet fees.

Sleep Inn & Suites
2855 NW Eden Bower Blvd.
Roseburg, OR 97470

541-464-8338
There is a pet fee of $7 per day.

Salem Dog Travel Guide
Accommodations

Salem

Holiday Inn Express
890 Hawthorne Ave SE
Salem, OR 97301
503-391-7000
There is a $15 one time pet fee.

Motel 6
1401 Hawthorne Ave NE
Salem, OR 97301
503-371-8024
There are no additional pet fees.

Phoenix Inn - Salem South
4370 Commercial St SE
Salem, OR 97302
503-588-9220
There is a $10 per day pet charge.

Red Lion Hotel
3301 Market St
Salem, OR 97301
503-370-7888
There is a $20 non-refundable pet fee.

Seaside Dog Travel Guide
Accommodations

Seaside

Best Western Ocean View Resort
414 N. Prom
Seaside, OR 97138
503-738-3334
There is a $15 per day pet fee. Pets are allowed
on the ground floor only.

Comfort Inn
545 Broadway Ave.
Seaside, OR 97138
503-738-3011
There is a pet fee of $7 per day.

Motel 6
2369 S Roosevelt (Hwy 101)
Seaside, OR 97138
503-738-6269
There are no additional pet fees.

Seaside Convention Center Inn
441 Second Ave
Seaside, OR 97138
503-738-9581
There is a $10.00 per day pet charge.

Beaches

Seaside

Del Rey Beach State Recreation Site
Highway 101
Seaside, OR
800-551-6949
There is a short trail to the beach. There is no day use fee. Dogs are allowed on the beach. They must be on a six foot or less leash at all times and people are required to clean up after their pets. On beaches located outside of Oregon State Park boundaries, dogs might be allowed off-leash and under direct voice control, please look for signs or postings. This park is located off U.S. Highway 101, 2 miles north of Gearhart.

Sisters Dog Travel Guide
Accommodations

Sisters

Comfort Inn
540 US 20 West
Sisters, OR 97759
541-549-7829
There is no pet fee. Pets may stay on the first floor only.

Springfield Dog Travel Guide
Accommodations

Springfield

Motel 6
3752 International Ct
Springfield, OR 97477
541-741-1105
There are no additional pet fees.

The Dalles Dog Travel Guide
Accommodations

The Dalles

Quality Inn Columbia River Gorge
2114 W. 6th
The Dalles, OR 97058

541-298-5161
There is a pet fee of $10 per day.

Tillamook Dog Travel Guide
Beaches

Tillamook

Cape Lookout State Park
Highway 101
Tillamook, OR
503-842-4981
This is a popular beach during the summer. The beach is a short distance from the parking area. It is located about an hour and half west of Portland. Picnic tables, restrooms (including an ADA restroom), hiking trails and campgrounds are available at this park. There is a $3 day use fee. Leashed dogs are allowed on the beach. Dogs are also allowed on hiking trails and campgrounds. They must be on a six foot or less leash at all times and people are required to clean up after their pets. On beaches located outside of Oregon State Park boundaries, dogs might be allowed off-leash and under direct voice control, please look for signs or postings. This park is located off U.S. Highway 101, 12 miles southwest of Tillamook.

Cape Meares State Scenic Viewpoint
Highway 101
Tillamook, OR
800-551-6949
The beach is located south of the scenic viewpoint. The viewpoint is situated on a headland, about 200 feet above the ocean. According to the Oregon State Parks Division, bird watchers can view the largest colony of nesting common murres (this site is one of the most populous colonies of nesting sea birds on the continent). Bald eagles and a peregrine falcon have also been known to nest near here. In winter and spring, this park is an excellent location for viewing whale migrations. Picnic tables, restrooms and hiking are available at this park. There are no day use fees. Leashed dogs are allowed on the beach. Dogs are also allowed on hiking trails. They must be on a six foot or less leash at all times and people are required to clean up after their pets. On beaches located outside of Oregon State Park boundaries, dogs might be allowed off-leash and under direct voice control, please look for signs or postings. This park is located off U.S. Highway 101, 10 miles west of Tillamook.

Troutdale Dog Travel Guide
Accommodations

Troutdale

Motel 6
1610 NW Frontage Rd
Troutdale, OR 97060
503-665-2254
There are no pet fees. One pet is allowed per room. Pets must be leashed when outside the room and cannot be left alone in the room.

Waldport Dog Travel Guide
Beaches

Waldport

Beachside State Recreation Site
Highway 101
Waldport, OR
541-563-3220
Enjoy miles of broad sandy beach at this park or stay at one of the campground sites that are located just seconds from the beach. Picnic tables, restrooms (including an ADA restroom), and hiking are also available at this park. There is a day use fees. Leashed dogs are allowed on the beach. Dogs are also allowed on hiking trails and campgrounds. They must be on a six foot or less leash at all times and people are required to clean up after their pets. On beaches located outside of Oregon State Park boundaries, dogs might be allowed off-leash and under direct voice control, please look for signs or postings. This park is located off U.S. Highway 101, 4 miles south of Waldport.

Governor Patterson Memorial State Recreation Site
Highway 101
Waldport, OR
800-551-6949
This park offers miles of flat, sandy beach. It is also an excellent location for whale watching. Picnic tables and restrooms are available at this park. There are no day use fees. Dogs are allowed on the beach. They must be on a six foot or less leash at all times and people are required to clean up after their pets. On beaches located outside of Oregon State Park boundaries, dogs might be allowed off-leash and under direct voice control, please look for signs or postings. This park is located off U.S. Highway 101, 1 mile south of Waldport.

Warrenton Dog Travel Guide
Accommodations

Warrenton

Shilo Inn
1609 E Harbor Drive
Warrenton, OR 97146
503-861-2181
There is a $10 per day pet fee.

Beaches

Warrenton

Fort Stevens State Park
Highway 101
Warrenton, OR
503-861-1671
There are miles of ocean beach. Picnic tables, restrooms (including an ADA restroom), hiking and campgrounds are available at this park. There is a $3 day use fee. Leashed dogs are allowed on the beach. Dogs are also allowed on hiking trails and campgrounds. They must be on a six foot or less leash at all times and people are required to clean up after their pets. On beaches located outside of Oregon State Park boundaries, dogs might be allowed off-leash and under direct voice control, please look for signs or postings. This park is located off U.S. Highway 101, 10 miles west of Astoria.

Woodburn Dog Travel Guide
Accommodations

Woodburn

La Quinta Inn & Suites Woodburn
120 Arney Road NE
Woodburn, OR
503-982-1727
Dogs of all sizes are allowed at the hotel.

Yachats Dog Travel Guide
Accommodations

Yachats

Adobe Resort
1555 US 101
Yachats, OR
541-547-3141
There is a $10 per day pet charge.

Shamrock Lodgettes
US 101
Yachats, OR 97498
541-547-3312
Pets are allowed in cabins only. There is an additional $5 per day charge. All units are non-smoking and have fireplaces.

The Fireside Inn
Hwy 101
Yachats, OR
800-336-3573
Located on the coast, the Fireside is a pet-friendly facility that encourages pet owners to bring their companions with them to enjoy time away together. Each pet is charged $7 per night which includes a "Pet Pack" complete with self-contained pooper scoopers, towels to dry off after a romp in the water, and sheets to protect furniture and bedding in the guest rooms. All rooms are non-smoking. They also have handicapped accessible units. Dogs may not be left alone in the rooms.

Beaches

Yachats

Neptune State Scenic Viewpoint
Highway 101
Yachats, OR
800-551-6949
During low tide at this beach you can walk south and visit a natural cave and tidepools. Or sit and relax at one of the picnic tables that overlooks the beach below. Restrooms (including an ADA restroom) are available at this park. There are no day use fees. Dogs are allowed on the beach. They must be on a six foot or less leash at all times and people are required to clean up after their pets. On beaches located outside of Oregon State Park boundaries, dogs might be allowed off-leash and under direct voice control, please look for signs or postings. This park is located off U.S. Highway 101,

Yachats State Recreation Area
Highway 101
Yachats, OR
800-551-6949
This beach is a popular spot for whale watching, salmon fishing, and exploring tidepools. Picnic tables and restrooms are available at this park. There are no day use fees. Dogs are allowed on the beach. They must be on a six foot or less leash at all times and people are required to clean up after their pets. On beaches located outside of Oregon State Park boundaries, dogs might be allowed off-leash and under direct voice control, please look for signs or postings. This park is located off U.S. Highway 101 in Yachats.

Chapter 17

Washington Dog-Friendly Travel Guide

Aberdeen Dog Travel Guide
Accommodations

Aberdeen

Red Lion Inn
521 W Wishkah
Aberdeen, WA
360-532-5210
There are no additional pet fees.

Anacortes Dog Travel Guide
Accommodations

Anacortes

Anacortes Inn
3006 Commercial Ave
Anacortes, WA 98221
360-293-3153
There is a $10 per night pet fee.

Fidalgo Country Inn
7645 St Route 20
Anacortes, WA 98221
360-293-3494
There is a $20 per day pet charge. There are 2 pet rooms.

Bainbridge Island Dog Travel Guide
Beaches

Bainbridge Island

Fay Bainbridge State Park
Sunset Drive NE
Bainbridge Island, WA
360-902-8844
This park is located on the northeast side of Bainbridge Island on Puget Sound. On a clear day, you can see Mt. Rainer and Mt. Baker from the beach. Picnic tables, restrooms and campgrounds are available at this park. Leashed dogs are allowed on the beach. Pets are not permitted on designated swimming beaches. However, there is usually a non-designated swimming beach area as well. Dogs are also allowed at the campgrounds. They must be on a eight foot or less leash at all times and people are required to clean up after their pets. To get there from From Poulsbo, take Hwy. 305 toward Bainbridge Island. Cross the Agate Pass Bridge. After three miles, come to stoplight and big brown sign with directions to park. Turn left at traffic light onto Day Rd. NE. Travel approximately two miles to a T-intersection. Turn left onto Sunrise Drive NE, and continue to park entrance, about two miles away.

Bellingham Dog Travel Guide
Accommodations

Bellingham

Holiday Inn Express
4160 Guide Meridian
Bellingham, WA 98226
360-671-4800
There is a $10 one time pet fee.

Motel 6
3701 Byron
Bellingham, WA 98225
360-671-4494
There are no additional pet fees.

Blaine Dog Travel Guide
Beaches

Blaine

Birch Bay State Park
Grandview
Blaine, WA
360-902-8844
This beach, located near the Canadian border, offers panoramic coastal views. Picnic tables, restrooms (including an ADA restroom), and campgrounds (including ADA campsites) are available at this park. Leashed dogs are allowed on the beach. Pets are not permitted on designated swimming beaches. However, there is usually a non-designated swimming beach area as well. Dogs are also allowed in the campgrounds. They must be on a eight foot or less leash at all times and people are required to clean up after their pets. This park is located 20 miles north of Bellingham and ten miles south of Blaine. From the south take exit #266 off of I-5. Go left on Grandview for seven miles, then right on Jackson for one mile, then turn left onto Helweg. From the north take exit #266 off of I-5, and turn right onto Grandview.

Centralia Dog Travel Guide
Accommodations

Centralia

Motel 6
1310 Belmont Ave
Centralia, WA 98531
360-330-2057
There are no additional pet fees.

Chehalis Dog Travel Guide
Accommodations

Chehalis

Howard Johnson Inn
122 Interstate Ave.
Chehalis, WA 98532
360-748-0101
Dogs of all sizes are welcome. There is a $10 one time pet fee.

Clarkston Dog Travel Guide
Accommodations

Clarkston

Motel 6
222 Bridge St
Clarkston, WA 99403
509-758-1631
There are no additional pet fees.

Copalis Beach Dog Travel Guide
Accommodations

Copalis Beach

Iron Springs Ocean Beach Resort
P. O. Box 207
Copalis Beach, WA 98535
360-276-4230
Iron Springs is a 100 acre resort on the Washington Coast located halfway between Copalis and Pacific Beach. They offer individual cottages with fireplaces and great ocean views. The cottages are nestled among the rugged spruce trees on a low lying bluff overlooking the Pacific Ocean. They are located near miles of sandy beaches. There is a $12.00 per day charge for pets. There are no designated smoking or non-smoking cabins. They are located 130 miles from Seattle and 160 miles from Portland.

Beaches

Copalis Beach

Griffith-Priday State Park
State Route 109
Copalis Beach, WA
360-902-8844
This beach extends from the beach through low dunes to a river and then north to the river's mouth. Picnic tables and restrooms are available at this park. Dogs are allowed on the beach. They must be on a eight foot or less leash at all times and people are required to clean up after their pets. This park is located 21 miles northwest of Hoquiam. From Hoquiam, go north on SR 109 for 21 miles. At Copalis Beach, at the sign for Benner Rd., turn left (west).

Des Moines Dog Travel Guide
Beaches

Des Moines

Saltwater State Park
Marine View Drive
Des Moines, WA
360-902-8844
This state beach is located on Puget Sound, halfway between the cities of Tacoma and Seattle (near the Sea-Tac international airport). Picnic tables, restrooms and campgrounds are available at this park. Leashed dogs are allowed on the beach. Pets are not permitted on designated swimming beaches. However, there is usually a non-designated swimming beach area as well. Dogs are also allowed at the campgrounds. They must be on a eight foot or less leash at all times and people are required to clean up after their pets. To get there from the north, take exit #149 off of I-5. Go west, then turn south on Hwy. 99 (sign missing). Follow the signs into the park. Turn right on 240th at the Midway Drive-in. Turn left on Marine View Dr. and turn right into the park.

Everett Dog Travel Guide
Accommodations

Everett

Holiday Inn
101 128th St SE
Everett, WA 98208
425-337-2900
There is a $50 one time pet fee.

Motel 6
224 128th St SW
Everett, WA 98204

425-353-8120
There are no additional pet fees.

Federal Way Dog Travel Guide
Accommodations

Federal Way

La Quinta Inn & Suites Federal Way
32124 25th Avenue South
Federal Way, WA
253-529-4000
Dogs of all sizes are allowed at the hotel.

Beaches

Federal Way

Dash Point State Park
Dash Point Rd.
Federal Way, WA
360-902-8844
This beach offers great views of Puget Sound. Picnic tables, restrooms, 11 miles of hiking trails and campgrounds are available at this park. Leashed dogs are allowed on the beach. Pets are not permitted on designated swimming beaches. However, there is usually a non-designated swimming beach area as well. Dogs are also allowed on hiking trails and campgrounds. They must be on a eight foot or less leash at all times and people are required to clean up after their pets. This park is located on the west side of Federal Way in the vicinity of Seattle. From Highway 5, exit at the 320th St. exit (exit #143). Take 320th St. west approximately four miles. When 320th St. ends at a T-intersection, make a right onto 47th St. When 47th St. ends at a T-intersection, turn left onto Hwy. 509/ Dash Point Rd. Drive about two miles to the park. (West side of street is the campground side, and east side is the day-use area.)

Forks Dog Travel Guide
Accommodations

Forks

Kalaloch Ocean Lodge
157151 Hwy. 101
Forks, WA 98331
360-962-2271
Perched on a bluff, overlooking the Pacific Ocean, sits the Kalaloch Lodge located in Olympic National Park. The Olympic National Forest is also located nearby. Dogs are not allowed in the lodge, but they are welcome in the cabins. This resort offers over 40 cabins and half of them have ocean views. There are no designated smoking or non-smoking cabins. Thanks to one of our readers who writes "This is a great place where you can rent cabins situated on a bluff overlooking the Pacific Ocean. Great for watching storms pound the beaches and walking wide sand beaches at low tide. Near rain forest with wooded hikes and lakes throughout. Not all units allow dogs, but you can still get a good view." There is a $12.50 per day pet fee.

Gig Harbor Dog Travel Guide
Accommodations

Gig Harbor

Best Western Wesley Inn of Gig Harbor
6575 Kimball
Gig Harbor, WA 98335
253-858-9690
There is a $10 per day additional pet fee.

Grayland Dog Travel Guide
Beaches

Grayland

Grayland Beach State Park
Highway 105
Grayland, WA
360-902-8844
This 412 acre park offers beautiful ocean frontage and full hookup campsites (including ADA campsites). Leashed dogs are allowed on the beach. Dogs are also allowed at the campgrounds. They must be on a eight foot or less leash at all times and people are required to clean up after their pets. This park is located five miles south of Westport. From Aberdeen, drive 22 miles on Highway 105 south to Grayland. Traveling through the town, watch for park signs.

Hood River Dog Travel Guide
Accommodations

White Salmon

Inn of the White Salmon
172 W Jewett
White Salmon, WA 98672
509-493-2335

There is a $10 per day pet fee. All rooms are non-smoking.

Ilwaco Dog Travel Guide
Beaches

Ilwaco

Fort Canby State Park
Highway 101
Ilwaco, WA
360-902-8844
This park offers 27 miles of ocean beach and 7 miles of hiking trails. Enjoy excellent views of the ocean, Columbia River and two lighthouses. Picnic tables, restrooms (including an ADA restroom), hiking and campgrounds (includes ADA campsites) are available at this park. Leashed dogs are allowed on the beach. Dogs are also allowed on hiking trails and campgrounds. They must be on a eight foot or less leash at all times and people are required to clean up after their pets. This park is located two miles southwest of Ilwaco. From Seattle, Take I-5 south to Olympia, SR 8 west to Montesano. From there, take U.S. Hwy. 101 south to Long Beach Peninsula.

Kelso Dog Travel Guide
Accommodations

Kelso

Motel 6
106 Minor Rd
Kelso, WA 98626
360-425-3229
There are no additional pet fees.

Kennewick Dog Travel Guide
Accommodations

Kennewick

La Quinta Inn & Suites Kennewick
4220 West 27th Place
Kennewick, WA
509-736-3326
Dogs of all sizes are allowed at the hotel.

Richland

Red Lion Hotel
802 George Washington Way
Richland, WA 99352

509-946-7611
There are no additional pet fees.

Royal Hotel
1515 George Washington Way
Richland, WA 99352
509-946-4121
There is a $25 one time pet fee.

Kent Dog Travel Guide
Accommodations

Kent

Howard Johnson Inn
1233 North Central
Kent, WA 98032
253-852-7224
Dogs of all sizes are welcome. There is a $10 per day pet fee.

La Quinta Inn Kent
25100 74th Avenue South
Kent, WA
253-520-6670
Dogs of all sizes are allowed at the hotel.

Leavenworth Dog Travel Guide
Accommodations

Leavenworth

Howard Johnson Express Inn
405 Hwy 2
Leavenworth, WA 98826
509-548-4326
Dogs up to 75 pounds are allowed. There is a $12 per day pet fee. Pets may not be left unattended in the rooms.

Lopez Island Dog Travel Guide
Beaches

Lopez Island

Spencer Spit State Park
Bakerview Road
Lopez Island, WA
360-902-8844
Located in the San Juan Islands, this lagoon beach offers great crabbing, clamming and beachcombing. Picnic tables, restrooms, campgrounds and 2 miles of hiking trails are available at this park. Leashed dogs are allowed on the beach. Pets are not permitted on

designated swimming beaches. However, there is usually a non-designated swimming beach area as well. Dogs are also allowed on hiking trails and campgrounds. They must be on a eight foot or less leash at all times and people are required to clean up after their pets. This park is located on Lopez Island in the San Juan Islands. It is a 45-minute Washington State Ferry ride from Anacortes. Dogs are allowed on the ferry. Once on Lopez Island, follow Ferry Rd. Go left at Center Rd., then left at Cross Rd. Turn right at Port Stanley and left at Bakerview Rd. Follow Bakerview Rd. straight into park. For ferry rates and schedules, call 206-464-6400.

Mercer Island Dog Travel Guide
Parks

Mercer Island

Luther Burbank Park
2040 84th Avenue SE
Mercer Island, WA
206-205-7532
This 77 acre park offers great views of Lake Washington and is popular for boating and fishing. There are almost 3 miles of walking paths. Dogs on leash are allowed. There is also a special off-leash area for dogs located at the north end of the park. To get there from I-5, take I-90 East to Mercer Island and take the Island Crest Way exit (#7). At the top of the ramp, turn right on SE 26th Street. At the stop sign turn left on 84th Avenue SE and drive straight to the park after another stop sign at SE 24th Street.

Moclips Dog Travel Guide
Accommodations

Moclips

Ocean Crest Resort
4651 SR 109
Moclips, WA 98562
360-276-4465
There is a $15 per day pet fee. Pets are allowed in some of the units. All rooms are non-smoking.

Moses Lake Dog Travel Guide
Accommodations

Moses Lake

Best Western Hallmark Inn & Conf Center
3000 Marina Dr

Moses Lake, WA 98837
509-765-9211
There are no additional pet fees.

Motel 6
2822 Wapato Dr
Moses Lake, WA 98837
509-766-0250
There are no additional pet fees.

Mount Baker - Glacier Dog Travel Guide
Accommodations - Vacation Home Rentals

Glacier

Mt. Baker Lodging
7463 Mt. Baker Highway
Glacier, WA 98244
360-599-2453
Private vacation rental homes located at the gateway to Mt. Baker. There are a wide variety of rental homes to choose, from honeymoon getaways and family cabins, to accommodations for group retreats and family reunions. All properties are privately owned, unique and completely self-contained.

Mount Vernon Dog Travel Guide
Accommodations

Mount Vernon

Best Western College Way Inn
300 W College Way
Mount Vernon, WA 98273
360-424-4287
There is a $10 per day additional pet fee.

Best Western CottonTree Inn
2300 Market Place
Mount Vernon, WA 98273
360-428-5678
There is a $10 per day additional pet fee. Pets are allowed on the first floor rooms only.

North Cascades National Park Dog Travel Guide
Parks

Newhalem

North Cascades National Park
State Route 20
Newhalem, WA
360-856-5700

Dogs are allowed on one of the hiking trails, the Pacific Crest Trail. This scenic hiking trail runs through the park and is rated moderate to difficult. The trail is located off Highway 20, about one mile east of Rainy Pass. At the Bridge Creek Trailhead, park on the north side of the highway and then hike north (uphill) or south (downhill). A Northwest Forest Pass is required to park at the trailhead. The cost is about $5 and can be purchased at the Visitor's Center in Newhalem. For a larger variety of trails, including a less strenuous hike, dogs are also allowed on trails at the adjacent Ross Lake National Recreation Area and the Lake Chelan National Recreation Area. Both recreation areas are managed by the national park.

Oak Harbor Dog Travel Guide
Accommodations

Oak Harbor

Best Western Harbor Place
33175 SR20
Oak Harbor, WA 98277
360-679-4567
There is a $15 per day additional pet fee.

Beaches

Oak Harbor

Fort Ebey State Park
Hill Valley Drive
Oak Harbor, WA
360-902-8844
This 600+ acre park is popular for hiking and camping, but also offers a saltwater beach. Picnic tables and restrooms (including an ADA restroom) are available at this park. Leashed dogs are allowed on the saltwater beach. Dogs are also allowed on hiking trails and campgrounds. They must be on a eight foot or less leash at all times and people are required to clean up after their pets. To get to the park from Seattle, take exit #189 off of I-5, just south of Everett. Follow signs for the Mukilteo/ Clinton ferry. Take the ferry to Clinton on Whidbey Island. Dogs are allowed on the ferry. Once on Whidbey Island, follow Hwy. 525 north, which becomes Hwy. 20. Two miles north of Coupeville, turn left on Libbey Rd. and follow it 1.5 miles to Hill Valley Dr. Turn left and enter park.

Joseph Whidbey State Park
Swantown Rd

Oak Harbor, WA
360-902-8844
This 112 acre park offers one of the best beaches on Whidbey Island. Picnic tables, restrooms, and several miles of hiking trails (including a half mile ADA hiking trail) are available at this park. Leashed dogs are allowed on the beach. Pets are not permitted on designated swimming beaches. However, there is usually a non-designated swimming beach area as well. Dogs are also allowed on hiking trails. They must be on a eight foot or less leash at all times and people are required to clean up after their pets. To get there from the south, drive north on Hwy. 20. Just before Oak Harbor, turn left on Swantown Rd. and follow it about three miles.

Ocean Park Dog Travel Guide
Accommodations

Ocean Park

Coastal Cottages of Ocean Park
1511 264th Place
Ocean Park, WA 98640
360-665-4658
The cottages are located in a quiet setting and have full kitchens and fireplaces. There is a $5 per day pet charge. There are no designated smoking or non-smoking rooms.

Beaches

Ocean Park

Pacific Pines State Park
Highway 101
Ocean Park, WA
360-902-8844
Fishing, crabbing, clamming and beachcombing are popular activities at this beach. Picnic tables and a restroom are available at this park. Dogs are allowed on the beach. They must be on a eight foot or less leash at all times and people are required to clean up after their pets. This park is located approximately one mile north of Ocean Park. From north or south, take Hwy. 101 until you reach Ocean Park. Continue on Vernon St. until you reach 271st St.

Ocean Shores Dog Travel Guide
Accommodations

Ocean Shores

The Polynesian Condominium Resort
615 Ocean Shores Blvd
Ocean Shores, WA 98569
360-289-3361
There is a $15 per day fee for pets. Pets are allowed on the ground floor only.

Beaches

Ocean Shores

Damon Point State Park
Point Brown Avenue
Ocean Shores, WA
360-902-8844
Located on the southeastern tip of the Ocean Shores Peninsula, this one mile long beach offers views of the Olympic Mountains, Mount Rainer, and Grays Harbor. Picnic tables are available at this park. Dogs are allowed on the beach. They must be on a eight foot or less leash at all times and people are required to clean up after their pets. To get there from From Hoquiam, take SR 109 and SR 115 to Point Brown Ave. in the town of Ocean Shores. Proceed south on Point Brown Ave. through town, approximately 4.5 miles. Just past the marina, turn left into park entrance.

Ocean City State Park
State Route 115
Ocean Shores, WA
360-902-8844
Beachcombing, clamming, surfing, bird watching, kite flying and winter storm watching are all popular activities at this beach. Picnic tables, restrooms, and campgrounds (including ADA campgrounds) are available at this park. Leashed dogs are allowed on the beach. Dogs are also allowed at the campgrounds. They must be on a eight foot or less leash at all times and people are required to clean up after their pets. This park is located on the coast one-and-a-half miles north of Ocean Shores on Hwy. 115. From Hoquiam, drive 16 miles west on SR 109, then turn south on SR 115 and drive 1.2 miles to the park.

Olympia Dog Travel Guide
Accommodations

Olympia

West Coast Inn
2300 Evergreen Park Drive
Olympia, WA 98502
360-943-4000
There is a $45.00 one time pet fee.

Tumwater

Best Western Tumwater Inn
5188 Capitol Blvd
Tumwater, WA 98501
360-956-1235
There is a $5 per day additional pet fee.

Motel 6
400 W Lee St
Tumwater, WA 98501
360-754-7320
There are no additional pet fees.

Olympic National Park Dog Travel Guide
Attractions

Port Angeles

Olympic National Park
600 East Park Avenue
Port Angeles, WA
360-565-3130
Pets are not permitted on park trails, meadows, beaches or in any undeveloped area of the park. There is one exception. Dogs are allowed on leash, during daytime hours only, on Kalaloch Beach along the Pacific Ocean and from Rialto Beach north to Ellen Creek. For those folks and dogs who want to hike on a trail, try the adjacent dog-friendly Olympic National Forest.

Parks

Olympia

Olympic National Forest
1835 Black Lake Blvd. SW
Olympia, WA 98512
360-956-2402
Leashed dogs are allowed on the national forest trails. Of particular interest is the Mt. Mueller Trail which offers great views of the Strait of Juan de Fuca and the mountains. Maps for this 13 mile loop trail and other trails can be picked up for free at a Forest Ranger Station including the one located at 551 Forks Avenue South, Forks, Washington.

Pacific Beach Dog Travel Guide
Accommodations

Pacific Beach

Sandpiper Ocean Beach Resort

4159 State Route 109
Pacific Beach, WA 98571
360-276-4580
Thanks to one of our readers who writes "A great place on the Washington Coast with miles of sand beach to run." There is a $10 per day pet fee. All rooms are non-smoking.

Beaches

Pacific Beach

Pacific Beach State Park
State Route 109
Pacific Beach, WA
360-902-8844
The beach is the focal point at this 10 acre state park. This sandy ocean beach is great for beachcombing, wildlife watching, windy walks and kite flying. Picnic tables, restrooms (including an ADA restroom), and campgrounds (some are ADA accessible) are available at this park. Leashed dogs are allowed on the beach. Dogs are also allowed in the campgrounds. They must be on a eight foot or less leash at all times and people are required to clean up after their pets. This park is located 15 miles north of Ocean Shores, off SR 109. From Hoquiam, follow SR 109, 30 miles northwest to the town of Pacific Beach. The park is located in town.

Port Angeles Dog Travel Guide
Beaches

Port Angeles

Kalaloch Beach
Olympic National Park
Port Angeles, WA
360-962-2283
Dogs are allowed on leash, during daytime hours only, on Kalaloch Beach along the Pacific Ocean and from Rialto Beach north to Ellen Creek. These beaches are in Olympic National Park, but please note that pets are not permitted on this national park's trails, meadows, beaches (except Kalaloch and Rialto beaches) or in any undeveloped area of the park. For those folks and dogs who want to hike on a trail, try the adjacent dog-friendly Olympic National Forest. Kalaloch Beach is located off Highway 101 in Olympic National Park.

Poulsbo Dog Travel Guide
Accommodations

Poulsbo

Holiday Inn Express
19801 7th Avenue NE
Poulsbo, WA 98370
360-697-4400
There is a $10 one time pet fee.

Pullman Dog Travel Guide
Accommodations

Pullman

Holiday Inn Express
1190 SE Bishop Blvd
Pullman, WA 99163
509-334-4437
There are no additional pet fees. Pets are allowed in the first floor rooms.

Richland Dog Travel Guide
Accommodations

Richland

Motel 6
1751 Fowler St
Richland, WA 99352
509-783-1250
There are no additional pet fees.

San Juan Island Dog Travel Guide
Accommodations

Friday Harbor

Blair House Bed and Breakfast
345 Blair Street
Friday Harbor, WA 98250
360-378-5907
Blair House is located in Friday Harbor, Washington on San Juan Island, just five short blocks from the ferry landing. The two acre grounds are wooded and landscaped. The Blair House Cottage is 800 square feet of private living where you, your children and your pets are welcome. You will need to take a car ferry to the island.

The Inn at Friday Harbor

Friday Harbor, WA 98250
360-378-4000
There is a $50.00 one time pet fee. You need to

take a car ferry to the island

Attractions

Friday Harbor

San Juan Island National Historic Park
125 Spring Street
Friday Harbor, WA
360-378-2902
Leashed dogs are welcome on the hiking trails. Some of the trails are self-guided tours of the area and buildings. Dogs on leash are also allowed at South Beach, which is located at the American Camp. Dogs are not allowed inside the Visitor's Center.

Beaches

Friday Harbor

South Beach
125 Spring Street
Friday Harbor, WA
360-378-2902
Dogs on leash are allowed at South Beach, which is located at the American Camp in the San Juan Island National Historic Park..

Seattle Dog Travel Guide
Accommodations

Seattle

Alexis Hotel
1007 First Avenue
Seattle, WA 98104
206-624-4844
Well-behaved dogs up to 200 pounds are welcome at this pet-friendly hotel. The luxury boutique hotel offers both rooms and suites. Hotel amenities include complimentary evening wine service, 24 hour room service and an on-site fitness room. This hotel is located near the historic Pioneer Square and Pike's Place Market. There are no pet fees, just sign a pet liability form.

Crowne Plaza - Downtown
1113 6th Ave
Seattle, WA 98101
206-464-1980
There is a $75 refundable pet deposit. Dogs up to 75 pounds are allowed.

Hotel Monaco Seattle

1101 4th Avenue
Seattle, WA 98101
206-621-1770
Well-behaved dogs of all sizes are welcome at this pet-friendly hotel. The luxury boutique hotel offers both rooms and suites. Hotel amenities include complimentary evening wine service, complimentary high speed Internet access in all guest rooms, 24 hour room service and a 24 hour on-site fitness room. There are no pet fees, just sign a pet liability form.

Hotel Vintage Park
1100 Fifth Avenue
Seattle, WA 98101
206-624-8000
Well-behaved dogs of all sizes are welcome at this pet-friendly hotel. The luxury boutique hotel offers both rooms and suites. Hotel amenities include complimentary evening wine service, complimentary high speed Internet access, and 24 hour room service. There are no pet fees, just sign a pet liability form.

La Quinta Inn & Suites Seattle
2224 Eighth Ave.
Seattle, WA
206-624-6820
Dogs of all sizes are allowed at the hotel.

La Quinta Inn Sea-Tac - Seattle
2824 S 188th St
Seattle, WA
206-241-5211
Dogs of all sizes are allowed at the hotel.

Motel 6
20651 Military Rd
Seattle, WA 98198
206-824-9902
There are no additional pet fees. One well-behaved pet per room is permitted.

Motel 6 - Airport
18900 47th Ave S
Seattle, WA 98188
206-241-1648
There are no additional pet fees.

Pensione Nichols Bed and Breakfast
1923 1st Avenue
Seattle, WA 98101
206-441-7125
Thanks to one of our readers who writes: "A charming and very dog-friendly place to stay in downtown Seattle." Large dogs are allowed to stay here if they are well-behaved. This B&B also requires that you do not leave your dog in the

room alone. The Pensione Nichols is the only bed-and-breakfast located in the retail and entertainment core of downtown Seattle. Housed in a remodeled, turn-of-the-century building in the historic Smith Block, Pensione Nichols overlooks the Pike Place Market. This B&B has 10 guest rooms and suites (the suites have private bathrooms). Rates are approximately $75 (guest rooms) to $175 (suites). During the summer, there is a 2 night minimum.

Residence Inn Seattle Downtown
800 Fairview Ave N
Seattle, WA 98109
206-624-6000
There is a $10 per day pet charge.

The Sheraton Seattle Hotel and Towers
1400 Sixth Avenue
Seattle, WA 98101
206-621-9000
Dogs up to 80 pounds are allowed. There are no additional pet fees. You must sign a pet waiver.

Vagabond Inn by the Space Needle
325 Aurora Ave N
Seattle, WA 98109
206-441-0400
This motel is located just several blocks from the Space Needle, the waterfront and Washington St. Convention Center. The motel has a heated swimming pool and jacuzzi, 24 hour cable television and more. There is a $10 per day pet charge

W Seattle
1112 Fourth Avenue
Seattle, WA 98101
206-264-6000
Dogs of any size are allowed. There is a $25 per day additional pet fee.

Attractions

Kenmore

Kenmore Air Seaplanes
6321 Northeast 175th
Kenmore, WA 98028
800-543-9595
Well-behaved, leashed dogs are allowed on these seaplanes. Small dogs can sit on your lap. For larger dogs, you will need to purchase an extra seat. To board the seaplanes, you will need to walk up a step ladder. Since seaplanes are usually noisier inside than large commercial airplanes, the staff or pilot usually hands out

earplugs to help keep the noise down. Seaplanes fly lower than commercial airliners and therefore you are able to see a lot more sights than if you where flying at over at 30,000 feet. They offer many scheduled flight routes to or from Seattle including the San Juan Islands, Oak Harbor, Victoria and Vancouver. Or you and your pooch can try the 20 minute sightseeing tour of Seattle. Charter packages are also available. For trips to or from Canada, customs regulations apply. You can hop aboard their seaplanes at the Kenmore Air Harbor at 6321 N 175th Street in Kenmore, or at the Lake Union Terminal at 950 Westlake Avenue in Seattle.

Seattle

Emerald Country Carriages
Piers 55-56
Seattle, WA
425-868-0621
Emerald Country Carriages allows well-behaved dogs on their elegant horse and carriage rides. They offer both open and closed carriages which seat up to six. The standard tour includes the waterfront and Pioneer Square. You can catch one of their white and burgundy carriages on the waterfront, between Piers 55 and 56. The cost is about $35 for a standard 30 minute tour and an extra $10 if you make a reservation in advance.

Pike Place Market
First and Pike
Seattle, WA
206-682-7453
The popular Pike Place Market is a historic area that covers nine acres, has about 15 residential and retail buildings, and gets about nine million visitors per year. This marketplace offers fresh seafood (watch out for flying fish!), vegetables, fruit, flowers, cafes, shops, artists, street performers and more. The place might look familiar if you have seen the movie, "Sleepless in Seattle," which was filmed at this marketplace. Canines are welcome at the marketplace, but are not allowed inside the food stores or cafes.

Pioneer Square
First Street and Yesler Way
Seattle, WA

Pioneer Square is Seattle's oldest neighborhood. It is preserved as a National Historic District. Please note that dogs are not allowed on the Underground Tour at Pioneer Square. In this district, you can stroll through the area and see the historic buildings, or better yet, take an elegant horse and carriage ride from Emerald Country Carriages.

Seattle Center
Mercer Street and Broad St.
Seattle, WA
206-684-7200
The Seattle Center is a 74 acre urban park which was home to the 1962 World Fair. While your pooch cannot go into the buildings, he or she is allowed to walk around the center with you and spot out several points of interest. The famed Seattle Space Needle resides at the center and is always a good photo opportunity. You and your pooch can also visit the Sculpture Garden and watch jugglers, musicians, face painters, and more. Pets must be on leash. If you have a doggie that happens to be under 20 pounds, you can even carry him or her on the Seattle Monorail.

Washington State Ferries
Pier 52
Seattle, WA
206-464-6400
The Washington State Ferries is the nation's largest ferry system and the state's number one tourist attraction. This ferry service offers many ferry routes, including Seattle to Bainbridge Island, Seattle to Bremerton, Edmonds to Kingston, Anacortes to Friday Harbor (San Juan Islands), and Anacortes to Sidney in British Columbia, Canada. Please see our Washington State Ferry listing in our Victoria, British Columbia, Canada City Guide for customs requirements for both people and dogs. While leashed dogs are allowed on the ferry routes mentioned above, the following pet regulations apply. On the newer ferries that have outside stairwells, dogs are allowed on the car deck and on the outdoor decks above the car deck. If the ferry has indoor stairwells, dogs are only allowed on the deck where they boarded the ferry. For example, if your dog comes onto the ferry in your car, he or she has to remain on the car deck. If you walk onto the ferry with your dog, your pooch is allowed on the outside deck where you boarded but cannot go onto other decks. In cases where your pet has to remain on the car deck, you can venture to the above decks without your pet to get food at the snack bars. However, the ferry system recommends in general that you stay with your pooch in the car. For any of the ferries, dogs are not allowed inside the ferry terminals. Ferry prices for people and autos are determined by the route and peak times, but in general tickets for people can start under $10 round trip, and more for autos. Dogs ride free!

Beaches

Seattle

Sand Point Magnuson Park Dog Off-Leash Beach and Area
7400 Sand Point Way NE
Seattle, WA
206-684-4075
This leash free dog park covers about 9 acres and is the biggest fully fenced off-leash park in Seattle. It also offers an access point to the lake where your pooch is welcome to take a dip in the fresh lake water. To find the dog park, take Sand Point Way Northeast and enter the park at Northeast 74th Street. Go straight and park near the playground and sports fields. The main gate to the off-leash area is located at the southeast corner of the main parking lot. Dogs must be leashed until you enter the off-leash area.

Parks

Seattle

Discovery Park
3801 W. Government Way
Seattle, WA
206-386-4236
Discovery Park is located northwest of downtown Seattle. It has over 500 acres and is the city's largest park. It offers views of both the Olympic and Cascade mountain ranges. Dogs on leash are allowed on about 7 miles of trails except for beaches, ponds, wetlands and the Wolf Tree Nature Trail.

Sand Point Magnuson Park
7400 Sand Point Way NE
Seattle, WA
206-684-4075
The park is northeast of Seattle and is located across the lake from the city of Kirkland. This park has about 350 acres and is Seattle's second largest park. You will find over four miles of walking trails along Lake Washington, through grassy fields, trees and brush. Dogs are not allowed in the water at Lake Washington, except at the off-leash area.

Sand Point Magnuson Park Dog Off-Leash Area
7400 Sand Point Way NE
Seattle, WA
206-684-4946
This leash free dog park covers about 9 acres and is the biggest fully fenced off-leash park in

Seattle. It also offers an access point to the lake where your pooch is welcome to take a dip in the fresh lake water. To find the dog park, take Sand Point Way Northeast and enter the park at Northeast 74th Street. Go straight and park near the playground and sports fields. The main gate to the off-leash area is located at the southeast corner of the main parking lot. Dogs must be leashed until you enter the off-leash area.

Restaurants

Seattle

Il Bistro
93A Pike Street
Seattle, WA
206-682-3040
This Italian restaurant, located in Pike Place Market, has three outdoor tables where your well-behaved dog can lay next to you. The dinner menu includes seafood specials, pasta and more.

Ivar's Salmon House
401 NE Northlake Way
Seattle, WA
206-632-0767
There are several different outdoor areas where they serve food, and dogs are only allowed at the Fish Bar area.

Lombardi's Cucina
2200 N.W. Market Street
Seattle, WA 98107
206-783-0055
This restaurant offers traditional Italian cuisine. Well-behaved dogs are allowed at the outdoor tables. If they are busy, they will try to find a spot away from the crowd for your pooch.

Madison Park Cafe
1807 42nd Ave East
Seattle, WA
206-324-2626
Well-behaved, leashed dogs can accompany you to the outdoor tables at this French bistro. The restaurant is open on the weekends for brunch and Tuesday through Saturday for dinner. The dinner menu includes entrees like Lemon Parsley Raviolis, Lavender Honey Marinated Rack of Lamb, duck, and steak. Prices start at about $15 per entree.

Maggie Bluff's Marina Grill
2601 W. Marina Place
Seattle, WA
206-283-8322

This restaurant, open for breakfast and lunch, serves hamburgers, salads, pastas, and more. Dogs are allowed at the outdoor tables. Heaters are usually available.

McCormick and Schmick's
1200 Westlake Avenue North
Seattle, WA
206-270-9052
This restaurant is located on Lake Union and offers a variety of seafood. Enjoy views of downtown Seattle and Lake Union. Dogs are allowed at the outdoor tables on the lakeside deck.

Portage Bay Cafe
4140 Roosevelt Way NE
Seattle, WA 98105
206-547-8230
Open for breakfast and lunch, this cafe allows dogs are their outdoor tables. A children's menu is available.

Sister's Cafe
Pike Place Market
Seattle, WA
206-623-6723
Located in Pike Place Market, this cafe serves sandwiches and more. Dogs are allowed at the outdoor tables.

Stores

Seattle

Three Dog Bakery
1408 1st Avenue
Seattle, WA
206-364-9999
You can purchase all kinds of fresh home-made treats for your pooch at this dog cookie bakery.

Transportation Systems

Seattle

King County Metro
Regional
Seattle, WA
206-553-3000
Both small and large dogs are allowed on the street cars and buses. Small dogs that fit in their owner's lap ride for free. Large dogs are charged the same fare as their owner and should not occupy a seat. Large dogs should ride on the floor of the bus, preferably under the seat. If you

have a very large dog, it is up to the driver as to whether or not your dog will be allowed. One large dog per bus is allowed. Dogs must be leashed.

Seattle Area Dog Travel Guide
Accommodations

Issaquah

Motel 6
1885 15th Pl NW
Issaquah, WA 98027
425-392-8405
There are no additional pet fees.

Kirkland

Best Western Kirkland Inn
12223 NE 116th St
Kirkland, WA 98034
425-822-2300
There is a $50 refundable pet deposit. There are only a few non-smoking pet rooms so make a reservation early.

La Quinta Inn Bellevue - Kirkland
10530 NE Northup Way
Kirkland, WA
425-828-6585
Dogs up to 75 pounds are allowed at the hotel.

Motel 6
12010 120th Pl NE
Kirkland, WA 98034
425-821-5618
One well-behaved dog is allowed per room. Pets must be attended at all times.

Parks

Redmond

Marymoor Park and Off-Leash Area
6046 West Lake Sammamish Pkwy NE
Redmond, WA
206-296-8687
This park offers 640 acres of land for recreational activities. Some special areas in the park include a velodrome (for bicyclist training and racing), a climbing rock, a model airplane flying field, and the historic Willowmoor Farm. Dogs on leash are allowed at the park. There is also a 40 acre off-leash dog exercise area where dogs can run free while under voice control. To get there from I-5 or I-405, take State Route 520 east to the West

Lake Sammamish Pkwy exit. At the bottom of the ramp, go right (south) on W. Lake Sammamish Parkway NE. The park entrance is the next left at the traffic light.

Spokane Dog Travel Guide
Accommodations

Spokane

Budget Inn
E. 110 Fourth Avenue
Spokane, WA 99202
509-838-6101
There are no additional pet fees.

Cavanaughs River Inn
N 700 Division St
Spokane, WA 99202
509-326-5577
There are no additional pet fees.

Doubletree Hotel Spokane City Center
N. 322 Spokane Falls Ct
Spokane, WA 99201
509-455-9600
There is a $25 one time pet fee.

Doubletree Hotel Spokane Valley
North 1100 Sullivan Road
Spokane, WA 99220
509-924-9000
There is a $50 refundable pet deposit.

Howard Johnson Inn
South 211 Division St.
Spokane, WA 99202
509-838-6630
Dogs of all sizes are welcome. There is a $10 per day pet fee.

Motel 6
1508 S Rustle St
Spokane, WA 99224
509-459-6120
There are no additional pet fees. One well-behaved pet per room is allowed.

Motel 6
1919 N Hutchinson Rd
Spokane, WA 99212
509-926-5399
Well-behaved dogs are allowed at the hotel.

Tacoma Dog Travel Guide
Accommodations

Tacoma

Best Western Executive Inn
5700 Pacific Hwy E.
Tacoma, WA 98424
253-922-0080
There is a $25 one time pet fee per visit.

Best Western Tacoma Inn
8726 S. Hosmer St
Tacoma, WA 98444
253-535-2880
There is a $20 one time pet fee.

La Quinta Inn Tacoma
1425 E 27th St
Tacoma, WA
253-383-0146
Dogs of all sizes are allowed at the hotel.

Motel 6
1811 S 76th St
Tacoma, WA 98408
253-473-7100
There are no additional pet fees. Pets must be attended at all times.

Vancouver Dog Travel Guide
Accommodations

Vancouver

Comfort Inn
13207 NE 20th Ave.
Vancouver, WA 98686
360-574-6000
There is a pet fee of $10 per day.

Staybridge Suites
7301 NE 41st St
Vancouver, WA 98662
360-891-8282
There is a $50 refundable pet deposit and an additional pet fee of $10 per day.

Walla Walla Dog Travel Guide
Accommodations

Walla Walla

La Quinta Inn Walla Walla
520 North Second Street
Walla Walla, WA
509-525-2522
Dogs up to 50 pounds are allowed at the hotel.

Wenatchee Dog Travel Guide
Accommodations

Wenatchee

La Quinta Inn & Suites Wenatchee
1905 N. Wenatchee Ave
Wenatchee, WA
509-664-6565
Dogs of all sizes are allowed at the hotel.

Westport Dog Travel Guide
Beaches

Westport

Twin Harbors State Park
Highway 105
Westport, WA
360-902-8844
This beach is popular for beachcombing, bird watching, and fishing. Picnic tables, restrooms (including an ADA restroom), and campgrounds (includes ADA campgrounds) are available at this park. Leashed dogs are allowed on the beach. Dogs are also allowed at the campgrounds. They must be on a eight foot or less leash at all times and people are required to clean up after their pets. This park is located three miles south of Westport on Highway 105. From Aberdeen,

Westport Light State Park
Ocean Avenue
Westport, WA
360-902-8844
Enjoy the panoramic view at this park or take the easy access trail to the beach. Swimming in the ocean here is not advised because of variable currents or rip tides. Picnic tables, restrooms (including an ADA restroom), and a 1.3 mile paved trail (also an ADA trail) are available at this park. Leashed dogs are allowed on the beach. Dogs are also allowed on the paved trail. They must be on a eight foot or less leash at all times and people are required to clean up after their pets. This park is located on the Pacific Ocean at Westport, 22 miles southwest of Aberdeen. To get there from Westport, drive west on Ocean Ave. about one mile to park entrance.

Yakima Dog Travel Guide
Accommodations

Yakima

Holiday Inn Express

1001 East A Street
Yakima, WA 98901
509-249-1000
There is a $6 per day pet fee.

Motel 6
1104 N 1st St
Yakima, WA 98901
509-454-0080
There are no additional pet fees. Pets must be
attended at all times.

Chapter 18

British Columbia Dog-Friendly Travel Guide

100 Mile House Dog Travel Guide
Accommodations

100 Mile House

Ramada Limited
917 Alder Rd
100 Mile House, BC V0K 2E0
250-395-2777
There is a $5 per day additional pet fee. Pets are allowed but not in the lobby. Pet rooms all have outside entrances.

Abbotsford Dog Travel Guide
Accommodations

Abbotsford

Holiday Inn Express
2073 Clearbrook Rd
Abbotsford, BC V2T 2X1
604-859-6211
There is a $10 per day additional pet fee.

Ramada Inn
36035 N Parallel Rd
Abbotsford, BC V3G 2C6
604-870-1050
There is a $10 per day additional pet fee.

Campbell River Dog Travel Guide
Accommodations

Campbell River

Coast Discovery Inn and Marina
975 Shoppers Row
Campbell River, BC V9W 2C4
250-287-7155
All Coast Hotels have on hand extra pet amenities if you forget something. For dogs, they have extra doggy dishes, sleeping cushions, nylon chew toys and dog food. If your dog needs one of these items, just ask the front desk. There is a $10 per day additional pet fee.

Castlegar Dog Travel Guide
Accommodations

Castlegar

Days Inn
651-18th Street
Castlegar, BC V1N 2N1
250-365-2700
There is a $10 per day pet pet additional fee.

Chilliwack Dog Travel Guide
Accommodations

Chilliwack

Best Western Rainbow Country Inn
43971 Industrial Way
Chilliwack, BC V2R 3A4
604-795-3828
There is an $10 per day pet fee.

Comfort Inn
45405 Luckakuck Way
Chilliwack, BC V2R3C7
604-858-0636
There is a pet fee of $5 per day. Pets are allowed on the ground floor.

Courtenay Dog Travel Guide
Accommodations

Courtenay

Coast Westerly Hotel
1590 Cliffe Avenue
Courtenay, BC V9N 2K4
250-338-7741
All Coast Hotels have on hand extra pet amenities if you forget something. For dogs, they have extra doggy dishes, sleeping cushions, nylon chew toys and dog food. If your dog needs one of these items, just ask the front desk. There is a $10 per day additional pet fee.

Cranbrook Dog Travel Guide
Accommodations

Cranbrook

Best Western Coach House
1417 Cranbrook St N
Cranbrook, BC V1C 3S7
250-426-7236
There is a $10 per day pet fee.

Dawson Creek Dog Travel Guide
Accommodations

Dawson Creek

Ramada Limited
1748 Alaska Avenue
Dawson Creek, BC V1G 1P4
250-782-8595
There is a $10 per day additional pet fee.

Delta Dog Travel Guide
Accommodations

Delta

Best Western Tsawwassen Inn
1665 56th Street
Delta, BC V4L 2B2
604-943-8221
There is a $10 per day pet fee. A large well-behaved dog is okay.

Enderby Dog Travel Guide
Accommodations

Enderby

Howard Johnson Inn
1510 George St.
Enderby, BC
250-838-6825
Dogs of all sizes are welcome. There is a $5 per day pet fee.

Fort St John Dog Travel Guide
Accommodations

Fort St John

Best Western Coachman Inn
8540 Alaska Road
Fort St John, BC V1J 5L6
250-787-0651
There is a $15 per day additional pet fee.

Quality Inn
9830 100th Ave
Fort St John, BC V1J1Y5
250-787-0521
There is a one time pet fee of $15.

Grand Forks Dog Travel Guide
Accommodations

Grand Forks

Ramada Limited
2729 Central Ave (Hwy 3)
Grand Forks, BC V0H 1H2
250-442-2127
There is a $10 per day additional pet fee. Pets are not allowed on the furniture.

Hope Dog Travel Guide
Accommodations

Hope

Quality Inn
350 Old Hope Princton Way
Hope, BC V0X1
604-869-9951
There is no pet fee. Pets may not be left alone.

Kamloops Dog Travel Guide
Accommodations

Kamloops

Coast Canadian Inn
339 St. Paul Street
Kamloops, BC V2C 2J5
250-372-5201
All Coast Hotels have on hand extra pet amenities if you forget something. For dogs, they have extra doggy dishes, sleeping cushions, nylon chew toys and dog food. If your dog needs one of these items, just ask the front desk. There is a $10 per day additional pet fee.

Days Inn
1285 W Trans Canada Hwy
Kamloops, BC V2E 2J7
250-374-5911
There is a $10 per day pet fee. The hotel has several pet rooms.

Howard Johnson Inn
610 West Columbia Street
Kamloops, BC
250-374-1515
Dogs of all sizes are welcome. There are no additional pet fees.

Ramada Inn
555 West Columbia St
Kamloops, BC V2C 1K7
250-374-0358
There is a $10 per day additional pet fee.

Kelowna Dog Travel Guide
Accommodations

Kelowna

Coast Capri Hotel
1171 Harvey Avenue
Kelowna, BC V1Y 6E8
250-860-6060
All Coast Hotels have on hand extra pet amenities if you forget something. For dogs, they have extra doggy dishes, sleeping cushions, nylon chew toys and dog food. If your dog needs one of these items, just ask the front desk. There is an extra person charge for dogs which is $20 -$25 Cdn. per day.

Ramada Lodge Hotel
2170 Harvey Ave (Highway 97N)
Kelowna, BC V1Y 6G8
250-860-9711
There is a $10 per day additional pet fee. Pets must be attended at all times.

Kimberley Dog Travel Guide
Accommodations

Kimberley

Quality Inn
300 Wallinger Ave
Kimberley, BC V1A1Z4
250-427-2266
There is no pet fee.

Mission Dog Travel Guide
Accommodations

Mission

The Counting Sheep Inn
8715 Eagle Road, R.R. #3
Mission, BC V2V 4J1
604-820-5148
They are 60 minutes from Vancouver and 45 minutes from Bellingham, Washington. This is an elegant Bed and Breakfast in the country and dogs are allowed in one of their rooms, the Carriage Suite. Check out their great season packages.

Nanaimo Dog Travel Guide
Accommodations

Nanaimo

Best Western Northgate Inn
6450 Metral Drive

Nanaimo, BC V9T 2I8
250-390-2222
There is a $10 per day pet fee. Dogs are allowed on the first floor only.

Coast Bastion Inn
11 Bastion Street
Nanaimo, BC V9R 2Z9
250-753-6601
All Coast Hotels have on hand extra pet amenities if you forget something. For dogs, they have extra doggy dishes, sleeping cushions, nylon chew toys and dog food. If your dog needs one of these items, just ask the front desk. There is a $10 per day additional pet fee.

Ramada Limited on Long Lake
4700 N Island Hwy
Nanaimo, BC V9T 1W6
250-758-1144
There is a $20 one time pet fee.

Parksville Dog Travel Guide
Accommodations

Parksville

Best Western Bayside Inn
240 Dogwood Street
Parksville, BC V9P 2H5
250-248-8333
There is a $10 per day pet fee. The hotel has oceanside and mountain view rooms.

Penticton Dog Travel Guide
Accommodations

Penticton

Ramada Inn & Suites
1050 Eckhardt Ave West
Penticton, BC V2A 2C3
250-492-8926
There is a $10 per day pet fee.

Port Alberni Dog Travel Guide
Accommodations

Port Alberni

Coast Hospitality Inn
3835 Redford Street
Port Alberni, BC V9Y 3S2
250-723-8111
All Coast Hotels have on hand extra pet

amenities if you forget something. For dogs, they have extra doggy dishes, sleeping cushions, nylon chew toys and dog food. If your dog needs one of these items, just ask the front desk. There are no additional pet fees.

Quality Inn
4850 Bever Creek Rd
Port Alberni, BC V9Y7C8
250-724-2900
There is a refundable pet deposit $25. There is a pet fee of $10 per day. Non-smoking rooms are limited so please reserve early.

Powell River Dog Travel Guide
Accommodations

Powell River

Coast Town Centre Hotel
4660 Joyce Avenue
Powell River, BC V8A 3B6
604-485-3000
All Coast Hotels have on hand extra pet amenities if you forget something. For dogs, they have extra doggy dishes, sleeping cushions, nylon chew toys and dog food. If your dog needs one of these items, just ask the front desk. There is a $10 per day additional pet fee.

Prince George Dog Travel Guide
Accommodations

Prince George

Coast Inn of the North
770 Brunswick Street
Prince George, BC V2L 2C2
250-563-0121
All Coast Hotels have on hand extra pet amenities if you forget something. For dogs, they have extra doggy dishes, sleeping cushions, nylon chew toys and dog food. If your dog needs one of these items, just ask the front desk. There is a $10 per day additional pet fee.

Prince Rupert Dog Travel Guide
Accommodations

Prince Rupert

Coast Prince Rupert Hotel
118 6th Street
Prince Rupert, BC V8J 3L7
250-624-6711

All Coast Hotels have on hand extra pet amenities if you forget something. For dogs, they have extra doggy dishes, sleeping cushions, nylon chew toys and dog food. If your dog needs one of these items, just ask the front desk. There are no additional pet fees.

Quesnel Dog Travel Guide
Accommodations

Quesnel

Ramada Limited
383 St Laurent Ave
Quesnel, BC V2T 2E1
250-992-5575
One pet per room is permitted. There is a $7 per day additional pet fee.

Revelstoke Dog Travel Guide
Accommodations

Revelstoke

Best Western Wayside Inn
1901 Laforme Blvd
Revelstoke, BC V0E 250
250-837-6161
There are no additional pet fees.

Richmond Dog Travel Guide
Accommodations

Richmond

Comfort Inn Airport
3031 Number 3 Road
Richmond, BC V6X2B6
604-278-5161
There is a pet fee of $10 per day. Pets are allowed on the first floor.

Saanighton Dog Travel Guide
Accommodations

Saanighton

Quality Inn Waddling Dog
2476 Mt Newton Cross Rd
Saanighton, BC V8M2B
250-652-1146
There is a pet fee of $5 per day.

Salmon Arm Dog Travel Guide

Accommodations

Salmon Arm

Best Western Villager West
61-10th St SW
Salmon Arm, BC V1E 1E4
250-832-9793
There are no additional pet fees. A large well-behaved dog is okay.

Sicamous Dog Travel Guide
Accommodations

Sicamous

Sundog Bed and Breakfast
1409 Rauma Ave
Sicamous, BC V0E 2V0
250-833-9005
There is a $15 per night pet fee with $5 going to the local SPCA. There are two pet friendly rooms.

Surrey Dog Travel Guide
Accommodations

Surrey

Ramada Hotel & Suites
10410 158th St
Surrey, BC V4N 5C2
604-930-4700
There is a $10 per day pet fee.

Ramada Limited
19225 Hwy 10
Surrey, BC V3S 8V9
604-576-8388
There is a $10 per day pet fee per pet.

Valemount Dog Travel Guide
Accommodations

Valemount

Best Western Canadian Lodge
1501 5th Ave
Valemount, BC V0E 2Z0
250-566-8222
Dogs up to at least 75 pounds are allowed. There are no additional pet fees. The hotel has one non-smoking pet room.

Vancouver Dog Travel Guide

Accommodations

Coquitlam

Best Western Chelsea Inn
725 Brunette Avenue
Coquitlam, BC V3K 1C3
604-525-7777
There is an $20 per day pet fee.

Holiday Inn
631 Lougheed Highway
Coquitlam, BC V3K 3S5
604-931-4433
There is a $30 one time pet fee.

Pitt Meadows

Ramada Inn
19267 Lougheed Hwy
Pitt Meadows, BC V3Y 2J5
604-460-9859
Pets must be well-behaved. There are no additional pet fees.

Vancouver

Best Western Sands Hotel
1755 Davie Street
Vancouver, BC V6G 1W5
604-682-1831
Situated in Downtown Vancouver down the block from Stanley Park and across from English Bay Beach. 2 Lounges, Restaurant, Room Service, Fitness Room and Sauna. The pet fee is $10.00 per day. Pets receive a welcome doggy bag upon arrival, includes Pet Lovers Digest, treats and scoop bags.

Coast Plaza Suite Hotel at Stanley Park
1763 Comox Street
Vancouver, BC V6G 1P6
604-688-7711
All Coast Hotels have on hand extra pet amenities if you forget something. For dogs, they have extra doggy dishes, sleeping cushions, nylon chew toys and dog food. If your dog needs one of these items, just ask the front desk. There is a $20 per day additional pet fee.

Granville Island Hotel
1253 Johnston St
Vancouver, BC
604-683-7373
This hotel has a restaurant on the premises called the Dockside Restaurant. You can dine there with

your pet at the outoor tables that are closest to the grass. The hotel charges a $25 per night pet fee per room.

Metropolitan Hotel
645 Howe Street
Vancouver, BC
604-687-1122
There are no additional pet fees.

Pacific Palisades Hotel
1277 Robson Street
Vancouver, BC
604-688-0461
Well-behaved dogs of all sizes are welcome at this hotel which offers both rooms and suites. Amenities include workout rooms, an indoor swimming pool, and 24 hour room service. There is a $25 one time per stay pet fee and $5 of this is sent to the SPCA.

Quality Hotel Downtown
1335 Howe St
Vancouver, BC V6Z1R7
604-682-0229
There is a pet fee of $15 per day.

Ramada Inn
1221 Granville St
Vancouver, BC V6Z 1M6
604-685-1111
There is a $20 per day additional pet fee.

Residence Inn by Marriott
1234 Hornby St
Vancouver, BC
604-688-1234
There is a $75 pet fee per visit plus $5 per night for your pet

Sylvia Hotel
1154 Gilford St
Vancouver, BC
604-681-9321
There are no additional pet fees.

Attractions

Albion

Albion Ferry
off River Road
Albion, BC
604-467-7298
This ferry transports passengers and vehicles across the River, between Fort Langley and Albion. Crossing time is 10 minutes. Pets are allowed. If you walk onto the ferry with no car, your pet must be leashed. If your dog comes onto the ferry in your vehicle, he or she needs to stay in the car. This ferry is run by the Fraser River Marine Transportation company and is a subsidiary of TransLink. The ferry is located east of Vancouver.

Boston Bar

Hell's Gate Airtram
43111 Trans Canada Highway
Boston Bar, BC
604-867-9277
Come and visit the steepest non-supported air tram in North America. You will experience breath-taking views, above the river's fishways, in one of their comfortable 25 passenger air tram cabins. After the tram ride, walk over to the Salmon House Restaurant where you can enjoy mouth-watering salmon at the outdoor tables. For some dessert visit the Fudge Factory where they have over 30 flavors of homemade fudge. Also on the premises is the Patio Cafe, which is home to British Columbia's smallest outdoor pub. Your dog can even enjoy a nice cold drink of water from the "Pup Pub" bucket at the cafe. Dogs on leash are welcome in the air tram, at the outdoor restaurant and at the outdoor pub. This attraction is located about 2 and 1/2 hours from Vancouver off the Trans Canada Highway.

North Vancouver

Capilano Suspension Bridge and Park
3735 Capilano Road
North Vancouver, BC V7R 4J1
604-985-7474
This is Vancouver's oldest and most famous attraction which draws over 800,000 visitors each year. The park is home to the world's greatest suspension footbridge, which was original built in 1889. Today's bridge is the fourth bridge at this location. It spans 450 feet across and is 230 feet above the Capilano River. Located on the other side of the bridge is a West Coast rain forest. The forest is a popular attraction for visitors and offers trails that pass by trout ponds and old growth evergreens. The park's trails are located in the rain forest and some of the trails offer interactive displays that explain the local flora and fauna. Near the main entrance you can visit the Totem Park with over 25 authentic totem poles from the 1930s. Then stop by the Big House which features First Nations carvers who explain and demonstrate their skills, and techniques. Walk through the Story Centre, where you can pose

with the "tramps", view artifacts, antiques and hear "voices from the past". While there at the park, dine at the outdoor tables at either the Bridge House Restaurant or the Canyon Cafe and Logger's Grill. Dogs on leash are allowed everywhere except in the Trading Post Gift Shop and inside the restaurants. Tour greeters and guides are available at the park for complimentary history and nature tours from May to October. The bridge and park are open daily except for Christmas Day. Summer hours are 8:30am until dusk and winter hours are 9am to 5pm. This park is located just 10 minutes from downtown Vancouver. To get there, go through Stanley Park, over the Lions Gate Bridge and go north 1 mile on Capilano Road. From the Trans-Canada Highway, take the Capilano road exit and go north for a half a mile.

Rosedale

Minter Gardens
52892 Bunker Road
Rosedale, BC
604-794-7191
Enjoy a world class show garden with your pooch. This attraction has 11 beautifully themed gardens spread out over 32 acres. Leashed pets are welcome outside and owners need to clean up after their pets. The gardens are open daily from April to mid-October. They are located 90 minutes east of Vancouver. From Highway 1, take Exit 135.

Vancouver

AquaBus Ferries
230-1333 Johnston Street/Granville Island
Vancouver, BC
604-689-5858
Sightseeing cruises are available on these small ferries. The cruises last about 25 minutes and pass by a floating village, kayakers, tugboats towing barges, fishermen, sail boaters and more. No reservations are required. Cruises depart from the Granville Island dock every twenty minutes daily from 9am to 7pm. Well-behaved leashed dogs are welcome.

Granville Island

Vancouver, BC V6H 3S3
604-666-6655
Once home to industrial factories, this area is popular for it's public market, art studios, and restaurants. Pets are not allowed inside the public marketplace because of the food, but your pooch

can walk along the sidewalks and the Sea Wall with you. Along the sidewalks there are usually entertaining street performers. Dog-friendly establishments on Granville Island include the Granville Island Hotel, AquaBus ferries and a dog bakery called Woofles. Granville Island is located just south of downtown Vancouver.

Historic Gastown
Water Street
Vancouver, BC
604-683-5650
This historic area is where Vancouver was founded. Gastown is named after the man John "Gassy Jack" Deighton who opened his saloon in 1867 on a shoestring budget. He got his name "Gassy Jack" because he talked a lot. The locals called the place Gassy's Town which was later shortened to Gastown. You can find Gassy Jack's statue at the corner of Water and Carrall Streets. In Gastown, you and your pooch can walk on the cobble-stoned streets and view the Victorian architecture. Be sure to stop by the Gastown Steam Clock, which is the world's first steam-powered clock. It blows every 15 minutes. Also in Gastown you can watch street performers or visit a dog-friendly outdoor restaurant on Powell Street like Gassy Jack's Deli or Cafe Dolcino.

Historic Gastown Guided Walking Tours
Water and Carrall Streets
Vancouver, BC
604-683-5650
Take a free guided historic walking tour of Gastown with your well-behaved dog. The GBIS (Gastown Business Improvement Society) offers tours that highlight the history and architecture of Vancouver's birthplace. The tours are held each summer from mid-June through August at 2pm daily. Tours last about 90 minutes. Meet at Gassy Jack's statue, on the corner of Water and Carrall Streets.

Sam Kee Building
Pender Street
Vancouver, BC

Visit the second largest Chinatown in North American and take a look at the Sam Kee Building. This building is the world's thinnest office building according to the Guinness Book of World Records. The two-story building was built in 1913 and is only 6 feet wide. The back of the building is right next to another building and it visually looks like it is part of the other building. But look closely and you will see that is it actually only 6 feet wide. The second floor has an overhang that the owner added in order to increase office space. At one time this building housed thirteen little businesses. Today the building is still used for office space. It is located in Chinatown at the corner of Pender and Carrall Streets.

Victoria

BC Ferries
1112 Fort Street
Victoria, BC V8V 4V2
250-386-3431
Pets are allowed on most of the BC ferries, including the route from Vancouver to Victoria. This route departs from Tsawwassen which is south of Vancouver and arrives at Swartz Bay, which is north of Victoria. You will need to bring your car on the ferry in order to visit most of the dog-friendly places in Victoria. Dogs are only allowed on the open air car deck and must stay in the car or tied in a designated pet area. Owners must stay with their pets. The travel time for this route is approximately 1 hour and 35 minutes. Guide dogs and certified assistance dogs are not required to stay on the car decks.

Vancouver to Alaska Ferries
1112 Fort Street
Victoria, BC V8V 4V2
250-386-3431
While we do not recommend this route for pet owners because you cannot always be with your pet, here is some information about taking a ferry with your dog from Vancouver to Alaska. First take a BC Ferry from Port Hardy to Prince Ruppert via the Inside Passage. The ferry ride is about 15 hours. Dogs are allowed on the car decks and pet owners are not allowed to stay with their pets. You can still visit your pet about 4 to 5 times during the day only when crew members designate certain visiting times. From Prince Rupert in Canada to Seward in Alaska, you will need to take an Alaska State Ferry. This route takes about 4 days. Pets are required to have current health certificates within 30 days of travel. Pets must remain in your car or in your carrier, on the car decks only. People are not allowed to stay with their pets. The captain will announce "pet calls" so pet owners can take their pets out for a short walk onboard in the designated pet area. While there are usually three pet visitation times per day, it is entirely up to the captain. The captain's decision is based on the weather and other factors. On both ferries, there is a designated pet area where your pets can relieve themselves. Owners must clean up after their pets. Guide dogs and certified assistance dogs

are not required to stay on the car decks.

Beaches

Vancouver

Spanish Banks West
NW Marine Drive
Vancouver, BC
604-257-8400
This beach allows dogs off-leash. Dogs are allowed from 6am to 10pm. People are required to clean up after their dogs. The beach is located in the Queen Elizabeth District. It is off NW Marine Drive, at the entrance to Pacific Spirit Park.

Sunset Beach
off Beach Avenue
Vancouver, BC
604-257-8400
This bay beach allows dogs off-leash. Dogs are allowed from 6am to 10pm. People are required to clean up after their dogs. The beach is located in the Stanley District, near Beach Avenue, under the Burrard Bridge. It is behind the Aquatic Centre east of the ferry dock.

Vanier Park
Chestnut
Vancouver, BC
604-257-8400
This beach allows dogs off-leash. Dogs are allowed from 6am to 10am and then from 5pm to 10pm. People are required to clean up after their dogs. The beach is located in the Queen Elizabeth District. It is on Chestnut at English Bay.

Parks

Burnaby

Burnaby Lake Regional Park
Sprott Street
Burnaby, BC
604-294-7450
Dogs on leash are allowed at this park and on the trails. This park is popular for birdwatching. Be on the lookout for bald eagles, great blue herons, or even green-backed herons. Along the shoreline you might see beavers, ducks and turtles. For some good exercise, try one of the trails that circles the lake.

Burnaby Mountain Park

Centennial Way
Burnaby, BC
604-294-7450
Dogs on leash are allowed at this park and on the trails. The park offers mountain, water and city views from the top of Burnaby Mountain. You might even see some deer or bald eagles. To get there, take Lougheed Highway and turn north on Gaglardi Way to Centennial Way.

Central Park
Boundary Road
Burnaby, BC
604-294-7450
Dogs on leash are allowed at this park and on the trails. This park is an urban forest with douglas fir, western hemloc, poplar and maple trees. To get there, take the Trans Canada Highway to Boundary Road. Go south to get to the park.

Confederation Park
Willingdon Avenue
Burnaby, BC
604-294-7450
Dogs on leash are allowed at this park and on the trails. There is an off-leash area located north of Penzance Drive, roughly between Willingdon and Gamma Avenues. To get to the park, take Hastings Road and then go North on Willingdon Avenue.

Confederation Park Off-Leash Area
Willingdon Avenue
Burnaby, BC
604-294-7450
Dogs are allowed off-leash year-round in a designated area. The area is located north of Penzance Drive, roughly between Willingdon and Gamma Avenues. There will be signs posted indicating the off-leash area. The following off-leash codes apply: clean up after your pet, you must be present and in verbal control of your dog at all times, dogs must wear a valid rabies tag, no aggressive dogs allowed, and dogs must be leashed before and after using the off-leash area. Dogs on leash are allowed throughout Confederation Park.

Coquitlam

Colony Farm Regional Park
Colony Farm Road
Coquitlam, BC
604-224-5739
This park offers large open fields with wildflowers. It is a good birdwatching spot to find hawks and herons. Dogs on leash are allowed on the trails,

except for beaches or where posted. To get there, take the Trans Canada Highway (Highway 1) east. Take the Cape Horn Interchange to Highway 7 (Lougheed), then turn right onto Colony Farm Road.

North Vancouver

Capilano River Regional Park
Capilano Park Road
North Vancouver, BC
604-224-5739
This park offers lush forest trails and is also home to the Capilano Fish Hatchery. Dogs on leash are allowed on the trails, except for beaches or where posted. The park is located in North Vancouver, next to the Cleveland Dam.

South Burnaby

Burnaby Fraser Foreshore Park Off-Leash Area
Byrne Road
South Burnaby, BC
604-294-7450
From October through March, dogs are allowed off-leash in a designated area near the Fraser River. The area is located near the end of Byrne Road. The following off-leash codes apply: clean up after your pet, you must be present and in verbal control of your dog at all times, dogs must wear a valid rabies tag, no aggressive dogs allowed, and dogs must be leashed before and after using the off-leash area. Dogs on leash are allowed in the rest of the park, but not on the banks of the Fraser River.

Vancouver

Charleson Park Off-Leash Area
6th Avenue
Vancouver, BC
604-257-8400
Dogs are allowed off-leash year-round in the Grass Bowl from 6am to 10pm. At the Waterfall Pond, dogs are allowed off-leash before 10am and after 7pm from June through September. During the rest of the year, there are no restricted off-leash hours at the Waterfall Pond.

Pacific Spirit Regional Park
Southwest Marine Drive
Vancouver, BC
604-224-5739
This is a popular park for jogging and running. The park offers over 30 miles or 54 kilometers of

trails. Dogs on leash are allowed on the trails, except for beaches or where posted. There is also an off-leash area in this park which will be posted with signs.

Queen Elizabeth Park
Cambie Boulevard
Vancouver, BC
604-257-8400
This 130 acre (52 hectare) park has about 6 million visitors per year. The popular Quarry Gardens is located at the top of the hill in the park. This land used to be an actual quarry before it became a city park. Dogs are allowed in the park and on the walkways and trails, except where posted. Dogs must be on leash. The park is located off Cambie Boulevard and is surrounded by the following streets: Cambie Blvd., Kersland Dr., 37th Ave., Midlothian Ave., and 27th Ave.

Queen Elizabeth Park Off-Leash Area
37th Avenue and Columbia St.
Vancouver, BC
604-257-8400
Dogs are allowed off-leash from 6am to 10pm only in the designated area. The off-leash area is located at approximately 37th Avenue and Columbia Street.

Stanley Park
Georgia Street
Vancouver, BC
604-257-8400
This park is the largest city park in Canada and the third largest urban park in North America. It attracts about 8 million people per year. The park has 1,000 forested acres and offers miles of trails, including a 6.2 mile paved trail around the perimeter. On the north side of the park, you will get a view of Lion's Gate Bridge. This bridge connects Vancouver and North Vancouver and is similar in size to the San Francisco Golden Gate Bridge. Dogs are allowed in the park, except on beaches or where posted. Your dog is welcome to walk or jog with you on the trails. Stanley Park is located is just north of downtown Vancouver. To get there, take Georgia Street towards North Vancouver. Dogs must be leashed.

Restaurants

Coquuitlam

Bread Garden Bakery Cafe
2991 Lougheed Highway
Coquuitlam, BC

604-945-9494
This cafe is open for breakfast, lunch and dinner. For breakfast they serve breakfast sandwiches, pastries, fruit salads and smoothies. For lunch and dinner they offer pasta and rice bowls, salads, sandwiches, wrapps, smoothies and desserts. Well-behaved, leashed dogs are allowed at the outdoor tables.

Bread Garden Bakery Cafe
100 Schoolhouse Street
Coquitlam, BC V3K 6V9
604-515-0295
This cafe is open for breakfast, lunch and dinner. For breakfast they serve breakfast sandwiches, pastries, fruit salads and smoothies. For lunch and dinner they offer pasta and rice bowls, salads, sandwiches, wrapps, smoothies and desserts. Well-behaved, leashed dogs are allowed at the outdoor tables.

Vancouver

Andale's Mexican Restaurant
3211 Broadway West
Vancouver, BC V6K 2H5
604-738-9782
Well-behaved, leashed dogs are allowed at the outdoor tables.

Apple Deli
849 Davie Street
Vancouver, BC
604-669-1309
Well-behaved, leashed dogs are allowed at the outdoor tables.

Bread Garden Bakery Cafe
889 West Pender Street
Vancouver, BC V6C 3B2
604-638-3982
This cafe is open for breakfast, lunch and dinner. For breakfast they serve breakfast sandwiches, pastries, fruit salads and smoothies. For lunch and dinner they offer pasta and rice bowls, salads, sandwiches, wrapps, smoothies and desserts. Well-behaved, leashed dogs are allowed at the outdoor tables.

Cafe Dolcino
12 Powell Street
Vancouver, BC V6A 1E7
604-801-5118
This cafe serves breakfast all day as well as Italian food. The cafe has two outdoor tables. Well-behaved, leashed dogs are allowed at the outdoor tables.

Cafe II Nido
780 Thurlow Street
Vancouver, BC V6E 1V8
604-685-6436
This restaurant is open for lunch and dinner. Well-behaved, leashed dogs are allowed at the outdoor tables.

Dockside Patio Restaurant
1253 Johnston Street
Vancouver, BC V6H 3R9
604-683-7373
This restaurant is located in the pet-friendly Granville Island Hotel. They are open for breakfast, lunch and dinner. Well-behaved, leashed dogs are allowed at the outdoor tables that are closest to the grass. The patio offers great views of False Creek and Vancouver City's skyline.

Don Francesco Ristorante
860 Burrard Street
Vancouver, BC
604-685-7770
This restaurant offers Italian cuisine with a Mediterranean flair. Well-behaved, leashed dogs are allowed at the outdoor tables.

Gassy Jack Deli
26 Powell Street
Vancouver, BC V6A 1E7
604-683-1222
This deli serves Mediterranean and Indian fast food. Well-behaved, leashed dogs are allowed at the outdoor tables.

Hermitage Restaurant
115 - 1025 Robson Street
Vancouver, BC V6E 4A9
604-689-3237
This French Restaurant is located in downtown Vancouver on popular Robson Street. Well-behaved, leashed dogs are allowed at the outdoor tables. They recommend that you make a reservation in advance because the outdoor seating can fill up quickly.

Le Gavroche Restaurant
1616 Alberni Street
Vancouver, BC
604-685-3924
This French restaurant is located within walking distance of Historic Gastown and Stanley Park. Well-behaved, leashed dogs are allowed at the outdoor tables.

Quattro on Fourth

2611 West 4th Avenue
Vancouver, BC
604-734-4444
This upscale Italian restaurant offers soups, salads, pastas, seafood, beef and more. Well-behaved, leashed dogs are allowed at the corner outdoor tables. They recommend calling in advance to reserve a table.

West Vancouver

Beach House at Dundarave Pier
150 - 25th Street
West Vancouver, BC
604-922-1414
This restaurant specializes in fresh fish and shellfish dishes. Well-behaved, leashed dogs are allowed at the outdoor tables. They recommend that you make a reservation in advance because the outdoor seating can book up several days in advance.

Bread Garden Bakery Cafe
550 Park Royal North
West Vancouver, BC V7T 1H9
604-925-0181
This cafe is open for breakfast, lunch and dinner. For breakfast they serve breakfast sandwiches, pastries, fruit salads and smoothies. For lunch and dinner they offer pasta and rice bowls, salads, sandwiches, wrapps, smoothies and desserts. Well-behaved, leashed dogs are allowed at the outdoor tables.

Hot Dog Jonny's
#120 - 1425 Marine Drive
West Vancouver, BC
604-913-3647
This restaurant has been voted "Best Hot Dogs in Vancouver" by the Vancouver Sun and Georgia Straight Readers Choice Award. They serve a dozen different hot dogs and sausages including all-beef Kosher, pork, poultry, veggie and smokies. A complete list of all ingredients and nutritional data is included on their web site. They have a few tables outside where well-behaved, leashed dogs are welcome.

Stores

Vancouver

O.K. Boot Corral
205 Carrall Street
Vancouver, BC V6B 2J2
604-684-2668

Only well-behaved leashed dogs are allowed inside this store. They offer boots, hats, replica antique firearms, and accessories like belt buckles. The store is located in Historic Gastown.

Woofles Doggilicious Deli
1496 Cartright Street
Vancouver, BC
604-689-3647
This specialty pet store offers 100% natural homemade dog and cat treats, pet jewelry, and toys. They even host doggie weddings and doggie parties. The store is located on Granville Island in the Kids Market. They are open seven days a week. Dogs are welcome!

Transportation Systems

Vancouver

Translink (Ferry, Train, and Bus)
Regional
Vancouver, BC
604-953-3333
Small dogs in hard-sided carriers are allowed on the SeaBus (ferry), SkyTrain (train) and buses.

Victoria Dog Travel Guide
Accommodations

Saanichton

Quality Inn Wadding Dog
2476 Mt Newton Crossroad
Saanichton, BC
250-652-1146
There is a $5.00 per night dog fee.

Super 8 Victoria/Saanichton
2477 Mount Newton Crossroad
Saanichton, BC
250-652-6888
There is a $10 one time pet fee.

Wintercott Country House
1950 Nicholas Rd.
Saanichton, BC
250-652-2117
This bed and breakfast inn is located about 15 minutes from Victoria. Well-behaved dogs of all sizes are welcome. There is no pet fee.

Sidney

Best Western Emerald Isle
2306 Beacon Ave

Sidney, BC V8L 1X2
250-656-4441
There is a $20 one time pet fee per visit.

Cedarwood Motel
9522 Lochside Dr
Sidney, BC
250-656-5551
There is a $15 per day additional pet fee.

Victoria Airport Travelodge
2280 Beacon Ave
Sidney, BC
250-656-1176
There is a $10 per day additional pet fee.

Sooke

Gordon's Beach Farm Stay B&B
4530 Otter Point Road
Sooke, BC V0S 1N0
250-642-5291
A well-behaved dog is allowed in one of their suite rooms that has marble flooring. There is a $10 one time per stay pet fee.

Ocean Wilderness Country Inn
109 W Coast Rd
Sooke, BC
250-646-2116
There is a $15 pet fee per visit.

Sooke Harbour House
1528 Whiffen Spit Rd
Sooke, BC
250-642-3421
There is a $30 per night pet fee.

Victoria

Accent Inn
3233 Maple Street
Victoria, BC
250-475-7500
There is a $10 one time pet fee.

Annabelles Cottage B&B
152 Joseph Street
Victoria, BC V8S 3H5
250-384-4351
Both pets and children are welcome. There is a $10 one time per stay pet fee. The inn is located near Beacon Hill Park.

Coast Harbourside Hotel and Marina
146 Kingston Street

Victoria, BC V8V 1V4
250-360-1211
Coast Hotels have on hand extra pet amenities if you forget something. For dogs, they have extra doggy dishes, sleeping cushions, nylon chew toys and dog food. If your dog needs one of these items, just ask the front desk. There is a $20 per day additional pet fee.

Dashwood Seaside Manor
1 Cook Street
Victoria, BC
250-385-5517
There is a $25 per stay pet fee.

Executive House Hotel
777 Douglas Street
Victoria, BC V8W 2B5
250-388-5111
This downtown Victoria hotel offers a European ambience. The hotel is directly across from the Victoria Conference Centre, one block from the Inner Harbour, Royal BC Museum, National Geographic Theatre, shopping and attractions. Pets are welcome for $15 per night extra.

Harbour Towers Hotel
345 Quebec St
Victoria, BC
250-385-2405
There is a $15 per day additional pet fee.

Howard Johnson Hotel
310 George Rd. East
Victoria, BC
250-382-2151
Dogs up to 60 pounds are allowed. There is a refundable pet deposit required.

Howard Johnson Hotel
4670 Elk Lake Drive
Victoria, BC
250-704-4656
Dogs of all sizes are welcome. There is a $15 per day pet fee.

Ryan's Bed and Breakfast
224 Superior St
Victoria, BC
250-389-0012
There is a $10 per night pet fee.

Tally Ho Motor Inn
3020 Douglas St
Victoria, BC
250-386-6141
There are no additional pet fees.

Attractions

Anacortes

Washington State Ferries
2100 Ferry Terminal Rd
Anacortes, WA
206-464-6400
This ferry service offers many routes in Washington State, as well as a route from Sidney, near Victoria, to Anacortes in Washington. The ferry ride is about 3 hours long and the ferry carries both passengers and vehicles. You can also catch a ferry to Sidney from Friday Harbor, Washington, in the San Juan Islands. This ferry ride is about 1 hour and 15 minutes. While leashed dogs are allowed on the ferry routes mentioned above, the following pet regulations apply. On the newer ferries that have outside stairwells, dogs are allowed on the car deck and on the outdoor decks above the car deck. If the ferry has indoor stairwells, dogs are only allowed on the deck where they boarded the ferry. For example, if your dog comes onto the ferry in your car, he or she has to remain on the car deck. If you walk onto the ferry with your dog, your pooch is allowed on the outside deck where you boarded but cannot go onto other decks. In cases where your pet has to remain on the car deck, you can venture to the above decks without your pet to get food at the snack bars. However, the ferry system recommends in general that you stay with your pooch in the car. For any of the ferries, dogs are not allowed inside the ferry terminals. The ferries in Anacortes leave from 2100 Ferry Terminal Road. The ferries in Friday Harbor leave from 91 Front Street and the ferries in Sidney leave from 2499 Ocean Avenue. Reservations are recommended 48 hours or more in advance if you are bringing a vehicle. Because you will be crossing over an international border, identification for Customs and Immigration is required. U.S. and Canadian citizens traveling across the border will need proof of citizenship such as your passport or a certified copy of your birth certificate issued by the city, county or state/province where you were born. You will also need photo identification such as a current valid driver's license. People with children need to bring their child's birth certificate. Single parents, grandparents or guardians traveling with children often need proof or notarized letters from the other parent authorizing travel. Dogs traveling to Canada or returning to Canada need a certificate from their vet showing a rabies vaccination within the past 3 years. Dogs traveling to the U.S. or returning to the U.S. need to have a valid rabies vaccination certificate (including an expiration

date and vet signature). The certificate must show that the dog had the rabies vaccine at least 30 days prior to entry and within the past 12 months.

Vancouver Island

The Butchart Gardens

Vancouver Island, BC

Leashed dogs are allowed at this 50-acre show-place of floral finery offering spectacular views of gardens. You and your pup can stroll along meandering paths and expansive lawns. But Butchart Gardens does more than just allow dogs. These dog-friendly folks have placed running dog drinking fountains throughout the entire garden. Thanks to one of our readers for recommending this place. The Butchart Gardens is a must visit if you are on Vancouver Island!

Victoria

BC Ferries
1112 Fort Street
Victoria, BC V8V 4V2
250-386-3431
Pets are allowed on most of the BC ferries, including the route from Vancouver to Victoria. These ferries depart from Tsawwassen which is south of Vancouver and arrives at Swartz Bay, which is north of Victoria. Dogs are only allowed on the open air car deck and must stay in your car or tied in a designated pet area on the car deck. Owners must stay with their pets. The travel time for this route is approximately 1 hour and 35 minutes. Guide dogs and certified assistance dogs are not required to stay on the car decks.

Grandpas Antique Photo Studio
1252 Wharf Street
Victoria, BC V8W 1T8
250-920-3800
Create an old time photo in one of the following themes of your choice; The Old West, Victorian Era, Roaring 20's, Southern Belle, US Military and more. Most costumes fit over street clothing and fit all ages and sizes. Bring your well-behaved dog and include him or her in your photo. The studio is open from 10am to 10pm year-round. Prints are usually ready in 10 minutes.

Victoria Carriage Tours
Menzies and Belleville Street
Victoria, BC
250-383-2207
Take a guided horse and carriage tour of the waterfront, Beacon Hill Park, historical buildings and more. Choose from 30 minute to 90 minute tours. Prices start at $70 Canadian Dollars for the entire carriage which holds about 4 to 6 people. Well-behaved, leashed dogs are welcome. Carriages usually run from 9am until midnight, 7 days per week, weather permitting.

Victoria Express
Belleville Street
Victoria, BC
250-361-9144
This passenger ferry service runs between Port Angeles in Washington and Victoria. Crossing time is about one hour. Dogs are allowed and must be leashed. The ferries in Port Angeles leave from the Landing Mall on Railroad Avenue. The ferries in Victoria leave from the port on Belleville Street. Currency exchange is available at the Port Angeles Reservation Office. Their toll free number in the U.S. is 1-800-633-1589. Reservations are recommended. Because you will be crossing over an international border, identification for Customs and Immigration is required. U.S. and Canadian citizens traveling across the border will need proof of citizenship such as your passport or a certified copy of your birth certificate issued by the city, county or state/province where you were born. You will also need photo identification such as a current valid driver's license. People with children need to bring their child's birth certificate. Single parents, grandparents or guardians traveling with children often need proof or notarized letters from the other parent authorizing travel. Dogs traveling to Canada or returning to Canada need a certificate from their vet showing a rabies vaccination within the past 3 years. Dogs traveling to the U.S. or returning to the U.S. need to have a valid rabies vaccination certificate (including an expiration date and vet signature). The certificate must show that your dog has had the rabies vaccine at least 30 days prior to entry and within the past 12 months.

Beaches

Victoria

Beacon Hill Park Off-Leash Beach
Dallas Road
Victoria, BC
250-385-5711
Dogs are allowed off-leash at the gravel beach in Beacon Hill Park. People are required to clean up after their dogs. The beach is located in downtown Victoria, along Dallas Road, between

Douglas Street and Cook Street.

Parks

Saanich

Francis/King Regional Park
Munn Road
Saanich, BC
250-478-3344
There are many hiking trails in this park. One of the trails is the Elsi King Trail. This interpretive trail is accessible and also good for families with young children. Dogs must be leashed in all high use areas including the Elsi King Trail. Dogs may be allowed off-leash in other areas as long as they are under voice control. The park is located about 30 minutes from Victoria. Take the Trans-Canada Highway from Victoria and then take the Helmcken Road exit. Turn left onto Burnside Road West and then turn right on Prospect Lake Road. Keep left on Munns Road and it will lead to the park entrance on the right.

Sooke

East Sooke Regional Park
East Sooke Road
Sooke, BC
250-478-3344
This park offers miles of trails through forests and along the rugged coastline. Enjoy views of the Olympic Mountains and the Strait of Juan de Fuca. The trails are rated easy to challenging. Dogs are welcome at the park and on the trails, but not on the beaches during the summer. The park district recommends that you keep your pets on leash in all high use areas and that pets need to be under your control at all times. The park is located about one hour from Victoria. To get there, take the Trans Canada Highway from Victoria and take the Colwood exit. Follow Old Island Highway which turns into Sooke Road. Turn left onto Gillespie Road and then turn right onto East Sooke Road.

Victoria

Beacon Hill Park
Douglas Street
Victoria, BC
250-385-5711
Views from oceanside bluffs and wildflowers on slopes can both be enjoyed at this park. The interior of the park features manicured flowerbeds and bridges over streams. Dogs on leash are allowed. Dogs can be off-leash at the gravel beach located along Dallas Road, between Douglas and Cook Street.

Restaurants

Victoria

17 Mile House Pub and Restaurant
5126 Sooke Road
Victoria, BC V9C 4C4
250-642-5942
Well-behaved, leashed dogs are allowed at the outdoor tables that are closest to the lawn.

Baja Grill
1600 Bay Street
Victoria, BC V8R 2B6
250-592-0027
This Mexican restaurant allows well-behaved, leashed dogs at their outdoor tables.

Cafe Brio
944 Fort Street
Victoria, BC
250-383-0009
This restaurant serves West Coast contemporary food with a Tuscan hint. They focus on using local, certified organic produce whenever possible. Menu items include salads, pasta, seafood, meat, poultry and dessert. Reservations are recommended. Well-behaved, leashed dogs are allowed at the outdoor tables.

Gino Cappuccino
777 Royal Oak Drive
Victoria, BC V8X 4V1
250-727-7722
This coffee house welcomes dogs to their outdoor tables. They will even give your dog a bowl of water. Items on the menu include coffee, cappuccino, tea, Italian Sodas, steamed milk, bagels, muffins and scones.

Golden Saigon Vietnamese Restaurant
1002 Johnson Street
Victoria, BC V8V 3N7
250-361-0015
Well-behaved, leashed dogs are allowed at the outdoor tables.

Pagliacci's
1011 Broad Street
Victoria, BC V8W 2A1
250-386-1662
This Italian restaurant offers homemade pasta, focaccia bread, cheesecake and more. Well-

behaved, leashed dogs are allowed at the outdoor sidewalk tables.

Westbank Dog Travel Guide
Accommodations

Westbank

Holiday Inn
2569 Dobbin Rd
Westbank, BC V4T 2J6
250-768-8879
There is a $10 per day additional pet fee.

Whistler Dog Travel Guide
Accommodations

Whistler

Chateau Whistler Resort
4599 Chateau Blvd
Whistler, BC
604-938-8000
This is a 5 star resort. There is no weight limit for dogs. There is a $25 per night additional pet fee.

Coast Whistler Hotel
4005 Whistler Way
Whistler, BC V0N 1B4
604-932-2522
All Coast Hotels have on hand extra pet amenities if you forget something. For dogs, they have extra doggy dishes, sleeping cushions, nylon chew toys and dog food. If your dog needs one of these items, just ask the front desk. There is a $25 one time pet fee.

Residence Inn by Marriott
4899 Painted Cliff Road
Whistler, BC V0N 1B4
604-905-3400
Thanks to one of our readers who writes "Offers a fantastic outdoor playground for dogs, located slopeside in the trees... and the town of Whistler is dog friendly. The town even has "dog-sitters" available, who you can hire to walk and play with your dog if you need the service (while you are out skiing). They were great." There is a $25 per day pet charge.

Summit Lodge
4359 Main Street
Whistler, BC
604-932-2778
Well-behaved dogs of all sizes are welcome at this hotel. Amenities include a year-round heated outdoor pool and hot tub. There is a $15 per day pet charge.

Chapter 19

West Coast Beach Guides

California Listings

San Diego

North Beach Dog Run
Ocean Blvd.
Coronado, CA

This dog beach is located in the city of Coronado at the end of Ocean Blvd next to the U.S. Naval Station entrance. Park on the street and walk along the Naval Station fence until you reach the ocean and then bear right. There will be signs posted for the North Beach Dog Run.

La Jolla Shores Beach
Camino Del Oro
La Jolla, CA
619-221-8900
Leashed dogs are allowed on this beach and the adjacent Kellogg Park from 6pm to 9am. The beach is about 1/2 mile long. To get there, take Hwy 5 to the La Jolla Village Drive exit heading west. Turn left onto Torrey Pines Rd. Then turn right onto La Jolla Shores Drive. Go 4-5 blocks and turn left onto Vallecitos. Go straight until you reach the beach and Kellogg Park.

Point La Jolla Beaches
Coast Blvd.
La Jolla, CA
619-221-8900
Leashed dogs are allowed on this beach and the walkway (paved and dirt trails) from 6pm to 9am. The beaches and walkway are at least a 1/2 mile long and might continue further. To get there, exit La Jolla Village Drive West from Hwy 5. Turn left onto Torrey Pines Rd. Turn right on Prospect and then park or turn right onto Coast Blvd. Parking is limited around the village area.

Dog Beach
Point Loma Blvd.
Ocean Beach, CA
619-221-8900
Dogs are allowed to run off leash at this beach anytime during the day. This is a very popular dog beach which attracts lots and lots of dogs on warm days. To get there, take Hwy 8 West until it ends and then it becomes Sunset Cliffs Blvd. Then make a right turn onto Point Loma Blvd and follow the signs to Ocean Beach's Dog Beach.

Ocean Beach
Point Loma Blvd.
Ocean Beach, CA

619-221-8900
Leashed dogs are allowed on this beach from 6pm to 9am. The beach is about 1/2 mile long. To get there, take Hwy 8 West until it ends and then it becomes Sunset Cliffs Blvd. Then make a right turn onto Point Loma Blvd and follow the signs to Ocean Beach Park. A separate beach called Dog Beach is at the north end of this beach which allows dogs to run off-leash.

Fiesta Island
Fiesta Island Road
San Diego, CA
619-221-8900
On this island, dogs are allowed to run off-leash anywhere outside the fenced areas, anytime during the day. It is mostly sand which is perfect for those beach loving hounds. You might, however, want to stay on the north end of the island. The south end was used as the city's sludge area (mud and sediment, and possibly smelly) processing facility. The island is often used to launch jet-skis and motorboats. There is a one-way road that goes around the island and there are no fences, so please make sure your dog stays away from the road. About half way around the island, there is a completely fenced area on the beach. Please note that the fully enclosed area is not a dog park. The city of San Diego informed us that is supposed to be locked and is not intended to be used as a dog park even though there may occasionally be dogs running in this off-limits area.

San Diego County North

Cardiff State Beach
Old Highway 101
Cardiff, CA
760-753-5091
This is a gently sloping sandy beach with warm water. Popular activities include swimming, surfing and beachcombing. Dogs on leash are allowed and please clean up after your pets. The beach is located on Old Highway 101, one mile south of Cardiff.

Del Mar Beach
Seventeenth Street
Del Mar, CA
858-755-1556
Dogs are allowed on the beach as follows. South of 17th Street, dogs are allowed on a 6 foot leash year-round. Between 17th Street and 29th Street, dogs are allowed on a 6 foot leash from October through May (from June through September, dogs are not allowed at all). Between 29th Street and

northern city limits, dogs are allowed without a leash, but must be under voice control from October through May (from June through September, dogs must be on a 6 foot leash). Owners must clean up after their dogs.

Rivermouth Beach
Highway 101
Del Mar, CA

This beach allows voice controlled dogs to run leash free from September 15 through June 15 (no specified hours). Leashes are required during mid-summer tourist season from mid June to mid Sept. Fans of this beach are trying to convince the Del Mar City council to extend the leash-free period to year round. The beach is located on Highway 101 just south of Border Avenue at the north end of the City of Del Mar. Thanks to one of our readers for recommending this beach.

Anaheim - Orange County

Corona Del Mar State Beach
Iris Street and Ocean Blvd.
Corona Del Mar, CA
949-644-3151
This is a popular beach for swimming, surfing and diving. The sandy beach is about a half mile long. Dogs are allowed on this beach during certain hours. They are allowed before 9am and after 5pm, year round. Pets must be on a 6 foot or less leash. Tickets will be issued if your dog is off leash.

Huntington Dog Beach
Pacific Coast Hwy (Hwy 1)
Huntington Beach, CA
714-536-5486
This beautiful beach is about a mile long and allows dogs from dawn to dusk. Dogs must be on leash and owners must pick up after them. They are permitted off leash ONLY in the water and must be under control at all times. Dogs are only allowed on the beach between Golden West Street and Seapoint Ave. Please adhere to these rules as there are only a couple of dog-friendly beaches left in the entire Los Angeles area. The beach is located off the Pacific Coast Hwy (Hwy 1) at Golden West Street. Please remember to pick up after your dog... the city wanted to prohibit dogs in 1997 because of the dog waste left on the beach. But thanks to The Preservation Society of Huntington Dog Beach (http: //www.dogbeach.org), it continues to be dog-friendly. City ordinances require owners to pick up after their dogs.

Main Beach
Pacific Hwy (Hwy 1)
Laguna Beach, CA
949-497-3311
Dogs are allowed on this beach between 6pm and 8am, June 1 to September 16. The rest of the year, they are allowed on the beach from dawn until dusk. Dogs must be on a leash at all times.

Newport and Balboa Beaches
Balboa Blvd.
Newport Beach, CA
949-644-3211
There are several smaller beaches which run along Balboa Blvd. Dogs are only allowed before 9am and after 5pm, year round. Pets must be on a 6 foot or less leash and people are required to clean up after their pets. Tickets will be issued if your dog is off leash. The beaches are located along Balboa Blvd and ample parking is located near the Balboa and Newport Piers.

Los Angeles - Hollywood

Haute Dogs on the Beach
on the beach
Long Beach, CA
562-570-3100
Once a month, during the spring and summer months, a certain section of the beach is open to dogs. Between 300 to 450 dogs come to play leash free in the shore each time. The special once a month event is organized by a private citizen and his website is http: //www.hautedogs.org/. Take a look at his website for dates and times.

Long Beach Dog Beach Zone
between Roycroft and Argonne Avenues
Long Beach, CA

This is a new three acre off-leash dog beach zone during specified hours daily. This is the only off leash beach that we are aware of in Los Angeles County and one of the few in Southern California. The hours vary by season and are 6 - 9 am & 6 - 8 pm during the summer from Memorial Day to Labor Day. During the rest of the year the hours are 6 - 9 am & 4 - 6 pm. Dogs are not permitted on the beach at any other time other than the scheduled hours. Dogs must be under visual and voice control of the owners. You can check with the website http://www.hautedogs.org for updates and additional rules about the Long Beach Dog Beach Zone.

Leo Carrillo State Beach
Hwy 1
Malibu, CA
818-880-0350
This beach is one of the very few dog-friendly beaches in the Los Angeles area. In a press release dated November 27, 2002, the California State Parks clarified the rules for dogs at Leo Carrillo State Beach. We thank the State Parks for this clear announcement of the regulations. Dogs are allowed on a maximum 6 foot leash when accompanied by a person capable of controlling the dog on all beach WEST (up coast) of lifeguard tower 3 at Leo Carrillo State Park, Staircase Beach, County Line Beach, and all Beaches within Point Mugu State Park. Dogs are NOT allowed EAST of lifeguard tower 3 at Leo Carrillo State Beach at any time. And please note that dogs are not allowed in the tide pools at Leo Carrillo. There should be signs posted. A small general store is located on the mountain side of the freeway. Here you can grab some snacks and other items. The park is located on Hwy 1, approximately 30 miles northwest of Santa Monica. We ask that all dog people closely obey these regulations so that the beach continues to be dog-friendly.

Ventura - Oxnard

Hollywood Beach
various addresses
Oxnard, CA

This beach is located on the west side of the Channel Islands Harbor. The beach is 4 miles southwest of Oxnard. Dogs must be on leash and owners must clean up after their pets. Thanks to one of our readers for recommending this beach.

Oxnard Shores Beach
Harbor Blvd.
Oxnard, CA

This beach stretches for miles. If you enter at 5th Street and go north, there are no houses and very few people. Dogs must be on leash and owners must clean up after their pets. Thanks to one of our readers for recommending this beach.

Silverstrand Beach
various addresses
Oxnard, CA

This beach is located between the Channel Islands Harbor and the U.S. Naval Construction Battalion Center. The beach is 4 miles southwest

of Oxnard. Dogs must be on leash and owners must clean up after their pets. Thanks to one of our readers for recommending this beach.

Santa Barbara

Goleta Beach County Park
5990 Sandspit Road
Goleta, CA
805-568-2460
Leashed dogs are allowed at this county beach. The beach and park are about 1/2 mile long. There are picnic tables and a children's playground at the park. It's located near the Santa Barbara Municipal Airport in Goleta, just north of Santa Barbara. To get there, take Hwy 101 to Hwy 217 and head west. Before you reach UC Santa Barbara, there will be an exit for Goleta Beach.

Arroyo Burro Beach County Park
2981 Cliff Drive
Santa Barbara, CA
805-967-1300
Leashed dogs are allowed at this county beach and park. The beach is about 1/2 mile long and it is adjacent to a palm-lined grassy area with picnic tables. To get to the beach from Hwy 101, exit Las Positas Rd/Hwy 225. Head south (towards the ocean). When the street ends, turn right onto Cliff Drive. The beach will be on the left.

Arroyo Burro Off-Leash Beach
Cliff Drive
Santa Barbara, CA

While dogs are not allowed off-leash at the Arroyo Burro Beach County Park (both the beach and grass area), they are allowed to run leash free on the adjacent beach. The dog beach starts east of the slough at Arroyo Burro and stretches almost to the stairs at Mesa Lane. To get to the off-leash area, walk your leashed dog from the parking lot to the beach, turn left and cross the slough. At this point you can remove your dog's leash.

Rincon Park and Beach
Bates Road
Santa Barbara, CA

This beach is at Rincon Point which has some of the best surfing waves in the world. In the winter, it is very popular with surfers. In the summer, it is a popular swimming beach. Year-round, leashed dogs are welcome. The beach is about 1/2-1 mile long. Next to the parking lot there are picnic tables, phones and restrooms. The beach is in

Santa Barbara County, about 15-20 minutes south of Santa Barbara. To get there from Santa Barbara, take Hwy 101 south and go past Carpinteria. Take the Bates Rd exit towards the ocean. When the road ends, turn right into the Rincon Park and Beach parking lot.

Avila Beach

Avila Beach
off Avila Beach Drive
Avila Beach, CA
805-595-5400
This beach is about a 1/2 mile long. Dogs are not allowed between 10am and 5pm and must be leashed.

Olde Port Beach
off Avila Beach Drive
Avila Beach, CA
805-595-5400
This beach is about a 1/4 mile long. Dogs are not allowed between 10am and 5pm and must be leashed.

San Luis Obispo

Oceano Dunes State Vehicular Recreation Area
Highway 1
Oceano, CA
805-473-7220
This 3,600 acre off road area offers 5 1/2 miles of beach which is open for vehicle use. Pets on leash are allowed too. Swimming, surfing, horseback riding and bird watching are all popular activities at the beach. The park is located three miles south of Pismo Beach off Highway 1.

Lake Nacimiento Resort Day Use Area
10625 Nacimiento Lake Drive
Paso Robles, CA
805-238-3256
In addition to the campgrounds and RV area, this resort also offers day use of the lake. Dogs can swim in the water, but be very careful of boats, as this is a popular lake for water-skiing. Day use fees vary by season and location, but in general rates are about $5 to $8 per person. Senior discounts are available. Dogs are an extra $5 per day. Proof of your dog's rabies vaccination is required.

Pismo State Beach
Grand Ave.
Pismo Beach, CA
805-489-2684

Leashed dogs are allowed on this state beach. This beach is popular for walking, sunbathing, swimming and the annual winter migration of millions of monarch butterflies (the park has the largest over-wintering colony of monarch butterflies in the U.S.). To get there from Hwy 101, exit 4th Street and head south. In about a mile, turn right onto Grand Ave. You can park along the road.

Coastal Access
off Hearst Drive
San Simeon, CA

There is parking just north of the Best Western Hotel, next to the "Coastal Access" sign. Dogs must be on leash.

Gorda

Kirk Creek Beach and Trailhead
Highway 1
Gorda, CA
831-385-5434
Both the Kirk Creek Beach and hiking trails allow dogs. Pets must be leashed. You can park next to the Kirk Creek Campground and either hike down to the beach or start hiking at the Kirk Creek Trailhead which leads to the Vicente Flat Trail where you can hike for miles with your dog. The beach and trailhead is part of the Los Padres National Forest and is located about 25 miles south of Big Sur.

Sand Dollar Beach
Highway 1
Gorda, CA
805-434-1996
Walk down a path to one of the longest sandy beaches on the Big Sur Coast. This national forest managed beach is popular for surfing, fishing and walking. Dogs must be on leash and people need to clean up after their pets. There is a minimal day use fee. The dog-friendly Plaskett Creek Campround is within walking distance. This beach is part of the Los Padres National Forest and is located about 5 miles south of the Kirk Creek and about 30 miles south of Big Sur.

Willow Creek Beach
Highway 1
Gorda, CA
831-385-5434
Dogs on leash are allowed at this day use beach and picnic area. The beach is part of the Los Padres National Forest and is located about 35 miles south of Big Sur.

Big Sur

Pfieffer Beach
Sycamore Road
Big Sur, CA
805-968-6640
Dogs on leash are allowed at this day use beach which is located in the Los Padres National Forest. The beach is located in Big Sur, south of the Big Sur Ranger Station. From Big Sur, start heading south on Highway 1 and look carefully for Sycamore Road. Take Sycamore Road just over 2 miles to the beach. There is a $5 entrance fee per car.

Carmel

Carmel City Beach
Ocean Avenue
Carmel, CA
831-624-9423
This beach is within walking distance (about 7 blocks) from the quaint village of Carmel. There are a couple of hotels and several restaurants that are within walking distance of the beach. Your pooch is allowed to run off-leash as long as he or she is under voice control. To get there, take the Ocean Avenue exit from Hwy 1 and follow Ocean Ave to the end.

Carmel River State Beach
Carmelo Street
Carmel, CA
831-624-9423
This beach is just south of Carmel. It has approximately a mile of beach and leashes are required. It's located on Carmelo Street.

Garrapata State Park
Highway 1
Carmel, CA
831-649-2836
There are two miles of beach front at this park. Dogs are allowed but must be on a 6 foot or less leash and people need to clean up after their pets. The beach is on Highway 1, about 6 1/2 miles south of Rio Road in Carmel. It is about 18 miles north of Big Sur.

Monterey

Monterey Recreation Trail
various (see comments)
Monterey, CA

Take a walk on the Monterey Recreation Trail and experience the beautiful scenery that makes Monterey so famous. This paved trail extends for miles, starting at Fisherman's Wharf and ending in the city of Pacific Grove. Dogs must be leashed. Along the path there are a few small beaches that allow dogs such as the one south of Fisherman's Wharf and another beach behind Ghiradelli Ice Cream on Cannery Row. Along the path you'll find a few more outdoor places to eat near Cannery Row and by the Monterey Bay Aquarium. Look at the Restaurants section for more info.

Monterey State Beach
various (see comments)
Monterey, CA
831-649-2836
Take your water loving and beach loving dog to this awesome beach in Monterey. There are various starting points, but it basically stretches from Hwy 1 and the Del Rey Oaks Exit down to Fisherman's Wharf. Various beaches make up this 2 mile (each way) stretch of beach, but leashed dogs are allowed on all of them . If you want to extend your walk, you can continue on the paved Monterey Recreation Trail which goes all the way to Pacific Grove. There are a few smaller dog-friendly beaches along the paved trail.

Asilomar State Beach
Along Sunset Drive
Pacific Grove, CA
831-372-4076
Dogs are permitted on leash on the beach and the scenic walking trails. If you walk south along the beach and go across the stream that leads into the ocean, you can take your dog off-leash, but he or she must be under strict voice control and within your sight at all times.

Santa Cruz

Rio Del Mar Beach
Rio Del Mar
Aptos, CA
831-685-6500
Dogs on leash are allowed at this beach which offers a wide strip of sand. From Highway 1, take the Rio Del Mar exit.

Davenport Beach
Hwy 1
Davenport, CA
831-462-8333
This beautiful beach is surrounded by high bluffs and cliff trails. Leashes are required. To get to the beach from Santa Cruz, head north on Hwy 1 for

about 10 miles.

Manresa State Beach
San Andreas Road
Manresa, CA
831-761-1795
Surfing and surf fishing are both popular activities at this beach. Dogs are allowed on the beach, but must be leashed. To get there from Aptos, head south on Highway 1. Take San Andreas Road southwest for several miles until you reach Manresa. Upon reaching the coast, you will find the first beach access point.

East Cliff Coast Access Points
East Cliff Drive
Santa Cruz, CA
831-454-7900
There are many small dog-friendly beaches and coastal access points that stretch along East Cliff Drive between 12th Avenue to 41st Avenue. This is not one long beach because the water comes up to cliffs in certain areas and breaks it up into many smaller beaches. Dogs are allowed on leash. Parking is on city streets along East Cliff or the numbered avenues. To get there from Hwy 17 south, take the Hwy 1 exit south towards Watsonville. Take the exit towards Soquel Drive. Turn left onto Soquel Avenue. Turn right onto 17th Avenue. Continue straight until you reach East Cliff Drive. From here, you can head north or south on East Cliff Drive and park anywhere between 12th and 41st street to access the beaches.

Its Beach
West Cliff Drive
Santa Cruz, CA
831-429-3777
Your dog can go leash free from sunrise to 10am and 4pm until sunset. It is not a large beach, but enough for your water loving dog to take a dip in the water and get lots of sand between his or her paws. According to the sign, dogs are not allowed between 10am and 4pm. It is located on West Cliff Drive, just north of the Lighthouse, and south of Columbia Street. It is also across from the Lighthouse Field off-leash area. To get there, head south on Hwy 17. Take the Hwy 1 North exit, heading towards Half Moon Bay and Hwy 9. Merge onto Mission Street (Hwy 1). Turn left onto Swift Street. Then turn left on West Cliff Drive. The beach and limited parking will be on the right.

Seabright Beach
Seabright Ave
Santa Cruz, CA
831-429-2850

This beach is located south of the Santa Cruz Beach Boardwalk and north of the Santa Cruz Harbor. Dogs are allowed on leash. Fire rings are available for beach bonfires. It is open from sunrise to sunset. To get there from Hwy 17 south, exit Ocean Street on the left towards the beaches. Merge onto Ocean Street. Turn left onto East Cliff Drive and stay straight to go onto Murray Street. Then turn right onto Seabright Ave. Seabright Ave will take you to the beach (near the corner of East Cliff Drive and Seabright).

Twin Lakes State Beach
East Cliff Drive
Santa Cruz, CA
831-429-2850
This beach is one of the area's warmest beaches, due to its location at the entrance of Schwann Lagoon. Dogs are allowed on leash. The beach is located just south of the Santa Cruz Harbor where Aldo's Restaurant is located. Fire rings for beach bonfires, outdoor showers and restrooms are available. It is open from sunrise to sunset. To get there from Hwy 17 south, exit Ocean Street on the left towards the beaches. Merge onto Ocean Street. Turn left onto East Cliff Drive and stay straight to go onto Murray Street. Murray Street becomes Eaton Street. Turn right onto 7th Avenue.

Palo Alto - Peninsula

Blufftop Coastal Park
Poplar Street
Half Moon Bay, CA
650-726-8297
Leashed dogs are allowed at this beach. The beach is located on the west end of Poplar Street, off Highway 1.

Montara State Beach
Highway 1
Half Moon Bay, CA
650-726-8819
Dogs on leash are allowed at this beach. Please clean up after your pets. The beach is located 8 miles north of Half Moon Bay on Highway 1. There are two beach access points. The first access point is across from Second Street, immediately south of the Outrigger Restaurant. The second access point is about a 1/2 mile north on the ocean side of Highway 1. Both access points have steep paths down to the beach.

Surfer's Beach
Highway 1
Half Moon Bay, CA

650-726-8297
Dogs on leash are allowed on the beach. It is located at Highway 1 and Coronado Street.

Esplanade Beach
Esplanade
Pacifica, CA
650-738-7381
This beach offers an off-leash area for dogs. To get to the beach, take the stairs at the end of Esplanade. Esplanade is just north of Manor Drive, off Highway 1.

Bean Hollow State Beach
Highway 1
Pescadero, CA
650-879-2170
This is a very rocky beach with not much sand. Dogs are allowed but must be on a 6 foot or less leash. Please clean up after your pets. The beach is located 3 miles south of Pescadero on Highway 1.

San Francisco

Baker Beach
Golden Gate Natl Rec Area
San Francisco, CA

This dog-friendly beach in the Golden Gate National Recreation Area has a great view of the Golden Gate Bridge. The beach is located approx. 1.5 to 2 miles south of the Golden Gate Bridge. From Lincoln Avenue, turn onto Bowley Street and head towards the ocean. There is a parking lot next to the beach.

Fort Funston/Burton Beach
Skyline Blvd./Hwy 35
San Francisco, CA

This is a very popular dog-friendly park and beach. In the past, dogs have been allowed off-leash. However, currently all dogs must be on leash. Fort Funston is part of the Golden Gate National Recreation Area. There are trails that run through the dunes & ice plant from the parking lot above with good access to the beach below. It overlooks the southern end of Ocean Beach, with a large parking area accessible from Skyline Boulevard. There is also a water faucet and trough at the parking lot for thirsty pups. It's located off Skyline Blvd. (also known Hwy 35) by John Muir Drive. It is south of Ocean Beach. Thanks to one of our readers for this info. Expect to see lots and lots of dogs having a great time. But not to worry, there is plenty of room for

everyone.

Ocean Beach
Great Hwy
San Francisco, CA
415-556-8642
You'll get a chance to stretch your legs at this beach which has about 4 miles of sand. The beach runs parallel to the Great Highway (north of Fort Funston). There are several access points including Sloat Blvd., Fulton Street or Lincoln Way. This beach has a mix of off-leash and leash required areas. Thanks to the San Francisco Dog Owners Group (SFDOG) for providing the following information: Dogs must be on leash on Ocean Beach between Sloat Blvd and Stairwell #21 (roughly at Fulton). North of Fulton to the Cliff House and South of Sloat for several miles are still okay for off-leash dogs, however parts of these areas may be impassible at high tide. The Golden Gate National Rec Area (GGNRA) strictly enforces the on-leash area between Sloat and Fulton. They usually give no warning tickets ($50 fine). As with all other leash required areas, we encourage dog owners to comply with the rules.

Marin - North Bay

Doran Regional Park
201 Doran Beach Road
Bodega Bay, CA
707-875-3540
This park offers 2 miles of sandy beach. It is a popular place to picnic, walk, surf, fish and fly kites. Dogs are allowed but must be on a 6 foot or less leash and proof of a rabies vaccination is required. There is a minimal parking fee. The park is located south of Bodega Bay.

Agate Beach
Elm Road
Bolinas, CA
415-499-6387
During low tide, this 6 acre park provides access to almost 2 miles of shoreline. Leashed dogs are allowed.

Muir Beach
Hwy 1
Muir Beach, CA

Dogs on leash are allowed on Muir Beach with you. Please clean up after your dog on the beach. To get to Muir Beach from Hwy 101 take Hwy 1 North from the north side of the Golden Gate Bridge.

Point Reyes National Seashore

Olema, CA
415-464-5100
Leashed dogs (on a 6 foot or less leash) are allowed on four beaches. The dog-friendly beaches are the Limantour Beach, Kehoe Beach, North Beach and South Beach. Dogs are not allowed on the hiking trails. However, they are allowed on some hiking trails that are adjacent to Point Reyes. For a map of dog-friendly hiking trails, please stop by the Visitor Center. Point Reyes is located about an hour north of San Francisco. From Highway 101, exit at Sir Francis Drake Highway, and continue west on Sir Francis Drake to Olema. To find the Visitor Center, turn right in Olema onto Route 1 and then make a left onto Bear Valley Road. The Visitor Center will be on the left.

Upton Beach

Highway 1
Stinson Beach, CA
415-499-6387
Dogs not allowed on the National Park section of Stinson Beach but are allowed at Upton Beach which is under Marin County's jurisdiction. This beach is located north of the National Park. Dogs are permitted without leash but under direct and immediate control.

Sonoma

Cloverdale River Park

31820 McCray Road
Cloverdale, CA
707-565-2041
This park is located along the Russian River and offers seasonal fishing and river access for kayaks and canoes. There are no lifeguards at the beach area. Dogs are allowed, but must be on a 6 foot or less leash. They can wade into the water, but cannot really swim because pets must remain on leash. There is a $3 per car parking fee.

Healdsburg Memorial Beach

13839 Old Redwood Highway
Healdsburg, CA
707-565-2041
This man-made swimming beach is located on the Russian River. Dogs are allowed at this park, but must be on a 6 foot or less leash. They can wade into the water, but cannot really swim because pets must remain on leash. People are urged to swim only when lifeguards are present, which is usually between Memorial Day and

Labor Day. The beach area also offers picnic tables and a restroom. There is a $3 to $4 parking fee per day, depending on the season.

Sea Ranch Coastal Access Trails

Highway 1
Sea Ranch, CA
707-785-2377
Walk along coastal headlands or the beach in Sea Ranch. There are six trailhead parking areas which are located along Highway 1, south of the Sonoma Mendocino County Line. Access points include Black Point, Bluff Top Trail, Pebble Beach, Stengal Beach, Shell Beach and Walk on Beach. Dogs must be on a 6 foot or less leash. There is a $3 per car parking fee. RVs and vehicles with trailers are not allowed to use the parking areas.

Salmon Creek

Sonoma Coast State Beach

Highway 1
Salmon Creek, CA
707-875-3483
Dogs on leash are allowed at some of the beaches in this state park. Dogs are allowed at Shell Beach, Portuguese Beach and Schoolhouse Beach. They are not allowed at Goat Rock or Salmon Creek Beach due to the protected seals and snowy plovers. Please clean up after your pets. While dogs are allowed on some of the beaches and campgrounds, they are not allowed on any hiking trails at this park.

Jenner

Stillwater Cove Regional Park

22455 Highway 1
Jenner, CA
707-565-2041
This 210 acre park includes a small beach, campground, picnic tables, and restrooms. The park offers a great view of the Pacific Ocean from Stillwater Cove. Dogs are allowed on the beach, and in the campground, but they must be on a 6 foot or less leash. People also need to clean up after their pets. There is a $3 day use fee. The park is located off Highway 1, about 16 miles north of Jenner.

Gualala

Gualala Point Regional Park Beach

42401 Coast Highway 1
Gualala, CA

707-565-2041
This county park offers sandy beaches, hiking trails, campsites, picnic tables and restrooms. Dogs are allowed on the beach, on the trails, and in the campground, but they must be on a 6 foot or less leash. People also need to clean up after their pets. There is a $3 day use fee.

Mendocino

Big River Beach
N. Big River Road
Mendocino, CA
707-937-5804
This small beach is located just south of downtown Mendocino. There are two ways to get there. One way is to head south of town on Hwy 1 and turn left on N. Big River Rd. The beach will be on the right. The second way is to take Hwy 1 and exit Main Street/Jackson heading towards the coastline. In about 1/4-1/2 mile there will be a Chevron Gas Station and a historic church on the left. Park and then walk behind the church to the trailhead. Follow the trail, bearing left when appropriate, and there will be a wooden staircase that goes down to Big River Beach. Dogs must be on leash.

Van Damme State Beach
Highway 1
Mendocino, CA

This small beach is located in the town of Little River which is approximately 2 miles south of Mendocino. It is part of Van Damme State Park which is located across Highway 1. Most California State Parks, including this one, do not allow dogs on the hiking trails. Fortunately this one allows dogs on the beach. There is no parking fee at the beach and dogs must be on leash.

Fort Bragg

MacKerricher State Park
Highway 1
Fort Bragg, CA
707-964-9112
Dogs are allowed on the beach, but not on any park trails. Pets must be leashed and people need to clean up after their pets. Picnic areas, restrooms and campsites (including an ADA restroom and campsites), are available at this park. The park is located three miles north of Fort Bragg on Highway 1, near the town of Cleone.

Westport

Westport-Union Landing State Beach
Highway 1
Westport, CA
707-937-5804
This park offers about 2 miles of sandy beach. Dogs must be on a 6 foot or less leash at all times and people need to clean up after their pets. Picnic tables, restrooms (including an ADA restroom) and campsites are available at this park. Dogs are also allowed at the campsites, but not on any park trails. The park is located off Highway 1, about 2 miles north of Westport or 19 miles north of Fort Bragg.

Eureka

Samoa Dunes Recreation Area
New Navy Base Road
Samoa, CA
707-825-2300
The Bureau of Land Management oversees this 300 acre sand dune park. It is a popular spot for off-highway vehicles which can use about 140 of the park's acres. Dogs are allowed on leash or off-leash but under voice control. Even if your dog runs off-leash, the park service requests that you still bring a leash just in case. To get there, take Highway 255 and turn south on New Navy Base Road. Go about four miles to the parking area.

Arcata

Mad River Beach County Park
Mad River Road
Arcata, CA
707-445-7651
Enjoy walking or jogging for several miles on this beach. Dogs on leash are allowed. The park is located about 4-5 miles north of Arcata. To get there, take Highway 101 and exit Giuntoli Lane. Then go north onto Heindon Rd. Turn left onto Miller Rd. Turn right on Mad River Road and follow it to the park.

McKinleyville

Clam Beach County Park
Highway 101
McKinleyville, CA
707-445-7651
This beach is popular for fishing, swimming, picnicking and beachcombing. Of course, there are also plenty of clams. Dogs on leash are allowed on the beach and at the campgrounds.

There are no day use fees. The park is located off Highway 101, about eight miles north of Arcata.

Trinidad

Trinidad State Beach
Highway 101
Trinidad, CA
707-677-3570
Dogs are unofficially allowed at College Cove beach, as long as they are leashed and under control. The residents in this area are trying keep this beach dog-friendly, but the rules can change at any time. Please call ahead to verify.

Orick

Gold Bluffs Beach
Davison Road
Orick, CA
707-464-6101
Dogs are allowed on this beach, but not on any trails within this park. Picnic tables and campgrounds are available at the beach. Pets are also allowed at road accessible picnic areas and campgrounds. Dogs must be on a 6 foot or less leash and people need to pick up after their pets. The beach is located off Highway 101. Take Highway 101 heading north. Pass Orick and drive about 3-4 miles, then exit Davison Rd. Head towards the coast on an unpaved road (trailers are not allowed on the unpaved road).

Crescent City

Beachfront Park
Front Street
Crescent City, CA
707-464-9507
Dogs are allowed at park and the beach, but must be leashed. Please clean up after your pets. To get there, take Highway 101 to Front Street. Follow Front Street to the park.

Crescent Beach
Enderts Beach Road
Crescent City, CA
707-464-6101
While dogs are not allowed on any trails in Redwood National Park, they are allowed on a couple of beaches, including Crescent Beach. Enjoy beachcombing or bird watching at this beach. Pets are also allowed at road accessible picnic areas and campgrounds. Dogs must be on a 6 foot or less leash and people need to pick up after their pets. The beach is located off Highway

101, about 3 to 4 miles south of Crescent City. Exit Enderts Beach Road and head south.

Oregon Listings

Brookings

Harris Beach State Park
Highway 101
Brookings, OR
541-469-2021
The park offers sandy beaches for beachcombing, whale watching, and sunset viewing. Picnic tables, restrooms (including an ADA restroom) and shaded campsites are available at this park. There is a minimal day use fee. Leashed dogs are allowed on the beach. Dogs are also allowed at the campgrounds. They must be on a six foot or less leash at all times and people are required to clean up after their pets. On beaches located outside of Oregon State Park boundries, dogs might be allowed off-leash and under direct voice control, please look for signs or postings. This park is located off U.S. Highway 101, just north of Brookings.

McVay Rock State Recreation Site
Highway 101
Brookings, OR
800-551-6949
This beach is a popular spot for clamming, whale watching and walking. Picnic tables and restrooms are available at this park. There are no day use fees. Dogs are allowed on the beach. They must be on a six foot or less leash at all times and people are required to clean up after their pets. On beaches located outside of Oregon State Park boundries, dogs might be allowed off-leash and under direct voice control, please look for signs or postings. This park is located off U.S. Highway 101, just south of Brookings.

Samuel H. Boardman State Scenic Corridor
Highway 101
Brookings, OR
800-551-6949
Steep coastline at this 12 mile long corridor is interrupted by small sandy beaches. Picnic tables, restrooms (including an ADA restroom), and a hiking trail are available at this park. There are no day use fees. Leashed dogs are allowed on the beach. Dogs are also allowed on the hiking trail. They must be on a six foot or less leash at all times and people are required to clean up after their pets. On beaches located outside of Oregon

State Park boundries, dogs might be allowed off-leash and under direct voice control, please look for signs or postings. This park is located off U.S. Highway 101, 4 miles north of Brookings.

Gold Beach

Pistol River State Scenic Viewpoint
Highway 101
Gold Beach, OR
800-551-6949
This beach is popular for ocean windsurfing. There has even been windsurfing national championships held at this beach. Picnic tables and restrooms are available here. There are no day use fees. Dogs are allowed on the beach. They must be on a six foot or less leash at all times and people are required to clean up after their pets. On beaches located outside of Oregon State Park boundries, dogs might be allowed off-leash and under direct voice control, please look for signs or postings. This park is located off U.S. Highway 101, 11 miles south of Gold Beach.

Port Orford

Cape Blanco State Park
Highway 101
Port Orford, OR
541-332-6774
Take a stroll on the beach or hike on over eight miles of trails which offer spectacular ocean vistas. Picnic tables, restrooms, hiking and campgrounds are available at this park. There is a minimal day use fee. Leashed dogs are allowed on the beach. Dogs are also allowed on hiking trails and campgrounds. They must be on a six foot or less leash at all times and people are required to clean up after their pets. On beaches located outside of Oregon State Park boundries, dogs might be allowed off-leash and under direct voice control, please look for signs or postings. This park is located off U.S. Highway 101, 9 miles north of Port Orford.

Humbug Mountain State Park
Highway 101
Port Orford, OR
541-332-6774
This beach is frequented by windsurfers and scuba divers. A popular activity at this park is hiking to the top of Humbug Mountain (elevation 1,756 feet) . Picnic tables, restrooms, hiking and campgrounds are available at this park. There is a minimal day use fee. Leashed dogs are allowed on the beach. Dogs are also allowed on hiking trails and campgrounds. They must be on a six

foot or less leash at all times and people are required to clean up after their pets. On beaches located outside of Oregon State Park boundries, dogs might be allowed off-leash and under direct voice control, please look for signs or postings. This park is located off U.S. Highway 101, 6 miles south of Port Orford.

Bandon

Bullards Beach State Park
Highway 101
Bandon, OR
541-347-2209
Enjoy a walk along the beach at this park. Picnic tables, restrooms, hiking and campgrounds are available at the park. There is a minimal day use fees. Leashed dogs are allowed on the beach. Dogs are also allowed on hiking trails and campgrounds. They must be on a six foot or less leash at all times and people are required to clean up after their pets. On beaches located outside of Oregon State Park boundries, dogs might be allowed off-leash and under direct voice control, please look for signs or postings. This park is located off U.S. Highway 101, 2 miles north of Bandon.

Seven Devils State Recreation Site
Highway 101
Bandon, OR
800-551-6949
Enjoy several miles of beach at this park. Picnic tables are available at this park. There are no day use fees. Dogs are allowed on the beach. They must be on a six foot or less leash at all times and people are required to clean up after their pets. On beaches located outside of Oregon State Park boundries, dogs might be allowed off-leash and under direct voice control, please look for signs or postings. This park is located off U.S. Highway 101, 10 miles north of Bandon.

Coos Bay

Sunset Bay State Park
Highway 101
Coos Bay, OR
541-888-4902
This park offers sandy beaches protected by towering sea cliffs. The campgrounds located at the park are within a short walk to the beach. You will also find a network of hiking trails here and in two adjacent parks. Picnic tables and restrooms (including an ADA restroom) are available at this park. There is a minimal day use fee. Leashed dogs are allowed on the beach. Dogs are also

allowed on hiking trails and campgrounds. They must be on a six foot or less leash at all times and people are required to clean up after their pets. On beaches located outside of Oregon State Park boundries, dogs might be allowed off-leash and under direct voice control, please look for signs or postings. This park is located off U.S. Highway 101, 12 miles southwest of Coos Bay.

Florence

Carl G. Washburne Memorial State Park
Highway 101
Florence, OR
541-547-3416
This park offers five miles of sandy beach. Picnic tables, restrooms, hiking and campgrounds are available at this park. There is a day use fee. Leashed dogs are allowed on the beach. Dogs are also allowed on hiking trails and campgrounds. They must be on a six foot or less leash at all times and people are required to clean up after their pets. On beaches located outside of Oregon State Park boundries, dogs might be allowed off-leash and under direct voice control, please look for signs or postings. This park is located off U.S. Highway 101, 14 miles north of Florence.

Heceta Head Lighthouse State Scenic Viewpoint
Highway 101
Florence, OR
800-551-6949
Go for a walk above the beach or explore the natural caves and tidepools along the beach. This is a great spot for whale watching. According to the Oregon State Parks Division, the lighthouse located on the west side of 1,000-foot-high Heceta Head (205 feet above ocean) is one of the most photographed on the Oregon coast. Picnic tables, restrooms and hiking are available at this park. There is a $3 day use fee. Leashed dogs are allowed on the beach. Dogs are also allowed on hiking trails. They must be on a six foot or less leash at all times and people are required to clean up after their pets. On beaches located outside of Oregon State Park boundries, dogs might be allowed off-leash and under direct voice control, please look for signs or postings. This park is located off U.S. Highway 101, 13 miles north of Florence.

Yachats

Neptune State Scenic Viewpoint
Highway 101

Yachats, OR
800-551-6949
During low tide at this beach you can walk south and visit a natural cave and tidepools. Or sit and relax at one of the picnic tables that overlooks the beach below. Restrooms (including an ADA restroom) are available at this park. There are no day use fees. Dogs are allowed on the beach. They must be on a six foot or less leash at all times and people are required to clean up after their pets. On beaches located outside of Oregon State Park boundries, dogs might be allowed off-leash and under direct voice control, please look for signs or postings. This park is located off U.S. Highway 101,

Yachats State Recreation Area
Highway 101
Yachats, OR
800-551-6949
This beach is a popular spot for whale watching, salmon fishing, and exploring tidepools. Picnic tables and restrooms are available at this park. There are no day use fees. Dogs are allowed on the beach. They must be on a six foot or less leash at all times and people are required to clean up after their pets. On beaches located outside of Oregon State Park boundries, dogs might be allowed off-leash and under direct voice control, please look for signs or postings. This park is located off U.S. Highway 101 in Yachats.

Waldport

Beachside State Recreation Site
Highway 101
Waldport, OR
541-563-3220
Enjoy miles of broad sandy beach at this park or stay at one of the campground sites that are located just seconds from the beach. Picnic tables, restrooms (including an ADA restroom), and hiking are also available at this park. There is a day use fees. Leashed dogs are allowed on the beach. Dogs are also allowed on hiking trails and campgrounds. They must be on a six foot or less leash at all times and people are required to clean up after their pets. On beaches located outside of Oregon State Park boundries, dogs might be allowed off-leash and under direct voice control, please look for signs or postings. This park is located off U.S. Highway 101, 4 miles south of Waldport.

Governor Patterson Memorial State Recreation Site
Highway 101

Waldport, OR
800-551-6949
This park offers miles of flat, sandy beach. It is also an excellent location for whale watching. Picnic tables and restrooms are available at this park. There are no day use fees. Dogs are allowed on the beach. They must be on a six foot or less leash at all times and people are required to clean up after their pets. On beaches located outside of Oregon State Park boundries, dogs might be allowed off-leash and under direct voice control, please look for signs or postings. This park is located off U.S. Highway 101, 1 mile south of Waldport.

Depoe Bay

Fogarty Creek State Recreation Area
Highway 101
Depoe Bay, OR
800-551-6949
This beach and park offer some of the best birdwatching and tidepooling. Picnic tables and hiking are available at this park. There is a $3 day use fees. Leashed dogs are allowed on the beach. Dogs are also allowed on hiking trails. They must be on a six foot or less leash at all times and people are required to clean up after their pets. On beaches located outside of Oregon State Park boundries, dogs might be allowed off-leash and under direct voice control, please look for signs or postings. This park is located off U.S. Highway 101, 2 miles north of Depoe Bay.

Lincoln City

D River State Recreation Site
Highway 101
Lincoln City, OR
800-551-6949
This beach, located right off the highway, is a popular and typically windy beach. According to the Oregon State Parks Division, this park is home to a pair of the world's largest kite festivals every spring and fall which gives Lincoln City the name Kite Capital of the World. Restrooms are available at the park. Dogs are allowed on the beach. They must be on a six foot or less leash at all times and people are required to clean up after their pets. On beaches located outside of Oregon State Park boundries, dogs might be allowed off-leash and under direct voice control, please look for signs or postings. This park is located off U.S. Highway 101 in Lincoln City.

Roads End State Recreation Site
Highway 101

Lincoln City, OR
800-551-6949
There is a short trail here that leads down to the beach. Picnic tables are available at this park. There are no day use fees. Dogs are allowed on the beach. They must be on a six foot or less leash at all times and people are required to clean up after their pets. On beaches located outside of Oregon State Park boundries, dogs might be allowed off-leash and under direct voice control, please look for signs or postings. This park is located off U.S. Highway 101, 1 mile north of Lincoln City.

Neskowin

Neskowin Beach State Recreation Site
Highway 101
Neskowin, OR
800-551-6949
Not really any facilities (picnic tables, etc.) here, but a good place to enjoy the beach. Dogs are allowed on the beach. They must be on a six foot or less leash at all times and people are required to clean up after their pets. On beaches located outside of Oregon State Park boundries, dogs might be allowed off-leash and under direct voice control, please look for signs or postings. This park is located off U.S. Highway 101 in Neskowin.

Pacific City

Bob Straub State Park
Highway 101
Pacific City, OR
800-551-6949
This is a nice stretch of beach to walk along. Picnic tables and restrooms (including an ADA restroom) are available at this park. There are no day use fees. Dogs are allowed on the beach. They must be on a six foot or less leash at all times and people are required to clean up after their pets. On beaches located outside of Oregon State Park boundries, dogs might be allowed off-leash and under direct voice control, please look for signs or postings. This park is located off U.S. Highway 101 in Pacific City.

Cape Kiwanda State Natural Area
Highway 101
Pacific City, OR
800-551-6949
This beach and park is a good spot for marine mammal watching, hang gliding and kite flying. Picnic tables are available at this park. There are no day use fees. Dogs are allowed on the beach. They must be on a six foot or less leash at all

times and people are required to clean up after their pets. On beaches located outside of Oregon State Park boundaries, dogs might be allowed off-leash and under direct voice control, please look for signs or postings. This park is located off U.S. Highway 101, 1 mile north of Pacific City.

Tillamook

Cape Lookout State Park
Highway 101
Tillamook, OR
503-842-4981
This is a popular beach during the summer. The beach is a short distance from the parking area. It is located about an hour and half west of Portland. Picnic tables, restrooms (including an ADA restroom), hiking trails and campgrounds are available at this park. There is a $3 day use fee. Leashed dogs are allowed on the beach. Dogs are also allowed on hiking trails and campgrounds. They must be on a six foot or less leash at all times and people are required to clean up after their pets. On beaches located outside of Oregon State Park boundaries, dogs might be allowed off-leash and under direct voice control, please look for signs or postings. This park is located off U.S. Highway 101, 12 miles southwest of Tillamook.

Cape Meares State Scenic Viewpoint
Highway 101
Tillamook, OR
800-551-6949
The beach is located south of the scenic viewpoint. The viewpoint is situated on a headland, about 200 feet above the ocean. According to the Oregon State Parks Division, bird watchers can view the largest colony of nesting common murres (this site is one of the most populous colonies of nesting sea birds on the continent). Bald eagles and a peregrine falcon have also been known to nest near here. In winter and spring, this park is an excellent location for viewing whale migrations. Picnic tables, restrooms and hiking are available at this park. There are no day use fees. Leashed dogs are allowed on the beach. Dogs are also allowed on hiking trails. They must be on a six foot or less leash at all times and people are required to clean up after their pets. On beaches located outside of Oregon State Park boundaries, dogs might be allowed off-leash and under direct voice control, please look for signs or postings. This park is located off U.S. Highway 101, 10 miles west of Tillamook.

Rockaway Beach

Manhattan Beach State Recreation Site
Highway 101
Rockaway Beach, OR
800-551-6949
The beach is a short walk from the parking area. Picnic tables are available at this park. There are no day use fees. Dogs are allowed on the beach. They must be on a six foot or less leash at all times and people are required to clean up after their pets. On beaches located outside of Oregon State Park boundaries, dogs might be allowed off-leash and under direct voice control, please look for signs or postings. This park is located off U.S. Highway 101, 2 miles north of Rockaway Beach.

Manzanita

Nehalem Bay State Park
Highway 101
Manzanita, OR
503-368-5154
The beach can be reached by a short walk over the dunes. This park is a popular place for fishing and crabbing. Picnic tables, restrooms (including an ADA restroom), hiking and camping are available at this park. There is a $3 day use fee. Leashed dogs are allowed on the beach. Dogs are also allowed on hiking trails and campgrounds. They must be on a six foot or less leash at all times and people are required to clean up after their pets. On beaches located outside of Oregon State Park boundaries, dogs might be allowed off-leash and under direct voice control, please look for signs or postings. This park is located off U.S. Highway 101, 3 miles south of Manzanita Junction.

Oswald West State Park
Highway 101
Manzanita, OR
800-551-6949
The beach is located just a quarter of a mile from the parking areas. It is a popular beach that is frequented by windsurfers and boogie boarders. Picnic tables, restrooms, hiking, and campgrounds are available at this park. There are no day use fees. Leashed dogs are allowed on the beach. Dogs are also allowed on hiking trails and campgrounds. They must be on a six foot or less leash at all times and people are required to clean up after their pets. On beaches located outside of Oregon State Park boundaries, dogs might be allowed off-leash and under direct voice control, please look for signs or postings. This park is located off U.S. Highway 101, 10 miles

south of Cannon Beach.

Cannon Beach

Arcadia Beach State Recreation Site
Highway 101
Cannon Beach, OR
800-551-6949
This sandy ocean beach is just a few feet from where you can park your car. Picnic tables and restrooms are available at this park. There are no day use fees. Dogs are allowed on the beach. They must be on a six foot or less leash at all times and people are required to clean up after their pets. On beaches located outside of Oregon State Park boundries, dogs might be allowed off-leash and under direct voice control, please look for signs or postings. This park is located off U.S. Highway 101, 3 miles south of Cannon Beach.

Ecola State Park
Highway 101
Cannon Beach, OR
503-436-2844
According to the Oregon State Parks Division, this park is one of the most photographed locations in Oregon. To reach the beach, you will need to walk down a trail. Restrooms, hiking and primitive campgrounds are available at this park. There is a $3 day use fee. Leashed dogs are allowed on the beach. Dogs are also allowed on hiking trails and campgrounds. They must be on a six foot or less leash at all times and people are required to clean up after their pets. On beaches located outside of Oregon State Park boundries, dogs might be allowed off-leash and under direct voice control, please look for signs or postings. This park is located off U.S. Highway 101, 2 miles north of Cannon Beach.

Hug Point State Recreation Site
Highway 101
Cannon Beach, OR
800-551-6949
According to the Oregon State Parks Division, people used to travel via stagecoach along this beach before the highway was built. Today you can walk along the originial trail which was carved into the point by stagecoaches. The trail is located north of the parking area. Visitors can also explore two caves around the point, but be aware of high tide. Some people have become stranded at high tide when exploring the point! This beach is easily accessible from the parking area. Picnic tables and restrooms are available at this park. There are no day use fees. Dogs are allowed on the beach. They must be on a six foot

or less leash at all times and people are required to clean up after their pets. On beaches located outside of Oregon State Park boundries, dogs might be allowed off-leash and under direct voice control, please look for signs or postings. This park is located off U.S. Highway 101, 5 miles south of Cannon Beach.

Tolovana Beach State Recreation Site
Highway 101
Cannon Beach, OR
800-551-6949
Indian Beach is popular with surfers. There is a short walk down to the beach. Picnic tables are available at this park. There are no day fees. Dogs are allowed on the beach. They must be on a six foot or less leash at all times and people are required to clean up after their pets. On beaches located outside of Oregon State Park boundries, dogs might be allowed off-leash and under direct voice control, please look for signs or postings. This park is located off U.S. Highway 101, 1 mile south of Cannon Beach.

Seaside

Del Rey Beach State Recreation Site
Highway 101
Seaside, OR
800-551-6949
There is a short trail to the beach. There is no day use fee. Dogs are allowed on the beach. They must be on a six foot or less leash at all times and people are required to clean up after their pets. On beaches located outside of Oregon State Park boundries, dogs might be allowed off-leash and under direct voice control, please look for signs or postings. This park is located off U.S. Highway 101, 2 miles north of Gearhart.

Warrenton

Fort Stevens State Park
Highway 101
Warrenton, OR
503-861-1671
There are miles of ocean beach. Picnic tables, restrooms (including an ADA restroom), hiking and campgrounds are available at this park. There is a $3 day use fee. Leashed dogs are allowed on the beach. Dogs are also allowed on hiking trails and campgrounds. They must be on a six foot or less leash at all times and people are required to clean up after their pets. On beaches located outside of Oregon State Park boundries, dogs might be allowed off-leash and under direct voice control, please look for signs or postings.

This park is located off U.S. Highway 101, 10 miles west of Astoria.

Washington Listings

Ilwaco

Fort Canby State Park
Highway 101
Ilwaco, WA
360-902-8844
This park offers 27 miles of ocean beach and 7 miles of hiking trails. Enjoy excellent views of the ocean, Columbia River and two lighthouses. Picnic tables, restrooms (including an ADA restroom), hiking and campgrounds (includes ADA campsites) are available at this park. Leashed dogs are allowed on the beach. Dogs are also allowed on hiking trails and campgrounds. They must be on a eight foot or less leash at all times and people are required to clean up after their pets. This park is located two miles southwest of Ilwaco.From Seattle, Take I-5 south to Olympia, SR 8 west to Montesano. From there, take U.S. Hwy. 101 south to Long Beach Peninsula.

Ocean Park

Pacific Pines State Park
Highway 101
Ocean Park, WA
360-902-8844
Fishing, crabbing, clamming and beachcombing are popular activities at this beach. Picnic tables and a restroom are available at this park. Dogs are allowed on the beach. They must be on a eight foot or less leash at all times and people are required to clean up after their pets. This park is located approximately one mile north of Ocean Park. From north or south, take Hwy. 101 until you reach Ocean Park. Continue on Vernon St. until you reach 271st St.

Grayland

Grayland Beach State Park
Highway 105
Grayland, WA
360-902-8844
This 412 acre park offers beautiful ocean frontage and full hookup campsites (including ADA campsites). Leashed dogs are allowed on the beach. Dogs are also allowed at the campgrounds. They must be on a eight foot or less leash at all times and people are required to clean up after their pets. This park is located five miles south of Westport. From Aberdeen, drive 22 miles on Highway 105 south to Grayland. Traveling through the town, watch for park signs.

Ocean Shores

Damon Point State Park
Point Brown Avenue
Ocean Shores, WA
360-902-8844
Located on the southeastern tip of the Ocean Shores Peninsula, this one mile long beach offers views of the Olympic Mountains, Mount Rainer, and Grays Harbor. Picnic tables are available at this park. Dogs are allowed on the beach. They must be on an eight foot or less leash at all times and people are required to clean up after their pets. To get there from From Hoquiam, take SR 109 and SR 115 to Point Brown Ave. in the town of Ocean Shores. Proceed south on Point Brown Ave. through town, approximately 4.5 miles. Just past the marina, turn left into park entrance.

Ocean City State Park
State Route 115
Ocean Shores, WA
360-902-8844
Beachcombing, clamming, surfing, bird watching, kite flying and winter storm watching are all popular activites at this beach. Picnic tables, restrooms, and campgrounds (including ADA campgrounds) are available at this park. Leashed dogs are allowed on the beach. Dogs are also allowed at the campgrounds. They must be on a eight foot or less leash at all times and people are required to clean up after their pets. This park is located on the coast one-and-a-half miles north of Ocean Shores on Hwy. 115. From Hoquiam, drive 16 miles west on SR 109, then turn south on SR 115 and drive 1.2 miles to the park.

Copalis Beach

Griffith-Priday State Park
State Route 109
Copalis Beach, WA
360-902-8844
This beach extends from the beach through low dunes to a river and then north to the river's mouth. Picnic tables and restrooms are available at this park. Dogs are allowed on the beach. They must be on a eight foot or less leash at all times and people are required to clean up after their pets. This park is located 21 miles northwest of

Hoquiam. From Hoquiam, go north on SR 109 for 21 miles. At Copalis Beach, at the sign for Benner Rd., turn left (west).

Pacific Beach

Pacific Beach State Park
State Route 109
Pacific Beach, WA
360-902-8844
The beach is the focal point at this 10 acre state park. This sandy ocean beach is great for beachcombing, wildlife watching, windy walks and kite flying. Picnic tables, restrooms (including an ADA restroom), and campgrounds (some are ADA accessible) are available at this park. Leashed dogs are allowed on the beach. Dogs are also allowed in the campgrounds. They must be on a eight foot or less leash at all times and people are required to clean up after their pets. This park is located 15 miles north of Ocean Shores, off SR 109. From Hoquiam, follow SR 109, 30 miles northwest to the town of Pacific Beach. The park is located in town.

Port Angeles

Kalaloch Beach
Olympic National Park
Port Angeles, WA
360-962-2283
Dogs are allowed on leash, during daytime hours only, on Kalaloch Beach along the Pacific Ocean and from Rialto Beach north to Ellen Creek. These beaches are in Olympic National Park, but please note that pets are not permitted on this national park's trails, meadows, beaches (except Kalaloch and Rialto beaches) or in any undeveloped area of the park. For those folks and dogs who want to hike on a trail, try the adjacent dog-friendly Olympic National Forest. Kalaloch Beach is located off Highway 101 in Olympic National Park.

Federal Way

Dash Point State Park
Dash Point Rd.
Federal Way, WA
360-902-8844
This beach offers great views of Puget Sound. Picnic tables, restrooms, 11 miles of hiking trails and campgrounds are available at this park. Leashed dogs are allowed on the beach. Pets are not permitted on designated swimming beaches. However, there is usually a non-designated

swimming beach area as well. Dogs are also allowed on hiking trails and campgrounds. They must be on a eight foot or less leash at all times and people are required to clean up after their pets. This park is located on the west side of Federal Way in the vicinity of Seattle. From Highway 5, exit at the 320th St.exit (exit #143). Take 320th St. west approximately four miles. When 320th St. ends at a T-intersection, make a right onto 47th St. When 47th St. ends at a T-intersection, turn left onto Hwy. 509/ Dash Point Rd. Drive about two miles to the park. (West side of street is the campground side, and east side is the day-use area.)

Des Moines

Saltwater State Park
Marine View Drive
Des Moines, WA
360-902-8844
This state beach is located on Puget Sound, halfway between the cities of Tacoma and Seattle (near the Sea-Tac international airport). Picnic tables, restrooms and campgrounds are available at this park. Leashed dogs are allowed on the beach. Pets are not permitted on designated swimming beaches. However, there is usually a non-designated swimming beach area as well. Dogs are also allowed at the campgrounds. They must be on a eight foot or less leash at all times and people are required to clean up after their pets. To get there from the north, take exit #149 off of I-5. Go west, then turn south on Hwy. 99 (sign missing). Follow the signs into the park. Turn right on 240th at the Midway Drive-in. Turn left on Marine View Dr. and turn right into the park.

Seattle

Sand Point Magnuson Park Dog Off-Leash Beach and Area
7400 Sand Point Way NE
Seattle, WA
206-684-4075
This leash free dog park covers about 9 acres and is the biggest fully fenced off-leash park in Seattle. It also offers an access point to the lake where your pooch is welcome to take a dip in the fresh lake water. To find the dog park, take Sand Point Way Northeast and enter the park at Northeast 74th Street. Go straight and park near the playground and sports fields. The main gate to the off-leash area is located at the southeast corner of the main parking lot. Dogs must be leashed until you enter the off-leash area.

Bainbridge Island

Fay Bainbridge State Park
Sunset Drive NE
Bainbridge Island, WA
360-902-8844
This park is located on the northeast side of Bainbridge Island on Puget Sound. On a clear day, you can see Mt. Rainer and Mt. Baker from the beach. Picnic tables, restrooms and campgrounds are available at this park. Leashed dogs are allowed on the beach. Pets are not permitted on designated swimming beaches. However, there is usually a non-designated swimming beach area as well. Dogs are also allowed at the campgrounds. They must be on a eight foot or less leash at all times and people are required to clean up after their pets. To get there from From Poulsbo, take Hwy. 305 toward Bainbridge Island. Cross the Agate Pass Bridge. After three miles, come to stoplight and big brown sign with directions to park. Turn left at traffic light onto Day Rd. NE. Travel approximately two miles to a T-intersection. Turn left onto Sunrise Drive NE, and continue to park entrance, about two miles away.

Oak Harbor

Fort Ebey State Park
Hill Valley Drive
Oak Harbor, WA
360-902-8844
This 600+ acre park is popular for hiking and camping, but also offers a saltwater beach. Picnic tables and restrooms (including an ADA restroom) are available at this park. Leashed dogs are allowed on the saltwater beach. Dogs are also allowed on hiking trails and campgrounds. They must be on a eight foot or less leash at all times and people are required to clean up after their pets. To get to the park from Seattle, take exit #189 off of I-5, just south of Everett. Follow signs for the Mukilteo/ Clinton ferry. Take the ferry to Clinton on Whidbey Island. Dogs are allowed on the ferry. Once on Whidbey Island, follow Hwy. 525 north, which becomes Hwy. 20. Two miles north of Coupeville, turn left on Libbey Rd. and follow it 1.5 miles to Hill Valley Dr. Turn left and enter park.

Joseph Whidbey State Park
Swantown Rd
Oak Harbor, WA
360-902-8844
This 112 acre park offers one of the best beaches on Whidbey Island. Picnic tables, restrooms, and

several miles of hiking trails (including a half mile ADA hiking trail) are available at this park. Leashed dogs are allowed on the beach. Pets are not permitted on designated swimming beaches. However, there is usually a non-designated swimming beach area as well. Dogs are also allowed on hiking trails. They must be on a eight foot or less leash at all times and people are required to clean up after their pets. To get there from the south, drive north on Hwy. 20. Just before Oak Harbor, turn left on Swantown Rd. and follow it about three miles.

Lopez Island

Spencer Spit State Park
Bakerview Road
Lopez Island, WA
360-902-8844
Located in the San Juan Islands, this lagoon beach offers great crabbing, clamming and beachcombing. Picnic tables, restrooms, campgrounds and 2 miles of hiking trails are available at this park. Leashed dogs are allowed on the beach. Pets are not permitted on designated swimming beaches. However, there is usually a non-designated swimming beach area as well. Dogs are also allowed on hiking trails and campgrounds. They must be on a eight foot or less leash at all times and people are required to clean up after their pets. This park is located on Lopez Island in the San Juan Islands. It is a 45-minute Washington State Ferry ride from Anacortes. Dogs are allowed on the ferry. Once on Lopez Island, follow Ferry Rd. Go left at Center Rd., then left at Cross Rd. Turn right at Port Stanley and left at Bakerview Rd. Follow Bakerview Rd. straight into park. For ferry rates and schedules, call 206-464-6400.

San Juan Island

South Beach
125 Spring Street
Friday Harbor, WA
360-378-2902
Dogs on leash are allowed at South Beach, which is located at the American Camp in the San Juan Island National Historic Park.

Blaine

Birch Bay State Park
Grandview
Blaine, WA
360-902-8844

This beach, located near the Canadian border, offers panoramic coastal views. Picnic tables, restrooms (including an ADA restroom), and campgrounds (including ADA campsites) are available at this park. Leashed dogs are allowed on the beach. Pets are not permitted on designated swimming beaches. However, there is usually a non-designated swimming beach area as well. Dogs are also allowed in the campgrounds. They must be on a eight foot or less leash at all times and people are required to clean up after their pets. This park is located 20 miles north of Bellingham and ten miles south of Blaine. From the south take exit #266 off of I-5. Go left on Grandview for seven miles, then right on Jackson for one mile, then turn left onto Helweg. From the north take exit #266 off of I-5, and turn right onto Grandview.

Victoria

Beacon Hill Park Off-Leash Beach
Dallas Road
Victoria, BC
250-385-5711
Dogs are allowed off-leash at the gravel beach in Beacon Hill Park. People are required to clean up after their dogs. The beach is located in downtown Victoria, along Dallas Road, between Douglas Street and Cook Street.

British Columbia Listings

Vancouver

Spanish Banks West
NW Marine Drive
Vancouver, BC
604-257-8400
This beach allows dogs off-leash. Dogs are allowed from 6am to 10pm. People are required to clean up after their dogs. The beach is located in the Queen Elizabeth District. It is off NW Marine Drive, at the entrance to Pacific Spirit Park.

Sunset Beach
off Beach Avenue
Vancouver, BC
604-257-8400
This bay beach allows dogs off-leash. Dogs are allowed from 6am to 10pm. People are required to clean up after their dogs. The beach is located in the Stanley District, near Beach Avenue, under the Burrard Bridge. It is behind the Aquatic Centre east of the ferry dock.

Vanier Park
Chestnut
Vancouver, BC
604-257-8400
This beach allows dogs off-leash. Dogs are allowed from 6am to 10am and then from 5pm to 10pm. People are required to clean up after their dogs. The beach is located in the Queen Elizabeth District. It is on Chestnut at English Bay.

Chapter 20

California and Nevada RV Park and Campground Guides

North Coast Dog-Friendly RV Park and Campground Guide

Crescent City

Crescent City

Jedediah Smith Campground
Highway 199
Crescent City, CA
707-464-6101
This campground is located in the Jedediah Smith Redwoods State Park and offers 106 RV or tent sites in an old growth redwood forest. RVs must be 36 feet or less. Camp amenities include restrooms, showers, fire pits, dump station and bear-proof lockers. While dogs are not allowed on any park trails, they are allowed in the campground. They are also allowed to walk on or along Walker Road which is just west of the campground. Pets must be leashed and attended at all times. Please clean up after your pets.

Eureka

Eureka

Eureka KOA
4050 North Highway 101
Eureka, CA 95503
707-822-4243
Pets are allowed in the campgrounds and RV spaces, but not in the cabins. Well-behaved leashed dogs of all sizes are allowed. People need to clean up after their pets. There is no pet fee. Site amenities include 50 amp service available and cable TV and telephone service for an extra fee. Other amenities include a swimming pool open during the summer, hot tub/sauna, LP gas, snack bar and free modem dataport. They are open all year.

Garberville

Redway

Dean Creek Resort
4112 Redwood Drive
Redway, CA 95560
707-923-2555
Located on the Eel River, this campground is located just 3 miles from the Avenue of the Giants attraction. Riverfront sites are available for both RVs and tent camping. Many of the RV sites have full hookups with 50 amp service available. All sites have picnic tables and barbecue grills. Other amenities include a pool, spa, sauna, coin laundry, mini-mart, meeting room, game room, playground and restrooms. Pets are allowed but must be leashed at all times. The camp is open year round.

Gasquet

Gasquet

Panther Flat Campground
Highway 199
Gasquet, CA
707-442-1721
This campground is located in the Smith River National Recreation Area and is part of the Six Rivers National Forest. The campground offers 39 tent and RV sites. RVs up to 40 feet are allowed and there are no hookups. Amenities include flush restrooms, pay shower, potable water, picnic tables, grills, fishing and sites with river and scenic views. There is a $15 per night fee. Pets on leash are allowed and please clean up after them. The campsite is located 2.5 miles east of Gasquet on Highway 199.

Gualala

Gualala

Gualala Point Regional Park Campgrounds
42401 Coast Highway 1
Gualala, CA
707-785-2377
This dog-friendly park offers sandy beaches, hiking trails and 20 campsites. RVs are permitted and there is a dump station, but no hookups. Dogs are allowed but must be on a 6 foot or less leash and proof of a rabies vaccination is required.

Jenner

Jenner

Stillwater Cove Regional Park Campgrounds
22455 Highway 1
Jenner, CA
707-565-2041
This 210 acre park offers 17 campsites. RVs are permitted and there is a dump station, but no hookups. The park also features a small beach,

great views of the Pacific Ocean, picnic tables and restrooms. Dogs are allowed but must be on a 6 foot or less leash and proof of a rabies vaccination is required. The park is located off Highway 1, about 16 miles north of Jenner.

Leggett

Standish-Hickey State Recreation Area Campground
69350 Highway 101
Leggett, CA 95455
707-925-6482
This campground offers tent sites. Dogs are not allowed on the park trails, but they are allowed on a few fire roads. The fire roads are not passable during the winter because of the river, but are fine during the summer months. The fire roads are located near the campground and near the main swimming hole. Dogs are also allowed in the water. Pets must be on leash and please clean up after them. The park is located 1.5 miles north of Leggett on Highway 101.

Orick

Elk Praire Campground
Newton B. Drury Scenic Parkway
Orick, CA
707-464-6101
This campground is located in Prairie Creek Redwoods State Park. While dogs are not allowed on any park trails, they are allowed at this campground. There are 75 RV or tent sites which are next to a prairie and old growth redwood forest. RVs must be less than 27 feet. There are no RV hookups. Camp amenities include restrooms, showers, fire pits, dump station and bear-proof lockers. Located just north of the campground is Cal Barrel Road. Dogs can walk on or along this 3 mile gravel road. There are not too many cars that travel along this road. Pets must be leashed and attended at all times. Please clean up after your pet. The campsite is located on Newton B. Drury Scenic Parkway off Highway 101.

Freshwater Lagoon Spit Overnight Use Area
Highway 101
Orick, CA
707-464-6101

Dogs are allowed at this overnight use area and in the water. The overnight tent use is located south of the southern most vehicle access point. Amenities include picnic areas with grills, chemical toilets and fire pits. Vehicles are $10 per night and people are $3 per night. Fees are payable at the self-registration kiosks. Overnight stays are limited to 15 consecutive days. Pets must be leashed and attended at all times. Please clean up after your pet. This tent area is located 1 mile south of Orick on Highway 101.

Gold Bluffs Beach Campground
Davison Road
Orick, CA
707-464-6101
This campground is located in Prairie Creek Redwoods State Park. While dogs are not allowed on any park trails, they are allowed at this campground and the adjoining beach. There are 29 tent sites and 25 RV sites at the beach. RVs must be less than 24 feet long and 8 feet wide. There are no RV hookups. All sites are on a first-come, first-served basis. Camp amenities include restrooms, solar showers and fire pits. Pets must be leashed and attended at all times. Please clean up after your pets. The campground is located on Davison Road, off Highway 101.

Weott

Humboldt Redwoods State Park Campgrounds
Avenue of the Giants
Weott, CA
707-946-2409
There are several campgrounds located in this park including Albee Creek, Burlington and Hidden Springs Campgrounds. Tent and RV sites are available. There are no hookups. Camp amenities include picnic tables, fire rings, showers and flush toilets. While dogs are not allowed on the trails, they are allowed in the campgrounds and on miles of fire roads and access roads. These paths are used mainly for mountain biking, but dogs are allowed too. There are both steep and gently sloping fire roads. Some of the fire roads are located next to the Albee Creek Campground. Pets on leash are allowed and please clean up after them. The park is located along the Avenue of the Giants, about 45 miles south of Eureka and 20 miles north of Garberville.

Whitethorn

Whitethorn

Nadelos Campground
Chemise Mountain Road
Whitethorn, CA
707-825-2300
This campground offers 8 walk-in tent sites ranging from 50 to 300 feet from the parking lot. The sites are shaded by Douglas fir trees and are set along a small mountain stream. Campground amenities include picnic tables, vault toilets, drinking water and fire rings. Day use parking for the dog-friendly Chemise Mountain Trail is located at this campground. Sites are $8 per day with a maximum of 14 days per stay. Pets are allowed but must be leashed in the campground. To get there, take Highway 101 to Redway. Go west on Briceland/Shelter Cove Road for 22 miles and then head south on Chemise Mountain Road for 1.6 miles. Travel time from Highway 101 is about 55 minutes.

Wailaki Campground
Chemise Mountain Road
Whitethorn, CA
707-825-2300
This campground offers 13 tent and trailer sites along a small mountain stream amidst large Douglas fir frees. Day use parking for the dog-friendly Chemise Mountain Trail is located at this campground. Camp amenities include picnic tables, grills, water and restrooms. There are no RV hookups. Sites are $8 per day with a maximum of 14 days per stay. Pets are allowed but must be leashed in the campground. To get there, take Highway 101 to Redway. Go west on Briceland/Shelter Cove Road for 22 miles and then head south on Chemise Mountain Road for 1.7 miles. Travel time from Highway 101 is about 55 minutes.

Shasta Cascades Dog-Friendly RV Park and Campground Guide

Bucks Lake

Bucks Lake

Silver Lake Campground
Forest Road 24N29X
Bucks Lake, CA
530-283-0555
This campground is located in the Plumas National Forest and offers 8 campsites. They are on a first-come, first-served basis. The trailhead

for the Gold Lake Trail is located at this campground. In the campground dogs must be on leash. On the trails, dogs on leash or off-leash but under direct voice control are allowed. To get there from Quincy, go west 9.2 miles on Bucks Lake Road. Turn right on a gravel road, 24N29X (Silver Lake sign). Go 6.4 miles to the campground.

Happy Camp

Happy Camp

Norcross Campground
Elk Creek Road
Happy Camp, CA
530-493-1777
This 6 site campground is located in the Klamath National Forest at an elevation of 2,400 feet. Amenities include vault toilets. The campground is open from May to October. This campground serves as a staging area for various trails that provide access into the Marble Mountain Wilderness. The trails are used by hikers and horseback riders. Dogs must be leashed in the campground. On trails, pets must be either leashed or off-leash but under direct voice control. Please clean up after your pets. The campsite is located 16 miles south of Happy Camp on Elk Creek Road.

La Porte

La Porte

Little Beaver Campground
off La Porte Road
La Porte, CA
530-534-6500
This campground is located at the Little Grass Valley Reservoir Recreation Area in the Plumas National Forest. There are 120 campsites, some of which offer prime lakeside sites. Amenities include water, flush toilets, trailer space and an RV dump station. Dogs are allowed in the campgrounds, on trails and in the water. In the campground dogs must be on leash. On the trails, dogs on leash or off-leash but under direct voice control are allowed. Reservations for the campsites can be made by calling 1-877-444-6777. The campground is located 3 miles north of La Porte off La Porte Road.

Lake Shasta

Shasta Lake

Hirz Bay Campground
Gilman Road
Shasta Lake, CA
530-275-1587
This campground is located in the Shasta-Trinity National Forest at an elevation of 1,100 feet. The campground offers 37 tent and RV campsites. RVs up to 30 feet are allowed and there are no hookups. Amenities include drinking water, accessible restrooms, flush toilets and boat ramp. Fishing, swimming and boating are popular activities at the campground. The camp is open year round. To make a reservations, call 1-877-444-6777. Dogs are allowed in the lake, but not at the designated swimming beaches. Pets must be leashed and please clean up after them. The campground is located 10 miles from Interstate 5 on Gilman Road.

Lakehead

Lakehead

Lakeshore Inn & RV
20483 Lakeshore Drive
Lakehead, CA 96051
530-238-2003
This campground has tall pine and oak trees, and overlooks Shasta Lake. All of the RV and tent sites have electricity and water. Septic and cable TV are available at some of the sites. Amenities include a large swimming pool, mini store, gift shop, playground, picnic area, video game room, showers, laundromat, dump station and handicap bathrooms. Well-behaved dogs are welcome. Pets should be quiet and please clean up after them. There is a $1 per day pet fee.

Shasta Lake RV Resort and Campground
20433 Lakeshore Drive
Lakehead, CA 96051
530-238-2370
This RV resort and campground is located on Lake Shasta. The campground is on Shasta-Trinity National Forest land. RV and tent sites are available. RVs up to 60 feet are allowed. Amenities include hot showers, swimming pool, private boat dock, playground and more. Well-behaved leashed dogs are allowed. Please clean up after your pets.

Lassen National Park

Hat Creek

Hat Creek Campground
Highway 89
Hat Creek, CA
530-336-5521
This campground is located in the Lassen National Forest at an elevation of 4,300 feet. The camp offers 75 campsites. Camp amenities include water, fire rings, picnic tables and restrooms. Most sites are available on a first-come, first-served basis. Some sites can be reserved. Call 1-877-444-6777 to make a reservation. The camp is open from late April to October. Dogs on leash are allowed at the campground and on trails. Please clean up after your dog. The camp is located in Hat Creek on Highway 89.

Mineral

Lassen Volcanic National Park Campgrounds
PO Box 100
Mineral, CA 96063
530-595-4444
This park offers many campgrounds, with the largest campground having 179 sites. Tent and RV sites are available and trailers up to 35 feet are permitted. There are no hookups. All sites are on a first-come, first-served basis. Pets must be leashed and attended at all times. Please clean up after your pet. Dogs are not allowed on any trails or hikes in this park, but see our Lassen National Forest listing in Susanville for nearby dog-friendly hiking, sightseeing and additional camping.

Old Station

Cave Campground
Highway 89
Old Station, CA
530-336-5521
This campground is located in the Lassen National Forest near the Subway Cave where you and your pooch can explore an underground lava tube. The camp is at an elevation of 4,300 feet and offers 46 campsites. Camp amenities include water, fire rings, picnic tables and restrooms. Most sites are available on a first-come, first-served basis. Some sites can be reserved. Call 1-877-444-6777 to make a reservation. The camp is open from April to October. Dogs on leash are allowed at the campground and on trails. Please clean up after your dog. The camp is located near the intersection of Highways 44 and 89.

Shingletown

Mt. Lassen/Shingletown

7749 KOA Road
Shingletown, CA 96088
530-474-3133
Located at an elevation of 3,900 feet, this twelve acre campground offers both tent and RV sites in the pines. Maximum length for pull through sites is 60 feet. Sites have 30 amp service available. Other amenities include LP gas, free modem dataport, snack bar, swimming pool during the summer and a deli. Well-behaved leashed dogs of all sizes are allowed. People need to clean up after their pets. The campgrounds are open from seasonally from March 1 through November 30.

Lewiston

Lewiston

Lakeview Terrace Resort

Lewiston, CA
530-778-3803
This resort overlooks Lewiston Lake and features an RV park and cabin rentals. RV spaces feature pull through sites, tables and barbecues. Most of the pull through sites offer a lake view. Other amenities include a laundry facility, restrooms and showers. Well-behaved quiet leashed dogs are welcome, up to two pets per cabin or RV. Pets are not allowed in the swimming pool area and cannot not be left alone at any time, either in your RV or at the cabins. Please clean up after your pet. There is no pet fee if you stay in an RV space, but there is a $10 per day fee for pets in the cabins.

Likely

Likely

Blue Lake Campground

Forest Service Road 64
Likely, CA
530-233-5811
This campground is located along Blue Lake at 6,000 foot elevation in the Modoc National Forest. There are 48 RV and tent sites, several of which are located directly on the lake. RVs up to 32 feet are allowed and there are no hookups. Amenities include picnic tables, fire pits, vault toilets and piped water. A boat ramp is located near the campground. Rowboats, canoes and low powered boats are allowed on the lake. The 1.5 mile Blue Lake National Recreation Trail begins at this campsite. Dogs on leash are allowed at the campgrounds, on trails and in the water. Please clean up after your pets. The campground is usually open from June to October, weather permitting. There is a $7 per vehicle fee. The campground is located is 16 miles from the small town of Likely. From Highway 395 go east on Forest Service Road 64. At about 10 miles you will come to a road junction. Stay on Forest Service Road 64 for the remaining 6 miles.

Mill Creek Falls Campground

Mill Creek Rd.
Likely, CA
530-233-5811
This campground is located in the Modoc National Forest at an elevation of 5,700 feet. There are 19 RV and tent sites. There are no hookups. Amenities include picnic tables, fire pits, vault toilets and drinking water. The Clear Lake Trail begins here and provides access into the South Warner Wilderness. Dogs on leash are allowed at the campgrounds, on trails and in the water. Please clean up after your pets. The campground is usually open from June to October, weather permitting. There is a $6 per night fee. To get there from the town of Likely, go 9 miles east on Co. Rd. #64. Then go northeast on West Warner Road for 2.5 miles. Go east on Mill Creek access road for 2 more miles.

Quincy

Quincy

Pioneer RV Park

1326 Pioneer Rd.
Quincy, CA
530-283-0769
This pet-friendly RV park is located in the Sierra Nevada Mountains between Lassen National Park and Lake Tahoe. They have over 60 sites on 6.5 acres. RV sites have long wide pull through sites, picnic tables, 30 or 50 amp service and full hookups with satellite TV. Tent campers are also welcome. Other amenities include a laundry room, LP gas, rec room with modem hookup, big screen TV, books exchange and ping pong table. They are located about 1.5 miles from downtown Quincy and right next to a county park which has an Olympic size swimming pool and a playground. Well-behaved leashed dogs of all sizes are allowed. People need to clean up after their pets. There is no pet fee. The RV park is open all year.

Redding

Redding

Mountain Gate RV Park
14161 Holiday Road
Redding, CA 96003
530-275-4600
This RV park's amenities include full RV hookups, lighted grounds, large pull through sites, convenience store, video rentals, cable TV, pool, rec room with pool table, email station, laundry, showers, restrooms, dump station, easy I-5 access and pet areas. Well-behaved leashed dogs are allowed. Please clean up after your pets. The park is located 7 miles north of Redding. From the south, take Interstate 5 and exit at Wonderland Blvd. Turn right and then make the first right (Holiday Road) and go .5 miles south. From the north, take Interstate 5 to the second Wonderland Blvd (Mountain Gate) Exit and turn left. Cross over I-5 and make the first right (Holiday Road). Then go .5 miles south.

Tionesta

Tionesta

Eagle's Nest RV Park
off Highway 139
Tionesta, CA
530-644-2081
This RV park is located 24 miles south of the town of Tulelake and 2 miles off Highway 139. Amenities include 20 full hookup pull through sites, showers, restrooms, laundromat, clubhouse with pool table, satellite TV and a book exchange. Grassy tent sites are also available. Well-behaved leashed dogs are welcome. Please clean up after your pets.

Trinity Center

Trinity Center

Clark Springs Campground
Highway 3
Trinity Center, CA
530-623-2121
This campground is located in the Shasta-Trinity National Forest at an elevation of 2,400 fee. The campground offers 21 tent and RV campsites. RVs up to 25 feet are allowed and there are no hookups. Amenities include a swimming beach, boat ramp, drinking water, picnic sites, wheelchair access and flush toilets. Fishing, swimming, boating and hiking are popular activities at the campground. The Trinity Lakeshore trailhead is located here. The camp is open from the beginning of April to mid-September. To make a reservations, call 1-877-444-6777. The campground is located 18 miles north of Weaverville off Highway 3. Dogs are allowed on the trails and in the lake water but only on non-designated swimming areas. Pets must be leashed and please clean up after them.

Hayward Flat Campground
off Highway 3
Trinity Center, CA
530-623-2121
This campground is located on the west side of the East Fork arm of Trinity Lake in the Shasta-Trinity National Forest. The campground is at an elevation of 2,400 feet and offers 94 tent and RV campsites. RVs up to 40 feet are allowed and there are no hookups. Amenities include drinking water and flush toilets. Fishing, swimming and boating are popular activities at the campground. The camp is open from mid-May to mid-September. To make a reservations, call 1-877-444-6777. The campground is located 20 miles north of Weaverville and 2.5 miles off Highway 3. Pets must be leashed and please clean up after them.

Wyntoon Resort
Highway 3
Trinity Center, CA 96091

This 90 acre wooded resort is located at the north end of Lake Trinity and offers both RV and tent sites. The RV sites are tree shaded, have full hookups with 30 or 50 amp service and RVs up to 60 feet. Tent sites are located under pine and cedar trees and have picnic tables and barbecues. Other camp amenities include a swimming pool, clubhouse, snack bar, ping pong, showers and laundry facilities. Well-behaved leashed pets are always welcome. Please clean up after your pet. There is a $1 per day pet fee.

Tulelake

Tulelake

Indian Well Campground
1 Indian Well
Tulelake, CA 96134
530-667-2282
This campground, located in the Lava Beds National Monument, offers 40 campsites for tents

and small to medium sized RVs. Amenities include water and flush toilets. Campsites are available on a first-come, first-served basis. Pets must be leashed and attended at all times. Please clean up after your pet. Dogs are not allowed on any trails or hikes in this park, but see our Modoc National Forest listings in this region for nearby dog-friendly hiking, sightseeing and additional camping.

Medicine Lake Campground
Forest Service Road 44N38
Tulelake, CA
530-233-5811
This campground is located on the shores of Medicine Lake at 6,700 foot elevation in the Modoc National Forest. There are 22 RV and tent sites. RVs up to 22 feet are allowed and there are no hookups. Amenities include picnic tables, fire pits, vault toilets and potable water. Dogs on leash are allowed at the campgrounds and in the water. Please clean up after your pets. The campground is usually open from July to October, weather permitting. There is a $7 per vehicle fee. To get there from the junction of Highway 139 and Co. Rd. 97, go about 18.5 miles west on Co. Rd. 97. Turn right on Forest Service Road 44N75. Go 1 mile to Forest Service Road 44N38. Go another .5 miles and then turn right and follow the signs to the Medicine Lake Campground.

Upper Lake

Upper Lake

Sunset Campground
County Road 301/Forest Road M1
Upper Lake, CA
916-386-5164
This campground is located in the Mendocino National Forest and is managed by Pacific Gas and Electric. Camp amenities include 54 tables, 54 stoves, 12 toilets, water, trailer space and 27 grills. The Sunset Nature Trail Loop begins at this campground. The campground is open from about May to September. There is a $12 fee per campsite and an extra $1 per night per pet fee. Dogs on leash are allowed and please clean up after them. To get there from Upper Lake, take County Road 301 north for 31 miles.

Whiskeytown

Whiskeytown

Brandy Creek RV Campground

P.O. Box 188
Whiskeytown, CA 96095
530-246-1225
This campground is part of the Whiskeytown National Recreation Area which allows dogs on trails, in the lake and on non-swimming beaches only. The camp offers paved parking spots for RVs along an access road. There are no hookups and generators are allowed but not during the quiet time which is usually from 10pm to 6am. All sites are on a first-come, first-served basis. Dogs must be leashed and attended at all times. Please clean up after your pet. The campground is open all year.

Oak Bottom Campground
P.O. Box 188
Whiskeytown, CA 96095
530-359-2269
This campground offers tent sites next to Whiskeytown Lake. The campground is part of the Whiskeytown National Recreation Area which allows dogs on trails, in the lake and on non-swimming beaches only. The camp also offers RV sites but there are no hookups. Generators are allowed but not during the quiet time which is usually from 10pm to 6am. During the summer reservations are required and during the winter sites are on a first-come, first-served basis. Dogs must be leashed and attended at all times. Please clean up after your pet. The campground is open all year.

Wine Country Dog-Friendly RV Park and Campground Guide

Napa Valley

Calistoga

Napa County Fairgrounds Campground
1435 Oak Street
Calistoga, CA 94515
707-942-5111
Located at the fairgrounds, this campground offers 46 RV/tent sites. RV sites are parallel in the parking lot and tent sites are located on an adjacent lawn. RV sites have full hookups (some have sewer). Other amenities include restrooms, showers, potable water and disabled accessible. Dogs are allowed but must be on a 10 foot or less leash. Please clean up after your pet. The campground is open all year.

Sonoma

Guerneville

Fifes Guest Ranch
16467 Highway 116
Guerneville, CA 95446
707-869-0656
Located on 15 acres and among redwood trees, this guest ranch offers individual cabins, cottages and tent camping. Amenities include a pool, volleyball court, gym and onsite massages. Well-behaved dogs of all sizes are allowed in the campsites, cabins and cottages for an additional fee.

Santa Rosa

Spring Lake Regional Park Campgrounds
5585 Newanga Avenue
Santa Rosa, CA
707-785-2377
This 320 acre regional park with a 72 acre lake offers 27 campsites and miles of easy walking trails. RVs are permitted and there is a dump station, but no hookups. Dogs are allowed but must be on a 6 foot or less leash and proof of a rabies vaccination is required.

San Francisco Bay Area Dog-Friendly RV Park and Campground Guide

Marin - North Bay

Bodega Bay

Doran Regional Park Campgrounds
201 Doran Beach Road
Bodega Bay, CA
707-875-3540
Walk to the beach from your campsite! There are over 100 campsites in this park which features 2 miles of sandy beach. RVs are permitted and there is a dump station, but no hookups. Dogs are allowed but must be on a 6 foot or less leash and proof of a rabies vaccination is required.

Westside Regional Park Campgrounds
2400 Westshore Road
Bodega Bay, CA
707-875-3540
This park offers 38 campsites. RVs are permitted but there are no hookups. Fishing is the popular activity at this park. Dogs are allowed but must be on a 6 foot or less leash and proof of a rabies vaccination is required. To get there from

Highway 1, take Eastshore Road.

San Rafael

Samuel P. Taylor State Park Campgrounds
Sir Francis Drake Blvd.
San Rafael, CA
415-488-9897
This park offers campsites for tents and RVs up to 27 feet. There are no hookups. Amenities include water, tables, grills, flush toilets and showers. While dogs are not allowed on the hiking trails, they are allowed on the bike trail that runs about six miles through the park. The path is nearly level and follows the Northwest Pacific Railroad right-of-way. The trail is both paved and dirt and it starts near the park entrance. Dogs are also allowed in the developed areas like the campgrounds. Pets must be leashed and please clean up after your pet. The park is located north of San Francisco, 15 miles west of San Rafael on Sir Francis Drake Blvd.

Palo Alto - Peninsula

Pescadero

Butano State Park Campground
Highway 1
Pescadero, CA
650-879-2040
The campground in this park offers both tent and RV sites. RVs up to 27 feet are allowed an there are no hookups. Camp amenities include picnic tables, water and vault toilets. While dogs are not allowed on the park trails, they are allowed in the campground and on miles of fire roads. Mountain biking is also allowed on the fire roads. Pets must be on a 6 foot or less leash. Please clean up after them. The park is located on the San Mateo Coast off Highway 1. To get there go 4.5 miles southeast of Pescadero via Pescadero and Cloverdale Roads.

Gold Country Dog-Friendly RV Park and Campground Guide

Columbia

Columbia

49er RV Ranch
23223 Italian Bar Road
Columbia, CA 95310

209-532-4978
There are no additional pet fees.

Downieville

Downieville

Rocky Rest Campground
Highway 49
Downieville, CA
530-288-3231
This 10 site campground is located in the Tahoe National Forest at a 2,000 foot elevation. Amenities include piped water and vault toilets. There is a $16 per site fee. The North Yuba trailhead is located at this campground. Pets must be leashed in the campsite and please clean up after your pets. The campground is located on Highway 49, 7.5 miles west of Downieville.

Foresthill

Foresthill

Big Reservoir/Morning Star Campground
Foresthill Divide Road
Foresthill, CA 95631
530-367-2129
This campground is located in the Tahoe National Forest and offers 100 sites at an elevation of 4,000 feet. Amenities include piped water and vault toilets. The Sugar Pine Trail is located nearby. Fees are $18 to $25 per site, depending on proximity to the waterfront. Pets must be leashed in the campground. Please clean up after your pets. To get there from Foresthill, go 18 miles northeast on Foresthill Divide Road.

French Meadows Reservoir Campground
Mosquito Ridge Road
Foresthill, CA 95631
530-367-2224
Located in the Tahoe National Forest, this 75 site campground is at an elevation of 5,300 feet. The campground is next to the French Meadows Reservoir. Camp amenities include piped water and flush/vault toilets. Pets are allowed but must be leashed in the campground. The campsite is located 36 miles east of Foresthill on Mosquito Ridge Road. Call to make a reservation.

Robinson Flat Campground
Foresthill Divide Road
Foresthill, CA 95631
530-367-2224
This campground is located at an elevation of 6,800 feet in the Tahoe National Forest, near the Little Bald Mountain Trail. The campground offer 14 sites (7 family sites and 7 equestrian sites) on a first-come, first-served basis. Amenities include well water and vault toilets. There is no fee. Pet must be on leash in the campground. Please clean up after your pets. To get there, go 28 miles from Foresthill on Foresthill Divide Road to Robinson Flat.

Robinson Flat Campground
Foresthill Divide Road
Foresthill, CA 95631
530-367-2224
This campground is located at an elevation of 6,800 feet in the Tahoe National Forest, near the Little Bald Mountain Trail. The campground offer 14 sites (7 family sites and 7 equestrian sites) on a first-come, first-served basis. Amenities include well water and vault toilets. There is no fee. Pet must be on leash in the campground. Please clean up after your pets. To get there, go 28 miles from Foresthill on Foresthill Divide Road to Robinson Flat.

Nevada City

Nevada City

Lodgepole Campground
off Yuba Gap
Nevada City, CA
916-386-5164
This 35 site campground is located in the Tahoe National Forest and is managed by PG&E. The campsite is located at an elevation of 5,800 feet. Pets must be leashed in the campground and please clean up after them. To get there from I-80, take the Yuba Gap exit for .4 miles. Go around Lake Valley Reservoir for 1.2 miles. Then take right fork 2.5 miles.

South Yuba Campground
North Bloomfield Road
Nevada City, CA
916-985-4474
This campground has 16 sites for tents or RVs. Camp amenities include picnic tables, fire grills, piped water, pit toilets and garbage collection. There are no RV hookups. The campground is open from April to mid-October. The cost per site is $5 per night with a 14 day maximum stay. Sites are available on a first-come, first-served basis. The South Yuba River Recreation Area is located about 10 miles northeast of Nevada City. From Nevada City, take Highway 49 north to North

Bloomfield Road. Drive 10 miles to the South Yuba Recreation Area. From the one land bridge at Edwards Crossing, go about 1.5 miles on a dirt/gravel road to the campground and trailhead. Trailers and motorhomes should take Highway 49 and then turn right at the junction of Tyler Foote Road. At the intersection of Grizzly Hill Road turn right and proceed to North Bloomfield Road.

Plymouth

Plymouth

Far Horizons 49er Village
18265 Highway 49
Plymouth, CA 209-245-6981

This RV park is located in the wine and gold country of the Sierra Foothills and offers 329 shady RV sites. All sites have full hookups with water, sewer, 30 or 50 amp electricity and cable TV. Other amenities include two swimming pools, laundry, game room, and onsite deli and market. Well-behaved leashed dogs are welcome, up to three per site. There are no pet fees. Please clean up after your pet. The RV park is open all year.

Pollock Pines

Pollock Pines

Sly Park Campground
4771 Sly Park Road
Pollock Pines, CA 95726
530-644-2545
The wooded Sly Park Recreation Area offers 159 campsites at an elevation of 3,500 feet. Site amenities include a table, barbecue and fire ring. Camp amenities include water, vault and toilets. No hookups are available but there is a dump station at the park entrance. Pets on leash are allowed in the campground and on trails including the 8 to 9 mile trail which surround the lake. The campgrounds are open during the summer. Reservations are required.

Sierra Nevada Dog-Friendly RV Park and Campground Guide

Big Pine

Big Pine

Big Pine Creek Campground
Glacier Lodge Road
Big Pine, CA
760-873-2500
This 36 site campground is located in the Inyo National Forest at an elevation of 7,700 feet. Amenities include water and space for RVs. There are no hookups. For hiking, the trailheads for the Big Pine Canyon Trails are located here. The fee for a campsite is $13. The campground is open from about mid May to mid October. To make a reservation call 1-877-444-6777. Pets must be leashed while in the campground and please clean up after your pets. To get there from Highway 395, exit in Big Pine and go 11 miles west on Glacier Lodge Road.

Glacier Lodge RV Park
Glacier Lodge Road
Big Pine, CA
760-938-2837
This campground offers tent camping and some RV spaces with full hookups. Amenities include a general store and nearby hiking and fishing. Dogs are also allowed in the cabins for an extra $15 per pet per stay. The Big Pine Canyon trailheads are located here which offer miles of dog-friendly on or off-leash hiking trails. Pets must be leashed in the campground and please clean up after them. The campground is open from April through October. To get there from Highway 395, exit in Big Pine and go 11 miles west on Glacier Lodge Road.

Bishop

Bishop

Four Jeffrey Campground
South Lake Road
Bishop, CA
760-873-2500
This 106 site campground is located in the Inyo National Forest at an elevation of 8,200 feet. Amenities include water, space for RVs and a dump station. There are no hookups. For hiking, the Bristlecone Pine Forest is located nearby and offers many dog-friendly trails. The fee for a campsite is $14. The campground is open from about mid April to mid October. To make a reservation call 1-877-444-6777. Pets must be leashed while in the campground and please clean up after your pets. To get there from Bishop, take Highway 168 west and continue for 14 miles. Then go south on South Lake Road. Go one mile.

Crowley Lake

Crowley Lake

Crowley Lake Campground
Crowley Lake Drive
Crowley Lake, CA
760-873-2503
This campground is located in open high desert country at 7,000 feet and has 47 tent and RV sites available. Please note that there are no trees and the winds can be strong. The area overlooks Crowley Lake which is a popular site for fishing. The campground is usually open from late April until the end of October. Camp amenities include 4 pit toilets and pull through trailer spaces. There are no hookups. All sites are first-come, first-served. There are no fees but donations are appreciated. Dogs are allowed but please keep them under control. The closest convenience stores are located in Mammoth Lakes, about 10 miles north of the campground or at a very small store in the Crowley Lake area. To get there, take Highway 395 to the Crowley Lake exit. Go west through the Crowley Lake community for about 2 miles. At Crowley Lake Drive turn north and go about 2 miles.

Dinkey Creek

Dinkey Creek

Dinkey Creek Campground
Dinkey Creek Road
Dinkey Creek, CA
559-297-0706
This campground is next to Dinkey Creek in the Sierra National Forest. The campground is on a large sandy flat above the river and shaded by cedar and pine trees. It is at an elevation of 5,400 feet. There are 128 tent and RV sites. RVs up to 35 feet are allowed and there are no hookups. Amenities include piped water, flush toilets, picnic tables and grills. There are several trails that start at this campground. Dogs are allowed at the campgrounds, on trails and in the water but only at non-designated swimming beaches. Pets must be leashed and please clean up after them. To make a reservation call 1-877-444-6777. To get there, take Hwy 168 east from Clovis towards Prather. Continue through Prather to Shaver Lake. Just before you reach Shaver Lake turn right on the Dinkey Creek Road. Travel 11.7 miles east to the Intersection of the Dinkey Creek Road and the McKinley Grove Road. Continue north on the Dinkey Creek Road for 3/10 of a mile to the

Campground.

Graeagle

Graeagle

Lakes Basin Campground
County Road 519
Graeagle, CA
530-836-2575
This campground is located in the Plumas National Forest and offers 3 campsites. Amenities include water, vault toilets and trailer space. Located at this campground is the trailhead for the Grassy Lake Trail. In the campground dogs must be on leash. On the trails, dogs on leash or off-leash but under direct voice control are allowed. Reservations for the campsites can be made by calling 1-877-444-6777. The campground is located 9 miles southwest of Graeagle on County Road 519.

Independence

Independence

Goodale Creek Campground
Aberdeen Cutoff Road
Independence, CA
760-872-5000
This campground is located at a 4,000 foot elevation on a volcanic flow, next to Goodale Creek. It offers great views of the Sierra Nevada Mountains. There are 62 tent and RV sites available. The campground is usually open from late April to the end of October. There are no fees, no hookups and no drinking water. All sites are on a first-come, first-served basis. Be aware of rattlesnakes in the area, especially during the summer months. The closest convenience stores are located in the towns of Independence and Big Pine. Dogs are allowed at the campground, but please keep them under control. To get there from Independence, go 16 miles north on Highway 395. Then take Aberdeen Cutoff Road west for 2 miles.

Johnsondale

Johnsondale

Redwood Meadow Campground
off Mountain Road 50
Johnsondale, CA

559-539-2607

This campground is located in the Sequoia National Forest at an elevation of 6,100 feet. It is across the road from the Trail of a Hundred Giants. The campground offers 15 tent and small RV sites. RVs up to 16 feet are allowed and there are no hookups. Vault toilets are located at the camp. Ideal camping is from May to October. Pets must be leashed and attended at all times. Please clean up after your pet. The campsite is located about 45 miles northwest of Kernville. From Kernville, take State Mountain Road 99 north to Johnsondale. Go west on 50 to the Western Divide Highway turnoff. Go 2 miles to the campground.

June Lake

June Lake

Silver Lake Resort
Route 3
June Lake, CA
760-648-7525

This resort offers an RV park with full hookups. All sites are situated side by side and have a paved patio slab and picnic table. Amenities include general store, cafe, showers, restrooms, laundry room and picnic area. Well-behaved leashed pets are allowed in the RV park. They need to be walked outside of the park and please clean up after your pet in the Sierra National Forest. The resort is open from the end of April to mid-October. They are located on the shore of Silver Lake.

Kernville

Weldon

Isabella Lake KOA
15627 Highway 178
Weldon, CA 93283
760-378-2001

Located near the dog-friendly Isabella Lake, this campground offers both tent sites and RV spaces. Well-behaved leashed dogs of all sizes are allowed. People need to clean up after their pets. There is no pet fee. Site amenities include a maximum length pull through of 40 feet and 30 amp service available. Other amenities include LP gas, an entrance gate, free modem dataport, snack bar and a seasonal swimming pool.

Lake Tahoe

Lake Tahoe

Encore SuperPark Tahoe Valley
1175 Melba Drive
Lake Tahoe, CA 96150
877-717-8737

Located in South Lake Tahoe, this campground offers both tent sites and RV spaces. RV site amenities include full hookups with 30 or 50 amp service, cable and a picnic table. Other campground amenities include volleyball and tennis courts, seasonal heated outdoor pool, pool table, playground, video game center, general store, laundry facilities, modem hookup and even a dog run. Well-behaved leashed dogs are welcome. Please clean up after your pet. There is no pet fee.

South Lake Tahoe

Fall Leaf Campground
Fallen Leaf Lake Road
South Lake Tahoe, CA
530-543-2600

This campground is at a 6,377 foot elevation and is located in the Lake Tahoe Management Basin Unit of the National Forest. The camp offers 250 sites and 17 are available on a first-come, first-served basis. The maximum RV length allowed is 40 feet and there are no hookups. Amenities include water, flush toilets, fire rings, picnic tables and barbecues. There are miles of trails which begin at or near this campground. Pets on leash are allowed but not at the beach. Please clean up after your pets. The campground is open from Memorial Day weekend to the end of October. To get there from the intersections of Highways 89 and 50, take Highway 89 north about 2.5 to 3 miles. Then turn left on Fallen Leaf Lake Road. Access to the campgrounds is on a rough paved road. A regular passenger car will make it, but go slow. For reservations, call toll free at 1-877-444-6777.

Lake Tahoe South Shore KOA
760 North Highway 50
South Lake Tahoe, CA 96150
530-577-3693

This campground is located five miles from the lake and nine miles from the casinos. Located near Echo Creek, the camp is surrounded by pines and mountains. They offer both tent and RV sites. Maximum length for pull through sites is 60 feet. Sites have 30 amp service available. Other amenities include cable TV, LP gas, free modem dataport and a seasonal swimming pool. Well-behaved leashed dogs of all sizes are allowed.

People need to clean up after their pets. There is a $3.50 pet fee per dog. They are open seasonally from April 1 through October 15.

Tahoe City

Meeks Bay Campground
Highway 89
Tahoe City, CA
530-543-2600
This campground is at a 6,225 foot elevation and is located in the Lake Tahoe Management Basin Unit of the National Forest. The camp offers 40 tent and RV sites. The maximum RV length allowed is 20 feet and there are no hookups. Amenities include water, flush toilets, fire rings, picnic tables and barbecues. Pets on leash are allowed but not at the beach. Please clean up after your pets. The campground is open from Memorial Day weekend to the end of October. The camp is located on the west shore of Tahoe on Highway 89, about 10 miles south of Tahoe City. It is located near D.L. Bliss State Park. For reservations, call toll free at 1-877-444-6777.

Zephyr Cove

Zephyr Cove RV Park and Campground
460 Highway 50
Zephyr Cove, NV 89448
775-588-6644
This campground is located within minutes of South Lake Tahoe and Stateline. RV site amenities include full hookups, telephone lines and cable TV. RVs up to 40 feet can be accommodated. Tent sites are either drive-in or walk-in sites, some of which offer lake views. Well-behaved dogs on leash are allowed.

Lone Pine

Lone Pine

Lone Pine Campground
Whitney Portal Road
Lone Pine, CA
760-876-6200
This 43 site campground is located in the Inyo National Forest at an elevation of 6,000 feet. Water is available at the site. There is a $12 fee per campsite. The campground is open from the end of April to mid October. To make a reservation call 1-877-444-6777. Pets must be leashed while in the campground. Please clean up after your pets. From Highway 395 take Whitney Portal Road.

Tuttle Creek Campground
off Horseshoe Meadows Road
Lone Pine, CA
760-876-6200
This campground is located at 5,120 feet and is shadowed by some of the most impressive peaks in the Sierra Nevada Mountain Range. The camp is located in an open desert setting with a view of Alabama Hills and Mt. Whitney. There are 85 tent and RV sites, but no hookups. Amenities include 9 pit toilets and picnic tables. All sites are based on a first-come, first-served basis. This campground is managed by the BLM (Bureau of Land Management). Pets on leash are allowed and please clean up after them. To get there go 3.5 miles west of Lone Pine on Whitney Portal Road. Then go 1.5 miles south on Horseshoe Meadows Road and follow the sign to the campsite.

Long Barn

Long Barn

Fraser Flat Campground
Fraser Flat Road
Long Barn, CA
209-586-3234
At an elevation of 4,800 feet this campground offers forested sites on the South Fork of the Stanislaus River. There are 34 tent and RV sites with a maximum RV length of 22 feet. There are no hookups. Amenities include piped water, vault toilets, picnic tables and grills. All sites are on a first-come, first-served basis. Pets on leash are allowed and please clean up after them. This campground is located in the Stanislaus National Forest. To get there, drive 3 miles north of Highway 108 at Spring Gap turnoff (Fraser Flat Road).

Mammoth Lakes

Mammoth Lakes

Lake George Campground
Lake George Road
Mammoth Lakes, CA
760-924-5500
This 16 site campground is located in the Inyo National Forest at an elevation of 9,000 feet. It is located near several trails. Amenities include water. There are no hookups. The fee for a campsite is $14. The campground is open from about the mid June to mid September. The sites

are available on a first-come, first-served basis. Pets must be leashed while in the campground and please clean up after them. To get there from the intersection of Main Street and Hwy 203, take Lake Mary Road to the left. Go past Twin Lakes. You'll see a road that goes off to the left (Lake Mary Loop Rd.). Go past this road, you'll want the other end of the loop. When you come to another road that also says Lake Mary Loop Rd, turn left. Then turn right onto Lake George Road and follow it to the campground.

Lake Mary Campground
Lake Mary Loop Road
Mammoth Lakes, CA
760-924-5500
This 48 site campground is located in the Inyo National Forest at an elevation of 8,900 feet. It is located near several trails. Amenities include water. There are no hookups. The fee for a campsite is $14. The campground is open from about the beginning of June to mid September. The sites are available on a first-come, first-served basis. Pets must be leashed while in the campground and please clean up after them. To get there from the intersection of Main Street and Hwy 203, take Lake Mary Road to the left. Pass Twin Lakes and then you'll come to Lake Mary. Turn left onto Lake Mary Loop Road.

New Shady Rest Campground
Sawmill Cutoff Road
Mammoth Lakes, CA
760-924-5500
This 94 site campground is located in the Inyo National Forest at an elevation of 7,800 feet. It is located near several trails. Amenities include water. There are no hookups. The fee for a campsite is $13. The campground is open from about mid May to the end of October. The sites are available on a first-come, first-served basis. Pets must be leashed while in the campground and please clean up after them. To make a reservation call 1-877-444-6777. To get there from the Mammoth Visitor's Center, take Hwy 203 towards town. The first street on your right will be Sawmill Cutoff Road. Turn right and Shady Rest Park is at the end of the road.

Reds Meadow Campground
off Highway 203
Mammoth Lakes, CA
760-924-5500
This 56 site campground is located in the Inyo National Forest at an elevation of 7,600 feet. It is near the dog-friendly Devil's Postpile National Monument and hiking trails including the John Muir Trail. Amenities include water. There are no

hookups. The fee for a campsite is $15. The campground is open from about the mid June to mid September. The sites are available on a first-come, first-served basis. Pets must be leashed while in the campground and please clean up after them. From Highway 395, drive 10 miles west on Highway 203 to Minaret Summit. Then drive about 7 miles on a paved, narrow mountain road.

McGee Creek

McGee Creek

McGee Creek Campground
McGee Creek Road
McGee Creek, CA
760-873-2500
This 28 site campground is located in the Inyo National Forest at an elevation of 7,600 feet. The campsite is in an open area and adjacent to McGee Creek. Amenities include water, flush toilets and space for RVs. There are no hookups. For hiking, the McGee Creek Trail is located within a few miles from the campground. The fee for a campsite is $15. The campground is open from mid May to mid October. To make a reservation call 1-877-444-6777. Pets must be leashed while in the campground and please clean up after your pets. To get there from Highway 395, take the first exit after Crowley Lake. Go 2 miles heading south on McGee Creek Road to the campground.

Mono Lake

Lee Vining

Glass Creek Campground
Highway 395
Lee Vining, CA
760-873-2408
This 50 site campground is located in the Inyo National Forest at an elevation of 7,600 feet. It is located near several trails. There are no hookups or water. The fee for a campsite is $14. The campground is open from about the end of April to the end of October. The sites are available on a first-come, first-served basis. Pets must be leashed while in the campground and please clean up after them. The campground is located between Lee Vining and Mammoth Lakes on Highway 395. It is at the intersection of the highway and the Crestview CalTrains Maintenance Station, about one mile north of the Crestview Rest Area.

Onyx

Onyx

Walker Pass Campground
Highway 178
Onyx, CA
661-391-6000
This campground has 11 walk-in sites for Pacific Crest Trail hikers and two sites are available for vehicles. Drinking water is available from spring through fall. There are no hookups. Hitching racks and corrals are available for horses. There are no reservations or fees but donations are accepted. Dogs are allowed but need on leash while in the campground. To get there from Ridgecrest, go 27 miles west on Highway 178 to Walker Pass.

Riverton

Riverton

Ice House Campground
Ice House Road
Riverton, CA
530-644-2349
This 83 site campground is located in the Eldorado National Forest at an elevation of 5,500 feet. It is located near the Ice House Bike Trail. There are no hookups or water. Camp amenities include restrooms, water, picnic tables, swimming, bicycling, hiking and more. Pets on leash are allowed in the campground, on the trails and in the water. Please clean up after your pets. To make a reservation call 1-877-444-6777. To get there from Placerville, take Highway 50 east for 21 miles to Ice House Road turnoff. Turn left and go 11 miles north to the campground turnoff. Then go one mile to the campgrounds.

Wench Creek Campground
Ice House Road
Riverton, CA
530-644-2349
This campground is located in the Eldorado National Forest next to Union Valley Reservoir and offers 100 tent and RV campsites. There are no hookups. Camp amenities include restrooms, water, swimming, bicycling and hiking. Dogs are allowed in the campground, on the trails and in the water. Pets should be leashed and please clean up after them. To get there from Placerville, take Highway 50 east and go 21 miles to Riverton. Turn left on Ice House Road. Go about 19 miles north to the reservoir.

Sequoia National Park

Three Rivers

Sequoia and Kings Canyon National Park Campgrounds
47050 General Highway
Three Rivers, CA 93271
559-565-3341
This park offers many campgrounds which range in elevation from 2,100 feet to 7,500 feet. The Lodgepole, Dorst, Grant Grove and Atwell Mill campgrounds are located near giant sequoia groves. The Lodgepole campground, located at 6,700 foot elevation, is one of the largest camps and offers 250 sites. Tent and RV camping is available, with a maximum RV length of 35 feet. Amenities at this campground include a laundromat, deli, market, gift shop, pay showers, flush toilets and more. Some of the campgrounds are open all year. Pets must be leashed and attended at all times. Please clean up after your pet. Dogs are not allowed on any trails or hikes in this park, but see our listings in the towns of Johnsondale and Hume for details about nearby dog-friendly hiking, sightseeing and additional camping.

Shaver Lake

Shaver Lake

Camp Edison at Shaver Lake
42696 Tollhouse Road
Shaver Lake, CA 93664
559-841-3134
This campground is located at Shaver Lake in the Sierra National Forest and is managed by Southern California Edison. There are 252 campsites with electricity and free cable TV. Amenities include picnic tables, restroom with heated showers, laundromats, marina and general store. Dogs are allowed at the campgrounds, on trails and in the water but only at non-designated swimming beaches. Pets must be leashed and please clean up after them. There is a $4 per night per pet fee. To make a reservation call 559-841-3134.

Dorabelle Campground
Dorabella Street
Shaver Lake, CA
559-297-0706
This campground is next to Shaver Lake in the Sierra National Forest. Some of the sites have lake views and all of the sites have shade from

dense pines trees. The camp is at an elevation of 5,500 feet. There are 68 tent and RV sites. RVs up to 40 feet are allowed and there are no hookups. Amenities include water, vault toilets, picnic tables and grills. Be sure to bring some mosquito repellant. There are several trails here that provide access around the lake. Dogs are allowed at the campgrounds, on trails and in the water but only at non-designated swimming beaches. Pets must be leashed and please clean up after them. To make a reservation call 1-877-444-6777. To get there, take Hwy 168 east from Clovis to Shaver Lake. In Shaver Lake turn right on Dorabella St. (Just after the 76 gas station). Travel 5/10 of a mile to Dorbelle Campground.

Tom's Place

Tom's Place

East Fork Campground
Rock Creek Canyon Road
Tom's Place, CA
760-873-2500
This 133 site campground is located in the Inyo National Forest at an elevation of 9,000 feet. Amenities include water, flush toilet, picnic tables and space for RVs. There are no hookups. For hiking, there are several trailheads nearby including the Hilton Lakes and Little Lakes Valley trails. The fee for a campsite is $15. The campground is open from about the end of May to the end of September. To make a reservation call 1-877-444-6777. Pets must be leashed while in the campground and please clean up after them. To get there from Bishop, take Highway 395 north for about 30 miles. Take the Tom's Place exit and go 4 miles on Rock Creek Canyon Road.

Truckee

Truckee

Lakeside Campground
off Highway 89
Truckee, CA
530-587-3558
This 30 site campground is located in the Tahoe National Forest at an elevation of 5,741 feet. Camp amenities include vault toilets. There is no water. Sites are $12 per night. The campground is located next to the reservoir and activities include fishing and swimming. Pets must be leashed in the campground. To get there from I-80, take Highway 89 North to Prosser Reservoir. To make

a reservation call 1-877-444-6777.

Yosemite

Bass Lake

Lupine/Cedar Bluff Campground
off Road 222
Bass Lake, CA
559-877-2218
This campground is next to Bass Lake in the Sierra National Forest. It is at an elevation of 3,400 feet and offers shade from dense pine, oak and cedar frees. There are 113 campsites for tent and RV camping. RVs up to 40 feet are allowed and there are no hookups. Camp amenities include piped water, flush toilets, picnic tables and grills. The campground is open all year. A .5 mile trail called The Way of the Mono Trail, is located near this campground. Dogs are allowed at the campgrounds, on trails and in the water but only at non-designated swimming beaches. Pets must be leashed and please clean up after them. To make a reservation call 1-877-444-6777. To get there, Take Hwy 41 north from Fresno; continue thru Oakhurst to Road 222. Turn right on Road 222, travel east 3 miles and turn right (Road 222), continue for 3/10 of a mile a bear right again. Travel 3.5 miles around the south side of the Lake to Lupine Cedar Campground. Check in at the Bass Lake Campground office before heading to your campsite. The office is located at the west end of the lake near Recreation Point.

Groveland

Yosemite Pines RV Resort
20450 Old Highway 120
Groveland, CA 95321
209-962-7690
This 30 acre RV park offers sites with both full and partial hookups as well as tent sites. Well-behaved dogs on a 10 foot or less leash are allowed. There is no pet fee. Please clean up after your pets.

Yosemite National Park

Yosemite National Park Campgrounds
PO Box 577
Yosemite National Park, CA 95389
209-372-0200
There are 10 dog-friendly campgrounds to choose from at this national park. Pets are allowed in all campgrounds except Camp 4, Tamarack Flat, Porcupine Flat, all walk-in sites and all group

campsites. Most of the campgrounds allow both tents and RVs up to 40 feet, but there are no RV hookups. Generators can be used sparingly only between 7am and 7pm. Some of the campgrounds are open all year but all are open during the summer. Reservations should be made well in advance, especially during the summer season. While this national park does not allow dogs on most of the trails, there are still about 6-7 miles of both paved and unpaved trails that allow dogs. See our Yosemite National Park listing for more details. Dogs must be on a 6 foot or less leash and attended at all times. People must also clean up after their pets.

Central Coast Dog-Friendly RV Park and Campground Guide

Big Sur

Big Sur

Big Sur Campground and Cabins
Highway 1
Big Sur, CA
831-667-2322
This tent and RV campground is set amongst redwood trees along the Big Sur River. For RVs there are full hookups and some pull through sites. Camp amenities include a general store, playground, basketball court and more. Well-behaved leashed dogs of all sizes are allowed in the tent and RV sites but not in the cabins. Pets must be attended at all times. People need to clean up after their pets. They are located about 5 miles from the dog-friendly Pfieffer Beach and 2.5 miles from Big Sur Station. The campground is open all year.

Fernwood at Big Sur
Highway 1
Big Sur, CA
831-667-2422
Dogs are allowed at the campgrounds but not in the motel. RVs are permitted and there are hookups are available.

Ventana Big Sur Campground
Highway 1
Big Sur, CA
831-667-2712
This campground is nestled among trees and along a stream. RVs up to 22 feet are permitted but there are no hookups and generators cannot be used at any time. The campground is usually open from April through mid-October. Dogs are

allowed but should be kept quiet and on a leash at all times. There is a maximum of 2 pets per campsite.

Ventana Campground
Hwy One
Big Sur, CA
831-667-2712
This 40 acre campground, located in a redwood tree lined canyon, offers 80 camp sites nestled among the trees and along the edge of the stream. RV's are limited to 22 feet and there are no hookups. Well-behaved quiet leashed dogs of all sizes are allowed, maximum of two dogs per site. People need to clean up after their pets. There is a $5 per night pet fee per dog. The campground is open from mid-March through mid-October.

Carmel

Carmel

Carmel by the River RV Park
27680 Schulte Road
Carmel, CA
831-624-9329
This RV park is located right next to the river. Amenities include hookups, basketball court, recreation room and dog walk area. Per Monterey County's Ordinance, maximum length per stay from April through September is 14 days and from October through March is 8 weeks. Well-behaved quiet dogs of all sizes are allowed, up to a maximum of three pets. Pets must be kept on a short leash and never left unattended in the campsite or in your RV. People need to clean up after their pets. There is no pet fee. The owners have dogs that usually stay at the office. The RV park is open all year.

Gorda

Gorda

Kirk Creek Campground
Highway 1
Gorda, CA
831-385-5434
Located in the Los Padres National Forest, this campground is situated on an open bluff 100 feet above sea level and offers great views of the ocean and coastline. The beach is reached by hiking down from the campgrounds. The Kirk Creek trailhead is also located at the campground and leads to the Vicente Flat Trail which offers

miles of hiking trails. Dogs are allowed in the campgrounds, on the hiking trails, and on the beach but must be leashed. Be aware that there are large amounts of poison oak on the trails. RVs up to 30 feet are permitted but there are no hookups. The campground is located about 25 miles south of Big Sur.

Plaskett Creek Campground
Highway 1
Gorda, CA
831-385-5434
Located in the Los Padres National Forest, this campground is nestled among large Monterey Pine trees. The campsites are within walking distance of the dog-friendly Sand Dollar Beach. Dogs must be leashed in the campgrounds and on the beach. RVs are permitted in the campgrounds but there are no hookups. The campground is about 5 miles south of the Kirk Creek and about 30 miles south of Big Sur.

Hollister

Hollister

Casa de Fruita RV's Orchard Resort
10031 Pacheco Pass Highway
Hollister, CA 95023
408-842-9316
This RV park is located at a popular roadside orchard resort which features a fruit stand, store, 24 hour restaurant, zoo, rock shop, gold panning, children's train ride, children's playground and picnic areas. Amenities at the RV park include full hookups, pull through sites, shady areas, TV hookups and tent sites. Well-behaved leashed dogs are allowed. There is a $3 per night pet fee per pet. Please clean up after your pets. The resort is located on Highway 152/Pacheco Pass, two miles east of the Highway 156 junction.

King City

King City

San Lorenzo Regional Park
1160 Broadway
King City, CA 93930
831-385-5964
This campground is located in the dog-friendly San Lorenzo Park where leashed dogs are allowed on the hiking trails. Tent sites on grass and shaded RV spaces with full hookups are available. RVs up to 50 feet can be accommodated. Camp amenities include laundry

facilities, putting green, internet access kiosk, restrooms and showers. Well-behaved leashed dogs of all sizes are allowed in the campground, maximum of two dogs per site. Pets must be attended at all times. People need to clean up after their pets. There is a $2 per night pet fee per dog. The campground is open all year.

Salinas

Salinas

Laguna Seca Campground and RV Park
1025 Monterey Highway 68
Salinas, CA 93908
831-755-4895
The popular Laguna Seca raceway is the highlight of this park. The park also offers a rifle range and an OHV and Off-Highway Motocross Track. Dogs are not permitted on any of the tracks including the OHV area. Dogs on leash are allowed at the RV and tent campgrounds. RV sites are paved and offer hookups with up to 30 amp service. Tent sites are dirt pads with showers, telephones and a playground within walking distance. Camping fees are subject to change depending on events that are being held at the raceway. Call ahead for rates and reservations.

San Luis Obispo

Arroyo Grande

Lake Lopez Recreation Area Campground
6820 Lopez Drive
Arroyo Grande, CA 93420
805-788-2381
This campground has 354 campsites which overlook the lake or are nestled among oak trees. Full hookups are available at some of the sites. This lake is popular for fishing, camping, boating, sailing, water skiing, canoeing, bird-watching and miles of hiking trails ranging from easy to strenuous. The marina allows dogs on their boat rentals for an extra $10 fee. Other amenities at the marina include a laundromat, grocery store and tackle shop. Dogs must be leashed at all times and people need to clean up after their pets. Reservations for the campsites are accepted.

Bradley

Lake San Antonio Campground

2610 San Antonio Road
Bradley, CA
805-472-2311
The south shore of Lake San Antonio offers three camping areas with over 500 campsites and a picnic area. They have full hookups for RVs. The north shore provides shoreline camping and full hookup sites. The majority of campsites are available on a first-come, first-served basis, but there are a limited amount of individual and group reservation sites. Up to two dogs are allowed per campsite. Dogs are also allowed on miles of hiking trails and in the water. Pets need to be leashed and please clean up after them. There is a $2 per night pet fee.

Oceano

Pacific Dunes RV Resort
1025 Silver Spur Place
Oceano, CA 93445
888-908-7787
Walk to the dog-friendly sand dunes and beach from this campground. Well-behaved leashed dogs are welcome in the tent sites and RV spaces. Please clean up after your pet. There is no pet fee. The RV pull through or back-in sites offer full hookups including 50 amp service, water, electric, sewer hookups, cable TV and a picnic table. Other campground amenities include a volleyball court, pool table, basketball courts, horseback riding, barbecue facilities, bicycle and walking paths, general store, laundry facilities, lighted streets, restrooms/showers, modem hookup and a clubhouse.

Paso Robles

Lake Nacimiento Campgrounds
Lake Nacimiento Drive
Paso Robles, CA
805-238-3256
This campground offers over 400 campsites and RV sites have both full or partial hook ups. Dogs are allowed around and in the lake. Be careful about letting your dog get too far into the water, as there are many boats on the lake. Pets must be on leash and attended at all times. There is a $5 per day charge for dogs. The lake is located west of Hwy 101, seventeen miles north of Paso Robles. Take the 24th Street (G-14 West) exit in Paso Robles and proceed west on G-14 to the lake.

Lake Nacimiento Resort RV and Campgrounds
10625 Nacimiento Lake Drive
Paso Robles, CA

805-238-3256
Dogs are allowed in the campgrounds, but not in the lodge. RVs are permitted and the resort offers full hookups. Dogs can swim in the lake, but be very careful of boats, as this is a popular lake for water-skiing. Proof of your dog's rabies vaccination is required.

Pismo Beach

Pismo Coast Village RV Park
165 South Dolliver Street
Pismo Beach, CA 93449
805-773-1811
This 26 acre RV park is located right on the dog-friendly Pismo State Beach. There are 400 full hookup sites each with satellite TV. RVs up to 40 feet can be accommodated. Park amenities include a general store, arcade, laundromat, guest modem access in lobby, heated pool, bicycle rentals and miniature golf course. The maximum stay is 29 consecutive nights. Well-behaved leashed dogs of all sizes are allowed, up to a maximum of three pets. People need to clean up after their pets. There is no pet fee. The campground is open all year.

San Luis Obispo

El Chorro Regional Park Campground
Highway 1
San Luis Obispo, CA
805-781-5930
This campground offers 62 campsites for tent or RV camping. Some of the RV spaces are pull through sites and can accommodate RVs up to 40 feet . Most of the sites offer full hookups with electricity, water and sewer. All sites are available on a first-come, first-served basis. Use t he self-registration envelopes upon arrival. There are several hiking trails to choose from at this park, from hiking on meadows to walking along a creek. Dogs must be leashed at all times on the trails and in the campground. Please clean up after your pets. There is a dog park located in this regional park where your pooch can run leash free. To get to the park from Highway 101, head south and then take the Santa Rosa St. exit. Turn left on Santa Rosa which will turn into Highway 1 after Highland Drive. Continue about 5 miles and the park will be on your left, across from Cuesta College.

Santa Margarita

Santa Margarita KOA

4765 Santa Margarita Lake Road
Santa Margarita, CA 93453
805-438-5618
This campground is located near Santa Margarita Lake Regional Park which has miles of dog-friendly trails. Up to two dogs are allowed at each tent site, RV site and cabin. Pets cannot be left alone in the cabins. Well-behaved leashed dogs of all sizes are allowed. People need to clean up after their pets. There is no pet fee. Site amenities include a maximum length pull through of 35 feet and 30 amp service available. Other amenities include LP gas, an entrance gate and a seasonal swimming pool. They are open all year.

Santa Margarita Lake Regional Park Camping
off Pozo Road
Santa Margarita, CA
805-781-5930
Primitive boat-in sites are available at this park. This lake is popular for fishing, boating and hiking. Swimming is not allowed at the lake because it is a reservoir which is used for city drinking water. There is a seasonal swimming pool at the park. Hiking can be enjoyed at this park which offers miles of trails, ranging from easy to strenuous. Dogs must be leashed at all times and people need to clean up after their pets.

Solvang

Buellton

Flying Flags RV Park and Campground
180 Avenue of the Flags
Buellton, CA 93427
805-688-3716
There are no additional pet fees.

Watsonville

Watsonville

Santa Cruz/Monterey Bay KOA
1186 San Andreas Road
Watsonville, CA 95076
831-722-0551
This 20 acre campground offers both tent and RV sites. Well-behaved leashed dogs of all sizes are allowed in the campgrounds and RV spaces, but not in the lodge or cabins. People need to clean up after their pets. There is no pet fee. The camp is located within a short drive of the dog-friendly Manresa State Beach. Site amenities include a maximum pull through length of 50 feet and 50

amp service available. Other amenities include an available pavilion/meeting room, entrance gate, LP gas, free modem dataport, swimming pool, and hot tub/sauna. They are open all year.

Central Valley Dog-Friendly RV Park and Campground Guide

Bakersfield

Bakersfield

Orange Grove RV Park
1452 South Edison Road
Bakersfield, CA 93307
661-366-4662
This RV park is on a 40 acre orange grove, about eight miles east of Highway 99. Site amenities include pull through sites and 50 amp full utility hookups. Other amenities include a rig and car wash, a children's playground, oranges available from December through March, a swimming pool, laundry facilities, propane, TV/group meeting room and a country store. Well-behaved leashed dogs are welcome. They have a special pet walk area and there are no pet fees. Please clean up after your pet.

Shafter

Bakersfield KOA
5101 E Lerdo Highway
Shafter, CA 93263
661-399-3107
RV spaces and grassy tent sites are available at this campground. RV site amenities include a maximum length pull through of 70 feet and 50 amp service. Other campground amenities include a seasonal swimming pool, modem dataport, LP gas. Gas stations and 24 hour restaurants are within walking distance. Well-behaved leashed dogs of all sizes are allowed in the tent and RV sites, but not in the cabins. People need to clean up after their pets. There is no pet fee. The campground is open all year.

Clear Lake

Clearlake Oaks

Island RV Park
12840 Island Drive
Clearlake Oaks, CA 95423
707-998-3940
Located on a small island in Clear Lake, this RV park offers 30 full hookup sites and 4 tent sites. Amenities include laundry facilities, boat ramps and docks and hot showers. Well-behaved leashed dogs are allowed. Please clean up after them. The RV park is located .25 miles off State Route 20 on Island Drive. You will cross a bridge to get to the island. They do not accept credit cards.

Kelseyville

Clear Lake State Park Campgrounds
Soda Bay Road
Kelseyville, CA
707-279-4293
This park offers 149 campsites for RV or tent camping. There are no hookups. Amenities include picnic tables, restrooms, showers and grills. While dogs are not allowed on the trails or the swimming beaches at this park, they are allowed in the campgrounds and in the water at non-designated swim areas. One of the non-designated swim beaches is located between campgrounds 57 and 58. Pets must be on leash and please clean up after them. The park is located is 3.5 miles northeast of Kelseyville.

Lost Hills

Lost Hills

Lost Hills KOA
I-5 and Highway 46
Lost Hills, CA 93249
661-797-2719
RV spaces and grassy tent sites are available at this campground. RV site amenities include 50 amp service. Other camp amenities include a large seasonal swimming pool, playground, phone hookups, LP gas and showers. Gas stations and 24 hour restaurants are within walking distance. Well-behaved leashed dogs of all sizes are allowed. People need to clean up after their pets. There is no pet fee. The campground is open all year.

New Cuyama

New Cuyama

Selby Campgrounds
Soda Lake Road
New Cuyama, CA
661-391-6000
Primitive camping is available at this campground which is located at the base of the Caliente Mountains and near the dog-friendly Caliente Mountain Access Trail. There are 5 picnic tables and 4 fire pits, but no shade trees. There is no garbage pickup service, electricity or drinking water. Leave vehicles along the edge of the road, do not drive to your chosen campsite. Be aware of rattlesnakes in the area. Dogs on leash are allowed. Please clean up after your dog. The campground is located off Highway 166, about 14 miles west of New Cuyama, on Soda Lake Road. There will be signs.

San Juan Bautista

San Juan Bautista

Betabel RV Park
9664 Betabel Road
San Juan Bautista, CA 95045
831-623-2202
Located about 5 miles south of Gilroy, this RV park is set in the quiet countryside. RV sites offer full hookups with 30 or 50 amp service. Other amenities include a mini mart, seasonally heated pool, propane, club/meeting rooms, satellite TV, restrooms, showers and handicapped access. Well-behaved leashed dogs of all sizes are allowed. People need to clean up after their pets. There is no pet fee. The campground is open all year.

Mission Farms RV Park & Campground
400 San Juan Hollister Rd.
San Juan Bautista, CA
831-623-4456
Thanks to one of our readers for recommending this campground. The camp sites are $28 per night and there is a $2 pet fee.

Stonyford

Stonyford

Letts Lake Complex Campground
Forest Road #17N02

Stonyford, CA
530-934-3316
This campground is located in the Mendocino National Forest and is next to a 35 acre lake. Water-based activities include non-motorized boating, trout fishing and swimming. There are 22 campsites and camp amenities include toilets, fire rings, water and trailer space. The access road and camps are suitable for 16 to 20 foot camping trailers. The campground is at an elevation of 4,500 feet and is closed in the winter. There is a $8 per day campsite fee. Prices are subject to change. Dogs on leash are allowed at the campground, on trails and in the water at non-designated swimming areas only. The camp is located 19 miles west of Stonyford.

Los Angeles Dog-Friendly RV Park and Campground Guide

Malibu

Malibu

Leo Carrillo State Park Campground
Highway 1
Malibu, CA
818-880-0350
The campgrounds offer tent and RV camping near the beach. The campsites are located on the inland side of Highway 1. You can walk to the beach along a road that goes underneath the highway. Dogs on leash are allowed in the campgrounds and on a certain section of the beach. Please clean up after you pets. The campground is located on Highway 1, about 30 miles northwest of Santa Monica.

Piru

Piru

Lake Piru Marina
4780 Piru Canyon Road
Piru, CA 93040
805-521-1231
While dogs are not allowed in the water at Lake Piru, they are allowed on a boat on the water. This marina rents pontoon boats starting at $65 for 4 hours. Well-behaved dogs are allowed on the boats.

Olive Grove Campground
4780 Piru Canyon Road

Piru, CA 93040
805-521-1500
Located at Lake Piru, this campground allows well-behaved leashed dogs in the developed campgrounds, but not in the water. However, dogs are allowed on a boat on the water. The Marina rents pontoon boats and dogs are allowed on the rentals. Campsite amenities include laundry facilities, showers, water, picnic areas and dumping stations. Five of the RV sites have hookups. There is a $2 per day pet fee. Please clean up after your pets.

Orange County Dog-Friendly RV Park and Campground Guide

Anaheim

Anaheim

Canyon RV Park at Featherly
24001 Santa Ana Canyon Road
Anaheim, CA 92802
714-637-0210
This RV park is situated on the Santa Ana River surrounded by mature cottonwood and sycamore trees. They have 140 RV hookup sites. Other amenities include a playground and bike trails. This park is about 14 miles from Disneyland. Well-behaved leashed dogs are welcome for an additional $1 per day. Please clean up after your pets. The RV park is open all year.

Huntington Beach

Huntington Beach

Bolsa Chica State Beach Campground
Pacific Coast Highway
Huntington Beach, CA
714-377-5691
This campground offers RV sites with hookups. Most RVs can be accommodated, just let them know when making a reservation if your RV is over 25 feet. Pets on leash are allowed and please clean up after them. While dogs are not allowed on this state beach, they are allowed on several miles of paved trails that follow the coast. Dogs are also allowed at the adjacent Huntington Dog Beach. The campground is located on the Pacific Coast Highway between Golden West to Warner Avenue.

Newport Beach

Newport Beach

Newport Dunes Waterfront Resort
1131 Back Bay Drive
Newport Beach, CA 92660
949-729-3863
This RV resort offers 394 RV sites with hookups. Amenities include a playground, fitness center, bike trail, laundry facilities, general store, onsite cafe and pet walk. Up to two well-behaved dogs per site are allowed but must be leashed, never left unattended, kept inside your RV at night and not allowed at the beach or in the water.

Inland Empire Dog-Friendly RV Park and Campground Guide

Arrowbear

Crab Flats Campground
off Green Valley Road
Arrowbear, CA
909-337-2444
This San Bernardino National Forest campground is located at an elevation of 6,200 feet. It is a popular campsite and off-highway vehicle staging area. Off-road and hiking trails are located near this campground. Tent and small RV sites are available, with a maximum RV length of 15 feet. Sites are available on a first-come, first-served basis. Pets on leash are allowed and please clean up after them. To get there take 330 north and go through Running Springs and Arrowbear to Green Valley Road. Turn left and go about 4 miles to the Crab Flats Campground sign at Forestry (dirt road). Turn left and go about 4.5 miles.

Green Valley Campground
Green Valley Lake Road
Arrowbear, CA
909-337-2444
This 36 site campground is located in the San Bernardino National Forest. RVs up to 22 feet are allowed and there are no hookups. The lake offers fishing, swimming and boating. Trails are located nearby. Pets on leash are allowed and please clean up after them. To make a reservation, call 1-877-444-6777. To get there, take Highway 330 north. Go through Running Springs and Arrowbear to Green Valley Lake Road. Turn left and go about 6 miles to the campground.

Big Bear Lake

Holcomb Valley Campground
Van Dusen Canyon Road
Big Bear Lake, CA
909-866-3437
This tent and RV campground is located in the historic Holcomb Valley about a mile from the Belleville Ghost Town. See our listing under Big Bear Lake for more information about the ghost town. There is no water and no hookups at the campsite. Camp amenities include toilets. The sites are on a first-come, first-served basis. Pets are allowed but must be leashed and cannot be left unattended. Watch out for rattlesnakes, especially during the warm summer months. The campground is located in the San Bernardino National Forest. To get there from the northeast corner of Big Bear Lake, take Highway 38 east and turn left onto Van Dusen Canyon Road. Once on this road, you will travel about 4 to 5 miles on a dirt road. The campground will be on the left.

Holloway's RV Park
398 Edgemoor Road
Big Bear Lake, CA 92315
909-866-5706
This RV park offers large level sites with a nice view of Big Bear Lake. RV sites offer full hookups, tables, barbecues. and TV cable. Park amenities include a small convenience store, restrooms, showers, laundry room, playground with horseshoes, basketball and boat rentals. Dogs are allowed at the campgrounds and on the boat rentals. Pets must be leashed and please clean up after them.

Pineknot Campground
Bristlecone
Big Bear Lake, CA
909-866-3437
This 52 site campground is part of the San Bernardino National Forest. It is located at an elevation of 7,000 feet. There are both tent and RV spaces with a maximum RV length of 45 feet. Amenities include water, flush toilets and picnic areas. Pets must be on leash and cannot be left unattended. Please clean up after your pets. The campground is on Bristlecone near Summit Blvd. Call to make a reservation.

Serrano Campground
4533 North Shore Drive
Big Bear Lake, CA
909-866-3437

This campground, located within steps of Big Bear Lake, offers tent and RV sites with full hookups. Well-behaved leashed dogs are welcome. Dogs are allowed at the campground, on the trails and in the lake. Pets cannot be left alone in the campground. Please clean up after your pet. To make a reservation, call 1-877-444-6777. The camp is located 4.5 miles east of the dam on the north side of the lake.

Fawnskin

Fawnskin

Hanna Flat Campground
Rim of the World Drive
Fawnskin, CA
909-337-2444
This 88 site campground is located in the San Bernardino National Forest at an elevation of 7,000 feet. RVs up to 40 feet are allowed and there are no hookups. Amenities include picnic tables, fire rings, paved parking, flush toilets and trash dumpster. The Hanna Flat Trailhead is located at this camp. Pets on leash are allowed and please clean up after them. To make a reservation, call 1-877-444-6777. To get there take Highway 18 to Big Bear Lake Dam. Go straight, do not cross over the dam. Highway 18 becomes Highway 38. Go the Fawnskin Fire Station and turn left onto the Rim of the World Drive. Go about 2.5 miles on a dirt road to the campsite.

Lake Arrowhead

Lake Arrowhead

North Shore Campground
Torrey Road
Lake Arrowhead, CA
909-337-2444
This 27 site campground is located in the San Bernardino National Forest. RVs up to 22 feet are allowed and there are no hookups. The trailhead for the North Shore National Recreation Trail is located at this campground. Pets on leash are allowed and please clean up after them. To make a reservation, call 1-877-444-6777. The camp is located near the north shore of Lake Arrowhead, about two miles northeast of the village. To get there from the Lake Arrowhead Marina, go east on Torrey Road. At the first left, take the dirt road to Forest Road 2N25 to the trailhead.

Lakeview

Lakeview

Lake Perris Campgrounds
off Cajalco Expressway
Lakeview, CA
909-657-0676
This campground offers 434 campsites including two RV areas with full hookups. While dogs are not allowed in the lake or within 100 feet of the water, they are allowed on miles of trails including the bike trail that loops around the lake. Pets must be leashed and please clean up after them. The campground is located 11 miles south of Riverside. From Interstate 215 exit at Cajalco Expressway and head east. Call to make reservations.

Pomona

Pomona

Los Angeles/Fairplex KOA
2200 North White Avenue
Pomona, CA 91768
909-593-8915
Located about 30 miles from Disneyland and next to the Fairplex, this 12 acre campground offers both tent and RV spaces. RV site amenities include a maximum length pull through of 70 feet, 50 amp service and telephone service. Other campground amenities include a free modem dataport, snack bar, swimming pool, hot tub/sauna and pavilion/meeting room available. Well-behaved leashed dogs of all sizes are allowed for short term stays. For a one month stay or longer, they have certain size and breed restrictions. People need to clean up after their pets. There is no pet fee. The campground is open all year.

Rimforest

Rimforest

Dogwood Campground
Highway 18
Rimforest, CA
909-337-2444
This 93 site campground is located in the San Bernardino National Forest. RVs up to 22 feet are allowed and there are no hookups. Pets on leash are allowed and please clean up after them. To make a reservation, call 1-877-444-6777. To get

there go 20 miles northeast of San Bernardino on Highway 18. The camp is located less than mile from Rimforest and 3 miles from Lake Arrowhead.

San Dimas

San Dimas

East Shore RV Park
1440 Camper View Road
San Dimas, CA 91773
909-599-8355
This family RV park offers over 500 full hookup paved sites including some pull through sites. Site amenities include a grassy area, view sites, and full hookups with 20, 30 or 50 amp service. Park amenities include picnic areas, children's playground, laundry room, swimming pool, general store and market, video rentals, basketballs and volleyballs, email station, restrooms and 24 hour check-in. Well-behaved dogs are allowed in the RV park, but not in the tenting area. Pets must be leashed and please clean up after them. There is a $2 per day pet fee. This RV park is open year-round.

Temecula

Temecula

Lake Skinner Campground
Rancho California Road
Temecula, CA
909-926-1541
This campground offers tent and RV sites with full hookups. The campground is located in a 6,040 acre park which features a lake, hiking trails and equestrian trails. Dogs are allowed on the trails and in the campgrounds, but not in the lake or within 50 feet of the lake. Dogs must be on a 6 foot or less leash and please clean up after them. To get there, take Highway 15 to Rancho California Road and go north 10 miles.

Pechanga RV Resort
45000 Pala Road
Temecula, CA 92592
909-587-0484
This RV resort is located at the Pechanga Casino in Temecula.

Vail Lake Wine Country RV Resort
38000 Hwy 79 S
Temecula, CA 92592
909-303-0174
This RV resort is located in the country, about 15 minutes from Interstate 15. There are several hiking trails throughout the RV park where you can walk with your dog.

Victorville

Victorville

Victorville/Inland Empire KOA
16530 Stoddard Wells Road
Victorville, CA 92392
760-245-6867
This campground offers large shaded sites in the high desert. RV spaces and tent sites are available. RV site amenities include a maximum pull through length of 75 feet and 30 amp service. Other camp amenities include a seasonal swimming pool, free modem dataport, LP gas and pavilion/meeting room. Well-behaved leashed dogs of all sizes are allowed for short term stays. For a one month stay or longer, they have certain size and breed restrictions. People need to clean up after their pets. There is no pet fee. The

campground is open all year.

San Diego Dog-Friendly RV Park and Campground Guide

Cardiff

Cardiff

San Elijo State Beach Campground
Old Highway 101
Cardiff, CA
760-753-5091
This campground offers RV sites with limited hookups. RVs up to 26 feet can use the hookup sites and RVs up to 35 feet are allowed. They offer both inland and ocean view spaces. While dogs are not allowed at this beach, you can walk to the dog-friendly Cardiff State Beach. The beach is about 1 mile south of Cardiff.

Descanso

Descanso

Cuyamaca Ranch State Park
12551 Highway 79
Descanso, CA 92016
760-765-0755
Five cabins are available at Paso Picacho campground. The log cabins are 12 feet by 12 feet with a deck. Each cabin has bunk beds that sleep four (no mattresses, you must bring your own bedding.) Amenities at each cabin include a picnic table, fire ring, barbecue and room for a small tent. Restrooms with pay showers and water are located near each site. The fee is $15 per night. There is an eight person maximum per site. You may bring your own padlock if you wish to lock the cabin during your stay. Dogs are allowed in the cabin but must not be left unattended. Dogs are allowed on two of the paved fire road trails in this park. This park is located about 10 miles from the town of Julian.

Julian

Julian

Lake Cuyamaca
15027 Highway 79
Julian, CA 92036
877-581-9904

This campground has 40 RV sites with hookups and 14 tent sites located next a popular fishing lake. There is a 3.5 mile trail surrounding the lake. Dogs on leash are welcome both in the campground and on the trail, but they are not allowed in the water. People need to clean up after their pets. The campground does not take reservations, so all the sites are available on a first-come, first-served basis.

Pinezanita Trailer Ranch and Campground
4446 Highway 79
Julian, CA 92036
760-765-0429
They have a fishing pond, stocked with blue gill and catfish. You can find fishing tackle and bait in the Campground Registration Office. Dogs are not allowed in the cabins, but they are welcome to stay with you at your RV, trailer, or campsite. There is a $2 per day pet charge. Pets must be on a 6 foot or shorter leash at all times. Noisy pets are cause for eviction. Carry plastic bags or a pooper scooper and pick up after your pet.

Pine Valley

Pine Valley

Laguna Campground
Sunrise Highway
Pine Valley, CA
619-445-6235
This 104 site campground is located in the Cleveland National Forest. It is located at an elevation of 5,600 feet and offers both tent and RV sites. RVs up to 40 feet are allowed and there are no hookups. Flush toilets are at this campground. There is a $13 fee per site. To make a reservations, call 1-877-444-6777. Pets on leash are allowed and please clean up after them. To get there, take Interstate 8 to the Sunrise Highway exit. Go about 13 miles to the campground.

San Diego

San Diego

Campland on the Bay
2211 Pacific Beach Drive
San Diego, CA
858-581-4200
This RV park is located on Mission Bay, across the water from Sea World. RV sites have full hookups and some offer beach front, bay view or primitive locations. Amenities include boat slips, a

boat launch, store with a market, game room and a laundry room. Dogs are allowed in certain areas. They must be leashed and please clean up after them. There is a $3 per day pet fee.

Santa Ysabel

Santa Ysabel

Lake Henshaw Resort
26439 Highway 76
Santa Ysabel, CA
760-782-3487
Lake Henshaw Resort, located at a lake which rests at the foot of the Palomar Mountains, offers camping and RV hookups. There are 15 sites with full RV hook-ups and 85 mobile home park sites.Children and pets are welcome. Lake Henshaw is a great place for fishermen of all levels. This resort is located off Highway 76, north of Julian.

Desert Dog-Friendly RV Park and Campground Guide

Baker

Baker

Mohave National Preserve Campgrounds
72157 Baker Road
Baker, CA 92309
760-255-8800
This park offers two family campgrounds, the Mid Hills Campground and Hole-in-the-Wall Campground. Elevations range from 4,400 feet to 5,600 feet. The campgrounds offer tent camping and one camp offers spaces for RVs. There are no hookups. The campsites are usually booked during deer hunting season. Spaces are available on a first-come, first-served basis. Pets are allowed but should be leashed. Please clean up after your pet. Contact the park for campground locations and more details.

Barstow

Yermo

Barstow/Calico KOA
35250 Outer Highway 15 North
Yermo, CA 92398
760-254-2311

This campground is located in a desert setting and is about 3.5 miles from the dog-friendly Calico Ghost Town. RV spaces and tent sites are available. RV site amenities include a maximum pull through length of 70 feet and 50 amp service. Other camp amenities include a seasonal swimming pool, free modem dataport, LP gas, snack bar, pavilion/meeting room and dog walking area. Well-behaved leashed dogs of all sizes are allowed. People need to clean up after their pets. There is no pet fee. The campground is open all year.

Death Valley

Death Valley

Death Valley National Park Campgrounds
Highway 190
Death Valley, CA 92328
760-786-3200
There are 10 campgrounds to choose from at this park, ranging from 196 feet below sea level to 8,200 feet above sea level. The Emigrant campground, located at 2,100 feet, offers tent camping only. This free campground offers 10 sites with water, tables and flush toilets. The Furnace Creek campground, located at 196 feet below sea level has 136 sites with water, tables, fireplaces, flush toilets and a dump station. Winter rates are $16 per night and less for the summertime. There are no hookups and some campgrounds do not allow generators. The Stovepipe Wells RV Campground is managed by the Stovepipe Wells Resort and offers 14 sites with full hookups but no tables or fireplaces. See our listing in Death Valley for more information about this RV park. About half of the campgrounds are open all year. Pets must be leashed and attended at all times. Please clean up after your pets. Dogs are not allowed on any trails in Death Valley National Park, but they can walk along roads. Pets are allowed up to a few hundred yards from the paved and dirt roads.

Stovepipe Wells Village Campgrounds and RV Park
Highway 190
Death Valley, CA 92328
760-786-2387
In addition to the motel, this establishment also offers a campground and RV park with full hookups. The main building has a restaurant, saloon, gift shops and swimming pool. They are located in the Death Valley Nationa Park. Well-behaved leashed dogs are allowed.

Joshua Tree National Park

Twentynine Palms

29 Palms RV Resort
4949 Desert Knoll
Twentynine Palms, CA 92277
760-367-3320
This RV resort is located less than 10 minutes from the Joshua Tree National Park visitor center. RV sites include full hookups and shade trees. They can accommodate large motorhomes and trailers. Park amenities include a recreation hall, fitness room, tennis courts, shuffle board, heated indoor pool, laundry, showers and restrooms. You can stay for a day, a week or all winter. Pets on leash are welcome. There is no pet fee, just clean up after your dog.

Joshua Tree National Park Campgrounds
74485 National Park Drive
Twentynine Palms, CA 92277
760-367-5500
There are nine campgrounds at this park which range from 3,000 foot to 4,500 foot elevations. Many have no fees and offer pit toilets. Only a few of the campgrounds offer water and flush toilets. There are no hookups and generators are not allowed between the hours of 10pm and 6am.

Needles

Needles

Moabi Regional Park Campground
Park Moabi Road
Needles, CA
760-326-3831
This park has a campground with 35 RV sites with full hookups and unlimited tent sites. The sites are situated in the main section of the park and along 2.5 miles of shoreline. The park is located on the banks of the Colorado River and is popular for camping, fishing, boating, swimming and water skiing. Dogs can go into the water but they strongly advise against it because there are so many fast boats in the water. Dogs must be leashed and please clean up after them. This park is located 11 miles southeast of Needles on Interstate 40.

Needles KOA
5400 National Old Trails Highway
Needles, CA 92363
760-326-4207
Located in the desert on historic Route 66, this campground offers tent and RV spaces. Dogs are allowed in the cabins too. RV site amenities include a maximum length pull through of 75 feet and 50 amp service available. Other campground amenities include a seasonal swimming pool, seasonal deli open November through April, snack bar, modem dataport, and LP gas. Well-behaved leashed dogs of all sizes are allowed. People need to clean up after their pets. There is no pet fee. The campground is open all year.

Palm Springs

Indio

Indian Wells RV Resort
47-340 Jefferson Street
Indio, CA 92201
800-789-0895
This RV resort offers many amenities such as three swimming pools, two spas, shuffleboard courts, basketball courts, pavilion with gas grills, billiards, horseshoes, fitness area, library, modem hookup, putting green, laundry facility, computer center and even a dog run. Site amenities include full hook-ups with 50 amp service, electric, water, sewer, paved pad and patio, and phone service for stays of 30 days or longer. Well-behaved leashed dogs are welcome. Please clean up after your pet. There is no pet fee. The RV park is located about 20 minutes from Palm Springs.

Pearblossom

Pearblossom

South Fork Campground
Valyermo Road
Pearblossom, CA
661-296-9710
This 21 site campground is located in the Angeles National Forest an elevation of 4,500 feet. There are both tent and small RV sites. RVs up to 16 feet are allowed. Amenities include vault toilets. There are many hiking trails nearby including one which leads to the dog-friendly Devil's Punchbowl County Park. Pets on leash are allowed and please clean up after them. From Highway 138 in Pearblossom, turn south on Longview Road. Turn right on Avenue W which then becomes Valyermo Road. Go past the Forest Service Raner Station. About .25 miles after you cross the bridge, turn right and go about 2 miles to the campground.

Nevada Dog-Friendly RV Park and Campground Guide

Elko

Elko

Double Dice RV Park
3730 Idaho Street
Elko, NV 89801
775-738-5642
This RV park offers 140 full hookup sites which come with water, sewer, 30 or 50amp electric, instant phone and 43 channel TV hookups. They have 75 sites which are pull through sites and can accommodate rigs as long as 65 feet. Park amenities include a game room, laundry room, free email/web center and showers. Tent sites are also available. Well-behaved leashed dogs are welcome. Please clean up after your pets. There is a $1 per night pet fee.

Ely

Ely

Ely KOA
HC 10, Box 10800
Ely, NV 89301
775-289-3413
This campground offers cabins, shaded RV sites and grassy tent sites. RV site amenities include hookups with 50 amp service, cable TV and a maximum length pull through of 85 feet. Other amenities include a seasonal swimming pool, playground, food mart, LP gas and modem dataport. Well-behaved leashed dogs are allowed at the tent sites, RV sites and in the cabins. Please clean up after your pets. There are no pet fees unless you stay in a cabin and then there is a refundable pet security deposit. The park is open all year. They are located about 3 miles south of Ely on Highway 50/6.

Las Vegas

Las Vegas

Las Vegas International RV Resort
6900 East Russell Road
Las Vegas, NV
702-547-5777
This RV park is located just east of Boulder Highway, away from the freeway and airport noise. They are located two minutes away from the largest shopping complex in Las Vegas. The shopping center includes a Super Wal-Mart, Costco, Target, Galleria mall with many restaurants and a Petco. Amenities at the RV park include full hookups with 30 and 50 amp service, 24 hour video security at the entrance, direct dial phones at all sites, restrooms, pool, spa, business center, laundry facilities, clubhouse with a big screen TV, pool table, library, fitness area and more. Well-behaved leashed dogs are welcome. Please clean up after your pets. The park is located about 10-15 minutes from the Las Vegas Strip.

Las Vegas KOA at Circus Circus
500 Circus Circus Drive
Las Vegas, NV 89109
800-562-7270
This RV park is located right on the Las Vegas Strip, next to Circus Circus. There are 400 full hookup sites, a heated pool, Jacuzzi, video arcade, full service convenience store and dog run. Well-behaved leashed dogs are allowed. Please clean up after your pets. There is no pet fee. If you are coming from the south on I-15, exit Sahara Avenue traveling east (to the right). Go to the first stop light (Las Vegas Blvd.) and turn right. Go to the first stop light (Circus Circus Drive) and turn right. The entrance will be on the right.

Laughlin

Laughlin

Don Laughlin's Riverside RV Resort
1650 S. Casino Drive
Laughlin, NV 89029
800-227-3849
This RV park, located across the street from the Riverside Resort Hotel, offers 740 full hookup RV sites. Amenities include laundry facilities, showers, and 24 hour security. Well-behaved leashed dogs are allowed. Please clean up after your pets. There is no pet fee.

Mesquite

Mesquite

Virgin River RV Park
100 Pioneer Blvd.
Mesquite, NV 89027
800-346-7721
This RV park is located behind the Virgin River

520

Hotel and Casino. They offer full hookups, showers and laundry facilities. Well-behaved leashed dogs are allowed. Please clean up after your pets. There is no pet fee. The park is open all year.

Reno

Reno

Bonanza Terrace RV Park
4800 Stoltz Road
Reno, NV 89506
775-329-9624
This RV park is located in a quiet spot two miles north of downtown Reno off Highway 395. The Bonanza Casino is across the street from the RV park. RV sites include a gravel parking pad, up to 50 amp electric, water, sewer and phone line. RVs up to 40 feet are welcome. Well-behaved leashed pets accompanied by their owner are welcome. There is a $1 per night pet fee. Please clean up after your pet.

Reno KOA
2500 East 2nd Street
Reno, NV 89595
775-789-2147
This campground, located at the Reno Hilton, offers RV sites with 50 amp service and a maximum length pull through of 65 feet. Amenities include direct access to the Reno Hilton's heated pool and health club, meeting room, snack bar, LP gas and modem dataport. Well-behaved leashed dogs are welcome. Please clean up after your pets. There is no pet fee. The park is open all year. From the junction of Interstate 80 and Highway 395 (Exit 15), go south 1 mile on Highway 395 to Glendale Avenue. The KOA is located at the Reno Hilton.

Reno RV Park
735 Mill Street
Reno, NV 89502
775-323-3381
This RV park is located about 4 blocks from the casinos. They offer full hookups, restrooms, showers, 24 hour security, electric gates, propane available, recreation area, picnic area and more. Well-behaved leashed dogs are welcome. Please clean up after your pets. There is no pet fee.

Virginia City

Virginia City

Virginia City RV Park
Carson and F Streets
Virginia City, NV
775-847-0999
Located just two blocks from downtown Virginia City, this park offers 50 RV sites with full hookups. Amenities include phone equipped spaces, showers, swimming pool, tennis courts park access, onsite market and deli, video rentals, laundry facility, slot machines and tent camping. Well-behaved leashed dogs are allowed. Please clean up after your pets. Reservations are accepted for busy periods. The park is open all year.

Wendover

Wendover

Wendover KOA
651 North Camper Drive
Wendover, NV 89883
775-664-3221
This campground offers both RV and tent sites. RV site amenities include hookups with 50 amp service, cable TV and a maximum length pull through of 80 feet. Other amenities include a swimming pool, meeting room, LP gas, modem dataport and snack bar. Well-behaved leashed dogs are allowed. Please clean up after your pets. There is no pet fee. They are open all year. To get there from Interstate 80, take the West Wendover Exit 410 to Wendover Blvd. Turn right and go .25 miles to Camper Drive and turn left.

Winnemucca

Winnemucca

Model T RV Park
1130 West Winnemucca Blvd.
Winnemucca, NV
775-623-2588
This RV park is located in town within walking distance to many services. Amenities include full hookup sites, laundry facilities, seasonal pool, restrooms and showers. Well-behaved leashed pets are allowed. There is no pet fee, just please clean up after your pet. The RV park is part of the Model T Casino and Winnemucca Quality Inn. To get there, take Interstate 80 to Exit 176. Then drive east on Winnemucca Blvd. for three minutes.

Chapter 21

West Coast Highway Guides

Interstate 5 Accommodation Listings

Washington (Interstate 5)

Bellingham Listings

Bellingham

Holiday Inn Express	360-671-4800	4160 Guide Meridian Bellingham WA
Motel 6	360-671-4494	3701 Byron Bellingham WA

Mount Vernon Listings

Mount Vernon

Best Western College Way Inn	360-424-4287	300 W College Way Mount Vernon WA
Best Western CottonTree Inn	360-428-5678	2300 Market Place Mount Vernon WA

Everett Listings

Everett

Holiday Inn	425-337-2900	101 128th St SE Everett WA
Motel 6	425-353-8120	224 128th St SW Everett WA

Seattle Listings

Seattle

Crowne Plaza - Downtown	206-464-1980	1113 6th Ave Seattle WA
La Quinta Inn & Suites Seattle	206-624-6820	2224 Eighth Ave. Seattle WA
La Quinta Inn Sea-Tac - Seattle	206-241-5211	2824 S 188th St Seattle WA
Motel 6	206-824-9902	20651 Military Rd Seattle WA
Motel 6 - Airport	206-241-1648	18900 47th Ave S Seattle WA
The Sheraton Seattle Hotel and Towers	206-621-9000	1400 Sixth Avenue Seattle WA
W Seattle	206-264-6000	1112 Fourth Avenue Seattle WA

Kent Listings

Kent

La Quinta Inn Kent	253-520-6670	25100 74th Avenue South Kent WA

Federal Way Listings

Federal Way

La Quinta Inn & Suites Federal Way	253-529-4000	32124 25th Avenue South Federal Way WA

Tacoma Listings

Tacoma

Best Western Executive Inn	253-922-0080	5700 Pacific Hwy E. Tacoma WA
Best Western Tacoma Inn	253-535-2880	8726 S. Hosmer St Tacoma WA
La Quinta Inn Tacoma	253-383-0146	1425 E 27th St Tacoma WA
Motel 6	253-473-7100	1811 S 76th St Tacoma WA

Olympia Listings

Olympia

West Coast Inn	360-943-4000	2300 Evergreen Park Drive Olympia WA

Tumwater

Best Western Tumwater Inn	360-956-1235	5188 Capitol Blvd Tumwater WA
Motel 6	360-754-7320	400 W Lee St Tumwater WA

Centralia Listings

Centralia		
Motel 6	360-330-2057	1310 Belmont Ave Centralia WA

Chehalis Listings

Chehalis		
Howard Johnson Inn	360-748-0101	122 Interstate Ave. Chehalis WA

Kelso Listings

Kelso		
Motel 6	360-425-3229	106 Minor Rd Kelso WA

Vancouver Listings

Vancouver		
Comfort Inn	360-574-6000	13207 NE 20th Ave. Vancouver WA
Staybridge Suites	360-891-8282	7301 NE 41st St Vancouver WA

Oregon (Interstate 5)

Portland Listings

Portland		
Comfort Inn	503-682-9000	8855 SW Citizen Dr. Portland OR
La Quinta Inn Portland - Lloyd	503-233-7933	431 NE Multnomah Portland OR
Motel 6	503-238-0600	3104 SE Powell Blvd Portland OR
Sheraton Portland Airport Hotel	503-281-2500	8235 NE Airport Way Portland OR

Portland Area Listings

Lake Oswego		
Crowne Plaza	503-624-8400	14811 Kruse Oaks Dr Lake Oswego OR
Tigard		
Motel 6	503-620-2066	17950 SW McEwan Rd Tigard OR
Wilsonville		
Holiday Inn Select	503-570-8500	25425 SW 95th Ave Wilsonville OR

Woodburn Listings

Woodburn		
La Quinta Inn & Suites Woodburn	503-982-1727	120 Arney Road NE Woodburn OR

Salem Listings

Salem		
Holiday Inn Express	503-391-7000	890 Hawthorne Ave SE Salem OR
Motel 6	503-371-8024	1401 Hawthorne Ave NE Salem OR
Phoenix Inn - Salem South	503-588-9220	4370 Commercial St SE Salem OR
Red Lion Hotel	503-370-7888	3301 Market St Salem OR

Albany Listings

Albany		
La Quinta Inn & Suites Albany	541-928-0921	251 Airport Road SE Albany OR

Eugene Listings

Eugene		
Best Western Greentree Inn	541-485-2727	1759 Franklin Blvd Eugene OR
Best Western New Oregon Motel	541-683-3669	1655 Franklin Blvd Eugene OR
Eugene Hilton	541-342-2000	66 East 6th Avenue Eugene OR
La Quinta Inn & Suites Eugene	541-344-8335	155 Day Island Rd. Eugene OR
Motel 6	541-687-2395	3690 Glenwood Dr Eugene OR
Quality Inn & Suites	541-342-1243	2121 Franklin Blvd Eugene OR

| Ramada Inn | 541-342-5181 | 225 Coburg Rd Eugene OR |
| The Valley River Inn | 541-687-0123 | 1000 Valley River Way Eugene OR |

Cottage Grove Listings

Cottage Grove

Best Western - The Village Green	541-942-2491	725 Row River Rd. Cottage Grove OR
Comfort Inn	541-942-9747	845 Gateway Blvd. Cottage Grove OR
Holiday Inn Express	541-942-1000	1601 Gateway Blvd Cottage Grove OR

Rice Hill Listings

Rice Hill

| Best Western Rice Hill Inn | 541-849-2500 | 621 John Long Rd Rice Hill OR |

Roseburg Listings

Roseburg

Best Western Douglas Inn	541-673-6625	511 SE Stephens Roseburg OR
Comfort Inn	541-957-1100	1539 Mullholland Dr. Roseburg OR
Holiday Inn Express	541-673-7517	375 Harvard Blvd Roseburg OR
Motel 6	541-464-8000	3100 NW Aviation Roseburg OR
Sleep Inn & Suites	541-464-8338	2855 NW Eden Bower Blvd. Roseburg OR

Grants Pass Listings

Grants Pass

Best Western Grants Pass Inn	541-476-1117	111 NE Agness Ave Grants Pass OR
Comfort Inn	541-479-8301	1889 NE 6th St Grants Pass OR
Holiday Inn Express	541-471-6144	105 NE Agness Ave Grants Pass OR
La Quinta Inn & Suites Grants Pass	541-472-1808	243 NE Morgan Lane Grants Pass OR
Motel 6	541-474-1331	1800 Northeast 7th St Grants Pass OR

Medford Listings

Medford

Best Western	541-779-5085	1154 E Barnett Rd Medford OR
Doubletree Hotel	541-779-5811	200 N Riverside Medford OR
Motel 6	541-779-0550	2400 Biddle Rd Medford OR
Motel 6	541-773-4290	950 Alba Dr Medford OR
Reston Hotel	541-779-3141	2300 Crater Lake Hwy Medford OR

Ashland Listings

Ashland

Best Western Bard's Inn	541-482-0049	132 N Main Street Ashland OR
Best Western Windsor Inn	541-488-2330	2520 Ashland St Ashland OR
La Quinta Inn & Suites Ashland	541-482-6932	434 S. Valley View Road Ashland OR

California (Interstate 5)

Yreka Listings

Yreka

Ben-Ber Motel	530-842-2791	1210 S Main St Yreka CA
Best Western Miner's Inn	530-842-4355	122 East Miner Street Yreka CA
Days Inn	530-842-1612	1804 B Fort Jones Rd Yreka CA
Motel 6	530-842-4111	1785 S Main Street Yreka CA

Mount Shasta Listings

Dunsmuir

| Oak Tree Inn | 530-235-2884 | 6604 Dunsmuir Avenue Dunsmuir CA |
| Railroad Park Resort | 530-235-4440 | 100 Railroad Park Road Dunsmuir CA |

Travelodge	530-235-4395	5400 Dunsmuir Ave Dunsmuir CA
McCloud		
Stony Brook Inn	800-369-6118	309 Colombero McCloud CA
Mount Shasta		
Best Western Tree House Motor Inn	530-926-3101	111 Morgan Way Mount Shasta CA
Dream Inn Bed and Breakfast	530-926-1536	326 Chestnut Street Mount Shasta CA
Econo Lodge	530-926-3145	908 S. Mt. Shasta Blvd. Mount Shasta CA
Mount Shasta Ranch Bed and Breakfast	530-926-3870	1008 W. A. Barr Rd. Mount Shasta CA
Mountain Air Lodge	530-926-3411	1121 S Mount Shasta Blvd Mount Shasta CA
Swiss Holiday Lodge	530-926-3446	2400 S. Mt. Shasta Blvd. Mount Shasta CA
Weed		
Holiday Inn Express	530-938-1308	1830 Black Butte Drive Weed CA
Lake Shastina Golf Resort	530-938-3201	5925 Country Club Drive Weed CA

Lakehead Listings

Lakehead		
Sugarloaf Cottages Resort	800-953-4432	19667 Lakeshore Drive Lakehead CA
Tsasdi Resort Cabins	530-238-2575	19990 Lakeshore Dr. Lakehead CA

Lakehead		
Antlers Resort and Marina	530-238-2553	P.O. Box 140 Lakehead CA

Redding Listings

Redding		
Best Western Ponderosa Inn	530-241-6300	2220 Pine Street Redding CA
Comfort Inn	530-221-6530	2059 Hilltop Drive Redding CA
Fawndale Lodge and RV Resort	800-338-0941	15215 Fawndale Road Redding CA
Holiday Inn Express	530-241-5500	1080 Twin View Blvd Redding CA
La Quinta Inn Redding	530-221-8200	2180 Hilltop Drive Redding CA
Motel 6	530-221-1800	1640 Hilltop Dr Redding CA
Motel 6 - North	530-246-4470	1250 Twin View Blvd Redding CA
Motel 6 - South	530-221-0562	2385 Bechelli Ln Redding CA
Ramada Limited	530-246-2222	1286 Twin View Blvd Redding CA
Red Lion Hotel	530-221-8700	1830 Hilltop Drive Redding CA
River Inn	530-241-9500	1835 Park Marina Drive Redding CA
Shasta Lodge	530-243-6133	1245 Pine Street Redding CA

Redding		
Seven Crown Resorts Houseboats	800-752-9669	10300 Bridge Bay Road Redding CA

Anderson Listings

Anderson		
AmeriHost Inn	530-365-6100	2040 Factory Outlets Dr Anderson CA
Best Western Knight's Inn	530-365-2753	2688 Gateway Drive Anderson CA

Red Bluff Listings

Red Bluff		
Motel 6	530-527-9200	20 Williams Ave Red Bluff CA
Super 8	530-527-8882	203 Antelope Blvd Red Bluff CA
Travelodge	530-527-6020	38 Antelope Blvd Red Bluff CA

Corning Listings

Corning		
Best Western Inn-Corning	530-824-2468	2165 Solano Street Corning CA
Shilo Inn Suites	530-824-2940	3350 Sunrise Way Corning CA

Willows Listings

Willows

Best Western Gold Pheasant Inn	530-934-4603	249 North Humboldt Avenue Willows CA
Days Inn	530-934-4444	475 N Humboldt Ave Willows CA
Super 8	530-934-2871	457 Humboldt Ave Willows CA

Williams Listings

Williams

Comfort Inn	530-473-2381	400 C St Williams CA
Motel 6	530-473-5337	455 4th Street Williams CA

Dunnigan Listings

Dunnigan

Best Western Country	530-724-3471	3930 County Rd. 89 Dunnigan CA

Woodland Listings

Woodland

Motel 6	530-666-6777	1564 Main Street Woodland CA
Sacramento - Days Inn	530-666-3800	1524 East Main Street Woodland CA

Sacramento Listings

Sacramento

Candlewood Suites	916-646-1212	555 Howe Ave. Sacramento
Canterbury Inn Hotel	916-927-0927	1900 Canterbury Rd Sacramento
Motel 6	916-372-3624	1254 Halyard Dr Sacramento
Ramada Inn	916-487-7600	2600 Auburn Blvd Sacramento
Residence Inn by Marriott	916-920-9111	1530 Howe Ave Sacramento
Residence Inn by Marriott - South Natomas	916-649-1300	2410 West El Camino Avenue Sacramento
Sheraton Grand Sacramento Hotel	916-447-1700	1230 J Street Sacramento

Stockton Listings

Stockton

La Quinta Inn Stockton	209-952-7800	2710 West March Lane Stockton CA
Motel 6 - Southeast	209-467-3600	1625 French Camp Turnpike Rd Stockton CA
Motel 6 - West	209-946-0923	817 Navy Drive Stockton CA
Residence Inn - Stockton	209-472-9800	March Lane & Brookside Stockton CA
Travelodge	209-466-7777	1707 Fremont St Stockton CA

Lathrop Listings

Lathrop

Days Inn	209-982-1959	14750 South Harlan Rd Lathrop CA

Westley Listings

Westley

Days Inn	209-894-5500	7144 McCracken Rd Westley CA
Econo Lodge	209-894-3900	7100 McCracken Rd Westley CA
Super 8	209-894-3888	7115 McCracken Rd Westley CA

Santa Nella Listings

Santa Nella

Holiday Inn Express	209-826-8282	28976 W. Plaza Drive Santa Nella CA
Motel 6	209-826-6644	12733 S Hwy 33 Santa Nella CA
Ramada Inn	209-826-4444	13070 S Hwy 33 Santa Nella CA

Los Banos Listings

Los Banos

Days Inn	209-826-9690	2169 East Pacheco Blvd Los Banos CA
Sunstar Inn	209-826-3805	839 W. Pacheco Blvd Los Banos CA

Coalinga Listings

Coalinga

Motel 6	559-935-1536	25008 W Dorris Ave Coalinga CA
Pleasant Valley Inn	559-935-2063	25278 W Doris St Coalinga CA

Kettleman City Listings

Kettleman City

Super 8	559-386-9530	33415 Powers Drive Kettleman City CA

Lost Hills Listings

Lost Hills

Days Inn	661-797-2371	14684 Aloma St Lost Hills CA
Motel 6	661-797-2346	14685 Warren St Lost Hills CA

Buttonwillow Listings

Buttonwillow

Motel 6	661-764-5153	20638 Tracy Ave Buttonwillow CA
Super 8	661-764-5117	20681 Tracy Ave Buttonwillow CA

Gorman Listings

Gorman

Econo Lodge	661-248-6411	49713 Gorman Post Rd Gorman CA

San Fernando Valley Listings

Sylmar

Motel 6	818-362-9491	12775 Encinitas Ave Sylmar CA

Los Angeles - Hollywood Listings

Norwalk

Motel 6	562-864-2567	10646 E Rosecrans Ave Norwalk CA

Pico Rivera

Days Inn - Pico Rivera	562-942-1003	6540 S. Rosemead Blvd Pico Rivera CA

Santa Fe Springs

Motel 6	562-921-0596	13412 Excelsior Dr Santa Fe Springs CA

Universal City

Sheraton Universal Hotel	818-980-1212	333 Universal Hollywood Drive Universal City CA

Anaheim - Orange County Listings

Anaheim

Econolodge at the Park	714-533-4505	1126 West Katella Ave Anaheim CA
Embassy Suites Hotel	714-632-1221	3100 E. Frontera Ave Anaheim CA
Hawthorn Suites	714-635-5000	1752 S. Clementine Anaheim CA
Motel 6	714-956-9690	1440 N State College Anaheim CA
Staybridge Suites	714-748-7700	1845 S. Manchester Ave Anaheim CA

Buena Park

Motel 6	714-522-1200	7051 Valley View Buena Park CA

Irvine

La Quinta Inn East Irvine	949-551-0909	14972 Sand Canyon Avenue Irvine CA

La Mirada

Residence Inn - La Mirada	714-523-2800	14419 Firestone Blvd La Mirada CA

Orange

Motel 6	714-634-2441	2920 W Chapman Ave Orange CA
Residence Inn - Orange	714-976-7700	3101 W. Chapman Avenue Orange CA

Santa Ana

Motel 6	714-558-0500	1623 E First Street Santa Ana CA
Red Roof Inn	714-542-0311	2600 N Main Street Santa Ana CA

San Clemente Listings

San Clemente

Holiday Inn	949-361-3000	111 S. Ave. De Estrella San Clemente CA

San Diego County North Listings

Carlsbad

Inns of America	760-931-1185	751 Raintree Carlsbad CA
Motel 6	760-434-7135	1006 Carlsbad Village Dr Carlsbad CA
Motel 6	760-431-0745	750 Raintree Dr Carlsbad CA
Residence Inn - Carlsbad	760-431-9999	2000 Faraday Ave Carlsbad CA

Oceanside

Motel 6	760-941-1011	3708 Plaza Dr Oceanside CA
Ramada Limited	760-967-4100	1140 Mission Ave Oceanside CA

San Diego Listings

Chula Vista

Motel 6	619-422-4200	745 E Street Chula Vista CA

La Jolla

Andrea Villa Inn	858-459-3311	2402 Torrey Pines Rd La Jolla CA

National City

Super 8	619-474-8811	425 Roosevelt Ave National City CA

San Diego

Motel 6 - North	858-268-9758	5592 Clairemont Mesa Blvd San Diego CA
Sheraton Suites San Diego	619-696-9800	701 A. Street San Diego CA
Staybridge Suites	800-238-8000	6639 Mira Mesa Blvd San Diego CA

San Ysidro

Motel 6 - Border	619-690-6663	160 E Calie Primera San Ysidro CA

Interstate 10 Accommodation Listings

California (Interstate 10)

Los Angeles - Hollywood Listings

Arcadia

Motel 6	626-446-2660	225 Colorado Pl Arcadia CA

Los Angeles

Holiday Inn - Downtown	213-628-9900	750 Garland Ave @ 8th St. Los Angeles CA

Santa Monica

Loews Santa Monica Beach Hotel	310-458-6700	1700 Ocean Avenue Santa Monica CA

West Covina

Hampton Inn	626-967-5800	3145 E. Garvey Ave West Covina CA

Inland Empire Listings

Claremont

Ramada Inn	909-621-4831	840 South Indian Hill Blvd Claremont CA

Ontario

Marriott - Ontario Airport	909-975-5000	2200 E. Holt Blvd Ontario CA
Motel 6	909-984-2424	1560 E Fourth St Ontario CA

Pomona

Sheraton Suites Fairplex	909-622-2220	601 West McKinley Avenue Pomona CA

Rialto

Best Western Empire Inn	909-877-0690	475 W Valley Blvd Rialto CA

San Bernardino

Motel 6	909-825-6666	111 Redlands Blvd San Bernardino CA

Beaumont Listings

Beaumont

Best Western El Rancho Motor Inn	909-845-2176	480 East 5th Street Beaumont CA

Banning Listings

Banning

Super 8	909-849-6887	1690 W. Ramsey St Banning CA
Travelodge	909-849-1000	1700 W. Ramsey Street Banning CA

Palm Springs Listings

East Palm Canyon

Motel 6	760-325-6129	595 E Palm Canyon Dr East Palm Canyon CA

Indio

Holiday Inn Express	760-342-6344	84-096 Indio Springs Pkwy Indio CA
Palm Shadow Inn	760-347-3476	80-761 Highway 111 Indio CA
Quality Inn	760-347-4044	43505 Monroe Street Indio CA

North Palm Springs

Motel 6	760-251-1425	63950 20th Ave North Palm Springs CA

Palm Desert

Comfort Suites	760-360-3337	39-585 Washington St Palm Desert CA
Motel 6	760-345-0550	78100 Varner Rd Palm Desert CA

Palm Springs

Super 8 Lodge - Palm Springs	760-322-3757	1900 N. Palm Canyon Drive Palm Springs CA

Rancho Mirage

Motel 6	760-324-8475	69-570 Hwy 111 Rancho Mirage CA

Blythe Listings

Blythe

Best Western Sahara Motel	760-922-7105	825 W. Hobson Way Blythe CA
Holiday Inn Express	760-921-2300	600 W. Donion St Blythe CA

Arizona (Interstate 10)

Phoenix Listings

Phoenix

Holiday Inn - West	602-484-9009	1500 N 51st Ave Phoenix AZ
Holiday Inn Express Hotel & Suites	480-785-8500	15221 S. 50th St Phoenix AZ
Motel 6	602-267-8555	5315 E Van Buren Street Phoenix AZ
Quality Hotel & Resort	602-248-0222	3600 N 2nd Ave Phoenix AZ
Quality Inn South Mountain	480-893-3900	5121 E. La Puente Ave. Phoenix AZ
Quality Suites	602-956-4900	3101 N. 32nd St Phoenix AZ

Phoenix Area Listings

Goodyear

Holiday Inn Express	623-535-1313	1313 Litchfield Rd Goodyear AZ

Scottsdale

Motel 6	480-946-2280	6848 E Camelback Rd Scottsdale AZ

Tempe

La Quinta Inn Phoenix Sky Harbor Tempe	480-967-4465	911 South 48th Street Tempe AZ
Motel 6	480-968-4401	1720 S. Priest Drive Tempe AZ

| Motel 6 | 480-945-9506 | 1612 N Scottsdale Rd/Rural Rd Tempe AZ |
| Studio 6 | 602-414-4470 | 4909 South Wendler Dr. Tempe AZ |

Casa Grande Listings

Casa Grande

| Holiday Inn | 520-426-3500 | 777 N Pinal Ave Casa Grande AZ |

Tucson Listings

Tucson

Best Western Executive Inn	520-791-7551	333 West Drachman Street Tucson AZ
Clarion Hotel & Suites Santa Rita	520-622-4000	88 E. Broadway Blvd. Tucson AZ
Comfort Suites	520-295-4400	6935 S. Tucson Blvd. Tucson AZ
Motel 6 - 22nd Street	520-624-2516	1222 S Frwy Tucson AZ
Motel 6 - Airport	520-628-1264	1031 E Benson Hwy Tucson AZ
Motel 6 - Benson Hwy N	520-622-4614	755 E Benson Hwy Tucson AZ
Motel 6 - Congess St	520-628-1339	960 S. Freeway Tucson AZ
Motel 6 - North	520-744-9300	4630 W Ina Rd Tucson AZ
Studio 6	520-746-0030	4950 S. Outlet Center Dr Tucson AZ

Benson Listings

Benson

| Motel 6 | 520-586-0066 | 637 S. Whetstone Commerce Dr Benson AZ |

Wilcox Listings

Wilcox

| Best Western Plaza Inn | 520-384-3556 | 1100 W Rex Allen Dr Wilcox AZ |
| Motel 6 | 520-384-2201 | 921 N Bisbee Ave Wilcox AZ |

Interstate 15 Accommodation Listings

California (Interstate 15)

San Diego Listings

National City

| Super 8 | 619-474-8811 | 425 Roosevelt Ave National City CA |

San Diego

| La Quinta Inn San Diego - Rancho Penasquitos | 858-484-8800 | 10185 Paseo Montril San Diego CA |
| Residence Inn | 858-673-1900 | 11002 Rancho Carmel Dr San Diego CA |

San Diego County North Listings

Escondido

| Castle Creek Inn Resort | 760-751-8800 | 29850 Circle R Way Escondido CA |

Temecula Listings

Temecula

| Comfort Inn | 909-296-3788 | 27338 Jefferson Ave. Temecula CA |
| Motel 6 | 909-676-6383 | 41900 Moreno Rd Temecula CA |

Temecula

| Temecula Vacation Rental | 310-390-7778 | Call to Arrange. Temecula CA |

Inland Empire Listings

Claremont		
Ramada Inn	909-621-4831	840 South Indian Hill Blvd Claremont CA
Corona		
Motel 6	909-735-6408	200 N Lincoln Ave Corona CA
Rialto		
Best Western Empire Inn	909-877-0690	475 W Valley Blvd Rialto CA

Victorville Listings

Hesperia		
Days Suites	760-948-0600	14865 Bear Valley Rd Hesperia CA
Victorville		
Howard Johnson Express Inn	760-243-7700	16868 Stoddard Wells Rd. Victorville CA
Ramada Inn	760-245-6565	15494 Palmdale Road Victorville CA
Red Roof Inn	760-241-1577	13409 Mariposa Rd Victorville CA

Barstow Listings

Barstow		
Days Inn	760-256-1737	1590 Coolwater Lane Barstow CA
Econo Lodge	760-256-2133	1230 E. Main Street Barstow CA
Holiday Inn Express	760-256-1300	1861 W. Main St. Barstow CA
Motel 6	760-256-1752	150 N Tucca Ave Barstow CA
Ramada Inn	760-256-5673	1511 E Main Street Barstow CA
Super 8 Motel	760-256-8443	170 Coolwater Lane Barstow CA

Nevada (Interstate 15)

Las Vegas Listings

Las Vegas		
Best Western Nellis	702-643-6111	5330 East Craig Street Las Vegas NV
Comfort Inn	702-399-1500	910 E. Cheyenne Rd. Las Vegas NV
Hawthorn Suites-The Strip	702-739-7000	5051 Duke Ellington Way Las Vegas NV
La Quinta Inn Las Vegas - Nellis	702-632-0229	4288 N. Nellis Rd. Las Vegas NV
La Quinta Inn Las Vegas - Tropicana	702-798-7736	4975 South Valley View Las Vegas NV
Motel 6 - Tropicana	702-798-0728	195 E. Tropicana Ave Las Vegas NV
Residence Inn - Hughes Center	702-650-0040	370 Hughes Center Drive Las Vegas NV
Rodeway Inn & Suites	702-795-3311	167 E. Tropicana Ave Las Vegas NV

Overton Listings

Overton		
Best Western North Shore Inn	702-397-6000	520 N. Moapa Valley Blvd Overton NV

Interstate 40 Accommodation Listings

California (Interstate 40)

Barstow Listings

Barstow		
Days Inn	760-256-1737	1590 Coolwater Lane Barstow CA
Econo Lodge	760-256-2133	1230 E. Main Street Barstow CA
Holiday Inn Express	760-256-1300	1861 W. Main St. Barstow CA
Motel 6	760-256-1752	150 N Tucca Ave Barstow CA

| Ramada Inn | 760-256-5673 | 1511 E Main Street Barstow CA |
| Super 8 Motel | 760-256-8443 | 170 Coolwater Lane Barstow CA |

Needles Listings

Needles

Days Inn and Suites	760-326-5836	1215 Hospitality Lane Needles CA
Econo Lodge	760-326-3881	1910 N. Needles Hwy Needles CA
Motel 6	760-326-3399	1420 J St Needles CA
Super 8	760-326-4501	1102 E Broadway Needles CA
Travelers Inn	760-326-4900	1195 3rd Street Hill Needles CA

Arizona (Interstate 40)

Kingman Listings

Kingman

Best Western A Wayfarer's Inn	928-753-6271	2815 East Andy Devine Kingman AZ
Best Western King's Inn	928-753-6101	2930 East Andy Devine Kingman AZ
Days Inn East	928-757-7337	3381 E Andy Devine Kingman AZ
Motel 6	928-757-7151	3351 E Andy Devine Ave Kingman AZ
Quality Inn	928-753-4747	1400 E. Andy Devine Ave. Kingman AZ
Super 8 Motel	928-757-4808	3401 E. Andy Devine Kingman AZ

Grand Canyon Listings

Williams

| Holiday Inn | 928-635-4114 | 950 N. Grand Canyon Blvd Williams AZ |
| Motel 6 - Grand Canyon | 520-635-9000 | 831 W Rt 66 Williams AZ |

Flagstaff Listings

Flagstaff

Comfort Inn I-17 & I40	928-774-2225	2355 S Beulah Blvd. Flagstaff AZ
Holiday Inn	928-714-1000	2320 E Lucky Lane Flagstaff AZ
Howard Johnson Inn	800-437-7137	3300 E. Rt. 66 Flagstaff AZ
La Quinta Inn & Suites Flagstaff	928-556-8666	2015 South Beulah Blvd. Flagstaff AZ
Motel 6	928-774-1801	2010 E Butler Ave Flagstaff AZ
Sleep Inn	928-556-3000	2765 S. Woodlands Village Blvd. Flagstaff AZ

Woodlands Village

| Motel 6 | 928-779-3757 | 2745 S. Woodlands Village Woodlands Village AZ |

Winslow Listings

Winslow

Days Inn	928-289-1010	2035 W. Hwy 66 Winslow AZ
Econo Lodge	928-289-4687	I40 & Exit 253 North Park Dr Winslow AZ
Holiday Inn Express	928-289-2960	816 Transcon Lane Winslow AZ

Holbrook Listings

Holbrook

Best Western Adobe Inn	928-524-3948	615 W Hopi Dr Holbrook AZ
Best Western Arizonian Inn	928-524-2611	2508 Navajo Blvd Holbrook AZ
Comfort Inn	928-524-6131	2602 E. Navajo Blvd. Holbrook AZ
Holiday Inn Express	928-524-1466	1308 E Navajo Blvd Holbrook AZ
Motel 6	928-524-6101	2514 Navajo Blvd Holbrook AZ

Chambers Listings

Chambers

| Best Western Chieftain Inn | 928-688-2754 | Hwy 40 and Chambers Chambers AZ |

Interstate 80 Accommodation Listings

California (Interstate 80)

Vallejo Listings
Vallejo

Holiday Inn	707-644-1200	1000 Fairgrounds Dr Vallejo CA

Vacaville Listings
Vacaville

Residence Inn	707-469-0300	360 Orange Dr Vacaville CA
Super 8 Motel - Vacaville	707-449-8884	101 Allison Court Vacaville CA

Dixon Listings
Dixon

Super 8	707-678-3399	2500 Plaza Court Dixon CA

Davis Listings
Davis

Best Western University Lodge	530-756-7890	123 B Street Davis CA
Econo Lodge	530-756-1040	221 D Street Davis CA
Howard Johnson Hotel	530-792-0800	4100 Chiles Road Davis CA
Motel 6	530-753-3777	4835 Chiles Rd. Davis CA
University Inn Bed and Breakfast	530-756-8648	340 A Street Davis CA
University Park Inn & Suites	530-756-0910	1111 Richards Blvd. Davis CA

Sacramento Listings
North Highlands

Motel 6	916-973-8637	4600 Watt Ave North Highlands CA

Roseville

Best Western Roseville Inn	916-782-4434	220 Harding Blvd. Roseville CA
Oxford Suites	916-784-2222	130 N Sunrise Ave Roseville CA

Sacramento

Motel 6	916-372-3624	1254 Halyard Dr Sacramento CA
Sheraton Grand Sacramento Hotel	916-447-1700	1230 J Street Sacramento CA

Gold Country Listings
Auburn

Best Western Golden Key	530-885-8611	13450 Lincoln Way Auburn CA
Holiday Inn	530-887-8787	120 Grass Valley Highway Auburn CA
Travelodge	530-885-7025	13490 Lincoln Way Auburn CA

Truckee Listings
Truckee

The Inn at Truckee	530-587-8888	11506 Deerfield Drive Truckee CA

Truckee

Andrea's Grinnin Bear Cabin	530-582-8703	Call to Arrange. Truckee CA
Fore Paw Cottage	530-587-4082	14906 Davos Drive Truckee CA

Nevada (Interstate 80)

Reno Listings

Reno		
Days Inn	775-786-4070	701 E 7th Reno NV
Motel 6 - Livestock Center	775-786-9852	866 N. Wells Ave Reno NV
Motel 6 - West	775-747-7390	1400 Stardust Street Reno NV
Truckee River Lodge	775-786-8888	501 W. 1st Street Reno NV
Sparks		
Motel 6 - Airport/Sparks	775-358-1080	2405 Victorian Ave Sparks NV

Lovelock Listings

Lovelock		
Ramada Inn Sturgeon's Casino	775-273-2971	1420 Cornell Ave Lovelock NV

Winnemucca Listings

Winnemucca		
Best Western Gold Country Inn	775-623-6999	921 West Winnemucca Boulevard Winnemucca NV
Best Western Holiday Motel	775-623-3684	670 W. Winnemucca Blvd Winnemucca NV
Days Inn	775-623-3661	511 W. Winnemucca Blvd Winnemucca NV
Holiday Inn Express	775-625-3100	1987 W. Winnemucca Blvd Winnemucca NV
Motel 6	775-623-1180	1600 Winnemucca Blvd Winnemucca NV
Red Lion Inn & Casino	775-623-2565	741 West Winnemucca Boulevard Winnemucca NV
Santa Fe Motel	775-623-1119	1620 W. Winnemucca Blvd Winnemucca NV
Super 8	775-625-1818	1157 Winnomucca Blvd Winnemucca NV

Battle Mountain Listings

Battle Mountain		
Comfort Inn	775-635-5880	521 E. Front Street Battle Mountain NV

Elko Listings

Elko		
Best Western Gold Country Inn	775-738-8421	2050 Idaho Street Elko NV
Comfort Inn	775-777-8762	2970 Idaho St Elko NV
High Desert Inn	775-738-8425	3015 Idaho Street Elko NV
Motel 6	775-738-4337	3021 Idaho Street Elko NV
Red Lion Casino	775-738-2111	2065 Idaho Street Elko NV
Shilo Inn	775-738-5522	2401 Mountain City Highway Elko NV

Interstate 84 Accommodation Listings

Oregon (Interstate 84)

Portland Listings

Portland		
La Quinta Inn Portland - Lloyd	503-233-7933	431 NE Multnomah Portland OR
Sleep Inn	503-618-8400	2261 NE 181st Ave. Portland OR

Troutdale Listings

Troutdale		
Motel 6	503-665-2254	1610 NW Frontage Rd Troutdale OR

Hood River Listings

Hood River		
Best Western Hood River Inn	541-386-2200	1108 E. Marina Way Hood River OR

| Columbia Gorge | 541-386-5566 | 4000 Westcliff Dr Hood River OR |
| Vagabond Lodge | 541-386-2992 | 4070 Westcliff Dr Hood River OR |

The Dalles Listings
The Dalles

| Quality Inn Columbia River Gorge | 541-298-5161 | 2114 W. 6th The Dalles OR |

Pendleton Listings
Pendleton

Best Western Pendleton Inn	541-276-2135	400 SE Nye Ave Pendleton OR
Holiday Inn Express	541-966-6520	600 SE Nye Ave Pendleton OR
Motel 6	541-276-3160	325 SE Nye Ave Pendleton OR

LaGrande Listings
LaGrande

| Howard Johnson Inn | 541-963-7195 | 2612 Island Avenue LaGrande OR |

Baker City Listings
Baker City

| Quality Inn | 541-523-2242 | 810 Campbell St. Baker City OR |

Ontario Listings
Ontario

| Best Western Inn & Suites | 541-889-2600 | 251 Goodfellow Street Ontario OR |
| Motel 6 | 541-889-6617 | 275 NE 12th St Ontario OR |

Interstate 90 Accommodation Listings

Washington (Interstate 90)

Moses Lake Listings
Moses Lake

| Best Western Hallmark Inn & Conf Center | 509-765-9211 | 3000 Marina Dr Moses Lake WA |
| Motel 6 | 509-766-0250 | 2822 Wapato Dr Moses Lake WA |

Spokane Listings
Spokane

Howard Johnson Inn	509-838-6630	South 211 Division St. Spokane WA
Motel 6	509-459-6120	1508 S Rustle St Spokane WA
Motel 6	509-926-5399	1919 N Hutchinson Rd Spokane WA

Highway 1 Accommodation Listings (California)

Westport

Highway Guides - Please always call ahead to make sure an establishment is still dog-friendly.

Howard Creek Ranch Inn B&B	707-964-6725	40501 N. Highway 1 Westport

Fort Bragg
Beachcomber Motel	707-964-2402	1111 N. Main Street Fort Bragg
Cleone Gardens Inn	707-964-2788	24600 N. Hwy 1 Fort Bragg
Delamere Cottages	707-964-9188	16821 Ocean Drive Fort Bragg
Harbor View Seasonal Rental	760-438-2563	Call to arrange. Fort Bragg
Shoreline Vacation Rentals	707-964-1444	18200 Old Coast Hwy Fort Bragg

Mendocino
Coastal Getaways	707-937-9200	10501 Ford Street POB1355 Mendocino
Inn at Schoolhouse Creek	707-937-5525	7051 N. Highway 1 Mendocino
MacCallum House	707-937-0289	45020 Albion Street Mendocino
McElroys Cottage Inn	707-937-1734	Main and Evergreen Streets Mendocino
Mendocino Seaside Cottages	707-485-0239	10940 Lansing St Mendocino
Stanford Inn by the Sea	707-937-5615	44850 Comptche-Ukiah Rd Mendocino
Sweetwater Spa & Inn	707-937-4076	44840 Main Street Mendocino
Whitegate Inn Village Retreat	707-937-4892	P.O. Box 150, 499 Howard St. Mendocino

Gualala
Mar Vista Cottages	707-884-3522	35101 South Highway One Gualala
Ocean View Properties	707-884-3538	P.O. Box 1285 Gualala
Sea Ranch Vacation Homes	707-884-4235	P.O. Box 246 Gualala
Serenisea Vacation Homes	707-884-3836	36100 Highway 1 S. Gualala
Surf Motel	707-884-3571	39170 S. Highway 1 Gualala

Inverness
Rosemary Cottage	415-663-9338	75 Balboa Ave Inverness

Inverness Park
Apple Cottage Vacation Rental	415-663-2000	Call to arrange. Inverness Park

Point Reyes Station
Berry Patch Cottage	415-663-1942	P.O. Box 712 Point Reyes Station
Point Reyes Station Inn Bed and Breakfast	415-663-9372	11591 Highway One, Box 824 Point Reyes Station
Tree House Bed and Breakfast Inn	415-663-8720	73 Drake Summit, P.O. Box 1075 Point Reyes Station

San Francisco
Best Western Tuscan Inn	415-561-1100	425 Northpoint Street San Francisco
Campton Place Hotel	415-781-5555	340 Stockton Street San Francisco
Days Inn - Lombard St	415-922-2010	2358 Lombard Street San Francisco
Harbor Court Hotel	415-882-1300	165 Steuart Street San Francisco
Hotel Cosmo	415-673-6040	761 Post Street San Francisco
Hotel Juliana	415-392-2540	590 Bush Street San Francisco
Hotel Palomar	415-348-1111	12 Fourth Street San Francisco
Hotel Triton	415-394-0500	342 Grant Avenue San Francisco
Marina Motel - on Lombard Street	415-921-9406	2576 Lombard St. San Francisco
Monticello Inn	415-392-8800	127 Ellis Street San Francisco
Palace Hotel	415-512-1111	2 New Montgomery Street San Francisco
Prescott Hotel	415-563-0303	545 Post Street San Francisco
Residence Inn	650-837-9000	Oyster Point Blvd & 101 San Francisco
Serrano Hotel	415-885-2500	405 Taylor Street San Francisco
The Laurel Inn	415-567-8467	444 Presidio Ave. San Francisco
W San Francisco	415-777-5300	181 Third Street San Francisco

Half Moon Bay
Holiday Inn Express	650-726-3400	230 S Cabrillo Hwy Half Moon Bay
Ramada Limited	650-726-9700	3020 N Cabrillo Hwy Half Moon Bay

Highway Guides - Please always call ahead to make sure an establishment is still dog-friendly.

Santa Cruz
1600 West Cliff	408-266-4453	1600 West Cliff Drive Santa Cruz
Beach Bungalow Vacation Rentals	831-469-6161	Call to Arrange. Santa Cruz
Edgewater Beach Motel	831-423-0440	525 Second Street Santa Cruz
Guesthouse International	831-425-3722	330 Ocean Street Santa Cruz
Redtail Ranch by the Sea	831-429-1322	Call to Arrange. Santa Cruz

Watsonville
Best Western Inn	831-724-3367	740 Freedom Boulevard Watsonville
Red Roof Inn	831-740-4520	1620 West Beach Street Watsonville

Monterey
Bay Park Hotel	831-649-1020	1425 Munras Ave Monterey
Best Western Monterey Beach Hotel	831-394-3321	2600 Sand Dunes Drive Monterey
Best Western Victorian Inn	831-373-8000	487 Foam Street Monterey
El Adobe Inn	831-372-5409	936 Munras Ave. Monterey
Hyatt Resort	831-372-1234	1 Od Golf Course Rd Monterey
Monterey Fireside Lodge	831-373-4172	1131 10th Street Monterey
Motel 6	831-646-8585	2124 N Fremont St Monterey

Carmel
Carmel Country Inn	831-625-3263	P.O. Box 3756 Carmel
Carmel Tradewinds Inn	831-624-2776	Mission St & 3rd Ave. Carmel
Casa De Carmel	831-624-2429	Monte Verde & Ocean Ave Carmel
Coachman's Inn	831-624-6421	San Carlos St. & 7th Carmel
Cypress Inn	831-624-3871	Lincoln & 7th Carmel
Hofsas House Hotel	831-624-2745	San Carlos Street Carmel
Lincoln Green Inn	831-624-7738	PO Box 2747 Carmel
Sunset House	831-624-4884	Camino Real and Ocean Ave Carmel
The Forest Lodge Cottages	831-624-7055	Ocean Ave. and Torres St. (P.O. Box 1316) Carmel
Vagabond's House Inn B&B	831-624-7738	P.O. Box 2747 Carmel
Wayside Inn	831-624-5336	Mission St & 7th Ave. Carmel

Big Sur
Big Sur Vacation Retreat	831-624-5339 Ext 13	off Highway One Big Sur

San Simeon
Best Western Cavalier Oceanfront Resort	805-927-4688	9415 Hearst Drive San Simeon
Motel 6	805-927-8691	9070 Castillo Dr San Simeon
Silver Surf Motel	805-927-4661	9390 Castillo Drive San Simeon

Cambria
Cambria Pines Lodge	805-927-4200	2905 Burton Drive Cambria
Cambria Shores Inn	805-927-8644	6276 Moonstone Beach Dr. Cambria
Fogcatcher Inn	805-927-1400	6400 Moonstone Beach Drive Cambria

Morro Bay
Adventure Inn On The Sea	805-772-5607	1150 Embarcadero Morro Bay
Days Inn	805-772-2711	1095 Main Street Morro Bay
Pleasant Inn Motel	805-772-8521	235 Harbor Street Morro Bay

San Luis Obispo
Best Western Royal Oak	805-544-4410	214 Madonna Rd. San Luis Obispo
Motel 6 - South	805-541-6992	1625 Calle Joaquin San Luis Obispo
Sands Suites & Motel	805-544-0500	1930 Monterey Street San Luis Obispo

Highway Guides - Please always call ahead to make sure an establishment is still dog-friendly.

| Vagabond Inn | 805-544-4710 | 210 Madonna Rd. San Luis Obispo |

Pismo Beach
Motel 6	805-773-2665	860 4th St Pismo Beach
Oxford Suites	805-773-3773	651 Five Cities Drive Pismo Beach
Sandcastle Inn	805-773-2422	100 Stimson Avenue Pismo Beach
Sea Gypsy Motel	805-773-1801	1020 Cypress Street Pismo Beach

Arroyo Grande
| Best Western Casa Grande Inn | 805-481-7398 | 850 Oak Park Road Arroyo Grande |

Lompoc
Days Inn - Vandenberg Village	805-733-5000	3955 Apollo Way Lompoc
Motel 6	805-735-7631	1521 North H Street Lompoc
Quality Inn & Suites	805-735-8555	1621 N. H Street Lompoc

Goleta
| Motel 6 | 805-964-3696 | 5897 Calle Real Goleta |

Santa Barbara
Casa Del Mar Hotel	805-963-4418	18 Bath Street Santa Barbara
Fess Parker's Doubletree Resort	805-564-4333	633 E. Cabrillo Boulevard Santa Barbara
Montecito Del Mar	805-962-2006	316 W Montecito St Santa Barbara
Motel 6 - Beach	805-564-1392	443 Corona Del Mar Santa Barbara
Motel 6 - State	805-687-5400	3505 State St Santa Barbara
San Ysidro Ranch	805-969-5046	900 San Ysidro Lane Santa Barbara
Secret Garden Inn & Cottages	805-687-2300	1908 Bath Street Santa Barbara

Ventura
Best Western Inn of Ventura	805-648-3101	708 E. Thompson Blvd. Ventura
La Quinta Inn Ventura	805-658-6200	5818 Valentine Road Ventura
Motel 6	805-643-5100	2145 E Harbor Blvd Ventura
Vagabond Inn	805-648-5371	756 E. Thompson Blvd. Ventura

Oxnard
Casa Sirena Hotel and Resort	805-985-6311	3605 Peninsula Rd Oxnard
Radisson Hotel Oxnard	805-485-9666	600 E. Esplanade Drive Oxnard
Residence Inn by Marriott	805-278-2200	2101 West Vineyard Avenue Oxnard
Vagabond Inn	805-983-0251	1245 N. Oxnard Blvd. Oxnard

Santa Monica
| Le Merigot Beach Hotel and Spa | 310-395-9700 | 1740 Ocean Avenue Santa Monica |
| Loews Santa Monica Beach Hotel | 310-458-6700 | 1700 Ocean Avenue Santa Monica |

Highway 49 Accommodation Listings (California)

Downieville
Downieville Carriage House Inn	530-289-3573	110 Commercial Street Downieville
Downieville River Inn & Resort	530-289-3308	PO Box 412 Downieville, CA Downieville
Downieville River Inn and Resort	530-289-3308	121 River Street Downieville

Nevada City
| The Outside Inn | 530-265-2233 | 575 E. Broad Street Nevada City |

Grass Valley

Bear River Retreat and Lodge	530-346-0078	20010 Hwy 174 Grass Valley
Best Western Gold Country Inn	530-273-1393	11972 Sutton Way Grass Valley
Swan Levine House Bed and Breakfast	916-272-1873	328 South Church Street Grass Valley
Auburn		
Best Western Golden Key	530-885-8611	13450 Lincoln Way Auburn
Holiday Inn	530-887-8787	120 Grass Valley Highway Auburn
Travelodge	530-885-7025	13490 Lincoln Way Auburn
Coloma		
Golden Lotus Bed and Breakfast Inn	530-621-4562	1006 Lotus Road Coloma
Placerville		
Best Western Placerville Inn	530-622-9100	6850 Green Leaf Dr. Placerville
Drytown		
Old Well Motel	209-245-6467	15947 State Highway 49 Drytown
Jackson		
Amador Motel	209-223-0970	12408 Kennedy Flat Rd Jackson
Jackson Gold Lodge	209-223-0486	850 N. State Hwy 49 Jackson
Angels Camp		
Best Western Cedar Inn & Suites	209-736-4000	444 South Main Street Angels Camp
Columbia		
Columbia Gem Motel	209-532-4508	22131 Parrotts Ferry Rd Columbia
Sonora		
Best Western Sonora Oaks	209-533-4400	19551 Hess Avenue Sonora
Sonora Aladdin Motor Inn	209-533-4971	14260 Mono Way (Hwy 108) Sonora
Jamestown		
Quality Inn	209-984-0315	18730 SR 108 Jamestown
Royal Hotel Bed and Breakfast	209-984-5271	18239 Main Street Jamestown
The National Hotel	209-984-3446	18183 Main Street Jamestown

Highway 50 Accommodation Listings

California Listings

Rancho Cordova		
Inns of America	916-351-1213	12249 Folsom Blvd Rancho Cordova
Residence Inn by Marriott	916-851-1550	2779 Prospect Park Drive Rancho Cordova
Folsom		
Lake Natoma Inn	916-351-1500	702 Gold Lake Drive Folsom
Residence Inn	916-983-7289	2555 Iron Point Road Folsom
Cameron Park		
Best Western Cameron Park Inn	530-677-2203	3361 Coach Lane Cameron Park
Placerville		
Best Western Placerville Inn	530-622-9100	6850 Green Leaf Dr. Placerville
South Lake Tahoe		
Accommodation Station	530-542-5850	2516 Lake Tahoe Blvd. South Lake Tahoe
Alder Inn	530-544-4485	1072 Ski Run Blvd. South Lake Tahoe
Buckingham Properties Lake Tahoe	530-542-1114	Call to Arrange South Lake Tahoe
Colony Inn at South Lake Tahoe	530-544-6481	3794 Montreal Road South Lake Tahoe
Fireside Lodge	530-544-5515	515 Emerald Bay Rd. South Lake Tahoe

Inn at Heavenly B&B	530-544-4244	1261 Ski Run Boulevard South Lake Tahoe
Lake Tahoe Accommodations	800-544-3234	Call to Arrange. South Lake Tahoe
Salsa's Chalet	707-565-3740	South Lake Tahoe
Sandor's Chateau Motel	530-541-6312	1137 Emerald Bay Road South Lake Tahoe
South Lake Tahoe Vacation Rental	415-388-8170	Call to arrange. South Lake Tahoe
Stonehenge Vacation Properties	800-822-1460	Call to Arrange. South Lake Tahoe
Super 8 Motel	530-544-3476	3600 Lake Tahoe Blvd. South Lake Tahoe
Tahoe Keys Resort	530-544-5397	599 Tahoe Keys Blvd South Lake Tahoe
The Nash Cabin	415-759-6583	Shirley Avenue South Lake Tahoe

Nevada Listings

Carson City
Best Value Motel	775-882-2007	2731 S Carson St Carson City
Super 8 Motel	775-883-7800	2829 S. Carson Street Carson City

Fallon
Super 8	775-423-6031	855 W. Williams Ave Fallon

Ely
Best Western Main Motel	775-289-4529	1101 Aultman Ely
Best Western Park Vue	775-289-4497	930 Aultman Ely
Ramada Inn Copper Queen Casino	775-289-4884	805 Great Basin Blvd Ely

Highway 99 Accommodation Listings (California)

Red Bluff Listings
Red Bluff
Motel 6	530-527-9200	20 Williams Ave Red Bluff
Super 8	530-527-8882	203 Antelope Blvd Red Bluff
Travelodge	530-527-6020	38 Antelope Blvd Red Bluff

Chico Listings
Chico
Esplanade Bed & Breakfast	530-345-8084	620 The Esplanade Chico
Holiday Inn	530-345-2491	685 Manzanita Ct Chico
Motel 6	530-345-5500	665 Manzanita Ct Chico
Music Express Inn Bed and Breakfast	530-891-9833	1091El Monte Avenue Chico
Super 8	530-345-2533	655 Manzanita Ct Chico

Paradise
Lime Saddle Marina Houseboat Rentals	530-877-2414	Call to Arrange. Paradise

Oroville Listings
Oroville
Motel 6	530-534-7653	505 Montgomery St Oroville

Yuba City Listings

Yuba City

Comfort Inn	530-674-1592	730 Palora Ave Yuba City
Days Inn	530-674-1711	700 N Palora Ave Yuba City

Sacramento Listings

Sacramento

Candlewood Suites	916-646-1212	555 Howe Ave. Sacramento
Canterbury Inn Hotel	916-927-0927	1900 Canterbury Rd Sacramento
Motel 6	916-372-3624	1254 Halyard Dr Sacramento
Ramada Inn	916-487-7600	2600 Auburn Blvd Sacramento
Residence Inn by Marriott	916-920-9111	1530 Howe Ave Sacramento
Residence Inn by Marriott - South Natomas	916-649-1300	2410 West El Camino Avenue Sacramento
Sheraton Grand Sacramento Hotel	916-447-1700	1230 J Street Sacramento

Stockton Listings

Stockton

La Quinta Inn Stockton	209-952-7800	2710 West March Lane Stockton
Motel 6 - Southeast	209-467-3600	1625 French Camp Turnpike Rd Stockton
Motel 6 - West	209-946-0923	817 Navy Drive Stockton
Residence Inn - Stockton	209-472-9800	March Lane & Brookside Stockton
Travelodge	209-466-7777	1707 Fremont St Stockton

Tracy

Motel 6	209-836-4900	3810 Tracy Blvd Tracy

Stockton

Seven Crown Resorts Houseboats	800-752-9669	8095 Rio Blanco Road Stockton

Modesto Listings

Modesto

Best Western Town House Lodge	209-524-7261	909 16th Street Modesto
Red Lion Hotel	209-521-1612	1612 Sisk Rd Modesto
Vagabond Inn	209-577-8008	2025 W Orangeburg Ave Modesto

Turlock Listings

Turlock

Best Western Orchard Inn	209-667-2827	5025 N Golden State Blvd Turlock
Motel 6	209-667-4100	250 S Walnut Ave Turlock

Merced Listings

Merced

Best Western Sequoia Inn	209-723-3711	1213 V Street Merced
Motel 6	209-384-2131	1410 V St Merced
Super 8	209-384-1303	1983 E. Childs Ave Merced
Travelodge	209-722-6225	1260 Yosemite Park Way Merced
Vagabond Inn	209-722-2737	1215 R Street Merced

Chowchilla Listings

Chowchilla

Days Inn	559-665-4821	Hwy 99 & Robertson Blvd Chowchilla

Madera Listings

Madera

Best Western Madera Valley Inn	559-673-5164	317 North G Street Madera
Days Inn	559-674-8817	25327 Ave 16 Madera
Super 8	559-661-1131	1855 W. Cleveland Ave Madera

Fresno Listings

Fresno

Econo Lodge	559-485-5019	445 N Parkway Dr Fresno
Holiday Inn Express and Suites	559-277-5700	5046 N. Barcus Rd Fresno
Red Roof Inn - Hwy 99	559-276-1910	5021 N Barcus Avenue Fresno

Selma Listings

Selma

Best Western Selma Inn	559-891-0300	2799 Floral Avenue Selma

Visalia Listings

Visalia

Holiday Inn	559-651-5000	9000 W. Airport Drive Visalia
Super 8	559-627-2885	4801 W Noble Ave Visalia

Tulare Listings

Tulare

Best Western Town and Country	559-688-7537	1051 N Blackstone Ave Tulare
Days Inn	559-686-0985	1183 N Blackstone St Tulare
Howard Johnson Express Inn	559-688-6671	1050 E Rankin Ave Tulare
Motel 6	559-686-6374	1111 N Blackstone Dr Tulare

Delano Listings

Delano

Shilo Inn	661-725-7551	2231 Girard Street Delano

Bakersfield Listings

Bakersfield

Best Western Crystal Palace Inn & Suites	661-327-9651	2620 Buck Owens Blvd. Bakersfield
Best Western Hill House	661-327-4064	700 Truxton Avenue Bakersfield
Days Hotel and Golf	661-324-5555	4500 Buck Owens Blvd Bakersfield
Doubletree Hotel	661-323-7111	3100 Camino Del Rio Ct Bakersfield
La Quinta Inn Bakersfield	661-325-7400	3232 Riverside Drive Bakersfield
Motel 6	661-327-1686	1350 Easton Dr Bakersfield
Motel 6	661-366-7231	8223 E Brundage Lane Bakersfield
Motel 6	661-392-9700	5241 Olive Tree Ct Bakersfield
Ramada Inn	661-831-1922	830 Wible Rd Bakersfield
Residence Inn	661-321-9800	4241 Chester Lane Bakersfield
Rio Bravo Resort	661-872-5000	11200 Lake Ming Rd Bakersfield
Super 8	661-322-1012	901 Real Rd Bakersfield

Highway 101 Accommodation Listings

Washington (Highway 101)

Olympia Listings

Olympia

West Coast Inn	360-943-4000	2300 Evergreen Park Drive Olympia WA

Tumwater

Best Western Tumwater Inn	360-956-1235	5188 Capitol Blvd Tumwater WA
Motel 6	360-754-7320	400 W Lee St Tumwater WA

Forks Listings
Forks		
Kalaloch Ocean Lodge	360-962-2271	157151 Hwy. 101 Forks WA

Aberdeen Listings
Aberdeen		
Red Lion Inn	360-532-5210	521 W Wishkah Aberdeen WA

Oregon (Highway 101)

Astoria Listings
Astoria		
Red Lion Inn	503-325-7373	400 Industry St Astoria OR

Seaside Listings
Seaside		
Best Western Ocean View Resort	503-738-3334	414 N. Prom Seaside OR
Comfort Inn	503-738-3011	545 Broadway Ave. Seaside OR
Motel 6	503-738-6269	2369 S Roosevelt (Hwy 101) Seaside OR
Seaside Convention Center Inn	503-738-9581	441 Second Ave Seaside OR

Cannon Beach Listings
Cannon Beach		
Best Western Cannon Beach	503-436-9085	3215 S. Hemlock Cannon Beach OR
Surfsand Resort	503-436-2274	148 W. Gower Cannon Beach OR
The Haystack Resort	503-436-1577	3361 S. Hemlock Cannon Beach OR

Lincoln City Listings
Lincoln City		
Ester Lee Motel	541 996 3606	3803 S.W. HWY. 101 Lincoln City OR
Looking Glass Inn	541-996-3996	861 SW 51st Street Lincoln City OR
Looking Glass Inn	541-996-3996	861 SW 51st Street Lincoln City OR

Newport Listings
Newport		
Best Western	541-265-9411	3019 North Coast Hwy Newport OR
Hallmark Resort	541-265-2600	744 SW Elizabeth St Newport OR
La Quinta Inn & Suites Newport	541-867-7727	45 SE 32nd Newport OR
Shilo Oceanfront Resort	541-265-7701	536 SW Elizabeth St Newport OR

Yachats Listings
Yachats		
Adobe Resort	541-547-3141	1555 US 101 Yachats OR
Shamrock Lodgettes	541-547-3312	US 101 Yachats OR
The Fireside Inn	800-336-3573	Hwy 101 Yachats OR

Reedsport Listings
Reedsport		
Economy Inn	541-271-3671	1593 Highway Ave 101 Reedsport OR

Coos Bay Listings
Coos Bay		
Motel 6	541-267-7171	1445 Bayshore Dr Coos Bay OR

Bandon Listings
Bandon

Best Western Inn at Face Rock	541-347-9441	3225 Beach Loop Rd Bandon OR
Driftwood Motel	541-347-9022	460 Hwy 101 Bandon OR
Sunset Motel	541-347-2453	1755 Beach Loop Rd Bandon OR

Harbor Listings
Harbor

Best Western Beachfront Inn	541-469-7779	16008 Boat Basin Rd Harbor OR

California (Highway 101)

Crescent City Listings
Crescent City

Gardenia Motel	707-464-2181	119 L Street Crescent City CA
Super 8	707-464-4111	685 Hwy 101 S. Crescent City CA
Town House Motel	707-464-4176	444 US Highway 101 South Crescent City CA

Arcata Listings
Arcata

Best Western Arcata Inn	707-826-0313	4827 Valley West Boulevard Arcata CA
Hotel Arcata	707-826-0217	708 Ninth Street Arcata CA
Quality Inn	707-822-0409	3535 Janes Rd Arcata CA
Super 8	707-822-8888	4887 Valley W. Blvd Arcata CA

Eureka Listings
Eureka

Best Western Bayshore Inn	707-268-8005	3500 Broadway Eureka CA
Discovery Inn	707-441-8442	2832 Broadway Eureka CA
Motel 6	707-445-9631	1934 Broadway Eureka CA
Quality Inn	707-443-1601	1209 Fourth Street Eureka CA
Ramada Inn	707-443-2206	270 5th Street Eureka CA
Red Lion Hotel	707-445-0844	1929 Fourth Street Eureka CA
The Eureka Inn	707-442-6441	518 Seventh Street Eureka CA
Fortuna		
Super 8	707-725-2888	1805 Alamar Way Fortuna CA

Fortuna Listings
Fortuna

Best Western Country Inn	707-725-6822	2025 Riverwalk Drive Fortuna CA

Miranda Listings
Miranda

Miranda Gardens Resort	707-943-3011	6766 Avenue of the Giants Miranda CA

Ukiah Listings
Ukiah

Days Inn	707-462-7584	950 North State St Ukiah CA
Motel 6	707-468-5404	1208 S State Street Ukiah CA

Marin - North Bay Listings
Novato

Inn Marin	415-883-5952	250 Entrada Drive Novato CA
Travelodge	415-892-7500	7600 Redwood Blvd Novato CA

San Francisco Listings

San Francisco

Best Western Tuscan Inn	415-561-1100	425 Northpoint Street San Francisco CA
Campton Place Hotel	415-781-5555	340 Stockton Street San Francisco CA
Days Inn - Lombard St	415-922-2010	2358 Lombard Street San Francisco CA
Harbor Court Hotel	415-882-1300	165 Steuart Street San Francisco CA
Hotel Cosmo	415-673-6040	761 Post Street San Francisco CA
Hotel Juliana	415-392-2540	590 Bush Street San Francisco CA
Hotel Palomar	415-348-1111	12 Fourth Street San Francisco CA
Hotel Triton	415-394-0500	342 Grant Avenue San Francisco CA
Marina Motel - on Lombard Street	415-921-9406	2576 Lombard St. San Francisco CA
Monticello Inn	415-392-8800	127 Ellis Street San Francisco CA
Palace Hotel	415-512-1111	2 New Montgomery Street San Francisco CA
Prescott Hotel	415-563-0303	545 Post Street San Francisco CA
Residence Inn	650-837-9000	Oyster Point Blvd & 101 San Francisco CA
Serrano Hotel	415-885-2500	405 Taylor Street San Francisco CA
The Laurel Inn	415-567-8467	444 Presidio Ave. San Francisco CA
W San Francisco	415-777-5300	181 Third Street San Francisco CA

Palo Alto - Peninsula Listings

Belmont

Motel 6	650-591-1471	1101 Shoreway Rd. Belmont CA

Burlingame

Embassy Suites	650-342-4600	150 Anza Blvd. Burlingame CA
Vagabond Inn	650-692-4040	1640 Bayshore Highway Burlingame CA

Millbrae

Clarion Hotel	650-692-6363	250 El Camino Real Millbrae CA

Mountain View

Residence Inn by Marriott	650-940-1300	1854 W El Camino Real Mountain View CA
Tropicana Lodge	650-961-0220	1720 El Camino Real Mountain View CA

Palo Alto

Motel 6	650-949-0833	4301 El Camino Real Palo Alto CA
Sheraton Palo Alto Hotel	650-328-2800	625 El Camino Real Palo Alto CA

Redwood City

Hotel Sofitel	650-598-9000	223 Twin Dolphin Dr Redwood City CA

San Carlos

Inns of America	650-631-0777	555 Skyway Road San Carlos CA

South San Francisco

Howard Johnson Express Inn	650-589-9055	222 South Airport Blvd. South San Francisco CA
La Quinta Inn South San Francisco	650-583-2223	20 Airport Blvd South San Francisco CA
Motel 6	650-871-0770	111 Mitchell Ave. South San Francisco CA
Vagabond Inn	650-589-9055	222 S. Airport Blvd South San Francisco CA

San Jose Listings

San Jose

Doubletree Hotel	408-453-4000	2050 Gateway Pl San Jose CA
Hilton San Jose	408-287-2100	300 Almaden Blvd San Jose CA
Motel 6	408-436-8180	2081 N 1st Street San Jose CA
Motel 6 - South	408-270-3131	2560 Fontaine Rd San Jose CA

Santa Clara

Marriott Hotel	408-988-1500	2700 Mission College Blvd Santa Clara CA
Motel 6 - Santa Clara	408-241-0200	3208 El Camino Real Santa Clara CA

Sunnyvale

Residence Inn - SV I	408-720-1000	750 Lakeway Sunnyvale CA
Residence Inn - SV II	408-720-8893	1080 Stewart Dr Sunnyvale CA
Summerfield Suites	408-745-1515	900 Hamlin Court Sunnyvale CA
Woodfin Suite Hotel	408-738-1700	635 E. El Camino Real Sunnyvale CA

San Luis Obispo Listings

Arroyo Grande

Best Western Casa Grande Inn	805-481-7398	850 Oak Park Road Arroyo Grande CA

Atascadero		
Motel 6	805-466-6701	9400 El Camino Real Atascadero CA
Pismo Beach		
Motel 6	805-773-2665	860 4th St Pismo Beach CA
Oxford Suites	805-773-3773	651 Five Cities Drive Pismo Beach CA
Sandcastle Inn	805-773-2422	100 Stimson Avenue Pismo Beach CA
Sea Gypsy Motel	805-773-1801	1020 Cypress Street Pismo Beach CA
San Luis Obispo		
Best Western Royal Oak	805-544-4410	214 Madonna Rd. San Luis Obispo CA
Motel 6 - South	805-541-6992	1625 Calle Joaquin San Luis Obispo CA
Sands Suites & Motel	805-544-0500	1930 Monterey Street San Luis Obispo CA
Vagabond Inn	805-544-4710	210 Madonna Rd. San Luis Obispo CA

Santa Maria Listings

Santa Maria		
Best Western Big America	805-922-5200	1725 North Broadway Santa Maria CA
Motel 6	805-928-8111	2040 N Preisker Lane Santa Maria CA

Solvang Listings

Buellton		
Motel 6	805-688-7797	333 McMurray Rd Buellton CA
Rodeway Inn	805-688-0022	630 Ave of Flags Buellton CA
Solvang		
Royal Copenhagen Inn	800-624-6604	1579 Mission Drive Solvang CA

Santa Barbara Listings

Carpinteria		
Motel 6	805-684-6921	4200 Via Real Carpinteria CA
Motel 6 - South	805-684-8602	5550 Carpinteria Ave Carpinteria CA
Goleta		
Motel 6	805-964-3696	5897 Calle Real Goleta CA
Santa Barbara		
Casa Del Mar Hotel	805-963-4418	18 Bath Street Santa Barbara CA
Fess Parker's Doubletree Resort	805-564-4333	633 E. Cabrillo Boulevard Santa Barbara CA
Montecito Del Mar	805-962-2006	316 W Montecito St Santa Barbara CA
Motel 6 - Beach	805-564-1392	443 Corona Del Mar Santa Barbara CA
Motel 6 - State	805-687-5400	3505 State St Santa Barbara CA
San Ysidro Ranch	805-969-5046	900 San Ysidro Lane Santa Barbara CA
Secret Garden Inn & Cottages	805-687-2300	1908 Bath Street Santa Barbara CA

Ventura - Oxnard Listings

Camarillo		
Motel 6	805-388-3467	1641 E Daily Dr Camarillo CA
Oxnard		
Casa Sirena Hotel and Resort	805-985-6311	3605 Peninsula Rd Oxnard CA
Radisson Hotel Oxnard	805-485-9666	600 E. Esplanade Drive Oxnard CA
Residence Inn by Marriott	805-278-2200	2101 West Vineyard Avenue Oxnard CA
Vagabond Inn	805-983-0251	1245 N. Oxnard Blvd. Oxnard CA
Ventura		
Best Western Inn of Ventura	805-648-3101	708 E. Thompson Blvd. Ventura CA
La Quinta Inn Ventura	805-658-6200	5818 Valentine Road Ventura CA
Motel 6	805-643-5100	2145 E Harbor Blvd Ventura CA
Vagabond Inn	805-648-5371	756 E. Thompson Blvd. Ventura CA

San Fernando Valley Listings

Thousand Oaks		
Motel 6	805-499-0711	1516 Newbury Rd Thousand Oaks CA
Thousand Oaks Inn	805-497-3701	75 W. Thousand Oaks Blvd. Thousand Oaks CA
Woodland Hills		
Vagabond Inn	818-347-8080	20157 Ventura Blvd. Woodland Hills CA

Highway 395 Accommodation Listings (California and Nevada)

Alturas

Best Western Trailside Inn	530-233-4111	343 North Main Street Alturas
Hacienda Motel	530-233-3459	201 E 12th St Alturas

Susanville

Budget Host Frontier Inn	530-257-4141	2685 Main St Susanville
River Inn	530-257-6051	1710 Main St Susanville

Reno

Days Inn	775-786-4070	701 E 7th Reno
Holiday Inn	775-786-5151	1000 E. 6th St. Reno
Motel 6 - Livestock Center	775-786-9852	866 N. Wells Ave Reno
Motel 6 - Virginia/Plumb	775-827-0255	1901 S. Virginia St Reno
Motel 6 - West	775-747-7390	1400 Stardust Street Reno
Residence Inn by Marriott	775-853-8800	9845 Gateway Drive Reno
Rodeway Inn	775-786-2500	2050 Market Street Reno
Truckee River Lodge	775-786-8888	501 W. 1st Street Reno
Vagabond Inn	775-825-7134	3131 S. Virginia St. Reno

Carson City

Best Value Motel	775-882-2007	2731 S Carson St Carson City
Super 8 Motel	775-883-7800	2829 S. Carson Street Carson City

Coleville

Andruss Motel	530-495-2216	106964 Highway 395 Coleville

Bridgeport

Best Western Ruby Inn	760-931-7241	333 Main Street Bridgeport

Lee Vining

Inn at Lee Vining	760-647-6300	45 2nd St Lee Vining
Murphey's Hotel	760-647-6316	51493 Hwy 395 Lee Vining

Mammoth Lakes

Crystal Crag Lodge	760-934-2436	P.O. Box 88 Mammoth Lakes
Discovery 4 Condominiums	760-934-6410	Call to Arrange. Mammoth Lakes
Edelweiss Lodge	760-934-2445	1872 Old Mammoth Road Mammoth Lakes
Mammoth Ski and Racquet Club	760-934-7368	Call to Arrange. Mammoth Lakes
Motel 6	760-934-6660	3372 Main St Mammoth Lakes
Shilo Inn	760-934-4500	2963 Main Street Mammoth Lakes
Travelodge	760-934-8240	54 Sierra Blvd. Mammoth Lakes
Villa De Los Pinos #3	760-722-5369	3252 Chateau Rd Mammoth Lakes

Bishop

Best Western Bishop Holiday Spa Lodge	760-873-3543	1025 North Main Street Bishop
Comfort Inn	760-873-4284	805 N. Main Street Bishop
Motel 6	760-873-8426	1005 N Man Street Bishop
Rodeway Inn	760-873-3564	150 E Elm Street Bishop
Vagabond Inn	760-873-6351	1030 N Main Street Bishop

Big Pine

Big Pine Motel	760-938-2282	370 S Main St Big Pine
Bristlecone Motel	760-938-2067	101 N. Main St. Big Pine

Independence

Best Western Prairie Inn	620-331-7300	3222 West Main Independence
Comfort Inn East	816-373-8856	4200 South Noland Rd. Independence
Independence Courthouse Motel	760-878-2732	157 N Edwards Street Independence
Ray's Den Motel	760-878-2122	405 N Edwards St Independence
Wilder House Bed & Breakfast	760-878-2119	325 Dusty Lane Independence

Lone Pine

Alabama Hills Inn	760-876-8700	1920 South Main Lone Pine
Best Western Frontier Motel	760-876-5571	1008 South Main Street Lone Pine

Olancha

Ranch Motel	760-764-2387	2051 S Highway 395 Olancha

Ridgecrest

Motel 6	760-375-6866	535 S China Lake Blvd Ridgecrest

Canadian Highway 1 and 5 Accommodation Listings (British Columbia)

Vancouver Listings

Coquitlam

Holiday Inn	604-931-4433	631 Lougheed Highway Coquitlam BC

Pitt Meadows

Ramada Inn	604-460-9859	19267 Lougheed Hwy Pitt Meadows BC

Surrey Listings

Surrey

Ramada Hotel & Suites	604-930-4700	10410 158th St Surrey BC
Ramada Limited	604-576-8388	19225 Hwy 10 Surrey BC

Abbotsford Listings

Abbotsford

Holiday Inn Express	604-859-6211	2073 Clearbrook Rd Abbotsford BC
Ramada Inn	604-870-1050	36035 N Parallel Rd Abbotsford BC

Chilliwack Listings

Chilliwack

Best Western Rainbow Country Inn	604-795-3828	43971 Industrial Way Chilliwack BC
Comfort Inn	604-858-0636	45405 Luckakuck Way Chilliwack BC

Hope Listings

Hope

Quality Inn   604-869-9951   350 Old Hope Princton Way Hope BC

Kamloops Listings
Kamloops

Coast Canadian Inn   250-372-5201   339 St. Paul Street Kamloops BC
Days Inn   250-374-5911   1285 W Trans Canada Hwy Kamloops BC
Howard Johnson Inn   250-374-1515   610 West Columbia Street Kamloops BC
Ramada Inn   250-374-0358   555 West Columbia St Kamloops BC

Salmon Arm Listings
Salmon Arm

Best Western Villager West   250-832-9793   61-10th St SW Salmon Arm BC

Sicamous Listings
Sicamous

Sundog Bed and Breakfast   250-833-9005   1409 Rauma Ave Sicamous BC

Revelstoke Listings
Revelstoke

Best Western Wayside Inn   250-837-6161   1901 Laforme Blvd Revelstoke BC

Please always call ahead to make sure an establishment is still dog-friendly.

Please always call ahead to make sure an establishment is still dog-friendly.

Please always call ahead to make sure an establishment is still dog-friendly.

Please always call ahead to make sure an establishment is still dog-friendly.

Please always call ahead to make sure an establishment is still dog-friendly.

Please always call ahead to make sure an establishment is still dog-friendly.

Notes

California Regions

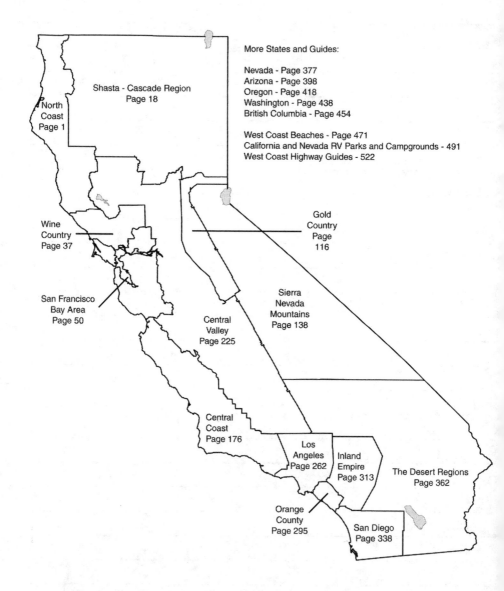

Shasta - Cascade Region
Page 18

North
Coast
Page 1

Wine
Country
Page 37

San Francisco
Bay Area
Page 50

Gold
Country
Page
116

Sierra
Nevada
Mountains
Page 138

Central
Valley
Page 225

Central
Coast
Page 176

Los
Angeles
Page 262

Inland
Empire
Page 313

The Desert Regions
Page 362

Orange
County
Page 295

San Diego
Page 338

More States and Guides:

Nevada - Page 377
Arizona - Page 398
Oregon - Page 418
Washington - Page 438
British Columbia - Page 454

West Coast Beaches - Page 471
California and Nevada RV Parks and Campgrounds - 491
West Coast Highway Guides - 522